THE
PERSUASION
GAME

www.amplifypublishinggroup.com

The Persuasion Game: The Influence Peddlers to the Trump Administration Who Jeopardized America

©2024 Chad Lewis. All Rights Reserved. No part of this publication may be reproduced, stored in a retrieval system or transmitted in any form by any means electronic, mechanical, or photocopying, recording or otherwise without the permission of the author.

Although the author and publisher have made every effort to ensure that the information in this book was correct at press time, the author and publisher do not assume and hereby disclaim any liability to any party for any loss, damage, or disruption caused by errors or omissions, whether such errors or omissions result from negligence, accident, or any other cause. The publisher and the author assume no responsibility for errors, inaccuracies, omissions, or any other inconsistencies herein. All such instances are unintentional and the author's own.

For more information, please contact:
Amplify Publishing, an imprint of Amplify Publishing Group
620 Herndon Parkway, Suite 220
Herndon, VA 20170
info@amplifypublishing.com

Library of Congress Control Number: 2024919615

CPSIA Code: PRV1124A

ISBN-13: 979-8-89138-418-7

Printed in the United States

To truth seekers everywhere.

CHAD LEWIS

THE PERSUASION GAME

THE **INFLUENCE PEDDLERS** TO THE **TRUMP ADMINISTRATION** WHO JEOPARDIZED AMERICA

CONTENTS

INTRODUCTION ix

PART I: TURKEY

CHAPTER 1: Halkbank 1
CHAPTER 2: Turkish Lobbying in the United States 7
CHAPTER 3: Building Access to DC Gatekeepers 13
CHAPTER 4: Heritage, Donations and US Politics 21
CHAPTER 5: Target #1 33
CHAPTER 6: Interference into the Halkbank Investigation ... 49

PART II: THE CLANDESTINE OPERATIONS OF RUDY GIULIANI AND LEV PARNAS

CHAPTER 7: The Emergence of the Dynamic Duo 71
CHAPTER 8: Shadow Diplomacy in Venezuela 77
CHAPTER 9: The Beginning of Ukrainegate 85
CHAPTER 10: Quid Pro Quo with Ukrainian Prosecutors 93
CHAPTER 11: The Pivot 101
CHAPTER 12: Freedom Gas 115
CHAPTER 13: Removing the Obstacles 125
CHAPTER 14: Modus Operandi 149

PART III: THE GLOBAL CONTEXT

CHAPTER 15: Russia Inc. 157
CHAPTER 16: The Tug-Of-War Against the West 167

PART IV: RUSSIAN INFLUENCE OPERATIONS IN THE UNITED STATES

CHAPTER 17: The Kremlin's Groundwork 189
CHAPTER 18: The Digital Strategy 195
CHAPTER 19: Campaign Infiltration 207
CHAPTER 20: The Streams of Influence 239

PART V: CONSEQUENCES

CHAPTER 21: The Imperfect Wheels of Justice 255
CHAPTER 22: Trump's Fight for the White House 263

EPILOGUE 283
THE INTEGRATED TIMELINE 287
ENDNOTES 339
ABOUT THE AUTHOR 507

INTRODUCTION

Lobbying has existed in the United States since its very beginning. However, it only started to become regulated in the middle of the twentieth century, with the rise of dissemination of Nazi propaganda in America. In 1938 Congress passed the Foreign Agents Registration Act that required representatives of foreign interests to report their activities to the US government. After the end of World War II and then the Cold War, its enforcement became rare, adherence to it was somewhat discretionary, and it remained unaltered for decades. Lobbying, for both foreign and domestic clients, became the epitome of political corruption in the United States.

During his 2016 presidential campaign, Donald Trump vowed to drain the influence peddling swamp in Washington, DC. However, during his time in the White House, he did the exact opposite. An outsider to the political establishment, he had an image of a dealmaker and a tough boss. Those traits manifested during Trump's presidency as his disregard for the established government guidelines, quid pro quos, and extortion tactics became normalized.

The Oval Office was a pilgrimage destination for people within Trump's orbit who sought to monetize their proximity to the president by promoting foreign and corporate interests. One person who uniquely positioned himself was Rudy Giuliani. Despite not having an official position in the administration, as the private attorney to the president of the United States, he gained access to high-level government officials. On the other hand, he had a consulting business with clients all over the world. Combining those with his decades-long experience and connections at the Department of Justice, Giuliani placed himself in a sweet spot to run his parallel version of the State Department while also having the president's ear. As a consequence, he became the perfect target to foreign dictators and criminals who sought to escape American justice.

The election of Trump coincided with building challenges for authoritarian rulers in the world. In the middle of 2016, Turkish president Recep Tayyip Erdogan narrowly survived a coup attempt. He reacted by implementing massive purges in the public sector, silencing dissent, and subjugating all the branches of the government to his rule. In another corner of the world, Venezuelan strongman Nicolas

Maduro fought against the public demands for his recall by deploying the military onto protesters.

Meanwhile, Russian dictator Vladimir Putin had been under increasing Western pressure for his forced annexation of the Crimean Peninsula in Ukraine two years prior. All of them were strongly criticized by the West. The United States, with its stance as the upholder of the international rule of law, was the major irritant for the autocrats who sought to stay in power forever and pilfer their countries' wealth for their own enrichment. By late 2016, united by their shared enmity toward America, the leaders of Russia, Venezuela, Turkey, and Iran had started forging an unofficial autocratic alliance to alleviate the US economic and judicial pressure.

With the surprise election of Donald Trump, the autocrats saw an opening and seized the moment to deploy their envoys to find inroads into the Trump orbit. Eventually, those envoys found their way to Giuliani and his associates, Lev Parnas and Igor Fruman. Driven by avarice and vanity, while leveraging their VIP access, the three emerged as the central gatekeepers into the Trump administration. Whether they understood it or not, they had also become cogs in a larger global game that America's adversaries were playing.

Throughout Trump's presidency, Giuliani and his associates clandestinely advocated for the dismissal of criminal cases that the US Department of Justice had opened on Turkish, Venezuelan, and Ukrainian billionaires. The trio also plotted to provide a safe haven for the Venezuelan dictator in the United States, while the State Department condemned his brutal attacks on his countrymen. They also pressured Ukrainian officials on behalf of Trump, which, on the flip side could also benefit the Kremlin. All the while, Parnas and Fruman had their own energy-related interests on the side, which had more relevance to their actions than was publicly known at the time.

Free of restrictive government rules and regulations, Giuliani and his associates used persuasion, coercion, and disinformation to achieve their goals in a way used by autocrats. Over time, their schemes spilled into the government apparatus, eroding the rule of law, public trust in American institutions, and steering the United States onto a dangerous path away from democracy, but toward Trump-led autocracy modeled after the likes of Turkey, Venezuela, and Russia.

PART I
TURKEY

CHAPTER 1

HALKBANK

THE CURIOUS CASE OF REZA ZARRAB

THE ARREST

On March 19, 2016, FBI agents arrested[1] a Turkish Iranian businessman in Miami International Airport. His name was Reza Zarrab, and he arrived to Florida with his family to visit Disney World with over $100,000 in petty cash.[2] He certainly was not a regular tourist.

Two days later Preet Bharara, the lead prosecutor of the Southern District of New York (SDNY), unsealed an indictment that charged Zarrab and two other persons with laundering around $20 billions' worth of illicit Iranian oil proceeds.[3]

The SDNY identified Zarrab, in his early thirties, as the main operator of that money-laundering scheme. By the time of his arrest, Zarrab had already amassed enormous wealth, owning about twenty properties, seven sea vessels, seventeen luxury cars, a large collection of firearms, and art worth millions.[4]

Zarrab began his career early; in his twenties he became the co-owner of an investment company based in the United Arab Emirates (UAE).[5] Over the years Zarrab's money-laundering operation grew into a global empire. From his office in Trump Towers in Istanbul,[6] Zarrab's organization moved around massive funds to and from Iran.

THE MONEY-LAUNDERING SCHEME

In early 2012 Reuters reported that there was a suspicious spike of gold exports from Turkey to Iran.[7] In March of that year, Turkey had sent to its isolated neighbor $480 million worth of gold, thirty times more than what had been exported the previous year. By July 2012 the exports of gold increased to a staggering sum of $1.8 billion. Those spikes correlated directly with the timing of sanctions that the United States and the European Union imposed on Iran in an attempt to curb its nuclear weapons development program and force its government to the negotiating table.[8] In January 2012 the United States sanctioned Iran's central bank. In June that same year, the United States banned international banks from processing oil-related transactions with Iran.

After the Turkish media pointed out the soaring gold exports, the flow of the precious metal to Iran was rerouted through the United Arab Emirates.[9] A number of travelers flying from Turkey to Dubai carried suitcases with up to fifty kilos of gold bullion worth millions. Reportedly, in a swift hike from $7 million worth of gold imported from Turkey to the UAE in July 2012, the number increased to $1.9 billion in August.[10] Meanwhile, the exports of gold from Turkey directly to Iran decreased to $180 million. Much of that illicit gold trade was operated[11] by Reza Zarrab.[12] However, carrying gold bullion in suitcases wasn't feasible in the long term, so a more intricate solution was devised.

In a nutshell, Zarrab's money-laundering scheme[13] worked as follows.[14] Iranian oil was sold to Turkey. The proceeds were then held in an account at Halkbank, a Turkish bank partially owned by the government. Reza Zarrab bribed Turkish officials and the Halkbank management to facilitate transfers of the illicit Iranian money to his shell companies in Turkey, the United Arab Emirates, and Iran. While being transferred, the funds could be broken down into smaller batches, converted into gold, or exchanged from one currency to another to disguise the origins of the money. That operation was vast. According to the SDNY prosecutors:[15]

Zarrab claimed, that at one point, which he described as before the imposition of the American embargo, he was exporting a ton of gold a day . . . Even using a price of $300 per ounce of gold, an amount below the lowest price per ounce of gold in the past 15 years, Zarrab's daily export of one ton of gold a day would be valued at $9,600,000, or approximately $3.5 billion in gold exports per year.

Furthermore, according to Zarrab, $3.5 billion in exports was less than 40% of the value of his annual exports . . . Zarrab asserted that he is responsible for approximately 25 billion Turkish lira in exports, or more than $11 billion.

In 2013, noticing the large imports of gold to Iran, the United States imposed sanctions on Iranian gold trading in an attempt to close yet another loophole that allowed Iran to maintain its oil revenue stream.[16] In response Zarrab and his team pivoted to using overpriced food and medicine bills to back up the money transfers.[17] By the time the funds were ready to be used by Iran, they would have changed hands so many times that it would be almost impossible to track them back to their illegal origin.

When later explaining the complex structure of the laundering process to US prosecutors, Zarrab identified Halkbank as the key element of the scheme.[18] The bank was allowed to legally process Iranian transactions only related to items that were exempt from sanctions, namely, food, medicine, and medical equipment. If

Iran attempted to use the funds for other purposes, Halkbank was supposed to block the transaction. Instead, Halkbank officials gave a green light to Zarrab's laundering scheme in exchange for bribes, which went all the way to the top of the Turkish government.[19]

The SDNY indictment outlined that Reza Zarrab had bribed the general manager of Halkbank and gave millions of dollars to Turkish ministers—of economic affairs, of EU affairs, and of interior, the last of whom was responsible for domestic law enforcement.[20]

Reza Zarrab, who eventually pleaded guilty to running the money-laundering scheme,[21] also admitted that he had donated significant funds to a Turkish charity organization named Togem-Der that was founded by the First Lady of Turkey Emine Erdogan. According to a news article attached to the SDNY filings,[22]

> President Recep Tayyip Erdogan's spouse, Emine Erdogan, was the founder of the organization and their daughters, Sümeyye Erdogan and Esra Albayrak, are among the benefactors . . . It was alleged Zarrab bribed ministers—for citizenship for his family members and trade help from banks, among other things—and Erdogan's son, Bilal. . . .
>
> After attending the Togem-Der conference, Zarrab began providing financial assistance to the organization on a monthly basis, asserted his lawyer. "His financial contributions to Togem-Der alone totaled approximately $850,000 in 2013, approximately $1 million in 2014, and approximately $2.3 million to date in 2016."

Zarrab's further testimonies revealed that Turkish president Recep Tayyip Erdogan was also implicated in the scheme:[23]

> Mr. Zarrab testified that it was Zafer Caglayan, Turkey's economy minister at the time, who said Mr. Erdogan had directed the two banks, Ziraat Bank and VakifBank, to participate in the scheme. Mr. Caglayan "told me that Mr. Prime Minister had given approval for this work," Mr. Zarrab said through an interpreter, referring to the Iranian trade.

It was clear that the SDNY investigation into Zarrab was of such a magnitude, implicating not only the Turkish state bank and government ministers but also the country's president, that it would become a very important piece of US-Turkey relations.

THE TURKISH SCANDAL

Reza Zarrab's arrest in the United States was not the first time he had been charged with money laundering. In December 2013 he was among the fifty-two people arrested by the Turkish police in a sweeping raid[24] that led to a large corruption scandal.[25] It incriminated government ministers, multiple businessmen connected to its then prime minister Recep Tayyip Erdogan,[26] and a Halkbank executive.[27] The Turkish media circulated details of the investigation,[28] such as large sums of cash found in arrested people's homes, including millions of dollars[29] stashed in shoeboxes.[30]

After these initial arrests, Prime Minister Erdogan sought to deflect the accusations of government corruption and instead pushed a narrative that his party had become a victim of a judicial coup.[31] He also claimed that the investigations into Erdogan's allies were orchestrated by the followers of Fethullah Gülen,[32] a cleric who lived in exile in the United States and whom Erdogan portrayed as his archnemesis. Within days of the arrests, Erdogan moved to contain the scandal by replacing several ministers within his cabinet, including some who were directly implicated in the fast-moving scandal.[33] However, when the investigation approached Erdogan's family, the prime minister changed his tactics.

Multiple audiotapes of purported police wiretaps of Erdogan and his son dated from December 17, 2013, were released on social media.[34] On those tapes a man who was believed to have been Erdogan told his son to get rid of the money at the house. Around that time the Turkish media reported[35] that both Erdogan's sons were involved in the corruption scheme and were targets of an upcoming second wave of arrests.[36]

That second wave never happened as, layer by layer, the judicial officials leading the investigation were removed from their positions. The day after the first raid, the deputy chief of the financial crimes unit was fired.[37] Almost a week later, seventy police officers were fired or reassigned, along with the chief of the Istanbul police force.[38] On December 26, 2013, the head prosecutor leading the corruption investigation was removed.[39] Around that time the Turkish government introduced new regulation that required prosecutors to inform the country's chief prosecutor about their investigations of corruption and armed organizations.[40] That change, in effect, was designed to undermine any investigations into high-level cabinet officials and removed a mechanism to hold them accountable.[41] Then in early January 2014, Prime Minister Erdogan issued a decree that removed 350 police officers in Ankara from their positions, including the chiefs of the units that investigated financial crimes, smuggling, and organized crime, effectively paralyzing the corruption investigation as a whole.[42]

Shortly thereafter, the arrested persons, including Reza Zarrab,[43] were released from Turkish prison.[44] By May 2014 the corruption case against Zarrab and others in Turkey had been dismissed.[45] However, in a couple of years, the investigation of the Turkish-Iranian money laundering scheme resurfaced in the United States and gained international coverage. *The Atlantic* called it "The Biggest Sanctions-Evasion Scheme in Recent History."[46]

If the SDNY criminal case continued on, Erdogan, at a minimum, risked losing face. In a worse scenario, he and his family members could lose their money, power, and freedom. To bury that investigation, the Turkish president deployed all the imaginable tools in his toolbox, launching a multilayered influence campaign that included US lobbying firms, covert intermediaries, and Turkish cultural groups in Washington, DC.

CHAPTER 2

TURKISH LOBBYING IN THE UNITED STATES

ERDOGAN'S PLIGHT

The year 2013 was tumultuous for Turkey and its prime minister, Recep Tayyip Erdogan. His government withstood two waves of massive protests, during which the demonstrators accused Erdogan and his administration of corruption. The first wave started in May 2013, when a small group of environmental activists gathered[1] in Gezi Park in central Istanbul to protest against its demolition and replacement with commercial real estate.[2] When the authorities responded with disproportionate police aggression, more people joined the activists, driving what initially was a small protest into a monthslong nationwide movement against the government's oppression of its people.[3]

A few months later, in December 2013, a wide-ranging government corruption scandal erupted, implicating businessmen close to Erdogan's orbit, his cabinet officials, his sons, and Erdogan himself. While he responded by ousting the prosecutors investigating the case, the Turkish people took their outrage to the streets, demanding Prime Minister Erdogan's resignation.[4] Similar to what he did during the Gezi Park protests, he reacted by, once again, using brutal force against the demonstrators.[5]

Despite the mass protests and accusations of corruption, Recep Tayyip Erdogan elevated his position from prime minister to president after winning the 2014 election in Turkey.[6] By that time his image had been tarnished by his government's aggressive crackdown on demonstrators, the corruption scandal, the subsequent purge of the police force, and the dismissal of the corruption case. His actions were more characteristic of a corrupt dictator than the leader of a democratic country.

In 2016 Erdogan's reputation was damaged further. After the spring arrest of money launderer Reza Zarrab in the United States, the question of Turkish government corruption was brought back to the front pages, this time in Western media. Then in July 2016, a faction within the Turkish military unsuccessfully attempted to force out Erdogan from power.[7] After surviving that coup attempt, Erdogan pushed back[8] by declaring a state of emergency[9] and squashing any attempt of dissent.[10] His government started silencing journalists who criticized him,[11] dismissed civil servants and educators en masse,[12] and jailed his political opposition.[13] In the following years, he would also restructure his country's judicial branch,[14] amend the constitution, and expand his presidential powers.[15]

All those actions created tension between Turkey and its Western allies. Foreign criticism, in turn, threatened to affect Erdogan's popularity and power at home. To improve his government's image, his administration started spending millions of dollars on foreign lobbying firms, with much of that effort focused in the United States, where prosecutors were advancing their investigation into the Turkish-Iranian money-laundering scheme.

US LOBBYING FIRMS

As Erdogan's political troubles in Turkey accumulated, he pointed fingers at his opposition. He singled out Fethullah Gülen, a Turkish cleric living in exile in the United States since 1999, as his archnemesis. Gülen still had a large following in Turkey, and Erdogan had accused him of being behind both the 2013 corruption investigations and the 2016 coup attempt. For those reasons, the Turkish government made its mission to persuade the United States to extradite Gülen back to Turkey. After the arrest of Reza Zarrab in America, Erdogan's administration added the gold trader's release to its requests to the US government.

The official way a foreign government can telegraph their wishes to the United States, in addition to diplomatic channels, is through lobbying firms, which, in turn, are required to report to the Department of Justice a description of services rendered to foreign interests and the payments received.[16] Those reports are regulated by the Foreign Agents Registration Act (FARA) and are mandatory for all lobbyists representing foreign interests, with the exception of diplomatic, humanitarian, or cultural activities and legal representation within boundaries of judicial proceedings.

FARA originated in 1938,[17] when, on the cusp of the Second World War, US Congress passed a piece of legislation that sought to defang subversive activities by Nazi Germany and socialist Russia. Its purpose has been to bring transparency to foreign lobbying while protecting the United States from malign foreign influence that aims to undermine the integrity of American institutions, national security, and the rule of law. While FARA regulations were revised at the end of the Cold War, by the mid-2010s they had become largely outdated and rarely enforced. Around that time the Turkish government began to hire several lobbying firms in the United States to restore its image[18] and persuade the American government to send Gülen and Zarrab back to Turkey.

Up until 2014 the Turkish government had worked primarily with one lobbying firm, called the Gephardt Group.[19] However, as a result of the events of 2013, the Turkish government started expanding its pool of lobbyists. In 2014 the Gephardt Group hired several subcontractors including the law firm Greenberg Traurig,[20] which was supposed to "gather information about legislative activities and oversight hearings in the House and Senate" and "develop and utilize contacts at the State and Defense Departments, and the National Security Council." In 2015 the Turkish government signed an additional lobbying contract with Amsterdam & Partners,[21] which, with its own team and more subcontractors,[22] pushed to discredit Fethullah Gülen's image in the United States and lobbied for his extradition.[23]

The arrest of Reza Zarrab in the United States in March 2016 created additional pressure on Recep Tayyip Erdogan and was another reason to expand his influence in the United States. The Turkish president personally pushed the Obama administration to release the gold trader. Those efforts proved futile.

As Donald Trump came into office in January 2017, the Turkish government sought to gain access to insiders close to the new president. One opportunity appeared with an introduction of the Turkish foreign minister to Brian Ballard, the head of a lobbying firm called Ballard Partners. At the time, Ballard was the chairman of the Trump Victory campaign in Florida[24] and had known Donald Trump for thirty years[25] and had lobbied for the Trump Organization since 2013.[26] As a whole Ballard was highly involved in conservative politics and fundraising, and in April 2017, he became a regional vice-chairman for the Republican National Committee.[27] In 2017 Ballard Partners signed lobbying contracts with the Turkish government[28] and Halkbank,[29] which together were worth around $5 million over the course of two years.[30]

In 2017, with Donald Trump entering office, the Gephardt Group bowed out of its lobbying contract for Turkey, and its former subcontractor, Greenberg Traurig, took over the services that included[31]

a. *Proposing and pursuing passage of legislation and other U.S. government action that promotes Turkey's interests and provides a positive image of Turks, Turkey, and the United States-Turkey relationship;*

b. *Preserving and enlarging the Congressional Caucus on Turkey and Turkish Americans;*

c. *Educating Members of Congress and the Administration on issues of importance to Turkey;*

d. *Promptly notifying Turkey of any action in Congress or the Executive Branch on issues of importance to Turkey;*

> e. Preparing brief analyses of developments in Congress and the Executive Branch on particular issues of concern to Turkey;
>
> f. Identifying official gatherings and social events to which Embassy personnel ought attend, including to the extent possible, obtaining the necessary invitations;
>
> g. Identifying and/or arranging speaking engagements locally and nationally for Embassy personnel or their appointed or suggested proxies in settings that will improve Turkey's image and advance its causes on Capitol Hill. Such would be, if so directed by Turkey, coordinated with Turkey's existing public relations service provider[s]; and
>
> h. Maintaining and forging alliances with other interest groups whose goals are similar to or shared by Turkey.

At the time, Greenberg Traurig had a clear advantage over the Gephardt Group. Rudy Giuliani, the former mayor of New York and a longtime friend of Donald Trump,[32] was serving as a senior advisor to Greenberg Traurig's executive chairman.[33] Giuliani was perfectly placed to potentially have easy access to the newly elected president and help Greenberg Traurig fulfill its contractual obligations with Turkey.

In February 2017, one month after Trump's presidential inauguration, while working at Greenberg Traurig, Rudy Giuliani, along with former US attorney general Michael Mukasey, joined Reza Zarrab's defense team.[34] Later that month Giuliani and Mukasey traveled to Turkey[35] to meet with the Turkish president to discuss Zarrab's case and to try to find a "diplomatic" solution to resolve it.[36] That trip raised a lot of brows and sent ripples through the US justice system. Judge Richard Berman, who oversaw the Halkbank case and whom Erdogan wanted removed,[37] commented on that trip in a 2018 interview:[38]

> *I knew the old Rudy . . . There seems to be somewhat of a disconnect between the old Rudy and the new Rudy . . . I am still stunned by the fact that Rudy was hired to be—and he very actively pursued being—the 'go-between' between President Trump and Turkey's President Erdogan in an unprecedented effort to terminate this federal criminal case.*

Judge Berman's concerns stemmed from Rudy Giuliani's failure to register as a foreign agent, as required by FARA. Although Greenberg Traurig had reported the contract with the Turkish government to the DOJ, all the individual lawyers who advocated for Turkish government's interests in the US needed to register their activities as well.

Giuliani's effort to mediate a diplomatic solution for Zarrab's case between

Erdogan and Trump administrations seemed to prove fruitless[39] when Zarrab, facing over a hundred years in prison,[40] pleaded guilty and agreed to cooperate with the investigation.[41] On November 21, 2017, as Zarrab was released from prison[42] to provide[43] state's evidence,[44] the Turkish government signed an agreement with King & Spalding,[45] a law firm from Atlanta, Georgia, to lobby the Department of Justice on Reza Zarrab's case.[46] The choice of King & Spalding did not seem accidental as its former partner Christopher Wray had recently become the director of the FBI.[47]

A week later Reza Zarrab appeared in court to testify against another Halkbank case defendant, Mehmet Hakan Atilla, and described in detail the bribes he paid to Turkish officials and the Halkbank executives.[48] Most importantly, Zarrab implicated President Erdogan in his money-laundering scheme.[49] After those revelations, Erdogan's government ramped up its spending on American lobbying firms, reaching around $10 million in 2018.[50] However, those lobbying firms were only one part of the multifaceted Turkish influence campaign in the United States.

CHAPTER 3

BUILDING ACCESS TO DC GATEKEEPERS

MICHAEL FLYNN AND OPERATION CONFIDENCE

In mid-July 2016, as the coup against Erdogan was unraveling in Turkey, Michael Flynn, a retired three-star general, gave a speech to a conservative group in Cleveland, Ohio.[1] In his address, he displayed support for the military coup plotters, accusing Erdogan's government of becoming increasingly Islamic based and arguing that the coup would drive Turkey toward a more pro-Western democratic model.

Two months later, on September 19, 2016, in an apparent change of heart, Flynn met in New York with Turkish officials who sought to keep Erdogan in power.[2] Those Turkish officials were Mevlut Cavusoglu, the country's foreign minister, and Berat Albayrak, the Turkish energy minister who also happened to be Erdogan's son-in-law. They were accompanied with a Turkish Dutch businessman, Ekim Alptekin.

Flynn brought to the meeting associates[3] from his consulting firm:[4] Bijan Kian, also known as Bijan Rafiekian, and James Woolsey, a former CIA director.[5] The Turks chose their contacts well. At the time, Flynn and Woolsey were advisors[6] to Donald Trump's campaign,[7] and Kian would later join the Trump transition team.[8]

The subject of the meeting was how to get Fethullah Gülen renditioned to Turkey,[9] or, as Woolsey would later describe it, "a covert step in the dead of night to whisk this guy away."[10] Since the attempt to topple Erdogan, the Turkish government had been heavily pressuring the United States to send Gülen back to Turkey and was getting impatient with the US Department of Justice,[11] which required a thorough investigation to determine whether the cleric's alleged misdeeds qualified him for extradition.[12]

Doubting the legality of an extrajudicial endeavor, Woolsey and his lobbyist wife, Nancye Miller, had a separate meeting the following day with Ekim Alptekin and another Turkish businessman, Sezgin Baran Korkmaz,[13] who both had connections to President Erdogan and acted[14] as unofficial Turkish intermediaries in the United States.[15] At that meeting Woolsey and Miller presented a less controversial solution, a $10 million lobbying contract to run a campaign in the United States against Fethullah Gülen.[16] The two claimed that they were equipped better than Flynn to persuade DC decision-makers to extradite Gülen. However, it was not their first proposal. Apparently, Miller and Woolsey had reached out to Korkmaz a month prior about the same subject and offered[17]

> *getting Washington insiders like then-Senator Jeff Sessions . . . to co-author articles on the situation in Turkey, engaging with influential lawmakers such as Republican Senator Bob Corker, and getting Woolsey on Fox News and CNN.*

Later Woolsey would claim that he had informed then vice president Joe Biden of the topic of the conversation.[18] However, he would seemingly omit the fact that he and his wife had twice pitched Turkish intermediaries to run what would be in effect a smear campaign on Gülen in exchange for millions of dollars.[19]

Ekim Alptekin chose to engage Michael Flynn and Bijan Kian for a significantly less sum. Through his Dutch firm, Inovo BV,[20] Alptekin hired the Flynn Intel Group for $600,000[21] to tarnish Gülen's reputation in the United States and then use it as an argument for his extradition.[22] The group dubbed their plot Project Truth,[23] but they later renamed it to Operation Confidence.[24]

On US Election Day, November 8, 2016, Michael Flynn, with editing assistance from Alptekin,[25] published an opinion piece demonizing Fethullah Gülen.[26] Contrary to the DOJ's[27] conclusions,[28] the op-ed characterized Gülen as a radical Islamic leader in the lens of Osama bin Laden and argued that Gülen's extradition would be within US national security interests.

Flynn and Kian's work for Alptekin was not just limited to an op-ed. After the September 2016 meeting, Kian visited[29]

> *a member of Congress and a congressional staffer in an attempt, among other things, to prompt congressional hearings on Gülen.*

In late December 2016, after Donald Trump's surprise victory in the presidential election, Michael Flynn, met again with Turkish government representatives in New York to, once again, discuss the extradition of Fethullah Gülen to Turkey.[30] Reportedly during that meeting,[31]

> *Flynn was offered upwards of $15 million, to be paid directly or indirectly, if he could complete the deal.*

Flynn, the future national security advisor, who was supposed to hold US principles and foreign policy interests as his highest priority, failed to report that highly inappropriate offer from representatives of a foreign country.[32] It would become public only months later,[33] after Flynn came under fire for lying to the FBI and resigned from his short-lived tenure at the Trump cabinet.

Flynn and Woolsey were among the highest people in the Trump orbit who were covertly cultivated by Turkish intermediaries and who were willing to monetize their closeness to Trump. However, they were not the only ones eager to serve as gatekeepers to DC and operate behind the veil of the official diplomatic arena to further Erdogan's goals.

LEV PARNAS AND THE BLACK SEA TYCOONS

A GATHERING IN KYIV

On a chilly evening in December 2016, a group of wealthy men gathered in an Asian-themed bar in Kyiv. Buddha Bar, as it was called, was owned by Igor Fruman,[34] a Ukrainian American businessman who once had been considered one of the richest people in Ukraine[35] and was believed to have connections to organized crime.[36] Fruman had special guests that night. One of them was Lev Parnas, whom Fruman had brought from the United States.[37]

A Brighton Beach native with Ukrainian roots,[38] Parnas was part of the New York criminal underworld in his late teens.[39] After the collapse of the Soviet Union, he traveled to Russia, Uzbekistan, and Ukraine, delivering goods and large amounts of cash.[40] Later in life he established dubious businesses[41] and accumulated large debts.[42] However, in 2016 Parnas appeared to have a turn of luck. A newly minted Republican donor,[43] Lev boasted about socializing at fundraising[44] events[45] with people connected to Donald Trump and later attending[46] the president-elect's invite-only[47] victory party[48] at the Hilton Hotel in Manhattan.

Another important guest at Buddha Bar that night was Mubariz Mansimov, also known as Mubariz Curbanoglu, an Azerbaijani-born Turkish shipping tycoon. Before becoming a Turkish citizen, Mansimov had reportedly been "an officer in the Soviet secret service" in his youth.[49] In Turkey Mansimov became close to Erdogan, so much so that he allegedly gifted the Turkish president a $25 million ship.[50] Mansimov also shared[51] Erdogan's support[52] for the Grey Wolves,[53] a Turkish ultraright movement[54] which had connections to organized[55] crime[56] and was under consideration to be designated by the European Union as a terrorist group.[57]

There was one more common thing Mansimov and the Turkish president shared. Like Erdogan, Mansimov reportedly was implicated in Reza Zarrab's scheme:[58]

The largest corruption investigations in Turkey's history, made public in December 2013, implicated Mansimov as well. His name surfaced when police raided the home of Barış Güler, the son of then-Interior Minister Muammer Güler and an associate of

> Reza Zarrab, an Iranian gold trader who often bribed the Turkish minister to promote and safeguard his illegal activities. Mansimov was already under investigation by the financial crimes department of the İstanbul Police Department, which conducted the investigation into Zarrab and his associates. The police, in their search of the home of Güler's son, found seven safes, a banknote counter and a ledger with names. One safe alone contained nearly $1.5 million as well as some euros and Turkish lira.
>
> In the ledger, Barış listed all the bribes he had taken not only from Zarrab but from other businesspeople. Mansimov's name was also in these notes. According to the testimony of Police Chief Yakub Saygılı, who coordinated the investigations, Barış was paid for his work to secure citizenship papers on behalf of Mansimov, and the ledger listed Mansimov as paying $20,000 for a single job.

The meeting in Kyiv wasn't accidental. Apparently, Mansimov was interested in using Lev Parnas's connections in the Trump world, specifically to the lobbyist Brian Ballard.[59]

THE WATERGATE HOTEL MEETING

In January 2017 Mubariz Mansimov and Lev Parnas met again, this time in Washington, DC. The day before Trump's inauguration, the two arranged a meeting at the Watergate Hotel for Turkish foreign minister Mevlut Cavusoglu and Brian Ballard. Parnas would later describe it as follows:[60]

> There were a lot of bodyguards, Turkish bodyguards . . . It was in a little restaurant. We went in. [Çavuşoğlu] was sitting in the restaurant with a couple of other Turkish dignitaries. . . .
>
> Mübariz introduced Brian Ballard as Trump's number one guy.

It appears that during the meeting the group discussed the Halkbank investigation as, a couple of days later, Mansimov would send a text message to Parnas with the name of the key Halkbank defendant in American custody, Reza Zarrab.[61]

After the meeting Parnas gave Mansimov tickets for Donald Trump's inaugural VIP ball,[62] which he ostensibly obtained from Brian Ballard.[63] Mansimov reciprocated by sending his private jet to Florida to pick up Parnas's sons and bring them to Ritz-Carlton Hotel located only blocks away from the White House.[64]

Whether or not Lev Parnas realized it at the time, Mansimov was a "cutout," an espionage term for a covert intermediary, who sought to clandestinely gain access to the incoming Trump administration and worked outside of official channels to advance the Turkish president's goals in the United States.

RNC DONORS' RETREAT

After the inauguration Mubariz Mansimov introduced Lev Parnas to another oligarch, Farkhad Akhmedov, who would replace Mansimov as an unofficial Turkish intermediary. Like Mansimov, Akhmedov was of Azerbaijani origin. He also was a former member of the Russian parliament[65] and had deep ties to both the Kremlin and to Turkey. According to an article from the Organized Crime and Corruption Reporting Project (OCCRP), an international network of investigative anticorruption journalists,[66]

> *Akhmedov has publicly claimed to have helped resolve international disputes between Turkey and Russia at least twice. In a 2016 interview with Russian state media outlet Sputnik, Turkish Foreign Minister Çavuşoğlu described Akhmedov as a valuable diplomatic go-between "who has worked closely with Putin and knows Putin well."*

It appears that Parnas and Akhmedov hit it off. Parnas spent several days on Akhmedov's 377-foot yacht[67] and accompanied him on a trip to Las Vegas,[68] where they met with a representative of an Armenian American criminal who had ties to the Turkish government.[69] Notably, in March 2017 Akhmedov went with Parnas to an RNC donors' retreat in Palm Beach, Florida.

Their access to the event was secured by Parnas's prior donation of $33,400 to the Republican National Committee (RNC)[70] At the event, Parnas and Akhmedov rubbed elbows with Republican dignitaries, highly influential donors, and RNC[71] officials[72] However, Akhmedov's presence there should have raised a big red flag for the organization. He was a foreign national who could not legally make political contributions in the United States. Moreover, he was a Russian oligarch, with ties to the Kremlin, being ushered into a prominent Republican event at the time when the US intelligence community was ringing the alarm on Russian influence operations during the 2016 election.

Instead, the RNC became a launch pad for Akhmedov to promote influence of various countries in the United States.

AKHMEDOV MEETS BRIAN BALLARD

After the RNC event, Lev Parnas and Farkhad Akhmedov flew on the oligarch's private jet to Washington, DC, to meet with Brian Ballard[73] Based on the messages between Parnas and Ballard, that were published by the OCCRP, the group discussed lobbying services for Turkey and Azerbaijan[74] Shortly thereafter Ballard Partners signed contracts with both[75] countries[76] Thus, Parnas and Akhmedov were the ones who brought Ballard Partners the Turkish lobbying contract that was mentioned in chapter 2. Parnas would later receive $45,000 from Ballard Partners for the introduction[77]

In August 2017 Ballard Partners added another Turkish client, Halkbank, with which Ballard Partners agreed to[78]

> *consult with the Client and advocate on its behalf those issues the Client deems necessary and appropriate before the U.S. Federal government, including but not limited to, representation before the Departments of Treasury, State, and Justice, and the Executive Office of the President. It shall further be the Firm's duty to inform Client of the developments in legislation and policy relevant to the Client's operations.*

To decipher Ballard Partners' scope of services, one needs to remember the predicament that Halkbank was in at the time. The Southern District of New York had previously charged Reza Zarrab and Halkbank officials with laundering money for Iran in violation of US sanctions. The sanctions component fell under the jurisdiction of the Department of the Treasury. The SDNY component fell under the jurisdiction of the Department of Justice. The fact that the case implicated a bank based in Turkey, a NATO ally, created potential national security ramifications and therefore fell under the jurisdiction of the State Department. The case was of such an importance that Erdogan's government believed that its resolution might require the involvement of the president of the United States, hence the mention of the executive office in Ballard Partners' contract.

All those clues indicated that the main goal of that contract was the release of Reza Zarrab and the dissolution of the Halkbank investigation at the Southern District of New York.

Ballard Partners' contract with Halkbank, despite being vague in scope, was still registered with the DOJ and thus was on their radar. However, there were actors of the Turkish government who sought to hide their operations from US authorities. For those purposes, they used other types of influence channels.

TIMELINE OF EVENTS RELATED TO LEV PARNAS AND TURKISH INTERMEDIARIES*

* See the full integrated timeline in appendix A.

October 12, 2016 - Lev Parnas went to a Trump fundraiser event in Florida. There, Lev Parnas crossed paths with Rudy Giuliani. The event was also attended by Brian Ballard.

October 24–27, 2016 - Lev Parnas made political contributions to twenty state Republican committees and a $33,400 donation to the Republican National Committee.

November 8, 2016 (US Election Day) - Lev Parnas was at Donald Trump's victory party at the Hilton Hotel in New York.

December 5, 2016 - Lev Parnas met Mubariz Mansimov in a nightclub in Kyiv, Ukraine. Mansimov reportedly asked Parnas to introduce him to Ballard Partners.

January 19, 2017 - Brian Ballard met with the Turkish foreign minister Mevlut Cavusoglu to discuss lobbying services for the Turkish government. The meeting was arranged by Lev Parnas and Mubariz Mansimov.

January 20, 2017 - Donald Trump entered office as the forty-fifth president of the United States. There were several inauguration parties. One of them, the Candlelight Dinner, was attended by Lev Parnas and Mubariz Mansimov.

Late January 2017 - Mubariz Mansimov introduced Lev Parnas to Farkhad Akhmedov, a Russian Azerbaijani oligarch with deep ties to the Russian government.

Early February 2017 - Lev Parnas accompanied Farkhad Akhmedov to Las Vegas, where they met with a representative of an Armenian American criminal who had ties to Mubariz Mansimov and to the Turkish government.

March 3–5 2017 - Lev Parnas and Farkhad Akhmedov attended the Republican National Committee donors' retreat in Palm Beach, Florida.

March 8, 2017 - Lev Parnas introduced Farkhad Akhmedov to Brian Ballard of Ballard Partners. They met in Washington, DC, to discuss a lobbying contract for Turkey.

May 11, 2017 - Ballard Partners signed a lobbying contract with Turkey ($125K/month). Lev Parnas was paid $45K for introducing Ballard Partners to the Turkish government.

August 21, 2017 - Ballard Partners signed a lobbying contract with Halkbank.

CHAPTER 4

HERITAGE, DONATIONS AND US POLITICS

THE TURKISH HERITAGE ORGANIZATION

Turkish intermediaries utilized a variety of tactics to expand their connections among influential Americans. One of the most efficient was through cultural and trade groups. Cultural groups were especially attractive as there was no hint of a mercantile or political interest but instead an appearance of a noble pursuit of the preservation and promotion of Turkish culture.

Several of those groups were established[1] by Ekim Alptekin,[2] one of the key figures in Turkish influencing in the United States, who recruited Michael Flynn. To the wider public, he was a Turkish Dutch businessman with a vast business empire that spanned across a number of countries.[3] He had aerospace, real estate, arms sales, energy, and consulting businesses in Turkey, the Netherlands, and the Middle East. Between 2015 and 2017, Ekim Alptekin served as the chairman of the Turkish-American Business Council (TAIK), which promoted bilateral trade and investments between the United States and Turkey.[4]

Around 2015 Alptekin moved to scale up the use of cultural organizations[5] and established another one called the Turkish Heritage Organization (THO) in Washington, DC.[6] On its website the organization described its purpose as "discussion and dialogue around Turkey's role in the international community and issues of importance in the US-Turkey bilateral relationship."[7] In plain English that meant the Turkish Heritage Organization, despite its misleading name, peddled the issues that were important for Erdogan and his government.

The founders of the Turkish Heritage Organization chose a fellow Turk, Halil Danismaz, to lead it. Before joining the organization, Danismaz was an executive at Turkish Airlines and acted as an informal personal attaché for Erdogan's son-in-law Berat Albayrak.[8] In 2016 Albayrak's emails were hacked and leaked by WikiLeaks.[9] Those emails revealed extensive communication between Albayrak and Danismaz. In his emails[10] Danismaz updated Albayrak on the progress of the

Turkish government's agenda in the United States, provided intelligence on Gülen's supporters, and discussed Albayrak's personal dealings in the States.[11]

Danismaz also offered ideas on how the Turkish government could use influence operations on US politicians. In around June 2012, he had emailed Albayrak a couple of presentations proposing that the Turkish government pay influencers to be camouflaged as journalists and get access to US government officials, thereby bypassing American FARA registration requirements and concealing the true nature of their influence operations.[12] Danismaz also suggested that those "journalists" could write pro-Turkey op-eds for the American public, and those editorials would cost less than hiring lobbying firms. Danismaz himself occasionally[13] wrote[14] op-eds that promoted views of Erdogan's government or criticized its opponents. According to the leaked emails, the talking points of those op-eds were defined by Berat Albayrak.[15]

Further, Albayrak instructed Danismaz to donate "up to $30,000"[16] to various political candidates in exchange for them releasing anti-Gülen statements. In other words, Albayrak, a Turkish official and Erdogan's son-in-law, directed Danismaz, the head of a Turkish cultural group, to corrupt US political candidates, offering them an illicit trade.

The Federal Election Commission (FEC) has records of Danismaz contributing in 2015 a total of $25,000 to various political action committees (PACs)[17] that were connected to the Turkish Coalition of America (TC-America), another Turkish cultural organization.[18] Those Turkish Coalition PACs collectively were able to donate over $510,000 to US political candidates.[19] Almost $300,000 were contributed to members of the House of Representatives,[20] including members of the bipartisan congressional Turkey Caucus,[21] which focused "on US-Turkey relations and issues that concern Turkish Americans" and worked closely with TC-America.[22]

Essentially, Danismaz's donations were bundled into a pro-Turkish PAC that was then used as a shell to make contributions to US candidates. Nevertheless, it appears that Danismaz followed Albayrak's instruction, thereby making straw donations,[23] or political contributions on the behalf or request of others, which is illegal in the United States. If the candidates were elected and they knew the purpose of those donations, they might feel the need to push for Turkish government interests.

One example of such influence was an effort to halt a resolution proposed in Congress that described Turkey's role in committing genocide against Armenians at the beginning of the twentieth century. That topic has been a continuous source of friction between the American and Turkish governments for decades, and the Turkish government had continuously opposed the resolution as hard as it could, deploying lobbyists and unofficial intermediaries to coax lawmakers. One of Albayrak's leaked emails that also included Erdogan's son, the members of the Turkish Heritage Organization, and an American lobbyist[24] who represented Turkey[25] demonstrated a coordinated effort to stop the resolution. The Turkish government was successful for years until the resolution was finally passed by Congress[26] at the end of 2019.[27]

In 2016, when the US government investigated Ekim Alptekin's clandestine efforts to peddle Turkish interests in Washington, DC, the Turkish Heritage Organization, which he founded, also came under a well-deserved scrutiny. Under the leadership of Danismaz, the organization, cloaked as a cultural charity, was deeply involved in advancing Turkish government interests in the United States without a FARA registration.

After being questioned by the FBI, Halil Danismaz left the group and fled to Turkey. So did Ekim Alptekin. In 2018 the latter was charged in absentia with a failure to register as a foreign agent while covertly promoting the Turkish government agenda in the United States.[28]

MURAT GÜZEL AND IMAAD ZUBERI

The Turkish Heritage Organization and its members were not the only ones peddling Turkish influence in the United States. The FBI also questioned a Turkish American businessman named Murat Güzel.[29] Güzel was the CEO of the Natural Food Group from Pennsylvania. He was an active member of the Turkish diaspora, attending events[30] organized by the Turkish Coalition of America,[31] and had been called by a diaspora magazine one of the most influential Turkish Americans.[32]

Indeed, he was. According to documents released by WikiLeaks, Güzel coordinated Turkish influence activities with Halil Danismaz and Berat Albayrak.[33] For example, Güzel exchanged emails with the two in early June 2013 about creating an alternative narrative about the Gezi Park protests that had erupted in Turkey a month prior. The strategy included writing opinion pieces in the US media outlets like *New York Times* and allegedly soliciting a former US congressman to write a pro-Turkey op-ed.[34]

Güzel was a board member of MUSIAD (Independent Industrialists and Businessmen Association, headquartered in Turkey)[35] and the treasurer of TASC[36] (Turkish American National Steering Committee, cochaired by Erdogan's cousin[37]). Both organizations were among the many Turkish cultural groups[38] that acted as Turkish government influence channels in the United States and conveyed a pro-Erdogan agenda.[39] For example, in 2018 Güzel, as a part of MUSIAD and TASC efforts, organized a press conference in Washington, DC, objecting US support to Syrian Kurds[40] and regurgitating Erdogan's claims that they were affiliated to the PKK Kurdish terrorist group.[41]

In 2020 TASC staged a campaign in the United States driving vans with TV screens and flying planes with banners commemorating the defeat of 2016 coup plotters and celebrating the "July 15, Victory of Turkish Democracy." The campaigns ran in New York, Washington, DC, and Saylorsburg, Pennsylvania, where Fethullah Gülen resided.[42]

Güzel was perfectly placed to advocate for Turkish government interests. He was a member of the Democratic National Committee[43] and had previously made hefty political contributions to Democratic candidates. The FEC website had over seven hundred donations made by Güzel from 2007 to 2021, with the total of $1.48 million worth of political contributions.[44] The largest share, $1.3 million, was donated between 2014 and 2018. Like Halil Danismaz, Güzel also made contributions to the Turkish Coalition USA PAC.[45]

In 2019 Murat Güzel was questioned by the FBI[46] but reportedly was granted immunity from US prosecution[47] in exchange for his testimony against another prolific political donor and a "mercenary fundraiser" named Imaad Zuberi.[48] At the time, Zuberi was under investigation for allegedly making a large amount[49] of straw donations[50] with money provided by his clients, including foreign ones, to establish connections to prominent US officials. In 2019 he confessed to the *New York Times*:[51]

> *To open doors, I have to donate.*

Prosecutors connected the two when they discovered that Güzel received a $50,000 check from Zuberi[52] and used his address for a 2015 donation to National Republican Congressional Committee.[53]

On his part, Zuberi used his DC connections to assist Turkish interests. In 2015 he had helped the Turkish ambassador to the United States bury a congressional resolution that opposed the erosion of human rights in Turkey.[54] That resolution could have potentially damaged Erdogan's party chances during the upcoming parliamentary elections.[55]

To solve the resolution issue, Zuberi offered the Turkish ambassador a chance to meet with the chairmen of the Foreign Affairs Committee outside official settings:[56]

> *Why don't you come to Los Angeles as my guest and I can have you meet both over dinner in private? . . . Let me know who else in the Foreign Affairs Committee you need help with? I know most of them on both sides.*

Indeed, Zuberi had cultivated his connections and made political[57] contributions[58] to the chairmen of the committee. He also donated to Senator Lindsey Graham (R-SC),[59] who was a member of the Senate Foreign Relations Committee, as well as a member of the Turkey Caucus.

Reportedly, Zuberi worked hard to halt the resolution, and one week before the Turkish election, he emailed a Turkish official:[60]

> *[Two Members of Congress] told me this will be delayed by a week 99% because they control the Foreign Affairs Committee. You . . . push me so hard I pushed . . . harder*

> than I have ever pushed them for anything ... Both asked me why I am pushing this hard for Turkey.

One of the reasons behind Zuberi's zeal was that he had been promised a free piece of land in Turkey for potential real estate projects.[61] It was not publicly known whether that promise was ever fulfilled, but Zuberi wouldn't have much opportunity to use it. In 2019 he would be charged with a FARA violation,[62] among other things, and would later be sentenced to twelve years in prison.[63] In contrast, Zuberi's pal Murat Güzel would remain free and continue appearing in the news about Turkish influence in the United States.[64]

RABIA KAZAN

WEALTHY TURKS AND TRUMP CAMPAIGN SURROGATES

Another apparent channel of influence was a Turkish national living in the United States named Rabia Kazan. Born to a conservative family,[65] a younger Kazan adhered to right-leaning views. She worked as a journalist at a Turkish right-wing newspaper[66] and allegedly was engaged to a member of the Grey Wolves ultranationalist movement,[67] Mehmet Ali Ağca, who had attempted to assassinate Pope John Paul II in 1981.[68]

As a former journalist, Kazan seemed to fit the profile of a clandestine Turkish intermediary that Halil Danismaz had recommended in a private email to Berat Albayrak.[69] Danismaz's idea was to "use front groups and operatives 'camouflaged' as journalists to gain access to Capitol Hill and the US security apparatus."[70] She did that within two years, rising from an unknown figure to a frequent visitor at the Trump International Hotel in Washington, DC, Congress, Mar-a-Lago, and the White House. Her ascent seemed to be part of a carefully crafted character whose purpose was to infiltrate pro-Trump MAGA (Make America Great Again) circles.

In April 2016 Rabia Kazan joined the advisory board[71] of the National Diversity Coalition (NDC),[72] a group founded by Michael Cohen, Trump's private attorney, to attract minority votes to the GOP frontrunner during the 2016 election.[73] The access to the NDC opened the doors for Kazan and catapulted her into the MAGA world. Her Instagram feed was filled with pictures of her with high-level Trump supporters.[74] Over time the people appearing in her Instagram posts grew more[75] prominent[76] in political influence and included congressmen, Trump's campaign team, his cabinet members, and his children.

Some of Kazan's newly obtained connections would later appear in Donald Trump's impeachment trials. Kazan herself would be tangentially connected to the first impeachment in connection to Ukraine through Robert Hyde, a Republican congressional candidate from Connecticut.[77] Kazan claimed that she had briefly dated Hyde,[78] around the time he was involved[79] in Giuliani and Parnas's illicit activities in Ukraine, which will be discussed in later chapters.

In June 2017 Rabia Kazan's associates from the NDC established the Urban Revitalization Coalition (URC), a nonprofit organization whose official purpose was to bring investment into unprivileged urban areas in the United States.[80] The group founder Pastor Darrell Scott had been[81] a longtime supporter of Donald Trump,[82] who reciprocated Scott's support by publicly endorsing the URC and signing an executive order to create investment opportunity zones in the United States.[83] The URC founders sought Kazan's assistance in fundraising[84] as she apparently came from wealth and had access to other prominent Turkish citizens and officials.[85] Kazan introduced the URC founders to the president of the Turkish-American Business Association/American Chamber of Commerce (TABA-AmCham), Ali Akat.[86]

In late April 2018 Ali Akat came to Washington, DC, and met with the URC founders, Darrell Scott and Kareem Lanier, ostensibly to promote commercial trade between the United States and Turkey during the Trump administration.[87] The group also discussed Turkish investments into the urban opportunity zones in America. Darrell Scott took his Turkish guest to landmark GOP locations including the Republican National Committee headquarters and the Eisenhower Executive Office Building, where the offices of the presidential administration staff are located.[88] Shepherded by Kazan and the URC officials, Akat also met with several congressmen,[89] including Pete Sessions, Joe Wilson, and Scott Perry. These three congressmen were then members of the bipartisan congressional caucus over the Turkish region.[90] During his trip Ali Akat also spent some time at the Trump International Hotel in Washington, DC,[91] and met several influential people from the MAGA world.[92]

After Akat's first visit to the United States, the URC founders tweeted about a potential $30 billion Turkish investment into US urban renewal areas and twenty-five thousand manufacturing jobs in return for US government tax incentives.[93] On his end, Ali Akat would later tell a Turkish reporter that US companies would be investing hundreds of millions of dollars into Turkey.[94]

There was an issue, though, with Darrell Scott being a part of arranging an international trade deal. The URC was a nongovernmental organization that had no authority to negotiate on behalf of the United States government. Commonly accepted foreign trade practices would require Akat to discuss the matter with the United States International Trade Administration (USITA). So Akat's meetings with the URC should be seen as intentionally held under the radar of regulators.

FIGURE 1. URC CASH GIVEAWAY ANNOUNCEMENT
SOURCE: NATIONAL DIVERSITY COALITION FACEBOOK PAGE

An exiled Turkish journalist commented on Akat's trip:[95]

> It's not possible Erdogan could not know . . . Even the smallest details of these things wouldn't happen without his knowledge . . . All businesses in the country, if allowed to operate, pay their dues to him, so to speak.

Despite the announcements about the joint projects,[96] there was no public record of any TABA-AmCham investment into American urban areas. However, Kazan was invited to join the URC, seemingly for introducing its founders to Akat.[97]

Ali Akat was not the only Turkish national whom Rabia Kazan connected to the URC. She also told *Salon* that she had introduced Darrell Scott and Kareem Lanier to Mehmet Nazif Günal,[98] a Turkish construction billionaire and founder of one of the top Turkish[99] government[100] contractors:

> Kazan said Scott and Günal had discussed millions of dollars in assets that Günal could no longer access in Saudi Arabia, and that Günal hoped that Scott could help convince Trump to lean on the Saudi king.

It appears that in exchange for an investment into the URC, Darrell Scott was willing to bring Günal's issue to President Trump. Once again, people with access to Trump sought to monetize it, and the Turks were eager to exploit it.[101] However, the URC effort was short lived. Its illicit activities, from holding cash giveaways events in black communities in support of Donald Trump[102] to soliciting investments from foreigners while not filing their tax returns,[103] attracted the attention of US authorities. As a result, in 2020 the IRS revoked the URC's tax-exempt status.[104] The URC also became a subject of an FBI investigation for violations of IRS regulations[105] and potential illegal foreign lobbying.[106]

Meanwhile, Rabia Kazan distanced herself from the URC, Darrell Scott, and Kareem Lanier and created her own organization, which she used as an influence vehicle.

THE MIDDLE EASTERN WOMEN'S COALITION

In 2007 Rabia Kazan released a book about Islamic violence against women.[107] In 2018, focusing on the same subject, Kazan founded the Middle Eastern Women's Coalition (MEWC)[108] to ostensibly increase awareness in the United States about sharia law and violence against women in the Middle East.[109] However, she stretched the issue, tying it to US domestic politics and attempting to exacerbate the cultural divide in America. In MEWC press releases, Kazan blamed former president Barack Obama for "encouraging" sharia law.[110] In her public speeches, Kazan claimed that she had "found Jesus"[111] and lavishly praised Donald Trump for hearing out the voices of Middle Eastern women.[112] All those talking points seemed to have been manicured to appeal to Christian Republican women who followed conservative media talking points and supported Donald Trump.

With her MAGA-appealing pitch and cosponsoring conservative female events,[113] Rabia Kazan became a keynote speaker at gatherings of Moms for America[114] and Virginia Women for Trump.[115] The efforts paid off as she gained access to influential MAGA women, socializing[116] with them[117] at the Trump International Hotel in DC and even joining the advisory board of Moms for America.[118]

Kazan also brought into the Middle Eastern Women's Coalition a conservative youth influencer, Christianné Allen, as the executive director of the coalition.[119] A few months later, Allen would become an assistant and spokesperson to Rudy Giuliani.[120]

Once she gained access to those influential women, Rabia Kazan used her wealth and connections in Turkey to ingratiate herself with them. In February 2019 Rabia Kazan took Martha Boneta, a conservative influencer from Virginia, to Turkey and paid for her three-night stay at a luxury hotel.[121] During that trip Kazan introduced Boneta to several wealthy Turkish people. One of them was Kazan's sister,[122] who was connected through her spouse to the Godiva chocolate empire. Another introduction was made to a Turkish billionaire named Rahmi Koç.[123] While in Turkey, Martha Boneta, with Kazan's help, arranged a call between Koç and Roger Stone,[124] a political trickster and long-term ally of Donald Trump.[125] By that time Stone had been implicated in the Russia investigation and was indicted by the DOJ.[126] He apparently had been fundraising for his legal expenses[127] and wanted Kazan and Koç to contribute.[128]

Martha Boneta reciprocated by opening her political circle to Kazan and introduced her to Michael Lindell, the CEO of MyPillow and an avid Trump supporter. Later Kazan would claim that, with Boneta's "encouragement," Kazan presented a diamond necklace worth $10,000 to Lindell's girlfriend.[129]

Years later Rabia Kazan would allege that the MAGA circle "used" her for money.[130] However, she herself utilized her wealth, or appearance thereof, to gain access to elite Trump supporters. She admitted to contributing $1,000 in cash to the NDC and donating $200 to one of the NDC members' congressional campaign,[131] despite being a foreign national and thus being[132] ineligible[133] to make political contributions in the United States. She also donated $2,800 to the Trump Victory PAC.[134]

Kazan disappeared from the MAGA world as quickly as she entered it. In the fall of 2019, Kazan accused Trump of being a racist.[135] It was not publicly revealed what made Kazan shift her position. A fallout between the United States and Turkey due to Erdogan's October 2019 attack on the Syrian Kurds[136] might have been one reason. Trump's first impeachment investigation gaining speed at the time[137] might have been another.

Whatever it was, it apparently was a subject of her conversation with the FBI.[138] Kazan would later tell a reporter that she reached out to the bureau after getting tired of online harassment. However, her own rise within MAGA circles was conspicuous enough and should have raised questions from the FBI.

What was her motive in expanding her access to Donald Trump's entourage and supporters, despite having no US citizenship and showing no ascertainable interest in US politics before 2016? Why did it take her over ten years between writing her sharia law book and speaking out about the cause? Why did she make lavish gifts to Martha Boneta and Michael Lindell's girlfriend, whom she barely knew? Why did she help solicit money for Roger Stone or the URC from Turkish billionaires? How did she get access to those billionaires in the first place? Also, how did she get access to Ali Akat, who was authorized by Turkey to negotiate large trade deals?

Although the US government did not charge Rabia Kazan for any crimes, her actions followed a playbook of other known covert Turkish intermediaries: using political contributions and a cultural cause to infiltrate GOP circles, as well as dating a MAGA insider, Robert Hyde, who around that time was involved in a plot in Ukraine.

Arguably, Kazan was more successful than others, reaching only one degree away of connection from Donald Trump. When placed in those GOP circles, Kazan could be a valuable asset for Turkish intelligence, being their eyes and ears at the Trump International Hotel in DC, Mar-a-Lago, US Congress, and the White House.

THE TURKISH INFLUENCE PLAYBOOK

The Turkish groups and influencers were just a small part of a multilayered influence operation[139] that was directed and funded by the Turkish government as a clandestine alternative to official diplomatic channels (figure 2). The influence operations were overseen by President Erdogan's most trusted men: his foreign minister Mevlut Cavusoglu and his son-in-law Berat Albayrak, who also was the minister of energy and the minister of finance at varying times. Coordinating lobbyists and cultural groups, Erdogan's henchmen systemically advanced his interests in the United States. Through informal events, political contributions, and Turkish-American PACs, Turkish intermediaries cultivated access to American politicians who could potentially be of use. The Turkish playbook also included soliciting op-eds to shape US public opinion.

In parallel, the intermediaries methodically built access to US elected officials, strategically targeting members of important committees, such as of foreign affairs, and the congressional Turkey Caucus, who were in a position to influence US policy. The goal was to then coax the lawmakers to intervene in decision-making to better accommodate whatever Erdogan wanted at that moment. That could be blocking a congressional resolution to recognize the Armenian genocide or muzzling criticism of the Erdogan government's human rights violations before an upcoming election in Turkey. Later, the intermediaries would make various attempts to persuade the US government to extradite Fethullah Gülen and to bury the US investigation into Reza Zarrab's money laundering.

With Donald Trump elected, Turkish intermediaries sought to penetrate Trump's circle, procuring access to anyone who was in the president-elect's orbit, including his campaign team members, his business partners, his advisors, and his children. In that effort Mubariz Mansimov and Farkhad Akhmedov, through Lev Parnas, gained access to Brian Ballard, a former Trump campaign finance manager, who had launched a lobbying firm in Washington. Ekim Alptekin recruited Michael Flynn, Trump's selected national security advisor, and, through Sezgin Baran Korkmaz, was introduced to James Woolsey, Trump's campaign advisor and a former director of the CIA. Rabia Kazan connected influential Turks to Trump surrogates. Finally, Turkey had a lobbying contract with Greenberg Traurig, where Donald Trump's future private attorney, Rudy Giuliani, was serving as the chairman's advisor.

Even after some of those Turkish intermediaries became incapacitated due to criminal charges, the overall effort continued unabated. Those who were compromised were replaced by others. For example, in 2018, after Ekim Alptekin's federal indictment in the United States,[140] TAIK, a Turkish trade group where Alptekin had served as the chairman, replaced him with a person named Mehmet Ali Yalcindag, who had previous connections to the Trump family through Trump Towers in Istanbul.[141] TAIK would also sign a lobbying contract with Mercury Public Affairs,[142] which employed Trump transition team's former communications director[143] Bryan Lanza.[144] By the time Donald Trump was sworn in as president, he was surrounded by people peddling Turkish interests and became the primary target of the Turkish influence operations.

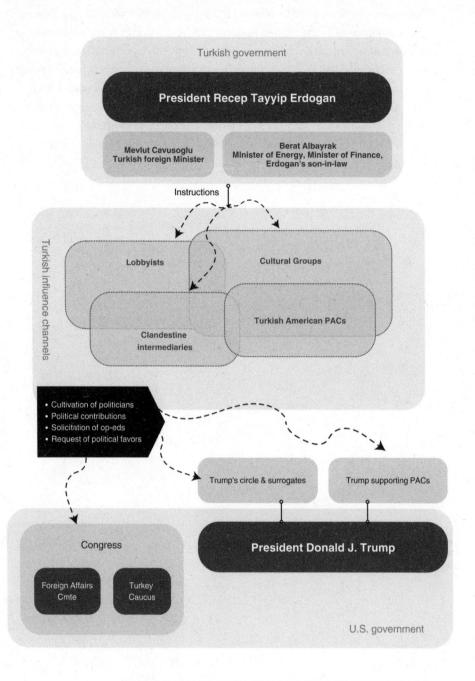

FIGURE 2. THE LAYERS OF TURKISH INFLUENCE IN THE UNITED STATES

CHAPTER 5
TARGET #1

THE CELEBRITY DEVELOPER

Before his presidential candidacy, Donald Trump was known for womanizing, lawsuits, real estate deals, and a reality TV show. He was the head of the Trump Organization, a real estate and brand management business that he had inherited from his father, Fred Trump. The organization operated a collection of businesses that included a vast number of hotels, apartment buildings, office buildings, and golf courses in the United States and abroad.[1]

Transitioning from his father's legacy, Donald Trump moved the Trump Organization's focus from middle-class residential property to luxurious condominiums and commercial real estate. Unlike his father, Donald Trump sought to market every deal as another reason to highlight how far he took his father's company. While Fred Trump built his residential real estate business locally in the New York area, his son's vision for the organization was to put the Trump name in lights globally.

By the time of Donald Trump's inauguration, his company had numerous foreign business interests and had investors from or attempted to do deals in more than dozen countries, including Turkey.[2]

TRUMP TOWERS IN TURKEY

In April 2012 both Donald Trump and his daughter Ivanka made appearances[3] at the launch of Trump Towers Mall in Istanbul.[4] The event was attended by then prime minister Erdogan, who made a speech and cut the ribbon.[5]

By 2016 the Trump Organization had reportedly been paid "up to $10 million"[6] in licensing fees for lending its name to the Turkish partners.[7] The construction was partially financed by the powerful Dogan family, who had interests in Turkish media, real estate, and energy sectors.[8]

Curiously, several characters who appeared in previous chapters were in some way or another connected to the Trump Towers in Istanbul. A son-in-law of the head of the Dogan empire, Mehmet Ali Yalcindag, would become the chairman of the Turkish-American Business Council, replacing Ekim Alptekin, who had fled the United States in the midst of being charged as a foreign agent. The first buyer who purchased eight apartments and a penthouse in Trump Towers Istanbul was Mubariz Mansimov,[9] the Turkish Azerbaijani shipping magnate who connected the Turkish foreign minister to Ballard Partners. Another familiar person who had an office in Trump Towers Istanbul was Reza Zarrab,[10] the key defendant and witness in the Halkbank investigation described in chapter 1.

TURKISH BUYERS IN MANHATTAN

In addition to the Trump Towers Istanbul project, in 2013 the Trump Organization was engaged in negotiations with Erdogan's son Bilal and son-in-law Berat Albayrak regarding real estate in Manhattan worth $28 million.[11] In an email exchange[12] shown in figure 3, Halil Danismaz, the president of the Turkish Heritage Organization who had been serving as Albayrak's henchman in the United States,[13] asked him and the younger Erdogan whether VakifBank could provide proof of funds to buy the property. To understand the importance of those emails, one needs to remember the context.

The email exchange happened in June 2013, six months before the bribery corruption scandal in Turkey, which would implicate Erdogan and his family, including Berat Albayrak.[14] The timing of the deal fit into the period when Reza Zarrab, one of the key figures of the scandal, was bribing Turkish officials[15] and donating large sums of money[16] to a charity led by Erdogan's wife.[17] VakifBank, which was supposed to provide the proof of funds for the Manhattan deal, was also part of Zarrab's money-laundering scheme,[18] reportedly under the personal direction of Erdogan.[19] Although it was not publicly known whether the Manhattan deal was finalized, the combination of the above factors and the notorious practice of laundering illicitly obtained money through purchasing real estate offered a distinct possibility that Berat Albayrak and Bilal Erdogan might have sought to convert illicit cash into a Trump-owned property.

Shortly after Donald Trump announced his presidential bid, the media questioned his ability to prioritize American foreign policy over his business interests abroad. Even his ally Steve Bannon, a far right strategist, seemed to be curious about that. In December 2015 Bannon interviewed Trump for Breitbart News, asking about his position on Turkey if elected president of the United States. Referring to Trump Towers in Istanbul, Donald Trump admitted that he had "a little conflict of interest."[20] His business ties to foreign powers, including Turkey, became a significant issue when Donald Trump unexpectedly won in November 2016.

From: danismaz@gmail.com
To: bilal.erdogan@gmail.com, beratalbayrak@gmail.com
Date: 2013-06-24 13:15
Subject: Fwd: NYC Building

315 W35th St. in icini gormeye gidecegim yarin ins.

Buradaki Vakifbank tan bir kagit almamiz mumkun mu? eski muduru (Yildirim
Eroglu) taniyordum ama yenisini tanimiyorum. Tanistirabilir misiniz? yarin
sabah kendisine bir selam vereyim.

Muhabbetle,

Halil

> Is it possible for us to get a paper from Vakifbank here? I knew the old manager (Yildirim Eroglu) but not the new one. Can you introduce me? Let me say hi to him tomorrow morning. Sincerely, Halil

P.S. pls read below. thanks
---------- Forwarded message ----------
From: Elena Baronoff <elenatrump@yahoo.com>
Date: Mon, Jun 24, 2013 at 10:28 AM
Subject: NYC Building
To: "danismaz@gmail.com" <danismaz@gmail.com>

Dear Halil,

Peter will be calling you shortly.
In the meantime, it looks like we are all set for tomorrow's appt but the
owner is insistent on seeing a proof of funds just to make sure he is
dealing with qualified buyers, which is very standard in this industry. Can
you request that your bank send you a letter stating that you are capable
of making a $28 million purchase?
I will call you soon. Today I am flying to Istanbul but I

TARGET #1   35

```
will always be
reachable while I am there via email/text/cell. Meanwhile,
Peter will be in
constant contact with you

Warm Regards,

Elena A. Baronoff
*International Ambassador of the City of Sunny Isles Beach
**Director of Sales & Marketing *
Lic. RE Broker

Trump International
18001 Collins Avenue, Sunny Isles Beach FL 33160
*M:* +1 305 213 3606 | *T:* +1 305 692 5778
www.miamitrumptowers.com | www.trumptowerscollection.com

P Please consider the environment before printing this e-
mail.
This e-mail, including attachments, is intended for the
person(s) or
company named and may contain confidential and/or legally
privileged
information. Unauthorized disclosure, copying or use of this
information
may be unlawful and is prohibited. If you are not the
intended recipient,
please delete this message and notify the sender.

--
*Halil I. Danismaz*
```

FIGURE 3. EMAIL EXCHANGE BETWEEN BILAL ERDOGAN AND A TRUMP INTERNATIONAL REAL ESTATE AGENT
SOURCE: WIKILEAKS

THE UNCONVENTIONAL PRESIDENT AND HIS STANCE TOWARD TURKEY

Donald Trump had a reputation of a belligerent bomb thrower[21] who reveled in any fight.[22] Trump had no prior experience in political office to build on. He was known to have an explosive personality and a collection of unapologetic business bankruptcies dating back to the 1980s.[23] His political identity was fairly unknown as, during his campaign, he often spoke vaguely of his political positions. At the same time, he used language with racial stereotypes, blaming ethnic groups and minorities for destroying America. Like former president Richard Nixon before him, Donald Trump amplified fears and anger inherent to some Americans and used those emotions as a political strategy. Trump's "America first" slogan was previously used by Charles Lindbergh, a pre–World War II celebrity pilot and a Nazi sympathizer. Trump echoed Lindbergh in his speeches and branded himself loosely with nationalist, populist, and isolationist ideas. Trump's presidential campaign was based on evoking nostalgia for "the good old days" and a pledge to "make America great again." It was also centered on a "fear of loss" of a past America. When it came to foreign policy, his ideas ran counter to the ideals set by Western democracies post–World War II, which focused on a stable global order based on free trade and the United States as the senior guarantor of the system.

After his unexpected electoral victory, Donald Trump's campaign tone was incorporated into American foreign policy. Candidate Trump's attacks on Mexican[24] and Muslim[25] immigrants were shaped into a family separation policy at the US border[26] and a partial Muslim ban[27] during Trump's presidency.

Donald Trump, constantly and without hesitation, attacked anyone who criticized his actions. He declared on numerous occasions that the media was the enemy of the American people and attacked public institutions such as the FBI, CIA, the powers of Congress, and the powers of the judicial branch. With constant fervor, the new president and his allies[28] promoted[29] conspiracy[30] theories[31] designed[32] to undermine public trust in established institutions.

Unsurprisingly, Donald Trump had a soft spot for authoritarian rulers. As former national security advisor John Bolton put it in his interview to *Foreign Policy* magazine,[33]

> *Trump was just taken with how [Chinese President] Xi [Jinping], [Russian President Vladimir] Putin, and Erdogan could just sort of do things in their respective countries and not have to account for it, so you could make a big gesture and forget the normal procedures of, in this case, law enforcement.*

John Bolton expanded on that point in a later interview to *Der Spiegel*:[34]

> *It seems more likely to me that Trump wanted to make an impression on Erdogan. It was part of his desire to do favors particularly for authoritarian leaders. He was trying to show Erdogan that he was going to do him a favor, perhaps in order to ask for a personal favor in return at some future date.*

Such an attitude by a US president would be a godsend for Erdogan. His government had already been trying to systemically influence the United States. One pressing issue was the extradition of Fethullah Gülen. Later the list expanded to demands for the US government to halt the ongoing Halkbank investigations and release Reza Zarrab. The Turkish government also had longer-term goals, such as the promotion of Turkey as a regional energy hub and the "de-escalation" of the conflict in Syria in terms favorable to Turkey. All those issues would be brought to Donald Trump's attention through lobbyists and Turkish intermediaries.

FETHULLAH GÜLEN

Fethullah Gülen, a Turkish cleric who had been living in a self-imposed exile in the United States since 1999, was once an ally of Recep Tayyip Erdogan. In the early 2000s, Erdogan's party, the AKP, and Gülen's movement worked together, advocating for the acceptance of Islamic values.[35] At the time, those views were considered in opposition to the modern Turkish state's secular values, which had been in place for decades. The Gülen movement, pushing the inclusion of Islamic values, expanded into a large network of schools and social organizations. The cleric himself gained a large number of followers in Turkey and beyond.

In 2013 the relationship between Erdogan and Gülen deteriorated and escalated into an archrivalry.[36] Gülen criticized Erdogan's government for its brutal suppression of the Gezi Park protesters throughout the summer of that year.[37] Erdogan, in apparent retaliation, threatened to close Gülen schools in Turkey.[38] The enmity reached a high point in December 2013, when the Turkish prosecutors charged several businessmen and government officials allied to Erdogan with running a large corruption scheme that would become the foundation of the Halkbank case. The investigation also implicated Erdogan and his family members. As the scandal spilled into public protests, Erdogan blamed the Gülen movement for orchestrating the investigation.

In July 2016 a part of the Turkish military unsuccessfully attempted to overthrow Erdogan's government. He, in turn, immediately blamed Fethullah Gülen as being the mastermind behind the coup attempt.

Even before July 2016, Erdogan's government had been trying[39] to persuade the US government[40] to have Gülen extradited to Turkey.[41] An American lobbying firm, Amsterdam & Partners, which was hired by Turkey in 2015,[42] had been[43] repeatedly[44] criticizing[45] Gülen[46] in US media months before the revolt against Erdogan. After the coup attempt, the Turkish government upped the ante and added more layers to its influence playbook, deploying Turkish cultural groups to run anti-Gülen smear campaigns, and considered more aggressive tactics, such as an outright abduction of the cleric from his home in Pennsylvania.[47]

As mentioned before, in September 2016 senior Turkish officials Mevlut Cavusoglu and Berat Albayrak met with Michael Flynn and James Woolsey to discuss the potential rendition of Gülen. At the time, Flynn was an important surrogate for the Trump campaign. Woolsey, the former CIA director, was a campaign advisor to the future president. On the day of US elections in November 2016, Michael Flynn wrote an op-ed in the *Hill*, where he portrayed Gülen as a terrorist supporter, calling the cleric "a shady Islamic mullah" and "radical Islamist."[48] That description did not match the official[49] US position[50] and raised eyebrows at the DOJ leading to investigations into Flynn's services for the Turkish government.

After numerous revelations implicating him in potential crimes, in February 2017 Michael Flynn was forced to resign his position as the national security advisor. The Fethullah Gülen issue was then picked up by Rudy Giuliani.[51] At the time, he worked at Greenberg Traurig, one of the law firms with lobbying contracts for the Turkish government. However, Giuliani couldn't legally advocate for Turkish interests as, unlike other Greenberg Traurig lawyers who were lobbying for Turkey, he had not registered as a foreign agent with the DOJ.[52] The only Turkey-related job that he was supposed to do was to provide a legal defense for Reza Zarrab, who had hired Giuliani as one of his attorneys. But seemingly, Giuliani was above those technicalities.

According to some White House officials, Giuliani pushed for the cleric's extradition so frequently that the issue became known among the staff as his "hobby horse."[53] According to *BuzzFeed News*, Rudy Giuliani went even further:[54]

> *First, Giuliani began publicly pushing pro-Erdogan policies on Fox News. As the year progressed, Giuliani began having private conversations with White House officials about Gülen. One White House official said that Giuliani was pushing the extradition of Gülen so aggressively, President Trump began to actually consider doing it.*
>
> *Giuliani's obsession with Gülen was apparently a genuine source of confusion for those around him. He reportedly began referring to the cleric as a "dangerous extremist," language ripped straight from far-right message boards and hyper-partisan media.*

The first two of Trump's chiefs of staff tried to limit Giuliani's access to the president out of apparent concern that Giuliani would bring his foreign clients' needs to the Oval Office, bypassing legal lobbying procedures, and that Trump would act on Giuliani's ideas.[55] Those concerns weren't unfounded.

In early 2017 President Trump seemingly acquiesced to Giuliani's requests, raising eyebrows among his staffs who questioned the legality of such an extradition. As one White House official put it:[56]

> *We're not going to arrest [Gülen] to do a solid for Erdogan.*

Donald Trump also ordered the Department of Education to investigate the activities of Gülen-affiliated schools in America. According to *Bloomberg*:[57]

> The White House suggested that the Education Department could investigate whether Gülen was laundering money through the schools, or could argue that the schools' ties to Gülen—a Muslim cleric—amounted to a religious affiliation and meant they couldn't receive federal funding.

The Department of Education refused citing discrimination against the Muslim charter school.[58]

Then in September 2017, the Turkish president pivoted by requesting to trade a pastor for a pastor: Turkish cleric Fethullah Gülen for American pastor Andrew Brunson, who had been arrested in Turkey in the fall of 2016 ostensibly for his connections to the Gülen movement:[59]

> You have a pastor too . . . You give us that one and we'll work with our judiciary and give back yours.

That request was not granted.

In late 2018 Erdogan tried another move. On October 2, 2018, Jamal Khashoggi, a *Washington Post* journalist and Saudi Arabian dissident, was killed in Turkey inside the Saudi consulate.[60] The Saudi government denied any involvement, while the Turkish government claimed to have some evidence proving otherwise. In the standoff between the two countries, Pres. Donald Trump sided with Saudi Arabia,[61] downplaying the evidence and the gravity of incident.[62] However, under pressure from Congress,[63] Trump begrudgingly requested that Turkey turn over any evidence they might have on Khashoggi's death.[64] Turkey, in turn, saw an opportunity to use the evidence as leverage to make the United States extradite Fethullah Gülen.[65]

Two weeks after Khashoggi's death, Secretary of State Mike Pompeo flew to meet with Erdogan in Ankara. At the meeting the "number one ask" of Turkish officials was the extradition of Gülen to Turkey.[66]

The White House reacted to the Turkish government's semitransparent attempts to publicly blackmail the United States by instructing the Department of Justice, the Federal Bureau of Investigations, and the Department of Homeland Security (DHS) to "examine legal ways of removing" Gülen.[67] Later in November the Turkish foreign minister, Mevlut Cavusoglu, made a public statement[68] that the Trump administration was "working on the extradition" of Gülen.[69]

In December 2018 the White House spokesperson, backing Cavusoglu's claim, stated that President Trump "would take a look at" the Gülen extradition topic.[70] US officials resisted the effort:[71]

> At first there were eye rolls, but once they realized it was a serious request, the career guys were furious.

Despite at least two sets of reviews ordered by the White House,[72] no action on the cleric's extradition would be made during Trump's presidency.[73]

The attempted blackmail scheme failed, and Turkey, under public pressure,[74] released the audiotape recording of Khashoggi's murder.[75]

ANDREW BRUNSON

Although Erdogan didn't succeed in having Gülen extradited, there were other people he sought to return to Turkey, and he had a bargaining chip to exchange for them, the detained American evangelical pastor Andrew Brunson. The Turkish government arrested Brunson in October 2016 and accused him of being a part of the Gülen movement.[76] US officials responded by publicly calling for his release. In mid-February 2017 seventy-eight members of Congress wrote an official letter to the Turkish president protesting his detention.[77] Later that month Erdogan met with Rudy Giuliani,[78] who represented Reza Zarrab, the key figure at the Halkbank case. Later it would be revealed that Giuliani had sought[79] to exchange Brunson[80] for the gold trader.[81] That effort failed.[82]

In July 2018 the Turkish government offered another candidate to swap for Brunson, Mehmet Hakan Atilla, a Halkbank official who had previously been arrested in the United States in relation to the SDNY investigation.[83] Those negotiations pulled Brian Ballard, a lobbyist whose firm represented Turkish and Halkbank interests in the United States, into the center of the effort to free Brunson. In late July Ballard met with Nick Ayers, the chief of staff to VP Mike Pence regarding "US-Turkey relations," as stated in Ballard's FARA report.[84]

Throwing more conditions on the table, the Turkish foreign minister asked US officials not only to release Atilla but also to "kill any investigation into Halkbank."[85] Trump's national security advisor, John Bolton, would later describe how the events unfolded in his book:[86]

> *The Turks, worried about escalating problems with America, wanted a way out, or so we thought, trying to wrap an exchange for Brunson into the Halkbank criminal investigation. This was at best unseemly, but Trump wanted Brunson out, so Pompeo and Mnuchin negotiated with their counterparts (Mnuchin because Treasury's Office of Foreign Assets Control was also looking into Halkbank). In three-way conversations, Mnuchin, Pompeo and I agreed nothing would be done without full agreement from the Justice Department prosecutors in the Southern District of New York, where the case involving over $20 billion Iran sanctions violations was pending. . . .*
>
> *. . . Trying this route to get Brunson's release was never going to work. Pompeo said, "The Turks just can't get out of their own way," but it was in fact Justice prosecutors who rightly rejected the deals worth next to nothing from the US government's perspective.*

That additional condition effectively killed the prisoner exchange talks.[87]

By that time, US officials had already started growing impatient. On July 26, 2018, President Trump and VP Mike Pence threatened to sanction Turkey unless Andrew Brunson was released.[88] The effort to free the pastor was not only limited to official channels but also seemingly went full steam through unofficial ones.

After the threat of sanctions, Brian Ballard was in communication with a person named Jay Sekulow, regarding "US-Turkey relations." In his FARA report, Ballard characterized Sekulow as the chief counsel of the American Center for Law and Justice.[89] It was a Christian-focused nonprofit organization that represented Andrew Brunson pro bono.[90] Curiously, Sekulow had also been one of Trump's personal attorneys since mid-2017[91] and had encouraged the president to raise the Brunson issue to Erdogan.[92]

On August 1, 2018, carrying out Trump and Pence's threats, the United States imposed sanctions on Turkey's justice minister and interior minister.[93] The announcement sent the Turkish lira into a tailspin.[94] The following week, on August 10, 2018, Trump doubled tariffs on Turkish aluminum and steel imported to the United States as a way to amp up the pressure.[95]

A month later another unofficial rescue effort emerged. In September 2018 Nancye Miller, the Washington lobbyist introduced in chapter 3, reportedly coordinated an effort to hold back-channel negotiations with President Erdogan to persuade him to release Andrew Brunson.[96] Apparently, Miller was too ill to travel to Turkey herself, but she had put together a peculiar team in her stead, which consisted of

- James Woolsey, Miller's husband, a former CIA director and a former advisor to Trump's transition team;[97]
- Sezgin Baran Korkmaz, a Turkish tycoon who provided his jet for the trip;
- Fr. James McCurry, a Franciscan priest; and
- Tommy Hicks Jr., the chairman of the America First Action super PAC,[98] a close friend of Donald Trump Jr., and a member of an equity investment fund with interests in the Texas energy industry.[99]

Nancye Miller, James Woolsey, and Sezgin Baran Korkmaz had already met in September 2016, when Miller and Woolsey proposed to Korkmaz that they run what would be in effect a smear campaign in the United States against Fethullah Gülen in exchange for $10 million.

The incongruous group embarked on a weeklong trip to Turkey but spent most of the time in a hotel while Miller was on the phone with Turkish representatives. However, on September 18, 2018, the group flew from Istanbul to Izmir. Tommy Hicks Jr. and Father McCurry reportedly went to visit Pastor Brunson while Woolsey and Korkmaz stayed behind on the jet.[100]

In parallel, in late September 2018, during the United Nations General Assembly in New York, where both President Trump[101] and President Erdogan[102] were giving addresses, Secretary of State Mike Pompeo and National Security Advisor John Bolton "advanced in discussions" for Brunson's release.[103] On September 21, 2018, around the time when Nancye Miller's team was in Turkey, Brian Ballard exchanged phone calls with Jay Sekulow and separately called to Vice President Pence's chief of staff, Nick Ayers, about "U.S.-Turkey relations." A month later, on October 11 and 12, Brian Ballard called and exchanged messages with Jay Sekulow again.[104] That last interaction was likely to share the news of Brunson's eventual release, which was officially announced on October 12, 2018.

The frequency of Ballard's communication with Ayers and Sekulow makes one wonder whether the lobbyist was the central middleman in the orchestration of Andrew Brunson's release. Were his actions coordinated with Nancye Miller's team? Or with John Bolton and other US officials who actually were supposed to be leading the negotiations? What, other than the lifting of the imposed sanctions, was offered in return for the release of the pastor?

After Brunson's release Trump tweeted:[105]

> *There was NO DEAL made with Turkey for the release and return of Pastor Andrew Brunson. I don't make deals for hostages. There was, however, great appreciation on behalf of the United States, which will lead to good, perhaps great, relations between the United States & Turkey!*

Considering that Turkey tried to trade Andrew Brunson for Fethullah Gülen, Reza Zarrab, or Mehmet Hakan Atilla, all of great value to Erdogan, it is hard to believe that Turkey would give up the American pastor without some type of concession in return. The official reason reportedly included "a commitment by the U.S. to ease economic pressure on Turkey."[106]

On October 14, 2018, two days after Brunson's release, Ali Akat, the president of the Turkish-American Chamber of Commerce, which, as described earlier, was at the time discussing a trade deal with the Urban Revitalization Coalition in the United States, said in an interview that[107]

> *fifteen U.S. companies, each with a minimum of $100 million to invest, are rolling up their sleeves to bring business to Turkey in the "first wave" of investment from the United States following the release of pastor Andrew Brunson.*

As John Bolton later described it, after Brunson was freed, "the light switch turned and it became a very good personal relationship between the two," referring to Trump and Erdogan.[108] On November 2, 2018, the sanctions on the Turkish ministers were lifted.[109] The steel tariffs that the United States had put on Turkey would be later cut in half.[110]

However, that thaw in the relationship between the two presidents would not last long.

THE WITHDRAWAL OF US TROOPS FROM KURDISH SYRIA

In October 2019 the relationship between Donald Trump and Recep Tayyip Erdogan hit another bump, this time over Syria. To understand the context of the friction, one needs to look back at the key historic points that led to it.

As a result of World War I, the Ottoman Empire broke into several countries. Left stateless was an ethnic group called the Kurds that populated areas within the borders of Turkey, Syria, Iran, Iraq, and Armenia.[111] For decades the Kurds living in Turkey sought greater autonomy within the Turkish state and the preservation of their culture and language. The Turkish government pushed back against Kurdish demands, forcing them to assimilate[112] and attacking areas predominantly populated by ethnic Kurds.[113] In the 1970s the Kurdish movement grew increasingly violent with the Kurdistan Workers' Party, or the PKK, which had over time committed on and off terroristic actions against the Turkish government.[114] As a result, Turkey,[115] along with the United States[116] and the European Union,[117] designated the PKK as a terrorist organization. At the same time, the Turkish state was condemned for extrajudicial violence against ethnic Kurds.[118] An estimated forty thousand people died as a result of the fighting.[119]

By 2013, exhausted by decades of violence, the Turkish government and the PKK had reached a ceasefire and entered negotiations to permanently halt the hostilities.[120] However, the timing couldn't be worse. Within months the region exploded from the escalation of the civil war in neighboring Syria and the overlapping emergence of a radical terrorist group, ISIS, in Iraq and Syria. In the coming years, both the Syrian civil war and the fight against ISIS became proxy conflicts, with countries forming coalitions with local infighting groups.[121]

The Syrian government was backed by Russian airpower and Iranian-affiliated forces on the ground that fought to maintain Syrian president Bashar al-Assad's power and influence in Syria.[122] On the opposing side, resistance groups, financed and armed by a majority Sunni Arab states and led by Saudi Arabia, formed a coalition army that became known as the Free Syrian Army (FSA).[123] Along with the Syrian Kurds, the Free Syrian Army fought Assad's forces, draining the government's manpower and resources over time. As the civil war continued, the fighting became more brutal. Assad's forces moved to a more defensive posture, protecting core government territories while pulling back from central and northeastern Syria, leading to a vacuum of control in those areas.

That vacuum was seized on by ISIS. The group had a radical interpretation of Islam where strict adherence to sharia law was to be maintained, violently if necessary, to build a worldwide movement. ISIS rapidly grew in influence, capturing both territory and military equipment in a fragmented Iraq and a war-torn Syria. The group declared itself an Islamic caliphate in its captured territories and called for its followers worldwide to defend it. ISIS became synonymous with brutal violence, murdering nonbelievers, raping young girls and women, and selling them into slavery. The group used social media to publicize beheadings of Westerners as a warning to those who might oppose them.

In response, the United States led an international coalition to destroy the Islamic State and drive its influence from both Syria and Iraq. In 2016 reports emerged of the United States equipping the Kurdish Free Syrian Army and the Kurdish YPG (People's Defense Units) and giving them air support against ISIS forces.[124] The Kurds, a stateless people of unique cultural beliefs, became the backbone of opposition to ISIS and its affiliations. The Kurdish fighters pushed ISIS-controlled territories back, drastically reducing its influence over Syrian lands.[125] The Kurds lost thousands of their people in the fight but became well known and respected by their partners in the anti-ISIS coalition.[126]

Over time, as the civil war continued in Syria, the Kurds moved to create an unofficial autonomous region in northern Syria, at the border with Turkey,[127] fighting both the Assad government and ISIS. Erdogan was resentful of the US-Kurdish alliance and the Kurdish settlements that emerged at the Syrian-Turkish border.[128] Despite being a part of the US-led Western coalition against ISIS, Turkey refused to fire on ISIS elements that were attacking Kurdish settlements.[129] During the war, citing potential connections of the Syrian Kurds and the PKK,[130] Turkey repeatedly[131] pressed[132] the United States to keep the Syrian Kurds at arm's length from the Syrian-Turkish border. To make their point, the Turkish military had launched several[133] incursions[134] into Syria to push the Kurds back. Trying to keep the peace, the U.S. had sought to create a buffer zone[135] using U.S. forces as a shield between the Turkish border and the Syrian Kurdish settlements to "deconflict" the dispute.

Still unhappy with that arrangement, in December 2018 the Turkish president asked his American counterpart to remove the US troops from the buffer zone in northern Syria. Per John Bolton's recollection:[136]

> On December 14, Trump and Erdogan spoke by phone. I briefed Trump beforehand on the situation in Syria, and he said, "We should get the hell out of there," which I feared he would also say directly to Erdogan.

Bolton's fears materialized when, five days after the phone call, President Trump announced an immediate withdrawal of American forces from Syria, claiming that ISIS had been defeated and that therefore US troops stationed in the country were unnecessary.[137] The abrupt announcement shocked both Trump's military advisors and other US officials.[138]

The following day Secretary of Defense James Mattis resigned in protest, expressing his opposition to the abandonment of the Syrian Kurds who had fought ISIS side by side with US forces.[139] In his resignation letter, Mattis underlined the importance of US allies to American national security, citing NATO support after September 11 and the seventy-four-nation anti-ISIS coalition in Syria and Iraq. He noted that the United States needed to be "clear eyed" about its adversaries.[140]

Several senators protested Trump's decision,[141] signing a letter that urged the president to reevaluate the withdrawal.[142] They argued that the ISIS threat had not been eliminated and that, if left unchecked, the terrorist organization could regroup and return in force. Lindsey Graham, one of the senators who had signed the letter, met with Donald Trump to discuss his order. After the meeting Graham told the press that the president had assured him that instead of withdrawing in thirty days, as was initially announced, US troops would leave Syria in an organized fashion.[143] Graham tweeted later that day:[144]

> *The President will make sure any withdrawal from Syria will be done in a fashion to ensure:*
>
> 1. *ISIS is permanently destroyed.*
>
> 2. *Iran doesn't fill in the back end, and*
>
> 3. *our Kurdish allies are protected.*

In January 2019 Lindsey Graham flew to Turkey to meet Erdogan and discuss with him a slower withdrawal of US forces in the region.[145] It seemed that Graham's efforts to arrange an organized withdrawal bore fruit, and the subject was shelved, with US troops gradually moving out military equipment from their bases in Syria.

However, several months later, in October 2019, after another phone call from the Turkish president, Donald Trump ordered the immediate withdrawal of the remaining US military.[146] As US forces rapidly abandoned the area, Turkish forces attacked Kurdish settlements along the Turkish border, ousting more than 160,000 Kurdish people from their homes.[147] President Erdogan warned the West against interfering in the Turkish offensive and threatened[148] to send millions of Syrian refugees sheltered in Turkey to Europe,[149] which, in turn, could pose a large political challenge for the EU.

During a press conference after his latest withdrawal order, Donald Trump tried to justify his abandonment of the Kurds by saying:[150]

> *They didn't help us in the Second World War. They didn't help us with Normandy, as an example.*

Not only was that comparison irrelevant, but it was also incorrect. Despite their ethnic group having no country of their own,[151] and therefore no state military,[152] some Kurdish people joined other countries' armies in the fight against the Nazi Germany.[153]

Trump's betrayal of America's Kurdish allies created immediate blowback in Congress, the press, and the greater foreign policy community.

Republican congresswoman Liz Cheney (R-WY) commented:[154]

> *Turkey is invading Syria in reported coordination with Russian-backed forces, ISIS terrorists are launching attacks in Raqqa, and thousands of ISIS fighters are biding their time in makeshift prisons . . . The U.S. is abandoning our ally the Kurds, who fought ISIS on the ground and helped protect the U.S. homeland.*

Republican Senate majority leader Mitch McConnell said at the time:[155]

> *A precipitous withdrawal of U.S. forces from Syria would only benefit Russia, Iran, and the Assad regime.*

Senator Lindsey Graham, once again, publicly opposed the Turkish invasion, condemning the Trump administration's choices and the Turkish government's actions. Graham also strongly suggested additional "veto proof" sanctions against Turkey if they did not relent from their Syrian invasion.[156]

After the intense bipartisan criticism, Trump made a U-turn on his previous position and tweeted:[157]

> *As I have stated strongly before, and just to reiterate, if Turkey does anything that I, in my great and unmatched wisdom, consider to be off limits, I will totally destroy and obliterate the Economy of Turkey (I've done before!).*

On October 9, 2019, Donald Trump attempted to rectify the situation by writing a letter to Erdogan. The letter started with "Let's work out a good deal!" and ended with "Don't be a tough guy. Don't be a fool!" Reportedly, the letter was "thoroughly rejected" by Erdogan and was thrown into the trash.[158]

When the letter did not yield the intended outcome, Trump imposed sanctions on three Turkish officials and increased steel tariffs to 50 percent,[159] like he had done during the negotiations to release Pastor Andrew Brunson.

Trump also tweeted:[160]

> *The United States will also immediately stop negotiations, being led by the Department of Commerce, with respect to a $100 billion trade deal with Turkey.*

Public critics labeled Trump's sanctions on Turkey as "toothless."[161]

In an effort to increase the pressure on the Turkish government, in mid-October the Trump administration surprised prosecutors at the Southern District of New York[162] by green-lighting the indictment of the Turkish Halkbank.[163] That was a significant step because prior charges were made on people, and previously the Attorney General had stonewalled the SDNY attempts to charge the bank itself.[164] The pressure tactics seemed to have worked, and by October 17, 2019, the Turkish intervention into Syria had ceased.

A week later, loosening the US stance, Trump lifted the sanctions on Turkey.[165] The reversal of the Halkbank indictment, however, would be not as simple and would take Trump more efforts to prevent the bank case from going forward.

CHAPTER 6

INTERFERENCE INTO THE HALKBANK INVESTIGATION

THE TESTIMONY OF REZA ZARRAB

As discussed in chapter 1, the Halkbank case was first prosecuted in Turkey in 2013. It led to massive public protests across the country against apparent government corruption. The magnitude of the case was enormous. It implicated numerous government officials, including then Turkish prime minister Erdogan and his family, as being complicit in an unprecedented $20 billion money-laundering scheme. Erdogan's immediate response to the emerging scandal was a reshuffling of the Turkish cabinet and the purging of police officers and prosecutors who had been investigating the case.

In 2014 the corruption case was silenced. The vast majority of the criminal charges were dropped. Reza Zarrab, the Iranian gold trader who had run the money-laundering operation, was set free, and the prosecutorial storm that could have taken down the Turkish government was swept away as if it never existed.

Two years later the Turkish money-laundering saga reappeared, this time in the United States. Justice Department authorities arrested Reza Zarrab as he arrived in Florida.[1] The following year, in March 2017, the FBI took into custody the deputy general manager for international banking at Halkbank, Mehmet Hakan Atilla, after he flew into New York.[2] Almost six months later, the SDNY indicted in absentia four more people, who included a former Turkish economic minister and two other Halkbank executives.[3]

Both Zarrab's and Atilla's court hearings were scheduled for late November 2017. By late October to early November, the news media started speculating that Zarrab might have turned state's evidence and was cooperating with the US government's investigation.[4] Journalists cited both his absence from preliminary hearings and details from prison records that stated that Zarrab had been released in early November.[5] Those assumptions turned out to be correct. Reza Zarrab pleaded guilty and agreed to testify against coconspirator Mehmet Hakan Atilla.[6]

Almost a month later, Zarrab appeared on the witness stand, providing a detailed

49

account of the money-laundering scheme and the names of the officials he bribed along the way to make the system work. The next day Zarrab shocked the jury and journalists in the audience by stating that Recep Tayyip Erdogan, while serving as Turkey's prime minister, personally gave an order for two other Turkish banks, VakifBank and Ziraat Bank, to process the funds in the scheme.[7] Along with Halkbank, these were among the largest banks in Turkey.[8]

Zarrab's claim of Erdogan's involvement in the scheme was corroborated by a former Istanbul police officer who stated during Atilla's trial that Erdogan was the "number one" target in the 2013 corruption investigation in Turkey.[9] After being removed from the investigation and being imprisoned during Erdogan's police purge, the officer fled Turkey with all the evidence he had gathered about the corruption case and handed those documents over to US prosecutors.[10]

During his testimony Zarrab also shared that after his release from a Turkish prison in 2014, he considered returning to the same trading scheme. Zarrab claimed that he was tacitly encouraged to do so by Berat Albayrak, Erdogan's son-in-law.[11] Zarrab ended his testimony with a story of what he believed was an assassination attempt while he was in prison. He assumed that it was a retaliation from the Turkish government for him agreeing to cooperate with US investigators.[12]

It seems that the Atilla hearings and Zarrab's testimony indeed stirred up a hornet's nest in Ankara. Days before the trial, Erdogan's government described it as a "clear plot against Turkey"[13] and announced an investigation into the American prosecutors handling the case.[14] The state media portrayed the trial as a fabrication by the Gülen movement[15] and yet failed to mention the part about Zarrab paying bribes to Turkish officials.[16] The day that Zarrab implicated Erdogan in his testimony, Turkish authorities, in apparent retribution, announced their intentions to seize the gold trader's assets.[17] Throughout the week of Zarrab's testimony, representatives of the Turkish government made bold statements about the deterioration of US-Turkish relations.[18] There was some truth to that. The Halkbank investigation threatened to snowball into a diplomatic crisis, and the situation was further exacerbated by Turkish officials.

In September 2017, a week after the SDNY indicted Erdogan's former Turkish minister of economy and a former Halkbank general manager,[19] the Turkish government announced a deal with Russia to purchase their S-400 air defense system.[20] By doing so, Turkey was seemingly sending a signal for the US government to intervene in the Halkbank investigations or risk losing Turkey as a strategic Middle Eastern ally that could turn toward the US adversary, Russia. That seemingly desperate gamble demonstrated the magnitude of geopolitical damage that could be caused by the $20 billion money-laundering case.

If the Halkbank investigation proceeded further, any additional prosecutions would have a cascading effect. Halkbank could be convicted and likely pay heavy fines. Turkey could suffer reputational damages on the world stage. Its banking institutions that were part of the money-laundering scheme could be cut off from the international banking system. That could, in turn, send Turkey into economic turmoil. But most important for the Turkish president, the investigations could impose a direct threat on Erdogan's power and freedom, as well as those family members implicated in the case. That was a big enough reason for Erdogan and his allies to pressure the US government to drop the case.

TURKISH PRESSURE

THE REQUESTS TO THE OBAMA ADMINISTRATION

In 2016 Erdogan asked then vice president Joe Biden, at least twice, to intervene in the investigation against Reza Zarrab. According to Biden's aide, in August 2016, when Biden flew to Turkey, Erdogan privately pressed the vice president to drop Reza Zarrab's criminal case; remove the incumbent SDNY attorney prosecuting the case, Preet Bharara; and fire the judge overseeing the case as a way to improve relations with Turkey.[21] The following month at the United Nations General Assembly gathering in New York, Erdogan again urged VP Biden[22] to release Zarrab and fire both the SDNY prosecutor and the judge overseeing the case.[23]

In October 2016 the Turkish justice minister reportedly requested US attorney general Loretta Lynch to return Reza Zarrab to Turkey but was denied.[24] Erdogan also brought up the Reza Zarrab issue during his last calls with Pres. Barack Obama, in December 2016 and again in early January 2017.[25] Neither President Obama nor his administration officials granted Erdogan's requests. However, with the new president coming into the White House, Erdogan had a new opening.

ERDOGAN'S REQUESTS TO DONALD TRUMP

The day after Donald Trump's victory in November 2016, Erdogan called to congratulate him.[26] Shortly after Donald Trump was sworn in as the forty-fifth president of the United States, his avid supporter Rudy Giuliani joined Reza Zarrab's legal team.[27] That gave Giuliani motive to repeatedly encourage the president and his administration officials to intervene in the matters that concerned the Turkish president the most, the return of Reza Zarrab and Fethullah Gülen to Turkey. As mentioned previously, Rudy Giuliani attempted to facilitate an exchange of his client for the American pastor Andrew Brunson, who was kept as a political hostage by the Turkish government.

Throughout 2017 Giuliani had been putting forth effort to persuade officials of the newly formed Trump administration to find a "diplomatic" solution and "lobbying anyone he could find in the government to get his guy [Zarrab] out."[28] To the dismay of his advisors, President Trump was receptive to Giuliani's pleas.

In a January 2021 interview, former secretary of state Rex Tillerson recalled that Rudy Giuliani and Michael Mukasey, a former US attorney general under George W. Bush, had repeatedly asked Tillerson to intervene in the Halkbank case, to which he replied:[29]

Y'all are barking up the wrong tree here because you're not going to find an agency in the government that is going to advise the government to do this.

Donald Trump had repeatedly signaled his interest in the resolution of the Halkbank investigation in the Turkish government's favor. Tillerson also told to *Foreign Policy* magazine[30]

that he was "not really sure that [Trump] understood the magnitude of the Halkbank case," and he tried to explain the gravity to the president, with no success.

John Bolton's account of Trump's actions was very similar:[31]

Despite being told what Halkbank was being investigated for, I'm still not certain he ever fully appreciated it was for violating U.S. sanctions against Iran and then committing financial fraud by lying about the violations... I don't think Trump ever fully internalized what the nature of the underlying charges was.

Trump was captivated by autocratic presidents and seemingly wanted to elevate himself to their level. Bolton characterized Trump's conversations with the Turkish president by suggesting that Trump would say something like:[32]

Oh, you need a favor, I'll do you a favor... I'm doing it for you personally.

Rex Tillerson had a similar opinion:[33]

That's what always made it very difficult in dealing with situations where the president seemed to want to grant relief to very authoritarian figures, whether it's Erdogan or [North Korean leader] Kim [Jong Un] or go down the list....

There were occasions where Erdogan would ask the president to do certain things and myself or others would intervene and explain to the president that it'd be not only difficult to do but potentially illegal to do so.

One such occasion happened in December 2018, when Trump and Erdogan discussed the Halkbank investigation during the G20 summit in Buenos Aires.[34] In his book the former national security advisor John Bolton described that meeting as follows:[35]

> Erdogan provided a memo by the law firm representing Halkbank, which Trump did nothing more than flip through before declaring he believed Halkbank was totally innocent of violating US Iran sanctions. Trump asked whether we could reach Acting US Attorney General Matt Whitaker, which I sidestepped. Trump then told Erdogan he would take care of things, explaining that the Southern District prosecutors were not his people, but were Obama people, a problem that would be fixed when they were replaced by his people.

He would end up fulfilling that promise, firing not one but two consecutive SDNY lead attorneys who were overseeing the Halkbank case.

THE FIRINGS OF THE US ATTORNEYS FOR THE SDNY

PREET BHARARA

The Southern District of New York is highly coveted by federal prosecutors and is considered the most prestigious. It has a history of high-profile prosecutions against organized crime figures, acts of terrorism, corruption in the public sphere, and financial crimes. Some of the notable cases include the prosecution of a Ponzi scheme financier, Bernie Madoff, and prosecutions related to the September 11 attack. The SDNY was central to investigating persons connected to the Halkbank money-laundering scheme. It is deemed the "Sovereign" District of New York for its reputation of relative free rein within the Department of Justice. Because of the scope of its cases, the appointments and removals of the key figures at the SDNY are closely followed by political and legal observers.

When Donald Trump was elected the president of the United States, all the federal US attorneys were getting ready to resign from their positions. Incoming presidents often replace federal attorneys with their own choices for the ninety-four federal district offices across the country. Usually, that process happens in an orderly fashion, with a seamless transition between administrations to avoid interruptions in investigations. The president nominates his choice for each federal district, and that choice then goes through a confirmation process in the Senate.

Like many other prosecutors, Preet Bharara, who had served as the US attorney for the SDNY since the beginning of the Obama administration, was preparing to be replaced. However, in late November 2016 the president-elect summoned Bharara to Trump Tower in New York and asked him to stay on as the lead prosecutor at the SDNY office.[36] Other people reportedly present at the meeting were Steve Bannon, who served as Trump's advisor, and Jared Kushner, the president-elect's son-in-law. According to Bharara's later recollection, during the meeting Donald Trump had asked the US attorney to write down his phone number on a Post-it sticker.[37] Later

Donald Trump would use that number to call Bharara at least three times.

The first two calls from Donald Trump to Preet Bharara came on December 12, 2016, and on January 18, 2017. As Donald Trump hadn't been sworn in as president yet and was still in the president-elect status, the prosecutor found it ethically acceptable to return Trump's calls. Bharara said in his podcast that he felt that Donald Trump's calls were his way of trying to "cultivate a relationship."[38]

Bharara passed the information about Trump's calls to Jeff Sessions, the attorney general in transition. Later Bharara would mention that, to his knowledge, Trump hadn't called any other lead federal prosecutors during the transition.[39]

On March 9, 2017, after Trump had been sworn in, his secretary left a voicemail on Bharara's phone asking him to call back. After a somewhat long deliberation and discussions with his peers, the prosecutor concluded that it would be inappropriate to return Trump's call. Bharara would later explain his decision as follows:[40]

So now I had this issue of whether or not to call the president of the United States back. And I presumed that the people would think, "Well, he's kind of your boss, he asked you to stay, you serve at the pleasure of the President, why don't just call him back?" And it's important to understand, that's not really how it works in the Justice Department. It's a little bit different and that there has to be not only independence, but the appearance of independence. And if something is happening, sort of behind the scenes and not through normal channels, it can look terrible, not just for the US attorney or the Attorney General or whoever, but for the President himself . . .

. . . I called Jeff Sessions' office and I spoke directly to Jody Hunt. Jody Hunt is the Chief of Staff to the Attorney General of the United States. And I said, "The President of the United States has called me, do you agree with me that I should decline to speak to the President of the United States?"

And Jeff Sessions' Chief of Staff said, "I agree with you."

So I called the [Trump] secretary back. It was about an hour and a half later, and I said, "I mean no disrespect to the President, but given guidelines and current circumstances and the agreement of Jeff Sessions' office, I don't think it's appropriate for me to speak directly to the President."

20 hours later, I was asked to resign.

I don't know if those two events are connected. We may never know, but the timing certainly is pretty odd.

The underlying reason behind Bharara's refusal to call back the president was the principle of the Justice Department's autonomy from the White House, which was introduced after former president Richard Nixon had attempted to use the DOJ for his own political interests.[41] Since then the common practice of communication between the members of the DOJ with the president has been through offices of the attorney general or the deputy attorney general.

Aside from the disregard of the interaction protocol by the president, as Preet Bharara pointed out, the timing of his calls was "pretty odd." At the time, a lot of meetings related to the Halkbank case, which Bharara's office was investigating, were happening in the background. The day after Donald Trump called to Preet Bharara for the second time, Brian Ballard, the lobbyist with close ties to the president, met with the Turkish foreign minister, Lev Parnas, and Mubariz Mansimov. Based on the text messages between Parnas and Mansimov, it appeared that during the meeting the groups had discussed Reza Zarrab's case.

Bharara's firing also came three weeks after Rudy Giuliani and Michael Mukasey went to Turkey to discuss with Erdogan a possible "diplomatic solution" for Zarrab's case. The day before Trump's last call to the prosecutor, Brian Ballard met with Parnas and Farkhad Akhmedov, the Russian oligarch who was acting as an intermediary for Turkey, to discuss a lobbying contract. Considering those events, one can't help but wonder whether Rudy Giuliani and Brian Ballard's meetings with Turkish officials were the animus behind Donald Trump's sudden change of heart and his decision to fire Preet Bharara.

GEOFFREY BERMAN

The position of the lead prosecutor at the SDNY was left open by the Trump administration for almost a year. Only in January 2018, then attorney general Jeff Sessions selected Geoffrey Berman as the interim US attorney for the SDNY.[42] Three months later, in April 2018, the judges of the Southern District of New York reappointed Berman for an indeterminate period or until there was another candidate picked by the president and approved by the US Senate.

Although Berman had previous experience at the SDNY, there were skeptics who were concerned that he was "Trump's puppet"[43] as before his appointment to the SDNY Berman had worked at Greenberg Traurig, the same law firm as Rudy Giuliani. However, Geoffrey Berman proved to be his own man when he later moved to investigate Trump's allies, including Rudy Giuliani and Steve Bannon. Berman's office would also investigate and charge Michael Cohen,[44] Imaad Zuberi,[45] Lev Parnas, Igor Fruman,[46] and Halkbank.[47]

In his book, *Holding the Line*, Geoffrey Berman described the Halkbank case as "a top priority since the day I took the job." Since his appointment and throughout the summer of 2018, the SDNY office had talked to the Halkbank lawyers. Berman wrote that the SDNY was willing to accept a deferred prosecution agreement, or DPA, that[48]

> required the bank to accept responsibility for its readily provable criminal conduct, cooperate with our office, accept a monitorship for some length of time, and agree to an unspecified monetary penalty reflective of its conduct. Those were the minimum parameters.

However, Turkish officials sought to have the Halkbank investigation dismissed entirely. As mentioned in the previous chapter, in July 2018 they tried to pressure the Departments of State and Treasury[49] to "kill" the money-laundering case in exchange for the release of the American evangelical pastor Andrew Brunson.[50] In November 2018 the Halkbank defense team brought their own version of the DPA that would allow the bank to "claim it was vindicated" and have the case closed.

The discussion of the case was happening at the highest levels of the US government. In mid-December 2018 Trump and Erdogan had a phone call where they discussed the Halkbank investigation. According to John Bolton's recollection:[51]

> Trump started by saying we were getting very close to a resolution on Halkbank. He had just spoken to Mnuchin and Pompeo, and said we would be dealing with Erdogan's great son-in-law (Turkey's Finance Minister) to get it off his shoulders. Erdogan was very grateful, speaking in English no less.

Probably unaware of those behind-the-scenes overtures, Geoffrey Berman decided to request permission from then acting attorney general Matthew Whitaker, who replaced the recently fired Jeff Sessions, to indict the bank.[52] Whitaker refused and reportedly attempted to stop the Halkbank investigation by ordering the case closed. However, Justice Department officials declined to follow through on the acting AG's request as they assumed that Whitaker would be replaced with someone else.[53]

That someone else was William Barr, who was confirmed as attorney general of the United States in mid-February 2019. Shortly after his confirmation, the new AG met with Berman and told him that he would take Berman's opinion on the Halkbank case "under advisement."[54] Berman had hoped that William Barr would run the Department of Justice without political interference and protect the integrity of its investigations. However, it turned out that Barr had a different approach.

Berman wrote in his book that shortly after his first meeting with Attorney General Barr, he discovered that Halkbank lawyers were talking directly to high-level officials within the DOJ, thereby bypassing the SDNY.[55] Berman implied that he perceived an unusual amount of interest in the Halkbank case, which was evidenced by the pressure that Attorney General Barr tried to apply on Berman. Later it became clear to him that the administration wanted special treatment for the Turkish bank.

That special treatment directive came all the way from the top. In April 2019 Donald Trump tasked AG William Barr and Secretary of Treasury Steven Mnuchin to intervene in the Halkbank case[56] and "handle" the issue.[57] A couple of months later, on June 10, 2019, Attorney General Barr called Berman and told him that the Trump administration had assigned Barr as the "point person" to oversee SDNY's Halkbank case.[58] The following day William Barr reportedly met with representatives of the Turkish Ministry of Justice. Berman was not informed of the meeting, nor was he invited.[59] That was highly irregular and inappropriate, considering his office was prosecuting the case.

Days later, on June 14, 2019, Halkbank lawyers, emboldened by their direct access to Main Justice, requested a "global resolution" with the SDNY. Berman considered it an agreement that could exonerate the bank and shield Turkish officials potentially implicated in the scheme from any future prosecution.[60]

Berman's answer was no.[61]

Shortly thereafter Attorney General Barr summoned Berman to Washington, DC, to discuss the Halkbank investigation and pressed Berman to accept the "global resolution."[62] Berman strongly opposed the settlement proposal:[63]

> *Barr raised the possibility that rather than grant official immunity to individuals, we could give them a side letter, a non-prosecution agreement that would not have to be disclosed to the court.*
>
> *... He wanted SDNY to do something completely off the record—to draft an agreement with the bank as well as bank and government officials that would be invisible to the public and the court.*
>
> *I replied that this would be a corruption of the process. It would be a "fraud on the court" to hide part of a resolution with the bank. I don't think he appreciated that comment very much.*

Returning from the meeting, Berman shared his frustration about Barr's proposal with his peers, arguing against letting the perpetrators go without any concessions.[64]

Former secretary of state Rex Tillerson later shared his sentiment on the case in an interview with *Foreign Policy* magazine:[65]

> *It's both the precedent and the fact that if you're not willing to prosecute these guys for these the most egregious violations under sanctions laws, then what are you going to do in the future, with anybody?*

Berman said that around that time he had received a tip[66] that if he kept his stance favoring the prosecution of Halkbank, then he would be replaced by Ed O'Callaghan,[67] a DOJ official who had previously led the National Security Division at the DOJ[68] and whom Berman considered a "Barr loyalist."[69]

After the standoff between William Barr and Geoffrey Berman, the Halkbank case "was taken away" from the SDNY and given to the National Security Division at the DOJ.[70] That, like other decisions of Attorney General Barr regarding the Halkbank case, was highly irregular. His actions might be explained by the pressure that he was coming under from President Trump, who, in turn, had been repeatedly bombarded by requests to drop the Halkbank investigation from Erdogan and many others.

Between June and October 2019, SDNY prosecutors didn't have access to the Halkbank case. Then the Trump administration's stance on the Halkbank case suddenly changed. Berman described the events in his book as follows:[71]

> *Then something unexpected, and, in light of all that occurred previously, bizarre, occurred on October 15. Barr called me and said the team should put the Halkbank case in the grand jury that day so we could be in a position to indict.*

That sudden shift was caused by a situation that was unfolding along the Turkish-Syrian border described in the previous chapter. In early October 2019, Turkish president Erdogan called Donald Trump and demanded that the United States remove its military forces that were stationed near Syrian Kurds. Against the recommendations of his advisors, Trump acquiesced to Erdogan's demands by ordering the immediate withdrawal of US forces from the area. That cleared the way for Turkish troops to launch their attack against the Syrian Kurds on October 9, 2019.

After strong bipartisan congressional backlash, President Trump rapidly inverted his position and demanded Turkey stop its invasion. On October 14, 2019, under pressure from Congress, Trump imposed sanctions on Turkey. The next day the United States increased its leverage on Turkey when the DOJ indicted Halkbank.

During all that standoff, there was another saga unraveling at the time. The Congress had opened an impeachment investigation on Donald Trump's actions related to Ukraine, which will be described later in this book. The impeachment process would dominate the media landscape for the following months. It undoubtedly was Donald Trump's main concern, leaving the Halkbank case a matter of lower priority.

Then in early 2020, leaks from John Bolton's book manuscript cast a shadow on Donald Trump's presidential decisions and his interactions with foreign powers. In his book Bolton brought more attention to the Halkbank case and its handling by Donald Trump and Attorney General Barr. Despite the Trump administration's numerous attempts to block the book from being published,[72] it was scheduled for release on June 23, 2020.

In parallel Trump's administration started making unexpected moves at the SDNY. On June 19, 2020, Attorney General Barr summoned Geoffrey Berman to a meeting. Berman recollected his conversation with Barr as follows:[73]

> "I want to make a change in the Southern District," Barr said at just about the same moment I lowered myself onto the chair. That's how he started. There were no pleasantries. He continued by saying that he wanted me to resign my position and take an open position at Main Justice—chief of the Civil Division. He said that would create an opening for Jay Clayton, who was chairman of the Securities and Exchange Commission, to be nominated for SDNY. . . .
>
> . . . I told Barr that I had no interest in the position he was offering and that I intended to stay in the job. He then, predictably, lifted the hammer. "If you do not resign from your position, you will be fired, and that will not be good for your résumé and future job prospects."

It seemed as if Attorney General Barr wanted to replace Berman with an ally. Barr was offering him a secure alternative, expecting Berman wouldn't complain. Barr's move seemed familiar to Berman. The attorney general had previously used similar tactics to oust the US attorney in Washington, DC, Jessie Liu. Her office had been investigating core Trump allies Roger Stone and Michael Flynn. Barr had offered her a job in the Treasury Department if she resigned her position as US attorney. Liu agreed. As her replacement, the DOJ suggested Ed O'Callaghan,[74] the same person who was considered to replace Berman at the SDNY in mid-2019, before settling for another close ally of Barr.[75]

Within weeks of Liu's resignation, there were dramatic changes in the cases of two Trump allies that she had overseen as DC district attorney. In early February 2019 a DOJ filing overrode the line prosecutor's seven to nine year sentencing recommendation[76] for the convicted Roger Stone and instead suggested that the court apply a less "excessive" sentence.[77] In response all four prosecutors handling Stone's investigation withdrew from the case.[78] Days later Attorney General Barr ordered a review of the DOJ's case against Michael Flynn despite Flynn already having pleaded guilty twice in court.[79] Around that same time, Donald Trump withdrew Jessie Liu's nomination for the undersecretary of the Treasury Department, effectively taking her out of the legal equation.[80]

Sensing that Barr's actions toward him echoed Liu's removal in DC, Geoffrey Berman refused to resign and declined Barr's offer at the DOJ Civil Division. That same day Barr returned with another suggestion:[81]

> Barr called me later that same afternoon with a new idea: Would I want to be chairman of the Securities and Exchange Commission, the job Clayton would be vacating?
>
> . . . And there was another big stumbling block Barr was conveniently ignoring: It was not his to offer. He didn't have the power to appoint me or anyone else chairman of

> the SEC. The person holding down that position is nominated by the president and confirmed by the Senate.

Berman declined that offer as well. At the end of the call, the attorney general promised to call Berman back the following day. However, that evening Barr released a statement that explained Berman was resigning and that he would be replaced with Jay Clayton,[82] an attorney from the SEC who lacked sufficient prosecutorial experience required to lead the office. Until Clayton could be confirmed by the Senate, Attorney General Barr offered that Craig Carpenito, the US attorney for New Jersey who already oversaw federal prosecutions in his own district, would also serve in the interim at the SDNY.

It seemed that Barr was trying to apply the tactics he used in DC now at the SDNY: to smoothly replace Berman with a loyal person, then intervene in the cases that could affect Donald Trump and his allies. Geoffrey Berman later explained the situation in an interview with *Stanford Lawyer* magazine:[83]

> *I was concerned not so much with the nomination of Jay Clayton, but more with who was going to take the spot of acting U.S. attorney during the interim period between my resignation and the confirmation. That's what I was primarily focused on—doing everything I could to ensure that the office's investigations would continue uninterrupted in the months prior to the election. A few months earlier the attorney general arranged for the U.S. attorney in D.C. to resign and replaced her not with her deputy but with someone from outside that office who was a senior adviser to the attorney general. I suspected that that was exactly what the attorney general wanted to accomplish in the Southern District and I was committed to stopping that from happening.*

Berman reacted to Barr's announcement of his resignation by issuing his own statement the same day:[84]

> *I learned in a press release from the Attorney General tonight that I was "stepping down" as United States Attorney. I have not resigned, and have no intention of resigning, my position, to which I was appointed by the Judges of the United States District Court for the Southern District of New York. I will step down when a presidentially appointed nominee is confirmed by the Senate. Until then, our investigations will move forward without delay or interruption. I cherish every day that I work with the men and women of this Office to pursue justice without fear or favor—and intend to ensure that this Office's important cases continue unimpeded.*

With that statement, Berman threw down the gauntlet. He called out Barr's insinuation that he had resigned in agreement with the attorney general. One could decipher the between-the-lines message that Berman was sending to Barr as "If you're going to fire me, you have to do it the right way, not put in someone to do your bidding."

Seemingly caught red-handed, the following day Attorney General Barr released a public letter accusing Geoffrey Berman of making a "public spectacle" and informing him that Berman had been removed from his position by presidential order.[85] The letter also included that Berman's deputy, Audrey Strauss, would take over Berman's duties.

In that short public standoff, after Barr's agreement to follow the lines of succession, on June 20, 2020, Berman agreed to step down:[86]

> *In light of Attorney General Barr's decision to respect the normal operation of law and have Deputy U.S. Attorney Audrey Strauss become Acting U.S. Attorney, I will be leaving the U.S. Attorney's Office for the Southern District of New York, effective immediately. It has been the honor of a lifetime to serve as this District's U.S. Attorney and a custodian of its proud legacy, but I could leave the District in no better hands than Audrey's. She is the smartest, most principled, and effective lawyer with whom I have ever had the privilege of working. And I know that under her leadership, this Office's unparalleled AUSAs [assistant US attorneys], investigators, paralegals, and staff will continue to safeguard the Southern District's enduring tradition of integrity and independence.*

Public critics suspected obstruction of justice in Berman's dismissal and drew parallels to Donald Trump's firing of the FBI director James Comey in May 2017[87] after Comey told Congress that the FBI was looking into the president and his campaign team for a potential conspiracy with the Russian government.[88]

There was no conclusive explanation given to the public by the White House or by the Department of Justice that justified US attorney Berman's sudden dismissal. On July 9, 2020, Geoffrey Berman testified to Congress about his firing where he illuminated Barr's pressure campaign to force him to quit.[89] His public firing also led to questions of the president's potential improper interference at the Department of Justice.[90] Donald Trump himself said he was "not involved" in Berman's firing[91] despite the fact that he was the only one who could fire the SDNY attorney. However, while the president had the power to fire the US attorney, doing so with corrupt intent would have been illegal.

Two years after his firing, Berman would release a book in which he would imply that his persistence with the Halkbank investigation might have been the reason. Also, at the time of Berman's firing, the SDNY was handling several cases that could potentially lead to Donald Trump. One of the people was the president's private attorney, Rudy Giuliani, who was probed for foreign lobbying,[92] as well as his associates Lev Parnas and Igor Fruman, indicted for their political donations. All of them were, at some point, part of Turkey's attempts to obstruct the prosecution of Halkbank. Any of those investigations could implicate Donald Trump, jeopardizing his chances for his reelection to a second term in 2020.

The day after Berman was fired, John Bolton gave an interview in which he shared his thoughts on Trump's willingness to intervene in the SDNY's investigation of the Halkbank case:[93]

> So if this had been a U.S. financial institution, we would've toasted them, and quite properly so. So it was not a case where Halkbank was being treated by the U.S. attorney for the Southern District of New York more harshly than an American bank. It was just really looking for the same kind of treatment.
>
> And the president said to Erdogan at one point, "Look, those prosecutors in New York are Obama people. Wait till I get my people in and then we'll take care of this." And I thought to myself—and I'm a Department of Justice alumnus myself—"I've never heard any president say anything like that. Ever."
>
> Now ultimately, I think Attorney General Barr got the prosecution of Halkbank that they deserved because the Turks wouldn't agree to anything like a reasonable settlement. So it turned out all right. But that's so far. That's how close we got. That's how close we got. And I find that disturbing . . . .
>
> [B]ut I tell ya, it did feel like obstruction of justice to me. The president has enormous power in the law enforcement area. The executive power is vested in the president.
>
> And the attorney general, as the Supreme Court said in the famous case, the attorney general is the hand of the president in fulfilling the president's duty to take care that the laws be faithfully executed. But that means faithful execution[,] means execution that's not politically motivated. And—this idea that you give Erdogan and his family, who use Halkbank like a slush fund—in exchange for, what?—some hope down the road of some other kind of treatment for Trump or the country—was very troubling.

TIMELINE OF THE EVENTS RELATED TO THE HALKBANK INVESTIGATION IN THE US*

*See the full integrated timeline in appendix A.

March 19, 2016 - Reza Zarrab, the Iranian gold trader at the center of in the Halkbank money-laundering scheme, was arrested in Miami, Florida, by the US government.

March 21, 2016 - The SDNY unsealed indictments of Reza Zarrab and two other people for conspiracy to evade US sanctions on Iran, money laundering, and bank fraud.

May 25, 2016 - The SDNY objected Reza Zarrab's request for bail and released a memorandum that implicated President Erdogan and other high-ranking Turkish officials in the Halkbank case.

August 24, 2016 - VP Joe Biden flew to Turkey to reassure American support for Erdogan's government after the coup attempt. According to his aide, Biden was privately pressed by Erdogan to drop the Halkbank case and remove SDNY attorney Preet Bharara to improve relations with Turkey.

September 21, 2016 - President Erdogan pressed Vice President Biden to release Zarrab and fire both the NY prosecutor Preet Bharara and the judge overseeing the case. Biden rejected the request.

October 2016 - The Turkish justice minister asked US attorney general Loretta Lynch to release Zarrab and return him to Turkey. The attorney general rejected the request.

November 30, 2016 - Donald Trump met with Preet Bharara in Trump Tower in New York City.

December 12, 2016 - Donald Trump called Preet Bharara for the first time.

January 18, 2017 - Trump International Hotel in Washington, DC, hosted an event with about forty foreign ambassadors and officials. The event was attended by the Turkish foreign minister Mevlut Cavusoglu, the incoming National Security Advisor Michael Flynn, and Rep. Devin Nunes.

January 18, 2017 - Donald Trump called Preet Bharara for the second time.

January 19, 2017 - Turkish foreign minister Mevlut Cavusoglu met with Brian Ballard to discuss a contract for lobbying services for the Turkish government. The meeting was arranged by Lev Parnas and Mubariz Mansimov.

January 22, 2017 - Mubariz Mansimov sent Lev Parnas a text with the name "Riza Zarrab."

February 24, 2017 - Rudy Giuliani contacted Preet Bharara to inform the prosecutor about his upcoming trip to Turkey. At the time, Giuliani was working at Greenberg Traurig.

Late February 2017 - Rudy Giuliani and former US attorney general Michael Mukasey met with President Erdogan in Turkey and allegedly discussed a "diplomatic solution" for Reza Zarrab's case.

March 1, 2017 - Greenberg Traurig signed a direct lobbying contract with the Turkish government. Before that Greenberg Traurig was a subcontractor of the Gephardt Group, which, in turn, provided lobbying services to the Turkish government.

March 3–5, 2017 - Lev Parnas and Farkhad Akhmedov attended the RNC donors' retreat in Florida.

March 8, 2017 - Lev Parnas and Farkhad Akhmedov flew to Washington, DC, to meet with Brian Ballard to discuss a lobbying contract with Turkey.

March 9, 2017 - Donald Trump called Preet Bharara for the third time.

March 11, 2017 - Pres. Donald Trump fired Preet Bharara.

March 27, 2017 - The FBI arrested Mehmet Hakan Atilla, deputy general manager for international banking at Halkbank. He was responsible for maintaining the bank's relationships, including its US correspondent accounts, and the bank's relationships with Iranian banks, including the Central Bank of Iran. The charges were brought by Preet Bharara's successor, Joon Kim.

March 27, 2017 - The news of Rudy Giuliani and Michael Mukasey joining Zarrab's legal team became public.

May 11, 2017 - Ballard partners signed a lobbying contract with Turkey, with a monthly fee of $125,000. Lev Parnas was paid $45,000 for introducing Ballard Partners to the Turkish government.

August 21, 2017 - Ballard Partners signed a lobbying contract with Halkbank.

September 6, 2017 - The SDNY expanded Reza Zarrab's indictment, adding charges of the former Halkbank general manager and the former Turkish minister of the economy.

September 12, 2017 - The Turkish government announced a deal to purchase the Russian-made S-400 air defense system.

October 26, 2017 - Reza Zarrab pleaded guilty to all counts and agreed to cooperate with the US authorities.

November 8, 2017 - Reza Zarrab was released from prison.

November 15, 2017 - The Turkish government inquired US officials about the location of Reza Zarrab.

November 18, 2017 - Turkey announced a probe into the US prosecutors handling the Halkbank investigations, accusing them of using fabricated documents.

November 21, 2017 - The Turkish government contracted King & Spalding, a law firm from Atlanta, Georgia, to advise Turkey on "US legislation including but not limited to regulatory and law enforcement matters."

November 29, 2017 - Reza Zarrab started testifying against Mehmet Atilla. Zarrab said that then prime minister Erdogan "personally ordered" two Turkish banks, Ziraat Bank and VakifBank, to be a part of the money-laundering scheme. (Ziraat Bank, VakifBank, and Halkbank are among the largest banks in Turkey.) Zarrab also said that his lawyers, Rudy Giuliani and Michael Mukasey, hadn't been successful in convincing Trump administration officials to negotiate a diplomatic resolution to his prosecution.

November 30, 2017 - Turkish authorities announced their intention to seize Zarrab's assets in Turkey.

December 21, 2017 - Pro-government Turkish media accused Judge Richard Berman, who was overseeing Atilla's trial, of being connected to the Fethullah Gülen movement.

January 3, 2018 - Halkbank executive Mehmet Hakan Atilla was found guilty.

January 3, 2018 - US attorney general Jeff Sessions announced Geoffrey Berman (not related to Judge Richard Berman) would serve as the interim US attorney at the SDNY.

January 9, 2018 - Turkish president Erdogan called the Halkbank investigation led by the SDNY prosecutors a "political coup attempt" against him.

May 16, 2018 - Mehmet Hakan Atilla was sentenced to thirty-two months in prison.

Mid to late July 2018 - The United States and Turkey almost reached an agreement to exchange Andrew Brunson for Mehmet Hakan Atilla. However, the talks halted when Turkey's foreign minister added the request to dismiss the Halkbank investigation in the United States.

December 1, 2018 - Erdogan and Trump met at the G20 summit in Buenos Aires, Argentina. According to John Bolton, Trump promised Erdogan at the meeting that he would take care of things in the Southern District and that "Obama people will be replaced by his people."

December 14, 2018 - Trump told Erdogan in a phone call that the US was "getting close to a resolution on Halkbank."

Around late December 2018–January 2019 – SDNY lead prosecutor Geoffrey Berman requested permission from the acting attorney general Matthew Whitaker to file criminal charges against Halkbank itself. Whitaker denied the request.

April 2019 - In a phone call with Erdogan, Trump reportedly told him that attorney general William Barr and secretary of treasury Steven Mnuchin would "handle" the Halkbank issue.

June 10, 2019 – Attorney General Barr informed SDNY attorney Geoffrey Berman that the Trump administration assigned Barr as a "point person" in the Halkbank investigation.

June 11, 2019 – Attorney General Barr met with representatives of the Turkish ministry of justice about the DOJ's prosecution of the Halkbank case.

June 14, 2019 - A Halkbank defense lawyer requested a "global resolution" that would indemnify the bank and any officials involved in the scheme. Berman refused.

June 17, 2019 - SDNY lead prosecutor Geoffrey Berman, traveled to Washington, DC, to discuss the Halkbank case with Attorney General Barr. According to the *New York Times*, "Mr. Barr pressed Mr. Berman to allow the bank to avoid an indictment by paying a fine and acknowledging some wrongdoing," Berman refused.

July 24, 2019 - After serving his prison sentence in the US, Mehmet Hakan Atilla returned to Turkey. He was "greeted at the airport with flowers and a hug" from

Berat Albayrak, as well as by the CEOs of Halkbank and Ziraat Bank. Three months later Atilla became the head of Turkey's Stock Exchange.

October 6, 2019 - President Trump had a call with President Erdogan where they discussed the withdrawal of US troops from Syria. President Trump acquiesced to President Erdogan's plan to invade northern Syria to attack the Kurdish settlements along the Turkish-Syrian border.

October 8, 2019 - President Trump ordered the rapid withdrawal of part of the US troops from northern Syria, opening the region up for a major Turkish incursion into Syria, to attack the Kurds along the border.

October 9, 2019 - After congressional pushback, President Trump sent a letter to President Erdogan about Turkey's invasion of the Kurds in Syria saying "Don't be a tough guy. Don't be a fool!" According to BBC, "President Erdogan received the letter, thoroughly rejected it and put it in the bin." Turkey launched its attack on the Syrian Kurds along the Turkish-Syrian border.

October 14, 2019 - President Trump imposed sanctions on Turkey to stop its incursion into Syria. Trump also announced the freezing of a potential "$100bn trade deal."

October 15, 2019 - The DOJ charged Halkbank with (1) conspiracy to defraud the United States, (2) conspiracy to violate the International Emergency Economic Powers Act (IEEPA), (3) bank fraud, (4) conspiracy to commit bank fraud, (5) money laundering, and (6) conspiracy to commit money laundering. The indictment was released during the Turkish incursion into Syria.

June 20, 2020 - SDNY lead prosecutor Geoffrey Berman was fired by President Trump.

June 23, 2020 – John Bolton released his book, in which he suggested that Trump's actions related to Halkbank could be an obstruction of justice.

July 2, 2020 - Judge Richard Berman ordered the Halkbank trial to be scheduled in March 2021.

PART II
THE CLANDESTINE OPERATIONS OF RUDY GIULIANI AND LEV PARNAS

CHAPTER 7

THE EMERGENCE OF THE DYNAMIC DUO

THE ASCENT OF LEV PARNAS

On October 9, 2019, the FBI arrested Lev Parnas and Igor Fruman at Dulles International Airport near Washington, DC.[1] The next day news headlines were flooded with questions of who those men were[2] and why they had one-way tickets to Austria on them.[3]

Ten days prior Parnas, Fruman, and Giuliani were subpoenaed by three House committees[4] in relation to their activities in Ukraine.[5] Parnas and Fruman were scheduled for deposition on October 10 and 11, 2019. Giuliani was requested to provide documents by October 15, 2019, and was reportedly planning to fly to Austria the same night as Parnas and Fruman.[6] However, after their arrest Giuliani decided to remain in the United States.

The main mystery was how Lev Parnas and Igor Fruman were connected to Rudy Giuliani and Donald Trump. Lev Parnas was born in Ukraine and moved to the United States with his family when he was a toddler. His parents settled in Brighton Beach, a New York enclave known for its post-Soviet immigrants. In his teens Lev Parnas became involved in the New York organized crime scene.[7] Still in his teens Parnas began traveling to Russia and the former Soviet republics, looking for business opportunities.[8] In his twenties he moved on to Florida.[9]

On the surface he was the epitome of success, driving luxury cars and living in wealthy areas such as Boca Raton and Sunny Isles in Florida.[10] However, his career in the Sunshine State proved to be erratic, with him being engaged in at least sixteen businesses over twenty years.[11] The scope of Parnas's activities was broad and included pump-and-dump[12] stock schemes,[13] computer gadgets,[14] movie production,[15] and insurance.[16] Many of those endeavors ended in lawsuits and accusations of fraud. Between 2004 and 2019, Parnas was a subject of several court rulings,[17] including two evictions due to his apparent inability to pay rent. During one rent payment dispute, Parnas had reportedly held a gun to his landlord's head while refusing to leave the property.[18]

Parnas's luck seemed to have turned, at least for a time, with the entrance of Igor Fruman into his life. Like Lev Parnas, Igor Fruman lived in Florida. Although he moved to the United States in the 1990s, Fruman maintained his connections in Ukraine and gained wealth through his ventures there. Fruman had been engaged in import/export, nightlife, and real estate businesses. He also co-owned Buddha Bar in Kyiv; a nightclub with a telling name, Mafia Rave; and luxury real estate in Odesa, Ukraine.[19] In 2011 he was deemed one of the two hundred richest people in Ukraine,[20] and his local connections spun from oligarchs and politicians to members of organized crime.[21]

Parnas claimed that he was acquainted with Fruman through Soviet-born expats circles but didn't know him well until 2016,[22] when Fruman allegedly approached Parnas with a business proposal.[23] From then on the two would venture into a cannabis business in Nevada,[24] liquified natural gas supply in Eastern Europe,[25] and a charity for a Jewish village in Ukraine.[26] For Parnas, Fruman's connections in Ukraine and post-Soviet countries would become an asset. In turn, Parnas would become Fruman's English-speaking guide into the MAGA world.

One would reasonably ask, "How did Lev Parnas enter the MAGA world in the first place?" In several of his interviews, Lev Parnas said[27] that in his teens he had sold Trump properties.[28] Parnas said he had mentioned this to Donald Trump to develop a connection to the Republican front-runner when they first met.[29] The date of that first encounter had not been established, but one of the earliest photos of Lev Parnas with Donald Trump was taken in March 2014 during a fashion show in Doral, Florida.[30]

The next summer Donald Trump announced his presidential bid. Parnas told in an interview that he learned of the news from his eldest son, who called him and said:[31]

> *Dad, I think one of your friends is running for President.*

Later, in October 2015, Parnas and his son booked tickets[32] to attend a Trump campaign rally in Florida.[33]

The following year, in October 2016, Lev Parnas and David Correia attended a Trump fundraiser.[34] Trump campaign surrogates, such as Rudy Giuliani and Brian Ballard,[35] were present as well.[36] Two weeks later Parnas, who had no previous political affiliations and had never donated to any candidates,[37] made various contributions totaling almost $100,000. He donated $50,000 to Trump Victory PAC and $2,700 to candidate Trump. He also made contributions worth $661.90 each to at least twenty state Republican committees and $33,400 to the Republican National Committee.[38]

Those donations catapulted Lev Parnas into Trump's circle and provided him inner access to the MAGA world. Parnas and his associates would be invited[39] to the Trump victory party in New York on election night.[40] He obtained tickets to

Donald Trump's inauguration and rubbed elbows with prominent GOP donors. In an interview Parnas claimed that he and other Trump donors "became a one big family." In the same interview, Parnas claimed that he and Rudy Giuliani became "good friends."[41]

RUDY GIULIANI

There was a stark contrast between Lev Parnas and Rudy Giuliani. Parnas seemed to run on the edges of the law, and Giuliani was an American icon with a reputation as a fierce fighter against organized crime.

After the 9/11 terrorist attack on the Twin Towers in New York, Rudy Giuliani, who was the city's mayor at the time, became known as "America's mayor" and a symbol of the country's resilience in the wake of the seemingly unfathomable tragedy. He was named *Time* magazine's Person of the Year in 2001[42] and made an honorary knight of the British Empire the following year.[43] Numerous additional awards followed. All doors seemed to be open to Rudy, perhaps even the American presidency.

Giuliani surely had the ambition and pedigree for the position. During the Reagan administration, Giuliani had served as an associate attorney general.[44] Later he became the lead prosecutor at the office of the Southern District of New York,[45] where he earned early fame for going after the Italian mafia.[46] Later he ran to become the mayor of New York, failing his first election before winning two consecutive terms. In 2000 Giuliani competed with Hillary Clinton for an open seat in the US Senate before withdrawing for medical reasons.[47]

After finishing his terms as New York's mayor, Giuliani started businesses in law, public speaking, security services, and investment banking.[48] His influence, acquired from the 9/11 tragedy, allowed him to get anyone on the phone, a clear benefit for his potential clients. Through his newly established companies, Giuliani was able to book speaking engagements and security consulting contracts with clients from Mexico,[49] Ukraine,[50] Russia,[51] and Qatar,[52] among others.

Capitalizing on his public image after 9/11, in 2007 Giuliani announced his presidential bid.[53] With the United States on the verge of an economic crisis and the country tiring of the wars in Afghanistan and Iraq, conservatives didn't seem to resonate with Giuliani's safety and security platform. After a weak showing in Republican primaries, Giuliani dropped out of the race.[54]

His former wife described Giuliani's state in the months that ensued as "clinical depression."[55] His moment in the spotlight seemed to have passed, and his relevance faded. That must have been devastating for Rudy, who was addicted to the "limelight and power."[56] Reportedly, he and his wife spent a month at Mar-a-Lago with Donald Trump while Rudy recovered from his failed presidential race.[57] A decade later, Giuliani's consoler would become the US president, and Rudy would, once again, find himself in the spotlight.

When Donald Trump announced his presidential campaign,[58] Rudy Giuliani was among the first high-profile people to endorse him.[59] Through the summer of 2016, Rudy Giuliani, while working at the law firm of Greenberg Traurig, constantly[60] appeared[61] on the campaign trail,[62] acting as a booster for Trump. He was a frequent guest across the news spectrum and, once again, was sought after for his opinions and sound bites as a Trump surrogate. After almost a decade of declined relevance, random speaking engagements, and infomercials,[63] Giuliani seemed to be back on the national stage.

When the GOP nominated Donald Trump as their party candidate, Rudy Giuliani was allocated a prime-time slot on the opening day of the Republican convention.[64] His speech was scheduled before the appearances of Melania Trump and Michael Flynn, indicating Giuliani's restored importance.

A month before the presidential election, the *Washington Post* released a decade-old tape in which Donald Trump could be heard denigrating women with lewd remarks.[65] The tape almost ended Trump's candidacy, with more than thirty Republicans, including Senate majority leader Mitch McConnell and House majority leader Paul Ryan, publicly condemning his remarks and requesting that Trump withdraw from the race.[66] The only person to publicly come to Trump's defense was Rudy Giuliani.[67] He argued that casual misogynistic talk did not necessarily lead to abusive actions, and therefore, it was just "locker room talk."[68] To everybody's surprise Donald Trump not only survived the media storm but also went on to win the election.

Trump's victory similarly elevated Rudy Giuliani's future public and private business prospects. He became a regular at the White House. In January 2017 President-Elect Trump announced that Giuliani would be an unofficial cybersecurity advisor to the incoming administration.[69] There were even talks about Giuliani becoming Trump's secretary of state,[70] director of national intelligence,[71] or attorney general.[72] That would have required his full financial disclosure, congressional scrutiny of his potential foreign conflicts of interest, and likely a bruising confirmation process in the Senate with strong Democratic opposition. Ultimately, Rudy would remain in private practice, thus avoiding any disclosures but, at the same time, ever present at the Trump White House.

THE CONVERGENCE

After the FBI arrested Lev Parnas and Igor Fruman, journalists were asking how in the world those two were connected to Rudy Giuliani. According to Parnas, his relationship with Giuliani went back to Donald Trump's election campaign.[73] On

October 12, 2016, Giuliani and Parnas crossed paths[74] at a Trump fundraiser in Florida.[75] On election night Lev Parnas, along with Rudy Giuliani and other Trump close supporters, was with Donald Trump and his family at the invite-only victory party in the Hilton Hotel in New York.[76] Parnas claimed that he and Giuliani ran into each other at many other Republican fundraising events and "grew close" after the election.[77]

Giuliani's version of introduction to his future associate was not time specific. The only thing that he divulged was that a "well-known investigator" had connected him to Parnas.[78]

In early 2017 both Rudy Giuliani and Lev Parnas worked in parallel, but seemingly separate, on projects related to the Turkish government. As mentioned previously, between January and March 2017, Lev Parnas facilitated meetings between DC lobbyist Brian Ballard and the Black Sea tycoons Mubariz Mansimov and Farkhad Akhmedov, who brought him to the Turkish foreign minister. One of the topics of those meetings was Reza Zarrab, the key defendant of the Halkbank investigation. As a result of those meetings, Ballard Partners would sign lobbying contracts with Turkey[79] and later Halkbank.[80]

Around that time Rudy Giuliani became part of Zarrab's defense team. In February 2017 Giuliani went to Turkey to meet with President Erdogan,[81] ostensibly to discuss the gold trader's case in hopes of finding a "diplomatic" solution.[82] That effort was not successful.

Giuliani and Parnas's parallel efforts on behalf of Turkish interests indicated that they were both part of the greater clandestine Turkish lobbying endeavor. It might be that this common Turkish cause brought Giuliani and Parnas together and was the beginning of their alliance. Later they and their circle would operate as a shadow State Department, attempting to exert their influence in various corners of the world through the White House.

For the rest of 2017, there were no public signs of convergence in Giuliani and Parnas's activities. The news trail picked up again in April 2018, when Parnas went to a dinner for important donors of the America First Action super PAC at the Trump International Hotel in Washington.[83] The dinner was also attended[84] by Rudy Giuliani,[85] who that month had become the president's private attorney,[86] and Giuliani's business partner[87] and Trump fundraiser[88] Roy Bailey.

After that event Parnas and Fruman made a hefty $325,000 contribution to the PAC. More fundraisers followed with more high-level introductions. One of them, in June 2018, was when Lev Parnas and Igor Fruman visited[89] another America First Action event.[90] There, Roy Bailey reportedly introduced Lev Parnas to a Florida-based shipping magnate named Harry Sargeant III.[91] Those new connections would in the future become key players in Giuliani and Parnas's foreign clandestine intrigues in Venezuela and Ukraine.

By August 2018, during the midterm election season, Rudy Giuliani and Lev

Parnas were crisscrossing the United States together in a private jet.[92] From then on the two would become practically inseparable. By the time of Parnas's arrest, his relationship with Giuliani was so deep that Rudy was the godfather of Parnas's youngest son.[93] Parnas's eldest son, Aaron, would intern at one of the offices of Greenberg Traurig, where Giuliani had served as an advisor to the chairman.[94] Aaron Parnas also claimed that he did research for Rudy Giuliani and was present at some conversations that Giuliani had with foreign clients.[95] One of those occurrences happened in September 2018, when Aaron Parnas found himself in a room with Rudy Giuliani and some of his allies at the Trump International Hotel in DC. The group gathered for a conference call with the Venezuelan dictator, Nicolas Maduro.

CHAPTER 8

SHADOW DIPLOMACY IN VENEZUELA

THE CALL WITH THE VENEZUELAN DICTATOR

In September 2018 Giuliani and his allies gathered in the BLT Prime room at the Trump International Hotel in Washington, DC. Aaron Parnas recollected the meeting in his exposé *Trump First*[1] as follows:

> Instead, there were eight individuals in the private room: my father, Igor Fruman, David Correia, Rudy Giuliani, Congressman Pete Sessions, his wife, and an aide. The eighth person was me.
>
> ... At this point, I still had little knowledge of what the meeting was about, outside of the general topic of "Venezuela." Congressman Sessions' arrival signaled to me that the topic of conversation was a lot more serious.
>
> ... My father then relayed the message that Harry Sargeant, a billionaire oil magnate who I had met a few times previously, was in Venezuela, traveling in a secured convoy on his way to meet with President Nicolás Maduro.
>
> ... Congressman Sessions, upon hearing that Harry Sargeant was in place, informed us that whatever phone he was going to use to call into Venezuela would be "burned." As he explained, the Central Intelligence Agency (CIA), would be listening into the phone call, and would therefore, have access to any present and future data on the device. Because of this, the device would have to be discarded after its use. Soon after, the Congressman's phone rang. It was go time. "Mr. President Maduro, It is an honor to speak with you tonight," exclaimed Sessions. When Rudy Giuliani heard Maduro's voice, he proceeded to leave the room, requesting that my father fill him in later on.

> ... On this phone call, Congressman Sessions intended to negotiate a deal for President Maduro to leave his post in Venezuela and to travel to the United States peacefully. Maduro, jokingly replied "I want to watch the Dallas Cowboys."
>
> ... Following the conversation in the BLT Prime room, the Congressman swore us to secrecy. He informed us that if anyone caught wind of the conversation, he, along with the current administration, would face political and personal turmoil.

Everything about that call was bizarre. Why was Pete Sessions, a Republican congressman from Texas, clandestinely talking to the Venezuelan president? Was Pete Sessions authorized to "negotiate a deal" with Maduro on behalf of the US government? Otherwise, who was Sessions speaking on behalf of? Why did Congressman Sessions use a burner phone to call the Venezuelan president instead of going through official channels? Why was Harry Sargeant III, a shipping magnate from Florida, meeting in person with Maduro? Why did the group want Maduro to move to the United States? What was Giuliani's role? How were Lev Parnas and Igor Fruman related to all that?

The answer to those questions might be related Venezuela's most prized resource: oil.

OIL DIPLOMACY

THE LIAISON BETWEEN PDVSA AND EXXON

In June 2017, a year and a half before the secret call to the Venezuelan president Nicolas Maduro, Rep. Pete Sessions received an email from the Venezuelan state oil company, the PDVSA, which solicited the congressman's assistance in arranging a meeting with Exxon Mobil,[2] which was located in Sessions's district in Texas.[3]

At the time, Exxon and the Venezuelan government were not on good terms. In 2007 the prior socialist president of Venezuela, Hugo Chavez, nationalized Exxon's assets in country that, according to some estimates, were worth $1.6 billion.[4] A decade later, with Venezuela in a deep economic crisis,[5] the government, now led by Chavez's successor, Nicolas Maduro, wanted to lure Exxon back in.[6]

Despite the old grudges between Exxon and the PDVSA, on July 31, 2017, the two companies found a way forward by signing a base agreement for Exxon to do business again in Venezuela's rich oil fields.[7] The timing of the deal could not be worse. The day before the contract was signed, Nicolas Maduro had pushed through a highly controversial referendum that would install a new governing body to change the constitution and replace Venezuela's increasingly oppositional legislative body.[8] The vote was marred by a continuing series of violent protests against Maduro's power grab.[9]

The US government responded by imposing[10] additional[11] rounds[12] of sanctions[13] on Venezuela in 2017 and 2018, citing systemic corruption and the ongoing violent repression of the political opposition. Those sanctions effectively halted Exxon's possibilities to work in the Venezuelan marketplace and put pressure on Congressman Sessions, who received political donations from the energy industry[14] and was acutely aware of its importance for his reelection bid. Sessions repeatedly[15] spoke out[16] against laws that could potentially harm energy companies in his district. According to the *Dallas Morning News*:[17]

> *He said that North Texas' successful business climate depends on companies knowing that there are public officials who "value who they are and who will support them."*
>
> *"We need to keep Dallas, Texas, leading-edge," said Sessions, who counts the oil and gas industry among his most generous campaign donors. "We need Hunt Oil here. And quite honestly, if you haven't figured it out, I'm for Exxon, too."*

In other words, in return for oil and gas industry donations, Pete Sessions might have felt an obligation to go an extra mile to support big energy companies within his constituency, including Exxon.

In late March 2018, President Trump signed an executive order for additional sanctions banning the use of Venezuelan-denominated digital currencies by US entities.[18] In early April 2018, Sessions was on a plane to Venezuela[19] to meet privately with President Maduro.[20] The meeting was reportedly attended by at least two other people. One was Sessions's former fellow congressman named David Rivera,[21] who, earlier that year, had signed a lobbying contract with the PDVSA[22] and would later be indicted[23] for failing to register as a foreign agent for Venezuela.[24] The second person at the meeting was Raul Gorrín, a Venezuelan media mogul.[25] Both Rivera and Gorrín were acting as the envoys of Maduro's interests in the United States and handpicked Pete Sessions as their liaison between the Venezuelan government and Exxon.[26]

THE MAGNATE

In November 2017 Harry Sargeant III, an energy and shipping magnate from Florida, traveled to Venezuela to meet government oil executives and "to see about buying some oil."[27] Sargeant, through Raul Gorrín, the media mogul mentioned above, was able to connect with PDVSA officials and the Venezuelan president himself, Nicolas Maduro. Throughout 2018 Harry Sargeant III continued negotiating with the Venezuelan government to "take over three dilapidated oil fields" in Venezuela. Apparently, those negotiations put Sargeant in the middle between the American and Venezuelan governments. In mid-2018 Nicolas Maduro wrote a letter to President

Trump and tasked Sargeant to deliver it. Sargeant attempted to hand over the letter during a fundraiser in New York in the summer of 2018 but wasn't successful.[28]

Then in September 2018, Sargeant traveled to Venezuela to meet with Nicolas Maduro. Pete Sessions and Rudy Giuliani's entourage were scheduled to join the discussion over the phone from Washington, DC. It was the secret call that Lev Parnas's son described in his book.

After that phone conversation, Rudy Giuliani came to the White House and met with the US national security advisor, John Bolton, pitching the idea to provide a "soft landing" for the Venezuelan dictator in the United States in exchange for Maduro's resignation. Bolton reportedly "vehemently rejected" the proposal.[29]

There were at least two issues with the Giuliani-Sessions-Sargeant shadow effort. The first one was that they, as a rogue group, had been engaged in a negotiation with an adversary foreign leader without coordination or approval from US policymakers. The second issue was that they were offering Maduro, the Venezuelan dictator who violated human rights and whom the US State Department had considered as egregiously corrupt,[30] a safe harbor in America. Maduro living in America with impunity would contradict the official US stance toward his regime and undermine the core principles of justice that America strives to adhere to.

But why would Giuliani, Sessions, and Sargeant clandestinely maneuver to remove Maduro in the first place? His authoritarian moves to suppress the Venezuelan people were the main factor impeding the lifting of the US sanctions off Venezuela. Amicably easing Maduro out of power could quickly bring a more democratic leader to Venezuela and, in turn, lead to the removal of layered US sanctions. With no sanctions in place, Sargeant and tangent American private interests could, once again, do business in Venezuela.

Despite no change in the US stance after the September call, within two months the Venezuelan government allowed Harry Sargeant's company,[31] Erepla Services, to sign a $500 million contract with the PDVSA.[32] Sargeant claimed that Maduro's permission was a token of goodwill to improve relations with America.[33] Another interpretation could be that Maduro gave Sargeant a proverbial carrot to incentivize the mogul to help persuade the US government to lift sanctions on Venezuela.

That move didn't work. In January 2019 the US government imposed a new layer of sanctions on the PDVSA,[34] effectively derailing Sargeant's business deal.[35] Exxon Mobil's 2017 contract with the PDVSA had a similar fate.

So throughout 2019 the group continued their Venezuelan endeavors.

PARALLEL EFFORTS IN 2019

In early 2019 Donald Trump's White House launched an initiative to squeeze Nicolas Maduro out of power by establishing connections to the Venezuelan opposition to support its leader, Juan Guaido.³⁶ The idea was to persuade the Venezuelan Supreme Court to rule that Maduro's 2018 election victory was fraudulent and legally deny him the presidency and instead install Guaido as the president of Venezuela. This effort went in combination with the Trump administration's "maximum pressure" sanctions package that eliminated many avenues of revenue for the Maduro government.³⁷ The end goal of those measures was to force Maduro from power in hopes that his removal would nudge Venezuela back to democracy.

The efforts failed when the Venezuelan Supreme Court judge who publicly opposed Maduro fled the country,³⁸ and those who supported the uprising were suppressed. On January 10, 2019, Nicolas Maduro was inaugurated as president of Venezuela for another term.³⁹

At the end of that month, the United States imposed another layer of sanctions on the PDVSA. The Venezuelan efforts to counter US sanctions continued on.

HARRY SARGEANT AND ROBERT STRYK

In the summer of 2019, Harry Sargeant partnered up with a DC lobbyist named Robert Stryk,⁴⁰ who had worked on the Trump election campaign⁴¹ and knew Rudy Giuliani.⁴² It seemed that, through Stryk, Harry Sargeant wanted to test the waters on the possibility of the administration changing its pressure policy on Venezuela.

In October 2019 Sargeant and Stryk traveled together to Caracas, Venezuela, to meet with Nicolas Maduro. The Venezuelan media mogul Raul Gorrín, who by that time had been indicted in the United States for the bribery of foreign officials,⁴³ also joined the meeting.⁴⁴ The group reportedly discussed a possibility of Stryk officially lobbying on behalf of Maduro's government in the United States. When Stryk filed the necessary paperwork⁴⁵ to the Department of Justice,⁴⁶ US lawmakers strongly pushed back against the lobbying initiative, causing Stryk and Sargeant to abandon it.⁴⁷

RUDY GIULIANI AND ALEJANDRO BETANCOURT LOPEZ

Meanwhile, there was yet another parallel effort by a different team to influence US policy toward Venezuela. In June 2019 Rudy Giuliani and Lev Parnas flew to London and met with Alejandro Betancourt Lopez,⁴⁸ a Venezuelan energy and construction executive with significant ties⁴⁹ to the Maduro regime.⁵⁰ They all met again in early August 2019, this time at Betancourt's villa near Madrid, Spain. Another person reported to have been present at that second meeting was Wilmer Guaido, the father of Juan Guaido,⁵¹ the Venezuelan opposition leader who was formerly backed by the US government against Maduro.

At the time, Betancourt was implicated in a DOJ investigation of a $1.2 billion money-laundering scheme from Venezuela into the Miami real estate.⁵² According to Lev Parnas, Betancourt had invited Rudy Giuliani onto his defense team.⁵³ Giuliani did not do that, at least not officially. However, after the meeting in Madrid, Rudy Giuliani, along with Betancourt's attorneys, sat down[54] with DOJ officials,[55] including attorney general William Barr,[56] to plead leniency in the Venezuelan mogul's case.[57] Giuliani argued that Betancourt, citing previous support of the Venezuelan opposition, sought clemency from the DOJ.[58]

Those actions aligned into an effort to establish a chain of quid pro quos that could simultaneously benefit the goal of replacing Maduro with Juan Guaido. The presence of Guaido's father at the meeting in Madrid suggested that Betancourt might have offered assistance in installing Juan Guaido as the next Venezuelan president, thus removing Nicolas Maduro. That could potentially serve as a catalyst for the United States to lift sanctions on Venezuela and allow American energy interests to access Venezuelan oil fields.

In the end the private efforts to ease Maduro out of power proved to be futile. One could argue that with more time Giuliani and his associates might have achieved their goal. However, in October 2019 the FBI arrested Giuliani's associates Lev Parnas and Igor Fruman, putting Giuliani and his circle under a magnifying glass.

At the time, there was little public information available about their dealings in Venezuela, and they would want to keep it that way. In contrast journalists unearthed a trove of information about the adventures of Giuliani, Parnas, and Fruman in Ukraine.

TIMELINE OF SHADOW DIPLOMACY IN VENEZUELA*

*See the full integrated timeline in appendix A.

June 8, 2017 - Congressman Pete Sessions received an email from the PDVSA asking for help arrange a meeting between the Venezuelan oil minister and the head of Exxon, in hopes of Exxon's investment into the Venezuelan oil production market.

July 30, 2017 – A constitutional referendum in Venezuela led to deadly mass protests.

July 31, 2017 - Exxon and the PDVSA signed a deal worth $259 million for Exxon to explore Venezuelan oil fields.

August 24, 2017 - US Department of the Treasury imposed sanctions that prohibited US banks from issuing long-term debt to the Venezuelan government and the PDVSA.

Late 2017/November 2017 - Raul Gorrín connected Harry Sargeant III to PDVSA officials. Harry Sargeant III went to Venezuela to meet with PDVSA officials "to see about buying some oil." There, he also met Maduro.

March 19, 2018 - US Department of the Treasury imposed new sanctions that banned US entities from using Venezuelan-denominated digital currencies.

On or around April 2, 2018 - Congressman Pete Sessions took an unofficial trip to Caracas and stayed at Raul Gorrín's luxury compound. On that trip Congressman Sessions met Pres. Nicolas Maduro. Both Raul Gorrín and David Rivera were present at the meeting.

May 20, 2018 - During the federal elections in Venezuela, Maduro won with 68 percent of the vote. The United States and a host of other countries rejected the result of the vote amid election improprieties, including fraud. The United States then backed a Venezuelan legislator, and opposition leader to Maduro, Juan Guaido, as the new president of Venezuela.

May 21, 2018 - The US imposed an additional layer of sanctions on Venezuela prohibiting the purchase of Venezuelan debt.

Summer 2018 - Harry Sargeant III attempted to deliver a letter from Nicolas Maduro to Donald Trump during a fundraiser in New York.

September 2018 - Harry Sargeant III met with Venezuelan president Nicolas Maduro in Caracas, Venezuela. Pete Sessions, sitting along with Lev Parnas, Igor Fruman, David Correia, and Aaron Parnas, called into that meeting. The call was focused on making a deal to allow Maduro to reside in the United States after resigning from the Venezuelan presidency.

September 2018 - Around the time of the call, Giuliani pitched Trump's national security advisor John Bolton about an alternative plan to ease Maduro from the office. Bolton "vehemently rejected" the plan.

November 2018 - Harry Sargeant III's Erepla Services LLC signed a contract with the PDVSA.

January 7, 2019 - A $500 million deal between Harry Sargeant III's Erepla Services LLC and the PDVSA was announced.

January 10, 2019 - President Maduro was inaugurated in Venezuela for his second term.

January 25, 2019 - The US imposed sanctions on the PDVSA.

Summer 2019 - Harry Sargeant III teamed up with Robert Stryk, a lobbyist connected to Rudy Giuliani. Sargeant and Stryk traveled to Venezuela to discuss the possibility of formal lobbying for Maduro in the US. The effort failed.

June 2019 - According to Lev Parnas, Giuliani and Parnas flew to London for an exhibition Yankees game and met Alejandro Betancourt Lopez, a Venezuelan oligarch who was under investigation as part of a $1.2 billion federal money-laundering case.

August 3, 2019 - Giuliani and Parnas met Betancourt a second time outside Madrid.

September 3, 2019 - Giuliani met with DOJ officials, reportedly to advocate for leniency for Betancourt.

CHAPTER 9

THE BEGINNING OF UKRAINEGATE

THE WHISTLEBLOWER COMPLAINT

On September 19, 2019, the *Washington Post*[1] and the *New York Times*[2] broke the news that a US intelligence official had filed a whistleblower complaint with the Intelligence Community inspector general (ICIG), whose role is to "conduct independent and objective audits, investigations, inspections, and reviews."[3] The complaint raised the alarm of Donald Trump and Rudy Giuliani's attempts to pressure the Ukrainian government.[4] The complaint stated that since early 2019 the US president and his allies had been trying to coerce the Ukrainian government to announce an investigation into Hunter Biden, the son of former vice president Joe Biden, who was potentially Donald Trump's main rival in the 2020 presidential race. The news spread like wildfire, with media outlets picking up the subject within hours.

The whistleblower defined Rudy Giuliani as "a central figure in this effort" and AG William Barr as seemingly "to be involved as well."[5] The report also mentioned two associates of Rudy Giuliani without providing names. Later those two would be identified as Lev Parnas and Igor Fruman.

The document described various activities that Giuliani and his associates were engaged in, including

- repeatedly meeting with Ukraine's prosecutor general, Yuri Lutsenko, and his allies;
- attempting to establish back-channel communications with the newly elected president of Ukraine, Volodymyr Zelensky;
- potential involvement of Rudy Giuliani in the dismissal of the US ambassador to Ukraine, Marie Yovanovitch.

However, the central subject of the whistleblower complaint was a call between Donald Trump and Volodymyr Zelensky that happened in late July 2019.

THE "PERFECT" CALL

On the morning of July 25, 2019, a dozen people joined a call between the presidents of the United States and Ukraine. On the American side, the officials who were listening in on the call included Secretary of State Mike Pompeo, White House staff, and members of the National Security Council (NSC).[6]

For calls with foreign leaders, presidential briefers would usually prepare a memo to provide context. Donald Trump notoriously lacked the patience for those several-page-long briefs and preferred flash cards.[7] He would often go off script and speak his mind. That appeared to be the case during his call with Zelensky.

After brief pleasantries Donald Trump cut to the chase:[8]

> *President Trump: I will say that we do a lot for Ukraine. We spend a lot of effort and a lot of time. Much more than the European countries are doing and they should be helping you more than they are. Germany does almost nothing for you . . . A lot of the European countries are the same way so I think it's something you want to look at but the United States has been very very good to Ukraine. I wouldn't say that it's reciprocal necessarily because things are happening that are not good but the United States has been very very good to Ukraine.*
>
> *President Zelensky: Yes you are absolutely right. Not only 100%, but actually 1000% . . . It turns out that even though logically, the European Union should be our biggest partner but technically the United States is a much bigger partner than the European Union and I'm very grateful to you for that because the United States is doing quite a lot for Ukraine. Much more than the European Union especially when we are talking about sanctions against the Russian Federation. I would also like to thank you for your great support in the area of defense. We are ready to continue to cooperate for the next steps. specifically we are almost ready to buy more Javelins from the United States for defense purposes.*
>
> *President Trump: I would like you to do us a favor though because our country has been through a lot and Ukraine knows a lot about it. I would like you to find out what happened with this whole situation with Ukraine, they say Crowdstrike . . . I guess you have one of your wealthy people . . . The server, they say Ukraine has it. There are a lot of things that went on, the whole situation. I think you're surrounding yourself with some of the same people. I would like to have the Attorney General call you or your people and I would like you to get to the bottom of it.*

To understand the gravity of Trump's requests, it's important to put them in context. At the time of the call, Volodymyr Zelensky had only been in office for two months. A former comedian, he was a newcomer with no political capital. His country had been at war with Russia since 2014. Ukraine, a small former Soviet republic, was under imminent threat of a large attack by its behemoth neighbor and needed all the military assistance it could get.

Earlier that year the US Congress had approved a $400 million military aid package for Ukraine[9] that needed to be delivered before September 30, 2019. Otherwise, the aid would expire.[10] In mid-July, at least a week before the call, President Trump had ordered his chief of staff, Mick Mulvaney, to withhold the aid to Ukraine.[11] With the military aid leverage held over the young Ukrainian president, Donald Trump hinted that for Ukraine to get the support they needed from the United States, Zelensky needed to submit to the American president's requests.

His first request was to look into CrowdStrike servers. The origins of that request stemmed from a long-running conspiracy theory that was propagated by Russian disinformation operations and amplified by Rudy Giuliani and Donald Trump as a counterargument to the allegations of Russian interference into the 2016 US presidential election. CrowdStrike was the firm hired by the Democratic National Committee to investigate the breach that happened in 2016. The firm established that Russian hackers were behind the cyberattack.[12] CrowdStrike then copied the electronic content of the compromised DNC servers and passed on the files to the FBI,[13] who were probing Russian interference into the US election.

However, Donald Trump falsely claimed[14] that after obtaining access to the DNC server, CrowdStrike moved the physical equipment to Ukraine because the founder of the firm was a wealthy Ukrainian.[15] Then according[16] to Donald[17] Trump,[18] CrowdStrike and Hillary Clinton's campaign refused to give the physical server to the FBI. Various versions of the theory claimed the DNC hacked its own servers,[19] framed Russia,[20] and hid the server in Ukraine, which, according to Trump and his allies, proved that Ukraine, not Russia, was behind the 2016 US election interference.

The Ukrainian president voiced a generic readiness for cooperation between the United States and Ukraine:

> President Zelensky: Yes it is very important for me and everything that you just mentioned earlier. For me as a President, it is very important and we are open for any future cooperation. We are ready to open a new page on cooperation in relations between the United States and Ukraine ... I would also like and hope to see him having your trust and your confidence and have personal relations with you so we can cooperate even more so. I will personally tell you that one of my assistants spoke with Mr. Giuliani just recently and we are hoping very much that Mr. Giuliani will be able to travel to Ukraine and we will meet once he comes to Ukraine ... I will make sure that I surround myself with the best and most experienced people. I also wanted to tell you that we are friends. We are great friends and you Mr. President have friends in our country so we can continue our strategic partnership. I also plan to surround myself with great people and in addition to that investigation, I guarantee as the President of Ukraine that all the investigations will be done openly and candidly. That I can assure you.

> President Trump: Good because I heard you had a prosecutor who was very good and he was shut down and that's really unfair. A lot of people are talking about that, the way they shut your very good prosecutor down and you had some very bad people involved. Mr. Giuliani is a highly respected man. He was the mayor of New York City, a great mayor, and I would like him to call you. I will ask him to call you along with the Attorney General. Rudy very much knows what's happening and he is a very capable guy. If you could speak to him that would be great. The former ambassador from the United States, the woman, was bad news and the people she was dealing with in the Ukraine were bad news so I just want to let you know that. The other thing, There's a lot of talk about Biden's son, that Biden stopped the prosecution and a lot of people want to find out about that so whatever you can do with the Attorney General would be great. Biden went around bragging that he stopped the prosecution so if you can look into it . . . It sounds horrible to me.

Within one spoken line of thought, Donald Trump mentioned several people who would become subjects of interest for journalists and investigators.

a. The prosecutor that Donald Trump mentioned was Ukraine's prosecutor general Yuri Lutsenko. He served in the previous presidential administration and, as a holdout, was expected to be replaced. Like in the United States, in Ukraine an incoming president would select and appoint his own cabinet officials across multiple departments. However, for some reason the American president expressed an interest that Zelensky keep Lutsenko as his top prosecutor.
b. In the next short phrase, Donald Trump made Rudy Giuliani his point man to manage the implementation of the favors that Trump had requested from Zelensky. Giuliani, as a private attorney for the president of the United States, would bypass official channels and instead create and run a shadow State Department loyal to the president. This move was highly irregular and indicated the scope of access and influence Rudy Giuliani had within the Trump administration.
c. The next person Trump mentioned was the former US ambassador to Ukraine Marie Yovanovitch. Earlier that year President Trump had fired the ambassador on short notice and without credible explanation. Some critics described her firing as a "political hit job."[21]
d. Eventually, Trump brought up his most important request: to force Ukraine to start an investigation into Joe Biden's son. The US president phrased it more subtly, that he wanted Ukraine to "look into" Joe Biden and his son's activities. Hunter Biden, the former vice president's son, had previously become central to conspiracy theories of Biden corruption. While his father was vice president with a US foreign policy portfolio including Ukraine, Hunter was a board member of a Ukrainian energy company called Burisma.[22] At relatively the same time in 2016, Vice President Biden recommended the Ukrainian president to

fire his prosecutor general Viktor Shokin,[23] whom both the United States and the EU perceived as corrupt.[24] Referring to that incident, Donald Trump and his allies then made multiple allegations that Joe Biden had suggested Shokin be fired because he was investigating Biden's son and the company that hired him.[25] However, that argument lacked merit as Shokin had, in fact, opposed investigating Burisma[26] and obstructed a British investigation into the company.[27]

There was another topic on that call that was largely overlooked by impeachment investigators or not discussed publicly: energy cooperation between the United States and Ukraine.

> President Zelensky: As to the economy, there is much potential for our two countries and one of the issues that is very important for Ukraine is energy independence. I believe we can be very successful and cooperating on energy independence with United States. We are already working on cooperation. We are buying American oil but I am very hopeful for a future meeting. We will have more time and more opportunities to discuss these opportunities and get to know each other better. I would like to thank you very much for your support.
>
> President Trump: Good. Well, thank you very much and I appreciate that. I will tell Rudy and Attorney General Barr to call. Thank you. Whenever you would like to come to the White House, feel free to call. Give us a date and we'll work that out.

President Zelensky brought up the subject of energy independence, presumably from Russia. Since 2014 the Kremlin has used energy blackmail against Ukraine, turning the flow of gas on and off to increase pressure and squeeze out territorial or political concessions. In those circumstances the prospects of Ukraine replacing Russian energy with American must have been a very attractive option.

Curiously, the official who represented the US government at Zelensky's May 2019 inauguration was then secretary of energy Rick Perry. When criticized for his pressure on Zelensky, Donald Trump would blame Rick Perry for asking him to place that call.[28] It would later be uncovered that the energy secretary did have some serious interest in Ukraine.[29]

The US president closed the phone call with a reminder that Rudy Giuliani and Attorney General Barr would follow up. Trump also dangled the possibility of Zelensky visiting the White House, a meeting that would represent American support for the Ukrainian government. The way the two sentences went back-to-back made it seem that one event was contingent on the other.

As the phone call progressed, some members of the National Security Council who were listening in on the conversation grew increasingly concerned.[30] Immediately after the call, one member, a top specialist on Ukraine, went to see the NSC legal counsel to discuss the potential implications of Trump's requests.[31] That might have caused a swift response from Trump's White House staff, who attempted to prevent the content of the call from leaking to the public. According to the whistleblower, White House lawyers were so alarmed by potential consequences that they ordered a "lock down" on all records, transcripts, and notes related to the call, hiding them in an electronic system that normally stored classified and highly sensitive information.[32] However, those were not the only attempts to contain the possible damage.

THE STANDOFF

Three days after the call with Zelensky, Donald Trump announced that his director of national intelligence, Dan Coats, would be replaced by a Trump ally, Congressman John Ratcliffe (R-TX).[33] After a media[34] uproar[35] about the congressman's lack[36] of qualifications[37] for the job, Ratcliffe withdrew his candidacy. Eleven days later the president announced the resignation of the deputy DNI, the second in line, and announced the appointment of a former chief of the National Counterterrorism Center, Joseph Maguire, as the acting DNI.[38]

At the time, the existence of the call between Trump and Zelensky, as well as its content, was not yet public, so those changes at the DNI looked to be a random reshuffling. In hindsight those firings appeared to be part of Trump's attempts to obstruct the flow of information about the call with Zelensky into the public. Ironically, the opposite happened. On August 12, 2019, the whistleblower filed the complaint that would set off a political firestorm.[39]

On August 15, 2019, Maguire became the acting director of national intelligence.[40] On his eleventh day on the job, he received the whistleblower complaint from the Intelligence Community inspector general, who, after reviewing the document for two weeks, concluded the complaint was credible and needed to be acted on. According to intelligence legal statute, Maguire had seven days to submit the complaint to congressional intelligence committees.[41] By the day of the deadline, on September 2, 2019, the acting DNI had not done so.[42]

After waiting for another week, the ICIG informed the House Intelligence Committee chairman, Adam Schiff, and its ranking member Devin Nunes of the existence of a whistleblower complaint that was withheld by the acting DNI Maguire.[43] That same day three House committees—of intelligence, of foreign affairs, and of oversight—launched an investigation.[44] Congressman Schiff demanded that the acting DNI turn over the whistleblower complaint. After not receiving the document within three days, the House Intelligence Committee subpoenaed Maguire.[45]

The office of the director of national intelligence responded by releasing a letter that stated that the whistleblower complaint "did not relate to any intelligence activity." The same letter stated that Joseph Maguire would not comply with the subpoena.[46]

Around that time, in his interview to CBS News, Rep. Adam Schiff commented on the acting DNI's refusal to release the whistleblower complaint as follows:[47]

> *No DNI—no director of national intelligence has ever refused to turn over a whistleblower complaint. And here . . . the significance is the inspector general found this complaint to be urgent, found it to be credible, that is they did some preliminary investigation, found the whistleblower to be credible, that suggests corroboration. And that it involved serious or flagrant wrongdoing. And according to the director of national intelligence, the reason he's not acting to provide it even though the statute mandates that he do so, is because he is being instructed not to. This involved a higher authority, someone above the DNI. Well there are only a few people . . . above the DNI . . .*
>
> *I can't go into the contents but I can tell you that at least according to the director of national intelligence, this involves an issue of privileged communications. Now that means it's a pretty narrow group of people that it could apply to that are both above the DNI in authority and also involve privileged communications. So, I think it's fair to assume this involves either the president or people around him or both. But at the end of the day if the director of national intelligence is going to undermine the whistleblower protections, it means that people are going to end up taking the law into their own hands and going directly to the press instead of the mechanism that Congress set to protect classified information. And that gravely threatens both our national security as well as a system that encourages people to expose wrongdoing. . . .*
>
> *. . . Yes, we're doing an investigation that will ultimately determine whether the president should be impeached.*

Within days the *Wall Street Journal* broke the news that during the July call with Volodymyr Zelensky, Donald Trump had pressured him to open an investigation into the Bidens.[48] Joe Biden and congressional investigators reacted[49] by demanding the release of the transcript of the call.[50] The House Speaker Nancy Pelosi released a public letter urging the Trump administration to comply with requests or deal with "a whole new stage of investigation."[51] Donald Trump responded[52] by stating that there was nothing wrong in that "perfect" call.[53]

Under pressure, a month and a half after the whistleblower complaint was filed, the acting DNI turned over the document to Congress and testified behind closed doors.[54] That was the very day the White House released the transcript of the call.[55]

However, the documents were delivered too late. By that time the House Speaker had already announced a formal impeachment inquiry into Pres. Donald Trump.[56] The investigation would reveal astonishing activities of some of Trump's allies in Ukraine and would lead to his first impeachment.

CHAPTER 10

QUID PRO QUO WITH UKRAINIAN PROSECUTORS

THE BLT TEAM

The whistleblower complaint not only included details of the call between Donald Trump and Volodymyr Zelensky but also mentioned Rudy Giuliani and his clandestine activities in Ukraine. The whistleblower did not describe the reasons behind Giuliani's activities in Ukraine. It would be later revealed that Giuliani and his team sought to find information that could discredit former vice president Joe Biden, whom Donald Trump perceived as a threat to his ardently sought reelection.

On December 6, 2018, on the sidelines of the White House Hanukkah party, Rudy Giuliani, Lev Parnas, and Igor Fruman met with President Trump and reportedly discussed a plan to create a scandal around former vice president Joe Biden using his son Hunter's work in Ukraine.[1] To implement the plan, they called in Giuliani's old colleagues, an opinion writer for a conservative media outlet, and a congressional assistant. Giuliani became the mastermind of the operation, which combined disinformation, political subterfuge, and overt extortion. Lev Parnas acted as an enforcer of Giuliani's orders, his unofficial envoy, and a translator of communications with Ukrainians.[2] Igor Fruman, using his Ukrainian business network, served as the guide to local officials and influential oligarchs. As the group frequently gathered at the BLT Prime Steakhouse at the Trump International Hotel in Washington, DC, Parnas referred to it as the BLT team.[3]

VICTORIA TOENSING AND JOE DIGENOVA

Two key members of the BLT team were Victoria Toensing and Joe diGenova, Rudy Giuliani's old friends from the Department of Justice. In the 1980s Victoria Toensing was the deputy assistant attorney general for the Criminal Division at the DOJ.[4] Her husband, Joe diGenova, was a US attorney for the District of Columbia.[5] After leaving the government, Toensing and diGenova established their own law firm in Washington, DC.[6]

In 2018 the couple was considered for positions in Donald Trump's legal team during the Mueller investigation.[7] However, because of a reported conflict of interest, they were unable to proceed.[8] Instead, they became frequent guests on Fox News, appearing on the channel over ninety times in 2019[9] and acting as Trump's informal advocates during the special counsel investigation.

According to Parnas, Toensing and diGenova were good friends with the newly sworn in attorney general William Barr,[10] which would become useful. By inviting Toensing and diGenova to the BLT team, Giuliani used them as his extensions for legal paperwork, for meetings with DOJ officials, and for appearing on TV as legal experts while advancing the objectives of the BLT team.

JOHN SOLOMON

Giuliani's strategy was to create as much negative press as possible around the Biden family, which would, in turn, increase the chances of Trump's reelection. For that purpose Giuliani enrolled an opinion columnist from the *Hill*, John Solomon. Rudy Giuliani would later recount his conversation with Solomon about the plan:[11]

> *I said, "John, let's make this as prominent as possible . . . I'll go on TV. You go on TV. You do columns."*

Solomon would write several opinion pieces at the *Hill* for the BLT team and serve as a press outlet for Giuliani's disinformation campaign.

DEREK HARVEY

Lev Parnas claimed that, from time to time, those meetings had also been attended by Derek Harvey,[12] a former staffer on Donald Trump's National Security Council[13] and later a senior aide to Rep. Devin Nunes (R-CA).[14] Although Nunes had at least one conversation with Parnas,[15] the congressman tried to be discreet[16] and occasionally deployed his aide, Derek Harvey, as his envoy.[17] Parnas asserted that Nunes was involved in the plot to find discrediting information on the Bidens' activities in Ukraine.[18] Nunes himself claimed that he was investigating alleged Ukrainian interference in the 2016 US election.[19] However, it was more likely that, along with the BLT team, Nunes sought to divert the public's attention from any connections between Donald Trump's campaign and the Russian interference in the 2016 election. Nunes had already shown himself to be a Trump loyalist when in 2017, while serving as the chair of the House Intelligence Committee that was investigating Russian disinformation operations, he had secretly shared information from that investigation with President Trump.[20]

The BLT team members, with the exception of Derek Harvey, were legally protected by privileged attorney-client agreements that functioned as a convenient shield from potential legal scrutiny of the group members. Toensing and diGenova were John Solomon's lawyers.[21] Giuliani and Parnas also claimed the possibility of attorney-client privilege,[22] citing Giuliani's previous consulting services for Parnas's company Fraud Guarantee.[23]

Together, the BLT team would embark on a complex operation of scouting in Ukraine for people who could assist in their effort to discredit the Bidens. Those people, in turn, would want favors from Giuliani and his team. The entire operation would turn into a complex web of quid pro quos, which are described in the following sections.

THE CULTIVATION OF UKRAINIAN PROSECUTORS

VIKTOR SHOKIN

The first person whom the BLT team members turned to for assistance was a former prosecutor general of Ukraine, Viktor Shokin. He already had personal animosity toward Joe Biden and was eager for vengeance.

Viktor Shokin was widely criticized by both Ukrainian and Western officials as being corrupt.[24] In 2015 the Obama administration, along with other Western countries,[25] was concerned that Ukraine's prosecutor general was protective of political elites and was a hindrance to anticorruption efforts.[26] Acting as the envoy of the administration, then-vice president Joe Biden demanded that the Ukrainian government fire Shokin in return for US financial aid.[27]

The sentiment was shared by Ukrainians as well. Shokin faced widespread public criticism.[28] In late 2015 and early 2016, Ukrainian protesters demanded[29] that then president Petro Poroshenko fire Shokin.[30] After some deliberation, on March 29, 2016, Ukrainian parliament ousted him from his position[31] with an overwhelming majority of 289 out of 305 votes.[32]

Lev Parnas would later claim that the idea to engage Shokin in the effort to discredit Joe Biden was suggested by Rep. Devin Nunes.[33] Interestingly enough, Nunes, along with his top aide, Derek Harvey, traveled to Europe from November 30 to December 3, 2018.[34] According to Parnas, during that trip Nunes and Harvey met with Shokin in Vienna, Austria.[35] Upon returning from the trip and around the time of the White House Hanukkah party, the congressman and his aide met with Parnas and solicited his assistance in "validating" their findings about the Bidens in Ukraine.[36] Shortly thereafter, in December 2018 Lev Parnas and Igor Fruman arranged a Skype call between Rudy Giuliani and Viktor Shokin.[37] Following the call the group reportedly started planning a trip for Shokin to the United States[38] to

> debrief him [Giuliani] here in front of [Senator] Mr. Lindsey Graham, and—certain other people like the attorney general.

The oddity of that effort was that Giuliani and Parnas, who operated in the shadows and held no official government positions, aimed to involve high-level US officials into their plot. Congressman Nunes at the time was the chair of the House Intelligence Committee while Senator Graham was the head of the Senate Judiciary Committee.

The obvious explanation to this activity was that Rudy Giuliani, Rep. Devin Nunes, and Sen. Lindsey Graham were conducting an unofficial clandestine probe without the knowledge of other members of the government. That would also explain why Nunes was secretive about his connection to the BLT team and used Harvey as a messenger. Years later Nunes would deny knowing Parnas[39] despite the existing[40] records[41] of at least one call between them and numerous messages between Parnas and Harvey.

Shokin was not able to meet Senator Graham and the attorney general as planned. The US Embassy in Ukraine denied Shokin's visa on "corruption grounds."[42] Upon hearing of the visa denial, Rudy Giuliani attempted to "revive it,"[43] reaching out to Donald Trump's attorney Jay Sekulow[44] and the State Department.[45] In a message to Lev Parnas, Giuliani wrote, "It's going to work I have no 1 in it,"[46] implying the president's involvement. Despite those efforts, Shokin did not get his visa and wasn't able to meet the US officials.

YURI LUTSENKO

If Viktor Shokin had the story to implicate the Bidens, Yuri Lutsenko, who succeeded him as Ukraine's prosecutor general, had the powers to open an investigation into it. Young and ambitious, Lutsenko was at the time known for his role in protests against pro-Russian presidents during the Ukrainian Orange Revolution in 2004 and Maidan Revolution in 2014.[47] He also had been incarcerated[48] for over two years[49] during Viktor Yanukovych's presidency, on charges that Lutsenko claimed were politically motivated,[50] and was pardoned in 2013.[51] After the dismissal of Viktor Shokin in 2016, Yuri Lutsenko, the folk hero of yesterday's protests, was offered the position of Ukraine's prosecutor general despite not having a law degree.[52]

Lutsenko had more luck with obtaining an American visa than Shokin and met with Rudy Giuliani and Lev Parnas in New York in January 2019.[53] Within Giuliani's office on Park Avenue, over the course of several days, Yuri Lutsenko laid out his version of Hunter Biden's complicity in Ukrainian corruption.[54] Lutsenko also alleged that some US Embassy employees in Ukraine were involved in a plot to smear Trump's campaign manager, Paul Manafort, in 2016.[55] Parnas claimed[56] that Lutsenko brought[57] to the meetings documents that he claimed proved Hunter Biden's corruption and Ukraine's, not Russia's, meddling in the 2016 US election.

Viktor Shokin joined the meetings by telephone. According to Lutsenko, during their first meeting, Rudy Giuliani called President Trump and "excitedly briefed" him on the information that Lutsenko had provided.[58] From then on Lev Parnas and Igor Fruman, who spoke Russian, which was commonly used in Ukraine, acted as go-betweens for Ukrainian officials and Giuliani's team. In late February 2019, Parnas and Fruman met with Ukraine's president, Petro Poroshenko, along with Yuri Lutsenko, and pressed them to announce an investigation into the Bidens and Ukraine's supposed "interference" into the 2016 US presidential election.[59]

In exchange for his assistance, Lutsenko requested a meeting with the attorney general of the United States. Lutsenko claimed that an American investment firm, Franklin Templeton, had laundered $7.5 billion from Ukraine.[60] Ukrainian officials reportedly had already attempted to recover the money from the investment firm and met with the FBI director during the Obama administration. However, at the time, the Ukrainians could not provide evidence to support their allegations.[61] Lutsenko wanted to revive the case and pitch the Trump administration's attorney general regarding the Franklin Templeton issue.

Lutsenko's second condition was to have the US ambassador in Ukraine Marie Yovanovitch removed from her position.[62] She was a strong supporter of the National Anticorruption Bureau of Ukraine, or NABU, the new investigative unit that was funded by the United States and European aid to tackle graft.[63] Established in the aftermath of Russia's invasion of Ukraine in 2014, NABU had broad[64] powers[65] to investigate corruption among members[66] of the country's government. In late 2017 NABU opened a corruption probe into Lutsenko.[67] Weeks later Lutsenko was accused of disrupting one of NABU's operations.[68] Soon the conflict between Lutsenko and NABU was shelved, but his resentment toward NABU remained. He believed that NABU was run by the US Embassy in Ukraine, and as a result, he developed a certain level of animosity toward Amb. Marie Yovanovitch.

It seemed that at the meetings in New York, Giuliani, Parnas, and Lutsenko had reached a common understanding, and each side delved into preparing their part of the deliverables. Lutsenko returned to Ukraine to search for more connections between Joe Biden and Burisma, the Ukrainian energy company. Rudy Giuliani and his team started thinking on how to arrange a meeting between Lutsenko and the US attorney general and devising a plan on how to get Ambassador Yovanovitch removed.

RETAINERS

At the time, Matthew Whitaker was the acting US attorney general, and Rudy Giuliani decided to not bring Lutsenko's requests to him. He instead preferred to wait until William Barr was confirmed as attorney general. Later Giuliani told a journalist from the *New Yorker*:[69]

> So I figured we'll wait, because I knew Barr would have the balls to deal with it.

Meanwhile, Giuliani drafted two retainer agreements. One was with the Ukrainian Ministry of Justice and another with Yuri Lutsenko that required them pay an advance of about $200,000 to Rudy Giuliani for him to help them present their Franklin Templeton case to US authorities.[70] After giving it another thought and thinking that "it would look bad," Giuliani decided against putting his own name on the agreements and instead referred the Ukrainians to the BLT team's lawyers, Victoria Toensing and Joe diGenova.[71]

With Lev Parnas's assistance, Toensing and diGenova negotiated a legal retainer contract with Yuri Lutsenko and his deputy. The contract negotiation went through several iterations. The April 12, 2019, version stated that for $25,000 per month over four months, the US lawyers would represent the Ukrainian prosecutor general and his deputy[72]

> in connection with recovery and return to the Ukraine government of funds illegally embezzled from that country and providing assistance to meet and discuss with the United States government officials the evidence of illegal conduct in Ukraine regarding the United States, for example, interference in the 2016 U.S. elections.

The subject of the agreement seemed left intentionally vague but included two key phrases. One was about the introduction of Lutsenko to US officials, presumably Attorney General Barr,[73] in an effort to recover funds that Lutsenko believed Franklin Templeton had laundered from Ukraine. Another referred to Ukraine's supposed interference into the 2016 presidential election, which was a tale that Rudy Giuliani and Donald Trump tried to solidify in American minds.[74]

Victoria Toensing and Joe diGenova also drafted an agreement with Viktor Shokin.[75] For $25,000 per month, the lawyers would represent him

> for the purpose of collecting evidence regarding his March 2016 firing as Prosecutor General of Ukraine and the role of then-Vice President Joe Biden in such firing, and presenting such evidence to U.S. and foreign authorities.

That arrangement did not make sense.

Shokin was providing evidence that happened to be very beneficial for the BLT team. Why would he be the one paying the money if he was the one providing services, unless there were other side services that Toensing and diGenova were providing to Shokin, or those he represented, that were not made public at the time?

A more important question that needs to be asked is "Why would Shokin and Lutsenko independently want to implicate their own government in attacking American elections when the US government had already definitively come to the conclusion[76] that the Russian government was the culprit?" Another question is "Where would Shokin and Lutsenko get the money to pay Toensing and diGenova?" as an official prosecutor general's salary in Ukraine would not be sufficient. If the money came from outside sources, who were the backers, and who would benefit from shifting the blame from Russia to Ukraine for meddling in the 2016 election?

SHOKIN'S INTERVIEW

By April 1, 2019, the BLT team produced an important piece of their anti-Biden campaign. Equipped with accounts of Shokin's firing and Burisma bank statements provided by Yuri Lutsenko, BLT team member and opinion writer John Solomon published an op-ed in the *Hill*.[77] The article implied that Joe Biden had covered up for his son's corruption in Ukraine. In the article Solomon claimed that the vice president had pressured the Ukrainian government into firing Shokin because he was investigating a large energy holding company named Burisma, where Biden's son was a board member. In fact, Viktor Shokin did exactly the opposite. In the view of the then-US Ambassador to Ukraine, Shokin's office had obstructed the investigation into Burisma,[78] and thereby protected its owner and the company.[79] In his narrative John Solomon omitted that fact, and instead built a twisted story.

Joe Biden's son Hunter Biden indeed was a board member at Burisma from May 2014[80] until April 2019.[81] In 2016 Joe Biden had indeed asked President Poroshenko to fire Shokin.[82] However, if Hunter Biden was guilty of profiting at Burisma from his father's position and if Vice President Biden took actions to shield his son, as Solomon claimed, why would the Bidens want to get rid of the prosecutor who, in fact, obstructed investigations on Burisma?

In reality Shokin's firing was caused by his obstruction to the implementation of Western-prescribed anticorruption reforms. Despite holes in Shokin's story, his claims were amplified by Rudy Giuliani and his associates as the foundation of their disinformation campaign against Joe Biden. Giuliani aimed to use that article as a stepping stone to trigger investigation into Joe Biden and his son in the United States and Ukraine.

Immediately after Shokin gave his interview to Solomon, Rudy Giuliani prepared a brief report for the secretary of state Mike Pompeo that included the testimonies of Viktor Shokin and Yuri Lutsenko about Hunter Biden and Marie Yovanovitch.[83] Giuliani said he had hoped that the report, combined with Solomon's article, would trigger an investigation into Joe Biden in the United States.[84] Years later Yuri Lutsenko would recall in an interview that he thought the public announcement of an investigation into the Bidens was more important to Rudy Giuliani than the investigation itself or its findings.[85]

In late April of 2019 all of Giuliani and his team's work came under risk of being lost. Ukraine had a presidential election, in which the incumbent, Petro Poroshenko, was defeated by a young comedian, Volodymyr Zelensky.[86] His victory meant that Lutsenko had little time left in his position as Ukraine's chief prosecutor before being replaced by the new administration. Those retainers negotiated by Toensing and diGenova, which were finalized two weeks before the Ukrainian election, would become meaningless and thus were left unsigned by Lutsenko and Shokin.[87]

Meanwhile, the BLT team pivoted from the Ukrainian prosecutors to looking for an introduction to Zelensky to proceed with their plan against Joe Biden.

CHAPTER 11

THE PIVOT

GIULIANI'S LEVERAGING

In early April 2019, when the Ukrainian presidential election runoff between Petro Poroshenko and Volodymyr Zelensky was announced, Lev Parnas started gathering information on people within Zelensky's circle, trying to establish a connection to him.[1] Meanwhile, feeling abandoned, Yuri Lutsenko grew bitter. In his communication with Parnas, Lutsenko vented his frustrations, accusing the Americans of being incapable of arranging a meeting for him with the US attorney general and removing the US ambassador to Ukraine.[2] On May 16, 2019, days before Zelensky's inauguration, Lutsenko gave an interview to Bloomberg News in which he claimed that there was "no evidence of wrongdoing" by the Bidens in Ukraine.[3] By doing so, Lutsenko contradicted his prior statements published by John Solomon. Later he would say that he decided to give this interview to Bloomberg to show that he was "not Giuliani's marionette."[4] But more probably, it was a futile attempt to keep his job as the prosecutor general at the new president's cabinet as, within the same interview, Lutsenko said that he was "ready to work" with Zelensky.[5]

Rudy Giuliani did not take Lutsenko's change of heart well and said that, by giving an interview to Bloomberg, he "undermined everything."[6] Through Lev Parnas he urgently demanded to talk to Lutsenko, with no apparent success.[7] With Lutsenko seemingly turning away from Giuliani and Parnas, they started exploring other ways to create noise around the Bidens and Ukraine's election interference investigations.

By early May 2019, Lev Parnas had established contact with one of Zelensky's advisors and sent him Rudy Giuliani's letter addressed to Zelensky.[8] It included a request for a meeting:[9]

> *In my capacity as personal counsel to President Trump and with his knowledge and consent, I request a meeting with you on this upcoming Monday, May 13th or Tuesday, May 14th. I will need no more than a half-hour of your time and I will be accompanied by my colleague Victoria Toensing, a distinguished American attorney who is very familiar with this matter.*

Giuliani, seemingly certain of a meeting with Zelensky, announced his trip to Ukraine and told the *New York Times*[10] of his intentions:

> *We're not meddling in an election, we're meddling in an investigation, which we have a right to do.*

The letter did not have its intended effect on Zelensky, and Giuliani texted to Parnas:[11]

> *This guy is cancelling the meeting I think? . . . I'm going to say I have been informed the people advising the PRES ELECT are no friends of the President [Trump].*

Volodymyr Zelensky was a political newcomer and needed strong support from the United States to hold off Russian aggression on the eastern Ukrainian border. Rudy Giuliani was well aware of these facts and was willing to leverage the appearance of the US president's support in exchange for an announcement of investigations into the Bidens and bogus claims of Ukrainian interference into the 2016 US presidential election.

Zelensky's inauguration was scheduled for May 20, 2019. US officials were preparing for VP Mike Pence to represent the United States at the event. However, Rudy Giuliani and Lev Parnas seemed to have intervened in that process.

Several months later, in his interview to Rachel Maddow from MSNBC, Parnas would recall his meeting with Zelensky's representative, Serhiy Shefir, a few days before the inauguration.[12]

> MADDOW: *It has been reported as far as we understand, from public reporting, that you conveyed to Mr. Shaffer the exact quid pro quo, that you wanted Zelensky to announce investigations into Joe Biden or military aid would not be released to Ukraine. Is that accurate?*
>
> PARNAS: *It was a little bit more than that. Basically, the message that I was supposed—that I gave Sergey Shaffer was a very harsh message. I was told to give it to him in a very harsh way, not in a pleasant way.*
>
> MADDOW: *Who told you to give it to him a harsh way?*
>
> PARNAS: *Mayor Giuliani, Rudy, told me after, you know, meeting with the president at the White House. He called me. The message was, it wasn't just military aid, it was all aid. Basically their relationships would be sour, that he would—that we would stop giving them any kind of aid that—*

MADDOW: Unless?

PARNAS: —unless that there was announcement made—it was several things. There were several demands at that point. A, the most important was the announcement of the Biden investigation.

MADDOW: Did you also convey to him that the U.S. government would stop showing support for Mr. Zelensky, that they wouldn't attend the inauguration? Or that—

PARNAS: That was—that was the biggest thing, actually. That was—that was the main—it wasn't—because at that time, you have to understand the way Ukraine is. For President Zelensky, winning on that platform, being a young president, and not really having any experience, the number one thing—and being at war with Russia at the time, the number one thing was not even aid, and I know it sounds crazy, but it was more support from the president.

MADDOW: Yes.

PARNAS: By having a White House visit, by having a big inauguration, by having all the dignitaries there. That was the key...

PARNAS: At our meeting, I was very, very stern. It was a heated conversation from our part to him, basically telling him what needs to be done. I mean, basically me. And at the—at—in the conversation, I told him that if he doesn't—the announcement was the key at that time because of the inauguration, that Pence would not show up. Nobody would show up to his inauguration.

MADDOW: Unless he announced an investigation into Joe Biden, no U.S. officials, particularly Vice President Pence would not come—

PARNAS: Particularly Vice President Mike Pence.

Seemingly, the ultimatum did not work on Zelensky's team. Parnas told Rachel Maddow in the same interview:

PARNAS: So, I called back and said no-go, and he—I remember Rudy going, OK, they'll see. Basically, the next day, Pence, to my awareness, Trump called up and said, to make sure Pence doesn't go there. So—

MADDOW: So, you believe that Mr. Pence's trip to the inauguration was canceled because they didn't agree—

> PARNAS: Oh, I know, 100 percent.
>
> MADDOW: —to announce an investigation into the Bidens?

Instead, the United States government was represented by a Trump cabinet member, secretary of energy Rick Perry, at the Zelensky inauguration.

OUTREACH TO IHOR KOLOMOISKY

Zelensky's election disrupted the BLT team's operation in Ukraine. Previous administration's officials, whom Giuliani and Parnas had been cultivating, were up for replacement, including the prosecutor general, Yuri Lutsenko. At the time of Zelensky's election, little was known about who he was going to appoint to the positions that were crucial for Giuliani and Parnas's purposes. So they started reaching out not only to Zelensky's campaign team but also to oligarchs, who had historically been perceived as kingmakers in Ukraine. Giuliani reportedly "looked at maybe 20 of these oligarchs" to find the ones who had "relevant information" that could help Giuliani's endeavors in Ukraine.[13]

One of them was Ihor Kolomoisky,[14] a Ukrainian billionaire[15] who was believed to be a major supporter of Zelensky's presidential campaign.[16] Like the other Parnas connections in Ukraine, Ihor Kolomoisky, a former governor of a region in eastern Ukraine, was a figure of significant influence. After his company PrivatBank was nationalized[17] by the Ukrainian government in 2016 on charges of fraud and money laundering of $5.5 billion,[18] Kolomoisky left Ukraine[19] and lived in self-imposed exile in Israel until 2019. In addition to being criminally charged in Ukraine, Kolomoisky was under an investigation in the United States[20] for using the proceeds of money laundered by PrivatBank to purchase at least twenty-two signature real estate buildings in the Midwest of the United States.[21]

Immediately after Zelensky's victory, Parnas and Fruman traveled to Israel to meet with Kolomoisky.[22] He later told the *New York Times* that Parnas and Fruman secured the meeting under a false pretense,[23] claiming a business opportunity related to liquified natural gas (LNG). During the conversation the duo, instead, requested Kolomoisky's assistance in arranging a meeting with Volodymyr Zelensky.[24]

That move didn't go well. Kolomoisky reportedly cut the meeting short:[25]

> "I told them I am not going to be a middleman in anybody's meetings with Zelensky," Kolomoisky said. "Not for them, not for anybody else. They tried to say something like, 'Hey, we are serious people here. Giuliani. Trump.' They started throwing names at me."

Kolomoisky returned to Ukraine in mid-May 2019 and gave an interview to local Ukrainian news in which he characterized Parnas and Fruman as "fraudsters."[26] Kolomoisky further claimed the duo boasted that they could arrange a visit from high-level US officials to Zelensky's inauguration for a $250,000 fee.[27]

In response to Kolomoisky's interview, Parnas and Fruman accused Kolomoisky of threatening their lives,[28] a claim that was picked up by Rudy Giuliani and shared on Twitter.[29] Despite a rough start, by mid-September 2019 Lev Parnas appeared to have patched his connection to Kolomoisky as the two started exchanging messages again.[30]

Years later Lev Parnas's lawyer would imply that Rudy Giuliani might have chosen to approach Kolomoisky because the oligarch had legal issues in the United States.[31] Giuliani had a track record of striking deals with foreign billionaires[32] who had been targeted by the US justice system.[33] Parnas claimed that Giuliani would offer the billionaires help with resolving their legal travails in the United States in exchange for their assistance in advancing Giuliani's goals.

Although Kolomoisky asserted that Parnas and Fruman had not discussed his legal issues in the United States with him, he mentioned that the duo had been talking to another exiled Ukrainian oligarch named Dmytro Firtash.[34] Fitting Giuliani's target profile, Firtash had been previously charged in the United States with bribery[35] and had been fighting extradition from Austria since 2014.[36] The BLT team apparently had been working in the United States to have the charges against Firtash dropped in exchange for his assistance in Giuliani's endeavors in Ukraine.[37]

Kolomoisky told the *New York Times* that if Parnas and Fruman had brought up the issue of Kolomoisky's investigation in America, he would have said:[38]

Let's watch Firtash and train on Firtash. When Firtash comes back here [to Ukraine], and everything is O.K., I will be your next client.

QUID PRO QUO WITH DMYTRO FIRTASH

WHO IS DMYTRO FIRTASH?

Dmytro Firtash seemingly was not Giuliani's first choice from his target oligarch list. In a March 2019 interview to the *Hill*, Giuliani denigrated Firtash:[39]

He is considered to be one of the close associates of [Semion] Mogilevich, who is the head of Russian organized crime, who is Putin's best friend . . . this guy [Firtash] who's considered to be one of the high-level, Russian organized crime members or associates.

Giuliani aptly described Firtash and what he represented. So how did the private lawyer of the president of the United States find common cause with him?

Dmytro Firtash is a Ukrainian oligarch with deep connections to the Kremlin and organized crime in Russia.[40] He rose from humble origins in Ukraine to become a power broker between Russian and Ukrainian political elites at the highest echelons.[41]

In 2020 a *NBC News* article, quoting a reputed Russian expert, characterized Firtash as more of a "purveyor of bribes than a proper businessman." The expert described Firtash as follows:[42]

> He has essentially been used by the Russians to buy political power in Ukraine . . . He's the person who has spent the most money on behalf of the Kremlin on Ukraine's politicians.

The expert was talking about the Party of Regions, which was financially backed by Firtash and headed by pro-Russian president Viktor Yanukovych.[43]

During Yanukovych's presidency Firtash served as an exclusive[44] buyer[45] of underpriced Russian gas that was then sold to Ukraine at a significantly higher markup. Fueled by loans of over $11 billion by the Russian-government-controlled Gazprombank,[46] Firtash went on a buying spree. In two years he amassed an empire that included downstream gas distribution across the country, fertilizer and titanium plants, multiple TV channels, and a bank, among other assets.[47]

Soon Firtash's empire spread beyond Ukraine.[48] Some of his dubious business practices were spotted by US authorities, and in 2013 Dmytro Firtash was charged by a Chicago federal court with bribery.[49] In March 2014 Firtash was arrested in Austria at the request of the FBI on international corruption and conspiracy charges.[50] Shortly afterward he was released on a bail of $174 million[51] that was paid by a Russian oligarch[52] and then embarked on a yearslong fight against extradition to the United States.

THE BLT TEAM MEETS FIRTASH

Two months after Giuliani had blasted Firtash in an interview, he flew to Paris and met with an executive of one of the oligarch's companies, with the apparent goal of seeking contact with the oligarch.[53] Lev Parnas explained his version of how the BLT team began to work with Firtash, claiming that in the spring of 2019 somebody from the "Firtash camp" reached out to the BLT team with a tip about the Mueller investigation.[54] Firtash's version was different. In an interview with the *New York Times*, he explained that Parnas and Fruman had "pitched" him, like they had done with Kolomoisky, an opportunity to sell LNG to Ukraine.[55] In June 2019 Lev Parnas and Igor Fruman flew to Vienna to meet with the oligarch.[56] It would be the first of many of the duo's trips to see Firtash.[57]

While Rudy Giuliani did not join them, he reportedly instructed his associates over the phone.[58] The notes taken by Parnas during that conversation would later be released to the American public during the first impeachment of Donald Trump (figure 4).[59]

Written on a notepad from the Ritz-Carlton Hotel in Vienna, it seemed to be a to-do list that Giuliani dictated to Parnas. The list included the effort to connect to Zelensky and "get Zelensky to announce" the investigation into the Bidens (notes #1 and #2).

The notes also mentioned a "package" that they wanted to take to DC (notes #3 and #4). This package may be related to a disinformation package about Ukraine that Rudy Giuliani and the BLT team had put together based on the information from Yuri Lutsenko and Viktor Shokin.[60] As mentioned earlier Giuliani had sent a package of his Ukraine theories to the secretary of state, Mike Pompeo, on White House letterhead.[61] It's possible that Rudy Giuliani considered putting together a similar package with Firtash's requests and delivering it to officials in DC.

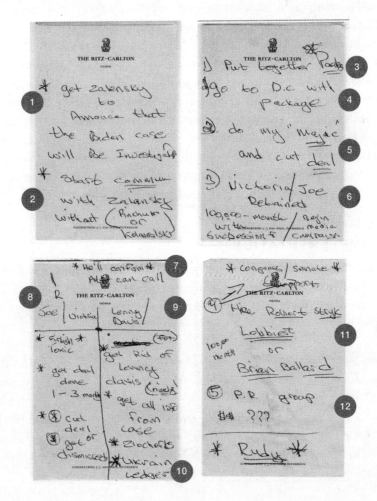

FIGURE 4. LEV PARNAS'S NOTES
SOURCE: HOUSE INTELLIGENCE COMMITTEE

Notes #6 and #8 covered the plans to engage Victoria Toensing and Joe diGenova, the same lawyer couple who signed retainer agreements to represent Yuri Lutsenko and Viktor Shokin. The intention was for Toensing and diGenova to replace Firtash's US-based lawyer Lanny Davis (note #9).

Note #10, the "Ukraine ledger," seemed to refer to Paul Manafort's black ledger[62] story.[63] Manafort, years before becoming Donald Trump's campaign manager in 2016, had done political consulting for Ukraine's pro-Russian president Viktor Yanukovych who had been financially backed by the country's oligarchs, including Firtash.[64] Ukraine's anticorruption forces later revealed that Manafort had received substantial payments from Yanukovych's party that were recorded in black ledgers.[65] However, he failed to report those payments in his US tax returns.[66] In an offshoot of the Mueller investigation, Manafort was convicted of a variety of crimes related to his previous activities as a consultant for the pro-Russian president.[67] Giuliani intended to twist Manafort's story into a tale of Ukraine's interference in the US election.

Giuliani and Parnas seemingly planned to lobby the US Congress as they discussed hiring lobbyists Robert Stryk and Brian Ballard (note #11), who were previously part of the influence efforts run by Venezuela and Turkey. In addition to pushing their Ukraine agenda to Congress, the secretary of state, and the Department of Justice, Giuliani and Parnas were planning a PR campaign (note #12) to spread the conspiracy to the wider American public. Essentially, those notes that Parnas took in Vienna were a road map to pivot the BLT team's Ukraine strategy after Zelensky's victory. The new plan included engaging with Dmytro Firtash.

THE IMPLEMENTATION

In June 2019 an Austrian court had approved the extradition of Firtash to the United States,[68] and he was reportedly considering the replacement of his US lawyers.[69] The BLT team seized that opportunity to offer their services. Years later Parnas would write his book:[70]

> *Our pitch was successful, Firtash agreed to hire Giuliani for $1 million. And $200,000 for me to be official translator and to be under the attorney-client privilege umbrella.*
>
> *When Giuliani ran the plan by the Boss, Trump's handlers were astonished. No, they answered unanimously, Giuliani could not represent a foreign billionaire who allegedly had strong ties to organized crime and a long history with Putin. It just wouldn't look good.*
>
> *Unfazed and determined, he employed a workaround. Giuliani hired Victoria Toensing and Joe diGenova—a husband-and-wife lawyer team who made their fame singing*

Trump's praises on Fox News—to be the official face of the operation, while he pulled the strings from behind the scenes. . . .

Firtash agreed to give Toensing a $1 million check for a retainer. Giuliani later told me that Toensing would share the money with him. Firtash got what he wanted, Giuliani and Trump got what they wanted and nobody but Trump's most inner circle was aware of any of it.

The goal was to make Firtash's legal[71] troubles[72] in the United States disappear. In exchange, Firtash was supposed to help Giuliani's BLT team with their crusade in Ukraine. Parnas described the plan to engage Firtash in his interview to MSNBC as follows:[73]

PARNAS: For us to be able to receive information from Firtash, we had to promise Firtash something.

MADDOW: Uh-huh.

PARNAS: So, for Firtash, it was basically telling him we knew his case is worthless here and that he's being prosecuted for no reason and that basically it could get taken care of. That—

MADDOW: That was your offer to Mr. Firtash.

PARNAS: Correct, correct.

MADDOW: That we can get this prosecution of you dropped.

PARNAS: Your extradition case, correct, yes. So, that was basically the situation at that point.

MADDOW: So the exchange with Mr. Firtash was going to be, you provide us information that would be detrimental to the public perception of the Mueller investigation, and we in turn will get your case dropped at the DOJ, so you won't get extradited to the United States anymore?

PARNAS: That's how it began.

MADDOW: Mr. DiGenova and Ms. Toensing were going to become lawyers to effectuate this trade?

> PARNAS: Correct.
>
> MADDOW: And you were supposed to broker this?
>
> PARNAS: Correct...
>
> MADDOW: The—announcing the Biden investigation and talking about getting Firtash off from this Department of Justice prosecution, these were connected?
>
> PARNAS: It was all connected. I mean, it was all—at the end of the day, it was all—the agenda was to make sure that the Ukrainians announced the Biden investigation.

Within a few weeks of meeting Parnas in Vienna, Firtash would dismiss his US-based lawyer and lobbyist, Lanny Davis, and instead hire Toensing and diGenova.[74] On July 23, 2019, Davis filed a FARA report about the termination of his services to Firtash.[75] It is safe to assume that Toensing and diGenova started representing the oligarch around that time.

In addition to a $1 million retainer to Toensing and diGenova[76] and $200,000 paid to Parnas for his "translation services,"[77] Firtash's company reportedly also paid for some of Giuliani, Parnas, and Fruman's travel expenses to Europe.[78] Further, in September 2019 Firtash, through a Russian bank account that belonged to one of his lawyers, would lend $1 million to Parnas's wife.[79]

As soon as Toensing and diGenova took over as Firtash's lawyers,[80] details of the oligarch's criminal case in the United States started leaking out to other members of the BLT team. Lev Parnas claimed that they had discovered that a member of the Special Counsel team had discussed a potential deal with the defense lawyers of Dmytro Firtash that included resolving his criminal case in exchange for information that might connect Donald Trump and his campaign to the Russian interference in the 2016 US election.[81]

On July 22, 2019, Solomon published a long article in the *Hill* in which he portrayed the Special Counsel team's move as conspiratorial and inappropriate.[82] However, it's not unusual for the DOJ to offer a deal to a defendant in exchange for his cooperation. Solomon also described Firtash's case in the United States as unsubstantiated, claiming that the oligarch was a victim of political persecution. This was yet another time when the *Hill* writer laundered disinformation that was beneficial to the BLT team's projects. In his article Solomon mentioned neither Firtash's connections to the Kremlin nor his own relationship with Giuliani, Toensing, and diGenova.

In late August Toensing and diGenova, as Firtash's new lawyers, met in person[83] with Attorney General Barr[84] and his colleagues to discuss the oligarch's case and "argue against the charges."[85] There was no immediate decision from the DOJ, and the BLT team continued their work.[86]

Soon thereafter, in late August, President Zelensky removed Yuri Lutsenko from the prosecutor general's position, thus cutting out the key player whom Giuliani and Parnas had been cultivating for months. With Lutsenko out of the equation, the BLT team shifted their focus onto Dmytro Firtash.

Toensing and diGenova also seemed to reach back to the former prosecutor general of Ukraine Viktor Shokin. On the request of Firtash's lawyers, the former prosecutor general wrote an affidavit to be submitted to an Austrian court in support of Firtash's extradition appeal to avoid US bribery charges.[87] In the affidavit Shokin claimed:[88]

> *Therefore, it is clear to me that certain US officials from President Obama's administration, in particular the US Vice-President Joe Biden, directly manipulated the political leadership of Ukraine on false pretext, in order to prevent DF [Dmytro Firtash] from returning to Ukraine, as they were so concerned about him re-establishing public life there.*

In his affidavit Shokin also regurgitated his baseless accusations of Biden's role in his firing:

> *The truth is that I was forced out because I was leading a wide-ranging corruption probe into Burisma Holdings ("Burisma"), a natural gas firm active in Ukraine, and Joe Biden's son, Hunter Biden, was a member of the Board of Directors. I assume Burisma, which was connected with gas extraction, had the support of the US Vice President Joe Biden because his son was on the Board of Directors.*

That last piece of information had nothing to do with Firtash's extradition case in Austria. However, including Shokin's statement about his firing within a formal affidavit and then inserting it into official court records provided Shokin's false claim a cover of legitimacy. It then could be quoted as a legal document and used by Giuliani and his team as a basis to manufacture dirt on the Bidens.

Shokin's affidavit was filed in an Austrian court under seal,[89] to be available for a judge but not for the public. However, within three weeks the document mysteriously found its way to John Solomon, who then weaponized it in another article published on September 26, 2019, on the *Hill*. Solomon presented the affidavit to his readers as solid proof of Biden's wrongdoing in Ukraine.[90]

The timing of that article was conspicuous. It was released around the same time the mainstream media published the transcript of the Trump-Zelensky call[91] and the text of the whistleblower complaint.[92] Combined, those two documents painted a picture that Donald Trump had sent Rudy Giuliani to act as the orchestrator of illicit activities in Ukraine. In effect, Rudy Giuliani was trying to deflect attention from Trump's impeachment by actively promoting a made-up narrative of Biden's alleged corruption.

While the congressional investigation into Donald Trump's misconduct toward Ukraine was gaining speed, Rudy Giuliani went onto ABC's *This Week* show and held a printed copy of Shokin's affidavit as a proof of Biden's corruption.[93] Giuliani continued to promote Viktor Shokin's allegations that he was unjustly fired under Joe Biden's pressure and pushed his affidavit in Fox News appearances in September,[94] October,[95] November,[96] and December of 2019,[97] as well as January[98] and February of 2020.[99]

Rachel Maddow, who interviewed Lev Parnas, summed up this Firtash–BLT team quid pro quo this way:[100]

> *So, a conservative journalist, John Solomon, and two Fox News lawyers, Joe diGenova and Victoria Toensing, and Rudy Giuliani and Lev Parnas are all involved, in Mr. Parnas telling, in an effort to enlist the help of a billionaire, Kremlin-connected, allegedly mobbed up oligarch, to help them pressure the Ukrainian government that they must announce investigations of Joe Biden.*

By the end of September, the BLT team's plot fell apart. On September 30, 2019, three House committees subpoenaed Giuliani, Parnas, and Fruman, requesting documents regarding their escapades in Ukraine.[101] Days later, in early October, Toensing and diGenova received news[102] that Attorney General Barr would not intervene in the Firtash case.[103] As Toensing and diGenova could not deliver their part of the bargain, they could not expect Firtash to make the Ukrainian government announce the investigations sought by the BLT team.

On October 9, 2019, Lev Parnas and Igor Fruman were arrested by the FBI agents at Dulles International Airport near Washington, DC, with one-way tickets to Vienna, Austria.

"I WILL BE THE HERO"

By late 2019 the congressional investigation into Donald Trump's conduct regarding Ukraine was gaining speed. With the arrest of Lev Parnas and Igor Fruman, who had been serving as Rudy Giuliani's foot soldiers, the probability of Giuliani himself being brought to justice had increased. Unwilling to comply with the congressional subpoena[104] that would reveal his actions in Ukraine, Giuliani instead pivoted to producing a "documentary" series that intended to serve several purposes.[105] Titled *The Ukraine Hoax: Impeachment, Biden Cash, and Mass Murder*, the series attempted to deflect the ongoing impeachment inquiry while smearing Joe Biden and discounting the Mueller investigation report that was released earlier that year.[106]

In early December 2019, Giuliani, accompanied by a production crew[107] from the right-wing channel One America News (OAN),[108] traveled to Hungary and Ukraine to conduct interviews with several Ukrainians for his documentary.[109] First, in Budapest Giuliani met with Yuri Lutsenko, the former prosecutor general of Ukraine.[110] Apparently, the two patched things up[111] after the fallout caused by Lutsenko's earlier interview to Bloomberg. The next day Giuliani and the OAN crew flew to Kyiv to meet with Viktor Shokin, the other former prosecutor general, and Konstantin Kulyk, Lutsenko's former deputy.[112] The prosecutors told the same stories they had provided earlier to John Solomon from the *Hill*, claiming Joe Biden's corruption in Ukraine and smearing former US ambassador in Ukraine Marie Yovanovitch.[113]

While in Kyiv, Giuliani also met with Andrii Derkach,[114] a former Ukrainian parliamentarian who, for over two decades, had been a member of the Party of Regions,[115] the pro-Russian political party financed by Dmytro Firtash. Another person interviewed for the documentary was Andrii Telizhenko, a former low-level diplomat at the Ukrainian Embassy in Washington, DC. Both Derkach and Telizhenko alleged that in 2016 the Ukrainian government, not Russian, interfered in the US election by conspiring with Democrats to promote Hillary Clinton and fabricating documents to incriminate Donald Trump's campaign manager, Paul Manafort.[116] Using those allegations, Giuliani aimed to disconnect Trump's name from Russia and direct the blame of election interference on Democrats and Ukraine.

OAN announced Giuliani's documentary in late December 2019, as Donald Trump's impeachment trial was reaching its final stage.[117] Both Giuliani[118] and Trump[119] then pushed the show on their Twitter accounts, driving it into the conservative media[120] ecosystem.[121]

The series aired in January 2020 and was immediately challenged by mainstream journalists,[122] who labeled it a propaganda piece.[123] Within days it disappeared from the network channels.

In August 2020 the director of the National Counterintelligence and Security Center would release a statement that flagged Andrii Derkach, one of the sources for Giuliani's documentary, as peddling disinformation to benefit the Kremlin.[124] A month later the US Department of the Treasury would sanction Derkach and his allies,[125] revealing that he was an agent of the Russian intelligence services and fed Giuliani disinformation to prevent Joe Biden from becoming president. The CIA would conclude that Derkach was involved in an effort to interfere into 2020 presidential election.[126]

It would also be revealed that when Giuliani was working on his documentary, US intelligence had warned[127] President Trump[128] that his private attorney was being targeted by Kremlin intermediaries. Trump shrugged the revelations off, commenting "That's Rudy."[129]

After the announcement of US sanctions targeting Derkach, Giuliani would try to downplay their connection and his own role in the attempt to undermine Biden's chances for the election.[130] The sham documentary that he produced would not have the intended effect neither on the election nor on the impeachment trial.

But in the fall of 2019, as pressure was mounting around him and Donald Trump, Giuliani was eager to fight back. When the congressional committees unveiled impeachment proceedings,[131] Giuliani exclaimed in an interview to the *Atlantic*:[132]

> *It is impossible that the whistle-blower is a hero and I'm not. And I will be the hero! These morons—when this is over, I will be the hero....*
>
> *I'm not acting as a lawyer. I'm acting as someone who has devoted most of his life to straightening out government ... Anything I did should be praised.*

Far from becoming a hero or being praised, Rudy Giuliani emerged during Donald Trump's first impeachment as the central player of a swirl of schemes in Ukraine. He was flagged as a key peddler of efforts to remove the US ambassador to Ukraine Marie Yovanovitch. The curious thing was that her removal was sought not only by the Ukrainian prosecutor, as Lev Parnas had claimed, but also by private energy interests who hoped to reap fortunes from Ukraine's gas industry.

CHAPTER 12

FREEDOM GAS

THE RUSSIAN GRIP ON NAFTOGAZ

THE RUSSIAN-UKRAINIAN MIDDLEMAN SCHEME

In 2019 Lev Parnas and Igor Fruman gained access to some of the most powerful Ukrainian oligarchs by pitching them on business opportunities related to liquified natural gas. Although the media paid more attention to their role in an effort to discredit Joe Biden, the duo had an additional endeavor in Ukraine that involved the country's national energy company, Naftogaz. Translated from Ukrainian, Naftogaz means "Petrogas." It's Ukraine's state-owned gas company that controls and operates the lion's share of the country's energy supply and infrastructure through a number of subsidiaries.

Before 2014 Naftogaz imported gas mainly from Russia. Naftogaz's large gas distribution artery also transported around 80 percent of Russia's gas exports to Europe.[1] Despite a gas codependence of buyer and seller between Russia and Ukraine, the relationship was not an easy one. It ebbed and flowed depending on who was the incumbent Ukrainian president and whether he adhered to a pro-Russian or a pro-Western policy. The Kremlin's favor, or lack thereof, was exercised through the supply of gas.

Dmytro Firtash, the Ukrainian oligarch described in the previous chapter, played a crucial role in the Russian-Ukrainian energy arrangement. In 2004, with the blessing of the Russian president, Vladimir Putin, and his closely allied Ukrainian counterpart, Leonid Kuchma, a newly created company, RosUkrEnergo (RUE), became the exclusive reseller of gas from the Russian state-owned Gazprom to Ukrainian Naftogaz.[2] RUE had no physical infrastructure of its own[3] yet acted as an intermediary between the two countries. Later it would be revealed that 50 percent of RosUkrEnergo was owned by Russian state-owned Gazprombank and 45 percent by Dmytro Firtash.[4] By some accounts, the scheme allowed RosUkrEnergo to make $2.5 billion per quarter by buying heavily discounted Russian gas and reselling it at a premium to Ukraine.[5] This scheme deprived Ukraine and Russia of state income while enriching the private owners of RUE, a needless intermediary.

In a few months, the arrangement was jeopardized by the 2004 election of Viktor Yushchenko as the president of Ukraine.

Yushchenko ran on a pro-Western platform, in opposition to then Ukrainian prime minister Viktor Yanukovych, whose campaign was seemingly[6] endorsed[7] by Russian president Vladimir Putin. The election race was highly contested with dirty tricks[8] that included the poisoning of the pro-Western candidate[9] and vote-counting irregularities.[10] Initially, the pro-Russian Yanukovych was declared the winner.[11] However, the Ukrainian Supreme Court ruled[12] that due to significant voting irregularities, the Ukrainian people would need to cast ballots again and choose between the two leading candidates, Yushchenko and Yanukovych.[13] As a result of the rerun, the pro-Western Viktor Yushchenko was elected as the next president of Ukraine.[14]

Shortly after Yushchenko was sworn in, his administration questioned the need of the Firtash middleman gas scheme.[15] To force Ukraine to adhere to the prior gas sales arrangement, Russia turned off the gas flow. Under pressure, Yushchenko submitted to the Kremlin's demands, and the scheme remained in place.[16]

Around the same time, a company controlled by Firtash started buying out Ukrainian regional gas distribution pipelines, giving him control over both the importation of gas and its downstream distribution to consumers.[17] In other words, Firtash's companies profited at two different tiers of gas distribution, both to and within Ukraine. RUE, serving as a middleman of a wholesale gas purchase from Russian Gazprom to Ukraine's Naftogaz, then distributed the gas through its federal pipelines into regions. Within the regions of Ukraine, most of the gas networks were owned and operated by private companies. By 2017 Firtash controlled[18] twenty of those local distribution companies throughout the country.[19]

In late 2008 the Ukrainian government embarked on another attempt to remove RUE from the Ukrainian supply chain and buy gas directly from Russia. After weeks of negotiations, several cutoffs of gas, and a spiteful increase of price by the Kremlin,[20] in 2009 Russia agreed to sell gas directly to Ukraine, eliminating the middleman,[21] but increased the gas sale price dramatically.[22]

The following year, in 2010, the Ukrainian people elected the pro-Russian candidate Viktor Yanukovych. His campaign and political party were financed by Dmytro Firtash.[23] The new funds brought in a more professional American political consultant, Paul Manafort, who ran Yanukovych's campaign and rebranded his image into that of a Western-like, polished politician.[24]

In turn, the new president reinstated Firtash as the middleman for the gas flow from Russia.[25] Further, the Russian-government-owned Gazprombank lent the oligarch over $11 billion that Firtash used in Ukraine to capture power over the country's infrastructure, media, and politics.[26] But that status quo would not last long as, in 2013, the Ukrainian people revolted against the Kremlin's hand in Ukrainian politics.

THE PARTITION OF UKRAINE

Located in the buffer area between the East and the West, Ukraine had grappled to reconcile its Soviet heritage and its European aspirations. The struggle was first apparent during the 2004 presidential election. The choice was between a pro-Western candidate, Viktor Yushchenko, and a pro-Russian one, Viktor Yanukovych. Ten years later the rift would spill into a war.

After becoming the Ukrainian president in 2010, Viktor Yanukovych attempted to appear as the keeper of the middle ground between Europe and Russia. However, in November 2013 he tipped his hand and exposed his true allegiances when he announced[27] a decision for Ukraine to pull back from an almost settled association agreement with the European Union.[28] Instead, he proclaimed that Ukraine would take a bailout loan from Russia.[29] This triggered what became known as the Maidan Revolution.

Throughout the winter many young Ukrainians took to the streets, condemning Yanukovych's decision and his perceived corruption.[30] In response, Ukrainian security forces violently assaulted the protesters,[31] killing dozens.[32] The situation spiraled out of control, with the demonstrators blaming the Yanukovych government for escalating the violence. Amid the chaos on the streets the government began to collapse.[33] On February 22, 2014, the Ukrainian parliament voted to remove President Yanukovych from his position[34] and two days later ordered his arrest for the "mass killing of civilians."[35] To avoid prosecution, Yanukovych fled[36] to Russia,[37] and an interim Ukrainian government took his place.

Shortly thereafter the new government reorganized, and Ukrainian prosecutors accused Yanukovych and his allies of stealing up to $100 billion worth of Ukrainian assets.[38] On March 5, 2014, the European Union began freezing funds believed to be related to corruption in Ukraine.[39] Days later, on March 13, Ukrainian oligarch Dmytro Firtash was arrested in Austria on bribery charges at the request of the US government.[40]

In parallel, after Yanukovych fled Ukraine, Russian forces, with insignias removed from their uniforms and equipment, invaded and occupied the Crimean Peninsula in southern Ukraine and annexed it at gunpoint.[41] A few weeks later, Russian-backed separatists declared the independence of areas in eastern Ukraine.[42] The Ukrainian government was in an impossible position of being attacked by its largest energy supplier. As Ukrainian forces fought back against Russian separatists, the Kremlin cut off the gas stream to Ukraine, and by extension to European buyers, applying pressure on the interim Ukrainian government to acquiesce to the demands of Russian separatists.[43]

Attempting to reclaim their territory, Ukrainian forces fought against the separatists for months. After significant Ukrainian losses,[44] on September 5, 2014, the government of Ukraine and the Russian-backed separatists signed a ceasefire deal, known as the Minsk Agreement.[45] It was a temporary solution that was meant to halt the advance of Russian forces. After a breakdown of that agreement and continued fighting, a second deal known as the Minsk II was brokered by Germany and France.[46] It was a strongly one-sided arrangement that included clauses beneficial to Russia,[47] namely, the political autonomy of the Russian-occupied Luhansk and Donetsk regions in eastern Ukraine, and a right for those regions to block Ukraine's foreign policy decisions, including joining the European Union or NATO. In exchange, Russian-backed separatists would stand down, effectively freezing the lines of the conflict.

Together, Minsk I and Minsk II served the purpose of stopping a full-scale Russian offensive into Ukraine. However, each party stalled the implementation of their obligations.[48] The deals, though, bought time for Ukraine to regroup. The region had remained in a simmering conflict for several years. The Russian strategy toward Ukraine since the "freezing" of the war had been to destabilize and delegitimize the interim Ukrainian government and its Western democratic aspirations.

Ukraine, with its economy devastated by the conflict, turned to the West for assistance. The European Union and the United States answered to the interim government's pleas with financial support. The International Monetary Fund (IMF) secured guaranteed loans for the Ukrainian government on several conditions,[49] one of which would be the introduction of strict anticorruption measures.[50]

To address those demands, the Ukrainian government set course to eradicate graft[51] by scrutinizing the activities of the oligarchs, establishing an anticorruption unit in the government,[52] and weeding out compromised officials from the country's apparatus. One of the most gargantuan efforts was focused on attempts to clean the country's energy industry of graft and separate it from politics.

As part of the Western financial package, the European Bank of Construction and Development lent $300 million to Naftogaz.[53] In exchange, the energy company agreed to establish a supervisory board of independent professionals to oversee structural reforms that, among other things, were designed to eliminate and prevent corrupt practices.[54] In 2017 the board included experts from Ukraine, France, Canada, the UK, and the United States.[55]

The new Ukrainian government and Naftogaz leadership sought to part from the old corrupt Kremlin-influenced ways and establish clean governance and transparent trade with Western partners. One of the people whom Naftogaz officials reached out to was the new US secretary of energy Rick Perry.[56] That endeavor would not turn out as the Naftogaz officials hoped for.

THE AMERICAN LNG PLOT

Fast forward to April 2017, Andriy Kobolev, the CEO of Naftogaz, and Yuri Vitrenko, the chief energy negotiator of Ukraine, sat down with US secretary of energy, Rick

Perry,[57] in his office in Washington.[58] The Ukrainian government was looking for a financial partner that could buy 49 percent of the equity in Naftogaz's pipeline system. It had previously transferred the lion's share of Russian gas to Europe and generated around $2 billion annually in transit fees.[59] Kobolev and Vitrenko presented that opportunity to Perry.[60]

Before becoming the US secretary of energy[61] in March 2017, Perry had served for fourteen years as the governor of Texas, the largest oil-producing state in the United States.[62] He also had served as a board member at Energy Transfer, a pipeline behemoth from Dallas, Texas.[63] So when the Naftogaz officials offered half of their pipeline infrastructure, Rick Perry was familiar with the business model and became interested in the opportunity.[64]

Since the beginning of his term as secretary of energy, Rick Perry had assumed a role of proselytizer for American liquified natural gas abroad, labeling it "freedom gas."[65] The gas-fracking boom in the United States made the country one of largest sources of LNG in the world. At the time, Perry's old company, Energy Transfer, had been planning to build an $11 billion gas terminal in a joint venture with Shell near Lake Charles in Louisiana.[66] The project was designed to have the capacity to liquify 16.45 million tons per year[67] and had already secured approval from the US government to export up to 2.33 billion cubic feet of gas daily.[68] The next step was to find clients.

Ukraine and Europe were heavily dependent on Russian natural gas for their energy needs and could potentially become welcoming markets for American LNG. American companies could ship the LNG to a Ukrainian gas hub, and the existing Ukrainian pipeline infrastructure could transport American liquified natural gas to both Ukrainian and European consumers.

If Perry's old company, Energy Transfer, were to supply gas to Ukraine, it would need logistics. All those billion cubic meters of liquified natural gas needed to be transported to Ukraine. That was where Lev Parnas, Igor Fruman, and Harry Sargeant III, the shipping magnate who was a part of the Venezuela endeavor, seemed to fit in. Sargeant had previously shipped fuel to US troops in Iraq and had the expertise that Parnas and Fruman needed to piggyback on Perry's plan, focusing on the shipping part.

Rick Perry's plan seemed noble enough, to sell American LNG to Ukraine and Europe as a counter to Russian supply with Kremlin's influence attached. However, he and his surrogates' methods would echo Russian corrupt practices. In the endeavor to implement his plan, Perry would pressure Ukraine's government to restructure Naftogaz's internationally approved anticorruption supervisory board, perceiving it as an obstacle to his plan. When the US ambassador to Ukraine Marie Yovanovitch and the CEO of Naftogaz, Andriy Kobolev, opposed[69] the restructuring of the Naftogaz board,[70] they would become[71] a hindrance[72] as well.

To make his freedom gas plan work, Perry seemed willing to take steps that countered American government interests and its official foreign policy. His actions would undermine the anticorruption efforts of the fledgling democracy. Contrary to their hopes, Ukrainian officials, instead of being liberated from the Kremlin's gas blackmail, would find themselves being pressured by Rick Perry and his allies.

UKRAINE'S NEW PARTNERS WITH A FAMILIAR PLAYBOOK

FIRST MOVES

In June 2017, two months after meeting with Naftogaz officials, Rick Perry had a second meeting with Ukrainian guests in his office. This time the Naftogaz CEO was accompanied by Ukraine's then president Petro Poroshenko and the country's minister of energy.[73] After that meeting Perry started probing the subject of Ukraine's energy sector more seriously.

As a part of his Ukraine research, Perry turned to Michael Bleyzer, a Houston-based investor whose company, SigmaBleyzer, had a diverse portfolio with stakes worldwide in agriculture, food, energy, telecommunications, and other sectors.[74] The two went way back. In 2009, while serving as the governor of Texas, Rick Perry had picked Michael Bleyzer to oversee a fund for tech start-ups.[75] Bleyzer and his wife were also among Perry's donors and had contributed at least $20,000 to his campaign.[76]

Bleyzer had been doing business between the United States and Ukraine for years and was one of the largest funders of the US-Ukraine Business Council, spearheading bilateral trade.[77] In one interview Bleyzer said that Perry had considered him "Mr. Ukraine"[78] and occasionally consulted with him about the country.

Around July 2017,[79] Bleyzer had been interacting with the US Department of Energy (DOE) staff about Ukraine and its energy industry.[80] Apparently, Bleyzer was interested in Ukraine's energy sector, particularly in hydrocarbon fields, from which petroleum and gas are sourced. On June 25, 2018, SigmaBleyzer announced that it was ready to invest $100 million into hydrocarbon exploration in Ukraine.[81] The press release stated that the decision was made after the heads of SigmaBleyzer, Aspect Holding, and Energy Transfer traveled to Ukraine to meet with an official from the country's Service for Geology and Deposits. The heads of those companies all had well-established relationships with Rick Perry.

SigmaBleyzer was Michael Bleyzer's company. In an interview with *Time* magazine, Bleyzer said that he was the one who brought the Energy Transfer executive to Ukraine and that the company's interest "had to do with Ukraine's gas-pipeline network."[82] Presumably, it was the same pipeline infrastructure that Naftogaz officials pitched to Rick Perry in April 2017.

Energy Transfer, as mentioned before, was a Texas company where Rick Perry had served as a board member before becoming the secretary of energy. The company's head, Kelcy Warren, had made generous[83] contributions[84] to Perry's 2015 presidential campaign,[85] by some accounts around $6 million.[86] While serving in the Trump administration, Perry had no apparent conflict of interest with his old company as he had given up his seat on the board and sold his Energy Transfer stock.[87]

The third company involved was Aspect Holding, which was founded by another Rick Perry ally, Alex Cranberg. He was an oil magnate who made numerous political contributions to the Republican Party[88] that, by 2019, had totaled over $3 million.[89] Cranberg had made contributions to Perry's presidential campaigns[90] and, in 2011, had lent his private jet to the candidate.[91]

In 2018, after Perry became the secretary of energy, Cranberg hired Perry's former campaign manager, Jeff Miller, to lobby for him in DC.[92] Seemingly, Miller and Cranberg maintained good relationship with Perry as they occasionally visited him at the Department of Energy, mostly using the VIP entrance.[93]

Thus, all three companies—SigmaBleyzer, Aspect Holdings, and Energy Transfer, whose heads had participated in the June 2018 meeting—were in one way or another connected back to Rick Perry.[94]

After SigmaBleyzer's investment announcement, the Ukrainian government started preparing documentation for bids to allocate its hydrocarbon fields for commercial exploration. The winners of the bids could explore the fields for decades and sell the proceeds to the domestic market in Ukraine or export to Europe using the country's transit pipelines. The initiative to begin the bidding process in the first place was credited to the US-Ukraine Business Council,[95] the trade group connected to Michael Bleyzer.[96]

In November 2018 the US-Ukraine Business Council organized[97] a bilateral energy panel in Kyiv to demonstrate the energy cooperation effort between the two countries.[98] By that time Rick Perry seemingly had already mapped out his freedom gas strategy. Speaking on a panel at that event, Secretary Perry described his vision of Ukraine becoming a gas hub as "the Texas of Europe."[99] According to his plan, the American LNG would be shipped from the United States through Poland, stored in Ukraine's gas storage facilities, and transported to western Europe.[100] It appeared that Perry also had a specific vendor in mind, which was to supply gas: his old company, Energy Transfer.[101]

The implementation of the plan would require Naftogaz, the main importer and transporter of gas in Ukraine, to select Perry's vendor. That decision could hardly be made without the agreement of the Naftogaz supervisory board.

RESETTING THE BOARD

In May 2019 Rick Perry, the secretary of energy, was sent to the inauguration of the newly elected Volodymyr Zelensky.[102] During that trip Perry pressed the new president to insert his allies into the Naftogaz supervisory board and gave him a list of names whom he saw as fitting candidates.[103] Observers of those actions later would note that they had the impression that Perry particularly aimed to replace an American member of the board, Amos Hochstein, who had worked closely with Vice President Biden during the Obama administration. Perry seemingly wanted to insert people "reputable in Republican circles."[104] Kurt Volker, in a message to another US diplomat, said that Perry wanted to include "2 senior US energy industry people" into the Naftogaz board.[105]

Perry would explain his actions by saying that the Ukrainians asked "for people who would be good to help either be on their board or consult with them in a global way."[106] The Ukrainians, however, perceived that Perry was trying to bypass the established process, in which the Naftogaz board was appointed by the Ukrainian Cabinet of Ministers. A person who had witnessed the incident said that he was appalled by Perry's actions as he deemed that the US government had "a higher ethical standard."[107]

One of the names on Perry's list was Michael Bleyzer, described previously.[108] If added to the Naftogaz board, Bleyzer could potentially steer the decision-making into a direction that could also benefit his own energy ambitions in Ukraine. Another person that Perry had recommended to Zelensky was a Houston-based oil businessman named Robert Bensh,[109] who had spent a little over a decade working in Ukraine's energy sector. During his time there, Bensh had served as an advisor to the minister of energy during the presidency of Russian-leaning Viktor Yanukovych.[110] Bensh had also reportedly held equity in a Ukrainian energy company[111] that, according to local[112] media,[113] belonged to Viktor Yanukovych's son.

In a 2020 interview, Bensh told a reporter that he hadn't been acquainted with Rick Perry until December 2018.[114] He recalled that around that time a friend had reached out to him about Perry's search for someone with experience in the Ukrainian energy sector. On Presidents' Day weekend, in February 2019, Perry met Bensh in a Houston airport and quizzed him on his views on Ukraine and its energy industry.[115] Apparently satisfied with Bensh's answers, three months later Perry would include Bensh's name on the list he gave to Ukraine's new president. Then in July 2019, Perry's aides introduced Bensh to Ukrainian officials who had come to Washington, DC.[116]

PAVING THE WAY

It's worth reminding that Perry's freedom gas project was unfolding at the same time as Rudy Giuliani and Lev Parnas were pressuring the Ukrainian government to announce investigations into the Bidens and alleged Ukraine's interference into the 2016 US presidential election. In July 2019 Ukrainian officials came to the United States in hopes of strengthening bilateral ties. Instead, they were pushed to do actions that could benefit the interests of Donald Trump and Rick Perry. Those tactics mirrored the Kremlin's playbook of extortion of Ukraine's energy industry.

On the morning of July 10, 2019, Andriy Yermak, Volodymyr Zelensky's chief of staff, and Oleksandr Danylyuk the chief of Ukraine's national security, met at the White House with several US officials,[117] including Rick Perry.[118] During the meeting Gordon Sondland, the US ambassador to the European Union, relaying Rudy Giuliani's talking points, pushed for the Ukrainian government to announce an investigation into the Bidens. John Bolton, US national security advisor who also attended the meeting, was flabbergasted by Sondland's statements to the Ukrainian officials and immediately cut the discussion short. Later Bolton would say that he didn't want to be a part of that "drug deal" and asked his deputy, Fiona Hill, to report the interaction he witnessed to National Security Council lawyers.[119]

The same night, Yermak and Danylyuk had dinner with Rick Perry's aides and Robert Bensh. At that meeting Bensh promoted the idea of selling American LNG to Ukraine and then transferring it to Europe, essentially telegraphing Perry's vision. Yermak and Danylyuk must've felt extremely bizarre being coaxed by Bensh, a former advisor to Yanukovych's administration, which in Ukrainian minds was associated with the Kremlin and corruption, especially considering that Ukraine was at war with Russia, and the officials came to the United States to seek support in their fight. Later Danylyuk the national security advisor to Zelensky, would recall that he thought the situation smelled "like trouble."[120]

Danylyuk's apprehensions were not unfounded. It seemed that Rick Perry wanted to insert Robert Bensh into the Naftogaz's supervisory board and, with him in place on the inside, to push Naftogaz to purchase American LNG from a specific supplier, a company named Louisiana Natural Gas Exports (LNGE), founded in June 2018 by a relative of Bensh. It had no assets or infrastructure, and to service Ukraine's energy needs, it was going to resell gas provided by Energy Transfer, Rick Perry's old company.[121] That arrangement resembled Dmytro Firtash's middleman scheme, in which his company, which also had no assets or infrastructure, bought gas from Russian Gazprom on a discount and then sold to Naftogaz with a high markup, splitting the profits between himself and his allies at Gazprom. For LNGE to be chosen as an energy supplier to Ukraine, the company would face understandable scrutiny from the Naftogaz supervisory board. That seemingly was the reason why Rick Perry pressed hard to reshuffle the Naftogaz supervisory board and have his own people installed in it.

LNGE's future role became apparent in late August 2019, when Rick Perry went to Warsaw with the purpose to "pave the way" for the transit of American LNG through Poland.[122] LNGE's CEO, Ben Blanchet, accompanied Rick Perry on the tripto Poland. Some members of Ukraine's delegation would later recollect that Perry and his staff, emboldened by their direct links to the powers in DC, pressed hard, saying, "If you want us as friends, you've got to do this."[123] Presumably, by "us" they meant the United States, and "this" was the deal with LNGE.

The US ambassador to Ukraine Marie Yovanovitch and the CEO of Naftogaz, Andriy Kobolev, both publicly[124] opposed[125] the restructuring of the supervisory board, arguing that the move would facilitate corruption. Their stance made them obstacles to the freedom gas plan, and thus they would need to be removed. If the reshuffling of the board was pushed by Rick Perry himself, the task of eliminating Ambassador Yovanovitch and Kobolev seemed to be assumed by Rudy Giuliani, Lev Parnas, and other members of the BLT team.

CHAPTER 13

REMOVING THE OBSTACLES

PARNAS AND FRUMAN'S ENERGY AMBITIONS

GLOBAL ENERGY PRODUCERS

Rick Perry was not the only person with ambitions to export American LNG to Ukraine. There was a rather large group of people who, in one way or another, became part of Perry's energy-related effort in Ukraine.

In April 2018 Lev Parnas and Igor Fruman registered a company named Global Energy Producers (GEP),[1] which, according to its business prospectus, strove to become the "largest exporter" of American LNG.[2]

Later that month Parnas and Fruman attended a dinner for VIP donors to Trump's America First Action super PAC at the Trump International Hotel in Washington, DC.[3] The duo seemingly hoped to develop contacts to advance their LNG interests in Ukraine.[4] The dinner was attended by influential Trump world insiders who could potentially facilitate Parnas and Fruman's goals. One of those people was Roy Bailey, Rudy Giuliani's very well-connected[5] business[6] partner.[7] Bailey had been a prominent GOP fundraiser with close ties to Texas politicians,[8] including former governor Rick Perry and Congressman Pete Sessions.

Bailey became a useful connection for Parnas and Fruman. He brought the duo to Capitol Hill to meet with his Texan friend Congressman Pete Sessions.[9] In June 2018 Bailey was said to have introduced Lev Parnas and Igor Fruman to Harry Sargeant III,[10] the shipping mogul who was previously mentioned in the Venezuela chapter. Sargeant worked with Giuliani and others behind the scenes to lift US sanctions from Venezuela to gain access to local oil fields.

Parnas, Fruman, and Sargeant apparently shared a common interest related to oil and gas sales to Ukraine and Europe. While Parnas and Fruman had the connections in Ukraine, they lacked experience in the energy sector. That missing piece was filled with Sargeant, who had decades of experience in the field. According to a publicly released memorandum, Parnas and Fruman's company, Global Energy Producers LLC, partnered up with Sargeant's Global Oil Management Group LLC to supply LNG to European markets[11] as an alternative to Russian gas. The venture ostensibly intended to gain access to the pipelines running through Europe and build an LNG terminal on the East Coast of the United States. While Parnas and Fruman traveled back and forth to Ukraine, combining their work on searching for dirt on the Bidens with their sidekick LNG project, Sargeant paid for some of the duo's travel expenses,[12] complaining, "Just getting expensive flying u guys everywhere LEV."[13]

PARALLEL EFFORTS

The talking points presented in the overview of Parnas and Fruman's company, Global Energy Producers,[14] echoed those of Rick Perry's pitch for freedom gas to Ukraine.[15] It also seemed that Rick Perry, Lev Parnas, and Igor Fruman were pushing parallel efforts to organize a coup at Naftogaz by reshuffling its supervisory board and replacing its CEO. However, the question is "Were their actions coordinated?"

There was no public data explicitly indicating it. Interestingly, after their later arrests, neither Lev Parnas, in[16] his[17] numerous[18] interviews,[19] nor Igor Fruman would mention their energy interest in Ukraine. Rick Perry would later deny any wrongdoing[20] and would refuse to comply with a congressional subpoena[21] when the US government started investigating the matters in Ukraine. However, all of them moved in the same circles that operated in Ukraine at the same time with the same goal, energy sales to Ukraine.

On one side, as described earlier, Rudy Giuliani and his BLT team were running the effort to smear Joe Biden and create a tale of Ukrainian interference in the US election. On the other side, Rudy Giuliani, as Donald Trump's personal envoy to Ukraine, inserted himself into governmental affairs related to Ukraine. One of those instances occurred when, after returning from Zelensky's inauguration, Rick Perry, along with Kurt Volker, US envoy to Ukraine, and Gordon Sondland, a US ambassador to the European Union, went to the White House[22] to report on their trip and discuss the possibility of arranging a meeting between the US and Ukrainian presidents.[23] President Trump did not seem very enthusiastic about the idea and referred Perry, Volker, and Sondland to Giuliani:[24]

> *Go talk to Rudy, he knows all about Ukraine.*

Rudy did not disappoint. On July 22, 2019, he had a call with Andriy Yermak, President Zelensky's chief of staff, pressing him to start investigations on the Bidens and on Ukraine's supposed "meddling" during the 2016 US election.[25] In exchange, Giuliani vouched to Yermak that he could persuade President Trump to favor Ukraine. Immediately after that conversation, Giuliani turned to Volker, asking him to arrange a call between President Trump and President Zelensky.[26] That call would happen three days later and would become the basis of the whistleblower complaint and Trump's first impeachment. Later, in an offhanded comment to the media, Donald Trump would blame his secretary of energy for suggesting the call in the first place:[27]

> *Not a lot of people know this but, I didn't even want to make the call. The only reason I made the call was because Rick asked me to. Something about an LNG [liquified natural gas] plant.*

On the call with Zelensky, Trump did not mention anything about an LNG plant but pressured the Ukrainian president to open an investigation into the Bidens and Ukraine's alleged meddling in the 2016 US election,[28] contrary to the US intelligence findings that had established Russia as the interfering country. However, Trump did express his displeasure with the US ambassador to Ukraine Marie Yovanovitch, which appeared to be in concert with Rick Perry and Lev Parnas's sentiments. As mentioned previously, she had opposed the restructuring of the Naftogaz supervisory board, while Rick Perry pressured Ukrainian officials to insert his own candidates into the board.

Gordon Sondland, one of the people who was present at the Oval Office meeting, would later testify that "everyone was in the loop" of what the Trump administration and the president's unofficial liaisons were doing in Ukraine.[29] Donald Trump's private attorney was at the very center of it. When asked about Rick Perry's plans about Naftogaz, Rudy Giuliani said, "I may or may not know anything about it."[30] Despite being coy about his knowledge of the American LNG and the Naftogaz saga, Giuliani played a crucial role in it. He had relentlessly campaigned for the removal of the US ambassador to Ukraine Marie Yovanovitch.

COLLATERAL DAMAGE

LOBBYING BEHIND THE SCENES

In late April 2018, Lev Parnas and Igor Fruman attended a VIP fundraiser for Trump donors in Washington, DC. At that event Parnas encouraged the president to remove Ambassador Yovanovitch, a longtime State Department official with deep expertise in Eastern Europe and Russia and the guardian of the anticorruption efforts in Ukraine. A recording released over a year later revealed the following exchange:[31]

> *Lev Parnas: I think if you take a look, the biggest problem there I think where you need to start is, we've got to get rid of the ambassador. She's still left over from the Clinton administration.*
>
> *Donald Trump: Where? The ambassador where? Ukraine?*

> Lev Parnas: Yeah. She's basically walking around telling everybody, "Wait, he's going to get impeached. Just wait."
>
> Donald Trump: Really?
>
> Lev Parnas: It's incredible...
>
> Lev Parnas: I don't have a name off back.
>
> Donald Trump: Get rid of her. Get her out tomorrow. I don't care, get her out tomorrow. Take her out, okay? Do it.

Days later, on May 9, 2018, Parnas and Fruman met with Congressman Pete Sessions in his office.[32] Reportedly, they had become acquainted at another fundraiser at Mar-a-Lago the previous month[33] and the duo pledged to donate $20,000 to Sessions's 2018 reelection campaign.[34] That same day as the meeting, Pete Sessions wrote a letter to the newly sworn in secretary of state, Michael Pompeo, advocating for the removal of Marie Yovanovitch:[35]

> I have received notice of concrete evidence from close companions that Ambassador Yovanovitch has spoken privately and repeatedly about her disdain for the current Administration in a way that might call for the expulsion of Ms. Yovanovitch as U.S. Ambassador to Ukraine immediately.
>
> I kindly ask you to consider terminating her ambassadorship and find a replacement as soon as possible."

The congressman's aide later testified to a grand jury that Parnas and Fruman also visited him in June 2018, and they were accompanied by another Giuliani associate, Roy Bailey, the congressman's "longtime friend."[36] At the end of that month, both Parnas and Fruman donated to Sessions $2,700 each.[37]

Pete Sessions admitted that he had met the duo several times and that they mostly talked about oil:[38]

> This was during the campaign, early in the campaign, and they did come by my office and I did meet them and I did meet them [sic] off the Hill and they did become contributors... That is not unusual for you to meet people who then become contributors. ... We talked about the ability for oil business... They're very interested in oil business. I'm from Texas, and I'm interested in it also.

The duo would maintain their connection with the Texas lawmaker and embark on their joint endeavor in Venezuela in the fall of that year.[39] Their clandestine call with the Venezuelan dictator Nicolas Maduro was described in chapter 8.

In November 2018, during the midterm elections, Sessions lost his congressional seat. According to an article from the *Daily Beast,* in late 2018 to early 2019, presumably after his defeat, Sessions was considered as one of the potential candidates to replace Yovanovitch as the US ambassador to Ukraine[40] despite having no expertise in the country.

A year later, during Donald Trump's first impeachment, Parnas would give an interview to MSNBC, claiming that the reason behind his efforts to have Marie Yovanovitch fired was a demand from Ukraine's prosecutor general Yuri Lutsenko in exchange for his opening an investigation into the Bidens.[41] However, Parnas failed to mention that he himself had considered Marie Yovanovitch a hindrance to his LNG goals[42] and had advocated for her removal months before working with Lutsenko, when he attended the VIP dinner for Trump donors in April 2018, and encouraged the president to "get rid of the ambassador."[43] Conveniently for Parnas, Lutsenko did indeed dislike the ambassador. She had openly supported NABU,[44] a Western-backed anticorruption unit in Ukraine that Lutsenko perceived as a competitor to his position.[45] Lutsenko also alleged that Yovanovitch had blocked his efforts to meet with the US attorney general.[46]

In January 2019, Rudy Giuliani and Lev Parnas met with Yuri Lutsenko for several days in New York. As mentioned in an earlier chapter, together, the group mapped out the steps to launch an effort to discredit the Bidens while also discussing the potential removal of Marie Yovanovitch. According to some accounts, Giuliani even persuaded President Trump to call in to a meeting with Lutsenko so that he could hear the information from the prosecutor firsthand.[47] That was when Donald Trump's interest to force investigations into the Bidens appeared to have converged with the energy goals of Rick Perry, Lev Parnas, and Harry Sargeant III, all of them focused on Ukraine.

President Trump had the executive power to remove the US ambassador to Ukraine. If Pete Sessions were to take her place, Rick Perry and Lev Parnas would have inserted an ally into a key position that could lean on the Ukrainian government for Parnas and Giuliani's requests. That, in turn, could help the parties interested in selling LNG to Ukraine as Perry would be one step closer to inserting his allies into Naftogaz's supervisory board. As a bonus Yovanovitch's removal would make Yuri Lutsenko happy, and he would agree to open an investigation into the Bidens. That, as a consequence, could tarnish Joe Biden's reputation and potentially eliminate Trump's main obstacle to his reelection. Shortly after their meeting in New York, the parties delved into the implementation of that multistep strategy.

THE SMEAR CAMPAIGN

Just Security, a website that focuses on the intersection of law and national security, reported that in mid-February 2019 Rudy Giuliani flew to Mar-a-Lago and coaxed the president to recall Marie Yovanovitch.[48] Around that time, a member of the BLT team, Victoria Toensing, checked in with Giuliani, asking whether there was an "absolute commitment for HER to be gone" that week,[49] presumably referring to the ambassador.

Toensing also had been exchanging messages with Lev Parnas on the Yovanovitch status:[50]

> **February 16, 2019**
> PARNAS: *Also really need to know status of madam A. While I'm here*
>
> TOENSING: *That's for Rudy to get tonight*
>
> **February 17, 2019**
> TOENSING: *Did Rudy come through? . . . Did he meet the guy re Amb?*
>
> PARNAS: *I am still waiting on that . . . Meeting with big guy in 4 hours . . .*
>
> PARNAS: *We just spoke all good thank you*
>
> TOENSING: *Was he successful re Amb*
>
> PARNAS: *this week*

The reason why Victoria Toensing was so interested in the removal of the ambassador was the fact that she and her husband, Joe diGenova, were, at the time, trying to get their retainer agreements with Lutsenko and Shokin signed. However, before signing the agreement and announcing the investigation on the Bidens, Lutsenko probably wanted Marie Yovanovitch removed first.

In response to Toensing's requests, Parnas wrote to her that the ambassador would be removed that week.[51] The bilingual Parnas served as the BLT team's connection to Lutsenko, who didn't speak good English. While intermediating between Toensing and Lutsenko, Parnas also had been coordinating an interview between Lutsenko and John Solomon, who, as mentioned earlier, wrote a story about Joe Biden and Viktor Shokin, a former prosecutor general of Ukraine. That article, then, was used as part of the disinformation campaign against Biden.

In a similar fashion and for a similar purpose, Yuri Lutsenko and John Solomon produced another scurrilous article. This time it was about Marie Yovanovitch, in which Lutsenko, attempting to paint the ambassador as corrupt, claimed that she had given him a "do-not-prosecute list."⁵² Published on March 20, 2019, the article caused an immediate pushback from the US government. The State Department vehemently denied Lutsenko's allegations, stating that the prosecutor general's accusations "intended to tarnish" the reputation of Marie Yovanovitch.⁵³

Two days after the publication of the Solomon interview and frustrated by the criticism from the US government that followed,⁵⁴ Lutsenko reached out to Parnas and vented:⁵⁵

> It's just that if you don't make a decision about Madam, you are bringing into question all my allegations. Including about B.

It appeared that Lutsenko referred to Ambassador Yovanovitch as "Madam." The "B" was likely a referral to Joe Biden or Burisma.

Despite the pushback from the State Department, the article was immediately picked up⁵⁶ by conservative media⁵⁷ and amplified by the BLT team and its surrogates.⁵⁸ On March 22 the BLT lawyer, Joe diGenova, appeared on Fox News and erroneously claimed that Trump had fired Ambassador Yovanovitch.⁵⁹ That same day Parnas sent a message to diGenova's wife, Victoria Toensing, that read, "Tell joe he was awesome my hero."⁶⁰

Parnas shared the *Hill* article and its Fox News spin-offs with a large number⁶¹ of people,⁶² including the Ukrainian prosecutors, shipping mogul Harry Sargeant III⁶³ and America First Action PAC finance director Joseph Ahearn.⁶⁴ Parnas asked Ahearn to share the articles with Donald Trump Jr., who later tweeted calls to fire the ambassador.⁶⁵ In a seemingly coordinated effort, a number of suspected inauthentic users shared Don Jr.'s post about the ambassador 7,320 times within the first forty-five minutes of it being published.⁶⁶ Some of those apparently fake users were later suspended by Twitter.⁶⁷

The BLT team's smear campaign on Yovanovitch followed the strategy that would become standard in spreading disinformation for their other projects. The routine process was that Giuliani concocted an argument that mixed partial truth with made-up accusations of misconduct.⁶⁸ That argument then was passed over to John Solomon, who wrote op-eds referring to "sources" that were selected by Giuliani.⁶⁹ When Solomon's articles were published, he, along with Rudy Giuliani, Victoria Toensing, and Joe diGenova, would interchangeably⁷⁰ appear⁷¹ on Fox News,⁷² amplifying the disinformation points written by Solomon. Finally, the articles, as well as the BLT team members' comments on them, would be picked up by people within Trump's orbit.⁷³ Such a strategy had a far-reaching cross-pollinating effect in creating the false narrative that Giuliani sought to spread.

By the end of March 2019, Rudy Giuliani had assembled a package that included clippings from Lutsenko's interview to Solomon, along with his allegations of the ambassador's obstruction of Lutsenko's work. Giuliani also tossed in a petty accusation of Yovanovitch blocking a visa for the former prosecutor Viktor Shokin, who couldn't join Lutsenko on his trip to New York. The accusatory information on Marie Yovanovitch was sandwiched in with Lutsenko's tall tale about Burisma and Joe Biden's son Hunter, who was on the board of Burisma. Rudy Giuliani packed all the files into a manila envelope that had the White House watermark and delivered the package to Secretary of State Mike Pompeo. To ensure the envelope received Pompeo's attention, Giuliani secured a call with the secretary of state on March 29, 2019.[74] Giuliani seemingly believed that the package contained enough proof to persuade Pompeo to fire Yovanovitch.

SURVEILLING THE AMBASSADOR

Another person whom Lev Parnas communicated with during his push to have the ambassador fired was a congressional candidate for Connecticut, Robert Hyde.[75] A devoted Trump supporter, Hyde had posted several photos of himself with people from the Trump orbit.[76] Within days of John Solomon's article coming out, Hyde sent Parnas ominous messages that implied that Hyde was in contact with someone doing physical surveillance of Marie Yovanovitch and could assist in arranging an abduction of the ambassador. Their exchanges from March 25 to 26, 2019, included the following:[77]

> HYDE: The address that you sent checks out
>
> HYDE: It's next to the embassy
>
> HYDE: They are willing to help if we/you would like a price
>
> HYDE: Guess you can do anything in the Ukraine with money . . . what I was told
>
> PARNAS: Lol
>
> HYDE: Update[:] she will not be moved[,] special security unit upgraded force on the compound[,] people are already aware of the situation[.] my contacts are asking what is the next step because they cannot keep going to check[,] people will start to ask questions
>
> HYDE: If you want her out they need to make contact with security forces

Although no harm was done to the ambassador by Robert Hyde's contacts, the fact that those messages were sent and weren't explicitly rebuffed by Lev Parnas illustrated the length people were willing to go to have Marie Yovanovitch removed.

Adding to the bizarreness of Robert Hyde's character, around that time, in early

2019 he reportedly dated Rabia Kazan,[78] the Turkish national who was described in chapter 4. She had infiltrated MAGA circles and connected influential Republicans to wealthy Turks, acting as a clandestine intelligence operative would. Was her relationship with Hyde genuine or part of a Turkish intelligence operation? Was she involved in the surveillance of Marie Yovanovitch? Those questions still remain unanswered.

"BOY I'M SO POWERFUL"

In April 2019 Volodymyr Zelensky's election became a black swan event for both the BLT team and Rick Perry, forcing them to quickly adapt their strategies. The members of the previous administration, who had been carefully cultivated, would have until early June to act, when the Zelensky administration would officially assume office.[79]

Three days before the Ukrainian presidential election, Yuri Lutsenko publicly retracted his allegations of Marie Yovanovitch giving him a "do-not-prosecute list."[80] Lutsenko's back-pedaling seemingly did not affect his communications with Parnas, and they continued to exchange messages.[81] Lutsenko had about six weeks left in office to announce the investigations. For him to do that, Marie Yovanovitch had to be removed as soon as possible.

Two days after Zelensky's election, Rudy Giuliani spoke to Donald Trump and, once again, asked him to sack the ambassador. After his call with the president, Giuliani exchanged the following messages with Parnas:[82]

> PARNAS: *Going to sleep my brother please text me if you have any news*
>
> GIULIANI: *He fired her again*
>
> PARNAS: *I pray it happens this time I'll call you tomorrow my brother*

Parnas's skeptical response can be explained by the fact that it was not the first conversation with President Trump about the ambassador, and every time he would agree to fire her, she would remain in place. However, this time Giuliani's arguments to President Trump seemed to have been more persuasive.

On April 24, 2019, Marie Yovanovitch received a call from a colleague in DC urging her to return to the United States because something was "going wrong."[83] On May 6, 2019, the US ambassador to Ukraine was officially removed from her position.[84]

Rudy Giuliani, in his excited messages to Parnas, exclaimed:[85]

> *Boy I'm so powerful I can intimidate the entire Ukrainian government . . . Please don't tell anyone I can't get the crooked Ambassador fired or I did three times and she's still there.*

In an unfathomable plot, private interests, with the help of the president's private attorney, managed to have a State Department official removed to advance their avaricious goals. The guardian of US foreign policy in Ukraine and a fervid supporter of its anticorruption program, Marie Yovanovitch was in the way of those who pursued LNG deals and sought to use Ukraine as a tool for Donald Trump's reelection. As such, she became collateral damage of their illicit play.

With Ambassador Yovanovitch removed, there was yet another person who opposed the changes within the Naftogaz board and could potentially obstruct the freedom gas plan. That person was Andriy Kobolev, the CEO of Naftogaz.

EFFORTS TO TOPPLE THE NAFTOGAZ CEO

PRESSURE ON KOBOLEV

On January 16, 2019, Ukrainian prime minister Volodymyr Groysman publicly called for a review of Naftogaz's contract with its CEO, Andriy Kobolev, citing exorbitant bonuses.[86] Kobolev responded to prime minister's pressure by arguing that Groysman main goal was to disrupt the governance structure of the Naftogaz supervisory board:[87]

> *If we go back to a situation when politicians have a say over the authority of the supervisory board, then we will end up going back to the darkest times of Naftogaz. . . . Why would Groysman make a public statement about something which is not within his authority and put public pressure on the supervisory board, which is designed not to take into account politics and public pressure? . . . This brings me to the conclusion that salary was not the object or major aim of this political request. Corporate governance was. What happens when supervisory boards are put under severe political pressure? They might resign. For Naftogaz, in a year of elections, the resignation of the supervisory board can mean a full reverse of all we have done so far.*

The US ambassador to Ukraine, Marie Yovanovitch, seemed to agree with Kobolev's assessment of the situation. Within days of Groysman's public statement she wrote him a letter warning that his suggested actions could undermine anticorruption efforts and serve Russia's interests.[88]

Curiously, on January 17, 2019, the day after Groysman's public statement, but before sending her letter, Marie Yovanovitch went to the Department of Energy, ostensibly to meet with Rick Perry.[89] The timing of the visit suggests that it might have been about Groysman, Naftogaz and Kobolev.

Several months later it would be revealed that Perry wasn't particularly fond of Kobolev as the Naftogaz CEO. Within his messages from June 2019 Kurt Volker, US envoy to Ukraine, would write:[90]

> I think Perry is the most negative—sees (Kobolyev) as obstructing both the upstream and downstream opening up of the market. . . Perry also wants 2 senior US energy industry people on an expanded board.

It appeared that Ukraine's prime minister's pressure on the Naftogaz CEO played right into Rick Perry's hands, who sought to install his allies onto the supervisory board. Yovanovitch and Kobolev's opposition to the forced changes within the board made them obstacles to the freedom gas efforts and set them on a collision course with Rick Perry's plan and those of his surrogates.

"SHIPLOADS" OF AMERICAN LNG

In January 2019 Naftogaz announced the creation of a new gas business division and appointed a person named Andrew Favorov as its head.[91] Favorov reportedly had been acquainted with Igor Fruman since staying in his hotel in Odesa years ago, and the two remained in contact on and off. When Favorov became the head of the gas division at Naftogaz, Fruman reached out to him, and the two agreed to meet at an energy conference in Houston, Texas, in March 2019.[92]

There, Andrew Favorov had dinner with Lev Parnas, Igor Fruman, and Harry Sargeant III. According to Favorov's recollection, the group discussed an opportunity to sell American liquified natural gas to Ukraine and distribute it through the Naftogaz pipeline network.[93] During the meeting the Americans emphasized their connections in high places. Parnas and Fruman mentioned their association with Rudy Giuliani. Harry Sargeant III reportedly said that he had regularly met President Trump at Mar-a-Lago.[94]

After dinner Parnas, Fruman, and Favorov continued their conversation at a bar. As founders of Global Energy Producers, Parnas and Fruman were reportedly eager to sell "100 shiploads" of American LNG to Ukraine. They also claimed that they had the "full backing" of the Trump administration[95] and that the president was going to remove Ambassador Yovanovitch.[96] Finally, Parnas and Fruman were planning to topple Naftogaz CEO, Andriy Kobolev, and replace him with someone amenable.[97] They offered that position to Favorov[98] in exchange for his assistance in purchasing liquified natural gas from their company.

Favorov later admitted that Parnas and Fruman, wearing golden chains and revealing bare chests, did not strike him as sophisticated political operatives. He could hardly believe that these two could influence the removal of the Naftogaz CEO, a process that would require the approval of Naftogaz's international supervisory board. Parnas and Fruman having a role in removing of Yovanovitch, a prominent State Department official, seemed to him similarly unlikely. Later Favorov would recall that he had felt uneasy about that plot and delicately left the meeting.

In the following weeks, Andrew Favorov received multiple messages from Igor Fruman. They would meet again in Washington, DC, in both late April and early May 2019.

On April 30, 2019, Favorov had dinner with Parnas, Fruman, and a representative of Sargeant's company. At the meeting the Naftogaz executive presented his ideas on sending American LNG to Ukraine.[99]

The following day Favorov, accompanied by the Naftogaz CEO, Andriy Kobolev, arrived for another meeting with Parnas and Fruman at the Trump International Hotel in Washington, DC. There, the Naftogaz officials were introduced to Jeff Miller and Tommy Hicks Jr.[100]

Miller was a former campaign manager to Rick Perry[101] and at the time was lobbying for energy companies.[102] One of his clients was Alex Cranberg's Aspect Holdings,[103] which was exploring hydrocarbon opportunities in Ukraine with Michael Bleyzer.

Tommy Hicks Jr. was introduced by Parnas as "the money guy."[104] Previously mentioned in chapter 5 as a member of a team that went to Turkey on an unofficial mission to rescue American pastor Andrew Brunson, Hicks, a native of Dallas, Texas, had also run an equity fund that had financial interests in the energy sector[105] and was a close friend of Donald Trump Jr.[106] By 2019 Hicks had left his position as chairman of Trump's America First Action PAC[107] and became a cochair of the Republican National Committee.[108] He also apparently occasionally dined with Parnas and Fruman.[109]

During the meeting with Favorov and Parnas, Miller and Hicks reportedly discussed the specifics of a potential deal, such as volumes and pricing of sending the American LNG to Ukraine through Poland. Favorov was skeptical about the viability of the plan and doubted Parnas and Fruman's ability to fulfill their claims.[110]

Then, on May 6, 2019, within a week from Andrew Favorov's meetings in DC, President Trump officially recalled Ambassador Yovanovitch.[111] Parnas immediately exchanged elated messages with various people both in Ukraine and the United States. Tommy Hicks Jr. and Harry Sargeant III were among them. Sargeant was particularly excited:[112]

PARNAS: *They just recalled her finally*

SARGEANT: *Awesome!!*

> PARNAS SENT AN ARTICLE ABOUT YOVANOVITCH TERMINATING HER WORK IN UKRAINE
>
> SARGEANT: *Split. Couldn't take phone away for 4 hours*
>
> PARNAS: *Lol...Me to[o]*

They must have felt that their LNG plan was coming along.

UNMASKING

When Ambassador Yovanovitch was suddenly recalled, Andriy Kobolev and Andrew Favorov's opinion about Parnas and Fruman changed. The next day Andriy Kobolev, Volodymyr Zelensky, and his aides met with Amos Hochstein, the US representative on the Naftogaz supervisory board. The meeting's official agenda was to discuss Ukraine's energy policy.[113] Instead, it ended up being about the pressure from Giuliani and Parnas.

Two weeks after the meeting, Amos Hochstein reached out to Fiona Hill,[114] a senior official on the US National Security Council and a prominent expert on Russia. She would later testify in Congress that Hochstein told her that the Ukrainians were very concerned and confused about Giuliani and his associates' efforts to open an investigation into Burisma and Hunter Biden, as well as their pressure to "change the composition of the Naftogaz board."[115]

That was the background context of Rick Perry's appearance at Volodymyr Zelensky's inauguration when he passed the new president a list of names whom he recommended for the Naftogaz supervisory board.[116] According to Associated Press reporting, attendees of the meeting had the "impression" that Perry wanted to replace the American board member Amos Hochstein with someone "reputable in the Republican circles."[117]

Three days after the inauguration, Rick Perry and the US envoys to Ukraine met with Donald Trump in the Oval Office and encouraged him to have a meeting with President Zelensky. Instead, the two presidents would have a call on July 25, 2019, which after the whistleblower's report would trigger the first Trump impeachment and derail the schemers' LNG aspirations.

Despite all the efforts to replace them, Andriy Kobolev and Amos Hochstein would remain in their position for several more months. However, the people who tried to remove them would face scrutiny in the United States.

THE OUTCOME OF THE LNG EFFORTS

LEV PARNAS AND IGOR FRUMAN

The whistleblower complaint about the call between Donald Trump and Volodymyr Zelensky would serve as a catalyst for the congressional investigation into everything that Trump's cabinet and its satellites were doing in Ukraine. In parallel, investigative journalists uncovered Lev Parnas and Rick Perry's apparent gas interests in Ukraine.

In the fall of 2019, Parnas and Fruman, along with Giuliani, were subpoenaed by three different House congressional committees in relation to their Ukraine schemes and their connection to President Trump.[118] Days later, Parnas and Fruman were arrested at an airport near Washington, DC, while trying to fly to Austria.[119] Apparently, Parnas and Fruman did not intend to comply with their subpoenas. *Rolling Stone* magazine reported that shortly after the committees issued them subpoenas, Lev Parnas sat down with John Dowd, a former member of Trump's legal team. Parnas claimed that, after some deliberation and a phone call with Trump's other personal attorneys, Jay Sekulow and Rudy Giuliani, the lawyers told Parnas not to comply with the subpoena.[120]

After Parnas and Fruman's arrest, Trump's legal team went into a full containment mode. Rudy Giuliani provided various quasi-legitimate reasons for his association with Lev Parnas and Igor Fruman.[121] Donald Trump, who had socialized with the duo at numerous fundraising[122] events,[123] distanced himself from Parnas and Fruman, claiming that he didn't know them.[124] That seemed unlikely, considering the president was aware of the criminal charges and gave his former lawyer, John Dowd, permission to represent the duo.[125] Shortly thereafter Kevin Downing, who had previously represented Trump's former campaign manager, Paul Manafort,[126] also joined Parnas and Fruman's defense team.[127]

Lev Parnas would later claim that Dowd and Downing, instead of working on defending him, were more focused on keeping him silent to protect the president.[128] By the end of October 2019, Lev Parnas had replaced Dowd and Downing with another criminal defense attorney[129] who had no affiliation with Donald Trump. With his new lawyer, Parnas immediately announced that he would comply with the congressional request[130] and started releasing information about his work with Rudy Giuliani and his encounters with the president.[131]

The US government charged Parnas and Fruman with campaign finance violations and with making straw donations to Republican candidates using funds that originated from foreign nationals, who were ineligible to make political contributions in the United States.[132] Those charges stemmed from their $325,000 donation to the America First Action PAC. The campaign documents stated that the contribution came from their company, Global Energy Producers;[133] however, it was wired[134] from another company.[135] Later that year Parnas and Fruman also made contributions to political candidates in Nevada[136] with funds provided by a Russian oligarch. Those donations violated the Federal Election Commission Act, which prohibits making political contributions on behalf of others.[137]

The SDNY prosecutors mentioned Ukraine[138] only in tangent with the removal of Marie Yovanovitch and made no mention of Parnas and Fruman's LNG ambitions. The first version of the indictment mentioned Pete Sessions under an alias, "Congressman-1," describing his role in the removal of the US ambassador to Ukraine.[139] After Sessions and his staff complied[140] with the SDNY subpoena,[141] references to him were removed from the second version of the duo's indictment.[142]

Needless to say, after Parnas and Fruman's arrest, the Global Energy Producers' Ukrainian LNG project was abandoned, and their partnership with Harry Sargent III seemingly fell apart.

RICK PERRY

A day after Parnas and Fruman's arrest, as a part of their impeachment inquiry, a number of congressional committees subpoenaed Rick Perry and requested a broad scope of documents related to his activities in Ukraine, Naftogaz, and connections to Rudy Giuliani and the BLT team.[143] The committees set the deadline for October 18, 2019. Despite Perry's initial bravado and announcement of his willingness to cooperate with Congress,[144] he refused to comply with the subpoena.[145] Perry told the *Wall Street Journal* that he had no plans to resign.[146] However, a day before his subpoena deadline,[147] Donald Trump proclaimed that Perry would be stepping down as the secretary of energy at the end of the year.[148]

When asked by journalists about his reported endeavor to reshuffle the Naftogaz board, Perry dismissed the subject as a "dreamed up story."[149] At the same time, the Department of Energy was "stonewalling"[150] congressional investigators who were trying to ascertain Perry's involvement. The congressional committees prioritized hearing out other officials and did not enforce Perry's subpoena. Only in September 2020 was a lone request from Sen. Ron Wyden (D-OR) sent to the inspector general of the Department of Energy, asking to investigate Perry's "role in pressuring Naftogaz."[151]

According to some accounts, prosecutors from the Southern District of New York might have probed the former energy secretary's involvement in Ukraine.[152] In late November to early December 2019, Naftogaz officials Andriy Kobolev and Andrew Favorov reportedly volunteered[153] to share[154] their side of the story to representatives of the SDNY. However, it seemed that the SDNY deemed there was not enough evidence to charge Perry and, in early 2020, dropped the investigation.[155] A former prosecutor who was interviewed by *Time* magazine theorized why the SDNY might have abandoned the case against Rick Perry:[156]

> *Criminal conflicts of interest are not charged all that frequently, because they can be hard to prove . . . It's got a relatively modest sentence. So often prosecutors will look at*

> that and say, "It's a lot of hard work to prove that, and it's not the biggest offense. So we're not going to take the time to go down that path."

After resigning as secretary of energy, Rick Perry rejoined the board of his old company, Energy Transfer.[157]

NAFTOGAZ AND PERRY'S CANDIDATES

Despite the scrutiny over the main facilitators of the freedom gas plan, the process continued on. In March 2020, weeks after Donald Trump was politically acquitted from his impeachment trial, the Ukrainian Cabinet of Ministers released an order appointing Robert Bensh, one of Rick Perry's candidates, to the Naftogaz supervisory board. Oddly, he was added as one of the representatives of the Ukrainian government, not as an independent expert like other Western members.[158] That same month Ukraine announced its intention to purchase six to eight billion cubic meters (bcm) of liquified natural gas from the United States.[159] Two months later Louisiana Natural Gas Exports and the Ukrainian government signed a memorandum of intent for supplies of American liquified natural gas to Naftogaz,[160] which could bring $20 billion worth of revenue to LNGE.[161] What was interesting and very disturbing was that the Ukrainian government had not announced a formal bidding contest and that LNGE seemed to secure the deal without competition.[162] Nor had LNGE gone through a vetting process by the US Department of Commerce, which is usually required for US companies that seek the US government's aid in foreign deals.[163]

Amos Hochstein, an American expert on the Naftogaz supervisory board, publicly criticized the Ukrainian government's decision to sign the memorandum with LNGE and to appoint Robert Bensh, one of its executives, to the Naftogaz board. Protesting against the LNGE arrangement and calling it a "sordid affair" in his resignation announcement, Hochstein left Naftogaz in October 2020.[164] Other independent board members also apparently opposed Bensh's presence at Naftogaz, citing his conflict of interest. In May 2021 Bensh would complain to the new CEO of Naftogaz about being excluded from board meetings.[165] However, his tenure there would not last long. In September 2021 other international members of the Naftogaz supervisory board would resign in protest,[166] effectively leading to its dissolution.[167]

The LNGE memorandum of intent would also be short-lived. As the 2020 presidential election in the United States had been approaching, the Ukrainian government seemingly decided to wait for the outcome of the election.[168] By 2022 the Ukrainian government abandoned the LNGE partnership and opted for another supplier of liquified natural gas from Canada.[169]

The project that interested Rick Perry in the first place, the sale of 49 percent of the Ukrainian pipeline infrastructure, also never materialized. In late 2019 the Ukrainian government decided against selling its transit pipelines.[170] Energy Transfer, whose head went to Ukraine in 2018 to scout out the opportunity, was left without any Ukrainian projects.

Michael Bleyzer, who had accompanied the Energy Transfer CEO to Ukraine and whom Rick Perry had included into the list he had given to Zelensky, didn't make it to the Naftogaz board. However, Bleyzer was one of the few winners in this energy saga. A week after Volodymyr Zelensky's inauguration, Ukrainian Energy LLC, a company jointly established by Bleyzer's and Cranberg's organizations, submitted a bid for the exploration of hydrocarbon fields in Ukraine.[171] In early July 2019, the Ukrainian government awarded the company the largest of five blocks on sale, with the other four being allocated to a Naftogaz subsidiary. The bid provided Ukrainian Energy LLC exclusive rights to explore petroleum on a 1,340-square-mile field for fifty years. Under the production sharing agreement (PSA), after recovering the invested capital, Bleyzer and Cranberg's company would split the profits with the Ukrainian government.[172]

In the end, Rick Perry's freedom gas dreams fell apart. Although SDNY prosecutors looked into the energy deals in Ukraine, they seemingly did not find enough evidence to charge Perry or his allies.[173] When subpoenaed by congressional investigators, Perry refused to testify and kept a low profile when sought after by journalists.[174] As a result, a substantial and perhaps a crucial piece in the Ukraine puzzle, the energy element, remained hidden from the public eye.

KEY EVENTS RELATED TO THE FREEDOM GAS EFFORT*

*See the full integrated timeline in appendix A.

October 23, 2015 - As one of the conditions of a $300 million loan from the European Bank of Reconstruction and Development, Naftogaz agreed to establish a supervisory board of independent professionals to oversee structural reforms that, among other things, would eliminate corruption.

April 2016 - Naftogaz formed its first supervisory board.

March 2, 2017 - Rick Perry became the secretary of energy.

April 19, 2017 - Rick Perry met with Andriy Kobolev, the CEO of Naftogaz, and Yuri Vitrenko, Kobolev's advisor, at Department of Energy headquarters. At the meeting the Naftogaz officials pitched a potential sale of 49 percent of the Ukrainian pipeline system.

June 20, 2017 - Rick Perry met with Pres. Petro Poroshenko at the Department of Energy headquarters. The CEO of Naftogaz, Andriy Kobolev, and Ukraine's minister of energy, Ihor Nasalyk, also attended the meeting. The same day Ukrainian president Poroshenko also met with President Trump.

July 21–22, 2017 - A Ukrainian American businessman, Michael Bleyzer, received an email from Rick Perry's chief of staff to come to the Department of Energy.

July 24, 2017 - Michael Bleyzer went to the Department of Energy.

March 3, 2018 - Igor Fruman attended a fundraising event at Mar-a-Lago for Donald Trump's reelection campaign.

April 2018 - Alex Cranberg, a founder of Aspect Holding, went to Rick Perry's office.

April 11, 2018 - Lev Parnas and Igor Fruman registered Global Energy Producers.

April 20, 2018 - Lev Parnas and Igor Fruman attended a fundraising event at Mar-a-Lago. Other people present at the event included Brian Ballard and a congressman from Texas, Pete Sessions. It seemed that Sessions and Parnas were introduced at that event. After that event the duo reportedly pledged to donate $20,000 to the campaign of Pete Sessions, who was running for a midterm reelection.

April 30, 2018 - Parnas and Fruman attended a dinner for VIP donors of America First Action PAC at the Trump International Hotel in Washington, DC. On a video from that event, Parnas could be heard mentioning that he was in a process of buying an energy company in Ukraine. At that dinner Parnas also nudged the president to fire Ambassador Yovanovitch.

May 9, 2018 - Parnas and Fruman visited Pete Sessions in his office. The same day, Sessions wrote a letter to the new secretary of state, Michael Pompeo, asking him to remove Marie Yovanovitch.

May 17, 2018 - Parnas and Fruman donated $325,000 to America First Action PAC.

May 23, 2018 - Yuri Lutsenko visited a UN event in New York and tried to set up a meeting with then attorney general Jeff Sessions. He claimed that his effort was blocked by the US ambassador to Ukraine, Marie Yovanovitch.

June 2018 - Lev Parnas, Igor Fruman, and David Correia visited Congressman Pete Sessions in his office. The group was reportedly accompanied by Roy Bailey.

Mid-June 2018 - Michael Bleyzer brought the head of Energy Transfer to Ukraine.

June 18, 2018 - Louisiana Natural Gas Exports Inc. (LNGE) was registered.

June 18-19, 2018 - Lev Parnas, Igor Fruman, and David Correia attended the America First Action PAC summit at the Trump International Hotel in Washington, DC. Roy Bailey said that at that event he introduced Parnas to Harry Sargeant III, a Florida-based shipping magnate.

June 25, 2018 - SigmaBleyzer announced that it was "ready to invest" $100M in Ukraine's energy. The announcement was made after a meeting of the heads of SigmaBleyzer, Aspect Holding, and Energy Transfer and an official from Ukraine's Geology and Mineral Resources Department.

June 25, 2018 - Lev Parnas and Igor Fruman donated to Pete Sessions $2,700 each.

November 6, 2018 - Pete Sessions lost his congressional seat during the midterm election. He reportedly became one of the candidates to replace US ambassador to Ukraine, Marie Yovanovitch.

November 12, 2018 - Rick Perry met with the Ukrainian prime minister Volodymyr Groysman in Kyiv, Ukraine. Andriy Kobolev, CEO of Naftogaz, also attended that meeting. The same day, Perry also met Ukraine's president Poroshenko.

In or around December 2018 - Robert Bensh received a call from an acquaintance who said that Rick Perry was looking for an expert on Ukraine's energy sector.

January 16, 2019 - The Ukrainian prime minister Volodymyr Groysman publicly called for a review of the contract with the Naftogaz CEO, Andriy Kobolev.

January 17, 2019 - Andrew Favorov was appointed as the head of the gas division. Shortly thereafter he reportedly received a message from Igor Fruman to have a chat.

January 17, 2019 - Amb. Marie Yovanovitch visited Rick Perry's office.

January 20, 2019 - Marie Yovanovitch wrote to Ukrainian prime minister, Volodymyr Groysman, objecting his statements about Naftogaz.

January 23-26, 2019 - Rudy Giuliani and Lev Parnas met with Ukraine's prosecutor general, Yuri Lutsenko, in New York. Lutsenko reportedly wanted to get Yovanovitch removed and was willing to help with the investigations in Ukraine. According to some accounts, Rudy Giuliani persuaded President Trump to call in to a meeting with Lutsenko so that he could hear the information from the prosecutor firsthand.

February 12, 2019 - Andriy Kobolev, CEO of Naftogaz, in his interview to the *Kyiv Post*, said that the government's attempt to curb the independence and authority of Naftogaz supervisory board would take Ukraine back to the "darkest times" of rampant corruption.

Around February 16–17, 2019 (Presidents' Day weekend) - Rick Perry met with Robert Bensh at an airport in Houston.

February 16–17, 2019 - Lev Parnas and Victoria Toensing, the BLT team lawyer, exchanged messages about the status of the removal of Marie Yovanovitch.

February 17, 2019 - Rudy Giuliani visited President Trump at Mar-a-Lago and advocated for the firing of Ambassador Yovanovitch.

March 5, 2019 - Marie Yovanovitch gave an anticorruption speech, in which she criticized the Ukrainian government for dragging its feet on anticorruption measures and called for the dismissal of Lutsenko's deputy for allegedly aiding some suspects in avoiding criminal charges.

Around March 11–15, 2019 - During an energy conference in Houston, Lev Parnas, Igor Fruman, and Harry Sargeant III met with Andrew Favorov, an executive at Naftogaz. According to Favorov, Parnas and Fruman discussed their interest in selling American LNG to Ukraine and wanted Favorov to unseat Kobolev as the head of Naftogaz to help them with their new venture.

March 20, 2019 - The *Hill* published John Solomon's article about Marie Yovanovitch, in which Lutsenko claimed that the ambassador gave him a "do-not-prosecute list." The article was immediately picked up and amplified by the BLT team and its surrogates.

March 22, 2019 - Lutsenko sent frustrated messages to Parnas, accusing him and his associates of inability to remove Marie Yovanovitch and implying that he couldn't announce an investigation into the Bidens as long as the ambassador held her position.

March 25–26, 2019 - Robert Hyde, a pro-Trump congressional candidate, sent Parnas messages that implied physical surveillance and a potential forced extraction of the US ambassador to Ukraine.

March 29, 2019 - Rudy Giuliani passed a disinformation package to Secretary of State Mike Pompeo. The package contained Shokin and Lutsenko's testimonies about the Bidens and Marie Yovanovitch.

April 18, 2019 - Yuri Lutsenko publicly retracted his statement about Yovanovitch giving him a "do not prosecute" list.

April 21, 2019 - Volodymyr Zelensky was elected as the new president of Ukraine.

April 23, 2019 - Rudy Giuliani spoke with Donald Trump and pressed him to remove Yovanovitch.

Around April 25, 2019 - The ambassador was told to return to the United States.

April 30, 2019 - Lev Parnas and Igor Fruman met with Andrew Favorov in Washington, DC. The meeting was also attended by a representative of a company owned by Harry Sargeant III.

May 1, 2019 - Parnas and Fruman met with Favorov and Kobolev at the Trump International Hotel in DC. During that meeting Parnas introduced the Naftogaz officials to
- Jeff Miller (a former campaign manager for Rick Perry and an energy lobbyist whose clients included Alex Cranberg) and
- Tommy Hicks Jr. (former chairman of Trump's America First Action PAC, cochair of the Republican National Committee, and an equity fund head with interest in the energy sector).

May 6, 2019 - The US ambassador to Ukraine, Marie Yovanovitch, was officially recalled at the request of President Trump. Lev Parnas exchanged excited messages about it with Harry Sargeant III and Tommy Hicks Jr.

May 7, 2019 - Volodymyr Zelensky, his aides, and the CEO of Naftogaz met with Amos Hochstein, American member on the Naftogaz supervisory board, to discuss the pressure they were experiencing from Giuliani and his associates.

On or around May 12, 2019 - Parnas met with Zelensky's aide, Serhiy Shefir and reportedly pressured him to announce investigations into the Bidens and the supposed Ukrainian interference into 2016 US election in exchange for VP Mike Pence attending Zelensky's inauguration.

May 16, 2019 - Ukrainian prosecutor general Yuri Lutsenko gave an interview to Bloomberg stating that there was not sufficient evidence to conduct an investigation on the Bidens in Ukraine, causing Rudy Giuliani's outrage.

May 20, 2019 - Rick Perry attended Volodymyr Zelensky's inauguration and handed over a list of names that he recommended as energy advisors for the new president and members of the Naftogaz supervisory board. The list included Michael Bleyzer and Robert Bensh.

May 22, 2019 - Amos Hochstein informed Fiona Hill, an official from the National Security Council, about the complaints from the Ukrainian officials on Giuliani's pressure campaign.

May 23, 2019 - Rick Perry, Kurt Volker (US envoy to Ukraine), and Gordon Sondland (US ambassador to the European Union) met with President Trump in the White House and advocated for him to have a meeting with Zelensky. Trump asked them to "talk to Rudy."

June 3, 2019 - Volodymyr Zelensky officially assumed office.

June 4, 2019 - Rick Perry attended a formal dinner in Ukraine along with other Western government officials.

June 19, 2019 - Kurt Volker sent a message to Bill Taylor, the US chargé d'affaires to Ukraine: "I think Perry is the most negative—sees (Kobolyev) as obstructing both the upstream and downstream opening up of the market."

July 1, 2019 - The Ukrainian government awarded oil and gas exploration fields to Michael Bleyzer, Rick Perry's ally.

July 10, 2019 - Ukrainian officials Andriy Yermak and Oleksandr Danylyuk had two meetings at the White House with US officials—John Bolton, Alexander Vindman, Rick Perry, Gordon Sondland, and Kurt Volker. Bolton called the first meeting a "drug deal" and asked Fiona Hill to report it to the National Security Council lawyer. The same evening, Yermak and Danylyuk met with Rick Perry's aides and Robert Bensh, during which Bensh pitched the officials the American LNG plan.

July 22, 2019 - Rudy Giuliani had a call with Zelensky's chief of staff, Andriy Yermak, and pressured him to start investigations on the Bidens and on Ukraine's "meddling" in the 2016 US election.

July 25, 2019 - Donald Trump had a call with Volodymyr Zelensky. That call would become the basis of a whistleblower complaint and lead to Trump's first impeachment.

August 31, 2019 - Rick Perry traveled to Poland to "pave the way for U.S. companies to ship gas to Ukraine via Poland." The CEO of LNGE, Ben Blanchet, accompanied Perry.

September 24, 2019 - In response to reports of Trump's phone call with Zelensky and the administration's failure to provide Congress with the whistleblower complaint, Speaker of the House Nancy Pelosi announced a formal impeachment inquiry of President Trump.

September 30, 2019 - Three House committees (Permanent Select Committee on Intelligence, Committee on Foreign Affairs, and Committee on Oversight and Reform) issued a request for the documents from Rudy Giuliani, Lev Parnas, and Igor Fruman.

October 9, 2019 - Lev Parnas and Igor Fruman were arrested at the Dulles Airport near Washington, DC.

October 10, 2019 - The US House Democrats subpoenaed Secretary of Energy Rick Perry and requested documents related to his activities in Ukraine. The deadline to provide the documents was set for October 18, 2019.

October 17, 2019 - A day before Perry was supposed to send the documents to Congress, Donald Trump announced that the secretary of energy would be stepping down. Perry refused to comply with the subpoena.

Late November - early December 2019 - Andriy Kobolev, CEO of Naftogaz, and Andrew Favorov, the head of Naftogaz gas division, voluntarily testified to the SDNY.

December 1, 2019 - Rick Perry left his position as secretary of energy.

December 13, 2019 - Naftogaz sued the Ukrainian government, claiming that the oil and gas fields were allocated for Bleyzer illegally.

January 1, 2020 - Rick Perry rejoined Energy Transfer's board.

February 5, 2020 - Donald Trump was acquitted in his first impeachment trial.

March 11, 2020 - Ukraine's Cabinet of Ministers signed an executive order appointing Robert Bensh onto the Naftogaz supervisory board as the representative of the Ukrainian government.

March 13, 2020 - The United States and Ukraine agreed on an annual supply of 6–8 bcm of American LNG.

May 27, 2020 - LNGE and Naftogaz signed a memorandum of supply of American liquified natural gas to Naftogaz. The twenty-year agreement was estimated to be worth $20 billion.

September 23, 2020 – Sen. Ron Wyden, the ranking member of the Senate Finance Committee, requested the inspector general for the Department of Energy to investigate Rick Perry's "role in pressuring Naftogaz."

October 8, 2020 - Ukrainian prosecutors announced an investigation into the Naftogaz management.

October 12, 2020 - Amos Hochstein resigned from the Naftogaz supervisory board, citing "slowdown in reform and creeping corruption" and the choice to work with LNGE.

April 28, 2021 - Ukraine's Cabinet of Ministers dismissed the Naftogaz board, then fired the CEO Andriy Kobolev and replaced him with his former advisor, Yuri Vitrenko.

CHAPTER 14

MODUS OPERANDI

THE SHADOW STATE DEPARTMENT

PERFECT PLACEMENT

With Donald Trump's ascent to the presidency, Rudy Giuliani was, once again, in a position of relevance and influence. He would play multiple roles, first as an advisor to Trump's transition team and later as a personal attorney to the president. When asked how much he was paid by Donald Trump, Giuliani responded:[1]

> *My other clients are paying me for the work I do for them. Nobody is paying me for a single thing I'm doing for Donald J. Trump.*

Many of those "other clients" were willing to pay a premium to the person who had the president's ear. In addition to his services to high-profile people from Turkey, Venezuela, and Ukraine who had been described earlier, Giuliani also catered to clients from Colombia,[2] Qatar,[3] Romania,[4] Armenia,[5] Uruguay,[6] Brazil,[7] Bahrain,[8] and possibly the Democratic Republic of Congo.[9] Those clients helped Giuliani make $9.5 million in 2017 and $5 million in 2018. In 2019 Giuliani claimed that over the years he had done security and legal consulting in more than eighty countries through his various companies.[10]

When challenged about potential conflicts of interest vis-à-vis his role with Donald Trump, Giuliani retorted:[11]

> *There's no conflict. What's the conflict? . . . I don't ask the president for anything for them ever. I've never represented them in front of the U.S. government. I don't peddle influence. I don't have to. I make a good deal of money as a lawyer and as a security consultant.*

However, Giuliani fully exploited his unique role. He had vast access to Donald Trump's government and operated his own parallel version of a shadow State

Department that consisted of lawyers, intermediaries, and propagandists. Some appointed officials admitted that they did not condone Trump's decision to have Giuliani involved,[12] yet nevertheless worked with him. Others argued that the President's private lawyer derailed the official U.S. policy towards Ukraine.[13] The president's private attorney, who had not gone through a Senate confirmation process or a background check, was not restricted by the stringent ethics rules[14] that require government officials to disclose their meetings with representatives of foreign governments and prohibit executive branch employees from taking advantage of their government position for personal monetary interests.[15] He had zero accountability and yet found himself in a position to direct US cabinet officials.

Aaron Parnas, the son of Giuliani's associate, described his observations of Giuliani's work in his book, *Trump First*:[16]

Once an individual was able to secure Rudy's help in their efforts, they passed the first hurdle in achieving legitimacy. Following step one, any individual seeking to effectuate personal foreign policy change would need people on the ground to help facilitate some of these conversations. This is where my father often came in. What began as others using Rudy to connect with the President, soon turned into Rudy utilizing my father to assist the President in his personal foreign policy objectives abroad. Through these actions, my father was able to facilitate conversations on the ground in Ukraine, Spain, and elsewhere, reporting directly to Rudy, who, in turn, reported directly to the President. These conversations likely were protected under the vaulted attorney-client privilege between Rudy and the President. Because of the President's tendency to recruit inexperienced private individuals to implement his personal policy campaigns, he is also able to quickly dispose of them if the campaigns ever become public. The frequency of Rudy's conversations with the President, in my opinion, made it nearly impossible for the President to be unaware of my father's actions abroad. I personally believe that if the public were to know the truth about this shadow State Department, the President would have been impeached not once, but multiple times—likely resulting in his removal from office. If witnesses were permitted in the President's impeachment trial, the public would have seen that the President utilized those around him to pursue his Trump First agenda, often at the detriment of the American people.

THE WEB OF QUID PRO QUOS

Giuliani's web of influence had a particular pattern where each of his projects consisted of multistep quid pro quos leading to government officials at the highest level, both in America and abroad. Many times those bargains included bending justice systems to their needs. Giuliani and his BLT team either weaponized prosecution or used the prospect of avoiding justice as a bait for others to serve their interests.

In doing so, they inevitably corrupted the rule of law in the countries they operated.

A prime example of that model was deployed in Ukraine, where to provide an advantage to President Trump, Giuliani's BLT team worked to hamstring his main political rival, Joe Biden. To achieve that, Giuliani's team tried to coax Ukraine's prosecutor general, Yuri Lutsenko, and strong-arm its newly elected president, Volodymyr Zelensky, into announcing an investigation into the Bidens. In exchange, Giuliani offered each foreign official a personalized deal. For Lutsenko, he agreed to arrange a meeting with Attorney General Barr[17] and to have Amb. Marie Yovanovitch removed.[18] For Zelensky, Giuliani promised to put in a good word to Trump on behalf of Ukraine.[19] If Zelensky refused, Giuliani had a backup plan of deploying the oligarch Dmytro Firtash to pull strings in Ukraine.[20] In return, the BLT team's lawyers were busy trying to persuade the US Department of Justice to drop Firtash's criminal case in America.[21]

Another multistep plot occurred in Venezuela, where Giuliani and his allies sought to create a situation that would allow US energy interests to explore the country's oil fields. For that, they first needed the US government to lift sanctions. That could be achieved by easing the Venezuelan dictator, Nicolas Maduro, out of power. After the BLT team's secret call with Maduro, Giuliani approached the national security advisor, John Bolton, encouraging the US government to provide a "soft landing" for the Venezuelan dictator in the United States.[22]

When that move didn't work, Giuliani seemed to have pivoted to building an arrangement with Venezuelan billionaire Alejandro Betancourt Lopez, who was implicated in a money-laundering scheme in the United States[23] and wanted to avoid charges. Giuliani, with Betancourt's lawyers, pleaded to DOJ officials,[24] including[25] Attorney General Barr,[26] that they provide leniency for the Venezuelan billionaire in return for Betancourt aiding Maduro's opponent, Juan Guaido.

Arguably, the most brazen of Giuliani's clandestine lobbying efforts was for Turkish interests. In the earliest days of Trump's presidency, Giuliani advocated that Trump officials extradite the Turkish cleric Fethullah Gülen so often that some White House officials called the issue Giuliani's "hobby horse."[27] While representing Reza Zarrab, the Turkish Iranian money launderer, Giuliani nagged then secretary of state Rex Tillerson in the Oval Office, asking him to intervene into Zarrab's criminal case.[28] By doing so, Rudy Giuliani technically lobbied on behalf of foreign interests directly connected to the president of Turkey.[29] This type of lobbying requires registration, pursuant to Foreign Agents Registration Act, which Giuliani didn't submit.[30] Some legal experts were baffled by his actions, with one stating:[31]

> There's an exemption for lawyers, but none of their activities can go outside of the courtroom ... Once you do something FARA would constitute as a political activity, just one thing, that would prevent you from being able to claim that exemption.

Rudy Giuliani's services to Reza Zarrab certainly went "outside of the courtroom."

Giuliani brought the discussion of Zarrab's case to the White House and traveled all the way to Turkey, where he met with Recep Tayyip Erdogan to seek a "diplomatic" solution.

In September 2018, as public[32] mentions[33] of Giuliani's foreign clients became more frequent, several Democratic senators wrote a request to the DOJ to probe his foreign connections:[34]

> We request that the Department of Justice review whether he is in compliance with [the Foreign Agents Registration Act], including whether he has an obligation to register any undisclosed political activities, has any delinquent filings, or has any deficiencies or abnormalities in his registration statements.

The senators' request didn't lead to any charges. One could ask why Giuliani wasn't held accountable for his clandestine lobbying. One of the reasons might have been that Giuliani, as a DOJ veteran, knew how to use loopholes in FARA regulations and shield himself from potential repercussions that his work for foreign clients could cause.

INSULATION

If anyone challenged Giuliani's connections, his tactic was to deny and deflect.[35] In controversial cases that could potentially blow back on him, Giuliani also avoided a paper trail that could tie him to his end clients. He often seemed to have insulated himself by having another friendly lawyer or an intermediary in between. For example, Giuliani reportedly drafted a retainer agreement for him to represent Yuri Lutsenko and Viktor Shokin, former Ukrainian prosecutor generals, in the United States.[36] However, after some consideration, Giuliani chose to ask other BLT lawyers, Victoria Toensing and Joe diGenova, to put their names on the retainer agreements.[37] Later Toensing and diGenova officially represented Dmytro Firtash while Giuliani orchestrated the BLT team members' actions related to the oligarch. Lev Parnas would write that Giuliani had initially planned taking on Firtash as his own client but, after a pushback from the White House, decided to have Toensing and diGenova to be the oligarch's official representatives.[38]

Giuliani also had no official contract with the Venezuelan billionaire Alejandro Betancourt Lopez. Instead, he was represented by Giuliani's old colleagues Jon Sale and Frank H. Wohl.[39] The two lawyers accompanied Giuliani to his meeting with the DOJ and Attorney General Barr[40] regarding Betancourt.[41] Deepening his insulation, Giuliani hired Jon Sale in the lead-up to Trump's first impeachment trial[42] and then claimed attorney-client privilege when asked about Betancourt.[43]

There were other situations when Giuliani and his surrogates had either legally represented each other or the same clients, again invoking attorney-client privilege. For example, Victoria Toensing and Joe diGenova were attorneys for John Solomon, the opinion writer for the *Hill* who disseminated the BLT team's disinformation. Giuliani also claimed attorney-client privilege with Lev Parnas,[44] citing legal representation, whenever questions about their connection were raised.[45] Certainly, on[46] many[47] occasions[48] Giuliani invoked that privilege with his most important client, Donald Trump.

Placed behind the layers of intermediaries and lawyers, Rudy Giuliani became a gray cardinal whose modus operandi included lobbying, extortion, disinformation, and webs of quid pro quos, often with obstruction of justice on one side and the weaponization of it on another. Giuliani, possessing this kind of power without official checks and balances, undermined the rule of law, sowed public distrust in institutions, and sabotaged elements of US foreign policy. In doing so, he jeopardized American democracy. Further, by promoting foreign interests, he became a cog in larger geopolitical plays.

PART III
THE GLOBAL CONTEXT

CHAPTER 15

RUSSIA INC.

THE CLOAKED ENVOY

As mentioned in the beginning of this book, in March 2017 Lev Parnas and Farkhad Akhmedov, a Russian oligarch and a former Russian government official, attended a retreat for the Republican National Committee donors in Florida.[1] The event, focused on raising funds for the 2018 midterm election,[2] was studded with high-level GOP donors.

Shortly after that event, Akhmedov and Parnas flew to Washington, DC, to meet with Brian Ballard. At the time, Ballard, who had run Trump's electoral campaign in Florida, was about to become the regional finance vice chair of the RNC[3] and was setting up a lobbying office in Washington, DC. According to text messages between Parnas and Ballard, the group discussed a lobbying contract between Ballard Partners and Turkey, as well as "putting $$$ in RNC."[4] That meeting would lead to Ballard Partners signing a lobbying contract with Turkey and another one with Halkbank.

There were several disturbing issues with Akhmedov's attendance at the RNC donors' retreat and his meeting with Brian Ballard. For starters, as a foreign national, Akhmedov was not eligible to make political contributions in the United States and thus had no chance of legitimately becoming an RNC donor. Also, in early 2017 there were several Russian oligarchs, deployed[5] by Vladimir Putin,[6] who clandestinely sought access to people within Donald Trump's orbit as part of Russia's broad influence campaign in the United States. As the Department of Justice started to probe Russia's interference into the 2016 presidential election, DC influencers started to shun Russian oligarchs,[7] likely fearing being caught up in the investigations.

One could reasonably wonder how Akhmedov managed to enter the world of the Republican elite without raising any red flags. The answer might lie in Parnas's messages to Ballard. In the same conversation as they discussed Akhmedov, Parnas encouraged Ballard to "close" lobbying contracts with Turkey and Azerbaijan. That suggested that Akhmedov might have used those two countries as proxies to present himself as an envoy of Turkey and Azerbaijan. He, indeed, had connections to those countries. Akhmedov was born in Azerbaijan and would be later given an award by the country's president for contributing into Russian-Azerbaijani relations.[8] Also, in

2016, just months before the GOP donor retreat, Akhmedov reportedly had acted as an agent of the Kremlin in patching up tensions with Turkey.[9] The oligarch's aid in arranging a lobbying contract between Turkey and Ballard Partners also had a side benefit of indirectly pulling Turkey closer to Russia.

Akhmedov, cloaked as a Turkish Azerbaijani envoy, with Parnas's help and an apparent prospect of a donation to the RNC, established a connection to Brian Ballard. Through that connection, Akhmedov achieved what other Kremlin-deployed oligarchs before him could not: he had gained access to Trump's orbit.

To understand the significance of that access, it's worthwhile to take a deeper look into the Kremlin's operations playbook both at home and abroad.

BEHIND THE IRON CURTAIN

Throughout the twentieth century, the Soviet Union, and later Russia, earned a reputation as a surveillance state due to its long history of spying on its own citizens and foreigners alike. Soviet intelligence tactics focused on intelligence gathering, the ruthless crackdown on independent thinking, and the promotion of a regimented communist ideology portraying itself as a social model superior to the "decadent" Western democratic and capitalist system. The indoctrination of Soviet society continued for decades as the Communist Party controlled all forms of domestic media. Generations of citizens were versed in Marxist-Leninist teaching and were taught to be suspicious of foreigners and the West. Those who questioned the Soviet government had to keep their thoughts to themselves or else suffer the consequences.

At the end of World War II, the Soviet government had occupied a number of adjacent countries in Eastern and Central Europe and forced them to join the communist bloc, led by the Soviet Union. Later these countries would be forced by the Kremlin into a strategic agreement known as the Warsaw Pact to oppose Western democratic states that had aligned themselves into a defensive coalition called the North Atlantic Treaty Organization, or NATO.

The Soviet government promoted communism abroad as a way of forging ideological alliances and projecting its power around the globe. The USSR played a zero-sum game against the West by dominating as many countries as possible with its eventual goal to diminish democracy as a model. In the United States, that pressure became known as the communist threat.

By the mid-1980s the Soviet system's command economy, which unlike the capitalist system was centralized, had fallen into malaise due to its inherent inefficiencies and overspending on military hardware. The state owned all means of production. In that dystopia the production of consumer goods was decided by the Soviet leadership as opposed to market demand. In time that model led to severe imbalances of supply and demand, causing deficits of some goods and abundance of others. The citizens understood that the system was failing, and yet they were unable to either openly criticize or correct it.

Some government officials sought to liberalize the system, seeking economic and political reform. This, in turn, created space for national identity movements in occupied Eastern European states, which further encouraged the dissolution of the Soviet system. Over the course of decades numerous communist officials in these occupied countries started showing insubordination to the Kremlin, as shown in the Hungarian uprising in 1956, and the Prague Spring in 1968. In the late 1980s, the population of some countries under the control of the Soviet system sought internal political reform. Other Soviet states would unilaterally declare independence from Moscow without retaliation. The Soviet Union's leader at the time, Mikhail Gorbachev, was himself facing increasing domestic economic and political crosswinds and had little political capital to face the growing instability within the Eastern European Soviet states.

The growing cracks in the system of what was widely believed to be an indestructible socialist state became readily apparent in August of 1991, when hard-liners, frustrated with Gorbachev's liberal reforms, attempted to remove him from power and sideline the democratic reformers' leader, Boris Yeltsin.[10] The coup failed but marked the beginning of a new era. While Gorbachev's power was waning, Yeltsin was on the rise. Four months later Gorbachev resigned, the Soviet Union was dissolved, and Boris Yeltsin became the first president of Russia.[11]

After the collapse of the Soviet Union, Americans stopped looking at Russia as a threat, and the collective West dramatically reduced defense spending.[12] There were timid hopes that Russia could become a democratic country. For a short period, after the lifting of the iron curtain, the Russian people felt an inebriating sense of freedom that they hadn't previously experienced. There was no government-imposed censorship. Borders were open, and the long-hated market capitalist model became more ubiquitous. However, with the new freedom also came chaos.

To transition the country from its autocratic communist past to a potentially democratic capitalist future, the new Russian government chose economic "shock therapy" instead of a gradual transition to a market economy.[13] With loose government oversight, the economy was metaphorically sent off a cliff, and the population was left on their own to figure out how to survive in the new Russia. It was the era of the audacious. Those who could adapt quickly found new possibilities.

The shock therapy created space for a new breed of businessmen who took advantage of the Yeltsin government's privatization program. In the years of this economic chaos, there was little regulation of state industries, and the control of those industries was up for grabs. Steel, aluminum, oil, and gas were among the most valuable resources for budding entrepreneurs to grasp. Those who could seize control over former Soviet assets needed muscle to protect them. With the country's law enforcement in disarray, businesses turned to organized crime figures for security in exchange for a fee. The penniless former policemen and security service officers became part of the business model by covering for mobsters and providing intelligence to oligarchs on their rivals.[14]

The end of the Soviet socialism and the beginning of Russian capitalism rearranged the social hierarchies and created an alliance of mobsters, oligarchs, and security service members who aspired for political power. The opportunity to attain that power presented itself in the late 1990s.

The 1998 Asian economic crisis devastated the Russian ruble as the government found itself unable to pay back its foreign debts and defaulted on its loans.[15] For the common person on the street, the default had numerous effects. It exacerbated an already high unemployment rate and caused significant delays in wages for workers, further impoverishing the population. Unsurprisingly, many people, disillusioned with the chaotic democratic capitalist experiment, longed for the perceived stability and order of the dead Soviet Union.

Public confidence in then president Boris Yeltsin was eroding.[16] His ability to govern was further questioned due to concerns about his health and alcohol problems, which became publicly[17] noticeable.[18] Sensing that his time was up, at the turn of the millennium, Boris Yeltsin announced his resignation and introduced his protégé, Vladimir Putin, as the acting president.[19]

EVOLUTION OF PUTIN'S RUSSIA

ASCENT TO POWER

Boris Yeltsin's announcement shocked people both in Russia and abroad. Journalists were asking the same question: "Who is Mr. Putin?"[20] Little was known about that soft-spoken person with a blank facial expression and little charisma. His rapid ascent to power was remarkable and indicated Putin's ability to maneuver politically.

Putin climbed the political rungs of power very quickly, moving from his position as a deputy mayor of Saint Petersburg in 1996 to working for the presidential administration in Moscow.[21] He was appointed the director of Russian security services in 1998 and became the prime minister of Russia in August 1999.[22]

One of the few early public appearances of Vladimir Putin happened shortly after his appointment as prime minister. In early September 1999, there were several bombings of residential buildings throughout the country.[23] Putin blamed Chechen terrorists for the attack and threatened to "wipe them out in the outhouse."[24] At the time, Chechnya was a de facto independent state that had successfully broken away after defeating Russian forces in a war of independence.[25] Putin's promise to retaliate for the bombings was, in fact, a declaration of war. That press conference thrust Putin from the shadows into the spotlight, giving him an image of a righteous terrorist fighter protecting the Russian people.[26] However, at the time, there was still very little known about Yeltsin's successor. In the hastily assembled March 2000 presidential elections, the acting president faced off with other more politically established contenders for the Russian presidency and needed to boost his image.

Weeks before the election, a book titled *First Person: An Astonishingly Frank Self-Portrait by Russia's President*[27] was released to the Russian public to shed more light on the mysterious protégé of Boris Yeltsin. The book contained his distilled biography and painted a picture of a straight-talking family man with a heightened sense of duty to his country. Along with childhood and family anecdotes, the book also told a story of a former KGB officer stationed in eastern Germany who, through his hard work, grew to become Russia's prime minister. The book seemed to have had its intended effect, and Vladimir Putin managed to win the election, becoming the second elected president of Russia.[28]

Vladimir Putin inherited a country that was failing in its transition to a market economy. Many Russians felt abandoned by the country's leadership. Putin reinvigorated the government as the Russian Army went to war with Chechnya. The Russian people offered support to their young president, who appeared as a leader who could straighten out the country. However, over the coming years, Putin's strong hand increasingly felt more like a tight grip.

THE GRIP

During the Yeltsin era, oligarchs had become accustomed to influencing politics. With Putin's rise to power, the oligarchs were given an implicit choice to either do business without meddling in politics or find themselves being investigated by the state.

Days after Vladimir Putin was sworn in as the president of Russia, a police squad raided the offices of a media company[29] whose owner, Vladimir Gusinsky, was critical of the new president.[30] Since its creation in 1993, Gusinsky's NTV broadcast channel had presented independent reports. During the first Russian-Chechen war in the mid-1990s, NTV journalists interviewed local people and rebels in Chechnya, providing coverage that sometimes contradicted what state officials were telling the Russian public.[31] After the 1999 bombings of the apartment buildings in several Russian cities, NTV published an investigation that implicated the Russian secret service involvement in those explosions.[32]

In the summer of 2000, Gusinsky was arrested.[33] Weeks later he was forced[34] to sell[35] NTV to Putin's allies,[36] who ensured that the channel would support the Putin government. Within a couple of years, virtually all media sources that had formerly belonged to oligarchs ceased to exist or were taken over by people close to Putin. After being released, Gusinsky immediately fled the country, never to return. He was not the only tycoon who was made an example. There were two other prominent oligarchs who fell under Putin's wrath.

One was Boris Berezovsky, an oligarch who had helped Vladimir Putin come to power as prime minister and the heir apparent to Boris Yeltsin.[37] During the 2000 presidential campaign, Berezovsky's TV channel, ORT Television, promoted Putin,[38] and as the oligarch later claimed, he had helped finance Putin's first election campaign.[39] However, during the first year of Putin's presidency, the two fell out. Berezovsky's TV channel criticized Putin over his response to a Russian submarine disaster that left 118 sailors dead.[40] Shortly thereafter, Russian authorities accused Berezovsky of money embezzlement[41] and arrested his associate,[42] forcing the oligarch to retreat to London.

Another oligarch was Mikhail Khodorkovsky, the owner of Yukos, one of the largest oil companies in Russia. During a meeting with Putin and other oligarchs in February 2003, Khodorkovsky confronted Putin on government corruption.[43] The subject was a known issue, but no one dared to admit it publicly. Later that year Khodorkovsky and his business partners were charged with tax evasion and sent to prison.[44] Khodorkovsky's oil company, Yukos, was auctioned off, with most of its assets bought by Russia's national oil company, Rosneft. Rosneft then became the largest oil company in the country, led by Igor Sechin,[45] an old colleague of Putin from the security services.

At the time, the public crackdown on oligarchs who had criticized Putin, including the takeover of their business assets, was often seen as holding robber barons accountable for the theft of the country's wealth in the 1990s.[46] That crackdown coincided with a decrease in the widespread public exposure of mobsters, who were not necessarily brought to justice but often reinvented[47] themselves,[48] donning business suits and calling themselves businessmen. That shift created a perception that Putin was taking steps to straighten out the country. The surviving oligarchs and businessmen with ties to organized crime were forced into a subservient role in Putin's Russia. The people who rose to the top and replaced the first generation of oligarchs often had connections to both the security services and Putin.[49]

As a whole, the security services were instrumental for Putin's ability to gain and maintain control over the country. Putin, in return, bestowed more authority on the Russian secret service, the FSB, and made it an omnipresent power behind his rule. The security services used their powers to surveil, discredit, or intimidate anyone who was deemed a threat to Putin's power.

The agency reported directly to the president without parliamentary oversight.[50] The FSB moved from a penniless agency during the Yeltsin era to the enforcer of the state,[51] just like its Soviet predecessor, the KGB. As a later director of the FSB put it, security service officers became the "new nobility."[52] Presumably, the new czar was Vladimir Putin.

As Putin's Russia coalesced, his government, the security service elite, the oligarchs, and organized crime amalgamated into one entity that could be best described as "Russia Inc.," with all showing undisguised obedience to the president.

THE FALL OF THE FAÇADE OF RUSSIAN DEMOCRACY

While Vladimir Putin's government had been restructuring the power hierarchy in both the political and economic realms, the country experienced a financial windfall from a commodities boom. Russia's main source of tax revenue, oil, tripled in value from 2003 to 2008.[53] As a result, the economy noticeably improved, and a thin layer of middle class started appearing across the country. At the time when other developing countries had their versions of prodemocratic color revolutions, the Russian state offered its citizens a tacit social contract. Putin's government would offer economic stability and a supply of consumer goods in exchange for the population's noninterference in politics.

That contract functioned well up to a certain point. As a result of the oil bonanza, the economy flourished. Ordinary people were, for the first time, able to afford cars, trips abroad, and apartments. However, economic growth was replaced with stagnation across the country during the great global recession of 2008–2009.[54] Even though the Russian government had built large financial reserves that protected the economy from a crash, oil prices took a noticeable dive at the end of 2008.[55] That fall trickled down to ordinary Russian citizens, who saw reduced salaries,[56] weren't paid on time,[57] and lost their jobs.[58] For many it was déjà vu, bringing back memories from the 1990s, where the well-connected prospered, and the rest were left to fend for themselves.

The falling incomes made the omnipresent kleptocracy more visible. Corruption spread from senior government officials to local policemen.[59] Graft could be found at all levels of Russian society, including education and healthcare systems.[60] Frustrations started to simmer within society. With the internet becoming widely used in Russian society, clear examples of government corruption started appearing in the still free Russian cyberspace.

By late 2011, during parliamentary elections, public frustration had reached a boiling point. Independent observers recorded[61] numerous irregularities[62] that resulted in the artificially inflated prevalence of Vladimir Putin's United Russia party. Those videos were uploaded on social media and spread like wildfire. Outraged Russian people took to the streets,[63] marking the beginning of a series of antigovernment protests, perhaps the largest since the collapse of the Soviet Union. Those protests were branded as the Bolotnaya Square protests, after the central gathering place in Moscow. Many of the protesters demanded fair elections and a "Russia without Putin."[64]

After serving two terms as president, followed by one term as prime minister, Putin was making a return for a third term as president. The urban and well-educated young middle class, along with older progressive thinkers, was disillusioned with the veneer of democracy in Russia. The protests continued for months, reaching their nadir in May 2012, when Putin was once again proclaimed president. The day before his inauguration, protesters gathered in Moscow, Saint Petersburg, and other large cities in Russia, chanting anti-Putin slogans. That weekend, on May 6 and 7, the police ramped up their forces and beat and arrested many protesters.[65] That weekend Putin shed any pretense of a democratic reformer and instead revealed his true nature of an autocrat willing to suppress his countrymen to stay in power.

Putin's government perceived the protests as a Russian version of the Ukrainian Orange Revolution or the Arab Spring, a prodemocratic movement that, if not suppressed, could topple him. The newly returned president blamed then US secretary of state Hillary Clinton for instigating the protests[66] after she pointed out "serious concerns" with the Russian election.[67] What followed in Russia was a classic crackdown on dissent and independent thinking that had been seen over and over in autocratic countries. Many protesters who took part at the Bolotnaya Square protests were charged with rioting and were imprisoned.[68] The Russian government would go on to ban protests.[69] The Kremlin publicly labeled NGOs and academic institutions with foreign funding that criticized the Russian government's actions as "foreign agents" in an attempt to weaken their credibility.[70]

The crackdown in Russia coincided with the democratic Maidan revolt in Ukraine. As described in previous chapters, Ukraine, for all intents and purposes, had been a country "captured" by the Kremlin and considered by Putin a colony of Russia, even after it gained its independence following the collapse of the Soviet Union. Its energy sector was heavily influenced by Russian intermediaries, primarily Dmytro Firtash, and the country's president Viktor Yanukovych rose to power with the backing of the Kremlin.[71] In late 2013 Yanukovych reneged on his prior promise to sign a long-negotiated EU association agreement[72] and instead favored a bailout loan from Russia.[73] Many Ukrainians responded by rallying against the decision, demanding that the Yanukovych government resign and Ukraine join the EU.[74] Like in Russia, the Maidan protesters organized through social media, using mostly VKontakte, the Russian copycat version of Facebook used predominantly throughout the two countries.

The trend was clear: social media platforms were a threat to the Kremlin's control of the country and needed to be neutralized. Over the following months, the Russian domestic security service, FSB, questioned the founder of VKontakte, Pavel Durov,[75] and pressured him to close protest groups both in Russia and Ukraine[76] and to give up the identities of the organizers.[77] In 2014 Durov was forced to flee the country,[78] and his company was taken over by a pro-Kremlin oligarch.[79]

In parallel with obtaining control over the largest social media network in Russia, the Kremlin established the Internet Research Agency, which later became commonly known as the Russian troll farm. One of the first mentions of the agency appeared in September 2013 on *Novaya Gazeta*,[80] one of the few independent Russian newspapers left. The article outlined that the new agency hired internet-savvy people to write comments on social media and news websites with a quota of one hundred comments a day using various fake social media accounts.[81] The topics were defined by the Kremlin. The comments praised Putin's government, while criticizing the Kremlin's opposition. In the article the *Novaya Gazeta* implied that the agency was connected to "Putin's chef," Yevgeny Prigozhin.[82] A decade later he would admit to being the founder of the agency.[83]

By late 2014 the Kremlin, through Putin's allies, expanded control over the information consumed by Russians. In addition to spreading propaganda to older citizens through TV and printed media,[84] the government now was molding the opinions of younger Russians in social media through government-curated online comments.[85]

If at home the Kremlin was able to suppress dissent, the pro-Russian president in Ukraine was not. As the Ukrainian Maidan protests turned into bloodshed, besieged and fearing for his life, the Ukrainian president, Viktor Yanukovych, fled to Moscow. Shortly thereafter, Russia's "little green men" appeared in Ukraine to take matters into the Kremlin's hands. Putin's regime wasn't willing to give up the lucrative gas scheme that helped Russian interests pilfer billions from Ukraine. Nor could Moscow allow Ukraine to become a democratic country, lest the democratic contagion spread to Russia and potentially destabilize Putin's regime. So as a solution, Russia forcefully annexed Crimea,[86] a peninsula in southern Ukraine, and armed pro-Russian separatists in the east of the country,[87] at the border with Russia, to fight by proxy against the new Ukrainian government.

To justify its aggression, the Kremlin deployed the novice Internet Research Agency trolls, who then[88] flooded[89] Russian, Ukrainian, and Western online media with made-up narratives[90] of discrimination[91] and violence against the Russian-speaking population in Ukraine. The Russian annexation of Crimea was also used domestically as a booster for Putin's declining image, with Russian state propaganda elevating a sense of glory that stoked patriotic fervor with the slogan "Крым Наш!" or "Crimea is ours!"[92]

In response to the annexation, the United States and other Western countries imposed sanctions on Russia. Kremlin propaganda responded by portraying Russia as an empire rising from its former humiliation of the 1990s while being besieged by the evil, morally corrupt West that wanted to prevent Russia from developing.[93] The rhetoric resembled that of the late Weimar Republic, which existed in Germany after the First World War. Following a humiliating surrender to its opponents and forced reparations, the Weimar Republic morphed into Nazi Germany under Adolf Hitler who used propaganda to blame "traitors" within the German government, as well as liberals, jews, and socialists for the World War I loss.[94] In an eerie similarity, Putin turned Russia into a more autocratic regime, using hate of others as a motivator.

Post-2014 the Putin regime started squeezing its most vocal critics and independent thinkers out of the country, while making others self-censure in fear of being targeted by the Russian state. Those who refused to abide by the new rules started to leave the country, leading to the largest brain drain Russia had experienced since the collapse of the Soviet Union.[95] Those who stayed and were vocal against the government were often beaten or arrested, to be shown as examples to instill fear and prevent others from voicing dissent.

One opposition leader, Boris Nemtsov,[96] was assassinated in front of the Kremlin. Another prominent opposition figure, Alexei Navalny, was poisoned,[97] arrested on trumped-up charges,[98] and would die in a Russian prison under questionable circumstances in 2024.[99] Those two were seen as potential challengers with enough political weight to mobilize the crowds against Putin. By kneecapping the opposition, the Kremlin attempted to drain all hope from anyone who harbored thoughts of public defiance.

As the next step, the Russian government passed new laws that further restricted its citizens' rights to expression,[100] as defined by the Russian Constitution, and tightened the Kremlin's control over information. By the mid-2010s the Kremlin stopped bothering to maintain the façade of democracy in Russia. It was clear that Putin had returned to the presidency to stay no matter the cost.

CHAPTER 16

THE TUG-OF-WAR AGAINST THE WEST

EXPORTING RUSSIAN DISINFORMATION

Vladimir Putin and his inner circle had been indoctrinated for decades in the KGB and had never shed their Cold War mentality. They had internalized the enmity toward the West and the urge for Russia to outdo the United States. That obsession was exacerbated by the inferiority complex of a fallen empire that wished to regain its former stature. All these factors drove Putin's aggressive foreign policy.

Putin's inner circle views the world under a distinct lens, separating the world into a binary construct of a "near abroad" and a "far abroad." The "near abroad" is comprised of countries adjacent to Russia that the Kremlin has sought to maintain a strong grip on. In this imperial mindset, all other countries, including the United States and the European Union, fall into the category of the "far abroad" with their own spheres of influence.

As countries adjacent to Russia asserted their own identity and started leaning toward Western democratic models, they inevitably pushed back against Moscow's influence. Putin perceived that as betrayal by Russia's vassal states and attempted to reassert the Kremlin's influence using a variety of methods, from disinformation and political manipulation to war. Blaming the West for the spread of democratic influence into what Putin considered his own fiefdom, he moved to retaliate by destabilizing the United States and the European Union.

In 2014, after Russia's invasion of Ukraine, the Kremlin came under wide criticism from the EU and the United States. That year the Kremlin propaganda machine began its attempts to rewire the minds of the West. As early as April of that year, Kremlin trolls, oftentimes masked as Westerners, sprung up en masse in comment sections of online articles.[1] Identifiable by their use of mediocre English, beset with grammar mistakes common for Russian speakers, the trolls sought to defend Russia and scorn Ukraine and its Western supporters.[2] By 2015 the trolls' English had improved, and they spread their comments to other polarizing topics, such as Syrian refugees entering Europe and the Brexit vote in the UK.

Adding another layer, the Kremlin expanded its state-sponsored propaganda channels, RT, or Russia Today, and Sputnik worldwide, broadcasting Kremlin-aligned talking points in various languages. It was a noticeable shift that marked the beginning of a new era in Russian foreign policy. The Kremlin moved against Western democratic countries by launching ambiguous warfare[3] that had a layered strategy of combining real world events, often with Russia as their architect, with disinformation and the coercion of foreign politicians to achieve overarching goals. Those goals were the destabilization of Russia's perceived foes. For a couple of years, it went largely unnoticed as Western governments failed to comprehend the gravity of the threat.

The Kremlin trolls overwhelmed unsuspecting authentic online news and social media users around the globe. Over time those real users unwittingly accepted the politically extreme talking points promoted by trolls, which, in turn, changed their perception of reality. By widening and deepening existing cultural divisions within targeted countries, the Kremlin trolls strengthened the political extremes and weakened the political center, in effect paralyzing them. Only in 2016, after the Brexit vote and the US presidential election, did the implications of Russian ambiguous warfare come into focus.

Over two years the Senate Intelligence Committee investigated Russian influence operations, and held five open hearings[4] for the American public that focused on exposing its industrial scale.[5] The committee also prodded Facebook, Instagram, Twitter, and other media platforms to take down thousands of inauthentic Russian users. Even though the social media companies removed many inauthentic users, they were quickly replaced by new ones that continued the Kremlin's efforts to create disinformation chaos.

Using its multilayered disinformation machinery combined with cyberattacks, energy diplomacy, arms sales, and military support, the Kremlin started to expand its foreign influence operations by supporting political leaders with extreme views in democratic countries while helping other autocratic rulers stay in power. The Kremlin intended to rearrange the balance of power by creating an alliance between Russia and similar autocracies to oppose the democratic West.

INFLUENCE IN EUROPE

Ever since Vladimir Putin first came to power, the Russian government had opposed former Soviet countries' efforts to join Western alliances. In 2008 Russia blocked Georgia from joining NATO by seizing control of its northern regions and creating a frozen conflict with no solution. In September 2013 Russia pulled Armenia away from signing the EU association agreement[6] in favor of joining the Russia-led rival Eurasian Customs Union.[7] Two months later the Kremlin also persuaded Ukrainian president Yanukovych to renege at the last minute on a long-negotiated EU association agreement in favor of a bailout loan from Russia.[8] After Ukrainians revolted against the scheme, Russian forces seized territory in Ukraine as a way of keeping a strategic foothold in the country.

In response, Western countries condemned Putin's aggression and imposed sanctions and trade embargoes on Russia.[9] The Kremlin reacted by launching its multifaceted campaign to destabilize the West. To sow discord in the European Union, the Kremlin started providing political and financial support to parties on both the extreme right and extreme left in a number of countries. Some of those political parties had worldviews aligned to Russia. Others simply served Russia's purpose. But most importantly, they could exacerbate divisions and destabilize Western governments.

For example, in *Austria* the Kremlin backed Heinz-Christian Strache and his right-wing Freedom Party.[10] The Kremlin had special interest in Austria as the country is home to Raiffeisen Bank, one of the largest European partners of the Russian state gas company, Gazprom. The bank's subsidiary, Raiffeisen Investment AG, had served as a financial hub for Dmytro Firtash's RosUkrEnergo[11] in the Russian-Ukrainian gas scheme, which was described in chapter 11. In March 2014, at the request of US prosecutors, the Austrian police arrested Firtash on bribery charges. His potential extradition to the United States could serve the Kremlin a damaging blow by removing a key operative from Ukraine.

Around the time of Firtash's arrest, members of the Austrian Freedom Party were invited as European tokens to "observe" the referendum on Russia's annexation of Crimea.[12] The Austrian politicians then gave interviews to RT[13] and Sputnik,[14] Russian propaganda outlets, assuring viewers of the legitimacy of the vote. In late 2016 the Freedom Party signed a cooperation agreement with Putin's United Russia Party.[15] Years later it would be revealed that Russian foreign influence operations targeted several members of the Freedom Party, including those who went to Crimea, offering them payments for their public statements and efforts to push the Kremlin's interests in the Austrian Parliament.[16]

It's not clear whether the Freedom Party members assisted the Kremlin in Firtash's case, but in April 2015, Austrian court denied the US request for Firtash's extradition. The United States appealed the decision, leading to a lengthy legal battle.

The Freedom Party leader Heinz-Christian Strache also attempted to mediate discussions between Russia and then president-elect Donald Trump by reaching out to his national security advisor in transition, Michael Flynn.[17] A year later Strache became the vice-chancellor of the country, with his party members overseeing Austria's foreign, interior, and defense ministries.[18] However, Strache's stint in the government was short lived. In May 2019 he resigned under scandal, after a video leaked to the public with him offering state contracts to a Russian woman in exchange for political donations.[19] The following month Austria approved Firtash's extradition to the United States[20] before it was blocked again by an Austrian court.[21]

In neighboring *Hungary* Vladimir Putin had cultivated the country's strongman prime minister, Viktor Orban.[22] In addition to their shared autocratic views on statesmanship, the leaders of the two countries had developed strong energy ties.[23] In January 2014 the countries suddenly announced cooperation on the revitalization of a Soviet-era nuclear power plant, with 80 percent of the project financed by Russia.[24] Going from being an old Putin critic, Orban turned into a staunch supporter,[25] criticizing EU sanctions on Russia[26] and modeling Hungary after Putin's illiberal democracy.[27]

In *France* the Kremlin supported Marine Le Pen's right-wing party, National Front,[28] which is known for its anti-immigrant, anti-EU, and anti-NATO stances. In 2014 a Czech affiliate of a Russian bank provided Le Pen's party a €9 million loan.[29] In 2017 the Kremlin unleashed its disinformation machine during France's national elections against Le Pen's main rival, Emmanuel Macron.[30] Seemingly in return for Russia's assistance, Le Pen supported Russia's annexation of Crimea and publicly stated that if she were elected president, she would lift sanctions on Russia.[31] Le Pen would also be useful to Putin as an advocate for France leaving the EU and NATO,[32] advancing Putin's goal to disintegrate the Western alliances.

For that specific purpose, in 2016 Kremlin trolls amplified pro-Brexit sentiments[33] in the *British* referendum that led to the separation of the United Kingdom from the European Union. Russian propaganda channels provided a platform for the leader of the far right UK Independence Party, Nigel Farage,[34] an outspoken advocate for leaving the EU. Russian media also elevated the profile of the former head of the left-wing Labor Party, Jeremy Corbyn,[35] who was known for his anti-NATO rhetoric.[36]

In the southern European country of *Montenegro*, as it sought to join NATO, Russian intelligence was involved in an outright coup attempt.[37] Together with Montenegrin opposition and Serbian nationalists, the conspirators reportedly plotted to attack the country's parliament on election eve, assassinate Montenegro's prime minister, and install pro-Kremlin officials.[38] The attempt failed, and in 2019 the plotters were sentenced to prison.

This is, by no means, a complete list of Russian meddling in European politics. The Kremlin has sought[39] clandestine[40] influence[41] in Italy, Germany, Greece, Spain, Serbia, and others. The news organizations controlled by the Russian government, RT and Sputnik, repeatedly provided platforms to fringe politicians in those countries and their parties. There were also cyberattacks on the German Bundestag,[42] British telecom companies,[43] and several Swedish media channels,[44] among others.[45] According to Western intelligence estimates, from 2014 to 2022, Russian intermediaries provided secret political contributions, transferred through shell companies, of over $300 million to individuals and organizations in the West in an effort to destabilize democracies.[46]

However, Europe was not the only target of prolific Russian influence as the Kremlin actively sought to remake the world in its authoritarian image.

RUSSIA AND IRAN'S ALLIANCE

Russia and Iran had had a complicated history through Soviet and post-Soviet times that vacillated depending on each country's political situation and the state of their relationships with the West. After the Second World War, Iran was a US ally and remained as such until the Islamic Revolution in 1979. Before it, the pro-Western government had been reforming the country toward a goal of modernization, leading to animosity among its conservative Islamic clerics and ripening the climate for a potential rebellion. The Islamic fundamentalists, who ousted the government, then sought to spread their revolution throughout the Middle East and further into the world. The Iranian Revolution surprised and concerned the Soviets[47] as they were fighting a war against Islamic insurgents in Afghanistan at the time. But primarily, the Soviets were upset that the Islamic Revolution marginalized their ideological allies, the Iranian Communist Party.[48]

The postrevolution Iranian theocratic government cultivated both anti-imperial and anti-Western rhetoric among its people[49] and had supported terrorist actions, financed proxy militia groups throughout the Middle East, and over decades assertively displayed prolonged aggression against Western interests in multiple countries, such as Israel, post–Saddam Hussein Iraq, and Saudi Arabia. Those collective actions over a forty-year period, paralleled by Iran's attempts to build a nuclear weapons program, led to a series of layered sanctions by Western governments.

In the late 1980s, as the USSR was falling into an economic abyss, it started selling arms to Iran.[50] That military trade was inherited by Russia after the collapse of the Soviet Union. However, in the 1990s, with Russia turning toward the West and improving ties with the United States, Yeltsin's administration scaled back its cooperation with Iran. In the 2000s Russia maintained formal diplomatic relations with Iran and sold small amounts of weapons but more often sided with the West and the United States, much to Iran's chagrin.

In 2010 the Russian government supported the UN ban on weapon sales to Iran due to its unwillingness to curb its nuclear proliferation program. Russia then backtracked from an arms deal with Iran that included an advanced air defense system, drawing Iran's ire as well as accusations of caving to Western pressure.[51] The Kremlin's withdraw from the deal drastically limited Iran's capacity to defend its nuclear facilities.

As part of the US endeavor to contain the Iranian nuclear program, the US Department of the Treasury sanctioned people[52] within the IRGC[53] as well as businesses believed to be controlled by the group to bring the government of Iran to the negotiating table. These US measures also involved secondary sanctions on the Iranian oil industry. Those secondary sanctions banned purchases of Iranian oil by US allies and prohibited both public and private financial institutions from aiding Iran in transactions related the purchase of Iranian oil. In 2013, noting an increased gold trade flowing to Iran,[54] Pres. Barack Obama expanded the sanctions by restricting the trade of precious metals, such as gold, with Iran.

The nuclear sanctions against Iran bit hard, depressing the value of their currency by half in the fall of 2013.[55] The country was cut off from significant transactions in the global financial system, and its economy was sent into a tailspin. Finding a way around Western sanctions, Iran entered into bilateral trade deals with several countries[56] outside the Western financial system. The most prominent was the Iranian-Turkish oil for gold trade, run by Reza Zarrab through Halkbank, as was described in chapter 1 of this book.

In time the Iranian government, dramatically weakened by its financial isolation from the world at large, was forced to the negotiating table. Between 2013 and 2015, Russia cooperated with the West in the negotiations with Iran. In July 2015 the United States, the UK, France, Germany, China, and Russia and Iran reached an agreement in what became known as the Joint Comprehensive Plan of Action, or JCPOA, commonly known as the Iran nuclear deal. According to the agreement, Iran would significantly decrease its nuclear research and production capabilities and allow oversight of its nuclear facilities by the United Nations' International Atomic Energy Agency inspectors.[57]

In exchange for Iran's compliance, the countries agreed to release $100 billion in Iranian assets[58] that had been previously frozen by the United States. The United States and the EU also lifted its nuclear-related sanctions on Iran,[59] including on oil transactions, with a provision that if any of the involved parties determined that Iran had broken the agreement, the sanctions would immediately snap back into place. Prior US sanctions unrelated to Iran's nuclear activity would remain in effect.[60]

At the time when the JCPOA was signed, some tectonic changes were happening in the Middle East, especially in Syria. Iran, despite its old grudges toward Russia, allied with the Kremlin to assist their mutual ally, Syrian dictator Bashar al-Assad.[61]

RUSSIA'S PROXY WAR IN SYRIA

THE BEGINNING

In 2015 Syria was deeply mired in a civil war that stemmed from large-scale protests that swept through several countries of the Arab world. That wave of protests became known as Arab Spring.

In 2011, like in other Middle Eastern countries at the time, the opponents of Syrian president Bashar al-Assad organized rallies seeking a regime change to his oppressive rule.[62] The government responded by deploying troops to violently suppress the demonstrators.[63] Angered by the government's actions, many members of the Syrian military defected from the army and formed an anti-Assad rebel group, the Free Syrian Army.[64] Joined by many common Syrians and armed reportedly by Saudi Arabia and Qatar, the rebels fought against regular Syrian Army units as the country spiraled into civil war.[65] Western countries condemned Syrian dictator Bashar al-Assad for violence against his own citizens.[66] Yet the United States, traumatized by the experience of several wars in the Middle East in the previous decade, was reluctant to directly intervene in the conflict.

However, in 2014 the conflict evolved when ISIS emerged and captured large swaths of Syrian and Iraqi land.[67] ISIS was bent on establishing a Sunni Islamic caliphate at the core of the Middle East. ISIS followers showed vicious brutality in attacking civilians in areas it controlled. Its leadership sought to create the caliphate by taking advantage of the chaos in Syria and a fragile Iraq, which was still recovering from a decade of violence. The rapid emergence of ISIS in Syria and Iraq, combined with its followers' frequent displays of brutality, led to the creation of a US-led coalition to eradicate ISIS-affiliated forces. Initially beginning with ten countries in September 2014,[68] the coalition would soon expand to at least sixty participants, including the United Kingdom, France, and Turkey.

As part of the anti-ISIS efforts, the United States started training[69] and arming[70] Syrian Kurds, who also opposed Assad's regime. That US-Kurdish alliance did not bode well with Turkish president Erdogan, who condemned the Western aid flowing to the Kurds.[71] That criticism stemmed from a historic conflict between the ethnic Kurdish minority who lived in Turkey and ethnic Turks. The Turkish-Kurdish conflict, which was described in chapter 5, became one of the main points in the evolution of the Syrian Civil War in the following years. The Turkish government aggressively sought to push the Syrian Kurds, who had been fighting for their lives against ISIS and Assad's forces, far away from the Turkish border.

By the time Russia entered the Syrian conflict, it had already become a fighting space of multiple coalitions with incompatible alliances.

ENTER RUSSIA

In September 2015 the Kremlin deployed Russian military forces to Syria, claiming to support the war against ISIS.[72] However, its priority was to help the Assad government remain in power. The Kremlin also supplied weapons to the Syrian Army and Iranian proxies while providing them[73] with air cover.[74] Russian air strikes targeted not only ISIS elements, but also anti-Assad rebel positions[75] and civilian mass gathering points such as schools,[76] hospitals,[77] and markets.[78]

Syrian people, who had been leaving the country since the beginning of the civil war, started to flee en masse to Europe to escape the growing violence. Some European countries that initially[79] supported[80] the Syrian refugees became overwhelmed[81] and faced[82] growing[83] opposition[84] from[85] right-wing[86] political parties. Over time, Western intelligence had come to believe that Russian forces in Syria were intentionally targeting civilian infrastructure[87] in an attempt to force the refugee migration toward Europe.[88] In parallel, Russian disinformation campaigns exacerbated antirefugee rhetoric in Europe.[89] Combined, those tactics aimed to destabilize European governments and empower fringe ultranationalist groups aligned to the Kremlin's interests.

The reason behind that move was an increasing enmity between the West and Russia due to the 2014 Russian invasion of Ukraine, its forced annexation of the Crimean Peninsula, and subsequent rounds of sanctions imposed on Russia by the United States and the EU. Putin sought to fight back by destabilizing Western countries, attempting to break up the Western consensus supporting the Ukrainian state, and diminishing areas of Western influence. As part of its multifaceted, ambiguous war against the West, the Kremlin began a campaign to replace the United States as the central power broker in the Middle East.

THE ASTANA PEACE PROCESS

In January 2017 the governments of Russia, Iran, and Turkey met in Astana, Kazakhstan, to coordinate their interests in Syria. Officials from Russia and Iran represented the Assad government's interests, and Turkish delegates represented some of the rebels who had been opposing Assad.[90] However, neither Kurdish-Syrian representatives[91] nor most of the Western coalition members[92] were asked to be present. Russia invited representatives from the United Nations and the incoming Trump administration,[93] albeit merely in an observer status.[94]

During the talks the parties discussed how to establish peace in Syria on their terms for the benefit of their interests. The key outcome of those negotiations was Turkey switching sides.[95] In the early years of the Syrian Civil War, Turkey had provided covert support for anti-Assad rebels and called for the dictator to step down.[96] Turkey's active involvement in Syria began in earnest with Turkey joining the US-led coalition in August 2015 and launching air strikes against ISIS positions.[97]

However, the Kremlin had found a simple solution to separate Turkey from the Western coalition. Aware of the Turkish animosity toward the Syrian Kurds, Russia and Iran had not invited them to the talks in Astana. Then with Putin's apparent tacit approval, Erdogan deployed the Turkish military to make intermittent attacks on the Syrian Kurdish settlements near the Turkish border.[98]

Ultimately, the Astana peace talks manifested two years later, in October 2019. As described in chapter 5, Syrian Kurdish settlements were buffered from Turkey by US military forces. After Turkish president Erdogan successfully pressured his American counterpart, Donald Trump, US forces rapidly withdrew from the Turkish-Syrian border.[99] Without American backing, the Syrian Kurds were forced to seek refuge with their former adversary, Assad's Syrian Army, to protect themselves from Turkish attacks.[100] Thus, Bashar al-Assad was freed from fighting a potent adversary that had been previously armed by the United States.

The abandoned US bases were quickly taken over by Turkish and Russian forces.[101] Russia had achieved its goals in Syria by reducing the American presence in the Middle East, keeping its ally Assad in power, and emerging as a power broker in the region with the crucial help of its newfound ally, Turkey.

TURKEY INC.

RUSSIA'S RAPPROCHEMENT WITH TURKEY

Like Russia, Turkey was once the center of a large empire that spanned from the Balkans to North Africa and into the Middle East. Longtime adversaries, the Russian and Ottoman Empires fought each other for centuries over territories surrounding the Black Sea.[102] The First World War served as a catalyst for the collapse of both of them. After the fall of the Russian czar, the forming Soviet Union managed to largely maintain its territories. In contrast, the collapse of the Ottoman Empire led to the creation of several smaller countries. At the end of the First World War, the former Ottoman capital itself, modern-day Istanbul, was occupied by British and French forces. Unwilling to live under occupation, former Ottoman army officers pushed back in resistance, leading to the Turkish War of Independence. As a result, the Turkish resistance leader, Mustafa Kemal Ataturk, became the founding father of modern Turkey. He envisioned his country transforming from a religious caliphate to a Western-modeled secular democracy.

Between the First and Second World Wars, Ataturk and then Soviet leader Vladimir Lenin built a pragmatic alliance based on common fear of the British and French Empires imposing their influence. The two leaders set similar trajectories to modernize their countries. They shed their former state religions, introduced mass education reforms, and attempted to industrialize. At the end of the Second World War, Lenin's successor, Joseph Stalin, had a different vision for the Soviet Union. He expanded its influence by occupying countries across Eastern Europe. That aggression changed the dynamic between Turkey and the USSR.

The Turkish government, feeling increasingly threatened by Soviet ambitions, sought support from the West and informally joined the Western bloc in February of 1945. A few years later, Turkey became a member of the newly formed North Atlantic Treaty Organization. For almost fifty years, Turkey would act as a bulwark against Soviet aggression in the Mediterranean and in the Middle East during the Cold War.

After the end of the Cold War and the collapse of the Soviet Union, Turkey and Russia slowly reestablished trade and energy ties.[103] In 2010 the countries signed an agreement for Russia to build a nuclear plant[104] estimated to be worth $22 billion[105] in the south of Turkey. That same year Turkey also introduced a visa-free regime for Russian citizens,[106] gaining millions of new tourists.[107] The two countries abandoned their adversarial Cold War sentiments, and the Black Sea neighbors seemed to be opened to a cooperative future.

The rapprochement continued undisturbed even when Turkey's fellow Black Sea neighbors, Georgia and Ukraine, were attacked by Russia in 2008 and 2014. Turkey, in a way, even benefited from Russia's conflict with Ukraine, which disrupted the flow of Russian gas to Europe. When the Kremlin sought to bypass Ukrainian transit routes, Turkey emerged as a potential energy hub. In December 2014 Putin and Erdogan announced the construction of the TurkStream pipeline, which would deliver Russian gas through a route under the Black Sea into Turkey and onward to southern Europe.[108] However, all those projects stumbled when Russia entered into the Syrian conflict in 2015.[109]

As mentioned previously, Russia and Turkey initially supported opposing sides in the Syrian Civil War. Turkey supported anti-Assad rebels and was a part of the US-led coalition that fought against ISIS.[110] Meanwhile, Russia, offering a false pretense to fight ISIS, instead constantly attacked anti-Assad rebels and civilian targets in the areas controlled by Assad's opposition.

Russia's involvement in the Syrian Civil War led to increasing tensions with Turkey. Russian aircraft operating in Syria had been repeatedly violating Turkish airspace for at least a month, causing criticism from Erdogan's government.[111] In November 2015 a Russian plane, once again, flew into Turkish airspace and, after several warnings, was shot down. The incident caused outrage in Russia and was called by Vladimir Putin "a stab in the back."[112] The Russian government responded by imposing sanctions on Turkish goods, canceling visa-free travel, and halting negotiations on the TurkStream pipeline project and the Russian-financed nuclear power plant.[113]

At the time, Russia supplied 60 percent of Turkey's natural gas[114] while also becoming its second-largest trading partner. With the Kremlin holding energy leverage, in June 2016 the Turkish president wrote[115] a letter[116] to his Russian counterpart, apologizing for shooting down the plane. Two months later, in an interview to a Russian propaganda outlet, the Turkish foreign minister would say that the idea for sending the letter came from Farkhad Akhmedov,[117] the same Russian oligarch mentioned earlier as an intermediary between Turkey and US lobbying firm Ballard Partners.[118] The Turkish foreign minister praised Akhmedov as a person who "knows Putin closely."[119] The letter seemingly had an effect on the Russian president as he shortly thereafter declared the closure of the "crisis chapter" with Turkey.[120] A month later another event occurred that decisively steered Turkey away from the West and closer to its eastern partner, Russia.

THE POSTCOUP PURGES

On July 15, 2016, parts of the Turkish military attempted to topple Erdogan and his government. Although the coup failed, a few hundred people were killed, and thousands more were injured throughout that night. The Turkish president survived the coup attempt and declared it "a gift from God" to build "a new Turkey."[121] Immediately thereafter Erdogan's government began to implement measures to cement his hold on power.

Even before the coup attempt, Erdogan had been tightening the screws on the Turkish populace, violently suppressing Gezi Park protesters in the summer of 2013, as described in chapter 2. After the eruption of a corruption scandal in December 2013 that implicated Erdogan and his family members, the Turkish government incarcerated the prosecutors and investigators probing the case. However, after the coup attempt, Erdogan had a plausible enough excuse to portray himself as the victim and use that to purge anyone who could oppose him.

In the coming years, Erdogan would remake the Turkish government into a verticalized system where he, as president, would have unprecedented power within the state, the courts, the media, and the nation's economy. In short, Erdogan's "new Turkey" would come to resemble Russia and become "Turkey Inc."

After the coup attempt, President Erdogan immediately declared a state of emergency.[122] What initially was supposed to last for three months continued on for two years.[123] During that period the government installed a curfew restricting civil gatherings[124] and presided over a massive purge of those who Erdogan said supported his toppling.[125] He blamed the coup attempt on the followers of his archrival Fethullah Gülen, a cleric who had lived in a self-imposed exile in Pennsylvania since 1999.

By early August 2016, under the anti-Gülenist aegis, Erdogan's government had fired about 21,700 officials from the Ministry of Education, suspended over 21,000 schoolteachers, forced 1,500 university deans to resign, fired over 9,000 police officers, and detained over 10,000 members of its military,[126] including its generals and admirals.[127] Erdogan's government also purged the Turkish justice system, removing about 4,000 judges and replacing them by less experienced loyalists.[128] According to a Reuters special investigation from 2020,[129]

> *At least 45% of Turkey's roughly 21,000 judges and prosecutors have three years of experience or less.*

With sycophants installed during the purge, the reshuffling of the Turkish justice system made it subordinate to the president and could be used as a weapon against both his real and perceived adversaries in the future.

At the same time, the Turkish government moved to control the influence of independent Turkish media by imprisoning opposition journalists[130] and forcing the closure[131] or sales of independent news outlets to Erdogan-friendly business owners.[132]

By January 2019 Turkey had become a country with one of the highest journalist incarceration rates in the world.[133] With Erdogan's government obtaining control over the majority of mainstream media, opposition candidates, journalists, and citizens moved online to express their opinions and frustration through social media.

In response, the Turkish government moved to squeeze out Turkish dissent from Twitter, Facebook, and Instagram. Even before the coup attempt, during the Gezi Park protests in mid-2013, the Turkish government deployed a team of six thousand "volunteers" to spread pro-government talking points online and combat anti-Erdogan sentiments[134] in tactics similar to the Kremlin trolls. After the coup attempt, the Turkish government's digital strategy evolved into a crackdown on social media, obliging them to open offices in Turkey,[135] attempting to force them to store their Turkish user data in Turkey,[136] and reserving the ability to take down content on the government's request.[137] The Turkish government also criminalized the spread of "disinformation" or whatever Erdogan didn't like.[138] If found guilty, offenders, who were mostly opposition candidates and journalists, could face up to three years in jail.

Erdogan's administration went even further, not only curtailing the political opposition and the media but also barring the general public from criticizing the president. The Turkish ruler began resorting to the usage of an old law that allowed the government to punish its citizens for "insulting the president." According to a Reuters article from October 2021,[139]

> *Since 2014, the year Erdogan became president, 160,169 investigations were launched over insulting the president, 35,507 cases were filed and there were 12,881 convictions.*

In parallel, the Turkish government moved to tamp down Erdogan's political opposition by targeting pro-Kurdish parties[140] that represented 20 percent of Turkey's population.[141] In November 2016 the Turkish government arrested eleven members of the largest Kurdish political party.[142] The purge extended into everything Kurdish, including politicians, teachers, culture, and language.[143] Erdogan's government attempted to equate all ethnic Kurds living both in Turkey and beyond to a Kurdish terrorist group, the PKK, and used it as an excuse for the persecution of all Kurds. Going further, the Turkish president ordered a large offensive against the Syrian Kurds, who, at the time, were fighting a life-and-death battle with elements of ISIS.

All those measures, implemented under the aegis of a righteous postcoup response, significantly diminished public dissent, weakened the political opposition, and strengthened Erdogan's grip over Turkey.

THE 2017 TURKISH CONSTITUTIONAL REFERENDUM

In parallel with the mass intimidation, Erdogan and his party launched a campaign to hold a constitutional referendum in April 2017[144] that was designed to eliminate the position of prime minister and centralize power around the president.[145] At the time, Turkey had a parliamentary system, with its prime minister holding more governing control than the president, who played more of a figurehead role. With the new constitutional changes, Erdogan, as president, could accumulate all the power and remain as the country's ruler for two additional presidential terms, lasting until 2029.[146] The proposed amendments were bundled into one single package, with no opportunity for citizens to compartmentalize the changes but to vote either "yes" or "no" for all of them.[147] The bundle, among other things, included a proposal that would significantly make it harder to investigate and remove the president.

As the referendum was happening under martial law, civil assemblies were not allowed. That meant the society could not openly discuss the potential ramifications of the proposed constitutional amendments or protest against them. While independent media was under government crackdown, Turkish state media, which was aligned with Erdogan and his party, promoted the "yes" vote and allocated very limited airtime to opponents of the referendum.[148]

On the day of the vote, in April 2017, Turkey's Supreme Board of Elections abruptly changed the rules and allowed uncertified votes to be accounted as legitimate.[149] Opposition and European election observers estimated[150] that as many as 2.5 million out of 47.5 million votes could have been potentially tampered with.[151] Considering that the number of those who had voted for the constitutional amendments was only 1.3 million higher than those who had opposed it,[152] there was a distinct possibility that tampering with 2.5 million votes might have swung the results. Independent observers and the opposition also cited irregularities such as ballot stuffing and voter intimidation.[153] By the end of the day, Turkey's Supreme Board of Elections pronounced the passage of the referendum, with a narrow majority of 51.4 percent voting in favor of the constitutional changes that cemented Erdogan's new presidential powers.[154]

A PUTINESQUE AUTOCRAT

All of Erdogan's actions after the July 2016 coup attempt resembled the authoritarian playbook. Surrounding himself with loyalists, he cracked down on his political opposition. His allies took control over large swaths of formerly independent media. He purged, then weaponized the justice system. Like his Russian counterpart, the Turkish president aspired for absolute authority. Like Putin, Erdogan presented himself as the restorer of lost imperial glory.

Immediately after the coup attempt, Erdogan chose to make his first trip abroad to Russia,[155] as opposed to any of Turkey's NATO allies. It marked the moment when

Erdogan seemingly turned from being a Western ally to a Putinesque autocrat. The Russian president was reportedly one of the first world leaders to express support to Erdogan after the coup attempt.[156] Kremlin-sponsored media also claimed that Russian intelligence had tipped off Erdogan of an imminent attempt to overthrow him.[157]

In contrast, Erdogan publicly argued that the West did not come to his rescue immediately[158] and that Western powers had wanted to oust him.[159] As proof, he cited Western criticism of the purges[160] after the coup[161] in conjunction with the European Union pausing talks about Turkey joining the EU.[162] The Turkish president also accused the United States of aiding the orchestration of the coup and blamed the US government for harboring Gülen.[163]

There was another bone of contention hidden underneath the Turkish president's anti-Western vitriol that would become the center of Erdogan's foreign policy vis-à-vis the United States and the greater West for years to come. Three months before the attempted coup, in March 2016, the United States arrested the Iranian Turkish gold trader Reza Zarrab in relation to the Halkbank money-laundering scheme. In late May of the same year, the US federal prosecutors who had indicted Zarrab released a memorandum that implicated President Erdogan and other high-ranking Turkish officials in the Halkbank case.[164]

In late August President Erdogan met with then US vice president Joe Biden, who had flown to Turkey to reassure the Turkish president of American support. During that bilateral meeting, Erdogan demanded that the United States extradite his archrival, Fethullah Gülen, and reportedly privately pressed Biden to drop the Zarrab case, fire the SDNY prosecutor, and remove the judge overseeing the case to improve relations with Turkey.[165] During a joint press conference, Vice President Biden spoke of the separation of powers between the branches of the US government,[166] seemingly signaling that Erdogan's requests would not be granted.

The US-Turkey feud escalated when in September 2017 the Southern District of New York unsealed additional criminal indictments against several Turkish government officials and Halkbank executives.[167] In an apparent tit-for-tat move, a week later the Turkish government announced its intention to purchase a Russian-made S-400 air defense system.[168] The deal was a clear sign of Erdogan's willingness to break from the West over the Halkbank investigation.

In response, the United States warned off Turkey from the purchase, suggesting that the Russian S-400 could compromise the capabilities of the F-35 aircraft[169] that Turkey had previously ordered from the United States and was waiting to be delivered. After almost two years of negotiations between the United States and Turkey, in which the Turkish government refused to cancel the Russian-Turkish arms deal, the United States would remove Turkey from the F-35 program.[170]

One could ask, "What was the risk?" The F-35 is America's next-generation stealth strike fighter with significant integrative technologies and continuously upgraded software. The technology in the fighter allowed it to act in heavily contested airspace while maintaining air superiority. The Russian-made S-400 was described at the time as "one of the best air defense systems."[171] Western military experts argued that the Russian military who serviced the S-400 in Turkey might gain access to the technical specifics of the F-35 fighter planes if they were to be delivered to Turkey.[172] With that access, Russian forces could decipher the aircraft's stealth signature and, in turn, make it vulnerable to Russian air defense systems and deprive American forces of their stealth advantage in a time of war. The Turkish government knew that the purchase of the S-400 system was subject to US CAATSA (Countering America's Adversaries through Sanctions Act) sanctions on the US trade partners who purchased substantial military equipment from Russia.[173] However, by agreeing to the Russian S-400 deal, Turkey signaled that if the United States were to pursue the Halkbank investigations, Erdogan would counter by turning Turkey, the country with the second-largest army in NATO after the United States, away from its Western allies.

The Russian-Turkish S-400 deal, combined with TurkStream and the Russian-financed nuclear power plant,[174] pulled Turkey toward Russia's orbit. Erdogan, like his Russian counterpart, seemed to have shed the veneer of democracy in Turkey and had chosen the path of corruption. The end of that path inevitably led to Erdogan's rapidly growing authoritarianism in Turkey. On paper Turkey would remain a member of NATO. In reality the Turkish president would take his country into the club of Russia's autocratic allies.

THE ALLIANCE OF RUSSIA AND VENEZUELA

COMRADE CHAVEZ

During the Cold War, the Soviet Union maintained a presence in Central America, using socialist Cuba as an outpost for power projection and surveillance in the Western Hemisphere. The most dangerous moment of that power projection happened in 1962, when the Soviet Union persuaded Cuban leader Fidel Castro to allow the placement of Soviet nuclear missiles on the island, less than one hundred miles from Florida. The standoff that ensued between the United States and the Soviet Union became known in history as the Cuban missile crisis. Although an outright conflict was averted, the Soviets continued to focus its surveillance activities on the Caribbean island on the United States up until the collapse of the Soviet Union.

In the early 1990s, Russian president Boris Yeltsin steered his government toward a less adversarial position with the United States. Bankrupt and unstable, Russia took large[175] loans[176] from the International Monetary Fund and opened the country to foreign investments to transition to a market economy. At the same time, the Russian government was trying to build a foundation for democracy in the country.

Undeniably, the Kremlin had significant issues to resolve at home before worrying about projecting its power overseas. However, things changed when Vladimir Putin became Russia's second president. He spent most of his first presidential term strengthening the government apparatus and the country's economy. Bolstered by rising oil revenues that replenished the treasury, Vladimir Putin was ready to build foreign relations from a position of strength and to once again utilize a country in the Western Hemisphere for Russian power projection.

Putin's ascent coincided with the election of socialist Hugo Chavez as the Venezuelan president in 1998.[177] A former military officer, Chavez ran on an anticorruption populist platform. Before the Chavez era, Venezuela had been a pro-Western capitalist democracy and a US ally, buying military equipment and letting American energy companies, such as Exxon Mobil and Chevron, explore its vast oil fields. However, through two successful constitutional[178] referendums,[179] Chavez set a new course to shift Venezuela from a capitalist democracy to a socialist dictatorship, with the government taking greater control over the country's economy[180] and abolishing term limits for the Venezuelan presidency.[181]

Ever since the discovery of black gold in Venezuela, the country had swung from prosperity to protests as global oil prices fluctuated. Over time the Venezuelan economy became increasingly focused solely on the production and export of oil and became the modern archetype example of the Dutch disease. When global oil prices increased, the Venezuelan people had buying power, which led to political stability. When prices were low, people could afford little, and the country had less financial and overall stability.

Instead of developing programs that could diversify the Venezuelan economy, Hugo Chavez chose short-term populist solutions. In the 2000s, with the oil prices soaring, the Chavez administration nationalized the Venezuelan assets of many Western oil companies,[182] including American Exxon and Dutch Shell,[183] which were absorbed by Petróleos de Venezuela SA, or PDVSA, the country's state oil conglomerate.[184] The PDVSA's profits, in turn, were doled out as subsidies for Chavez's populist social programs.[185] At the time, with no end in sight of the oil bonanza, Chavez could afford to implement his ideas of a socialist paradise and, at the same time, strengthen his domestic political position.

The nationalization of the foreign companies' assets and the increasing authoritarianism led to an exodus of investors from Venezuela, leading to tensions with European countries and the United States. The rift between Venezuela and America was exacerbated when, in 2006, the United States imposed an arms embargo in response to the Venezuelan government's purported support of neighboring Colombian terrorist guerrillas.[186] Within two months Hugo Chavez found a solution to the arms embargo by signing a series of arms deals with Russia.[187] The agreements included over fifty helicopters and more than twenty Russian fighter planes[188] to replace the aging American-made F-16 jets.

Russia also announced a licensing agreement for the construction of a factory to make Kalashnikov assault rifles near the Venezuelan capital. In addition to the arms deal, the two countries announced that a Russian oil company would build a gas pipeline in southern Venezuela and explore for oil in the Orinoco basin, the largest hydrocarbon deposit in Venezuela. At the time, the Russian president stated that the agreements with Venezuela were "not directed against other states."[189] However, the Kremlin shared Chavez's anti-Americanism, and Putin would seize the opportunity to reestablish an outpost in the Western Hemisphere.

Putin's power projection motives in Venezuela became more apparent in 2008. That year the United States offered support for Georgia, a former Soviet bloc country, in its bid to join NATO.[190] Putin considered Georgia to be in Russia's sphere of influence and, in response to NATO entreaties, invaded Georgia, occupying parts of its territory.[191] Putin knew that Georgia, as a country with an unresolved military conflict, would not be eligible to join the alliance.

As Russia's aggression in Georgia was condemned by the West and tensions escalated, the Russian government sent aircraft with nuclear capabilities to Venezuela as a show of power.[192] The message was clear: Putin was not going to tolerate American support in what he perceived as a Russian vassal state. It didn't matter if it was an independent country. As a counterbalance, Putin would increase Russia's presence in America's backyard, in Venezuela. Over the following years of the Chavez era, Russian arms supply to Venezuela would swell to $11 billion and would include tanks, fighter jets, and the S-300 air defense system.[193]

With the death of Hugo Chavez, Russian-Venezuelan relations entered a new phase.

THE DUTCH DISEASE TRAP

After Hugo Chavez died of cancer in 2013, Venezuela was left in the hands of its vice president, Nicolas Maduro.[194] However, Maduro's Venezuela did not enjoy the same oil profits reaped by Chavez. Between 2013 and 2016, oil prices decreased dramatically, plummeting from around $100 per barrel in 2013 to a little over $30 per barrel in 2016.[195] That was due to a combination of factors, including the expansion of fracking in the United States, the relief of oil sanctions on Iran, and the continued steady oil output by OPEC countries.[196] Such a steep dive was devastating for the Venezuelan economy, with 95 percent of its export revenue coming from oil.[197] It was a prime case example of what economists call the "Dutch disease,"[198] which refers to a situation that occurred in the Netherlands in the 1970s. The country discovered large deposits of natural gas, then built its economy around it to the detriment of other industries, becoming hostage to gas price fluctuations.

To make matters worse, the Venezuelan government had no safety net to weather the oil crisis as it had previously spent much of its sovereign wealth fund on social subsidies.[199] As a result, its economy started to collapse.[200] In response, the Venezuelan government started printing more money, leading to hyperinflation.[201] Then the situation snowballed into diminished consumer buying power and an unhappy electorate.

Since 2014 the Venezuelan people had been taking[202] their frustrations[203] to the streets,[204] protesting food and medical supply shortages, increased violence, hyperinflation, and corruption at the center of Maduro's government. By late 2016 Maduro faced mass protests demanding his recall.[205] His government was also on the brink of defaulting on its sovereign debt.[206] With Western investors previously alienated after the mass nationalization, the Venezuelan dictator turned again to Russia for financial support.

In November 2016 the Russian state oil company, Rosneft, lent $1.5 billion to its Venezuelan counterpart, the PDVSA. To guarantee the loan, the PDVSA used 49.9 percent of its US subsidiary called Citgo as collateral.[207] The money did not last long, and Venezuela borrowed more from Russia. By August 2017 the PDVSA had owed Rosneft $6 billion, and the Venezuelan government had a separate debt to Russia that had reached $17 billion.[208] As Venezuela struggled to pay back Russia, the countries restructured the deal to allow Venezuela to use oil as payment. Further, Venezuela covered a part of its debt by transferring a number of its valuable oil deposits to Russian control. As a result, Russia absorbed a significant share of the Venezuelan oil industry, including its foreign trade contracts that were a lifeline to the country's revenue.[209] In a further sign of increased energy cooperation, in March 2019 Venezuela announced the relocation of the PDVSA's European office from Lisbon to Moscow.[210]

At the time, Russian cash helped the Venezuelan government avert default on its national debt and keep Nicolas Maduro in power. However, cash was not the only form of support that Russia provided to Maduro's regime. Around the time of the presidential election in May 2018, Maduro, concerned about a possible assassination attempt, boosted his security by hiring Russian mercenaries, who guarded him for the following months.[211] The mercenaries were a part of the Wagner Group, which positioned itself as a private military company. However, Wagner was, in fact, an arm of the Kremlin run by Putin's ally Yevgeny Prigozhin and did the Kremlin's dirty work in different corners of the world while providing the Russian government with plausible deniability.[212] The presence of Russian mercenaries in Venezuela might have served not only to secure Maduro's power but also to enforce Russia's interests in Venezuela.

In a maneuver similar to one seen in Ukraine, Russia built significant leverage over the Venezuelan energy industry and kept its president in power, effectively capturing Venezuela as a state. From that captured state in America's backyard, the Kremlin intended to pressure the United States to diminish its support of former Soviet countries. Years later, during Donald Trump's first impeachment trial, a member of the US National Security Council, Fiona Hill, would describe a Russian ultimatum given to her as follows:[213]

> You stay out of Ukraine or you move out of Ukraine, you change your position on Ukraine, and, you know, we'll rethink where we are with Venezuela.

THE AUTOCRATIC ALLIANCE

In late 2016 Russia's efforts to cultivate relations with Iran, Venezuela, and Turkey seemingly paid off as those countries started cooperation with both Russia and one another in a variety of initiatives. As mentioned previously, Russia and Iran successfully pulled Turkey toward their interests in the Syrian conflict. Their peace talks in Astana, Kazakhstan, changed the dynamics of the Syrian Civil War, leading to the collapse of the ground forces of the Western coalition. The Assad regime was secure, and Russia's prominence as a middle power broker grew dramatically.

The Kremlin's new friend Erdogan started building diplomatic relations with Maduro. Both of them found common cause in overcoming their fragile political footing at home. Erdogan survived a coup attempt while Maduro closely averted a recall referendum.[214] In the months following, both would suppress opposition and change the fabric of their countries' constitution, staging[215] referendums[216] to cement their powers. In 2018 both[217] would be reelected[218] amid credible allegations of voting irregularities.

In October 2016 Turkey hosted a large energy conference that was attended by both the Russian and Venezuelan presidents.[219] One of the main discussion topics at the event was the falling oil prices[220] that hurt both Russia and Venezuela, whose economies strongly depended on oil. That plummeting was partially caused by the release of Iranian oil into the global market after the signing of the JCPOA nuclear deal and the West's subsequent lifting of oil-related sanctions.

There were one-on-one talks between the countries on the outskirts of the conference. Putin and Erdogan furthered their talks on the construction of the Russian-Turkish gas pipeline, TurkStream,[221] which had the potential of making Turkey a regional energy hub. Maduro and Erdogan announced an agreement to strengthen the relationship between their two countries.[222] Maduro and Putin talked about finding solutions to stabilize oil prices.[223] The Venezuelan dictator then took that issue to Iran's supreme leader, Ayatollah Ali Khamenei, whom Maduro visited immediately after the conference.[224]

All those meetings would become useful later, when those countries would help Venezuela skirt US sanctions. In 2018 Venezuela would send $900 million worth of gold to Turkey in exchange for a food program that was part of a corrupt money-laundering scheme for Venezuelan officials.[225] Russia would seem to be aiding Venezuela's money-laundering efforts, when in 2019 several reports would emerge of Russian airplanes carrying Venezuelan gold[226] and making stops at Dubai[227] and Cabo Verde.[228]

By April 2020 Maduro's government would set up a direct deal with Iran, sending the fellow pariah state gold in exchange for its help in reviving Venezuela's decrepit gasoline refineries.[229] In the following months, Iran would send to Venezuela tankers with fuel-refining chemicals[230] and food.[231] Meanwhile, the Venezuelan gold reserve would decrease by nineteen tons.[232] All these actions intentionally avoided the global financial system and aided the corrupt governments that sought to stay in power. In the years to come, the two autocracies would deepen their ties, signing long-term trade deals.[233]

Their enmity toward the West in general and the United States in particular was the key bonding factor among the members of the Russian-led autocratic alliance. The United States, with its stance as the upholder of the international rule of law, was a major irritant for the autocrats who sought to stay in power forever and pilfer their countries' wealth for their own enrichment. As the relationships of those four countries vis-à-vis the United States spiraled down, Russia, Iran, Venezuela, and Turkey forged an informal alliance to find ways to support one another in their revolt against the United States and the West as a whole.

PART IV

RUSSIAN INFLUENCE OPERATIONS IN THE UNITED STATES

CHAPTER 17

THE KREMLIN'S GROUNDWORK

THE "ILLEGALS"

After the end of the Cold War, the period of thaw between Russia and the United States lasted only a little over a decade, chilling again during Vladimir Putin's first presidential term. In 2003 the country of Georgia, which borders Russia, elected a Western-leaning government for the first time. The following year a neighboring Ukraine elected a prodemocratic president in what would later be called the Orange Revolution. The Kremlin blamed the United States for meddling in two former Soviet countries and thus overstepping into Russia's sphere of influence. The tension between the Kremlin and the White House increased again when in 2008 the United States publicly supported Georgia and Ukraine joining NATO.[1] As mentioned earlier, the Kremlin reacted by seizing parts of Georgia[2] and declaring its presence in the Western Hemisphere by deepening its relationship with the socialist government of Venezuela.[3]

When Barack Obama became the US president in 2009, he attempted to "reset" the relationship with the new Russian president, Dmitry Medvedev, who had temporarily replaced Putin. However, in June 2010 the US Department of Justice rounded up ten members of a Russian spy ring[4] who had been living in the United States as "sleeper" agents, assimilating in American society while secretly gathering intelligence for Moscow.[5] Americans might remember the story of a redhead, Anna Chapman, who was one of the ten spies caught by the FBI.[6] It was the largest public Russian spy incident since the Cold War.

The Russian spies operated in the United States as "illegals," that is, working without diplomatic cover from the Russian government. Most of them had assumed fake identities and built background stories over the years. Their goals included gaining access to people connected to the US government, from nuclear experts[7] to government officials, all the while collecting information on US policies vis-à-vis Russia and areas of Russian interests.[8]

After the Russian spies were returned to Russia in a prisoner swap in July 2010,[9] the Kremlin did not abandon its efforts to infiltrate the US government. The Russian government merely adapted its tactics and deployed another group, which included another redhead, Maria Butina.

THE GUN LOVERS

In April 2011 a Russian official named Alexander Torshin traveled to a convention organized by the National Rifle Association, or the NRA. At the time, Torshin was a Russian senator and the first vice-chairman of the Federation Council, the Russian analogue of the US Senate. At the event, Torshin was introduced to the then incoming NRA president, David Keene. Torshin appeared to be seeking Keene's "assistance to try and validate his efforts to reform gun laws in Russia,"[10] where gun rights were virtually nonexistent. The two bonded quite well, so much so that in a couple of years Keene would reschedule his birthday dinner to accommodate Torshin's schedule.[11]

Torshin's choice to target the NRA was not random. By the end of the twentieth century, the organization had become a Republican Party[12] kingmaker.[13] Its endorsement or criticism could make or break a Republican candidate's career. For a Russian official, a friendship with the head of the NRA would open access to US lawmakers, allowing Torshin and his protégé, Maria Butina, various ways to infiltrate Republican political circles in the coming years.

In 2012 Alexander Torshin became a life member of the NRA. The following year he invited Keene to a gun rights event in Moscow. The NRA president accepted the invitation and brought along Paul Erickson, a former GOP operative and lobbyist, to facilitate the trip. The event was hosted by Maria Butina. In 2011 Butina founded a Russian progun group[14] called the Right to Bear Arms.[15] She claimed that she didn't meet strong resistance from the government when she registered her group,[16] which was surprising considering Russia's strict gun regulations.[17] Butina praised her "good lawyers" to be the reason.[18] However, it was more likely that the Russian government officials who were her patrons and oligarchs who financially backed her organization were the ones to credit.[19]

At Butina's event Keene gave a speech about "the history of firearms restrictions and freedoms in the United States."[20] Other activities in Keene's Moscow itinerary included a visit to a museum, a dinner with Torshin and his wife, and reportedly a scheduled meeting with Vladimir Putin's spokesperson, Dmitry Peskov.[21]

After Keene's trip to Moscow, Maria Butina reached out to Paul Erickson and asked him to abstain from publicizing the photos from Keene and Torshin's private dinner. Butina claimed that it might harm Torshin's image in Russia.[22] But most probably, she didn't want the US public and authorities to know about the NRA director's fraternization with people so close to the Russian government.

As a next step in their infiltration, in December 2013 Butina and Torshin asked David Keene to solicit former ambassador to the United Nations and future Trump national security advisor, John Bolton, to record an address in support of Russian gun rights.[23] Bolton agreed, and Butina played the video of his speech[24] to Russian Duma officials.[25]

The following year Maria Butina flew to the United States to go to a NRA convention in Indianapolis, Indiana. She almost missed the event as her visa application to the United States was initially denied. However, the issue was resolved after David Keene personally pulled strings, leaning on an assistant to Congressman Ed Royce (R-CA),[26] the chairman of the House Foreign Affairs Committee.[27] Butina went to the event under the pretense of asking the NRA leadership "for advice and guidance" to advance the gun rights agenda in Russia.[28] However, her real purpose was to cultivate ties to the NRA leaders because it was, as Butina correctly perceived, a "central place and influence" within the Republican Party and "the largest sponsor of the elections to the US congress."[29]

The 2014 NRA trip was Maria Butina's first visit to the United States but not her last. In 2016 Butina moved to the United States to study at American University in Washington, DC.[30] While living in the heart of US politics and masquerading as a gun rights advocate, Butina developed a good relationship with the NRA president and then used the organization as a gateway to establish connections to American conservative influencers and Republican officials. From DC she reported to her mentor, Alexander Torshin, assessing, cultivating, and further infiltrating political circles.

THE CULTIVATION OF DONALD TRUMP

MISS UNIVERSE PAGEANT IN MOSCOW

While Butina and Torshin were building inroads to the NRA, Kremlin-connected oligarchs were cultivating Donald Trump. In January 2013 Aras Agalarov, a real estate mogul and contractor for Russian state projects, and his son, Emin, a pop singer, partnered up with Donald Trump to hold his Miss Universe beauty pageant in Moscow.[31] The venue of the event was owned by the Agalarovs, who reportedly invested $20 million into the Moscow edition of the contest.[32]

The event was scheduled for November 9, 2013. Donald Trump would later boast that "almost all of the oligarchs" attended the pageant,[33] along with "generals and top-of-the-government people."[34] Trump even extended a personal invitation to the Russian president, who reportedly "cancelled at the last minute" but sent a courtesy present.[35]

Donald Trump arrived on the eighth of November and spent almost thirty-eight hours in Moscow.[36] During his short stay, Trump appeared in Emin Agalarov's music video.[37] and gave an interview to MSNBC, during which he hinted at a run for the US presidency.[38] He also agreed with the Agalarovs to pursue a Trump Tower project in Moscow.

Immediately upon returning to the United States on November 11, Donald Trump tweeted:[39]

> @AgalarovAras I had a great weekend with you and your family. You have done a FANTASTIC job. TRUMP TOWER-MOSCOW is next. EMIN was WOW!

TRUMP TOWER IN MOSCOW

Donald Trump apparently had already attempted to build a Trump Tower in Moscow several times since the late 1980s.[40] The negotiations with the Agalarovs were "at least his fifth attempt."[41] However, the project seemed to have stalled by late November 2014.

Things changed in June 2015, when Donald Trump announced his presidential bid. Various Russians suddenly started reaching out to Donald Trump and his organization. In July Donald Trump received an invitation to Aras Agalarov's sixtieth birthday party,[42] including the dangled possibility to meet with Vladimir Putin.[43] Instead of attending the event, Trump sent a birthday note. In the following months, the Trump Organization received at least three unsolicited proposals to build a Trump Tower in Moscow.[44]

One of those proposals came from a former Trump business partner named Felix Sater,[45] a colorful Russian American with a criminal past.[46] In the mid-2000s Sater was a senior executive at the Bayrock Group, an investment group with Eurasian origins that reportedly owned a part of the Trump Soho real estate project in New York.[47] It seemed that the main purpose of those proposals was not the construction of the Trump Tower but an opportunity to establish a connection between Donald Trump and Vladimir Putin. The proposal was just a reason to open doors. Throughout 2015 and 2016, members of Donald Trump's inner circle and presidential campaign team received several outreaches offering to arrange a meeting between Trump and Putin.[48]

Seemingly flattered with the attention, while on the campaign trail, Donald Trump would occasionally praise the Russian president, confusing observers and the media.[49] Years later investigators would explain those pro-Putin comments as an attempt to indirectly advance the Trump Tower Moscow project.[50] With multiple offers on the table, Trump's team chose to proceed on the proposal of Felix Sater, who brought in a little-known Russian company as an investment partner. In October 2015, while running for the US presidency, Donald Trump signed a letter of intent for the Trump Tower Moscow project.[51]

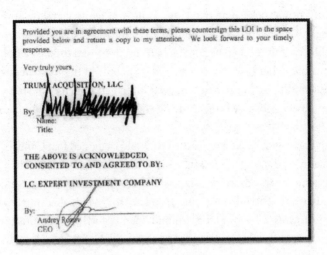

FIGURE 5. DONALD TRUMP'S SIGNATURE ON A LETTER OF INTENT FOR TRUMP TOWER IN MOSCOW
SOURCE: SENATE INTELLIGENCE COMMITTEE REPORT

Shortly thereafter, Felix Sater wrote an email to Michael Cohen, Trump's personal lawyer and a vice president at the Trump Organization, stating:[52]

> Buddy our boy can become President of the USA and we can engineer it. I will get all of Putins [sic] team to buy in on this, I will manage this process . . . Michael, Putin gets on stage with Donald for a ribbon cutting for Trump Moscow, and Donald owns the republican nomination. And possibly beats Hillary and our boy is in . . . We will manage this process better than anyone. You and I will get Donald and Vladimir on a stage together very shortly. That the game changer.

It seems both Michael Cohen and Felix Sater recognized the opportunity that a presidential campaign could bring to the Trump Organization. Regardless of the outcome of the election, the Trump brand stood to benefit from the campaign. Cohen would later claim that Trump considered the campaign the "greatest infomercial in political history"[53] and ran for office not necessarily to become the president but to promote the Trump Organization.

Felix Sater, who had been instrumental in moving things in Moscow, promised Michael Cohen to arrange financing for the Trump Moscow project from VTB Bank, one of the largest Russian banks that at the time had been sanctioned by the United States.[54] The discussions continued into 2016. Seemingly afraid to lose face in front of Trump, Cohen pressured Sater to push things faster.[55] Growing impatient, Cohen took matters into his own hands, and on January 11, 2016, he sent a cold email to the office of Putin's spokesman and close confidant, Dmitry Peskov. It showed the Trump Organization's interest in building a Trump Tower in Moscow. Within days Peskov's chief of staff reached back to Cohen and promised to "pass along" Cohen's notes ostensibly to her boss and other relevant people in the Russian government. Cohen appeared to be impressed how well informed the chief of staff was about the Trump Tower Moscow project. If she was that well informed, that meant so would be her superiors.[56]

Shortly thereafter, Felix Sater reached back and suggested that Cohen and Trump go to Russia to set the deal in motion. After some back-and-forth, Cohen and Sater settled on tying the travels to the Saint Petersburg International Economic Forum, or SPIEF, that was scheduled for June 16–18, 2016.[57] With Vladimir Putin giving the keynote address, the annual event had been branded as the most important economic event in Russia and attended by the various officials of the Russian government and Russia's business elite.[58]

The planning of the trip went as far as Michael Cohen emailing a copy of his passport to receive a Russian visa.[59] At the same time, back in the United States, candidate Trump was one of the last remaining Republican contestants, with his prospects increasing every day. By the end of May 2016, Trump had become the presumptive Republican nominee. At this point it must have become clear that, while running for office, Donald Trump could not travel to Russia, let alone consummate a business deal in a country so adversarial to the United States. On June 14, 2016, Michael Cohen and Felix Sater met in New York at Trump Tower, where Cohen declined the invitation to go to Russia.[60] As a result, the Moscow project fell apart.

While Cohen and Trump might have thought that they were capitalizing on the presidential campaign and leveraging Moscow to advance the Trump Tower project, it was quite the opposite. The Trump Tower Moscow project was the Kremlin's effort to establish a deep connection to the Republican frontrunner, to infiltrate both his organization and his presidential campaign, and, through incentives, to secure Trump's alignment with Russian interests. If the Kremlin could achieve all that and help Trump become president, Russia had a chance to diminish the US role in the world arena. If Donald Trump, a volatile narcissist with no political experience, ascended to power, the United States government could become dysfunctional to a point where it weakened America's role in crucial Western alliances, making them susceptible to Russian influence and giving the Kremlin a powerful advantage in its tug-of-war against the West.

CHAPTER 18

THE DIGITAL STRATEGY

THE AMERICAN DEPARTMENT AT THE TROLL FARM

Using the Trump Tower Moscow project as bait was only one of many facets in a larger plot to influence the 2016 US election. The next important step was to work the masses, to sway the American electorate to the direction that the Kremlin needed. For that purpose, Russia deployed its online trolls that it had been using to mold its own citizens.

In April 2014 the Internet Research Agency, or the IRA, also known as the troll factory and controlled by Putin's ally Yevgeny Prigozhin, created the "American department"[1] that focused on the US social media users. Around the same time, the IRA staff started writing comments in English on Western media websites. As early as May 2014, journalists noticed pro-Russia comments in mediocre English that appeared below the articles related to Russia and Ukraine.[2] As mentioned previously, those comments later expanded to the articles related to issues relevant for Europe, such as the migration crisis and Brexit. However, the most daring project of the Kremlin trolls was their operation to influence the hearts and minds of American voters.

In June 2014 two high-level members of the IRA took a research trip to the United States. They visited Nevada, California, New Mexico, Colorado, Illinois, Michigan, Louisiana, Texas, and New York. They sought to discover pain points within American politics, especially in swing states, that could sway voters from one direction of the political spectrum to another. In some states they met with grassroots political activists who explained their tactics to the Russians.[3]

By 2015 the IRA staff had developed a strategy on how to utilize social media functions to their advantage. Taking their tactics to the next level, IRA operatives created and curated issue-specific accounts on Facebook, Instagram, and Twitter. Those issues were focused on divisive social, cultural, racial, and political issues in the United States, such as immigration, gun rights, deep state conspiracies, police brutality, and gender identity. The fake pages and their engagement with real users were meticulously cultivated by the paid workers of the IRA, which was run with military discipline. Tardiness wasn't tolerated. The workers ought to fulfill their daily quotas of content generation with posts and comments without copying and pasting while striving to appear authentically American. The failure to do so led to fines.[4]

The workers received daily directions[5] to write content tailored to current events in the United States, as well as important holidays and commemorative dates.[6] In the spring of 2015, those daily instructions started including "tasks to discredit the image" of presidential candidates.[7] The main targets were Hillary Clinton and moderate Democratic and Republican candidates. The fringe candidates, Bernie Sanders and Donald Trump, were spared as the IRA management apparently "supported" them.[8]

Over time the content created by the Kremlin trolls reached tens of millions. According to Facebook estimations, just between 2015 and 2017:[9]

> as many as 126 million Americans on the social media platform came into contact with content manufactured and disseminated by the IRA.

That was around half of the US adult population[10] and about 60 percent of Facebook users in America at the time.[11] According to an article by *RBC*, a Russian business magazine that obtained internal information from the troll farm, a relatively small team of eighty people at the American department managed at least 118 issue-specific pages on Facebook, Instagram, and Twitter.[12] The largest of them are presented on figure 6.

Some of those social media pages not only made posts on the dedicated topics but also arranged rallies and engaged grassroots activists in the United States who supported the same issues. In the spring of 2015, the IRA tested the concept to see whether it was possible to organize a political rally from afar. For that purpose, the IRA created a Facebook event, choosing a location in New York City as a gathering point for the experiment, promising a free hot dog to those who would come.[13] On the day of the test event, the IRA operatives gathered in their office in Saint Petersburg, Russia, and observed through street cameras whether anyone showed up.[14] Those who came to the nonexistent event in hopes of winning a free hot dog might have been disappointed, but the Kremlin trolls found a new, efficient way to utilize social media in their influence work.

In May 2016 one of the IRA-run pages, Heart of Texas, organized an anti-Islamic protest in Houston, Texas.[15] Another page named United Muslims of America, also run by the IRA, scheduled a separate pro-Muslim rally for the same date at the same location.[16] Both groups had hundreds of thousands of followers on Facebook.[17] By doing so, the IRA intentionally pitted two diametrically opposed cultural groups against each other,[18] increasing the degree of polarization in the same community. Similar gatherings for two opposing groups were organized[19] in New York.[20]

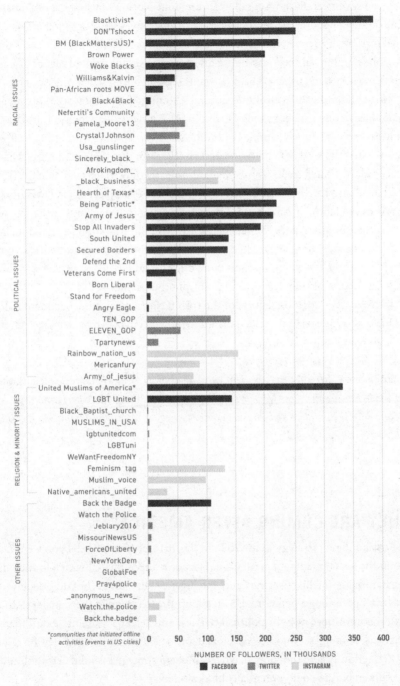

FIGURE 6. DIGITAL FOOTPRINTS OF THE TROLL FARM

SOURCE: *RBC* MAGAZINE

In August 2016 Russian moderators of a Facebook group called Being Patriotic organized seventeen flash mob rallies throughout Florida[21] in support of Donald Trump.[22] Masquerading as Americans, the IRA operatives sent Facebook messages to real pro-Trump activists and encouraged them to participate. In some cases the IRA trolls reimbursed the grassroots activists' expenses for printed materials and other marketing items, using US bank accounts registered with stolen American IDs.[23]

Throughout the 2016 election season, IRA-curated Facebook accounts organized rallies in other states as well,[24] including in Pennsylvania,[25] North Carolina,[26] and Minnesota.[27] These examples of online activities spilling into offline rallies demonstrated the level of penetration and engagement that the Kremlin trolls had achieved in the United States. Those events also clearly showed the goals that the IRA pursued in America. Its efforts aimed to help Donald Trump get elected, widening the tear in the fabric of American society, increasing internal conflict that could lead to destabilization of the United States. The Kremlin trolls overwhelmed social media and news sites with targeted messaging, further shifting authentic users' perception of reality, changing their convictions, and fertilizing impressionable brains for further disinformation and political propaganda.

In November 2016 the efforts of the troll farm's American department paid off. One of the employees described the moment when the US presidential election results were announced as follows:[28]

> On November 9, 2016, a sleepless night was ahead of us. And when around 8 a.m. the most important result of our work arrived, we uncorked a tiny bottle of champagne . . . took one gulp each and looked into each other's eyes . . . . We uttered almost in unison: "We made America great."

"THEY ARE COMING AFTER AMERICA"

The Russian digital strategy to interfere in the 2016 presidential election went far beyond the social media manipulation. Hacker teams affiliated with a branch of Russian military intelligence, the Chief Intelligence Directorate, or GRU, deployed a massive operation to penetrate US election infrastructure at the state level, the election committees of both political parties, and select presidential candidate campaigns. In doing so, the GRU developed for the Kremlin a detailed view on how the US election system functioned, what campaign strategies candidates used, and what vulnerabilities could potentially be exploited.

STATE ELECTION INFRASTRUCTURE HACKS

In mid-July 2016 Illinois election officials reached out to the FBI to report unusual activity in their network. During their investigation the FBI discovered that the state voter registration database had been hacked, and the personal information of over two hundred thousand voters had been downloaded from a database that contained names, addresses, partial social security numbers, and state IDs of fourteen million voters.[29] The FBI also identified several IP addresses that were later attributed to the affiliates of the GRU,[30] from which the hackers accessed Illinois voter registration infrastructure, and requested other states to check whether anyone from those IP addresses entered their networks. By late September 2016, election officials from twenty-one states had responded, confirming that some of those IP addresses made connections to their state election networks.[31] Years later the US Intelligence Community would conclude that Russian hackers might have targeted all fifty states and conducted research on "general election-related web pages, voter ID information, election system software, and election service companies."[32] A high-level US cybersecurity official described the Russian hackers' actions as[33]

> conducting the reconnaissance to do the network mapping, to do the topology mapping so that you could actually understand the network, establish a presence so you could come back later and actually execute an operation.

Members of the US Department of Homeland Security, or DHS, stated that the Russian hackers' scan reportedly had been so thorough that they "almost certainly could have done more" if they wanted to.[34] However, the US government found no direct evidence "that vote tallies were altered or that voter registry files were deleted or modified" by the Russian hackers.[35] As to the reasons why the hackers did not do more, the DHS theorized that the hacking operation[36]

> fits under the larger umbrella of undermining confidence in the election by tipping their hand that they had this level of access or showing that they were capable of getting it.

HILLARY CLINTON CAMPAIGN HACK

Starting in March 2016 and continuing for months onward, GRU hackers attempted to gain access to the email accounts of Hillary Clinton's campaign staff, sending phishing emails that appeared similar to Google security alerts or password change emails.[37] Eventually, they breached the mailbox of Clinton's campaign chairman, John Podesta, and proceeded to steal tens of thousands of his emails.[38] Those emails included campaign strategy, fundraising discussions, and team quarrels.[39] They also contained unflattering communication about Hillary Clinton's weaknesses as a politician,[40] her apparent change of position toward corporations,[41] and a possible conflict of interest between her potential presidency and the Clinton Foundation,[42] which was run by her husband, the former president Bill Clinton.

The Russian hackers apparently remained unnoticed by the campaign for months. In mid-June 2016 candidate Clinton said in an interview:[43]

> *So far as we know, my campaign has not been hacked into.*

She was gravely mistaken.

CLINTON EMAILS AND THE TRUMP CAMPAIGN

On June 3, 2016, eleven days before Clinton's interview, candidate Trump's son Donald Trump Jr. received an email that a Russian acquaintance was interested in passing over some compromising information on Hillary Clinton. The person in question was Emin Agalarov, the son of Aras Agalarov, who had sponsored Donald Trump's Miss Universe contest in Russia in 2013 and was one of the first contenders for the construction of a Trump Tower in Moscow. The email was written to Trump Jr. by Emin Agalarov's music agent from Britain. The email included the following:[44]

> *Emin just called and asked me to contact you with something very interesting.*
>
> *The Crown prosecutor of Russia met with his father Aras this morning and in their meeting offered to provide the Trump campaign with some official documents and information that would incriminate Hillary and her dealings with Russia and would be very useful to your father.*
>
> *This is obviously very high level and sensitive information but is part of Russia and its government's support for Mr. Trump—helped along by Aras and Emin.*
>
> *What do you think is the best way to handle this information and would you be able to speak to Emin about it directly?*

Donald Trump Jr. replied:[45]

> *If it's what you say I love it especially later in the summer. Could we do a call first thing next week when I am back?*

Later Donald Trump Jr. reached out to Emin Agalarov and, after some back-and-forth, agreed to meet with a "Russian government attorney" to discuss what the Russians had on Hillary Clinton.[46]

On June 9, 2016, Donald Trump Jr., Jared Kushner, and Donald Trump's campaign manager, Paul Manafort, met with a Russian lawyer, Natalia Veselnitskaya, and her associates in Trump Tower in New York.[47] Manafort later would recall that he told Trump Jr. at the time that people "coming from that part of the world" usually "have an agenda of their own."[48] Indeed, Veselnitskaya did. She did not tell the group about the hacked emails but claimed that some American investors laundered money both in the United States and in Russia and that some of that money went to the Clinton campaign. Then Veselnitskaya, in a convoluted way,[49] presented what she was really after, a veiled request for the United States to repeal the Magnitsky Act,[50] an act that passed in 2012 that permitted the sanctioning of specific people connected to human rights violations in Russia. By 2016, under that act, the United States had sanctioned thirty Russian[51] individuals[52] and targeted[53] people connected to Vladimir Putin. It appeared that, through Veselnitskaya, the Kremlin was telegraphing a request for the time when and if Donald Trump became the president of the United States.

Jared Kushner, confused and frustrated, asked whether Veselnitskaya had solid proof of the laundered money ending up in the Clinton campaign.[54] Veselnitskaya replied she could not trace the money in the United States, making her arguments moot for the discussion. After the meeting Kushner characterized it as a "waste of time."[55]

Apparently, Donald Trump took notice of Russia's attempts to assist his campaign. And a month after the Trump Tower meeting, on July 27, 2016, during one of his public speeches, he overtly signaled his interest in whatever the Kremlin had on Hillary Clinton by saying:[56]

> *Russia, if you're listening, I hope you're able to find the 30,000 emails that are missing. I think you will probably be rewarded mightily by our press.*

Russia might have indeed been listening. According to the Senate Intelligence Committee Report that would be released in 2020,[57]

> *Within five hours of Trump's statement, GRU hackers spearphished non-public email accounts of Clinton's personal office for the first time and targeted seventy-six email accounts hosted by the Clinton Campaign's domain.*

Two days later, on July 29, 2016, several media[58] outlets reported[59] that the Clinton campaign had been hacked by Russia's intelligence services.

THE DCCC AND DNC HACKS

By early April 2016, the GRU hacking team had already breached the network of the Democratic Congressional Campaign Committee, or the DCCC, a committee that provides informational, fundraising, and operational support for the election of Democrats into the US House of Representatives. First, the GRU hackers penetrated a DCCC employee's computer through a spear-phishing email, an email that appeared to be sent from a trusted source but was, in fact, designed to steal the user's credentials if the user clicked on links or buttons. The go-to designs that the Russian hackers used looked like Google password recovery or security alert emails. Then using the employee's credentials, the hackers obtained access to twenty-nine computers within the DCCC network and scanned its database for election strategy plans and political intelligence, including opposition research.[60]

Some of the DCCC users had access to the database of the Democratic National Committee, or the DNC, which provides support to Democratic candidates at the local, state, and national levels. Using the stolen DCCC credentials, the GRU hackers were able to access thirty computers within the DNC network[61] and, once again, scanned the entire database for election-related information that the Kremlin might find useful.[62]

By the summer of 2016, Russian hackers had copied and exported to their own servers over seventy gigabytes of information from the DCCC database[63] and thousands of DNC emails,[64] which included internal DNC communication about political donors and Democratic candidates' campaigns.[65] When US intelligence officials identified Russian hackers as those behind the DNC breach, the Kremlin denied any involvement.[66] Putin's chief internet advisor commented to the Russian media that probably "someone simply forgot the password."[67]

THE RNC HACK

In September 2016 Michael McCaul (R-TX), a Republican congressman and the chairman of the House Homeland Security Committee, said in an interview to CNN that the Russian hackers also penetrated the Republican National Committee:[68]

> WOLF BLITZER, CNN: *Is Russia trying to influence this U.S. election in order to get Donald Trump elected?*
>
> CONGRESSMAN MCCAUL: *Well, I think the question is, are they trying to influence or just trying to undermine our electoral process?*
>
> *I think the FBI director would tell you they are trying to just undermine the integrity of the process. It's important to note, Wolf, that they have not only hacked into the DNC, but also into the RNC. They are not discriminating one party against the other.*

> The Russians are basically—have hacked into both parties at the national level and that gives us all concern about what their motivations are.
>
> BLITZER: Mr. Chairman, I haven't heard about any Russian hacking of the Republican National Committee. I have heard a lot about the Democratic National Committee.
>
> But you're giving us new information. You're telling us that the Russians have hacked RNC e-mails and other documents?
>
> MCCAUL: Yes. They have hacked into the Republican National Committee.
>
> So, this is—again, they are not picking sides here, I don't think. They are hacking into both political parties.

The RNC immediately rebuffed McCaul's comment and denied any RNC hacks by the Russians.[69] McCaul then retracted his statement, saying that he "misspoke" and that he had meant to say that Republican political operatives were hacked, not the RNC.[70]

Months later, in January 2017, then FBI director James Comey testified in front of the Senate and said that the Russians had hacked into state-level Republican campaigns[71] and old RNC email domains[72] that weren't used anymore.[73] Comey added that the FBI found no evidence of hacking into the "current RNC."[74] Later it would be revealed that Russian hackers had also penetrated into the campaigns of at least two Republican presidential candidates, Lindsey Graham[75] and Marco Rubio.[76]

In one of his later Senate testimonies, FBI director Comey characterized Russia's actions by saying:[77]

> They're coming after America. They will be back.

WEAPONIZATION OF THE HACKED DATA

On June 8, 2016, two months after the Russian penetration of the DNC, the hackers' affiliates launched DCLeaks.com,[78] a website where they published thousands of stolen DNC emails. They also alleged that DCLeaks was "launched by the American hacktivists who respect and appreciate freedom of speech, human rights and government of the people."[79]

Six days later, CrowdStrike, the cybersecurity company hired by the DNC to investigate the hacks, ascribed them to Russia.[80] The GRU hackers, attempting to deflect attention from Russia, created a fake online persona named Guccifer 2.0[81] and portrayed it as a "lone hacker."[82] Through Guccifer 2.0 the GRU passed large archives of hacked data to WikiLeaks,[83] an online platform known for publishing leaked classified or confidential documents. WikiLeaks, as a well-known public platform, had a much larger reach than DCLeaks or Guccifer 2.0. It also had an easy search function for users to scan the entire WikiLeaks database for a specific word.

After receiving the archives from Guccifer 2.0, WikiLeaks started releasing portions of the hacked DNC and Clinton campaign emails on strategic dates to have "maximum impact."[84] The first trove of the DNC emails was released on July 22, 2016, three days before the Democratic National Convention, where the party would announce its official presidential nominee. Hillary Clinton and Bernie Sanders were the two contenders. The WikiLeaks release revealed emails from the DNC chair that disparaged a staffer who worked for Bernie Sanders[85] in what appeared to be bias by the DNC against Sanders's candidacy.[86] The publication of those emails was intended to create infighting among the Democratic candidates' supporters, as well as discredit and destabilize the DNC.

On October 7, 2016, the Obama administration formally accused Russia of hacking into the DNC and stealing and then publicly disseminating the stolen information.[87] That same day, a bombshell video of Donald Trump was published by the *Washington Post*.[88] In it, the Republican candidate made lewd remarks about "grabbing" women by their genitalia. Seemingly to pull the public attention away from Russia's hacking and the scandalous video about Trump, that same afternoon, WikiLeaks released[89] thousands[90] of emails[91] stolen from John Podesta, Clinton's campaign chair. To chip away at the Clinton campaign's credibility, Podesta's emails would continue to be published every day, right up until Election Day.[92]

The formal accusation and dueling releases turned up the heat on both Hillary Clinton and Donald Trump, who would face each other in the second presidential debate two days later, on October 9.[93] While posting of the trove of DNC and Clinton campaign emails continued, there was no parallel publishing of the RNC's hacked emails. Those who wondered why that was the case hypothesized that either the Russians did not find any valuable information on the RNC servers[94] or they kept it for some other use, such as a potential blackmail of Donald Trump and the Republican Party.[95]

The information published by WikiLeaks was then reinforced by Kremlin trolls using their web of disinformation personas.[96] However, they were not the only ones amplifying the WikiLeaks releases. Donald Trump's campaign, aware of the upcoming WikiLeaks publications, prepared press strategies before them.[97] The candidate himself also professed his "love" for WikiLeaks and repeatedly alluded to the hacked emails while campaigning.[98] Trump's longtime friend Roger Stone, who described himself as a "dirty-trickster,"[99] had been acting as the connector between WikiLeaks and the Trump campaign team, giving it advanced notice of what WikiLeaks might release next.[100] Meanwhile, the candidate's son Trump Jr. was communicating with WikiLeaks, which asked him to "push" its stories.[101]

Years later, in September 2020, after a lengthy investigation into Russian interference, Democratic senators who were a part of the bipartisan Senate Intelligence Committee would offer a view separate from their Republican colleagues, concluding:[102]

> *The Committee's bipartisan Report found that Russia's goal in its unprecedented hack-and-leak operation against the United States in 2016, among other motives, was to assist the Trump Campaign. Candidate Trump and his Campaign responded to that threat by embracing, encouraging, and exploiting the Russian effort. Trump solicited inside information in advance of WikiLeaks's expected releases of stolen information, even after public reports widely attributed the activity to Russia, so as to maximize his electoral benefit. The Campaign crafted a strategy around these anticipated releases to amplify the dissemination and promotion of the stolen documents. Even after the US. government formally announced the hack-and-leak campaign as a Russian government effort, Trump's embrace of the stolen documents and his efforts to minimize the attribution to Russia only continued. The Committee's Report clearly shows that Trump and his Campaign were not mere bystanders in this attack—they were active participants. They coordinated their activities with the releases of the hacked Russian data, magnified the effects of a known Russian campaign, and welcomed the mutual benefit from the Russian activity.*

CHAPTER 19
CAMPAIGN INFILTRATION

MARIA BUTINA

THE RUSSIAN "DIPLOMACY PROJECT"

While hacking into the DNC network, the Kremlin utilized similar penetration tactics in its attempts to infiltrate the GOP and the Trump campaign. Instead of the mass sending of spear-phishing emails, the Kremlin deployed a number of covert agents who, through extensive networking, sought access to the conservative political landscape. Once that access was established, Russian agents cultivated influential people, in hopes of coaxing them into doing Russia's bidding.

Maria Butina and her mentor, Alexander Torshin, who were introduced in chapter 17, were examples of those agents. Since at least 2011, Torshin, a Russian senator, had been building a relationship with members of the National Rifle Association.[1] Torshin introduced his assistant, Maria Butina, to then NRA president David Keene and his lobbyist wife, Donna Keene.[2] Like many in America, Torshin and Butina saw the NRA as potential kingmakers in conservative politics whose support or a lack thereof could define a political candidate's career. In the 2016 election cycle, the NRA would spend $54 million to elect Republicans, of which $30 million would be allocated in support of Donald Trump.[3]

In January 2015 Torshin became the deputy chairman of Russia's Central Bank.[4] As a result, Butina took over communication with Keene, who by that time had already finished his term as the NRA president[5] but still had a great deal of influence. In her twenties, masquerading as a Russian gun activist and using her female charm, Butina would be able to leverage her NRA contacts to advance deep into Republican circles (figure 7). Similar to Rabia Kazan, the Turkish clandestine intermediary described in chapter 4, Butina would gain access to the United States conservative elite, including congressmen and presidential candidates.[6]

In early 2015 Maria Butina devised a plan for a "diplomacy project" and presented it to her Russian handler, Alexander Torshin.[7] According to the plan, Butina intended to use her connection to David Keene to build an unofficial back channel of communication between the Kremlin and the next US president, whom she believed would be a Republican. If Butina succeeded, the Kremlin could attempt to covertly influence US policy toward Russia, which at the time was careening to a dark place. The Kremlin especially wanted to shake off the sanctions imposed on Russia by the United States after the annexation of the Crimean Peninsula.

In her presentation, Butina argued:[8]

> *The resulting state of affairs [between the Kremlin and the next US president] needs to be strengthened specifically in the current time period, before the 2016 presidential election. After the election, conducting negotiations on that level will be extremely problematic. The spokesperson [Butina] needs to participate in all the major upcoming RP [Republican Party] conferences (about once a month in various US cities [...]), to speak in the American media as an expert from Russia and to have constant contact with the RP leadership.*
>
> ***Also, it is important to note the large number of players from Russia who are interested in this matter—entrepreneurs and RF [Russian Federation] citizens who own businesses and property in the US.*** *If relations between the two countries do not improve and the process of imposing sanctions becomes harsher, Russian business will face a high risk of losing assets abroad.*
>
> *Thus, we propose to consider the issue of providing the spokesperson with financial support for attending the events mentioned above (a total budget of about $125,000) as well as separate meetings with interested parties (the MFA [Russian Ministry of Foreign Affairs], the Russian business representatives) in order to determine where the focus of Russian interests lies in cooperating with the US.*

Torshin and his superiors promptly approved Butina's plan, and she immediately proceeded to its implementation. As she would need to spend more time in the United States, she applied for a graduate school studies program[9] at American University in Washington, DC.[10] In 2016 she would be accepted and move to the United States on a student visa.[11]

EARLY INROADS INTO CONSERVATIVE POLITICS

In early 2015 Maria Butina reached out to David Keene and his wife, seeking their assistance in putting together a list of key GOP events and the names of expected important attendees. The Keenes not only provided a detailed list but also helped her obtain invitations to those events.[12] Throughout the spring and summer of 2015, Maria Butina and her boyfriend, Paul Erickson, toured the country, attending those GOP events.[13]

The two had met during Keene's 2013 trip to Moscow and became romantically involved, so much so that Erickson would financially contribute to her university tuition[14] and living expenses.[15] Despite moving in with him later, Butina would not[16] seem[17] particularly thrilled about Erickson, who was balding and almost twice her age. However, he had something Butina needed: deep connections into the conservative political circles.[18] Erickson was a GOP influencer with decades of involvement in Republican politics.[19] He had advised several Republican presidential candidates and was a board member of the company that organized the Conservative Political Action Conference,[20] or CPAC, an annual hard-core conservative extravaganza. Considering Paul Erickson's résumé and his deep connections, he would become extremely valuable to Butina in her pursuit to gain access to the movers and shakers of Republican politics.

With help from Paul Erickson and David Keene,[21] in April 2015 Maria Butina and Alexander Torshin attended an NRA event in Nashville, Tennessee.[22] At that event Keene introduced Torshin and Butina to Wisconsin governor and prominent conservative Scott Walker, who planned to run for president. Three months later Butina and Erickson went to Walker's presidential campaign announcement. After the event Butina prepared for Torshin a detailed assessment of Walker's chances of winning the Republican presidential nomination.[23]

In July 2015 Butina and Erickson traveled to Las Vegas for a libertarian event, FreedomFest.[24] Several presidential candidates, including Republican senator Marco Rubio and Donald Trump, were scheduled to appear there. In a Q and A session after Donald Trump's speech, Butina asked him about his views on Russia and sanctions. Trump replied:[25]

I know Putin, and I'll tell you what, we get along with Putin . . . I believe I would get along very nicely with Putin, okay? And I mean where we have the strength. I don't think you'd need the sanctions. I think we would get along very, very well.

While at FreedomFest, Butina also connected to Patrick Byrne,[26] the former CEO of Overstock and then backer of another presidential candidate, Sen. Rand Paul. Butina charmed Byrne, a bachelor in his fifties, with conversations about Russian literature and philosophy, and the two took romantic trips to several US cities[27] throughout the time when Butina was dating Erickson. The latter did not seem to mind. In an email to another Butina financial supporter, Erickson wrote:[28]

I'd like to add Byrne to the very small circle of Maria Butina college scholarship providers (you and I and an NRA poohbah are the founding trio). Byrne is a bachelor by choice and consequences of his intellectual gifts and limitations, but is now concerned with his mortality and family legacy. Since meeting Maria, he has found ever more creative ways to pitch a standing $1 million offer to her "to have a baby with him." He is utterly enamored of her imagined gene stock and believes that a baby would cement not only his familial line but also relations between our two nations . . . . I *think that he could be persuaded by men like you and me to support Maria in more concrete—if less carnal—terms.*

Byrne would later recall that during their encounters, Butina:[29]

spoke increasingly about meeting or seeking to meet people involved in the presidential campaigns of Hillary Clinton, Mr. Trump, Senator Ted Cruz of Texas and Senator Marco Rubio of Florida.

It was not known whether Byrne assisted her in her quest for access. However, Butina continued her prolific networking activity. Over the coming years, she would attend numerous conservative gatherings,[30] from informal dinners to prominent political events, such as CPAC and the NRA conventions, where she enjoyed VIP access that gave her the ability to meet with the events' speakers.[31] She used each event to methodically build her network and identify people whom she could exploit for her goals. US officials who had met Butina described her as "solicitous"[32] and "friendly, curious and flirtatious."[33] The people Butina crossed paths with included numerous prominent conservative influencers; US congressmen, including a member of the House Foreign Affairs Committee;[34] the head of Michigan Republican Party;[35] officials from the Department of the Treasury and the Federal Reserve;[36] and presidential candidates and their staff.[37] That was quite an impressive list for a grad student in her midtwenties.

TRIPS TO RUSSIA

The next layer of Maria Butina's diplomacy project was to interconnect influential groups of people in the United States and Russia through informal events. As part of that effort, in the summer of 2015, Butina reached out to Keene with a proposal to bring VIP members of the NRA to Moscow.[38] David Keene responded with a list of people whom he would consider for the trip. Butina also asked Paul Erickson to identify people to invite to Moscow, emphasizing that she was interested only in those who were politically influential. The final list included both the former and the incoming NRA presidents, an NRA fundraiser, the CEO of the Outdoor Channel, and a Milwaukee County sheriff,[39] who would later become a Trump campaign surrogate.[40] To persuade some of them to join the trip, Butina suggested a potential business deal with a Russian arms manufacturer[41] and a possibility of meeting the Russian president, Vladimir Putin, or even his potential appearance in a documentary by the Outdoor Channel.[42]

The people whom Butina and Torshin planned to invite from the Russian side were also of high caliber. The list included the "leading media oligarch in all of Russia"; the head of a prominent PR firm; the former director of Russia's internal security service, FSB; Russia's foreign minister; and the deputy prime minister, who was under the US sanctions.[43] All were close allies of Vladimir Putin.

In December 2015 Torshin and Butina, along with Russian officials and oligarchs, welcomed the NRA dignitaries to Moscow.[44] The fact that Butina, a purported gun rights activist from a country where gun rights were nonexistent, could arrange meetings with the Russian officials at the highest level did not seem to raise any suspicions among the NRA members. Apparently, no one fathomed that she could possibly be a cog in the Russian intelligence system.

Meanwhile, by successfully connecting ranking NRA members and influencers to Russian policymakers, Butina implemented another part of her diplomacy project. In doing so, both Butina and Torshin gained a higher profile within the Russian government, and their further activities would be coordinated and approved by the Russian Ministry of Foreign Affairs.

The NRA trip also served as a "launching pad" to advance Butina's infiltration into the next political level.[45] One of the NRA members on the Moscow trip agreed to introduce Butina and Torshin to the leadership of the US National Prayer Breakfast, an annual invitation-only event in Washington, DC, that brings together America's highly influential political, religious, cultural, and business elites. Since the 1950s the event has been consistently attended by both incumbent and former presidents, congressmen, and US cabinet members.[46] It was a perfect opportunity to cultivate ties to America's elite, and Butina and Torshin leveraged all their connections to get invitations to the 2016 and 2017 National Prayer Breakfast events.[47]

The NRA members were not the only influential Americans whom Butina and Torshin met in Russia. In 2015 David Keene asked Torshin to meet with Congressman Dana Rohrabacher (R-CA) to discuss cooperation possibilities between Washington and Moscow.[48] Torshin agreed and met with Rohrabacher in Russia. As what frequently seemed to happen around Butina and Torshin, the newfound connection to Representative Rohrabacher would then open even more doors to other well-placed people.

RUSSIAN-AMERICAN FRIENDSHIP DINNERS

Another avenue for connecting the Kremlin's agents to powerful Americans arose when one of Paul Erickson's "oldest friends in politics" and a "Rockefeller heir," George O'Neill Jr., started hosting regular informal Russian-American "friendship dinners."[49] On several occasions Butina and Erickson asked O'Neill to invite hand-picked Americans whom the couple deemed influential. One such example was Patrick Byrne, whom Butina and Erickson had met at the FreedomFest libertarian conference. In his July 2016 email to O'Neill, Erickson proposed the following:[50]

> *Patrick Byrne, the founding CEO of Overstock.com, met Maria last July at Freedom Fest in Las Vegas and has been stalking her ever since ... [he] supports "our" vision of a new dawn of relations between the two countries. He ... would find it effortless to attend a monthly dinner in Washington with whomever of our original cast might wish to dine at a given time ... Maria VERY much wants you two to meet to compare your genius level IQ's.*

Erickson characterized those dinners as events attended by "Russian banking oligarchs" and boasted that "no one else is dealing with the Kremlin at this high a level today."[51]

DONALD TRUMP'S CAMPAIGN

In May 2016 Donald Trump became the Republican Party's presumptive presidential nominee.[52] That same month he secured an endorsement by the NRA.[53] Immediately, Butina, Erickson, and Torshin reached out to their contacts to gain access to people within Donald Trump's campaign. That effort didn't prove successful.[54] However, Butina and Torshin, while attending an NRA convention in Louisville, Kentucky, ran into the son of the future president Donald Trump Jr. and took a photo with him.[55]

Butina and Erickson tenaciously continued their efforts to reach Trump campaign officials, and another opportunity arose at a dinner hosted by Rep. Dana Rohrabacher, where Erickson met Sam Clovis, a senior advisor to the Trump campaign. After the dinner Erickson sent an email to Clovis stating that he had "been developing a back-channel to the Kremlin for the past couple of years."[56] Clovis reportedly ignored the email.

Butina, Erickson, and Torshin also considered approaching the Trump campaign's foreign policy advisor, Carter Page,[57] who had seemed sympathetic to Russia. However, that sympathy brought unwanted media[58] scrutiny[59] to Page, leading to his ouster from the campaign.[60]

Butina then targeted J. D. Gordon, a former senior foreign policy advisor to the Trump campaign. She would meet with him at a bar, invite him to one of O'Neill's Russian-American friendship dinners, and later go with him to a rock concert.[61]

In late October 2016, Butina reported to Torshin the following:[62]

> *I talk to all of Trump's Russia advisors. There are three of them. They do not have any other contacts at the RF [Russian Federation]. Just you and I. At the same time, I am working in a group that is writing proposals to him on foreign policy strategy. I have a couple of people on his staff.*

Two weeks later Donald Trump won the US election. After seeing the initial results, Maria Butina wrote to Alexander Torshin:[63]

> *I'm going to sleep. It's 3 am here. I am ready for further orders.*

In the next days, Butina prepared two papers for Torshin and the Russian Ministry of Foreign Affairs, in which she laid out an action plan to influence the Trump administration. Essentially, her strategy distilled was to expand on her existing conservative connections in hopes of establishing unofficial channels of communication between the Kremlin and the Republican Party. She also suggested organizing a conference that would look like a "private initiative" to build Russian-American relations.[64]

Meanwhile, Butina's boyfriend, Paul Erickson, reportedly worked behind the scenes to join Trump's transition team[65] but was blocked due to issues with his security clearance. That didn't discourage the Russian-American power couple, and they continued their efforts to network at one of the Trump's inauguration balls.[66]

THE NATIONAL PRAYER BREAKFAST 2017

As their next goal, Butina and Torshin aimed to meet with Pres. Donald Trump at the National Prayer Breakfast in February 2017. As mentioned previously, it was a large event that gathered America's business, cultural, and political elite at one location. The organizers presented it as dedicated to "the person and principles of Jesus, with a focus on praying for leaders of our nation and from around the world."[67] However, critics described the event as[68]

> *an international influence-peddling bazaar, where foreign dignitaries, religious leaders, diplomats and lobbyists jockey for access to the highest reaches of American power.*

Capitalizing on her established connections within the NRA and the 2016 National Prayer Breakfast and dangling the possibility of Putin's attendance, Butina obtained tickets to the 2017 National Prayer Breakfast for a group of fifteen Russian nationals, which included former Kremlin staffers, business executives, a head of a Russian university, and a mayor of a Siberian town. All of them were cleared by Russia's Ministry of Foreign Affairs to attend the event. Butina described the Russian delegates to Erickson as "VERY influential in Russia" and that they were "coming to establish a back channel of communication."[69] That was a brazenly open move, considering that in early 2017 the US investigations into Russian interference were gaining steam and increasingly more public attention.

On the eve of the official National Prayer Breakfast event, the Russians attended another "friendship dinner" hosted by George O'Neill.[70] Butina's boyfriend, Paul Erickson, suggested that O'Neill invite members of Congress to join the gathering by highlighting the profile of the Russian attendees and their closeness to the Russian president. Among those who agreed to attend was Rep. Dana Rohrabacher (R-CA),[71] the same congressman who had previously met Torshin in Russia in both 2015 and 2016.

During the National Prayer Breakfast, Butina and Torshin were scheduled to meet Donald Trump, a courtesy arranged by the event's leadership. However, the meeting was canceled at the last moment. Butina explained the mishap as "overbooking" of the president's schedule. White House security provided an alternative reason. They reportedly discovered Torshin's connections to Russian organized crime and advised against the meeting.[72]

BUTINA'S FALL

In November 2016, days after the presidential election, Butina had a birthday party in a DC bar where she reportedly bragged about her connections to the Trump campaign and high-level Russian officials.[73] That declaration apparently drew attention. By that time she had already been under surveillance by the FBI for months.[74] It seemed that in the summer of 2017 Butina became aware of her potential legal trouble as, around that time, she retained a lawyer.[75]

In April 2018 the FBI seized Butina's electronic devices from her apartment in DC.[76] The FBI also searched Paul Erickson's home in South Dakota, where they found a handwritten note that read, "How to respond to FSB offer of employment?"[77] suggesting that he had been courted by the Russian intelligence services.

The FBI arrested Butina in July 2018,[78] and five months later, she pleaded guilty to acting as an unregistered Russian agent.[79] The US government was clear in their assessment of Butina's actions and the damage she had caused America. US prosecutors believed[80] that she had connections to the Russian intelligence.[81] FBI officials accused her of being involved in an effort to identify and recruit Americans who could work for Russian intelligence,[82] that is, in addition to the information she had gathered during numerous conservative events and passed over to Torshin. The judge overseeing her case described Butina's actions as "a threat to our country's democratic institutions"[83] and sentenced[84] her to eighteen months in prison.

The following year Butina was deported to Russia,[85] where she became a member of the Russian Parliament.[86] Butina's mentor and handler, Alexander Torshin, was sanctioned by the US government in April 2018.[87] Butina's boyfriend, Paul Erickson, was indicted in February 2019 for money laundering and wire fraud,[88] found guilty, and was sentenced to seven years in prison.[89] However, he was never charged with any crimes in connection with Maria Butina. In early 2021, on the last day of his presidency, Donald Trump pardoned Paul Erickson.[90]

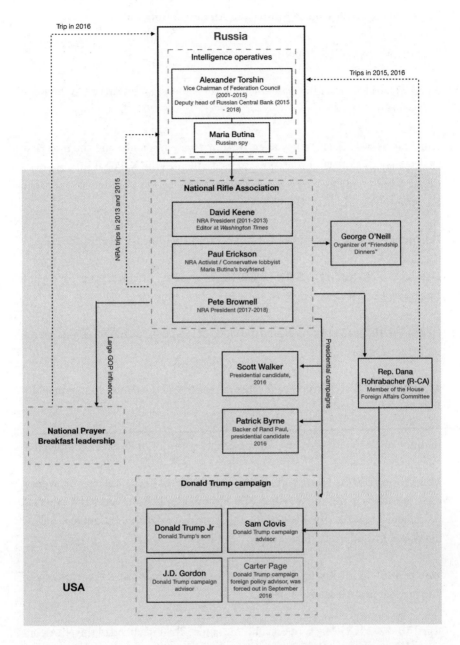

FIGURE 7. INFILTRATION OF CONSERVATIVE POLITICS BY MARIA BUTINA AND ALEXANDER TORSHIN

Key events related to Maria Butina and Alexander Torshin*

*See the full integrated timeline in appendix A.

April 22, 2011 - Maria Butina founded a Russian progun group called the Right to Bear Arms.

April 28–May 1, 2011 - Alexander Torshin, Russian senator and the first vice-chairman of the Russian Federation Council, attended the National Rifle Association convention in Pittsburgh, Pennsylvania, where he was introduced to the then incoming NRA president, David Keene.

February 10, 2012 - Alexander Torshin became a lifetime member at the NRA.

October 31–November 1, 2013 - David Keene and Paul Erickson traveled to a gun rights event in Moscow, which was hosted by Maria Butina.

December 10, 2013 - Butina played the video of John Bolton's progun rights speech to Russian Duma officials.

April 25–27, 2014 - Maria Butina attended the NRA convention in Indianapolis, Indiana.

January 20, 2015 - Torshin became the deputy governor of Russia's Central Bank.

Mid-February 2015 - Maria Butina reached out to David Keene and his wife, seeking their assistance in putting together a list for important GOP events and expected prominent attendees. The Keenes not only provided a detailed list but also helped her obtain invitations to those events.

March 2015 - Maria Butina devised a plan for a "diplomacy project" and presented it to her handler, Alexander Torshin.

April 10–12, 2015 - Maria Butina and Alexander Torshin attended the NRA convention in Nashville, Tennessee, where they were introduced to Wisconsin governor and 2016 Republican presidential candidate, Scott Walker. At a dinner before that event, Torshin and Butina met with officials from the Federal Reserve and the Department of the Treasury and a member of the House Foreign Affairs Committee.

July 11, 2015 - Maria Butina and Paul Erickson traveled to Las Vegas for a libertarian event, FreedomFest. At that event Butina asked Donald Trump about his views on Russia and sanctions. Trump replied that he would "get along very nicely with Putin" and that sanctions weren't necessary. While at FreedomFest, Butina also connected to Patrick Byrne, the former CEO of Overstock and then backer of presidential candidate Rand Paul.

August 3, 2015 - Rep. Dana Rohrabacher (R-CA) traveled to Russia and met with Alexander Torshin.

December 8–13, 2015 - Ranking NRA members visited Moscow, where they met several Russian officials.

February 4, 2016 - Torshin and Butina attended the National Prayer Breakfast.

April 2, 2016 - Rep. Dana Rohrabacher (R-CA) went to Russia and met with Torshin once again.

May 4, 2016 - Donald Trump became the presumptive Republican nominee.

May 20, 2016 - Torshin and Butina attended the NRA convention in Louisville, Kentucky, and "ran into" Donald Trump Jr. At that event the NRA endorsed Donald Trump.

July 12, 2016 - Representative Rohrabacher organized a dinner in Washington, DC, where Erickson met Sam Clovis, a senior member of Trump's campaign team. After the dinner Erickson sent him an email stating that he had been "developing a back-channel to the Kremlin for the past couple of years."

July 18, 2016 - Butina prepared a forecast on the election outcome for the Russian Ministry of Foreign Affairs and sent it to Torshin. She also pondered approaching Carter Page.

July 23, 2016 - Erickson sent an email to O'Neill about inviting Patrick Byrne, the CEO of Overstock, to the future friendship dinners and including him into Butina's "scholarship fund."

August 2016 - Butina moved to the United States to study at American University of International Service in Washington, DC.

September 28, 2016 - Butina encountered J. D. Gordon, a former senior advisor to the Trump campaign, then invited him to O'Neill's friendship dinner.

October 18, 2016 - Butina and J. D. Gordon went to a rock concert.

October 20, 2016 - Butina reported to Torshin that she had gained access to three members of the Trump campaign.

November 8, 2016 - Election Day. Donald Trump was elected the US president. Butina wrote to Torshin, "Waiting for your orders."

November 10–11, 2016 - Butina prepared for Torshin and the Russian Ministry of Foreign Affairs two papers about the next steps of influence on the Trump administration.

November 12, 2016 - At her birthday party in DC, Butina bragged about having access to the Trump campaign.

November 15, 2016 - Butina received invites to the next National Prayer Breakfast for more than a dozen of Russian delegates.

January 31, 2017 - The Russian delegation attended a "friendship dinner" organized by O'Neill.

February 1, 2017 - Butina and Torshin were scheduled to meet with Donald Trump at the National Prayer Breakfast. The meeting was canceled at the last minute.

June–July 2017 - Butina retained a law firm in the United States.

November 2017 - The Senate Finance Committee reached out to Butina about her connections to Alexander Torshin.

April 6, 2018 - Alexander Torshin was sanctioned by the United States.

April 25, 2018 - The FBI seized Butina's electronic devices.

April 2018 - Butina testified to the Senate Intelligence Committee.

July 15, 2018 - Butina was arrested in Washington, DC.

December 13, 2018 - Butina pleaded guilty to acting as an unregistered agent for Russia.

February 6, 2019 - Paul Erickson was indicted for money laundering and wire fraud.

> **April 26, 2019** - Butina was sentenced to eighteen months in prison, including time served.
>
> **October 25, 2019** - Butina was deported to Russia.
>
> **January 20, 2021** - Erickson was pardoned by Donald Trump.
>
> **October 2021** - Butina became a member of the Russian Parliament.

THE TARGETING OF CARTER PAGE

"MALE-1"

As mentioned earlier, Maria Butina and Alexander Torshin sought to find sympathetic Americans of influence and incentivize them toward Russian goals. One of the people they targeted was Carter Page, a foreign policy advisor to Donald Trump's campaign. However, Butina and Torshin were not the first Russians who were interested in Page.

Between 2008[91] and 2013,[92] Page reportedly had been in contact with members of Russia's foreign intelligence agency, or the SVR, an acronym for the Russian title of the service, Sluzhba Vneshney Razvedki. When in 2013 FBI agents warned him that the Russian operatives intended to use him as an informant,[93] Carter Page did not seem surprised and responded that the Kremlin likely kept tabs on him since his time in Moscow.[94] Between 2004 and 2007, Page worked in the Moscow office of the financial firm Merrill Lynch, focusing on the nexus between the Russian banking and energy sectors, a niche of great wealth and opportunity for those at the center of it. A graduate from the US Naval Academy,[95] a holder of a master's degree in national security studies from Georgetown University, an MBA from New York University,[96] and a PhD from a university in London,[97] Page had a pedigree that could attract attention from Russian secret services.

Russia's domestic security service, the FSB, routinely tracks foreigners who live in Russia[98] to spot counterintelligence and national security threats. If the FSB deems a person potentially threatening to the Kremlin regime, such as outspoken journalists, academics, or diplomats, the secret services may deploy intimidation[99] tactics[100] to silence them or force them to leave Russia. The FSB also seeks to identify those foreigners who can become potential assets. First, FSB operatives assess[101] a person's knowledge, convictions, and worldview. If its agents consider a person suitable, the FSB may attempt to turn a person into an asset of the Russian security services. Carter Page seemingly belonged to the latter group.

In 2008, upon returning to the United States, Page founded an energy consulting firm named Global Energy Capital LLC. His company board included a deputy financial director of Gazprom,[102] one of the largest Russian state-owned energy companies. That same year he also signed up to volunteer for Sen. John McCain's presidential campaign.[103] Curiously enough, in that time Page was approached by Russian foreign intelligence officers, who would cultivate him for years.[104]

In January 2015 prosecutors at the SDNY charged the Russian intelligence agents[105] who were in contact with Page,[106] with one of them pleading guilty to acting as unregistered foreign agents for Russia later that year.[107] The FBI affidavit attached to the case referred to an unidentified "Male-1"[108] and included a conversation between two SVR agents who described "Male-1" as an overeager asset who wanted to "earn lots of money"[109] and could be fooled with empty promises. A couple of years later, investigative journalists would identify Carter Page as "Male-1" from the FBI affidavit.[110]

ADVISOR TO THE TRUMP CAMPAIGN

The arrest of Page's Russian contacts did not discourage him from seeking involvement in Russia-related affairs. On the contrary, from December 2015 to February 2016, he worked through his network of contacts to join the Trump campaign's foreign policy advisory team, stressing his experience in Russia and the need for a "change of direction in U.S.-Russia relations."[111]

In parallel, the Trump campaign had been gaining steam. Despite winning popular support among grassroots conservatives, the campaign struggled to attract political heavyweights in necessary advisory positions. It was most evident that it lacked foreign policy and national security expertise and was heavily criticized for it by the media. Under pressure, in March 2016 Sam Clovis, a senior Trump campaign advisor, hastily conjured together a foreign policy team.[112] Clovis did a Google search on potential candidates and, after finding "no immediate land mines" in their records, vetted them for the advisory positions to the campaign. Clovis later admitted that he and the campaign were "desperate to get the press off our backs." Page, due to his background, was considered the Russian expert among them.[113]

Shortly after Trump revealed the names of his new policy advisors, journalists did their own research on Page and discovered that none of the prominent experts on Russia were aware of him.[114] The Trump campaign press secretary would later explain the reasons behind adding Page as follows:[115]

> *I think there was an understanding that this group [National Security Advisory Committee] was put together when nobody wanted to be associated with our campaign or our candidate . . .*

> I think describing him [Page] as an "adviser" is inaccurate. I don't know who he was advising, but he was not advising the candidate or the policy team. . . . He was just a person whose name got slapped on a list for a committee because we didn't have anybody else.

Page immediately came under media scrutiny due to his seemingly pro-Russian foreign policy positions. Bloomberg highlighted his connections to Gazprom.[116] The *National Review*, a conservative journal, labeled him as an "out-and-out Putinite."[117] They were not wrong. Page's views on US-Russian relations struck a divergent cord from most Western-based Russian analysts and mirrored the Kremlin's position.

Since early 2016, even before joining the Trump team, Carter Page wrote unsolicited emails to Clovis with his views and suggestions for Trump's policy toward Russia. One of the first emails, written in January 2016, included the following:[118]

> I spent the past week in Europe and have been in discussions with some individuals with close ties to the Kremlin. The possible game-changing effect which Mr. Trump could have in bringing the end of the new Cold War that Obama and George W Bush managed to create in recent years has literally brought a new exceptionally high level of optimism in Moscow and across the country. Given the essential strategic position that Russia has in the world as a permanent member of the UN Security Council, etc., the effect of Mr. Trump could be nothing short of monumental. Through my discussions with these high level contacts, it is their belief that a direct meeting in Moscow between Mr Trump and President Putin could be arranged.

During the six months that Page was on the foreign policy team, he repeatedly boasted about his connections in Russia and suggested that candidate Trump should go to Moscow.[119]

PAGE'S SPEECHES IN RUSSIA AND HIS SEPARATION FROM THE CAMPAIGN

The news of Carter Page joining Trump's foreign policy advisory team seemingly put him back on the Kremlin's radar. Shortly after the public announcement of his new position, Page received an invitation to give a graduation commencement speech in Moscow at the New Economic School in July 2016. The campaign cleared him to appear at the event on the condition that Page would only speak as a private person and not as a campaign representative. However, the whole reason why the school was interested in Page, offering to pay for his travels to Moscow, was his access to the Trump campaign.[120]

Carter Page ended up giving speeches at the New Economic School in July and later in December 2016. Each of his appearances was used for Russian propaganda[121] and hyped by local influencers.[122] The Russian media presented Page as a high-level Trump advisor and a "famous American economist."[123] His name appeared[124] in articles alongside Arkady Dvorkovich, the Russian deputy prime minister, and Igor Sechin, the head of Rosneft, Russia's state-owned oil company. Both men are among the most powerful people in Russia. Dvorkovich was present both times that Page went to New Economic School in Moscow,[125] artificially elevating Page's status and creating the optics of two presidential advisors working together to thaw Russian-American relations.

After his trip, Page sent an email to the Trump campaign staff stating that he had received "incredible insights" from meeting Russian officials. Later, when subpoenaed by the Senate Intelligence Committee and asked about those "insights," Page would say in his testimony that he did not remember the high-level encounters and that his statements might "have been an exaggeration."[126] However, when pressed, he would admit that he had met with members of the Russian presidential administration.[127]

Page's July 2016 speech in Russia created[128] additional[129] concerns[130] in the international press. Journalists were curious about what Donald Trump's foreign policy advisor was doing in Moscow at the time when the GRU hackers were attacking the DNC.[131] Later it would be revealed that, in August-September 2016, Page had also traveled to Hungary[132] to meet with an advisor to Viktor Orban,[133] the country's prime minister and a staunch supporter of Vladimir Putin.

Page had a number of unauthorized media appearances as a key Trump advisor that led campaign staff to consider him a liability.[134] On September 25, 2016, the Trump campaign publicly began distancing itself from Carter Page before forcing him off the campaign entirely.[135] The following month, the FBI began surveilling Page.[136] After Trump's electoral victory, Page attempted to join the transition team by reaching out to his campaign contacts, to no avail.[137]

Several months later, Carter Page became one of the focal points of the US government's Russian interference investigations. While many others shunned additional publicity, Page was eager to step into the spotlight. In more than a dozen interviews with news media, Page consistently played coy while denying any wrongdoing.[138] In November 2017 Page testified to the House Intelligence Committee. During the questioning he was elusive, consistently evading direct answers.[139]

Although Carter Page was not charged with any crimes, he undeniably pushed foreign policy views that aligned with or offered benefit to the Kremlin. Like Maria Butina and other Russian agents, throughout 2016 Carter Page advocated for Donald Trump meeting Vladimir Putin in person. He thrust himself into the campaign to build a higher personal profile, and like many others with access to Trump's orbit, he sought to capitalize on it.

THE CULTIVATION OF GEORGE PAPADOPOULOS

In March 2016, along with Carter Page, the Trump campaign added George Papadopoulos to its token foreign policy advisory team.[140] Papadopoulos, an ambitious twenty-eight-year old,[141] positioned himself as an energy expert who focused on the Middle Eastern and Mediterranean regions. However, as Donald Trump signaled that his foreign policy would aim to improve US-Russian relations, Papadopoulos was eager to appear knowledgeable in that area as well despite, as he would later admit, being "a complete wannabe when it came to the U.S.-Russia relationship."[142]

What happened next to Papadopoulos was a prime case example of Russian intelligence tradecraft utilizing[143] "useful idiots,"[144] or unwitting accomplices, to achieve their goals. Papadopoulos was subject to traditional intelligence tactics including cultivation by academics, businessmen, or honey traps of beautiful women attempting to coerce and incentivize for the Kremlin's advantage.

In mid-March 2016, shortly after accepting a role in the Trump campaign's foreign policy team, George Papadopoulos traveled to Rome. There, he was introduced to Joseph Mifsud,[145] a British Maltese professor who was affiliated with a number of European universities[146] and frequently[147] attended[148] the Valdai Discussion Club, a Kremlin-supported think tank that hosts annual gatherings attended by Vladimir Putin. When he learned about Papadopoulos's new role in the Trump campaign, Mifsud embarked on a charm offensive,[149] signaling that he could help Papadopoulos connect to the Russian government. To back his claims, Mifsud introduced Papadopoulos to two Russians, Olga Polonskaya and Ivan Timofeev.[150] The two were supposed to assist in arranging a meeting between Donald Trump and Vladimir Putin.

Mifsud presented Olga Polonskaya as a relative to the Russian president,[151] which Papadopoulos perceived as her being "Putin's niece."[152] Later, running a Google search, Papadopoulos discovered that Putin didn't have any siblings.[153] She most likely served as an attractive face to coordinate between Papadopoulos and whomever she represented on the Russian end. Later Papadopoulos would admit that, in person, Polonskaya barely spoke English, but her text messages were almost fluent, suggesting that likely someone else had been writing them for her. The communication bloomed to the point that the two exchanged over seventy messages in one day in October 2016.[154]

The other person introduced to Papadopoulos, Ivan Timofeev, was an executive at the Russian International Affairs Council (RIAC). Cofounded by the Russian Ministry of Foreign Affairs,[155] RIAC looked more like a wheelhouse of Russian foreign policy. Its board included Vladimir Putin's spokesperson and Russian diplomats[156] while its members were prominent Russian officials, pro-Kremlin academics, businessmen, and media executives.[157]

From March to November 2016, Papadopoulos continued to occasionally meet with Mifsud while also communicating with Polonskaya and Timofeev. The main topics of their discussions were attempts to arrange a meeting between Donald Trump and Vladimir Putin or for Trump's advisors to come to Russia.[158] Papadopoulos, without expertise on Russia yet eager to promote himself within the Trump campaign, picked up on the idea of a meeting between Trump and Putin and started bombarding campaign members with emails advocating for arranging it. His zeal was noticed by and sparked a tacit rivalry with Carter Page, who himself was touting his Russian connections to the Trump campaign. On one call Page told Papadopoulos to "stop showing off."[159] Papadopoulos did not.

In late April 2016, three months before the media first reported on the hack on the Clinton campaign,[160] Mifsud told Papadopoulos that Russia had "dirt" on her. Papadopoulos would later suggest in a FBI interview that he might have passed that knowledge over to his most frequent contact in the campaign, Sam Clovis.[161]

Within a couple of weeks, Papadopoulos also shared that information with Australian diplomats over drinks in London. One of those diplomats reported the story to his superiors, who then contacted the FBI.[162] That report would, in part, trigger an FBI investigation into Papadopoulos, Russian actions during the 2016 election, and the possibility of coordination between the Russian government and the Trump campaign.[163]

By mid-May, after Donald Trump had become the presumptive Republican nominee, Joseph Mifsud made a bold move by pushing himself as a European liaison for the Trump campaign. In his email to Papadopoulos, Mifsud laid out his vision:[164]

1. *We will continue to liaise through you with the Russian counterparts in terms of what is needed for a high level meeting of Mr. Trump with the Russian Federation.*

2. *I will set up interviews for you with IL Giornale and Corriere della Sera in Italy focusing on Mr. Trump's foreign policy perspectives.*

3. *If provided with key speaking/highlighted points I will use them in the next European Council on Foreign Relations meeting to be held in June in The Hague.*

4. *I will liaise with the European Parliament about the possibility of an invitation to Brussels for Mr. Trump.*

5. *Once updated, I can use specific points during the campaign to be turned into articles in the European media—I can also be a central point if you wish to sustain key agreed foreign policy and diplomatic points for the campaign in Europe and the Middle East (I am often asked to chair important debates e.g. the Doha Forum and other fora in Morocco/Bahrain etc.)*

> 6. I am extremely keen to support Mr. Trump's campaign in foreign policy issues with Europe, the Middle East and North Africa—and wish to do so from Europe and also with my links inside the USA (e.g. the Washington Diplomatic community and publications).
>
> 7. If needed, I can also prepare and sign op-eds sustaining Mr. Trump's campaign.
>
> 8. Once the campaign gets started—I would be keen to be on any shows as a "neutral" opinion maker and expert in support of Mr. Trump vis-à-vis global issues.
>
> 9. I am also extremely interested in following Mr. Trump throughout some of his campaign trail and reporting back to European media as an "independent" opinion maker.
>
> 10. I am open to any suggested action plans which the team might wish to make now and the future and to contribute with my knowledge to the campaign—from the inside or the outside.

Mifsud reiterated his requests to serve as a surrogate for the Trump team in July and later in November, right after the election. While pretending to seek to represent the Trump campaign in the European Union, Mifsud's emails suggested that he was more interested in collecting intelligence. In a July email to Papadopoulos, Mifsud wrote that, as a campaign liaison, he "would also need to be briefed periodically on all foreign affairs."[165] If that were to happen, there was no doubt those briefings would end up with the Russian government.

There is no publicly known information on whether Papadopoulos conveyed Mifsud's requests to the campaign. Papadopoulos himself was increasingly on thin ice with some of the campaign members who were getting tired of his unauthorized public comments[166] related to Russia.[167] As a result, some factions of the Trump team tried to sideline Papadopoulos.[168] Despite that infighting, in November 2016 Papadopoulos attempted to join the Trump administration, aiming at a position on the National Security Council or, as a fallback option, the "special envoy and coordinator for international energy affairs."[169]

During that time a person named Sergei Millian, who was the president of the Russian-American Chamber of Commerce[170] and claiming to have "insider knowledge and direct access to the top hierarchy in Russian politics," encouraged Papadopoulos to join Trump's transition team. Previously, Millian had invited Papadopoulos to an energy conference in Moscow and offered to introduce him to "top energy experts in Russia and Europe." Millian also suggested that he could make speaking arrangements for Papadopoulos.[171]

According to Papadopoulos's wife, after Trump's election Millian had even offered

Papadopoulos a business deal that included a thirty-thousand-dollar monthly salary if he joined the Trump transition team. Papadopoulos would later tell the FBI that when he told Millian that he didn't intend to seek employment at Trump's team, Millian's attitude turned from "cordial" to cold.[172] The timing and tone of Millian's words suggested that Russian interests had intended to turn Papadopoulos into an informant.

Shortly after Donald Trump's inauguration in January 2017, Papadopoulos was interviewed by the FBI. During the interview he falsely claimed that he had met Mifsud before joining the Trump campaign.[173] Nine months later he pleaded guilty to lying to the FBI.[174] In September 2018, after working with the Special Counsel, Papadopoulos was sentenced to fourteen days in prison, a $9,500 fine, two hundred hours of community service, and one year of probation.[175] In late December 2020, as Donald Trump was leaving the White House, he pardoned George Papadopoulos.[176]

PAUL MANAFORT

BECOMING A POLITICAL GURU

In March 2016 Donald Trump's campaign hired Paul Manafort, a veteran political consultant and lobbyist, as its convention manager.[177] Within two months he would be promoted to campaign chairman and its chief strategist. He had decades of experience as a political consultant for the Republican establishment and immense technical knowledge of campaigning.[178] His work included multiple presidential campaigns, from Ronald Reagan to Bob Dole.[179]

In the 1980s Manafort rose to be one of the most influential people in Washington, DC. Together with other young and bold political consultants, including Roger Stone, who was previously mentioned in the WikiLeaks "hack and leak" episode, Manafort established an unorthodox method of projecting influence in Washington, DC.[180] Through one of Manafort's firms, his team helped political candidates get elected. Their method was to develop elaborate polling to understand psychological profiles of the electorate and attune their candidate's image and platform. Meanwhile, they sought to discredit opposing candidates.[181] Although standard practice in modern politics, those tactics were a novelty in a world before social media.

Through another firm, also controlled by Manafort, his team started lobbying for corporate interests, reaching out to the same politicians Manafort helped elect, and asking for favors. By doing so, Manafort and his partners revolutionized lobbying, creating a continuous cycle of helping elect officials and then targeting them to advance their corporate clients' interests. In years following, Manafort expanded his lobbying reach to foreign clients, sometimes with unsavory reputations. His firm consulted for foreign autocratic leaders,[182] including presidents for life and rebel militia leaders, becoming known in DC as "the torturers' lobby."[183] Unsurprisingly, the more compromised his clients were, the more they were willing to pay.

Manafort was one of the early architects of the DC swamp, rife with influence peddling for special interests, that Donald Trump would pledge to drain. His 1980s model of lobbying would become increasingly prevalent and later flourish during the Trump era. People who had helped Donald Trump get elected, such as Brian Ballard, would then turn around and lobby his administration.

A DECADE IN UKRAINE

By the mid-2000s fate had brought Paul Manafort to pro-Kremlin oligarchs. Through an heir of the Rothschild banking dynasty, Manafort was introduced to Oleg Deripaska,[184] a Russian aluminum magnate and one of the richest people in the world. Deripaska had amassed his wealth by winning the so-called aluminum wars,[185] a ruthless brawl among businessmen competing for the control of the aluminum industry in early post-Soviet Russia. The fight left a long trail of unexplained deaths[186] that contributed to Deripaska's reputation as an oligarch tied to Russian organized crime.[187]

In 2004, when he met Manafort, Deripaska, whose aluminum empire included businesses worldwide, had a potential problem boiling in Ukraine. The country had just tilted toward the West with the election of a pro-European presidential candidate, Viktor Yushchenko, who had defeated Russia's preferred presidential candidate, Viktor Yanukovych. The election of Yushchenko potentially jeopardized[188] Deripaska's business assets in the country[189] as, while campaigning, the new president had spoken openly about cracking down on Ukraine's endemic corruption.[190]

Deripaska, who was believed[191] to be one of Vladimir Putin's pocket businessmen,[192] aimed to keep the Kremlin's influence in Ukraine intact. So he introduced Manafort to a group of pro-Kremlin Ukrainian oligarchs who were the primary backers of Viktor Yanukovych and his Party of Regions.[193] The party lacked popular support and was deservedly seen as a corrupt pro-Russian "party of oligarchs."[194] As if confirming that image, in July 2005 Yanukovych's Party of Regions signed a partnership agreement with Putin's political party, United Russia.[195] Around that time, with the parliamentary elections in Ukraine approaching, the oligarchs met with Manafort in Moscow[196] and vouched to pay his company $20 million[197] if he could improve the electoral outlook for Viktor Yanukovych and his Party of Regions.

As his first step, Manafort drafted a memo to Deripaska, in which he laid out his vision for Viktor Yanukovych and his party to win using Western political tools and tactics.[198] Aware that Yanukovych was backed by the Kremlin and that his party's victory would benefit Russia, Manafort also stated:[199]

> We are now of the belief that this model can greatly benefit the Putin Government if employed at the correct levels with the appropriate commitment to success . . . [The effort] will be offering a great service that can re-focus, both internally and externally, the policies of the Putin government.

What Manafort was offering to the Kremlin was a road map for a political influence campaign in Ukraine using subtle Western techniques that would not be openly challenged by the West. If the tactics worked in Ukraine, they could be duplicated in any other country where Russia sought to wield its influence.

As Manafort spoke neither Russian nor Ukrainian, he hired a Russian-military-trained linguist, Konstantin Kilimnik, who would later become his protégé as a strategist[200] and his right hand in the region.[201] Manafort reportedly called him a "powerful little dude"[202] as the five-foot-tall[203] Kilimnik apparently had deep access to both the Russian and Ukrainian business elite. Years later the Mueller investigation[204] and the US Senate Intelligence Committee[205] would conclude that Kilimnik was a Russian intelligence officer.

Manafort's meticulously thought-out campaign for modernizing the Party of Regions was effective,[206] winning it 32 percent of the seats within the Ukrainian parliament in 2006.[207] It was an astonishing achievement, considering that in the 2002 parliamentary elections a joint coalition of the Party of Regions and four other parties[208] had gained a meager 12 percent.[209] Paul Manafort's next task was to remake the image of an inarticulate and uncharismatic Viktor Yanukovych and get him elected as Ukraine's president. It was not an easy task, but Manafort managed to polish Yanukovych up by dressing him in Western-style suits[210] and writing eloquent speeches for him.[211] The effort was successful, and Yanukovych won the 2010 presidential election. With Yanukovych in power, Manafort's firms then turned to lobby the EU[212] and the United States[213] on behalf of Yanukovych and his government, albeit without registering with FARA for the US part.[214]

In 2014 a second pro-European democratic revolution occurred in Ukraine. After violent protests against his perceived corruption, Pres. Viktor Yanukovych fled to Russia. The interim government opened an investigation into the fugitive president, and his financial assets worldwide were subsequently frozen. Yanukovych's Party of Regions attempted a comeback under a new name, the Opposition Bloc, with the help of Manafort.[215] However, the oligarchs, who had showered him with over $75 million before the revolution,[216] couldn't pay him for his last job.[217] By 2015 Paul Manafort's political machine in Ukraine was shattered, his benefactor was in exile, and his revenue stream had dried out.

FROM POLITICAL INFLUENCE TO BUSINESS ENDEAVORS

While working for Viktor Yanukovych and the Party of Regions, Paul Manafort's team also provided political consulting services directly to Russian oligarch Oleg Deripaska. According to the Senate Intelligence Report from 2020:[218]

> *Manafort and Deripaska used to meet regularly and had a number of different projects ongoing. This included a political influence program which Deripaska financed. As part of this program, Manafort worked on influence efforts in Central Asia, Cyprus, Georgia, Guinea, Montenegro, and elsewhere in Europe. . . .*
>
> *Deripaska used an offshore entity to pay Manafort and his firm tens of millions of dollars for this and other work, including at least $25 million in 2008 alone.*

However, Manafort's relationship with Deripaska evolved beyond political consulting and into business deals. In 2007 Manafort created an investment fund called Pericles, which was registered in the Cayman Islands. Its sole investor was a company that belonged to Oleg Deripaska.[219] The fund's reported purpose was to make investments throughout Eastern Europe, but its only investment was $19 million into a telecommunications company in Odesa, Ukraine.[220]

In 2008, due to the global financial crisis, Deripaska's former $28 billion net worth[221] plummeted to $3.5 billion,[222] forcing the oligarch to ask the Kremlin for a bailout.[223] As a result, Deripaska pressured Manafort to return the $19 million[224] he had invested into Pericles.[225] Either unable or unwilling to pay back, Manafort went into hiding from Deripaska for years.[226] Having no luck in retrieving the money amicably, in December 2014 Deripaska filed a legal petition in a Cayman Island court accusing Manafort and his team of expropriating the $19 million.[227] It was clear that Deripaska wasn't going to let go of the debt.

Within months Manafort, citing emotional breakdown, surrendered himself into a psychiatric hospital in Arizona. He found himself at the bottom of a financial and emotional well,[228] with his political consulting income from Ukraine halted and him owing millions to a Russian oligarch connected to organized crime. He urgently needed a solution.

THE TROJAN HORSE WITHIN THE TRUMP CAMPAIGN

To remedy his situation, Paul Manafort grew determined to join Donald Trump's presidential campaign. Manafort had an apartment in Trump Tower in New York and was acquainted with the candidate. They weren't close, but they had common friends, to whom Manafort reached out in early 2016 to get their help in securing a position within the campaign. He offered to work for free, explaining the move to his team that the work within the Trump campaign, albeit unpaid, would be "good for business,"²²⁹ resurrecting Manafort's business profile in America and guaranteeing big future paydays as a political consultant. If Manafort could get Trump elected, he would have a successful track record within the most sophisticated election system, the United States. With Trump's victory Manafort could not only restore his relevance but also potentially get any presidential candidate in the world as a client.

Immediately after joining the campaign, Manafort sent memos about his appointment on Trump's team to his former Ukrainian colleague Konstantin Kilimnik for him to relay the news to the Ukrainian oligarchs and most importantly to his former patron Oleg Deripaska. In the memos Manafort informed the oligarchs about his new position and relayed "his willingness to consult on Ukrainian politics in the future."²³⁰ The subtext was that with his new job Manafort had gained more leverage, which could be used to help him reconcile his old debts and maybe even win more contracts.

Like in the good old Ukrainian days, Konstantin Kilimnik reentered Manafort's orbit, acting as Manafort's liaison to the oligarchs. Shortly after sending out the memos, Manafort asked Kilimnik how they could use Manafort's new role to "get whole" with Deripaska.²³¹ In early May 2016, the two met in New York for a brainstorming session.²³²

After that meeting Manafort directed his deputy to periodically give polling and campaign strategy information to Kilimnik,²³³ which Kilimnik reportedly passed to Russian intelligence services.²³⁴ That information included Trump's performance in eighteen swing states, broken down city by city.²³⁵ It was incredibly valuable data. Equipped with that insight, the Kremlin could target social media users from those cities by deploying its internet trolls and manicuring their messaging at a local level to sway them to vote for Trump.

Within his communications with Kilimnik, Manafort also stated his willingness to provide a private briefing to Deripaska regarding the Trump campaign, with a tacit understanding that Deripaska would pass over the information to the Kremlin or the Russian intelligence. It appeared that the polling data Manafort provided was appreciated, and by early August, Kilimnik informed him that Deripaska's lawsuit regarding the $19 million "had been dismissed."²³⁶

Throughout the campaign Manafort extensively communicated with Kilimnik, sharing his thoughts and ideas on the Trump campaign strategy. Kilimnik shared some of those ideas with his other associates, asserting that if Donald Trump followed Manafort's guidance, he had a real chance of becoming the president.²³⁷

Kilimnik also confided with an associate that Manafort had a "clever plan of screwing Clinton." Years later, while piecing together the Russian interference campaign, the Senate Intelligence Committee would conclude that Kilimnik might "have been connected to the GRU's hack and leak operation" related to the DNC and Hillary Clinton's emails.²³⁸ Adding more weight to that conclusion, journalists would discover that in March 2016, around the time when Russian hackers gained access to the Clinton campaign emails, and when Manafort joined the Trump team, he made a strange visit to the WikiLeaks founder who had been hiding within the Ecuadorian embassy in London to avoid extradition to the US.[239] Only a few months later, WikiLeaks would begin releasing troves of emails from Hillary Clinton's campaign.

Besides Trump campaign polling data, Manafort and Kilimnik discussed a "Ukrainian Peace Plan"[240] that could allow the Kremlin to turn Russian-occupied areas in eastern Ukraine into a semiautonomous region, with Viktor Yanukovych as its leader. All that was needed for the implementation of the plan was a "wink (or a slight push)" from Donald Trump and the United States positioning itself as an unbiased mediator. According to Kilimnik's email to Manafort,[241]

> *DT could have peace in Ukraine basically within a few months after inauguration.*

Later Manafort would admit that the proposed "peace plan" was, in fact, an attempt for Russia to secure "backdoor" influence in Ukraine. After running initial polling, Manafort and his team would conclude that eastern Ukrainians were not fond of Yanukovych, and the endeavor fell apart.[242]

THE RECKONING

In the middle of August 2016, the *New York Times* published a story about ledgers that contained handwritten accounts of cash paid out by the Kremlin-backed Ukrainian Party of Regions. Manafort's name reportedly appeared in them twenty-two times, with payments that totaled $12.7 million over five years.[243] The Trump campaign, which by that time had also been deflecting press reports about Carter Page and George Papadopoulos's Russian connections, seemingly could not take more accusations of its exposure to the Kremlin. Shortly after the revelation, Paul Manafort was forced to resign from the campaign.[244] However, he remained in contact with Donald Trump and his inner circle, sending suggestions to capitalize on the WikiLeaks releases, speaking to Donald Trump on election night, and emailing Don Jr. claims that Ukraine was the one interfering in the 2016 US presidential election. After the election Manafort lobbied behind the scenes to install his contacts into the Trump administration.[245]

By mid-2017 the circle had started closing around Manafort and his activities were investigated by the Special Counsel team. In June 2017 Manafort retroactively registered at FARA, declaring his lobbying work for Ukraine from years ago.[246] The following month the FBI executed a search warrant at his house in Virginia, seeking his financial documents.[247]

In October 2017 Paul Manafort was indicted[248] and a year later was found guilty of multiple crimes,[249] including tax fraud and bank fraud related to his work in Ukraine. The Special Counsel offered a cooperation agreement that Manafort accepted. As part of that agreement, Manafort admitted his illegal foreign lobbying[250] and pleaded guilty to money laundering, conspiracy against the United States, and conspiracy to obstruct justice. However, Manafort was later found to be "repeatedly lying"[251] in his testimony and was denied the benefits of his plea deal. At the end of this saga, Paul Manafort received a 7.5-year prison sentence[252] along with an asset forfeiture estimated to be worth over $42 million.[253]

In December 2020, during his last days in the White House, Donald Trump would pardon Manafort[254] and order the return of some of his previously confiscated assets.[255] Manafort's Ukrainian Russian colleague Konstantin Kilimnik would be indicted by the Special Counsel[256] and sanctioned by the US government[257] but remain out of US reach, residing in a safe haven near Moscow.[258]

Despite Manafort's short stint within the Trump campaign, he had by far, the highest value for the Kremlin. By the time he resigned, Manafort had become Donald Trump's campaign manager, who knew every minute detail of the strategy with complete access to ever-changing internal campaign polling data. Unlike Carter Page and George Papadopoulos, Manafort had previously worked for years with Kremlin surrogates and was well aware of how Russian intelligence and political influence operations worked. And yet to have his multimillion-dollar debts written off, Paul Manafort gave the Russian government valuable insight into the Trump campaign during the 2016 election.

THE RUSSIAN ENVOYS

AMBASSADOR KISLYAK

Immediately after the 2016 election, the Kremlin deployed its henchmen to the United States to establish back-channel communications with the Trump transition team.[259] Between November 2016 and January 2017, a stream of people that included Russian officials, oligarchs, and US businessmen who had worked in Russia attempted to make inroads to the Trump transition team.[260] One of their apparent targets was Trump's incoming national security advisor, Michael Flynn,[261] who had already had previous contact with Russian government officials.

In 2013, while serving as the director of the Defense Intelligence Agency (DIA), he had traveled to Moscow for an official meeting with his Russian counterpart at Russian military intelligence headquarters. The meeting was arranged with the help of the Russian ambassador to the United States, Sergey Kislyak. A year later Flynn was fired from his position at the DIA[262] for temper issues.[263] He then transitioned to the private sector, providing consulting[264] services.[265]

In December 2015 Flynn returned to Moscow,[266] where he gave a paid speech[267] at the tenth anniversary gala for the Kremlin's state-owned propaganda outlet Russia

Today (RT).²⁶⁸ At the dinner he was seated right next to the Russian president, Vladimir Putin.²⁶⁹ As a former military official, Michael Flynn was required to obtain a prior approval from the Pentagon for his RT appearance and the $45,000 speaker's fee that came with it.²⁷⁰ He failed to do so.²⁷¹ After his trip to Moscow, Flynn remained in contact with Russian ambassador Kislyak.²⁷²

In late November 2016, Sergey Kislyak walked into Trump Tower in New York for a meeting with Michael Flynn and Trump's son-in-law, Jared Kushner. Kislyak spoke about a possibility of Russian generals briefing the Trump transition team on Syria while Kushner conveyed the incoming administration's interest in resetting US-Russian relations. However, Kushner, sensing that Kislyak did not have the direct line to Putin, asked to be introduced to someone who did.²⁷³

If Kushner avoided further contacts with the ambassador, Flynn was more open. After the Trump Tower meeting, Sergey Kislyak and Michael Flynn spoke again by phone in December 2016,²⁷⁴ shortly after the Obama administration had announced sanctions on Russia for its interference in the US election.²⁷⁵ During the call Flynn attempted to smooth things over. He suggested to Kislyak that Moscow not further escalate tensions so that the two countries could "have a better conversation" after Donald Trump's inauguration.²⁷⁶ By doing so, Flynn mirrored the president-elect's message that downplayed the importance of Russia's attack on the 2016 election. It also was a sign that the president-elect and his national security advisor didn't see the importance of the Kremlin's actions that wreaked havoc on the United States. After all, Russia's efforts seemed to have helped Trump get into the White House.

In the same call, Ambassador Kislyak also relayed the Kremlin's messages to the incoming administration. One was to arrange a video call between Vladimir Putin and Donald Trump the day after the inauguration so that Putin could both congratulate Trump on his electoral victory and discuss the Syrian Civil War. Kislyak's other message extended an invitation to the Trump administration to send representatives to the Russian-sponsored Syrian peace talks in Astana, Kazakhstan. As described in chapter 16, the Kremlin had gathered a coalition as an alternative to the existing Western one that focused not so much on the elimination of ISIS but instead on coordinating efforts to keep the Syrian dictator, Bashar al-Assad, in power. Obama administration officials had not been invited.²⁷⁷ Days after the Kislyak-Flynn call, the Russian president issued an uncharacteristic public statement proclaiming that Russia would abstain from any additional response to US sanctions.²⁷⁸

On January 12, 2017, Kislyak followed up with Flynn about the Astana talks offer, to which Flynn responded that a team was being assembled for the trip.²⁷⁹ However, no American officials would go to the Russian-led summit²⁸⁰ because that same day the *Washington Post* published an article about Flynn's clandestine calls with the Russian ambassador,²⁸¹ turning up the heat under the incoming Trump administration. The US media reacted²⁸² by²⁸³ questioning²⁸⁴ whether Flynn, as a member of the transition team, had a right to speak on behalf of the US government, let alone suggest undoing the current administration's position toward Russia's interference. When brought into the spotlight, Flynn denied discussing US sanctions with Kislyak both in his statements to the press[285] and privately to the incoming vice president, Mike Pence,[286] putting himself and the administration in a compromising position vis-à-vis the Kremlin.

Flynn repeated his false narrative during the interview with FBI agents that happened shortly after Trump's inauguration.[287] The problem for Flynn was that, as the FBI had regularly surveilled the Russian ambassador, they had a recording of the call between Kislyak and Flynn[288] that proved that he wasn't telling the truth to the investigators.[289] By lying to the FBI, the national security advisor committed a federal crime. Flynn's plight was further complicated by an ongoing FBI investigation into his potential ties to the Turkish government[290] that started following his pro-Turkish op-ed[291] on the Election Day that was mentioned in chapter 3.

In February 2017, twenty four days into his tenure in the Trump administration, Michael Flynn would be fired from his position as the national security advisor to the president of the United States.[292] After that, Flynn's career and reputation would only go downhill. He would retroactively file FARA registration with the Department of Justice for his Turkish lobbying[293] and lie about details within it.[294] He would also plead guilty to lying to the FBI about his conversations with Kislyak[295] and agree to cooperate with Robert Mueller's investigation into Russian interference.[296] The judge overseeing Flynn's case would later state that Flynn "sold his country out,"[297] apparently referring to his meetings with Turkish interests and their monetary offers. In mid-2019 Flynn would change his attorneys, hiring a new lawyer, Sidney Powell,[298] who would aid Flynn in attempting to withdraw from his guilty plea.[299] Shortly thereafter, with William Barr becoming the new attorney general, the Justice Department would unsuccessfully[300] attempt[301] to drop Michael Flynn's case for opaque reasons.

THE OLIGARCHS

A month after the US election, Putin convened a meeting[302] with a group of fifty Russian oligarchs[303] and "suggested" that they establish contact with the Trump transition team to prevent any potential US sanctions on the oligarchs' businesses. As Putin's "suggestions" were considered veiled directives, the failure to follow through on them could have negative consequences.[304] To avoid that, several oligarchs embarked on a quest to find inroads to the Trump transition team.

Some of them came close to Donald Trump. One of the oligarchs had a meeting with Trump's son-in law, Jared[305] Kushner,[306] in December 2016. Another oligarch used an intermediary to hire Trump's private attorney, Michael Cohen,[307] for consulting. Other oligarchs combed through their network to find people to connect with Trump's inner circle but hit a wall as the Russian interference investigations in the United States gained speed.[308]

However, one of Putin's envoys, Kirill Dmitriev, seemed to advance the most. Dmitriev oversaw Russia's $10 billion sovereign wealth fund (RDIF)[309] and used his investment contacts to gain access to Trump's transition team. Dmitriev contacted George[310] Nader,[311] an informal emissary of the United Arab Emirates and Saudi Arabia, to set up a meeting. Nader then introduced Dmitriev to Erik Prince,[312] the former owner of a private military company[313] that had numerous US government contracts. At the time, Prince had been acting as an unofficial surrogate[314] and advisor[315] to the Trump campaign.

Several days before Donald Trump's inauguration, Dmitriev, Nader, and Prince met in the Seychelles islands. Dmitriev wasn't impressed with Prince and felt that he was not high enough in the transition team to affect policy.[316] Prince, on his side, reported the discussions to Steve Bannon,[317] Trump's chief strategist. Later Bannon would deny knowing anything about the meeting in the Seychelles islands. Despite his denials, the data from his mobile service provider showed that Prince and Bannon exchanged "dozens of messages" during that period.[318] However, both of their phones contained no text messages[319] before[320] March 2017.

In parallel to the meeting with Prince, Kirill Dmitriev hedged his bets by reaching out to Rick Gerson, an equity fund manager and a friend of Jared Kushner. Dmitriev caught Gerson's attention by dangling a possibility of a joint investment project between the RDIF and Gerson's fund. Over several phone calls, the two discussed conditions that would need to be in place for a joint project to happen. As part of their discussion, the two developed a "reconciliation plan" for the United States and Russia. On January 17, 2017, Dmitriev consolidated those thoughts into one text and sent it over to Gerson.[321] That text, presented below, shed some light on why the Kremlin had been so relentlessly trying to establish a contact with the Trump team:

Resending the 5 point plan with proper numbering of points :):

Rick, here are some preliminary thoughts (including yours:)) on US Russia cooperation per our earlier discussion—we believe that is [sic] is a win-win approach. I plan to be in the US January 27-30 to further discuss with you and the most senior relevant people from the US side:

1. *Jointly fighting terrorism and significantly enhancing our coordination in that area.*
   - *setting up military coordination and joint actions in Syria*
   - *resuming work of intelligence agencies of info sharing on terrorism*
   - *a joint special forces mission where together US and Russia takes out a key ISIS person or place or frees an area then announces it after*
   - *a massive joint humanitarian effort in Syria. A joint project to fund and build hospitals and emergency medical centers in Syria in both rebel and*

> govt areas or at least to jointly flood both areas with medical supplies and basic food. Especially medical and nutrition for children

2. *A serious anti-WMD joint effort to reduce WMD by US and Russia and prevent WMD terrorism across nuclear, biological, and chemical weapons. Jointly going after and reducing the odds of nuclear terrorism security as the profound risk to the world. Rick is involved with the Nuclear Threat Initiative which Warren Buffett funds and is chaired by former Senator Sam Nunn who was chairman of the armed services committee. This group already has high level Russian involvement so it's an easy place to collaborate in a high profile way.*

3. *Developing win win economic and investment initiatives that will be supported by both electorates.*
   - *a visit by top US businesses to Russia to highlight existing US successes in Russia and joint future opportunities;*
   - *joint RDIF fund with OPIC to support US investment in Russia to make US businesses competitive vs subsidized Chinese businesses in Russia*
   - *Russian company builds a plant with RDIF financing to serve the US market in the US Midwest creating real jobs for a hard hit area with high unemployment. US production by foreign companies a focus of the new administration*
   - *highlighting benefits of US Russia business cooperation through media*

4. *Having an honest and open and continual dialogue on differences and concerns*
   - *resolving Ukraine crises through fulfillment of Minsk agreements and ensuring Ukraine fulfills its obligations*
   - *working group between the State Department and Russian Ministry of Foreign affairs to address key differences*

5. *Ensuring there is proper communication and trust among all of the key people from each side*
   - *a small group with 2–3 people from each side authorized to finalize an action plan for a major improvement in the US Russia relationship*
   - *coordination across major agencies and government bodies to achieve tangible impact in the next 9–12 months*
   - *well prepared meeting between the two leaders with several breakthroughs on key issues as per above.*

At first glance, if looked at as a stand-alone document, the plan could seem to propose noble pursuits. However, when evaluated within the context of other things that the Kremlin and its operatives were doing in the United States and worldwide at the time, one could spot a number of red flags.

As Dmitriev acted at the direction of the Russian president, it is safe to believe that these points were approved by Vladimir Putin. At the time when Dmitriev sent this plan to Gerson, on January 17, 2017, Russia was preparing for the Astana talks, which would begin a week later with the purpose of keeping the Syrian dictator, Bashar al-Assad, in power. As mentioned previously, the Kremlin had been supporting Assad for years, attacking civilian targets, such as hospitals and markets in rebel-held territory.[322] With that context Russia's offers for a joint humanitarian effort with the United States sounded hypocritical at best.

The next point from Dmitriev's plan, about a large investment into a plant in the US Midwest, could indeed create jobs. However, it would also provide leverage for Russian interests to influence local lawmakers, which, in turn, could affect US-Russia relations.

The following phrase of the proposal focused on "resolving" the conflict in Ukraine. When juxtaposed with Konstantin Kilimnik's "Ukraine peace plan," it showed how disingenuous Dmitriev's plan was. As mentioned previously, Kilimnik's plan, which he discussed with Paul Manafort, aimed for the Kremlin to take over eastern Ukraine and install Viktor Yanukovych as its ruler. Dmitriev's stated plan, fulfilling the Minsk agreements, would have the same impact, effectively giving Russia a veto over Ukraine's foreign and domestic policy.

Rick Gerson, who was seemingly unaware of the broader context of Russia's actions, adapted Dmitriev's message into a formal document, then gave it to Jared Kushner, who, in turn, passed it to Steve Bannon and Rex Tillerson, Trump's secretary of state. It's not known whether Bannon or Tillerson responded to the proposal; however, Gerson's communication with Dmitriev ended by the end of March 2017 as their investment project seemed to stall.[323]

Kirill Dmitriev and other oligarchs before him were yet another part of the Kremlin's multilayered disruptive strategy, which is laid out in figure 8. Through a combined push of multiple cyberattacks, industrial-scale disinformation operations on social media, and dozens[324] of clandestine intermediaries,[325] the Kremlin worked to elevate Donald Trump and provide Russia an opportunity to reset relations with the United States in its favor. A challenge to that reset occurred when, in December 2016, US intelligence concluded that Russia had systematically interfered in the US election[326] and the FBI started probing the Kremlin's actions. Trump would react by continuously criticizing the investigation[327] and trying to hinder it.[328] After the revelations both the House and the Senate Intelligence Committees had multiple open- and closed-door hearings on the subject.

During one of those hearings, then FBI director James Comey confirmed that the agency had been looking into potential coordination between Russia and the Trump campaign.[329] Shortly thereafter, President Trump fired Comey[330] in an attempt to halt the probe. However, by doing so, he triggered the appointment of Robert Muller, who would become the special counsel to oversee the investigation into both Russia's actions and potential cooperation between the Kremlin and the Trump campaign.[331]

One would think that the DOJ probe would curb the Kremlin's malicious activities. That couldn't be farther from the truth. Under the spotlight the Kremlin simply redirected its influence. It was hardly a coincidence that in early 2017 Russian-connected oligarchs Mubariz Mansimov and Farkhad Akhmedov, who appeared to represent Turkish interests, met with Lev Parnas in an attempt to access Trump's orbit. Neither they nor Lev Parnas would be mentioned in the Mueller investigation[332] or the Senate intelligence reports[333] about the Russian interference in the 2016 US election. However, they played a part in the next wave of the Kremlin's influence operations in the United States that Russia now wielded through proxy countries.

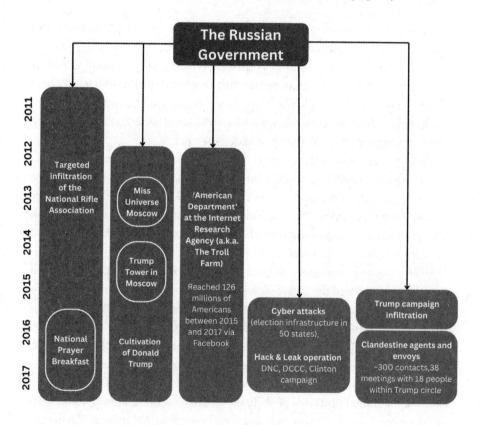

FIGURE 8. LAYERS OF RUSSIAN INFLUENCE IN THE UNITED STATES, 2011–2017

238 THE PERSUASION GAME

CHAPTER 20

THE STREAMS OF INFLUENCE

THE EVENTFUL YEAR

The 2016 US election cycle was starkly different from previous ones. The temperature of the political discourse online was reaching the boiling point. The country was simmering with rallies supporting opposing candidates.

In the background Russia was waging its massive election interference operation, further electrifying the already charged air. Kremlin trolls were methodically spreading disinformation and sowing divide among Americans both on social media and on the streets. Russian military intelligence hacked and released troves of emails that discredited the Democratic Party and its presidential candidate, Hillary Clinton.

The main reason for the Kremlin's cyber wrath against the United States was the sanctions imposed by America and its Western allies on Russia after its invasion of Ukraine and the annexation of the Crimean Peninsula in 2014. Those sanctions undermined Russia's economy, thereby putting a strain on Vladimir Putin's image in Russia.

Russia's autocratic allies, Turkey and Venezuela, had their own wish lists in the United States. As laid out in Part I of this book, surviving a coup attempt, the Turkish president Recep Tayyip Erdogan sought to have the man he blamed for its organization, Fethullah Gülen, extradited from the United States to Turkey. Erdogan also wanted back Reza Zarrab, the key defendant in the SDNY money-laundering case that implicated the Turkish president and his family members.

Meanwhile, on the other side of the world, the Venezuelan president Nicolas Maduro had been facing calls to resign. With the country's economy in free fall, large crowds were protesting perceived corruption, endemic inflation, and food shortages. Several of his cabinet officials had been sanctioned by the United States for human rights violations. Some had their foreign assets frozen and visas to America restricted.[1] The Maduro government sought to have those sanctions and restrictions lifted.

In October 2016 the presidents of Russia, Turkey, and Venezuela gathered in Istanbul for an energy summit, which was described in chapter 16. After that event the three countries, united by their shared loathing of America, increased their cooperation to counter US pressure in their respective areas of interest. The Russian state oil company, Rosneft, provided a $1.5 billion loan to its Venezuelan counterpart, the PDVSA, which used 49.9 percent of its US subsidiary Citgo as a collateral.[2] Turkey, turning away from its Western partners, found a common cause with Russia in Syria.

On November 8, 2016, Russia, Turkey, Venezuela, and other foreign countries that had faced pressure under the Obama administration received news that brought them a prospect that could turn the tides. The American public elected Donald Trump as their president.

DEEPENING THE SWAMP

Immediately after Donald Trump's election victory, foreign powers started seeking inroads to his transition team. As Trump started fundraising for his inauguration, various foreign players seized the opportunity to secure tickets to the festivities by making large donations[3] either directly or through[4] intermediaries.[5]

In late December 2016, three weeks after the Venezuelan PDVSA had secured a $1.5 billion loan from Russian Rosneft, the PDVSA's subsidiary in the United States Citgo donated $500,000 to Donald Trump's inauguration, although the firm reportedly had not contributed to previous presidential inaugurations.[6] A couple of months later, on behalf of the Venezuelan government, Citgo and its intermediaries would lay the groundwork for a $50 million lobbying contract with a former congressman from Florida, David Rivera.[7]

Another large donation of $900,000 to Trump's inaugural committee came from Imaad Zuberi,[8] the "mercenary" fundraiser described in chapter 4. He would later admit that part of the donation funds came from foreign sources and would be convicted of FARA violations.[9]

One of the people who paid Imaad Zuberi to obtain tickets to the inauguration was Murat Güzel,[10] an executive at two Turkish cultural groups in the United States who was mentioned in Part I of this book. Güzel reportedly paid $50,000 to Zuberi for tickets, which did not materialize. Years later, while under investigation by the SDNY regarding his donation to the Trump inauguration, Zuberi would write a backdated refund check to Güzel to make it look like it was issued before the SDNY subpoena.[11]

In contrast, Zuberi was able to obtain a ticket for his more prominent Turkish connection, the country's foreign minister, Mevlut Cavusoglu.[12] Just before Donald Trump's inauguration, Mevlut Cavusoglu had met with Lev Parnas, Mubariz

Mansimov, and Brian Ballard to discuss a lobbying contract between Turkey and Ballard Partners.[13] The Turkish foreign minister also attended an inaugural breakfast meeting at the Trump International Hotel[14] on January 18, 2017, where Michael Flynn, the incoming national security advisor, and Rep. Devin Nunes, the chair of the House Committee on Intelligence, were present.[15]

The inauguration events were also attended by Lev Parnas, who claimed to have obtained his tickets through Brian Ballard,[16] the vice-chairman of the inaugural committee. Parnas also managed to secure tickets for Mubariz Mansimov, an Azerbaijani oligarch with ties to Turkish president Erdogan who was allegedly implicated in Reza Zarrab's money-laundering scandal.[17] Another person accompanying Parnas and his family to the inauguration was Roman Nasirov,[18] then head of Ukraine's tax service who will be described in more detail later in this chapter. At one VIP inaugural ball, Parnas apparently connected with more powerful people, including other oligarchs from post-Soviet countries.

Lev Parnas's connection to Mubariz Mansimov would soon lead to the introduction to Farkhad Akhmedov,[19] a Russian Azerbaijani oligarch and a former Russian senator. In March 2017 the two would attend a VIP retreat for RNC donors after Parnas had donated $33,400 to the committee.[20] Cloaked as a Turkish-Azerbaijani envoy, Akhmedov would mingle with prominent GOP donors at a time when other Russian oligarchs were stonewalled due to the FBI's investigation into election interference.

Another interesting example of a donor connected to foreign nationals was an Iraqi American businessman named Wadie Habboush. His family's energy consulting and investment company, the Habboush Group, did business both in the United States and Turkey.[21] In January 2017 Habboush's father donated $334,000 to the Republican National Committee and $666,000 to Trump's inauguration, which were reportedly the elder Habboush's first political contributions in the United States.[22] Those donations opened the doors to Trump's inaugural ball[23] and the RNC donors' retreat, which the younger Habboush attended.[24]

After the inauguration, in early February 2017, Habboush would use his connections to randomly[25] appear[26] at the White House to meet with National Security Council officials. The following day he would sit down[27] with Trump's senior advisor, Steve Bannon. During the meetings Habboush would claim to have connections to Venezuelan president Maduro and the country's minister of foreign affairs[28] and advocate for the easing of US sanctions on Venezuela.[29]

Similar to Parnas, Habboush would bring to the RNC donor event a Turkish envoy, a construction mogul named Emrullah Turanli.[30] He was one of President Erdogan's "closest associates"[31] and among the high-profile businessmen who were[32] arrested[33] during the December 2013 corruption scandal in Turkey in connection to Reza Zarrab's bribery and money-laundering scheme. As such, similar to Erdogan, Turanli might have been equally interested in halting Zarrab's criminal case in the United States.

Notably, there was a common thread between Lev Parnas, Farkhad Akhmedov, and Wadie Habboush. Each of them peddled the interests of not one but several countries, overlapping between Russia, Turkey, and Venezuela. The presence of those three intermediaries at high-level political events in the United States gave the impression that those countries, which had already moved to form an informal autocratic alliance, also tried to cross-promote their interests to Donald Trump's White House in a seemingly coordinated fashion. That makes sense, considering that the reports of Russian interference investigations were gaining more public coverage in the beginning of Donald Trump's presidency.

However, at the time of inauguration, there were some Russians and Kremlin proxies who had managed to get invitations to Trump's inaugural festivities. For example, Maria Butina, the Russian spy cloaked as a gun activist, attended one of the balls with her GOP-connected boyfriend, Paul Erickson.[34] Paul Manafort, the ousted Trump campaign manager, attended the events,[35] as well as his former patron Serhiy Lyovochkin,[36] one of the Ukrainian oligarchs[37] who had previously financed his political consulting work in Ukraine.[38] Manafort's protégé, Russian intelligence agent Konstantin Kilimnik, also obtained tickets[39] to one of the balls through a straw donor[40] but decided[41] to skip[42] the event at the last moment. Natalia Veselnitskaya, the lawyer who had met with Donald Trump Jr. and Jared Kushner at Trump Tower in the summer of 2016, was seen at an inaugural party hosted by Rep. Dana Rohrabacher (R-CA).[43]

Not everyone who sought to attend Trump events was able to. There was Pavel Fuks, a Russian Ukrainian oligarch with large business interests in Russia who had paid $200,000 to a lobbyist for inauguration tickets[44] but was apparently duped and instead had to watch the ceremony from a bar in Washington, DC.[45] Months later Fuks would hire a better-connected person, Rudy Giuliani,[46] ostensibly to lobby for the Ukrainian city of Kharkiv in the United States.[47]

These numerous attempts to gain access were a small glimpse of all the foreign outreaches to people within Trump's orbit. Those who were closest to the president stood to benefit the most and sought to streamline the influence peddling. For instance, a month after the inauguration, Colony NorthStar, an investment firm founded by Thomas Barrack, the head of Trump's inaugural committee, developed a strategy to connect foreign businesses to the US government.[48] The memo prepared by Barrack's firm stated:[49]

> "Contact"—"Cultivation"—"Conversion" should be the mantra and objective of Colony NorthStar's international program in DC and internationally;
>
> Building a subtle brand in DC and internationally is yet another cornerstone needed for the DC operations. The key is to strategically cultivate domestic and international relations while avoiding any appearance of lobbying. Done properly the international

> program can be the fundamental building block that ties all of the pieces of the Washington, DC, program together.

Another person from the inaugural committee, Brian Ballard, established a Washington, DC, office for his lobbying firm and signed a record number of corporate and foreign clients within its first year.[50] He would later be described as the "most powerful lobbyist" in Trump's Washington.[51]

Pres. Donald Trump, who had pledged to drain the political swamp of interest peddling,[52] instead provided oxygen for the pay-for-play lobbyists and their clients.[53]

ALL THE WAYS TO GIULIANI AND PARNAS

TURKISH INTERESTS

As described in Part I of this book, Turkish interests had been cultivating people close to Donald Trump even before the election. In the fall of 2016, Turkish intermediaries had discussed with Michael Flynn and James Woolsey, the former CIA director who was the advisor to Trump's transition team, the possibility of an extrajudicial extraction of Fethullah Gülen from Pennsylvania and his delivery to Turkey.[54] By the end of the year, the Turks persuaded Flynn to publish an op-ed openly critical of Gülen.[55] They also reportedly offered the incoming national security advisor $15 million for his assistance to have the cleric extradited to Turkey.[56] However, by mid-January 2017 Flynn's position in the White House was becoming increasingly tenuous as the reports of his clandestine calls with the Russian ambassador started appearing in the press. By mid-February Flynn was fired, and the Turkish intermediaries needed to find another insider within the Trump orbit.

Rudy Giuliani became that person. Within days of Flynn's firing, Giuliani was on a plane flying to Turkey to privately meet with President Erdogan to discuss a "diplomatic solution" for the release of Reza Zarrab from US government custody.[57] On March 1, 2017, after Giuliani's trip to Turkey, Greenberg Traurig, where he worked at the time, signed a direct lobbying contract with the Turkish government.[58] Previously, the firm had served as a lobbying subcontractor to another one that provided services to Turkey. At the end of March, it was revealed that Giuliani had joined Reza Zarrab's already expansive legal team.[59]

Meanwhile, Lev Parnas, Mubariz Mansimov, and Farkhad Akhmedov had been serving as intermediaries between Brian Ballard and Turkish officials. In May 2017 Ballard Partners signed a lobbying contract with the Turkish government. In August of that year, the firm also added Halkbank,[60] the bank used by Reza Zarrab in his money-laundering scheme, as its client.

While the Turkish government gained access to two influential lobbying firms,

Rudy Giuliani and Lev Parnas found themselves in positions to enable clandestine high-level access to policymakers in Washington, DC.

VENEZUELAN INTERESTS

As mentioned in chapter 8, Rudy Giuliani and Lev Parnas would become part of a secret call with the Venezuelan president Nicolas Maduro. However, there were many other interconnected events that preceded that call.

The Maduro government entrusted a Venezuelan media mogul named Raul Gorrín to set up influence channels in the United States. In February 2017 Gorrín reached out to a former Florida congressman, David Rivera. By March 7, 2017, Rivera had prepared a draft for a $50 million lobbying contract between his firm and the US-based PDVSA subsidiary Citgo[61] and sent it to Gorrín for him to pass it over to the Venezuelans.[62] After several iterations, in late March 2017 Rivera's firm, Interamerican Consulting, signed the contract for unspecified "strategic consulting services" with PDV USA, another American subsidiary of the PDVSA.[63] Five years later Rivera would be arrested for obscuring the true nature of his services and failing to report his representation of Venezuelan government interests to the DOJ as required by law.[64] Rivera's indictment would argue that although Rivera signed a contract with a US subsidiary of the Venezuelan state oil company, his actions were, in fact, directed by the Venezuelan president and his government. The indictment would also state:[65]

> *The ultimate goal of these efforts was to garner political support in the United States for a normalization of relations between the United States and Venezuela, to include resolving a legal dispute between U.S. Oil Company 1 and Venezuela and preventing the United States from imposing additional economic sanctions against President Maduro and other members of his regime.*

"U.S. Oil Company 1" was most likely Exxon Mobil, a Texas-based global oil conglomerate that had previously done extensive business in Venezuela until its government decided to nationalize Exxon's assets.[66]

Immediately after signing the contract, in early April 2017, Rivera and his associate arranged a meeting between Texas congressman Pete Sessions,[67] who represented the district where Exxon was headquartered, and Venezuela's foreign minister in New York. After the meeting Rivera wrote to Sessions that the Venezuelan "President and First Lady have sent down orders"[68] to coordinate the communication with Exxon only through the congressman and Raul Gorrín.[69]

The further development of events was described in chapter 8. In the summer of 2017, Pete Sessions assisted the PDVSA and Exxon to resolve their differences, with the two oil behemoths signing a $259 million deal.[70] However, the agreement was hindered by additional[71] US sanctions[72] imposed[73] on Venezuela in July and August of 2017, which gave Rivera more reason to keep charging the Venezuelans.

In parallel, at the end of June 2017, Raul Gorrín, through the US subsidiary of his Venezuelan Globovision television corporation, hired Ballard Partners,[74] allegedly for finding "expansion opportunities" in the US market.[75] Ballard Partners would report lobbying both Congress and the White House to advance Gorrín's TV channel's goals.[76] However, experts found it odd that Ballard sought to lobby Congress or the White House for TV licensing that could have been resolved by obtaining approval from the Federal Communications Commission.[77] Considering Gorrín's active role as Maduro's intermediary in the United States, it was quite possible that the $800,000 lobbying contract[78] was yet another attempt to gain closer access to Trump's officials. Ballard Partners, on its end, did not file FARA registration at the DOJ for its services for Gorrín as the contract was signed not with a foreign entity, but with the US subsidiary of Venezuelan Globovision.[79]

Brian Ballard, in turn, reportedly introduced Gorrín to Harry Sargeant III, the shipping mogul from Florida. With Gorrín's help, Sargeant was able to meet with PDVSA officials and Venezuelan president Nicolas Maduro[80] in late 2017 to discuss his company's access to some Venezuelan oil fields.[81]

Several months later, both Pete Sessions and Harry Sargeant would turn to Rudy Giuliani and Lev Parnas for assistance. Their joint effort would culminate in a September 2018 clandestine call with Nicolas Maduro that unsuccessfully sought to provide a safe retirement for the Venezuelan dictator in the United States[82] with no application of justice for the crimes that he and his government had committed against the Venezuelan people.

PRO-KREMLIN UKRAINIANS

There was another group of foreigners who were eager to gain access to Donald Trump's circle: Ukrainians who either had business ties to Russia or were connected to the pro-Kremlin Party of Regions. After former president Viktor Yanukovych fled to Russia in early 2014, the new Ukrainian administration under Petro Poroshenko pledged to eradicate corruption. He publicly declared the "deoligarchization" against those who had corruptly benefited during the Yanukovych era. One of the instruments to attempt to tackle the omnipresent graft was the creation of the National Anticorruption Bureau of Ukraine financed by Western aid. By late 2016 NABU was investigating several former and incumbent politicians,[83] as well as oligarchs. As a result, it faced enormous pushback from highly influential people who had exploited the deeply rotten system for years. Those people could benefit from weakened US support to Ukraine's anticorruption measures and, like many other foreign interests, sought to find access to the incoming Trump administration.

At the time, Paul Manafort, who had previously worked with the pro-Kremlin oligarchs, was no longer part of the Trump team and faced a criminal investigation, so the Ukrainians needed to find other conduits into US political circles. Both Rudy Giuliani and Lev Parnas would fill in the niche that was vacated by Manafort.

While in Kyiv in early December 2016, Lev Parnas met with the head of the Ukrainian tax service named Roman Nasirov.[84] Later that month Parnas and Nasirov traveled to Mar-a-Lago[85] to see President-Elect Donald Trump.[86] A month later Nasirov attended Donald Trump's inauguration ceremony,[87] staying at the same hotel as Parnas.[88] In an apparent quid pro quo for Parnas's guidance, Nasirov helped arrange a $10 million loan[89] for a business project in Saint Louis that was connected to Lev Parnas.[90]

As is common among people seeking access to Trump, there was something that Nasirov needed from the new administration. In early 2017 he was under criminal investigation led by NABU in Ukraine for assisting a former member of the Party of Regions in embezzling state funds.[91] Shortly after the inauguration, Nasirov signed a lobbying contract with Ballard Partners for the firm to "advocate before the U.S. government."[92] The contract didn't appear within the FARA registry[93] as Nasirov hired Ballard through another, presumably American, law firm. Brian Ballard would later state that, although he received $200,000, he didn't "do any work" for Nasirov,[94] probably due to Nasirov's arrest in Ukraine in March 2017.[95]

Another person who sought to gain access to Donald Trump's orbit was Pavel Fuks, the Russian Ukrainian oligarch who had paid a lobbyist to obtain inauguration tickets but didn't receive them.[96] Curiously, Fuks had already crossed paths with Donald Trump years earlier. Before moving to Ukraine, Fuks was a real estate developer in Russia who, in the mid-2000s, had negotiated with Donald Trump about building a Trump Tower in Moscow until the talks fell apart.[97]

In 2017, Pavel Fuks hired Rudy Giuliani for what he would later describe as lobbying services in the United States for the city of Kharkiv and Ukraine.[98] Fuks also stated that, through Giuliani, he wanted to convey to the American establishment that Ukraine was "a good country and that people can do business with us."[99] Giuliani rebuffed that claim,[100] arguing that Fuks had contracted his security firm to provide consulting for the city of Kharkiv in Ukraine.

Those early connections to pro-Kremlin Ukrainians would later pave the way to more famous Giuliani and Parnas escapades in Ukraine, which were described in Part II of this book. In the following years, with Rudy Giuliani rising to the position of President Trump's private attorney and Lev Parnas serving as Giuliani's foot soldier, the duo would become the key gatekeepers into the Trump world for various special interests, both foreign and domestic.

THE WEB OF INFLUENCE

By late 2018 Rudy Giuliani and Lev Parnas had become inseparable. They were crisscrossing the United States on private jets[101] during the midterm elections and flying to Paris,[102] London,[103] and Madrid[104] to meet with their foreign clients. Giuliani positioned himself into a unique spot to assist them. On one side he acted as advisor, fixer, and spokesperson to the president of the United States, all pro bono. On the other side, with Parnas at his side, Giuliani emerged as the central conduit into and out of the Trump world.

As presented in this book, they ran a massive number of projects that, at a macro level, constituted an overlapping covert web of influence presented in the diagram on figure 9.

1-2 In the early days of the Trump presidency, Lev Parnas served as a conduit for Turkish intermediaries by connecting them to Brian Ballard, who then signed lobbying contracts with Turkey and Halkbank. Coincidentally or not, within days of Ballard's first meeting with Farkhad Akhmedov, Donald Trump, under questionable circumstances, fired the lead prosecutor at the SDNY, Preet Bharara, who had been spearheading the Halkbank investigation.[105] Two years later Trump would fire another SDNY prosecutor, Geoffrey Berman, who had insisted on pressing charges against Halkbank.[106]

In parallel to Parnas, Giuliani advocated for a "diplomatic" solution between Turkey and the United States[107] that entailed releasing his client, Reza Zarrab, in exchange for the return of the US evangelical pastor Andrew Brunson. Giuliani even brought the issue to the Oval Office and, with the tacit approval of President Trump, unsuccessfully pressured then secretary of state Rex Tillerson to intervene.[108] Another topic of Giuliani's frequent conversations at the White House was the extradition of Erdogan's archnemesis, Fethullah Gülen, from the United States.[109] Giuliani, despite promoting those Turkish interests has not registered with the DOJ as a Turkish foreign agent.

3-4 In 2018 and 2019, Rudy Giuliani, Lev Parnas, Pete Sessions, and Harry Sargeant were pushing a clandestine effort to ease Venezuela out of US sanctions that could, in turn, allow US energy interests to gain access to Venezuelan oil fields. The initial plan was to amicably persuade Maduro to step down by offering him safe retirement in the United States. When Giuliani brought that plan to the White House, then national security advisor John Bolton "vehemently rejected" the idea.[110]

Giuliani's team then pivoted to entering into a quid pro quo with Alejandro Betancourt Lopez, a Venezuelan mogul who was under investigation in the United States for money laundering. Betancourt seemed to have offered to help the Venezuelan opposition leader Juan Guaido to replace Maduro, thus providing a fresh face in Venezuela that Giuliani and his allies needed. In exchange Betancourt wanted Giuliani's assistance in the United States to have the investigation dropped.[111] Executing his part of the deal, in early September 2019, Giuliani met with the U.S. attorney general William Barr[112] and other DOJ officials and asked them for leniency on Betancourt's behalf.[113]

5-6 While Giuliani and Parnas's activities in Turkey and Venezuela were episodic, their escapades in Ukraine continued for years during the Trump presidency, starting with their connections to the head of Ukraine's tax service, Roman Nasirov, and Russian Ukrainian oligarch Pavel Fuks, who were mentioned earlier.

7-8 In 2018 Lev Parnas and his associate, Igor Fruman, embarked on an LNG endeavor in Ukraine, seemingly paralleling Secretary of Energy Rick Perry's freedom gas project. On one hand, Perry pressured Ukrainian officials to install his allies onto the supervisory board of the state energy company, Naftogaz.[114] On the other hand, Parnas and Fruman worked behind the scenes to replace the Naftogaz CEO with someone amenable to promote their goals.[115] The two of them also pushed to have the US ambassador to Ukraine Marie Yovanovitch removed from her position,[116] seeing her as a hindrance to their LNG goals.[117] Giuliani also took an active part in that plot, promoting the ambassador's firing to Secretary of State Mike Pompeo and Pres. Donald Trump. Another person involved in the concerted effort to oust the ambassador was Rep. Pete Sessions, who, immediately after meeting Lev Parnas in his office, wrote a letter to Mike Pompeo advocating for Yovanovitch's removal.[118]

Yovanovitch was also a thorn on Rick Perry's side as she opposed the changes in the Naftogaz management structure and its supervisory board, presciently arguing that such a move could potentially undermine anti-corruption efforts made in the Ukrainian gas sector.[119] Her removal and replacement with a friendly face, such as Pete Sessions, whose name was reportedly "circulated inside and outside the administration" as a candidate for her position,[120] could potentially benefit both Perry and Parnas's LNG goals.

9-10 Arguably, the most egregious scheme in Ukraine was the "mission"[121] that Giuliani and Parnas received from President Trump. The goal was to smear the former US vice president Joe Biden and his son Hunter Biden, who had been a board member of a Ukrainian company called Burisma. Throughout

2019 the duo worked on a campaign to coerce the Ukrainian government to announce an investigation on Hunter Biden's role in Burisma and to then use the investigation as a core piece to tarnish Joe Biden's campaign for 2020 presidential election. The overall effort was complemented by the dissemination of disinformation in the United States through op-eds[122] written by John Solomon[123] at the *Hill* and media appearances by Rudy Giuliani.[124]

To achieve their goals in Ukraine, the duo engaged the country's prosecutor general, Yuri Lutsenko, and one of Ukraine's most influential oligarchs, Dmytro Firtash. For their assistance each had received a personalized offer from Giuliani and Parnas. Lutsenko was promised a meeting with the US attorney general and to have Ambassador Yovanovitch removed from her post. The last part also conveniently served Parnas's LNG goals. Firtash, who had been previously charged in the United States for bribery and was battling extradition from Austria, was promised assistance to fight off his criminal case in the United States. For a $1 million retainer fee from Firtash,[125] the BLT lawyers, Victoria Toensing and Joe diGenova, met with[126] Attorney General Barr[127] and advocated for the dismissal of Firtash's criminal case in the United States.

Giuliani and Parnas's schemes in Ukraine came to an abrupt halt in the fall of 2019, when a whistleblower complaint describing the notorious call between Donald Trump and the Ukrainian president Volodymyr Zelensky was released to the public.[128] In that call Trump had attempted to strong-arm Zelensky into announcing an investigation into the Bidens and Ukraine's alleged election interference. That call would not only become the triggering event for Donald Trump's first impeachment but also provide clues to a broad array of shadow schemes operated by Rudy Giuliani, Lev Parnas, and their BLT teammates.

At the end of September 2019, Giuliani, Parnas, and Fruman were subpoenaed by three House committees investigating Trump's pressure on the Ukrainian government.[129] Within days Parnas and Fruman would be arrested. Their indictment would reveal that, on top of their already wide range of activities, in 2018 the two had also sought to obtain cannabis production licenses in various US states.[130] To facilitate those licenses, Parnas and Fruman made political contributions to candidates in targeted states. The money for donations was provided by a Russian businessman, Andrey Muraviev, who was their partner in the cannabis venture. In other words, Parnas and Fruman were making political contributions on behalf of another person, or straw donations, which are illegal.

With his associates arrested and his patron, Pres. Donald Trump, facing an impeachment trial, Rudy Giuliani was in a tricky position. Because of his association to Parnas and Fruman, he faced scrutiny both in the Congress and potentially at the SDNY. The only person who could save Giuliani was Donald Trump, but to do that, he needed to stay in power.

To remedy Trump's travail, Giuliani, once again, turned to Ukraine. As the impeachment hearing were progressing, he worked on a "documentary" that accused Ukraine of interfering in the 2016 election. The main sources of those claims were Andrii Derkach and Andrii Telizhenko, Ukrainian officials connected to Russian intelligence services.[131] The main goal of the documentary was to deflect public attention away from the impeachment trial and denounce the findings of the Mueller investigation, which had definitively proved the existence of Russia's massive influence operation against the United States during the 2016 presidential election. That was a very revealing moment. In an attempt to save his skin, Rudy Giuliani was willing to seek assistance from Russia, a country openly adversarial to America. By promoting the disinformation provided by Kremlin operatives, he knowingly aided and abetted Russia's efforts to destabilize the US political system. In a wry twist, Russian interests, once again, were indirectly helping Donald Trump, this time to avoid impeachment and remain in power.

The investigations of late 2019 revealed the extent of the multilayered persuasion game of illicit lobbying and the exchange of favors among people close to Donald Trump. That endless circle of corruption and obstruction of justice stemmed from the insatiable greed for money and power. But that cycle significantly corroded the rule of law both within the United States and abroad. It also went against official US foreign policy and jeopardized US national security while enormously benefiting foreign powers.

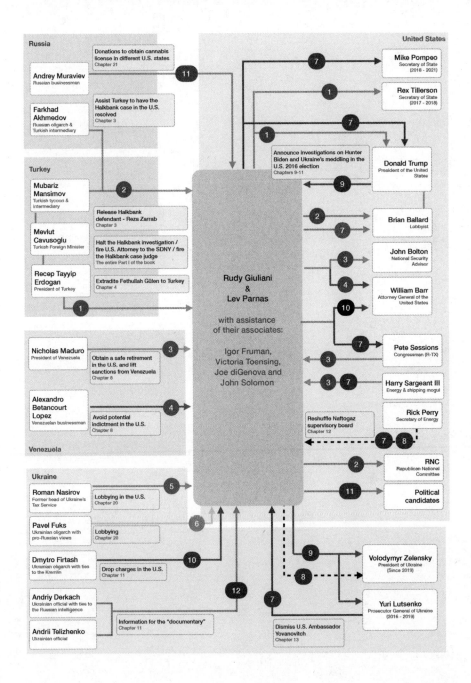

FIGURE 9. RUDY GIULIANI AND LEV PARNAS'S INFLUENCE PROJECTS

THE STREAMS OF INFLUENCE 251

PART V
CONSEQUENCES

CHAPTER 21

THE IMPERFECT WHEELS OF JUSTICE

PARNAS AND FRUMAN

STRAW DONATION CHARGES

On September 9, 2019, the chairmen of the House Foreign Relations Committee, House Intelligence Committee, and House Oversight Committee announced investigations into Donald Trump and Rudy Giuliani's efforts to pressure the Ukrainian government.[1] A wave of subpoenas followed, with the committees issuing one to Rudy Giuliani, Lev Parnas, and Igor Fruman and directing the documents to be provided by October 14, 2019.[2]

Instead of complying with the subpoenas, Parnas, Fruman, and Giuliani booked flights to Austria. On October 9, 2019, Parnas and Fruman were arrested[3] while boarding a flight to Vienna in Dulles Airport outside Washington, DC.[4] Giuliani, who had also planned to fly to Austria later that day,[5] remained in America after his associates' arrest.

SDNY prosecutors charged Lev Parnas, Igor Fruman, and their associate, David Correia, with campaign finance violations[6] that stemmed[7] from their $325,000 donation to America First Action PAC. The PAC's own documents had stated that the contribution came from Parnas and Fruman's company, Global Energy Producers;[8] however, it was wired from another[9] firm's[10] bank account. The SDNY also charged them with making straw donations to Republican candidates[11] using $1 million originating from a Russian national, Andrey Muraviev,[12] who was ineligible to make political contributions in the United States. Parnas and Correia were separately charged with defrauding investors of their other company named Fraud Guarantee,[13] which ironically was supposed to provide insurance for investment fraud.

However, the SDNY indictments didn't reflect the full scope of Parnas and Fruman's use of political contributions. From 2016 to 2018, the duo[14] donated[15] at least $900,000 to the Republican Party and its political candidates (figure 10).[16] Those contributions then provided them with access to donor retreats and new fundraiser events, which Parnas and Fruman exploited to expand their access. Then when the time was right, they could ask for favors from politicians they supported. Those could be requests for the benefit of Parnas and Fruman's business endeavors, such as the LNG project in Ukraine or the cannabis business in the United States. The two could also peddle issues important to people who provided the funds. While the SDNY indictment mentioned Russian businessman Andrey Muraviev as the source of Parnas and Fruman's donations, investigative journalists uncovered several other people who gave large sums to the two.

As mentioned previously, in January 2017[17] Roman Nasirov,[18] the head of Ukraine's tax service, reportedly helped Parnas obtain a $10 million loan for a business project in Saint Louis.[19]

In early 2018 Igor Fruman took out a $3 million mortgage loan[20] from a group of people that included a Russian American couple whose son[21] was a high-level executive at Yandex,[22] the largest Russian IT company that was perceived[23] by its[24] critics[25] as the Kremlin's surveillance tool.[26] The legal documents for the loan were arranged by a real estate lawyer from Florida[27] who, according to a DC government ethics watchdog, the Campaign Legal Center,[28] specialized in

working with foreign real estate buyers and advising realtors on how to avoid federal requirements aimed at disclosure of foreign buyers who use shell companies to launder money.

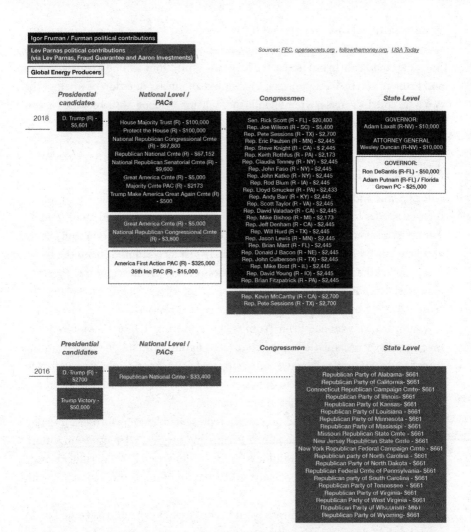

FIGURE 10. DONATIONS OF LEV PARNAS AND IGOR FRUMAN/IGOR FURMAN (2016-2018)
SOURCES: FEC.GOV, OPENSECRETS.ORG, FOLLOWTHEMONEY.ORG, CLC

Then in the summer of 2018, Parnas and Fruman launched[29] a shady[30] fundraising[31] campaign for Anatevka,[32] a Jewish refugee village in Ukraine. The funds were to be collected by American Friends of Anatevka, a charity organization[33] in New York where the two were board members.[34] Bloomberg News[35] and the *Times of Israel*[36] also pointed out that many of Anatevka's donors were highly influential. Some of them were oligarchs[37] from post-Soviet countries; others had[38] ties[39] to the Russian[40] government.[41]

In 2019, while the BLT team lawyers advocated for the dismissal of Dmytro

Firtash's criminal case, Parnas and his wife received[42] a $1 million loan that was wired from a Russian bank account that belonged to Firtash's lawyer.[43]

One couldn't help but notice the Russian connections among many of Parnas and Fruman's financial supporters. That raised an uneasy question of whether the two were cogs in a greater Kremlin influence scheme all along, with unlimited access the US president's private attorney.

PARNAS'S REVOLT

After Parnas and Fruman's arrest, media outlets reported detailed accounts of their escapades in Ukraine and their connections to Rudy Giuliani and President Trump. While Giuliani provided convoluted reasons for his association with Parnas and Fruman,[44] President Trump immediately distanced himself from the two,[45] downplaying the importance of multiple photos in which they appeared together. However, behind the scenes, Trump's legal machinery was working to contain the crisis. Lawyers from Trump's orbit were deployed to aid Parnas and Fruman's defense.

John Dowd, who had been Trump's lawyer during the Russian interference investigation,[46] became their legal counsel to fight off the subpoenas[47] from the three House committees that were investigating Trump and Giuliani's conduct in Ukraine. For that, Dowd had to obtain[48] Trump's personal consent[49] to avoid any accusations of potential conflict of interest.

Kevin Downing, who had previously represented Trump's former campaign manager Paul Manafort,[50] also joined Parnas and Fruman's defense team.[51] Both Dowd and Downing, after consulting with Rudy Giuliani and Trump's other private attorney, Jay Sekulow, reportedly advised Parnas and Fruman not to comply with the subpoenas.[52]

Shortly thereafter, Lev Parnas would claim that Dowd and Downing's main priorities had been to protect the president and silence Parnas.[53] As a result, by the end of October 2019, he switched to another criminal defense attorney, Joseph Bondy,[54] who had no apparent affiliation with Donald Trump. Fruman, on the other hand, picked SDNY alumnus Todd Blanche, who had also previously represented Paul Manafort.[55] Those choices defined Parnas and Fruman's diametrically opposing legal defense tactics. While Fruman remained silent, Parnas took a public stance against Giuliani and Trump.

While SDNY prosecutors and journalists scrutinized Parnas, Fruman, and others connected to them, multiple House committees were investigating Donald Trump's actions regarding Ukraine. In late October 2019, after hiring his new lawyer, Parnas announced that he would comply with the congressional subpoena[56] that requested information about his work with Rudy Giuliani and his encounters with the president. Around the same time, Giuliani covertly called Parnas's new lawyer, Joseph Bondy, encouraging him to call back to Giuliani's burner phone number.[57]

In January 2020 Lev Parnas turned over to the investigative committees a trove of documents, photos, and select communication excerpts regarding his involvement in the shadow schemes in Ukraine.[58] However, Parnas left out the information about his LNG effort. Others who were mentioned in the subpoenas either[59] refused[60] to comply[61] or claimed[62] to not have any relevant information. In January 2020 Parnas, seeking to present a carefully curated story of his involvement, also gave interviews to MSNBC[63] and CNN,[64] presenting himself a changed man who realized that he had been brainwashed, used, and then abandoned by Rudy Giuliani and Donald Trump.

Curiously, in those interviews Parnas did not mention anything about his involvement in the Turkish influence effort to halt Reza Zarrab's case or the call with the Venezuelan president. Only in September 2020 did he come out publicly about his role in connecting Turkish intermediaries to GOP circles.[65] The following month Parnas's son, Aaron, published *Trump First*, a book in which he described the Venezuela call in minute details.[66] Revealing as those accounts might be, they did not lead to any additional criminal charges.

By the end of the SDNY investigations in 2021, Lev Parnas, Igor Fruman, and their associate, David Correia, either pleaded[67] guilty[68] or were found guilty[69] of making straw donations and defrauding investors.

ABOVE THE LAW

The concurrence of Parnas and Fruman's criminal case with the Trump impeachment investigation brought attention to Pete Sessions and Rick Perry. Sessions appeared in the first version of Parnas and Fruman's indictment as "Congressman-1."[70] SDNY prosecutors mentioned in the document that Parnas and Fruman had each donated $2,700 to Pete Sessions. Also, according to the indictment:[71]

> *These contributions were made for the purpose of gaining influence with politicians so as to advance their own personal financial interests and the political interests of Ukrainian government officials, including at least one Ukrainian government official with whom they were working. For example, in or about May and June 2018, PARNAS and FRUMAN committed to raise $20,000 or more for then-sitting U.S. Congressman ("Congressman-1"), who had also been the beneficiary of approximately $3 million in independent expenditures by Committee-1 during the 2018 election cycle.*
>
> *. . . At and around the same time PARNAS and FRUMAN committed to raising those funds for Congressman-1, PARNAS met with Congressman-1 and sought Congressman-1's assistance in causing the U.S. Government to remove or recall the then-U.S. Ambassador to Ukraine (the "Ambassador").*

After Sessions and his staff agreed to comply with the SDNY subpoena,[72] the prosecutors issued a superseding indictment[73] from which they, for reasons unknown, took out references of Sessions's role in the removal of Marie Yovanovitch and that his campaign had received $3 million from Committee-1, which was later identified as Trump's America First Action PAC.[74]

Congressman Sessions also was never held accountable for his involvement in the rogue effort to provide safe retirement for the Venezuelan dictator in the United States. The "political and personal turmoil"[75] that Sessions was concerned about after his clandestine call with Nicolas Maduro in September 2018 never materialized.

Investigative journalists[76] also uncovered[77] that US secretary of energy Rick Perry had been spearheading an effort to replace the Naftogaz supervisory board members with his allies while, in parallel, Lev Parnas seeded efforts to topple the company's CEO. The day after Lev Parnas was arrested, the House committees subpoenaed Rick Perry.[78] Despite his earlier claims that he would cooperate with the investigation,[79] as the due day approached, the Department of Energy proclaimed that Perry would not comply.[80] The day before Perry was supposed to provide the documents to Congress, Donald Trump announced that Rick Perry would resign from his position as the secretary of energy.[81] Although the slow wheels of justice had eventually caught up with Lev Parnas and Igor Fruman, their apparent higher-positioned coconspirators averted accountability.

UNDER PRESSURE

While Rudy Giuliani's associates, one by one, began to face scrutiny, he, too, felt the increasing pressure. In early August 2019, SDNY prosecutors started probing Giuliani's efforts in Ukraine.[82] By the end of 2019, the SDNY was conducting an investigation into Giuliani's potential illegal foreign lobbying for both Turkish and Ukrainian interests in violation of the Foreign Agents Registration Act.[83] Several news sources reported at the time that various undisclosed entities, including Ballard Partners,[84] received subpoenas regarding their communication and payments to Rudy Giuliani and his companies.[85] According to the *Wall Street Journal*,[86] those subpoenas listed several crimes that Giuliani was being investigated for:

> Obstruction of justice, money laundering, conspiracy to defraud the United States, making false statements to the federal government, serving as an agent of a foreign government without registering with the Justice Department, donating funds from foreign nationals, making contributions in the name of another person or allowing someone else to use one's name to make a contribution, along with mail fraud and wire fraud.

Giuliani angrily responded to the SDNY investigation:[87]

> *If they're investigating me, they're assholes. They're absolutely assholes if they're investigating me.*

The SDNY investigation would last for two years. Within its scope, in April 2021 the FBI would execute search warrants at Rudy Giuliani's and Victoria Toensing's homes,[88] seizing their electronic devices.[89] However, in late 2022 the SDNY would announce[90] that criminal charges on Giuliani for foreign lobbying would not be "forthcoming."[91] Years later an FBI whistleblower would[92] file a complaint[93] with the Senate Judiciary Committee, claiming that his superiors stymied investigations into Rudy Giuliani that the agent had led in cooperation with the SDNY.

However, back in late 2019, Rudy Giuliani was under enormous pressure, with every aspect of his life being scrutinized by journalists and investigators. Witnesses[94] who[95] testified[96] during Trump's impeachment trial painted a damning picture. One of them described how former national security advisor John Bolton had aptly characterized Giuliani as a "human hand grenade who's going to blow everybody up" with his scheming in Ukraine.[97] The common theme of all those testimonies was that Rudy Giuliani and his associates were central to the extortion of the Ukrainian government on President Trump's behalf.

Also, the symbiosis between Giuliani and Trump, which had benefited them both, was in jeopardy. If either of them were brought to justice, they would likely both sink. On one hand, if Rudy Giuliani, as President Trump's private lawyer was indicted, that could reflect on Donald Trump himself. At minimum that could threaten his reelection, and at maximum, Trump could be implicated in Giuliani's crimes. But as long as he remained president, Trump could potentially intervene into the investigations that focused on Giuliani, like he would later do for his other allies, Michael Flynn,[98] Paul Manafort, and Roger Stone.[99]

On the other hand, President Trump, who was the key for Giuliani's ability to land wealthy foreign clients, was at the brink of a potential impeachment. Without Trump as president, Giuliani could lose his access, his clients, and his place in the public spotlight. But most importantly, he could also lose protection for his possible crimes if Trump was removed from power.

So, to salvage public opinion about Donald Trump and counter the ongoing inquiries, Giuliani hastily conjured up a documentary about Joe Biden in Ukraine.[100] In the film, former Ukrainian prosecutors Viktor Shokin[101] and Yuri Lutsenko,[102] as well as Kremlin-connected Ukrainian officials Andrii Derkach[103] and Andrii Telizhenko,[104] provided pieces of "evidence" in an attempt to discredit the Democratic candidate for president. The film aired in early December 2019 on One America News, an ultraconservative media platform. Later, after allegations[105] of false[106] information[107] being provided[108] in the movie, it was removed from the OAN YouTube channel.

Meanwhile, the effort to impeach Donald Trump was reaching its final stage.

In late December 2019, after a bitter debate, the House of Representatives voted in favor of impeaching the president.[109] After the Christmas recess, the Senate would take up the impeachment trial.

Early signs indicated that the Senate Republicans were not interested in an impeachment. Instead, they supported a partisan victory and thus in Donald Trump's acquittal. Sen. Lindsey Graham, the head of the Judicial Committee, vowed to do everything in his power to make the trial "die quickly."[110] When Democratic senators called for hearing the testimonies from witnesses,[111] such as John Bolton and Lev Parnas, Republican senators fiercely blocked those attempts.

On February 5, 2020, Senate Democrats voted in favor of the impeachment, and all but one Republican senator voted against.[112] The two-thirds majority of the senators' votes needed for the conviction of the president was not met, and Donald Trump was acquitted.[113] Despite overwhelming evidence of his abuse of power, extortion, and bribery, Donald Trump was given a get-out-of-jail-free card by the GOP. People within the party used varied excuses to justify their acquittal votes.[114] Some claimed he was innocent.[115] Others argued the impeachment was rushed.[116] Another group still agreed that the president acted improperly but that the actions were not serious enough to impeach him.[117] Last, one senator claimed that, like a good schoolboy, Donald Trump had "learned his lesson."[118]

Democratic senators disagreed. After the acquittal, a group of them published an op-ed in the *Washington Post* with a prescient observation:[119]

> *No one can seriously argue that President Trump has learned from this experience. This was not the first time he solicited foreign interference in his election, nor will it be the last. As we said during the trial, if left in office, the president will not stop trying to cheat in the next election until he succeeds. . . .*
>
> *Because of the impeachment process, voters can now stand forewarned of the lengths to which the president will go to try to secure his reelection, violating the law and undermining our national security and that of our allies.*

They could not imagine just how far Donald Trump and his allies would go to keep him in power.

CHAPTER 22

TRUMP'S FIGHT FOR THE WHITE HOUSE

DIMINISHING CHANCES

A DISASTER TEST

Immediately after surviving the impeachment, Donald Trump faced another test. The spring of 2020 was a period of anxious uncertainty worldwide including the United States due to the outbreak of the novel coronavirus. At the time, there was neither a working vaccine nor a proven treatment to tackle the pathogen. In an attempt to stifle the rising number of COVID-19 cases, many states imposed restrictions on public gatherings and then moved to full lockdowns. Those restrictions triggered a chain reaction that caused many businesses to lose revenue and fire staff, sending unemployment to numbers not seen in decades. The United States, like the rest of the world, was in health crisis, which brought along an economic one. Americans were desperate for information and a solution. They expected their president to provide leadership and guidance to help the public navigate the uncharted waters.

During the first years of Donald Trump's presidency, the US government's machinery rode on the inertia of institutional memory and processes established over decades. The COVID-19 pandemic, though, was a unique situation that required the government to gather all its competence to handle the crisis. With Donald Trump as president, that task turned out to be much harder.

When the first cases of COVID-19 appeared in America, Donald Trump intentionally dismissed any potential health threat,[1] claiming that the virus would miraculously go away.[2] During a campaign rally in February 2020, he downplayed the threat of COVID-19, describing it as a "new hoax" devised by Democrats.[3] As the number of cases and deaths increased, Trump continuously claimed that his administration was handling the pandemic "perfectly."[4] To his advisors' shock, he recommended that the public treat COVID-19 with unproven drugs[5] or with an injection of bleach.[6]

Trump's rhetoric was more characteristic of autocrats, who often engage on boisterous showmanship when times are smooth. However, when a real disaster occurs and threatens to diminish their popularity, they struggle to control the narrative and instead react by attempting to suppress any critical voices.

In April–May 2020, some Americans took their pent-up frustration to the streets, demanding the end of the lockdowns and other COVID-19 restrictions.[7] The initiative was encouraged by President Trump, who tweeted a call to "liberate" various states[8] where Democratic governors maintained stay-at-home orders. On April 30, 2020, an armed conservative militia group, taking the president's call literally, occupied the Michigan Capitol building.[9] Trump characterized the incident as "very good people" wanting to "get their lives back."[10]

In late May of 2020, the country's attention shifted to another wave of protests on the opposite end of the political spectrum after Minneapolis police officers caused a death of an African American man named George Floyd.[11] The incident, recorded by bystanders, showed a white policeman kneeling on the neck of a distressed Floyd, who gasped for breath. The video spread like wildfire throughout social media. The next day people gathered in Minneapolis to voice their dissent against what they perceived as racial injustice.[12] The cause was quickly picked up nationwide, and by early June, protests had reached over 550 locations throughout the country.[13] In stark contrast to his support for the antilockdown protests, this time President Trump advocated for the suppression of the civil rights–fueled unrest by floating the use of active US military units.[14] That created a whole new set of concerns about the Trump administration's selective approach to the rights of the two groups, one that supported him and the other that, he believed, did not. By mid-2020 it was clear that growing portions of the American public had become dissatisfied with Trump, driving his poll numbers down.[15]

THE BOOKS

Trump's reelection chances were further threatened by a tell-all book written by his former national security advisor, John Bolton. A few months after his firing by the president, several news outlets announced that Bolton was writing a book[16] about his time in the Trump administration.[17] By the end of December 2019, he had submitted his book manuscript for prepublication review.[18] Under monthslong pressure from the White House, the National Security Council evaluated the manuscript to make sure it didn't contain any classified information.[19] Trump threatened that Bolton would have a "very strong criminal problem" if the book was published. Apparently picking up on Trump's remarks, the Department of Justice under AG Bill Barr sued Bolton, claiming that the book still contained classified details and thus had national security ramifications.[20] Despite the administration's push to suppress the book, in mid-June 2020 the judge overseeing the case ruled in Bolton's favor, allowing it to be released.[21]

On June 23, 2020, Bolton's book *The Room Where It Happened: A White House Memoir*[22] was placed on the shelves of bookstores throughout the country. In that book Bolton depicted President Trump as impulsive, incompetent, and self-serving, with little regard for American foreign policy interests. He also provided a wider perspective on Trump and Giuliani's schemes in Ukraine while lamenting the number of US officials pulled into the plot.[23] In another storyline Bolton described how Trump had promised the Turkish president to intervene in the Halkbank case.[24] Both subjects not only marred Trump but also put a spotlight on Rudy Giuliani, who at the time was under investigation by the SDNY for his clandestine activities in both Ukraine and Turkey.[25] In a move that seemed hardly coincidental, three days before the book's release, Attorney General Barr and President Trump forced the SDNY lead prosecutor, Geoffrey Berman, to resign. Bolton reacted to Berman's firing, characterizing it as obstruction of justice.[26]

On September 15, 2020, two weeks before the first presidential debate, another book was released, this time from a longtime *Washington Post* journalist, Bob Woodward. Focused on the Trump presidency, his book *Rage* included a February 2020 interview in which the president acknowledged the deadliness of coronavirus[27] despite publicly stating otherwise at the time.[28] The revelation of Trump's duplicity came as the United States passed the tragic milestone of two hundred thousand COVID-19 deaths,[29] causing another round of questions of the Trump administration's handling of the pandemic.[30]

PLAYING DIRTY

Donald Trump and his allies attempted to remedy his declining ratings in several ways. Since early 2020 Trump had been continuously sowing doubt in the legitimacy and safety of mail-in ballots in the upcoming presidential election.[31] Preying on the fact that most citizens weren't versed in the safeguards built into the mail-in voting process, the president claimed that they were easy to manipulate and could be "stolen out of mailboxes."[32] Some members of the administration, including AG William Barr, repeated the president's points on mail-in voting.[33] The claim was also echoed and amplified within conservative media.[34] That disinformation campaign was a countermeasure to Democrats' efforts to promote the use of mail-in ballots as a safer alternative to in-person voting during the pandemic.[35]

In contrast, by mid-2020 Trump started pushing to outright postpone[36] the election,[37] combining claims that mail-in ballots were unreliable and that in-person voting was dangerous during the pandemic. Aware of his low polling against Biden[38] and preparing the ground for the possibility of a loss, Trump tweeted:[39]

> With Universal Mail-In Voting (not Absentee Voting, which is good), 2020 will be the most INACCURATE & FRAUDULENT Election in history. It will be a great

> embarrassment to the USA. Delay the Election until people can properly, securely and safely vote???

As Election Day approached, Donald Trump clearly understood that his reelection chances were slim. Yet he signaled his intention to cling to the presidency at all costs. During a press conference in late September 2020, when asked about a peaceful transition of power in case of a loss, President Trump retorted:[40]

> Well, we're going to have to see what happens. . . .
>
> We'll want to have—get rid of the ballots and you'll have a very—we'll have a very peaceful—there won't be a transfer, frankly. There'll be a continuation.

Meanwhile, Rudy Giuliani continued his crusade on discrediting Joe Biden and his family. A month before the 2020 election, Trump's private attorney made headlines again, claiming that he had come into possession of the contents of a laptop that allegedly belonged to Hunter Biden and contained evidence of his corruption in Ukraine.[41] At no surprise, the conspiracy was picked up by Trump supporters[42] and amplified through social media,[43] creating fury among conservatives days before the election.

THE ELECTION

On election night the mood in the White House was tense but optimistic. It was a tight race, with Donald Trump and Joe Biden showing very close results in the early hours of the vote count. Things changed when around 11:00 p.m. Fox News called Arizona, an expected Republican stronghold, for Joe Biden. According to Trump advisors, the president turned "increasingly unhappy"[44] as the prospect of him losing the election became more probable. As panic grew, a reportedly inebriated Rudy Giuliani suggested that the president should just proclaim victory[45] despite the objections of other Trump aides.[46] Siding with his private attorney, at around 2:30 a.m., while votes were still being counted, the president issued a public statement:[47]

> This is a fraud on the American public. This is an embarrassment to our country. We were getting ready to win this election. Frankly, we did win this election. We did win this election . . .
>
> We want the law to be used in a proper manner. So we'll be going to the US Supreme Court. We want all voting to stop. We don't want them to find any ballots at four o'clock in the morning and add them to the list. Okay?

On November 5, while US election workers were still sifting through the unprecedented number of mail-in ballots[48] spurred by the COVID-19 pandemic, Donald Trump once again called for the halt of the vote counting.[49] Despite the sitting US president's early attempt to obstruct the democratic process, the counting continued, and days later, Joe Biden would be proclaimed the winner of the 2020 presidential election.[50]

RESHUFFLING THE DECK

On election night, as the scale of the presidential race tilted toward Joe Biden, Donald Trump and Rudy Giuliani grew desperate. They were running out of time and were willing to resort to extreme measures. Considering the dubious steps they had already taken in Ukraine to gain advantage in the reelection and the pressure they were under in late 2020, one couldn't expect that Trump and Giuliani would concede gracefully. However, few could imagine that the supposed leader of the free world and his private attorney would be willing to violate the Constitution so blatantly as to jeopardize the very foundation of American democracy, the peaceful transfer of power.

Within days of the election, in a move characteristic of autocrats, the president replaced competent experts who challenged the veracity of statements with sycophants by assigning Rudy Giuliani as the head of his campaign legal team and dismissing those who tried to persuade him to concede. Giuliani brought his old allies onto the team. Two familiar faces on it were Joe diGenova and Victoria Toensing,[51] who had previously assisted Giuliani in his schemes in Ukraine. Another prominent member of the team was Sidney Powell,[52] a Dallas lawyer who had previously served as a defense attorney for the disgraced and convicted former Trump national security advisor, Michael Flynn.[53] The new team intended to challenge the election results using an array of Giuliani's dubious methods. Other Trump allies, such as former secretary of energy Rick Perry and Texas congressman Pete Sessions, who had previously appeared in this book, were also tangentially connected to the larger effort to overturn the election results.

As the head of the Trump legal team, Rudy Giuliani resorted to his usual tricks of disinformation, intimidation, and the bending of the rule of law. The multilayered scheme to overturn the election results led by Rudy Giuliani is presented in figure 11. From the get-go, Giuliani's team pursued two parallel, but later overlapping, efforts. One was to claim a national conspiracy of election fraud against his client and then to use those claims to persuade officials and legislators in battleground states to subvert their election results to Trump's advantage. Over time the team's strategy morphed into a second effort to disrupt the electoral process by attempting to replace legitimate state electors with Trump-aligned "alternate" ones.

In a fashion that had become familiar since the beginning of his presidency, Donald Trump bulldozed officials who challenged the veracity of his statements. Those who disagreed with Trump or refused to submit to his pressure were either smeared in social media, removed from their positions, or chose to resign. One such example was Chris Krebs, the head of the Cybersecurity and Infrastructure Security Agency (CISA), created by the Trump administration[54] and tasked with protecting the US election from outside interference. On November 11, 2020, his agency issued a formal statement that "the November 3rd election was the most secure in American history."[55] A few days later, Donald Trump, who had been pushing an opposing narrative, fired him, claiming that the CISA's statement was "highly inaccurate."[56]

Another unexpected victim of Trump's rage was AG William Barr, who had often been the president's attack dog. Barr's last act of loyalty was his approval of investigations into election fraud while the vote count was still ongoing. That action violated the DOJ's standing policy of holding off any election-related investigations until the end of the vote count.[57] By the end of November, no evidence had been found to support Trump's claims of mass election fraud, and so, on December 1, 2020, Barr publicly announced that the DOJ had "not seen fraud on a scale that could have effected a different outcome in the election,"[58] causing Trump's rage.[59] By mid-December Barr had reached his limit with the president's false indignance and submitted his resignation. Meanwhile, Trump continued to charge forward in his attempts to overturn the election.

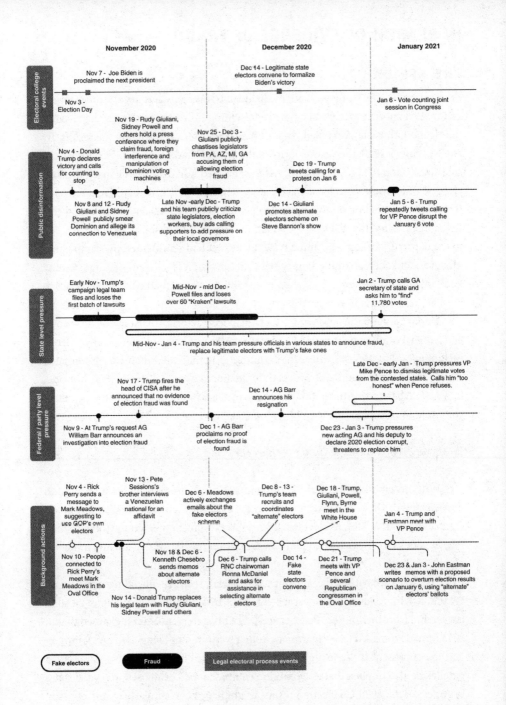

FIGURE 11. A LAYERED TIMELINE OF TRUMP'S EFFORTS TO OVERTURN 2020 ELECTION RESULTS

IN SEARCH OF EVIDENCE OF FRAUD

THE AFFIDAVITS

Before announcing Rudy Giuliani as the head of his campaign legal team, Donald Trump had another group of lawyers representing his campaign. Immediately after the election, those lawyers filed lawsuits in several states challenging the results. By late November 2020, the vast majority of the lawsuits had been dismissed for lack of substance,[60] and the ballot recounts that they had requested didn't[61] change[62] the state election outcomes. With legal challenges going nowhere, it was apparent to many that all the conventional tools to challenge the election results had been exhausted. Refusing to accept the reality of the situation, Trump kept pushing the effort, leading to the departure of some prominent law firms that had represented the campaign.[63] The president then reshuffled his remaining campaign legal team betting on Rudy Giuliani and his motley crew,[64] who were willing to use unconventional tactics to keep Donald Trump in power.

Under Giuliani the new team, which included Victoria Toensing, Joe diGenova, and Sidney Powell, sought to fuel public outrage by appearing on conservative media, including on Fox News,[65] where they continuously reiterated their unsubstantiated claims about voter fraud and vouched to file more lawsuits. Despite their bravado, they had no basis to legitimately claim fraud. In a rare moment of truth, Rudy Giuliani confessed in private to one Republican official:[66]

We've got lots of theories, we just don't have the evidence.

With no credible proof of election tampering, Trump's legal team scoured to find their own. They used two affidavits as the basis for their massive disinformation campaign about a "stolen" election. Both sources were connected to Congressman Pete Sessions (R-TX), who had played a significant role in Rudy Giuliani's influence operations both in Venezuela[67] and Ukraine[68] through 2018 and 2019.[69]

The first affidavit source, a former Venezuelan security official named Leamsy Salazar, was interviewed on November 13, 2020, by William Lewis Sessions, a Dallas lawyer and a brother of Rep. Pete Sessions.[70] In his statement Salazar claimed that in 2013 he had witnessed how Smartmatic voting software was being used on Dominion voting equipment in Venezuela to deliver desirable election results.[71] Drawing a parallel, he also implied that as Dominion equipment had been used in several states in America, the 2020 US election results might have been similarly tampered with. Salazar's theory was[72] quickly[73] debunked[74] by independent experts and also Trump's own staff. However, the Giuliani legal team kept using the affidavit in public as evidence of a conspiracy. Interestingly, Lewis Sessions would later say that Salazar's interview had been solicited by "a person working with Sidney Powell's legal team,"[75] which suggested that the affidavit might have been "manufactured" by the Trump legal team.

The second affidavit was produced by Joshua Merritt,[76] a former member of a far right militia group[77] and an employee at Allied Security Operations Group, or ASOG, a private contracting group from Texas, comprised of former military intelligence officials with conservative leanings. ASOG had previously worked with Pete Sessions in an unsuccessful attempt to challenge his midterm election loss in 2018.[78] Sessions also had personally known Merritt and attempted to lend him credibility by referring to him as a "top, top computer forensic expert."[79] Merritt declared to have uncovered corruption in the 2020 election and that the voting equipment was "certainly compromised by rogue actors, such as Iran and China."[80] In a later interview, Merritt would say that Trump's team took his suspicions at face value, did no background checks, and used them as a predicate for their claims of a stolen election.[81]

Trump's legal team member Sidney Powell attempted to keep Merritt's identity secret while describing him as a "military intelligence expert"[82] and affording him qualifications he didn't have. Merritt had never finished his military intelligence training and instead had spent a decade in the army, working mostly as a vehicle mechanic.[83] The document he provided also didn't hold up under scrutiny as its findings lacked a coordinated methodology.[84] However, that did not stop Powell from using Merritt's false affidavit to spread the election fraud story.

THE "KRAKEN" LAWSUITS

Equipped with the two dubious affidavits, Trump's legal team gathered for a press conference on November 19, 2020.[85] In a speech that would mark the true beginning of the "stolen election" myth, Sidney Powell combined Salazar's and Merritt's claims and announced that foreign powers had interfered in the 2020 election by manipulating voting equipment, leading to Joe Biden's victory.[86] Powell used Salazar's and Merritt's affidavits not only as the foundation of Donald Trump's "big lie" about the stolen election but also as the basis for a new batch of sixty-two lawsuits that were filed by the Giuliani legal team[87] throughout the battleground states where Donald Trump had lost. The end goal was to prevent the certification of the states' election results. Powell characterized filing those lawsuits as "releasing the kraken,"[88] referring to a mythical sea monster that destroyed ships.

Despite the dreadful nickname, the lawsuits didn't pose much threat. They were hastily prepared, containing a myriad of mistakes and inaccuracies.[89] Very soon all but one of them were dismissed for lack of factual evidence.[90]

PRESSURE ON STATE OFFICIALS

In parallel, starting in late November, Rudy Giuliani embarked on a public roadshow to speak in front of state lawmakers in Pennsylvania,[91] Arizona,[92] Georgia,[93] and

Michigan.[94] Those spectacle hearings were broadcast live to the public, and Giuliani used them to boost the election fraud claims. His main audience was not the legislators but Americans who voted for Trump. During the meetings Giuliani publicly chastised the state officials, accusing them of allowing fraud in their electoral process, calling their state elections a "sham,"[95] and claiming the existence of "five . . . six . . . seven . . . hundred thousand of illegal votes."[96] Those public accusations were part of a strategy that aimed to galvanize Trump supporters, who, in turn, could then pressure state legislators to tip their state election results toward Donald Trump.

Trump and Giuliani wanted battleground state officials to proclaim election fraud in their states based on the speculation and hearsay that the president and his attorney presented as fact. In turn, those proclamations could then be used as justification to not certify Biden's electors in those states. Those efforts failed.

After the battleground states certified Biden's electors in mid-December, Trump and his allies then moved to pressure[97] state[98] officials[99] to decertify[100] those legally authorized electors while plotting with "alternate" Trump-aligned electors to flip their states' election results from Biden to Trump. Such actions, if followed through, would nullify the will of the voters.

As, one by one, officials in those states refused, Trump and Giuliani then resorted to intimidation tactics. They repeatedly vilified state legislators and election workers in their public appearances and social media. In some states Trump's campaign bought TV ads calling the public to pressure governors to "inspect" the voting equipment. By doing so, the president and his lawyer instigated the MAGA faithful to push state officials on Trump's behalf. As a result of those efforts, more than a dozen state legislators and election workers were continuously harassed both by phone and email. They and their family members received death threats. Trump's supporters gathered outside the officials' homes and, in some cases, of their relatives.[101]

Donald Trump and his team were especially vicious in Georgia. It was a historically Republican state, and Joe Biden's victory margin there was one of the slimmest in the country,[102] with the difference between the two candidates being 11,779 votes out of almost 5 million. That made Georgia the perfect target for a barrage of harassment from President Trump and his entourage.

Shortly after the election, Rudy Giuliani and Donald Trump started spreading false accusations of ballot stuffing by two Georgia election workers, a mother and a daughter.[103] The issue was amplified[104] online[105] by pro-Trump influencers, and soon thereafter these election workers started receiving death threats.[106] The end goal of that smear campaign was to make the election workers falsely "confess"[107] to committing election fraud and use that confession to persuade Georgia officials to sway the election results in Trump's favor. Trump himself repeatedly attempted[108] to coerce[109] the governor of Georgia into calling a special session to overturn the state's election results.

As the office of Georgia secretary of state, Brad Raffensperger, resisted, Donald

Trump's surrogates increased the pressure. Part of it came from Donald Trump Jr., who strong-armed Georgia Republican senators who were running for reelection to support the effort to overturn the results in exchange for the president's endorsement.[110] The senators obliged by calling for Raffensperger's resignation.[111] On another occasion Sen. Lindsey Graham (R-SC) called Raffensperger and inquired about absentee ballots,[112] which the secretary of state perceived as a veiled request to "toss" out legitimate absentee ballots.[113] The harassment of Georgian officials culminated on January 2, 2021, when Donald Trump personally called Brad Raffensperger, cajoling him with implicit threats to "find" 11,780 votes,[114] the exact amount that would give him a one-vote advantage over Joe Biden.

As Raffensperger and officials in other states continued to stand their ground, Trump's team devised a parallel scheme that they sought to implement in Georgia and other battleground states.

THE "ALTERNATE" ELECTORS PLOT

ELECTORAL PROCEDURES

As their "kraken" lawsuits failed to gain traction in state after state, Trump and his allies adopted a parallel scheme that involved the disruption of the electoral college and the violation of the Electoral Count Act. Together, these constitutional mandates outline the presidential election and vote-counting procedures. To understand the Trump team's actions, it's important to describe the rules of the electoral process.

Every four years in early November, the United States holds a presidential election. People cast their votes either in person or by mail. With the exception of Maine and Nebraska, each state allots all of its electoral college votes to the candidate with the most votes. There are 538 electors,[115] who are allocated across the states in proportion to the number of members of Congress for each state. For example, in 2020, New York, which had 27 House representatives[116] and 2 senators, was allocated 29 electoral votes.[117] The small state of Rhode Island, which had 2 House representatives[118] and 2 senators, was allocated 4 electoral votes.[119] Those electors must meet certain requirements and be officially approved with a certificate of ascertainment by either its secretary of state or its governor. A presidential candidate who wins a total of 270 or more of the 538 electoral votes wins the election.

In mid-December all the state electors convene at locations designated by their state constitutions to certify the votes. Those certified votes are then sent to Congress and the National Archives. By law,[120] on January 6 Congress counts the electoral college votes and legitimizes the election results. The vice president has a ceremonial role in presiding over the counting process, with no right to intervene.

Things get less straightforward if none of the presidential candidates reaches the 270-electoral-vote threshold. In that case it is up to the House of Representatives to choose the president and for the Senate to select the vice president.[121] That was what Donald Trump and his allies were trying to achieve. They attempted to capitalize on the fact that the general public lacked familiarity with the intricacies of the electoral process and to use their claims of fraud as cover to disrupt the electoral vote count and to push the final decision for the next president of the United States to the House of Representatives.

THE EVOLUTION OF THE SCHEME

The day after the election, the president's chief of staff, Mark Meadows, received a text message that read:[122]

> HERE's an AGRESSIVE [sic] STRATEGY: Why can t [sic] the states of GA NC PENN and other R controlled state houses declare this is BS (where conflicts and election not called that night) and just send their own electors to vote and have it go to the SCOTUS [the Supreme Court of the United States].

The sender was the former secretary of energy Rick Perry, who had previously appeared in this book as one of the people pushing for American LNG sales to Ukraine. This time the former secretary of energy advocated for ignoring the will of American voters in several states and "just" send their own Republican state electors to choose Donald Trump.

Almost a week after Perry sent the text message, two Texas businessmen connected to him went to the White House.[123] In a follow-up email the next day, one of them mentioned:[124]

> [President Trump] liked the plan we presented to use a parallel path of state legislators.

The email also included a suggestion to have "4+ MONSTER RALLY—TRIALS"[125] with

> [t]ens of thousands of Trump voters staring up at the GOP state legislators from their districts who ALONE control which slate of electors their state will submit.

Later that month Rudy Giuliani did exactly that, holding public spectacles in Pennsylvania,[126] Arizona,[127] Georgia,[128] and Michigan,[129] during which he chided state legislators for supposed election fraud. Those early messages and emails suggested that Rick Perry and his allies seemed to have been the origin of the plot to use alternate electors.

By late November to early December 2020, battleground state officials had refused to submit to Trump's pressure, the DOJ had refuted allegations of mass fraud, and Sidney Powell's kraken lawsuits were being dismissed. At that moment the scheme to push alternate electors became the core strategy of Trump's team. However, that scheme evolved over time. Two people crucial in that evolution were Kenneth Chesebro and John Eastman, both outside legal advisors to Trump's legal team. Between the two of them, they wrote[130] several[131] memos[132] for the White House and Trump's team[133], offering recommendations[134] and scenarios[135] of how to disrupt the election certification process.

In his memo to a Trump campaign lawyer from December 6, 2020, Kenneth Chesebro laid out his vision as follows:[136]

> *It seems feasible that the Trump campaign can prevent Biden from amassing 270 electoral votes on January 6, and force the Members of Congress, the media, and the American people to focus on the substantive evidence of illegal election and counting activities in the six contested States, provided three things happen:*
>
> a. *All the Trump-Pence electors meet and vote, in all six contested States, and send in the certificates containing their votes, in compliance with federal and state statutes, on December 14;*
>
> b. *There is pending, on January 6, in each of the six States, at least one lawsuit, in either federal or state court, which might plausibly, if allowed to proceed to completion, lead to either Trump winning the State or at least Biden being denied the State (of course, ideally by then Trump will have been awarded one or more of the States); and*
>
> c. *On January 6 in a solemn and constitutionally defensible manner, consistent with clear indications that this what the Framers of the Constitution intended and expected, and consistent with precedent from the first 70 years of our nation's history, Vice President Pence, presiding over the joint session, takes the position that it is his constitutional power and duty, alone, as President of the Senate, to both open and count the votes, and that anything in the Electoral Count Act to the contrary is unconstitutional.*

This was the first time when the idea of preventing Joe Biden from reaching the 270-electoral-vote threshold was proposed. As described above, according to the electoral college rules, 270 was the minimum amount of votes required to be proclaimed the winner. Chesebro proposed the creation of alternate pro-Trump electors in six battleground states of Arizona, Georgia, Michigan, Nevada, Pennsylvania, and Wisconsin. Trump's team would add a seventh state, New Mexico.[137]

Three days later Chesebro would send the Trump team step-by-step instructions of how those alternate electors would need to convene, directing them to follow as many requirements as possible to uphold the illusion of legitimacy and even suggesting that the alternate electors meet on the same day as the legitimate electors, on December 14. Weaving in the pending kraken lawsuits into his theory, Chesebro suggested that alternate Trump electors would be legitimized if any of those lawsuits were ruled in Trump's favor.[138] The last point of the memo implied that on January 6 the vice president, as the president of the Senate, could himself open the electoral votes and decide what to do with them despite the fact that the action would discard the will of the voters and violate the Electoral Count Act.

A week later, on December 13, Chesebro sent Giuliani an email outlining his vision of the vice president's role in the scheme and bringing forward ideas on how to leverage social media and the courts:[139]

> *The bottom line is I think having the President of the Senate firmly take the position that he, and he alone, is charged with the constitutional responsibility not just to **open** the votes, but to **count** them—including making judgments about what to do if there are conflicting votes—represents the best way to ensure:*
>
> 1. *that the mass media and social media platforms, and therefore the public, will focus intensely on the evidence of abuses in the election and canvassing; and*
>
> 2. *that there will be additional scrutiny in the courts and/or state legislatures, with an eye toward determining which electoral votes are the valid ones.*

On January 2 Kenneth Chesebro forwarded that email to John Eastman,[140] who built on Chesebro's ideas to create a six-page memo that included a multivariable scenario for January 6. Eastman offered a scheme that he believed could deliver a victory for Trump. It looked as follows:[141]

> *VP Pence opens the ballots, determines on his own which is valid, asserting that the authority to make that determination under the 12th Amendment, and the Adams and Jefferson precedents, is his alone (anything in the Electoral Count Act to the contrary is therefore unconstitutional).*
>
> i. *If State Legislatures have certified the Trump electors, he counts those, as required by Article II (the provision of the Electoral Count Act giving the default victory to the "executive"-certified slate therefore being unconstitutional). Any combination of states totaling 38 elector votes, and **TRUMP WINS**.*
>
> ii. *If State Legislatures have not certified their own slates of electors, VP Pence determines, based on all the evidence and the letters from state legislators calling*

> into question the executive certifications, decides to count neither slate of electors. (Note: this could be done with he gets to Arizona in the alphabetical roster, or he could defer Arizona and the other multi-slate states until the end, and then make the determination). At the end of the count, the tally would therefore be 232 for Trump, 222 for Biden. Because the 12th Amendment says "majority of electors appointed," having determined that no electors from the 7 states were appointed..., **TRUMP WINS.**
>
> iii. *Alternatively, VP Pence determines that because multiple electors were appointed from the 7 states but not counted because of ongoing election disputes, neither candidate has the necessary 270 elector votes, throwing the election to the House. IF the Republicans in the State Delegations stand firm, the vote there is 26 states for Trump, 23 for Biden, and 1 split vote.* **TRUMP WINS.**

Eastman's memo outlined specific calculations of alternate electoral votes required to take Biden's vote count below 270, while giving advantage to Trump. Under Eastman's assumptions both candidates would have less than 270 votes, and the election of the president would then be delegated to the House, according to the electoral college rules.[142] Alternatively, the decision-making could also be returned to the states where local officials would need to decertify Biden electors and instead certify Trump's alternate ones. At the time, twenty-six out of fifty states were controlled by Republicans, and Eastman implied that if those states stood "firm" with Trump, they could flip the Biden votes.

Chesebro's and Eastman's proposals were unconstitutional, and they both[143] knew it.[144] Trump's alternate electors scheme was not legitimate as the alternate electors were neither representative of the states' actual election results nor approved by their state governments. The vice president had no power to single-handedly toss out the votes of the American people. His role was merely ceremonial. However, those factors did not hinder Trump and his team's efforts.

PUTTING THE PIECES INTO PLAY

THE "ALTERNATE" TRUMP ELECTORS

Donald Trump and his team fully embraced Kenneth Chesebro and John Eastman's ideas. On December 6, the same day when Chesebro sent his key memo to the White House, President Trump called the RNC chairwoman Ronna McDaniel to solicit her assistance in recruiting alternate electors.[145] John Eastman, who was also on the call, alleged that those "contingent" electors would be used only if any of the ongoing lawsuits filed by the Trump campaign were ruled in his favor.[146]

Immediately afterward, Trump's team started assembling alternate electors in the seven battleground states of Arizona, Georgia, Michigan, Nevada, New Mexico, Pennsylvania, and Wisconsin. The argument that Trump's team used to persuade those persons to participate as alternate electors was the same they had used with the RNC chairwoman, that their votes were contingent on the outcome of the lawsuits in their state.[147] Nevertheless, Trump's team asked those electors to falsely claim in written certificates that they were duly elected and qualified.[148] Some of those alternate state electors, namely, in Pennsylvania and New Mexico, had some misgivings and included a caveat that they could be considered legitimate only if courts had decided as such.[149]

As instructed by Chesebro, to maintain the illusion of legitimacy, the alternate electors convened on December 14, the same day the genuine electors certified their votes. Chesebro also directed the alternate electors to gather in the same state buildings as the genuine ones. Some alternate electors complied, entering the premises under false pretenses.[150] Others considered staying overnight in their State Senate Building to avoid being spotted.[151] After the December 14 gatherings, similar to legitimate state electors, the Trump alternate ones also sent their votes to Congress and the National Archives,[152] to be counted on January 6.

Kenneth Chesebro and Rudy Giuliani coordinated[153] every[154] step taken by the alternate electors. Around the time when the alternate electors clandestinely convened, members of Trump's team publicly endorsed the effort. On December 14 Rudy Giuliani went on an ultraconservative show hosted by Trump ally Steve Bannon and claimed that alternate electors were signed in as a contingency.[155] That same day a senior Trump campaign official appeared on Fox News, mirroring Giuliani's claims.[156] By doing so, they planted the concept of Trump alternate electors into supporters' heads as yet another layer of the "big lie." Throughout December Trump allies would continue instilling the thought of the "stolen" election in conservative minds, feeding them false hopes that it was still possible to keep Donald Trump in the White House.

"BE THERE, WILL BE WILD"

On December 18, 2020, some of Trump's most controversial allies surprisingly appeared at the White House.[157] Leading the group was Sidney Powell. She was accompanied by former Trump national security advisor, Michael Flynn, who by that time had been pardoned by Trump despite lying to the FBI about his calls with the Russian ambassador. The third person with them was Patrick Byrne, the former CEO of Overstock who had a relationship with the previously mentioned Russian spy Maria Butina. As the group assembled in the Oval Office, White House lawyers rushed in to make sure that the president didn't make any hasty decisions. Later Rudy Giuliani and Mark Meadows joined the meeting as well.

To put this meeting into context, it occurred four days after the legitimate state electors convened in all fifty states and confirmed Joe Biden as the winner of the 2020 election.[158] By that time most of Trump's advisors had told him that it was time to concede.[159] The Department of Justice had already announced that they did not find any evidence of mass electoral fraud,[160] and the courts had already dismissed almost all the kraken lawsuits filed by Trump's legal team.[161]

However, Powell, Flynn, and Byrne came to the White House to persuade Donald Trump to continue fighting. The trio pushed ideas of seizing voting equipment with the help of the National Guard and appointing Sidney Powell as a special counsel to oversee an investigation of alleged voter fraud.[162] They even brought a draft of an executive order for Trump to sign.[163]

The flabbergasted White House lawyers vehemently opposed the plan.[164] They kept asking Powell whether she had any evidence to back her claims of fraud, to which she retorted that she could prove her theories when she had the voting machines seized.[165] The meeting quickly turned into a shouting match[166] that almost escalated into a fistfight between Flynn and a White House lawyer.[167]

After a nearly six-hour-long standoff, Powell's idea of declaring martial law and seizing voting machines was shut down. However, another idea had emerged: to have a Trump supporter rally in Washington, DC, on January 6 while Congress would be counting the electoral votes. That rally could create an illusion of mass public dissent against Joe Biden's electoral victory. It also could apply pressure on members of Congress and on Vice President Pence to comply with the Trump team's plan of using their alternate electors to drive down Joe Biden's electoral vote count below 270.

Giuliani, Powell, Flynn, and Byrne left the White House after midnight. Shortly thereafter, Donald Trump tweeted a call for his followers to come to Washington, DC, on January 6, 2021, ending it with "Be there, will be wild!"[168]

"JUST SAY THE ELECTION WAS CORRUPT"

In late December another group crucial for the implementation of the alternate electors scheme gathered in the Oval Office. On the night of December 21, eleven Republican congressmen, mostly from the battleground states, arrived to the White House.[169] Other people present at the meeting were VP Mike Pence; Trump's chief of staff, Mark Meadows; and the omnipresent Rudy Giuliani. The main subject on the agenda was developing an action plan for the January 6 congressional joint session. At the meeting John Eastman, one of the architects of the plot, argued that if they managed to reduce Joe Biden's electoral votes below 270, the decision on the next president could be delegated to the House of Representatives.[170] If that were to happen, Trump would need assistance from those congressmen present at the meeting.

In the days following, President Trump sought to persuade the new leadership of the Department of Justice to aid his cause. As mentioned previously, in mid-December AG William Barr had submitted his resignation to the president. Barr's deputy, Jeffrey Rosen, became the new acting attorney general. Starting from Rosen's very first day, Trump barraged the acting attorney general with requests to announce an investigation, floated the idea of the DOJ seizing voting equipment, and peppered Rosen with conspiracy claims of election fraud. During a tirade on one of their calls, the president told the acting attorney general:[171]

> Just say the election was corrupt and leave the rest to me and the Republican Congressmen.

That phrase revealed that Donald Trump wanted to use a DOJ statement as fuel for his election fraud claims and to equip Republican congressmen with an argument for any potential debate during the joint session in Congress on January 6.

As the acting attorney general continued to refuse to be a part of Trump's desperate effort to cling to power, the president threatened to replace him with an obscure DOJ official who could be more compliant. The standoff between Trump and Rosen culminated on the evening of January 3, when several top DOJ officials met with the president at the White House and threatened to resign en masse if he appointed a sycophant as the head of the Justice Department.[172] Only under the threat of mass resignation did Trump back down.

Running out of options, the president pivoted to increasing the pressure on his vice president, who Trump believed was his last chance to stay in the White House.

THE PENCE CARD

As mentioned previously, Trump's team had been given recommendations from outside legal advisors, Kenneth Chesebro and John Eastman, to enroll Mike Pence into their alternate electors scheme. They falsely argued in their[173] memos[174] that the vice president had the ultimate power to intervene in the counting of the electoral votes during the joint congressional session on January 6. By introducing competing sets of votes from several states, they aimed to push Pence to either ignore both sets of electors or outright choose Trump's alternate electors. The overarching objective was to reject Biden's electoral votes in seven states, thereby reducing his electoral college vote count below 270. Then they planned to either delegate the voting to the House of Representatives or return the election decision to the states.

In the first case, in which the decision-making would be delegated to the House of Representatives, Trump hoped to rely on the Republican congressmen whom he had met with in late December. In the second case, Trump's team would need to persuade state officials to certify Trump's alternate electors. In either case, the end goal was to deliver a victory for Donald Trump.

Pence's team had independently been searching for clarification of the legal guidelines of his role during the electoral vote-counting session.[175] By early January Pence's team had solidified their view that his role was only ceremonial and that, thus, he had no power to toss out electoral votes. However, Trump kept telling the public otherwise and pushed Pence to collaborate. At a New Year's event on January 1, 2021, the two had an argument, and Trump didn't hold back. Pence later would recall the president's words as:[176]

> *You're too honest... Hundreds of thousands are gonna hate your guts... People are gonna think you're stupid.*

Through the morning of January 6, Donald Trump kept trying to persuade Mike Pence to follow the Trump team's plan.[177] As personal pleas did not seem to work, Trump and his allies incited the public against Pence to escalate the pressure. The president repeatedly tweeted unsubstantiated claims of a stolen election[178] and calls for Pence to "do the right thing."[179] Steve Bannon and his podcast guests, one of them being John Eastman, discussed the January 6 scenario and Pence's purported role in it.[180]

Concerned of the disinformation that was actively spread by Trump and his allies,[181] Pence felt compelled to release his own statement. On January 6, minutes before the beginning of the joint session in Congress, he issued a public letter[182] vowing to follow his role as defined by the Constitution and the Electoral Count Act, which did not bestow on him any powers to intervene in the counting of electoral votes. At the end of that tumultuous day, the vice president would uphold his constitutional duty and ignore the alternate electors' counterfeit certificates, bringing the alternate electors plot to an end.

JANUARY 6

President Trump and his allies saw the joint congressional session on January 6, 2021, as the event that would define whether he would stay in the White House. All their efforts since the November election led to that point. Throughout the winter holiday season, Trump's allies promoted the January 6 rally and energized MAGA fans by feeding them false claims. Pushed by various Trump supporters on social media, it spread like wildfire.[183]

Following Donald Trump's siren call to Washington, a crowd of far right groups mobilized at the Ellipse near the White House on the night before January 6.[184] That night Trump's allies, old and new, went onstage to galvanize the crowd. The event speakers included[185] Trump's friend Roger Stone, disgraced former national security advisor Michael Flynn, and former Trump campaign advisor George Papadopoulos, all of whom had been convicted in connection to Russia's 2016 election interference.

However, they all had[186] been[187] pardoned[188] by Donald Trump before Christmas. The speakers portrayed Donald Trump as an unjustly targeted messiah who had fought for the American people. They used common polarization tactics of "us vs. them," labeling those who asserted that Trump had won as "patriots" and those who believed that he had lost as "traitors."

In the early morning of January 6, Donald Trump set the focus of the day by tweeting:[189]

> States want to correct their votes, which they now know were based on irregularities and fraud, plus corrupt process never received legislative approval. All Mike Pence has to do is send them back to the States, AND WE WIN. Do it Mike, this is a time for extreme courage!

As the day progressed, MAGA celebrities, one after another, took to the stage, stoking the protesters to march on the Capitol. In his speech Rudy Giuliani alluded to the "stolen" election and called for the rally goers to "have trial by combat."[190] At noon Donald Trump gave a long speech that called for Vice President Pence to "have the courage to do what he has to do."[191] He closed his speech by urging his supporters to walk to the Capitol and "give them [Republicans] the kind of pride and boldness that they need to take back our country."[192]

Shortly after 2:00 p.m., protesters who had been marching toward the Capitol and breaking through police lines breached the Capitol building. At 2:24 p.m., just hours after the vice president had released his public letter, Donald Trump tweeted:[193]

> Mike Pence didn't have the courage to do what should have been done.

That tweet added more fuel to the fire. Chanting, "Hang Mike Pence!"[194] and "Bring out Pence!"[195] the MAGA mob stormed into the Capitol building,[196] prompting lawmakers to evacuate under physical threat.[197] Vice President Pence and his family, who were also in the building, missed the mob by a few feet.[198] Outside, another group of Trump supporters installed makeshift gallows,[199] making their threats to execute the vice president seem acutely real.

As hell broke loose within the Capitol building, Pres. Donald Trump, despite many requests from his advisors to soothe the attackers' rage,[200] "gleefully" watched[201] the chaos unravel.[202] When told that the protesters were calling for Pence to be hanged, Trump reportedly replied that perhaps he deserved that.[203] Trump apparently needed to stay in power so much that he was willing to sacrifice his vice president's life and US democracy.

EPILOGUE
AMERICA... INC.?

January 6, 2021, turned out to be a manifestation of Donald Trump's presidency. Fueling the crowd with lies and hatred and aided by complicit conservative allies, Donald Trump and Rudy Giuliani unleashed the mob to attack the very symbol of American democracy. The insurrection was the natural outcome of the never-ending persuasion games that occurred during Trump's presidency.

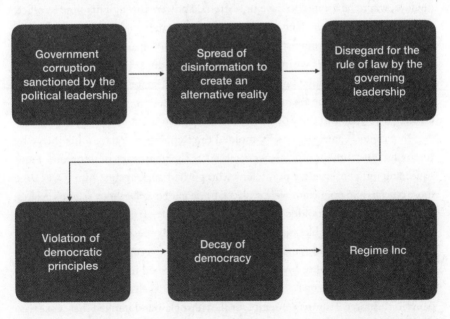

FIGURE 12. PATH TO REGIME INC.

In his fierce effort to stay in power, Donald Trump steered the United States onto the path that had been previously taken by Vladimir Putin, Recep Tayyip Erdogan, and Nicolas Maduro, all of whom were trapped into their presidencies by their corruption, insatiable greed, and the fear of prosecution if their power was lost. They all, over time, have transformed their countries into a version of Regime Inc., taking very similar steps (figure 12).

Commonly, the leaders' personal corruption trickled down into their countries' government systems and elites. When Russians, Turks and Venezuelans started speaking up against their rulers, their governments suppressed independent media and deployed disinformation tactics, deflecting opposing voices and creating an alternative reality for those who were less informed. To keep pilfering their countries' resources without any criminal repercussions, Putin, Maduro, and Erdogan, installed sycophants as justice system officials. Through sham elections and referendums, the strongmen have secured their positions in power until the end of their lives, even if it brought economic decay to their countries and oppression to ordinary people.

Through their years in power the presidents of Russia, Venezuela and Turkey have consistently crippled the core principles of democracy - of free speech, of open and fair elections, and of equal application of the rule of law. Their countries eventually evolved into autocratic regimes that were ran as corporations, subject to the will of one individual at the top.

Similar to those dictators, Trump sought to run the United States as his own fiefdom, where he aspired to have unrestrained power. Through his time in office, the media repeatedly challenged the veracity of his statements, and in retort Trump relentlessly lambasted mainstream news while spreading alternative narratives in an attempt to cloak his various episodes of misconduct. The constant spread of falsehoods by the president and his allies had the ultimate goal of corrupting the public's mind. Over time Trump's narrative shifted his followers' perception of reality, creating a new view of the world centered on the adoration of Trump.

In parallel, Trump gradually molded the Republican Party in his image by removing government officials who served as the guardrails of democracy and squeezing out conservative politicians who pushed back against him. Over time those officials and politicians were replaced by people complacent to Trump's desires.

As he gradually molded Washington to his taste, Trump's disregard for the rule of law grew more blatant. In the beginning of his presidency, Donald Trump professed that he would remake Washington by eliminating the corruption of the ruling elite. At the end of his term, he openly pardoned his allies who had been found guilty of misdeeds related to the Kremlin's 2016 election meddling. Those pardons displayed Trump's contempt for the rule of law and implied that those who were loyal to him could skirt justice.

The United States has become a highly polarized country where the quiet voice of reason has been frequently silenced by emotional diatribes in the name of Donald Trump. It has reached the tipping point, about which the first president of the republic, George Washington, had warned us about in his farewell address:[1]

> *The alternate domination of one faction over another, sharpened by the spirit of revenge natural to party dissension, which in different ages and countries has perpetrated the most horrid enormities, is itself a frightful despotism. But this leads at length to a more formal and permanent despotism. The disorders and miseries which result gradually incline the minds of men to seek security and repose in the absolute power of an individual, and sooner or later the chief of some prevailing faction, more able or more fortunate than his competitors, turns this disposition to the purposes of his own elevation on the ruins of public liberty.*

Although Trump lost the 2020 election, his MAGA movement has marched on. He continues to wield enormous influence over his supporters and the Republican Party. Trump's cumulative actions left the conservative establishment infected with MAGA populism and, if allowed to continue, would undoubtedly lead to breaks in the constitutional framework of American democracy. If Trump returns to the White House, he may never leave it and may well become the despot George Washington so presciently wrote about.

Today America is at a crossroads. One path leads to the continued rule of a democratic republic with a legal system striving for common justice. If the United States submits to Donald Trump, it will follow the darker path that leads to our country's eventual transformation into America Inc. Making the right choice between those two paths is not a mere moral crusade but a practical imperative for the preservation of democracy for our future generations.

APPENDIX A
THE INTEGRATED TIMELINE

This timeline combines all relevant events across the United States, Turkey, Russia, Ukraine, and Venezuela.

2011

April 22, 2011 - Maria Butina, a Russian progun activist, founded[1] a group called the Right to Bear Arms.[2]

April 28–May 1, 2011 - Alexander Torshin, Russian senator and the first vice-chairman of the Russian Federation Council, attended the National Rifle Association convention in Pittsburgh, Pennsylvania, where he was introduced to the then incoming NRA president, David Keene.[3]

2012

February 10, 2012 - Alexander Torshin became a lifetime member at the NRA.[4]

2013

May 28, 2013–August 20, 2013 - Gezi Park protests[5] spread through Turkey, where antigovernment protesters spoke against the Turkish government's censorship of free speech and media, as well as the growing authoritarianism of Erdogan's rule. In response, the government pressured the Turkish media not to cover the unrest and used excessive force against protesters.[6] Because of the Turkish government's aggressive response, the EU halted Turkey's membership negotiations.[7]

June 4–9, 2013 - Members of a number of Turkish American cultural groups exchanged emails about writing op-eds and countering the existing news coverage narrative with their versions of Gezi Park protests. The group's coordinator was Murat Güzel, a Turkish American businessman. People in the email exchange included Erdogan's son-in-law Berat Albayrak and his henchman, Halil Danismaz.[8]

June 24, 2013 – A Trump Organization real estate agent exchanged emails with Halil Danismaz about a purchase of real estate in Manhattan for $28 million. Danismaz forwarded the email to Berat Albayrak and Bilal Erdogan, a son of the Turkish prime minister Erdogan.[9]

October 31–November 1, 2013 - NRA president David Keene and a former GOP operative, Paul Erickson, flew to a gun rights event in Moscow, which was hosted by Maria Butina.[10]

November 8–10 2013 - Donald Trump traveled to Moscow[11] for the Miss Universe beauty pageant. The event was financed by Russian oligarch Aras Agalarov. After that event Trump hinted at constructing a Trump Tower in Moscow with the Agalarovs.[12]

November 21, 2013 - People in Ukraine started protesting[13] against the decision of their president, Viktor Yanukovych, to halt Ukraine's association agreement talks with the European Union[14] in favor of a loan from the Russian government.[15] That decision triggered what became known as the Maidan Revolution

December 2013 - At the request of Russian spy Maria Butina and her handler, Alexander Torshin, NRA president, David Keene, asked then former US Ambassador to the United Nations John Bolton to record an address for the Russian Duma that advocated for gun rights.[16] Bolton recorded a video[17] that was later played by Butina to Russian officials.[18]

December 17, 2013 - Turkish police arrested fifty-two officials and businessmen, including Reza Zarrab, an Iranian Turkish gold trader, in connection to a large government corruption scheme.[19] The scheme also threatened then prime minister Recep Tayyip Erdogan. On a recording that was leaked into the public, a person sounding like Prime Minister Erdogan warned his son of ongoing police raids and instructed him to get rid of a large amount of cash kept at home.[20] The scandal led to anticorruption protests that lasted over a week.[21] In response to the scandal, Erdogan replaced ten cabinet members[22] and fired several police unit chiefs.[23]

2014

January 7, 2014 - The Turkish government dismissed more than 350 police officers including the chiefs of financial crime, antismuggling, and organized crime units.[24]

February 22, 2014 - Ukrainian president Viktor Yanukovych fled to Russia amid mass protests against him.[25]

February 27, 2014 - The "little green men," who were later revealed to be Russian special forces, appeared in the Crimean Peninsula to "protect" pro-Kremlin protesters.[26] It would begin a long war between Russia and Ukraine.

February 28, 2014 - Reza Zarrab was released from a Turkish prison[27] after the Turkish government dropped the charges against him. Zarrab would continue trading gold[28] until his arrest in the United States in 2016.

March 7, 2014 - The first known public photo of Lev Parnas with Donald Trump was taken at Ivanka Trump's fashion event in Florida and was posted on Facebook.[29]

March 13, 2014 - Dmytro Firtash, a Ukrainian oligarch with deep Russian connections, was arrested in Austria at the request of the United States.[30]

April 2014 - The Internet Research Agency created the "translator project," also known as the "American department."[31] In the following years, the IRA would produce disinformation at an industrial scale for American social media users.

April 25–27, 2014 - Maria Butina attended an NRA convention in Indianapolis, Indiana.[32]

April 30, 2014 - The Pentagon announced[33] that in the upcoming months Michael Flynn, after being accused of insubordination[34] and bad management style, would be relieved of his position as the director of the Defense Intelligence Agency. He would officially leave the position in August 2014.[35]

June 16, 2014 - The Russian government cut off gas exports to Ukraine in the midst of the conflict in eastern Ukraine.[36] By doing so, the Kremlin also cut off gas that flowed to Europe through the vast Ukrainian gas pipeline network, hoping that the EU would lean on Ukraine to submit to Russia's demands.

June 2014 - Two high-level members of the Russian Internet Research Agency took a scouting trip to the United States. They sought to find out divisive issues and pain points of American culture, especially in swing states, that could sway voters from one direction of the political spectrum to another. In some states they met with grassroots political activists, who explained their tactics to the Russians.[37]

August 10, 2014 - Recep Tayyip Erdogan won the presidential election in Turkey.[38]

August 12, 2014 - Greenberg Traurig registered as a foreign agent of Turkey[39] as a subcontractor for the Gephardt Group,[40] another lobbying firm.

August 28, 2014 - Recep Tayyip Erdogan was sworn in as the Turkish president.[41]

October 2014 - Michael Flynn, along with Bijan Kian,[42] founded the Flynn Intel Group,[43] a firm that provided consulting services and intelligence research.

October 17, 2014 - Turkish prosecutors dismissed public corruption investigations[44] involving Halkbank.

December 2014 - Russia and Turkey signed an agreement to build an underwater gas pipeline, TurkStream, that would bypass Ukraine and go from Russia through Turkey into southern Europe.[45]

2015

January 20, 2015 - Alexander Torshin became the deputy chairman of Russia's Central Bank.[46]

Mid-February 2015 - Maria Butina reached out to former NRA president David Keene and his wife, seeking their assistance in putting together a list of key GOP events and the names of expected important attendees. The Keenes not only provided a detailed list but also helped Butina obtain invitations to those events.[47]

Spring 2015 - The Internet Research Agency management's daily instructions started including "tasks to discredit the image" of presidential candidates.[48] The main targets were Hillary Clinton and moderate Democratic and Republican candidates. In contrast, the fringe candidates Bernie Sanders and Donald Trump were spared as the IRA management apparently "supported" them.[49]

Spring 2015 - The IRA ran a test political rally from afar by creating a Facebook event, putting a location in New York as a gathering venue, and promising a free hot dog to those who would come.[50] Observing the event through street cameras from their office in Saint Petersburg, Russia, the IRA established the possibility of creating events remotely.[51]

March 2015 - Maria Butina devised a plan for a "diplomacy project" and presented it to her mentor, Alexander Torshin.[52]

April 10–12, 2015 - Maria Butina and Alexander Torshin attended an NRA convention in Nashville, Tennessee,[53] where they were introduced to Wisconsin governor Scott Walker. At a dinner before that event, Torshin and Butina met officials from the US Federal Reserve and Treasury Department and a member of the House Foreign Affairs Committee.[54]

June 16, 2015 - Donald Trump announced his 2016 presidential campaign.[55]

July 11, 2015 - Maria Butina and Paul Erickson traveled to Las Vegas for a libertarian event, FreedomFest.[56] After Donald Trump's speech, Butina asked him about his views on Russia and sanctions.[57] Trump replied that he would "get along very nicely with Putin" and that sanctions weren't necessary. While at FreedomFest, Butina also connected to Patrick Byrne,[58] the former CEO of Overstock and then backer of presidential candidate Sen. Rand Paul.

July 13, 2015 - Maria Butina and Paul Erickson traveled to Scott Walker's presidential campaign announcement event.[59] Afterward, Butina prepared for Torshin a detailed assessment of Walker's chances of winning the Republican presidential nomination.[60]

July 22, 2015 - Russian oligarch Aras Agalarov invited Donald Trump to his sixtieth birthday party. Trump politely declined to attend.[61]

August 3, 2015 - Rep. Dana Rohrabacher (R-CA) met with Alexander Torshin in Russia.[62]

August 28, 2015 - The Turkish government signed a lobbying contract with Amsterdam & Partners.[63]

September 2015 - Trump's private lawyer, Michael Cohen, received two proposals for the construction of a Trump Tower in Moscow.[64]

September 2015 - The Russian government deployed military forces to Syria to support the Assad regime in the Syrian Civil War.[65]

October 23, 2015 - In exchange for a $300 million loan from a European bank, the Ukrainian government agreed to establish a supervisory board of independent professionals to oversee structural reforms at Naftogaz, the country's state gas company, as a measure to eliminate corruption.[66]

November 2, 2015 - Michael Cohen sent to a Russian contact[67] a letter of intent signed by Donald Trump[68] for the construction of a Trump Tower in Moscow.

November 24, 2015 - Turkish military forces shot down a Russian fighter plane along the borders of Syria and Turkey.[69] That incident cooled down the relationship between Russia and Turkey,[70] which recovered in mid-2016[71] with mediation assistance[72] from a Russian oligarch and former senator, Farkhad Akhmedov.[73]

December 8–13, 2015 - A group of ranking NRA members traveled to Moscow, where they met with several Russian officials.[74]

December 9–12, 2015 - Michael Flynn traveled to Moscow to speak at an event hosted by the Russian propaganda channel, RT. He was paid over $45,000 for his appearance.[75]

2016

January 11, 2016 - Michael Cohen reached out directly to the office of the Russian president's spokesperson, Dmitry Peskov, seeking assistance with the Trump Tower project in Moscow.[76]

January 19, 2016 - It was announced that former New York mayor Rudy Giuliani and his colleague Marc Mukasey would be leaving the law firm of Bracewell & Giuliani to join Greenberg Traurig.[77]

January 20, 2016 - Amsterdam & Partners, which had a lobbying contract with the Turkish government, subcontracted Mercury Public Affairs[78] to lobby the US government to investigate organizations connected to Fethullah Gülen, Erdogan's declared archnemesis who had been living in self-imposed exile in the United States for decades.

February 4, 2016 - Alexander Torshin and Maria Butina attended the National Prayer Breakfast,[79] a high-level annual event in Washington, DC, that gathered international political, business, and religious elites.

February 2016 - Michael Flynn began acting as an advisor to candidate Trump.[80]

March 2016 - Hackers from Russian military intelligence, also known as the GRU, started breaching Hillary Clinton's campaign.[81] They stole tens of thousands of the campaign chair's emails.[82]

March 19, 2016 - The US government arrested Iranian gold trader Reza Zarrab,[83] who was the focal point in the Halkbank money-laundering scheme.

March 21, 2016 - The SDNY issued indictments for three people, including Reza Zarrab, for conspiracy to evade US sanctions on Iran, money laundering, and bank fraud.[84]

Around March 21, 2016 - George Papadopoulos and Carter Page joined the Trump campaign foreign policy advisory team.[85]

March 29, 2016 – Donald Trump's campaign announced that Paul Manafort had become the campaign's convention manager.[86]

April 2016 - A former Turkish journalist, Rabia Kazan, joined[87] the National Diversity Coalition advisory board.[88] The NDC was a group founded by Michael Cohen, Trump's private attorney, to attract minority votes to candidate Trump during the 2016 campaign.

April 2016 - Ukraine's Naftogaz formed its first international supervisory board.[89]

April 2, 2016 - Rep. Dana Rohrabacher (R-CA) went to Russia and met with Alexander Torshin once again.[90]

April 12, 2016 - Russia's GRU hacking team breached the Democratic Congressional Campaign Committee network.[91]

May 2016 - The Russian Internet Research Agency organized two events for two confronting groups, a pro-Muslim and an anti-Muslim, in Houston, Texas, for the same time and at the same location.[92] By doing so, the IRA intentionally pitted those groups against each other,[93] increasing the degree of polarization in the same community.

May 4, 2016 - Donald Trump became the presumptive Republican presidential nominee.[94]

May 20, 2016 - Alexander Torshin and Maria Butina attended an NRA convention[95] where the NRA endorsed Donald Trump.[96] Around that event Torshin and Butina ran into Donald Trump Jr.[97]

May 25, 2016 - The SDNY objected to Reza Zarrab's request for bail and released a memorandum that implicated President Erdogan and other high-ranking Turkish government officials in the Halkbank case.[98]

Summer of 2016 - GRU hackers copied and exported[99] to their own servers[100] over seventy gigabytes of information from the DCCC database and tens of thousands of DNC emails, which included internal DNC communication about political donors[101] and Democratic candidates' campaigns.[102]

June 3, 2016 - Donald Trump Jr. received an email with a request for a Russian lawyer to meet him. The email claimed that the lawyer had potentially compromising information on Hillary Clinton.[103]

June 8, 2016 - Affiliates of the Russian hackers launched DCLeaks.com, a website where they published thousands of the stolen DNC emails. They also claimed that DCLeaks was "launched by the American hacktivists who respect and appreciate freedom of speech, human rights and government of the people."[104]

June 9, 2016 - Paul Manafort, Jared Kushner, and Donald Trump Jr. met with Russian lawyer Natalia Veselnitskaya and her associates with an expectation of obtaining damning information on Hillary Clinton.[105] Instead, Veselnitskaya indirectly asked

Trump's team to repeal the Magnitsky Act, which would lift sanctions of several Russian officials.

June 14, 2016 - The DNC hack[106] became public and was ascribed to Russia.[107] To deflect attention from Russia, GRU hackers created a fake online persona named Guccifer 2.0, portraying it as a "lone hacker."[108]

Around June 27, 2016 - President Erdogan wrote a letter to Vladimir Putin, apologizing for the Turkish downing of the Russian plane.[109] Acting as an intermediary between the two countries, Russian oligarch Farkhad Akhmedov[110] was the one who suggested[111] to Erdogan to write the letter.

Mid-July 2016 - Illinois election officials reported unusual activity in their network to the FBI. During their investigation the FBI discovered that Russian hackers had gained access to the state voter registration database that contained names, addresses, partial social security numbers, and state IDs of fourteen million voters.[112]

July 15, 2016 - Fractions of the Turkish military unsuccessfully attempted a coup against President Erdogan.[113] Mass government crackdowns followed, with nearly 160,000 detained,[114] including at least 10,000 soldiers[115] and 2,745 judges.[116] A week later the Turkish government declared a state of emergency[117] that would last for years.

July 15, 2016 - Michael Flynn gave a speech to a conservative group in Cleveland, Ohio, where he expressed support to the Turkish military and their attempt to topple Erdogan.[118]

July 16, 2016 - Paul Erickson sent an email to Sam Clovis saying that he had been "developing a back-channel to the Kremlin for the past couple of years."[119]

July 18, 2016 - Butina prepared a forecast on the election outcome for the Russian Ministry of Foreign Affairs and sent it to Torshin. In her message she also pondered approaching Trump campaign foreign policy advisor Carter Page.[120]

July 22, 2016 - WikiLeaks released the first tranche of the DNC emails, containing the DNC chair's disparaging comments about one of the Democratic presidential candidates' staffers.[121]

July 23, 2016 - Paul Erickson sent an email to a "Rockefeller heir," George O'Neill, who hosted Russian-American friendship dinners, about inviting Patrick Byrne, the CEO of Overstock.[122]

July 25-28, 2016 - The Democratic Party held its national convention,[123] at which Hillary Clinton was announced as its official presidential nominee.[124]

July 27, 2016 - Donald Trump publicly urged Russia to find "30,000 missing emails" that belonged to Hillary Clinton.[125] Within hours, the GRU hackers attacked seventy-six email accounts registered at the Clinton campaign's domain.[126]

August 2016 - The IRA organized seventeen flash mob rallies throughout Florida[127] in support of Donald Trump.[128] Masquerading as Americans, the IRA operatives sent Facebook messages to real pro-Trump activists and encouraged them to participate. In some cases the IRA trolls reimbursed the grassroots activists' expenses for printed materials and other marketing items, using US bank accounts registered with stolen American IDs.[129]

August 2016 - Maria Butina moved to the United States to study at American University of International Service in Washington, DC.[130]

August 2, 2016 - Turkish president Erdogan accused the West of orchestrating the coup attempt against his government.[131]

August 9, 2016 - President Erdogan traveled to Saint Petersburg, Russia, to meet with Russian president Putin and reset the relationship between two countries. It was Erdogan's first international trip since the coup attempt.[132]

August 9, 2016 - The Flynn Intel Group signed a $600,000 contract with Inovo BV, a company controlled by Turkish businessman Ekim Alptekin.[133]

August 14, 2016 - The *New York Times* published an article that revealed Paul Manafort's undeclared $12.7 million payments from pro-Kremlin oligarchs in Ukraine.[134] Within days the news[135] was[136] picked up[137] by other media outlets.

August 19, 2016 - Paul Manafort was forced to resign from the Trump campaign after reports of his undeclared income from Ukraine appeared in the media.[138]

August 24, 2016 - VP Joe Biden flew to Turkey to reassure American support for Turkey after the coup attempt against President Erdogan. According to Biden's aide, President Erdogan privately pressed the vice president to drop the Halkbank case and remove the lead SDNY prosecutor, Preet Bharara, as a way to improve the relations with Turkey.[139]

September 2016 - Republican congressman Michael McCaul (R-TX), who was also the chairman of the House Homeland Security Committee, said in an interview to CNN that the Russian hackers also penetrated the Republican National Committee. The RNC denied it, and McCaul later retracted his statement.[140]

September 1, 2016 - Hundreds of thousands of Venezuelans protested against Maduro's government, calling for a referendum to recall him.[141]

September 19, 2016 - Michael Flynn met with Mevlut Cavusoglu, Turkish foreign minister, and Berat Albayrak, then Turkish energy minister (and Erdogan's son-in-law), to discuss how to get Fethullah Gülen extradited to Turkey. Ekim Alptekin, Bijan Kian (Flynn's associate and a member of Trump's transition team), and James Woolsey (ex-CIA director) were also present at the meeting. Afterward, James Woolsey allegedly informed then vice president Joe Biden about the meeting.[142]

September 20, 2016 - James Woolsey and his lobbyist wife, Nancye Miller, met with Ekim Alptekin and Sezgin Baran Korkmaz at Peninsula Hotel in New York.[143] At the meeting Woolsey and Miller pitched a $10M contract for their lobbying services.[144]

September 21, 2016 - On the outskirts of the United Nations General Assembly, President Erdogan met with Vice President Biden and, once again, pressed to release Zarrab and fire both the New York prosecutor Preet Bharara and the judge overseeing the case.[145]

September 22, 2016 - The Venezuelan National Election Council ruled[146] that a referendum for Maduro's recall would be held months later than requested by the Venezuelan opposition.[147] Unsatisfied with the ruling, Venezuelans went to protest on the streets.[148] Maduro characterized the call for a referendum as a coup attempt.[149]

September 28, 2016 - Maria Butina encountered J. D. Gordon,[150] a former senior foreign policy advisor to the Trump campaign, then invited him to a Russian-American friendship dinner.[151]

Late September 2016 - Election officials from twenty-one US states responded to the FBI, confirming that some of the IP addresses that attacked the Illinois election system also made connections to their state election networks.[152]

October 7, 2016 - The Turkish government arrested American pastor Andrew Brunson, accusing him of connections to Fethullah Gülen.[153]

October 7, 2016 - The Obama administration formally accused Russia of hacking into the DNC and stealing and disseminating the stolen information.[154] That same day a bombshell video of Donald Trump making lewd remarks about women[155] appeared in the media.[156] Later that day WikiLeaks began releasing thousands of emails stolen from John Podesta,[157] the chairman of Hillary Clinton's campaign. While turning public attention away from Russia, the leaks turned up the heat for both Hillary Clinton and Donald Trump, who faced each other in the second presidential debate two days later.

October 10, 2016 - Amid layers of sanctions from Western democracies and calls for a referendum for his removal,[158] Venezuelan president Nicolas Maduro went on his first trip to Turkey[159] for the World Energy Congress.[160] There, he met with Turkish president Erdogan[161] and Russian president Vladimir Putin.[162] After that meeting the ties between the governments of Russia, Turkey, and Venezuela would strengthen, leading to the formation of an unofficial autocratic alliance that would coordinate[163] trade[164] outside the Western commercial network[165] and arrange their version of "peace talks" on Syria.[166]

October 12, 2016 - Lev Parnas went to a Trump fundraiser in Florida,[167] where he reportedly crossed paths with Rudy Giuliani.[168] The event was also attended by Brian Ballard.

October 18, 2016 - Maria Butina and J. D. Gordon went to a rock concert.[169]

October 20, 2016 - Maria Butina emailed Alexander Torshin, claiming that she had access to three members of the Trump campaign.[170]

October 24–27, 2016 - Lev Parnas, who had no prior history of political contributions, donated to twenty state Republican committees and a $33,400 donation to the Republican National Committee. He also donated $50,000 to Trump Victory PAC and $2,700 to candidate Trump. The total amount of contributions made by Parnas within three days was almost $100,000.[171]

October 2016 – The Turkish justice minister asked US attorney general Loretta Lynch to release Zarrab and return him to Turkey.[172] The attorney general rejected the request.

November 6, 2016 - WikiLeaks released more than eight thousand stolen DNC emails.[173]

November 8, 2016 (US Election Day) - Michael Flynn published an op-ed in the *Hill* in support of the Turkish government and portraying Fethullah Gülen as similar to Osama bin Laden.[174] At the time, Michael Flynn was not registered with the DOJ as a Turkish lobbyist.

November 8, 2016 (US Election Day) - As the states called the election for Donald Trump, Butina wrote to Torshin, "I am ready for further orders."[175]

November 9, 2016 - The Internet Research Agency staff in Saint Petersburg, Russia, gathered for a toast and proclaimed, "We made America great!"[176]

November 10-11, 2016 - Maria Butina prepared for Alexander Torshin and the Russian Ministry of Foreign Affairs two papers about the next steps of influence on the Trump administration.[177]

November 12, 2016 - While celebrating her birthday party in DC, Butina reportedly bragged about having access to the Trump campaign.[178]

November 15, 2016 - Maria Butina received invitations to the annual National Prayer Breakfast for more than a dozen of Russian delegates.[179]

November 30, 2016 - President-Elect Donald Trump met with the US attorney from the SDNY, Preet Bharara, reportedly asking him to stay in his position.[180]

November 30, 2016 - The PDVSA, the Venezuelan state oil company, signed a $1.5 billion loan deal with Rosneft, the Russian state oil company, in which the PDVSA used 49.9 percent of its US subsidiary Citgo as a collateral.[181]

November 30, 2016 - Michael Flynn, a senior Trump advisor, and Jared Kushner, Trump's son-in-law, met with the Russian ambassador to the US, Sergey Kislyak, at Trump Tower.[182]

December 5, 2016 - Lev Parnas and Igor Fruman met with Mubariz Mansimov in Fruman's nightclub in Kyiv. Mansimov reportedly asked Parnas to introduce him to the lobbying firm Ballard Partners.[183] During the same trip, Parnas was reportedly also met Roman Nasirov, the head of Ukraine's tax service.[184]

December 12, 2016 - President-Elect Donald Trump made his first of three direct calls to the US attorney for the SDNY, Preet Bharara.[185]

December 16, 2016 - Lev Parnas and Roman Nasirov went to Mar-a-Lago to see Donald Trump.[186]

December 19, 2016 - Russian president Putin had a meeting[187] with a group of 50 oligarchs and directed them to establish back-channel communications with the Trump transition team.[188]

Late December 2016 - Michael Flynn, while serving in Trump's transition team, reportedly was offered $15 million by Turkish representatives in New York to help Fethullah Gülen get extradited from the United States.[189]

December 22, 2016 - Citgo, a US subsidiary of the Venezuelan state-owned PDVSA, donated $500,000 to the Trump inauguration.[190] That donation came three weeks after the PDVSA borrowed $1.5 billion from Russian Rosneft, using almost 50 percent of Citgo as a collateral.[191]

December 23, 2016 - Russian ambassador Sergey Kislyak called Michael Flynn to discuss Russia's views on peace in the Middle East.[192]

December 29, 2016 - The United States introduced new sanctions on Russian security services and individuals and expelled thirty-five Russian diplomats in response to Russia's interference in the 2016 US presidential election.[193]

That same day Michael Flynn spoke with the Russian ambassador about the US sanctions[194] and asked Russia "not to escalate the situation."[195] During the call the Russian ambassador also asked Flynn to send representatives to Astana, Kazakhstan, for peace talks organized by Russia. The talks, focused on resolving the Syrian Civil War, were scheduled for the end of January 2017. Obama administration officials had not been invited.[196]

December 31, 2016 - Russian ambassador Kislyak called Michael Flynn back to inform him that Russia had agreed not to retaliate to US sanctions.[197]

End of 2016 - Michael Flynn closed his consulting firm, the Flynn Intel Group,[198] as he was transitioning to the national security advisor position.

December 2016–early January 2017 - President Erdogan, during his phone calls with the outgoing President Obama, asked him to drop Reza Zarrab's criminal case.[199]

2017

January 2017 - The head of the Ukrainian tax service, Roman Nasirov, helped Lev Parnas obtain a $10 million loan[200] for a real estate project[201] in Saint Louis that Lev Parnas was a part of. Parnas also had attempted to raise $100 million from Russian oligarch Farkhad Akhmedov for the same project.[202]

Around that time Roman Nasirov would indirectly hire Ballard Partners through a US law firm,[203] thus allowing Ballard to avoid registering that contract as required by FARA.

January 10, 2017 - FBI director James Comey testified in front of the Senate and said that the Russians had hacked into state-level Republican campaigns[204] and old RNC email domains[205] that weren't used anymore.[206] Comey added that the FBI found no evidence of hacking into the "current RNC."[207]

January 11-12, 2017 - Erik Prince, the founder of a US-based private military group, and Kirill Dmitriev, the head of Russia's direct investment fund and one of the oligarchs deployed by Putin, met[208] in the Seychelles[209] islands[210] for back-channel discussions between the Russian government and Donald Trump's inner team. Upon returning to the United States, Prince reported the meeting with Dmitriev to Steve Bannon,[211] Trump's senior advisor.

January 12, 2017 - Russian ambassador Kislyak called Flynn to follow up on the invitation about the Syrian Civil War peace talks in Astana, Kazakhstan. Flynn responded that a team was being assembled for the trip.[212]

January 17, 2017 - One of Trump's inaugural events, the Chairman's Global Dinner, took place in Washington, DC.[213]

January 18, 2017 - The Turkish foreign minister Mevlut Cavusoglu attended an inaugural breakfast meeting at the Trump International Hotel[214] on January 18, 2017, where Michael Flynn, the incoming national security advisor, and Rep. Devin Nunes, the Chair of the House Committee on Intelligence were presen.[215] It is unclear if the Turkish foreign minister, Flynn, and Nunes had a private face time.

January 18, 2017 - President-Elect Donald Trump called SDNY lead attorney, Preet Bharara, for the second time,[216] two days before his inauguration.

January 19, 2017 - Lev Parnas and Mubariz Mansimov arranged a meeting between Brian Ballard and the Turkish foreign minister, Mevlut Cavusoglu, to discuss a contract for lobbying services for the Turkish government. At the time, Ballard was the chairman of Trump Victory and the finance chief of the Trump campaign in Florida.[217] He also was a vice-chairman of the inauguration committee. Three days after the meeting, Mansimov sent Parnas a text with the name "Riza Zarrab."[218]

January 19, 2017 - Donald Trump's inaugural committee hosted the candlelight dinner at Union Station in Washington, DC.[219] The event was attended by Turkish foreign minister Mevlut Cavusoglu,[220] Lev Parnas, and Mubariz Mansimov.[221]

January 20, 2017 – Donald Trump entered office as the forty-fifth president of the United States.[222]

January 23-24, 2017 - The Russian government organized peace talks in Kazakhstan that focused on the Syrian Civil War.[223] The talks would be the beginning of Astana peace process[224] that would change the dynamics of the players in the conflict by elevating Russia and Turkey and by diminishing the roles of the United States and other Western countries.

January 24, 2017 - Michael Flynn sat down with the FBI agents for a voluntary interview in which he lied about his communications with the Russian ambassador.[225]

January 26, 2017 - Acting US attorney general Sally Yates warned Trump White House officials about Michael Flynn being potentially compromised by the Russian government.[226]

January 27, 2017 - President Trump had dinner with FBI director James Comey, during which Trump requested "loyalty" from Comey.[227]

January 31, 2017 - A Russian delegation attended a private Russian-American friendship dinner in Washington, DC.[228]

Late January 2017 - Mubariz Mansimov introduced Lev Parnas to Farkhad Akhmedov, a Russian Azerbaijani oligarch with deep ties to the Russian government.[229]

February 1-2, 2017 - Russian spy Maria Butina and her handler, Alexander Torshin, attended the National Prayer Breakfast. Butina and Torshin were scheduled to meet Donald Trump during the event, a courtesy arranged by the event's leadership. However, their meeting was canceled at the last moment. Allegedly, White House security advised against the meeting due to findings that connected Torshin to Russian organized crime.[230]

Early February 2017 - Lev Parnas accompanied Russian oligarch Farkhad Akhmedov to Las Vegas.[231]

February 8–9, 2017 - Wadie Habboush, an Iraqi American businessman whose father had donated[232] $334,000 to the Republican National Committee and $666,000 to Trump's inauguration, randomly[233] appeared[234] at the White House and requested to talk to National Security Council officials. Habboush was accompanied by a close friend of Donald Trump Jr. The next day Habboush reportedly met with Steve Bannon to discuss easing up US sanctions on Venezuela.[235]

February 13, 2017 - National security advisor Michael Flynn resigned from his position[236] after public scrutiny of his phone calls with the Russian ambassador and his lying to the FBI and Vice President Pence about those phone calls.

February 14, 2017 - Pres. Donald Trump privately asked FBI director James Comey to go easy on Michael Flynn.[237] The conversation was immediately written into memos by Comey.[238]

February 24, 2017 - Rudy Giuliani contacted Preet Bharara,[239] the lead prosecutor at the SDNY who was handling the Halkbank investigation, about his upcoming trip to Turkey on behalf of Reza Zarrab, the defendant in the Halkbank case.[240] At the time, Giuliani was serving as an advisor to the chairman of Greenberg Traurig, a law firm that had been lobbying for Turkey since 2014.[241]

Early 2017 - Rudy Giuliani and Michael Mukasey, former attorney general who also was in Zarrab's defense team, pressed Secretary of State Rex Tillerson to help them persuade the Justice Department to drop the criminal case against Reza Zarrab.[242] The meeting occurred in the Oval Office in President Trump's presence.[243] Tillerson refused.[244]

March 3–5, 2017 - The Republican National Committee gathered its donors at a retreat in Palm Beach, Florida. The event was attended by Lev Parnas, Farkhad Akhmedov,[245] Wadie Habboush, and Emrullah Turanli,[246] a Turkish construction mogul[247] with ties[248] to Erdogan and implicated[249] in Reza Zarrab's money-laundering scheme.

March 7, 2017 - Michael Flynn retroactively registered[250] his company as a foreign agent[251] for Turkey. Later he would admit that the information in the FARA registration form contained falsehoods.[252]

March 7, 2017 - The head of the Ukrainian Tax Service, Roman Nasirov, was arrested in Ukraine.[253] He was accused of using his public office to assist a former member of the Ukrainian parliament to embezzle $75 million. Nasirov was released on bail shortly after his arrest.

March 7, 2017 - David Rivera, a former Florida congressman turned lobbyist, drafted a $50 million lobbying contract with Citgo[254] and sent it to Venezuelan media mogul Raul Gorrín, who acted as an unofficial envoy of the Venezuelan government in the United States.[255]

March 8, 2017 - Lev Parnas and Farkhad Akhmedov flew to Washington, DC, to meet with Brian Ballard to discuss a lobbying contract with Turkey,[256] which would be signed in May 2017.[257] Three months later, Ballard Partners would sign another lobbying contract with Halkbank.[258]

March 9, 2017 - President Trump called SDNY lead attorney Preet Bharara for the third time. Bharara declined to speak to him as Donald Trump had already been sworn in as the president of the United States, and direct conversation between the US attorney and the president would have undermined the independence of the judicial branch and ethical rules of the DOJ.[259]

March 11, 2017 - President Trump fired Preet Bharara.[260]

On or around March 21, 2017 - Former Florida congressman David Rivera, through his firm, Interamerican Consulting, signed a $50 million lobbying contract with PDV USA, an American subsidiary of the Venezuelan national oil company, the PDVSA.[261] However, Rivera reportedly did not register as foreign agent for his consulting work.[262] Rivera received $15 million between March and June 2017.

March 27, 2017 - The FBI arrested Mehmet Hakan Atilla, deputy general manager for international banking at Halkbank who oversaw the bank's US correspondent accounts and its relationships with Iranian banks, including the Central Bank of Iran. The charges, brought by Preet Bharara's successor at the SDNY, Joon Kim, included conspiracy to evade US sanctions against Iran, bank fraud, and other offenses.[263]

March 27, 2017 - The information of Reza Zarrab hiring Rudy Giuliani and Michael Mukasey became public.[264]

March 30, 2017 - Secretary of State Rex Tillerson traveled to Turkey and met with Turkish foreign minister Mevlut Cavusoglu, who brought up Reza Zarrab's case[265] and accused the recently fired SDNY lead prosecutor, Preet Bharara, of "being a pawn of anti-Turkish forces."[266]

Around April 2, 2017 - David Rivera, Texas congressman Pete Sessions, and the Venezuelan foreign affairs minister met in New York to discuss the normalization of ties between Venezuela and the United States.[267]

April 16, 2017 - Turkey held a constitutional referendum that reallocated significant powers to the position of the president, including ability to interfere in the judicial affairs.[268]

April 19, 2017 - Trump administration secretary of energy, Rick Perry, met with Andriy Kobolev, the CEO of Naftogaz, and Yuri Vitrenko, Kobolev's advisor, at the Department of Energy headquarters.[269] At the meeting the Naftogaz officials presented an opportunity of a potential sale of 49 percent of the Ukrainian pipeline system.[270]

May 2017 - Pavel Fuks, a Ukrainian oligarch with ties to the Kremlin, hired Rudy Giuliani.[271] Fuks claimed that Giuliani was to lobby for Ukraine in the United States,[272] while Giuliani alleged that the purpose of the contract was security consulting for the city of Kharkiv in eastern Ukraine.[273]

May 9, 2017 - President Trump fired FBI director James Comey.[274]

May 11, 2017 - Ballard Partners signed a lobbying contract with Turkey[275] for a monthly fee of $125,000.[276] Lev Parnas was paid $45,000 for introducing Ballard Partners to the Turkish government.[277]

May 16, 2017 - President Trump met with President Erdogan in the White House. Later that day Erdogan's security guards violently attacked anti-Erdogan protesters who appeared near the Turkish Embassy in Washington, DC.[278] Donald Trump did not publicly comment on the incident.[279]

May 17, 2017 - The US Department of Justice appointed Robert Mueller as a special counsel to investigate Russian interference in the 2016 US election.[280]

June 8, 2017 - Rudy Giuliani met with Ukrainian president Petro Poroshenko and Prosecutor General Yuri Lutsenko.[281] At the meeting they reportedly discussed a project in Kharkiv initiated by a Ukrainian Russian oligarch, Pavel Fuks.[282]

June 8, 2017 - The Venezuelan state oil company, PDVSA, sent an email to Congressman Pete Sessions asking for help in arranging a meeting between the Venezuelan oil minister and the head of Exxon,[283] in hopes of luring Exxon back into the Venezuelan oil market.

June 16, 2017 - Venezuelan mogul Raul Gorrín, through a US subsidiary of his media company, hired Ballard Partners to "lobby for his Globovision television corporation."[284] The Globovision–Ballard Partners contract was reportedly worth $800,000.[285] Later Gorrín would claim that Ballard had also introduced him to Harry Sargeant III,[286] a shipping magnate from Florida who would become one of the main figures of Venezuelan influence peddling in the United States.

June 20, 2017 - US secretary of energy, Rick Perry, met with Pres. Petro Poroshenko at the Department of Energy headquarters. The CEO of Naftogaz, Andriy Kobolev, also attended the meeting.[287] Later that day Ukrainian president Poroshenko also met with President Trump.[288]

The same day Rick Perry also met with US ambassador to Ukraine Marie Yovanovitch.[289]

June–July 2017 - Maria Butina retained a law firm in the United States.[290]

July 16, 2017 - Millions of Venezuelan people voted in an unofficial[291] referendum objecting[292] to Maduro's intention to rewrite the constitution.

July 21–22, 2017 - Michael Bleyzer, a Ukrainian American businessman, received an email from Rick Perry's chief of staff inviting him to the Department of Energy. Bleyzer went there two days later.

July 30, 2017 - Nicolas Maduro's government arranged a vote to create the constituent assembly,[293] which was filled with Maduro's allies and planned to rewrite the Venezuelan constitution[294] to cement Maduro's rule. The event led to deadly mass protests.[295]

July 31, 2017 - Exxon and the PDVSA signed an energy deal worth $259 million.[296]

August 21, 2017 - Ballard Partners signed a lobbying contract with Halkbank.[297] This was in addition to another lobbying contract with the government of Turkey that Ballard Partners had signed in May 2017.

August 24, 2017 - The US Department of the Treasury imposed sanctions that prohibited US banks from issuing long-term debt to the Venezuelan government and the PDVSA.[298]

September 6, 2017 - The SDNY indicted former Halkbank executives and a former Turkish minister of the economy in relation to Reza Zarrab's case. The SDNY charged them with[299]
- conspiring to use the US financial system to conduct hundreds of millions of dollars' worth of transactions on behalf of the government of Iran and other Iranian entities, which were barred by United States sanctions;
- lying to US government officials about those transactions;
- laundering funds in connection with those illegal transactions, including millions of dollars in bribe payments to facilitate the scheme; and
- defrauding several financial institutions by concealing the true nature of these transactions.

September 12, 2017 - In seeming retaliation to the SDNY's indictments of former Halkbank executives and Turkish officials, Erdogan's government announced a deal to purchase the Russian-made S-400 air defense system.[300] The United States would later respond by removing Turkey from the F-35 fighter jet program, citing the risk of the leak of proprietary US technology to Russia.[301]

October 6, 2017 - Venezuelan president Nicolas Maduro met with Turkish president Recep Tayyip Erdogan in Ankara, Turkey.[302]

October 26, 2017 - Reza Zarrab pleaded guilty to all counts (fraud, money laundering, and violations of the US sanctions on Iran) and agreed to cooperate with the US government.[303]

Late 2017 - Raul Gorrín connected Harry Sargeant III, a Florida-based shipping magnate, to PDVSA officials.[304]

November 2017 - Shipping mogul Harry Sargeant III went to Venezuela "to see about buying some oil" and met with President Maduro.[305]

November 2017 - Igor Fruman and Rabbi Moshe Reuven Azman established the American Friends of Anatevka in Brooklyn, New York. The organization was registered as a 501(c)(3) tax-exempt charity.[306]

November 2017 - The Senate Finance Committee reached out to Maria Butina about Alexander Torshin.[307]

November 8, 2017 - Reza Zarrab was released from prison in exchange for his cooperation with the ongoing Halkbank investigations.[308]

November 10, 2017 - Roman Nasirov was indicted again in Ukraine.[309]

November 15, 2017 - The Turkish government inquired about the location of Reza Zarrab after he was released from a US prison.[310]

November 21, 2017 - The Turkish government contracted King & Spalding, a law firm from Atlanta, Georgia, to advise Turkey on "U.S. legislation including but not limited to regulatory and law enforcement matters."[311] The company choice might not have been accidental as, several months prior, one of the law firm's former partners, Christopher Wray, became the director of the FBI.[312]

November 29–30, 2017 - Reza Zarrab testified in US court against Mehmet Atilla,[313] another Halkbank defendant, during which he said that then prime minister Erdogan "personally ordered"[314] the routing of illicit funds through two Turkish banks, Ziraat Bank and VakifBank, which, along with Halkbank, are among the largest banks in Turkey.[315] Zarrab also said that his lawyers, Rudy Giuliani and Michael Mukasey, hadn't been successful in persuading Trump administration officials to negotiate a diplomatic resolution for his release.[316]

November 30, 2017 - Turkish authorities announced their intention to seize Zarrab's assets in Turkey.[317]

December 1, 2017 - Former Trump national security advisor, Michael Flynn, pleaded guilty to lying to the FBI about his conversations with the Russian ambassador to the United States, Sergey Kislyak. Flynn also pleaded guilty to providing false information in his retroactive FARA registration as a foreign agent of Turkey.[318]

2018

January 3, 2018 - US attorney general Jeff Sessions announced that Geoffrey Berman would be the interim lead prosecutor at the SDNY.[319] The position had been vacant for almost a year. Berman's term would later be extended by unanimous judicial appointment on April 25, 2018.[320]

January 3, 2018 - Halkbank executive Mehmet Hakan Atilla was found guilty in US federal courts of conspiring to evade US sanctions on Iran and money laundering.[321]

January 9, 2018 - President Erdogan said in an address to the Turkish parliament that the Halkbank investigation led by the SDNY was a "political coup attempt" against him.[322]

March 3, 2018 - Igor Fruman attended a Trump fundraising event at Mar-a-Lago.[323]

March 13, 2018 - President Trump fired his secretary of state, Rex Tillerson,[324] who would be later replaced by CIA director Mike Pompeo.[325]

March 19, 2018 - The US Department of the Treasury imposed new sanctions on Venezuela, banning the use of Venezuelan-denominated digital currencies by US entities.[326]

April 2018 - Alex Cranberg, energy businessman and the founder of Aspect Holding, went to Rick Perry's office.[327]

April 2018 - Maria Butina testified to the Senate Intelligence Committee.[328]

On or about April 2, 2018 - Congressman Pete Sessions took the unofficial trip to Caracas, Venezuela,[329] and stayed at a luxury compound that belonged to Raul Gorrín,[330] the Venezuelan media mogul who had been serving as a clandestine envoy for Venezuelan president Nicolas Maduro. During that trip Sessions had a meeting with Maduro, which was also attended by Raul Gorrín and David Rivera, the former Florida congressman turned lobbyist.[331]

April 6, 2018 - Maria Butina's handler, Alexander Torshin, was sanctioned by the United States.[332]

April 11, 2018 - Lev Parnas and Igor Fruman registered a company named Global Energy Producers.[333]

April 18, 2018 - President Erdogan announced that the Turkish general elections that were scheduled for November 2019 would be brought forward to June 2018.[334]

April 19, 2018 - Rudy Giuliani became one of Donald Trump's private attorneys.[335]

April 20, 2018 - Lev Parnas and Igor Fruman attended a fundraising event at Mar-a-Lago. Other people present at the event included Brian Ballard and Congressman

Pete Sessions.³³⁶ After that event Parnas and Fruman reportedly pledged to donate $20,000 to Pete Sessions's midterm reelection campaign.³³⁷

April 25, 2018 - Darrell Scott of the Urban Revitalization Coalition introduced Ali Akat, the president of the Turkish-American Business Association and head of the Turkish-American Chamber of Commerce, to GOP operatives and congressmen. Akat was introduced to Darrell Scott by Rabia Kazan.³³⁸

April 25, 2018 - The FBI seized Maria Butina's electronic devices.³³⁹

April 30, 2018 - Ali Akat posted a photo of himself at the Trump International Hotel in Washington, DC. In his Instagram post, Akat thanked Lara Trump, Ivanka Trump, and Darrell Scott for hosting Akat's visit to the United States.³⁴⁰

April 30, 2018 - Lev Parnas attended a VIP dinner for America First Action super PAC donors at the Trump International Hotel in DC. The dinner was also attended by the president's son Donald Trump Jr., his close friend and RNC fundraiser Tommy Hicks Jr., and Giuliani's business partner, Roy Bailey.³⁴¹

During that meeting Parnas mentioned his energy business aspirations in Ukraine and claimed that US Ambassador to Ukraine Marie Yovanovitch publicly criticized President Trump. Donald Trump reacted to the remark by publicly ordering the firing of Ambassador Yovanovitch.³⁴²

May 9, 2018 - Parnas and Fruman met with Congressman Pete Sessions in his office.³⁴³ The same day Sessions wrote a letter to Secretary of State Mike Pompeo seeking the dismissal of Ambassador Yovanovitch.³⁴⁴

May 9, 2018 - Ron DeSantis, who was running to be the governor of Florida at the time, approached Lev Parnas at the Trump International Hotel in Washington, DC, reportedly telling Parnas that "he was told"³⁴⁵ to meet Parnas because he "was very close with Donald Trump."³⁴⁶

May 9, 2018 - Rabia Kazan became a partner at the Urban Revitalization Coalition.³⁴⁷ According to Kazan, she didn't have any experience for the position but was appointed anyway for introducing URC founders, Darrell Scott and Kareem Lanier, to Ali Akat and wealthy Turkish people.

May 15, 2018 - Aaron Investments I, a company owned by Lev Parnas, received $1,260,329.80 from a real estate lawyer in Florida.³⁴⁸ The original source of the funds was a $3 million[349] mortgage loan[350] received against Igor Fruman's real estate from a Russian American couple.

May 16, 2018 - Mehmet Hakan Atilla, the former deputy general manager for international banking at Halkbank, was sentenced to thirty-two months in the United States for violating the US sanctions on Iran.[351]

May 17, 2018 - Lev Parnas and Igor Fruman donated $325,000 to the Trump-supporting America First Action super PAC. The money was sent from Aaron Investments I, but Parnas claimed the contribution was made by Global Energy Producers, another company he and Fruman owned.[352]

May 20, 2018 - Nicolas Maduro was reelected with 68 percent of the votes.[353] The United States and several other countries rejected the election result, claiming improprieties and fraud. The United States then backed Venezuelan legislator and opposition leader Juan Guaido as the recognized president of Venezuela.

May 21, 2018 - The United States imposed an additional layer of sanctions on Venezuela prohibiting the purchase of Venezuelan debt, as well as the use of Venezuelan debt as collateral by US entities.[354]

May 23, 2018 - Ukrainian prosecutor general Yuri Lutsenko visited a United Nations event in New York and tried to set up a meeting with then attorney general Jeff Sessions. Lutsenko claimed that his effort was blocked by the US ambassador to Ukraine, Marie Yovanovitch.[355]

Summer 2018 - Shipping mogul Harry Sargeant III attempted to deliver a letter from Venezuelan president Maduro to Donald Trump during a political fundraiser in New York.[356]

June 2018 - Lev Parnas, Igor Fruman, and David Correia, accompanied by Roy Bailey, visited Congressman Pete Sessions in his office.[357]

Mid-June 2018 - Michael Bleyzer, Rick Perry's friend and the founder of SigmaBleyzer, a Houston-based billion-dollar investment group, brought the head of Energy Transfer to Ukraine.[358] Energy Transfer was the firm where Rick Perry served as a board member both before and after holding the position of the secretary of energy.

June 18, 2018 - Louisiana Natural Gas Exports Inc. was registered.[359] This company would later be selected as the one to sell US LNG to Ukraine.[360] It had no assets and infrastructure but was supposed to buy gas from Energy Transfer and then resell it to Ukraine.

June 18–19, 2018 - Lev Parnas, Igor Fruman, and David Correia attended the America First Action super PAC summit at the Trump International Hotel in Washington, DC.[361] Roy Bailey said that, at that event, he introduced Lev Parnas to energy shipping mogul Harry Sargeant III.[362]

June 21, 2018 - Lev Parnas donated $50,000 to Ron DeSantis's gubernatorial campaign.[363]

June 22, 2018 - Judge Richard Berman, who was overseeing the Halkbank case, raised concerns about Rudy Giuliani's efforts to have it terminated.[364]

June 24, 2018 - During a snap election in Turkey, Erdogan was reelected president, with expanded powers cemented by the constitutional referendum held the year prior.[365]

June 25, 2018 - SigmaBleyzer announced that it was "ready to invest" $100M in Ukraine's energy sector.[366] The announcement was made after the Head of the State Service for Geology and Deposits of Ukraine met with the heads of SigmaBleyzer, Aspect Holding, and Energy Transfer, all of whom had[367] connections[368] to Rick Perry.

June 25, 2018 - Lev Parnas and Igor Fruman each donated $2,700 to Congressman Pete Sessions's reelection campaign.[369]

July 9, 2018 - Venezuelan president Maduro and Turkish president Erdogan met in Turkey.[370]

July 15, 2018 - Maria Butina was arrested in Washington, DC, on the suspicion of acting as a Russian agent.[371]

Mid–late July 2018 - The United States and Turkey almost reached an agreement to exchange Andrew Brunson, the American evangelical pastor, for Mehmet Hakan Atilla, the former Halkbank official arrested in the United States in relation to the SDNY investigation. However, the talks halted when Turkey's foreign minister added a demand to dismiss the Halkbank investigation in the United States.[372]

July 24, 2018 - Brian Ballard, while representing Turkey and Halkbank, had an in-person meeting[373] with the chief of staff of VP Mike Pence, Nick Ayers.[374]

July 25, 2019 - The Campaign Legal Center filed a complaint with the Federal Election Committee regarding Parnas and Fruman's $325,000 donation to America First Action super PAC.[375] Parnas and Fruman hired Greenberg Traurig to defend them and their company, Global Energy Producers, in the FEC investigation.[376]

July 26, 2018 - President Trump and Vice President Pence publicly threatened to impose sanctions on Turkey for the country's continued detention of Pastor Andrew Brunson.[377]

July 2018 - The US Treasury Department expressed concerns that Venezuelan gold shipments to Turkey might be ending up in Iran.[378]

Between July and October 2018 - Brian Ballard called six times to Jay Sekulow,[379] one of the personal attorneys to Donald Trump[380] and the counsel to a Christian NGO that represented the detained pastor Andrew Brunson.[381]

August 2018 - Venezuela and Turkey set up a joint mining company to explore gold in Venezuela.[382]

August 1, 2018 - The United States imposed sanctions on two Turkish officials in retaliation for the continued imprisonment of Pastor Andrew Brunson.[383]

August 10, 2018 - President Trump doubled tariffs on aluminum and steel imported from Turkey to the United States to turn up the pressure on the Turkish government to release Pastor Andrew Brunson.[384]

September 2018 Energy shipping mogul Harry Sargeant III met with Venezuelan president Nicolas Maduro in Caracas, Venezuela.[385] Congressman Pete Sessions, Rudy Giuliani, Lev Parnas, and others joined that meeting via a phone call.[386] On the call the group discussed a possible "soft landing" for Maduro in the United States in the case of his willingness to leave the Venezuelan presidency.

September 2018 - Around the time of the call with Nicolas Maduro, Rudy Giuliani talked to Trump's national security advisor, John Bolton, about Giuliani's alternative plan to ease Maduro from office. Bolton "vehemently rejected" the plan.[387]

September 2018 - Rudy Giuliani, Lev Parnas, and Igor Fruman recorded a video[388] congratulating Rabbi Moshe Azman, the head rabbi of Anatevka,[389] a Ukrainian village for Jewish refugees. Lev Parnas and Igor Fruman were board members of an American charity established to raise funds for the village.[390] Rudy Giuliani would become Anatevka's honorary mayor.[391]

About September 14–21, 2018 - Former CIA director James Woolsey, Trump backer Tommy Hicks Jr., and a Franciscan priest, Fr. James McCurry, went to Turkey on a private weeklong trip to hold talks about the release of Pastor Andrew Brunson. The trip reportedly was organized by Nancye Miller, a lobbyist married to Woolsey. According to OCCRP, Miller had been in communication with the office of Turkish president Recep Tayyip Erdogan before the trip.[392] The transportation for the trip was provided by Sezgin Baran Korkmaz, a Turkish tycoon who would be later charged in the United States with money laundering.[393]

September 16, 2018 - Rudy Giuliani, Lev Parnas, and Harry Sargeant III attended the Dallas Cowboys vs. New York Giants game at the Arlington, Texas, stadium.[394]

On or around September 25, 2018 - During the United Nations General Assembly in New York, Secretary of State Mike Pompeo and National Security Advisor John Bolton "advanced in discussions" for Pastor Andrew Brunson's release.[395]

September 28, 2018 - Congress passed a spending bill that included $250 million in military aid for Ukraine. The bill was signed by President Trump. Per the legislation, the money needed to be disbursed by September 30, 2019.[396]

October 12, 2018 - The Turkish government released Pastor Andrew Brunson from Turkish detention.[397]

October 13, 2018 - President Trump tweeted that there was "no deal" made for Brunson's release.[398]

October 14, 2018 - Ali Akat, the president of the Turkish-American Business Association and head of the Turkish-American Chamber of Commerce, announced in an interview that[399]

fifteen U.S. companies, each with a minimum of $100 million to invest, are rolling up their sleeves to bring business to Turkey in the "first wave" of investment from the United States following the release of pastor Andrew Brunson.

November 1, 2018 - The US Department of the Treasury imposed another layer of sanctions on Venezuela, this time on the sales of Venezuelan gold to US entities.[400]

November 2, 2018 - President Trump lifted the US sanctions that were imposed on Turkish ministers in response to the detention of Andrew Brunson in Turkey.[401]

November 5, 2018 - The US Department of the Treasury reimposed sanctions on the purchases of Iranian oil.[402] President Trump temporarily granted a six-month waiver to Turkey, among eight other countries, to allow the purchase of Iranian oil products.[403]

November 6, 2018 - During the midterm elections in the United States, Ron DeSantis was elected as the governor of Florida,[404] and Pete Sessions lost his congressional seat.[405] Lev Parnas and Fruman made political contributions to both of them.

November 7, 2018 - Pres. Donald Trump fired AG Jeff Sessions and replaced him with Matthew G. Whitaker as the interim attorney general.[406]

November 12, 2018 - Secretary of Energy Rick Perry met with the Ukrainian prime minister, Volodymyr Groysman and the CEO of Naftogaz, Andriy Kobolev, in Kyiv, Ukraine,

The same day Perry also met with Petro Poroshenko, then president of Ukraine, and discussed "reforms to Ukraine's energy sector."[407]

November 20, 2018 - The Southern District of Florida indicted in absentia the Venezuelan media mogul Raul Gorrín for money laundering.[408]

Around November 28, 2018 - According to Rudy Giuliani, one of his former SDNY colleagues reached out to him, claiming that former VP Joe Biden was implicated in Ukraine's interference in the 2016 US election.[409]

November 30–December 3, 2018 - Congressman Devin Nunes (R-CA) and his assistant, Derek Harvey, reportedly met with Viktor Shokin, former Ukraine's prosecutor general, in Vienna, to seek information on the Bidens in Ukraine.[410]

November–December 2018 - Acting Attorney General Whitaker reportedly attempted to stop the Halkbank case from going forward and ordered the case to be closed, but Justice Department officials declined to follow through the acting AG's request.[411]

In or around December 2018 - Robert Bensh, a Houston-based oil businessman with experience in Ukraine, received a call from an acquaintance who said that Rick Perry was looking for an expert on Ukraine's energy sector.[412]

December 1, 2018 - President Erdogan and President Trump met at the G20 summit in Buenos Aires, Argentina, and discussed the Halkbank case.[413] According to John

Bolton, during that meeting Trump promised Erdogan that he would replace "Obama people" in the Southern District of New York with his own.[414]

December 3, 2018 - President Erdogan traveled to Venezuela and became the first Turkish president to visit the country.[415]

Shortly after December 3, 2018 - Derek Harvey and Lev Parnas met at the Trump International Hotel in DC to talk about the Bidens and allegations of Ukraine's interference in the 2016 US election. According to Parnas, around that time he had a phone conversation with Congressman Devin Nunes, who asked Parnas for assistance to "validate" the information that Nunes had obtained from Shokin.[416]

December 6, 2018 - President Trump met with Rudy Giuliani, Lev Parnas, and Igor Fruman at the White House Hanukkah party and reportedly discussed a scheme to create a scandal around Biden and Ukraine.[417]

Late 2018 - Lev Parnas and Igor Fruman arranged a Skype call between Rudy Giuliani and Viktor Shokin,[418] the former Ukrainian prosecutor general who had allegedly met with Congressman Devin Nunes in Vienna.

December 12, 2018 - Trump signed an executive order establishing the White House Opportunity and Revitalization Council.[419] The order could benefit the Urban Revitalization Coalition.

December 13, 2018 - Maria Butina pleaded guilty to acting as an unregistered agent for Russia.[420]

December 14, 2018 - During a phone call, President Trump told President Erdogan that the United States was "getting close to a resolution on Halkbank."[421] During that same phone call,[422] Donald Trump agreed[423] to withdraw US forces from Syria within thirty days. That decision was beneficial for Turkey as Turkish forces would later repeatedly[424] attack[425] Kurdish settlements[426] along the Turkish-Syrian border, which had previously been under the protection of the US military.

December 18, 2018 - Michael Flynn's business associates, Bijan Kian and Ekim Alptekin, were charged with illegally lobbying for Turkey.[427]

December 19, 2018 - President Trump, despite objections from his national security advisors, announced the immediate withdrawal of US forces from Syria.[428] The following day Secretary of Defense Jim Mattis would resign in deep protest of the withdrawal.[429]

Sometime in 2018 - Rabia Kazan, a former Turkish right-wing journalist turned MAGA ambassador, founded the Middle Eastern Women's Coalition. The first Instagram post for its account appeared on December 15, 2018.[430]

2019

January 7, 2019 - Reuters reported a $500 million deal between Harry Sargeant III's company Erepla Services LLC and the Venezuelan state oil company, the PDVSA.[431]

January 8, 2019 - The US Department of the Treasury sanctioned Venezuelan media mogul Raul Gorrín for corruption and bribery.[432]

January 10, 2019 - Venezuelan president Nicolas Maduro was sworn in for his second term as president amid serious allegations of election fraud.[433]

January 16, 2019 - The Ukrainian prime minister, Volodymyr Groysman, publicly called for a review of the contract with Naftogaz CEO, Andriy Kobolev.[434]

January 17, 2019 - Andrew Favorov was appointed as the head of the Naftogaz gas division. Shortly thereafter, he reportedly received a message from Igor Fruman to have a chat.[435]

January 17, 2019 - The US ambassador to Ukraine, Marie Yovanovitch, visited Rick Perry's office.[436]

January 19, 2019 - Sen. Lindsey Graham (R-SC), privately flew to Turkey on a commercial flight and met with President Erdogan to discuss American-Turkish foreign relations.[437]

Around January 2019 - SDNY lead prosecutor, Geoffrey Berman, requested permission from Acting Attorney General Matthew G. Whitaker to file criminal charges against the institution of Halkbank itself. Whitaker denied the request.[438]

January 20, 2019 - The US ambassador to Ukraine, Marie Yovanovitch, wrote a letter to Ukrainian prime minister Volodymyr Groysman objecting to his statements about Naftogaz and warning that the proposed changes could invite corruption.[439]

January 25–26, 2019 - Lev Parnas and Igor Fruman arranged for Rudy Giuliani to meet the Ukrainian prosecutor general, Yuri Lutsenko, in New York.[440] Lutsenko claimed that he had evidence of Hunter Biden's corruption.[441] During the meeting with Lutsenko, Rudy Giuliani reportedly "excitedly" spoke to President Trump to share the findings.[442]

January 28, 2019 - The United States imposed sanctions on the Venezuelan state oil company, the PDVSA, banning most US companies from doing business with it.[443]

January–February 2019 - The Ukrainian prosecutor general, Yuri Lutsenko, asked Rudy Giuliani to represent Ukraine and him personally. Giuliani drew up two retainer agreements worth a total of $500,000.[444] He would later change his mind,[445] and his name in the retainers would be replaced[446] by his allies Victoria Toensing and Joe diGenova.[447]

February 2, 2019 - Rabia Kazan sponsored an event for the Virginia Women for Trump with Trump's ally Roger Stone as the keynote speaker.[448]

February 6, 2019 - GOP operative and Maria Butina's boyfriend, Paul Erickson, was indicted for money laundering and wire fraud.[449]

February 12, 2019 - Rudy Giuliani met with Ukraine's prosecutor general, Yuri Lutsenko, in Warsaw, Poland.[450]

February 12, 2019 - Andriy Kobolev, the CEO of Naftogaz, said in an interview to the *Kyiv Post* that the government's attempt to curb the independence and authority of the Naftogaz supervisory board would take Ukraine back to the "darkest times" of rampant corruption.[451]

February 14, 2019 - William Barr was confirmed as attorney general of the United States.[452]

Around February 16–17, 2019 (Presidents' Day weekend) - Rick Perry met with Robert Bensh, an oil businessman with experience in Ukraine, at an airport in Houston.[453]

February 16–17, 2019 - Lev Parnas and Victoria Toensing, the BLT team lawyer, exchanged messages about the status of the removal of Marie Yovanovitch.[454]

February 17, 2019 - Rudy Giuliani visited Donald Trump at Mar-a-Lago and advocated for the removal of Ambassador Yovanovitch.[455]

February 2019   Ukraine's minister of internal affairs warned the US ambassador to Ukraine, Marie Yovanovitch, that he had been approached by Rudy Giuliani and his associates who were plotting to have her fired.[456]

Late February 2019 - Lev Parnas and Igor Fruman met with then Ukrainian president Poroshenko and Prosecutor General Yuri Lutsenko in Kyiv. During that meeting Parnas and Fruman pressed Poroshenko to announce an investigation into Ukraine's alleged interference in the 2016 US election in exchange for an invitation to the White House.[457]

February 2019 - Rabia Kazan took Martha Boneta, a prominent MAGA influencer from Virginia, to Turkey and introduced her to a Turkish billionaire with connections to Erdogan. Boneta, in turn, arranged a call between the billionaire and Roger Stone, who attempted to persuade the billionaire to financially contribute to Stone's legal expenses.[458]

March 5, 2019 - Marie Yovanovitch gave an anticorruption speech, in which she criticized the Ukrainian government of dragging its feet on anticorruption measures and called for the dismissal of Lutsenko's deputy for allegedly aiding some suspects in avoiding criminal charges.[459]

March 11–15, 2019 - Lev Parnas, Igor Fruman, and Harry Sargeant III traveled to Houston, meeting with Andrew Favorov, an executive at Naftogaz. According to Favorov, Parnas and Fruman discussed their interest in selling American LNG to Ukraine and wanted Favorov to become the head of Naftogaz to help with the new venture. Favorov recounted that Sargeant claimed he had regular meetings with President Trump, who had allegedly expressed his "full support" of the LNG sales plan. According to Favorov, during those meetings Parnas mentioned that efforts to remove US ambassador Yovanovitch were underway.[460]

March 20, 2019 - The *Hill* released John Solomon's interview with Ukraine's prosecutor general, Yuri Lutsenko, in which Lutsenko announced that he was opening investigations into Ukraine's alleged interference into the 2016 US election.[461] On the same day, the *Hill* published another article in which Lutsenko claimed that Marie Yovanovitch gave him a "do not prosecute" list.[462]

March 22, 2019 - Lutsenko sent frustrated messages to Parnas, accusing him and his associates of inability to remove Marie Yovanovitch and implying that he couldn't announce an investigation into the Bidens as long as the ambassador remained in her position.[463]

March 22, 2019 - Special Counsel Robert Mueller submitted his report on Russia's interference to AG William Barr,[464] who would withhold it from the public for almost a month.[465]

March 25–26, 2019 - Robert Hyde, a pro-Trump congressional candidate, sent Parnas messages that implied physical surveillance of Ambassador Yovanovitch and her potential forced extraction.[466]

March 28, 2019 - Rudy Giuliani passed a disinformation packet about Ukraine and the Bidens to Secretary of State Mike Pompeo. The disinformation packet contained testimonies obtained from Viktor Shokin and Yuri Lutsenko.[467]

March 2019 - Rabia Kazan reportedly gifted a $10,000 necklace to the girlfriend of Michael Lindell, the founder of MyPillow company.[468]

April 2019 - During a phone call, President Erdogan, once again, asked President Trump to drop the Halkbank case. Trump responded by telling Erdogan that AG William Barr and Treasury Secretary Steven Mnuchin would "handle" the Halkbank issue.[469]

April 1, 2019 - John Solomon published an article about Joe Biden and the former Ukrainian prosecutor general Viktor Shokin. It alleged that Biden had corruptly pushed the Ukrainian government to oust Shokin.[470]

April 5, 2019 - Six former ambassadors to Ukraine wrote a letter to the State Department objecting to the smear campaign against Amb. Marie Yovanovitch.[471]

April 7, 2019 - Rudy Giuliani said on Fox News that he wanted the Department of Justice to look into Biden's dealings in Ukraine.[472]

April 12, 2019 - Victoria Toensing and Joe diGenova sent a draft of a $125,000 retainer agreement, which they took over from Rudy Giuliani, to Yuri Lutsenko and his subordinate, Konstantin Kulyk.[473]

April 14–16, 2019 - The Trump International Hotel in Washington, DC, hosted the Thirty-Seventh Annual Conference on U.S.-Turkey Relations.[474] The gathering was organized by the Turkish-American Business Council and its new chair, Mehmet Ali Yalcindag, who had previous connections to the Trump family through Trump Towers in Istanbul.[475] Before leading TAIK, Yalcindag had served as an executive at the Turkish branch of Yandex, the largest Russian internet company.[476]

The event was attended by Berat Albayrak, President Erdogan's son-in-law and then Turkish finance minister, who, with Jared Kushner's help, met with President Trump and asked him to halt sanctions on Turkey for its purchase of the Russian-made S-400 air defense system.[477]

April 15, 2019 - Victoria Toensing and Joe diGenova sent a $125,000 retainer agreement to Viktor Shokin.[478]

April 18, 2019 - Ukrainian prosecutor general Yuri Lutsenko retracted the public statement he had previously made to John Solomon at the *Hill* about Ambassador Yovanovitch giving him a "do not prosecute" list.[479]

April 18, 2019 - The Department of Justice publicly released the Special Counsel's report on Russia's interference in the 2016 US election.[480]

April 21, 2019 - A TV comedian, Volodymyr Zelensky, defeated the incumbent Ukrainian president, Petro Poroshenko, in the presidential election.[481]

Around April 22–24, 2019 - Lev Parnas and Igor Fruman traveled to Israel to meet[482] Ihor Kolomoisky,[483] a Ukrainian Israeli oligarch, seeking his help to reach out to the newly elected president of Ukraine, Volodymyr Zelensky.

April 23, 2019 - Rudy Giuliani met with President Trump and asked him to remove Amb. Marie Yovanovitch, and Trump, once again, agreed to fire her.[484]

On or around April 25, 2019 - Ambassador Yovanovitch returned to the United States after a warning phone call.[485]

April 26, 2019 - Donald Trump appeared on Fox News and accused Ukraine of interfering in the 2016 US election.[486]

April 26, 2019 - Maria Butina was sentenced to eighteen months in prison, including time served.[487]

April 30, 2019 - Lev Parnas and Igor Fruman met with Andrew Favorov, the head of the Naftogaz gas division, in Washington, DC. The meeting was also attended by a representative of a company owned by energy shipping mogul Harry Sargeant III.[488]

May 1, 2019 - Parnas and Fruman met with Andrew Favorov and the CEO of Naftogaz, Andriy Kobolev, at the Trump International Hotel in DC.[489] During that meeting Parnas introduced the Naftogaz officials to

- Jeff Miller, a former campaign manager for Rick Perry and an energy lobbyist whose clients included Alex Cranberg, and
- Tommy Hicks Jr., the former chairman of Trump's America First Action PAC,[490] cochair of the Republican National Committee,[491] and the head of an equity fund with interest in the energy sector.[492]

May 6, 2019 - Amb. Marie Yovanovitch was officially recalled from her position in Ukraine.[493] Lev Parnas sent messages to Tommy Hicks Jr. and Harry Sargeant III, letting them know of her recall.[494]

May 7, 2019 - Harry Sargeant III responded to Lev Parnas by texting, "Split. Couldn't take phone away for 4 hours."[495]

May 10, 2019 - Rudy Giuliani announced that he was going to Ukraine to urge its government to investigate Joe Biden.[496] That same day Giuliani sent a letter through Parnas to the newly elected Ukrainian president, Volodymyr Zelensky, requesting a meeting.[497]

May 11, 2019 - Rudy Giuliani canceled his planned trip to Ukraine and issued a public statement, accusing Zelensky of having in his team "enemies of the United States."[498]

On or around May 12, 2019 - Lev Parnas pressured[499] Zelensky's aide, Sergey Shaffer,[500] to announce an investigation into the Bidens in exchange for Mike Pompeo's appearance at Zelensky's inauguration.

May 16, 2019 - Ukrainian prosecutor general Yuri Lutsenko gave an interview to Bloomberg stating that there was not sufficient evidence to conduct an investigation on the Bidens in Ukraine,[501] causing Rudy Giuliani's outrage.[502]

May 20, 2019 - Volodymyr Zelensky was inaugurated as Ukraine's new president. US secretary of energy Rick Perry attended the inauguration instead of VP Mike Pence, who was initially announced to attend. While in Ukraine, Perry gave Zelensky a list of names that Perry recommended as candidates for the Naftogaz advisory board. The list included Michael Bleyzer and Robert Bensh.[503]

May 21, 2019 - Rudy Giuliani met in Paris with Moshe Azman, the rabbi of Anatevka, a Ukrainian village for Jewish refugees. The rabbi proclaimed Giuliani as Anatevka's honorary mayor and gave him a symbolic key to the village.[504] During the same trip, Giuliani met with Yuri Lutsenko's deputy,[505] ostensibly in hopes of using him as Lutsenko's replacement after the fallout caused by the prosecutor's interview to Bloomberg.

May 23, 2019 - Rick Perry, Kurt Volker (US envoy to Ukraine), and Gordon Sondland (US ambassador to the European Union) met with President Trump in the White House and encouraged him to have a meeting with President Zelensky. Trump directed them to "talk to Rudy" to arrange it. [506]

May 2019 - Rabia Kazan quit the advisory board of the National Diversity Coalition.[507]

Summer 2019 - Harry Sargeant III, energy shipping mogul, and Robert Stryk, a lobbyist connected to Rudy Giuliani,[508] traveled to Venezuela to discuss a possibility of formally lobbying for the Venezuelan government in the United States. The effort failed.[509]

Summer 2019 - Lev Parnas's son, Aaron, interned at Greenberg Traurig.[510]

June 3, 2019 - Volodymyr Zelensky officially assumed office.[511]

June 4, 2019 - Rick Perry attended a formal dinner in Ukraine[512] along with other Western government officials.[513]

June 10, 2019 - AG William Barr called the SDNY lead prosecutor, Geoffrey Berman, and told him that the Trump administration had assigned Barr as a "point person" to oversee the Halkbank case.[514]

June 11, 2019 - Attorney General Barr met with representatives of the Turkish Ministry of Justice regarding the Halkbank case. Strangely, SDNY lead prosecutor Geoffrey Berman, who was handling the case, was not invited.[515]

June 11, 2019 - Ukraine's president, Volodymyr Zelensky, sent a motion to the Verkhovna Rada (Ukraine's parliament) to dismiss Yuri Lutsenko as the prosecutor general.[516]

June 14, 2019 – Halkbank defense lawyers requested a "global resolution" from the SDNY. Berman would later describe it as a "toothless DPA," or deferred prosecution agreement, that would allow the bank and all involved in the money laundering to avoid accountability. Berman's answer was no.[517]

June 17, 2019 - Attorney General Barr summoned Berman to Washington, DC, to discuss the Halkbank investigation[518] and pressed Berman to accept the global resolution.[519] Berman refused.

June 18, 2019 - The US Department of Defense approved a $250 million military aid package for Ukraine.[520]

June 19, 2019 - Kurt Volker, the US envoy to Ukraine, sent a message to Bill Taylor, the US chargé d'affaires to Ukraine, about Rick Perry's misgivings about Naftogaz CEO Andriy Kobolev.[521]

June 25, 2019 - An Austrian court approved the extradition of Dmytro Firtash,[522] a Ukrainian oligarch, to the United States based on the charges of bribery.

Around June 29–30, 2019 - Rudy Giuliani and Lev Parnas flew to London[523] for a Yankees exhibition game and met with Alejandro Betancourt Lopez,[524] a Venezuelan tycoon who was a person of interest in a US-based $1.2 billion money-laundering case.[525] Probably during the same trip, Giuliani and Parnas met[526] with[527] a person connected to Dmytro Firtash.

June 2019 - The Halkbank case "was taken away" from the SDNY and given to the National Security Division at the DOJ.[528]

Around June–July 2019 - SDNY lead prosecutor Geoffrey Berman received a tip[529] that if he kept his stance of advocating for the Halkbank prosecution, then he would be replaced by Ed O'Callaghan,[530] a DOJ official who had previously led[531] the National Security Division at the DOJ and was considered a "Barr loyalist."[532]

July 1, 2019 - The Ukrainian government awarded oil and gas exploration fields to Michael Bleyzer, Rick Perry's ally.[533]

July 10, 2019 - Two Ukrainian officials, Andriy Yermak and Oleksandr Danylyuk, had two meetings at the White House with US officials—John Bolton, Alexander Vindman, Rick Perry, Gordon Sondland, and Kurt Volker. During the first meeting, Sondland reportedly offered to the Ukrainian officials an exchange: an invitation for Zelensky to the White House in return for the Ukrainian government announcing an investigation into the Bidens. Bolton referred to it as a "drug deal" and asked his colleague, Fiona Hill, to report the conversation to the National Security Council lawyer.[534]

That same evening Yermak and Danylyuk met with Rick Perry's aides and Robert Bensh, during which Bensh pitched the Ukrainian officials the American LNG plan.[535]

During that trip Andriy Yermak reportedly asked Kurt Volker to introduce him to Rudy Giuliani.[536]

July 18, 2019 - President Trump ordered a halt of military aid to Ukraine.[537]

July 22, 2019 - Rudy Giuliani had a call with Zelensky's chief of staff, Andriy Yermak, and pressured him to start investigations on the Bidens and on Ukraine's alleged "meddling" in the 2016 US election.[538]

July 22, 2019 - John Solomon released an article on the *Hill* about an outreach from Special Counsel Mueller's team to Ukrainian oligarch Dmytro Firtash during the Russian election interference investigations. The article implied that doing so was somehow improper.[539]

July 23, 2019 - Lanny Davis, a lawyer who had been representing Firtash in the United States, filed a FARA report about halting his services to the oligarch.[540] The next day *Time* magazine received news that Firtash had hired Giuliani allies Victoria Toensing and Joe diGenova.[541] Lev Parnas was hired as a "translator" go-between.[542]

July 24, 2019 - One of the people sentenced in relation to the Halkbank case, Mehmet Hakan Atilla, finished serving his prison sentence in the United States and returned to Turkey.[543] Later that year Atilla became the head of Turkey's stock exchange.[544]

July 25, 2019 - President Trump called President Zelensky and asked him not to dismiss Prosecutor General Lutsenko and suggested that Ukraine should do a favor for the United States by announcing investigations into the Bidens and into Ukraine's alleged interference into the 2016 US election.[545] That call triggered Trump's first impeachment trial. Trump later said that he had called Zelensky because Rick Perry, the secretary of energy, had asked him to.[546] Perry confirmed that, saying that he urged Trump to call Zelensky to discuss the issues "related to energy and the economy."[547]

August 2, 2019 - Rudy Giuliani and Lev Parnas met Andriy Yermak, President Zelensky's chief of staff, in Madrid.[548] During the meeting Giuliani and Parnas, once again, asked the new Ukrainian government to investigate the Bidens and Ukraine's alleged interference in the 2016 US election.[549]

August 3, 2019 - Giuliani and Parnas met with Alejandro Betancourt Lopez, the Venezuelan mogul, in his villa outside Madrid.[550]

August 5, 2019 - President Trump signed an executive order imposing additional sanctions on Venezuela.[551]

August 12, 2019 - The office of the inspector general of the Intelligence Community received a whistleblower complaint about events surrounding President Trump's phone call with President Zelensky.[552]

August 26, 2019 - Victoria Toensing and Joe diGenova met with Attorney General Barr,[553] seeking the dismissal of Dmytro Firtash's criminal case in the United States.[554]

August 29, 2019 - Ukraine's prosecutor general, Yuri Lutsenko, was replaced with a new one.[555]

August 31, 2019 - US energy secretary Rick Perry went to Warsaw, Poland,[556] with the purpose of facilitating the shipping of American gas to Ukraine through Poland's pipelines.[557] The CEO of LNGE, Ben Blanchet, accompanied Perry.[558]

September 2019 - Lev Parnas's wife, Svetlana Parnas, received a $1 million loan from a lawyer representing Dmytro Firtash. The money was wired from a Russian bank account.[559]

September 3, 2019 - Rudy Giuliani met with the DOJ officials,[560] including Attorney General Barr,[561] to ask for leniency for Venezuelan mogul Alejandro Betancourt Lopez, whom he had met in Madrid a month before.[562]

September 9, 2019 - The US inspector general of intelligence sent a letter to Congressmen Adam Schiff and Devin Nunes, who led the House Intelligence Committee. The ICIG alerted them to the existence of an "urgent" and "credible" whistleblower complaint. The letter disclosed that, despite the ICIG's assessment, the acting director of national intelligence, Joseph Maguire, did not believe he was required to transmit the complaint to Congress.[563]

September 9, 2019 – Three House committees launched investigations into President Trump and Rudy Giuliani's efforts to pressure the Ukrainian government to assist with Trump's reelection campaign by investigating the Bidens. The chairmen of the House Foreign Relations Committee, the House Intelligence Committee, and the House Oversight Committee sent letters to the White House and State Department announcing their investigation.[564]

September 10, 2019 - President Trump fired his national security advisor, John Bolton.[565]

September 11, 2019 - US military aid to Ukraine that had previously been withheld by Trump was released.[566]

September 24, 2019 - In response to reports of Trump's phone call with Zelensky and the Trump administration's failure to provide Congress with the whistleblower complaint, the Speaker of the House, Nancy Pelosi, announced a formal impeachment inquiry.[567]

September 25, 2019 - The White House released the transcript of the July 25, 2019, call between Donald Trump and Volodymyr Zelensky.[568]

September 26, 2019 - The whistleblower complaint was released.[569]

September 26, 2019 - John Solomon published an article on the *Hill* about an affidavit written by the former Ukrainian prosecutor general Viktor Shokin, in which he claimed that he was fired unfairly due to Joe Biden's corrupt attempt to protect his son Hunter.[570] Using that affidavit, Rudy Giuliani attempted to create negative press coverage around Joe Biden[571] while deflecting news of the investigations into Donald Trump's actions in Ukraine, which had been increasingly dominating news headlines.

September 30, 2019 - Three House committees (Permanent Select Committee on Intelligence, Committee on Foreign Affairs, and Committee on Oversight and Reform) issued a request for documents from Rudy Giuliani, Lev Parnas, and Igor Fruman. The committees directed the documents to be provided by October 14, 2019.[572]

Early October 2019 - Attorney General Barr declined to intervene in Dmytro Firtash's criminal case.[573]

October 3–November 16, 2019 - Current and former Trump administration officials with knowledge of Trump and Giuliani's Ukraine activities were questioned behind closed doors by members of the House Intelligence, Foreign Affairs, and Oversight Committees.[574]

October 6, 2019 - President Trump had a call with President Erdogan, during which they discussed Erdogan's demand for the withdrawal of US troops from Syria.[575]

October 8, 2019 - The White House officially refused to cooperate with the impeachment investigation.[576]

October 8, 2019 - President Trump ordered the rapid withdrawal of US troops from northern Syria,[577] opening up the region for a major Turkish incursion into Syria to attack the Kurds along the border.

October 9, 2019 - Trump's withdrawal of the US forces embedded with the Syrian Kurds in northern Syria caused both Democratic and Republican lawmakers to speak[578] out[579] against the president's decision. The US forces had fought alongside the Kurds against ISIS and the Bashar al-Assad regime and were the backbone of the Western coalition ground forces in the fight against ISIS.

After the criticism, President Trump changed his position and sent a letter to President Erdogan[580] about Turkey's invasion of the Kurds in Syria, saying, "Don't be a tough guy. Don't be a fool!" Erdogan reportedly tossed that letter into a trash can.[581] Turkey launched its attack on the Syrian Kurds along the Turkish-Syrian border.

October 9, 2019 - The FBI arrested Lev Parnas and Igor Fruman at Dulles Airport near Washington, DC.[582] The duo was on their way to Austria. Before their arrest Rudy Giuliani had told a journalist that he was also planning to fly to Austria.[583]

October 10, 2019 - Three House committees subpoenaed Secretary of Energy Rick Perry, requesting documents related to his activities in Ukraine.[584] The deadline to provide the documents was set for October 18, 2019.[585]

October 11, 2019 - The former US ambassador to Ukraine Marie Yovanovitch testified in front of the investigating committees behind closed doors.[586]

October 14, 2019 - The former White House top Russia advisor Dr. Fiona Hill testified in a closed-door session.[587]

October 14, 2019 - President Trump imposed sanctions on Turkey over its incursion into Syria,[588] increasing US steel tariffs on Turkey to 50 percent.[589] Trump also sanctioned several Turkish officials from the Ministries of Defense, Energy, and Interior.[590] Further, Trump announced the halting of trade negotiations between the two countries worth $100 billion. Some members of Congress called those sanctions "toothless."[591]

October 15, 2019 - The SDNY announced charges against Halkbank.[592] Before that the US government had charged only the people related to the $20 billion money-laundering scheme. This time it was the bank, where the Turkish government was the majority shareholder. The charges included (1) conspiracy to defraud the United States, (2) conspiracy to violate the International Emergency Economic Powers Act, (3) bank fraud, (4) conspiracy to commit bank fraud, (5) money laundering, and (6) conspiracy to commit money laundering.

October 16, 2019 - Ballard Partners terminated its lobbying contract with Halkbank.[593]

October 17, 2019 - VP Mike Pence traveled to Turkey to meet with President Erdogan[594] and persuaded him to halt the Turkish offensive in Syria.

October 17, 2019 - A day before Rick Perry was supposed to send the documents to Congress, Donald Trump announced that the secretary of energy would be stepping down.[595] Perry refused to comply with the subpoena.[596]

October 23, 2019 - President Trump removed all the sanctions he had imposed on Turkey after the Turkish incursion into Syria earlier that month.[597]

October 25, 2019 – Russian spy Maria Butina was deported to Russia.[598]

November 1, 2019 - Rudy Giuliani called Lev Parnas's new lawyer, Joseph Bondy, urging him to call back to Giuliani's "soon to be gotten rid of" number.[599]

November 13, 2019 - Turkish president Erdogan visited the White House.[600]

November 13–21, 2019 - Current and former Trump administration[601] officials[602] publicly[603] testified[604] before the House Intelligence Committee during Donald Trump's first impeachment hearings.

Late November–early December 2019 - Andriy Kobolev, CEO of Naftogaz, and Andrew Favorov, the head of Naftogaz gas division, voluntarily[605] testified[606] to the SDNY.

Early December 2019 - Giuliani, accompanied by a production crew[607] from the right wing channel, One America News (OAN)[608], traveled[609] to Hungary and Ukraine to conduct interviews with several Ukrainians for his documentary.

December 1, 2019 - Rick Perry left his position as secretary of energy.[610]

December 13, 2019 - Naftogaz sued the Ukrainian government, claiming that the oil and gas fields were allocated for Michael Bleyzer's company illegally.[611]

December 18, 2019 - The US House of Representatives debated and voted in favor of impeaching President Trump.[612] The next step would be to send the articles of impeachment for voting in the Senate.

2020

January 1, 2020 - After leaving his position as the secretary of energy, Rick Perry rejoined the board of Energy Transfer.[613]

January 8, 2020 - TurkStream, the Russian-Turkish gas pipeline that was laid from Russia to southern Europe through the Black Sea and into Turkey, entered into service.[614]

January 15, 2020 - The articles of impeachment were delivered from the House of Representatives to the Senate.[615]

February 3, 2020 - Sen. Ron Wyden, the ranking member of the Senate Finance Committee, requested documents from Attorney General Barr about his involvement in the Halkbank case.[616]

February 5, 2020 - The Senate voted to acquit President Trump on the counts of abuse of power and obstruction of Congress.[617]

March 11, 2020 - Ukraine's Cabinet of Ministers signed an executive order appointing Robert Bensh, Rick Perry's candidate, onto the Naftogaz supervisory board.[618]

On or around March 13, 2020 - The United States and Ukraine agreed on an annual supply of six to eight billion cubic meters of American LNG.[619]

Around April 20, 2020 - The Venezuelan government started sending gold to Iran in exchange for Iranian assistance in reviving Venezuelan refineries.[620]

May 27, 2020 - LNGE and Naftogaz signed a memorandum for the prospect of sales of American liquified natural gas to Naftogaz.[621] The twenty-year agreement[622] was estimated to be worth $20 billion.[623]

June 16, 2020 - Despite the Trump White House attempts to halt the release of John Bolton's book and the DOJ's lawsuit against the former national security advisor, the judge ruled in Bolton's favor, allowing the book to be published.⁶²⁴ Multiple senior Trump advisors characterized Bolton as a traitor.⁶²⁵ President Trump suggested that Bolton would have a "very strong criminal problem" if he published the memoir.⁶²⁶

June 19, 2020 - AG William Barr met with SDNY lead prosecutor Geoffrey Berman. Later that day Barr announced that Berman would be "stepping down."⁶²⁷ Berman publicly disagreed with the attorney general's characterization and refused to resign unless the leadership succession of the SDNY went through proper channels.⁶²⁸

June 20, 2020 - President Trump officially fired Geoffrey Berman.⁶²⁹ After a dispute between Barr and Berman about the line of succession to lead the SDNY, Attorney General Barr acquiesced to Berman's demand to follow the line of succession⁶³⁰ instead of appointing a loyalist. Berman's deputy, Audrey Strauss, took over the leadership at the SDNY.⁶³¹

June 21, 2020 - In an interview with ABC News, former national security advisor John Bolton described President Trump's multiple conversations with Turkish president Erdogan. Bolton explained that Erdogan wanted to "take the pressure off Halkbank" and that Trump had obstructed US justice to accommodate his Turkish counterpart.⁶³²

June 23, 2020 - John Bolton's book was released.⁶³³ In it he described, among other things, Donald Trump's apparent willingness to obstruct justice in the Halkbank case.⁶³⁴

July 2, 2020 - Judge Richard Berman, who was presiding over the Halkbank case, ordered the scheduling of the Halkbank trial for March 2021.⁶³⁵

September 10, 2020 - *Politico* wrote that Robert Bensh, a candidate offered to Zelensky by Rick Perry, was "set to join" the Naftogaz supervisory board "pending final paperwork."⁶³⁶

September 11, 2020 - Ukraine's minister of energy announced that LNGE was refusing to cooperate with Ukraine on the supply of liquified gas.⁶³⁷

September 17, 2020 - The SDNY released a superseding indictment of Lev Parnas, Igor Fruman, David Correia, and Andrey Kukushkin.⁶³⁸ This version, unlike the first version of the indictment, did not include any reference to "Congressman-1,"⁶³⁹ who was identified as Rep. Pete Sessions (R-TX).⁶⁴⁰ The first version of the indictment stated that Parnas and Fruman had committed to donate $20,000 to Sessions and that America First Action PAC, to which Parnas and Fruman had donated $325,000, had contributed $3 million to Sessions's 2018 reelection campaign.⁶⁴¹

September 18, 2020 - An attorney for Halkbank requested the dismissal of the US case, claiming that the bank was immune from prosecution because of the Turkish bank's "sovereign immunity." The judge did not grant the request, and the trial remained scheduled for March 1, 2021.[642]

September 23, 2020 - Sen. Ron Wyden requested that the inspector general of the Department of Energy investigate Rick Perry's "role in pressuring Naftogaz."[643]

October 8, 2020 - Ukrainian prosecutors announced an investigation into the Naftogaz management.[644]

October 12, 2020 - Amos Hochstein, a US member at the international Naftogaz supervisory board, resigned from it, protesting the decision to work with LNGE.[645]

October 16, 2020 - Turkey test-fired the Russian-made S-400 air defense system.[646]

November 3, 2020 - US Election Day.

November 4, 2020 - Donald Trump declared victory, even though the votes were still being counted.[647]

November 4, 2020 - Rick Perry sent text messages to Mark Meadows suggesting the use of "alternate" electors in the swing states where Trump lost.[648]

November 4, 2020–mid November 2020 - Trump's campaign legal team filed[649] and lost[650] the first batch of lawsuits to challenge the election results.

November 6, 2020 - Greenberg Traurig discontinued its lobbying contract with Turkey.[651]

November 7, 2020 - Joe Biden was widely proclaimed as the elected forty-sixth President of the United States.[652]

November 9, 2020 - Under pressure from President Trump, AG William Barr announced an investigation into election fraud.[653] That violated the DOJ's policy of holding off any election-related investigations until the official end of the vote count.[654]

November 10, 2020 – Two businessmen connected to Rick Perry went to the White House.[655] The next day they sent a follow-up email stating that President Trump agreed with the alternate electors plan. The email also suggested the need to hold large public trials in four battleground states.[656]

November 13, 2020 - Lewis Sessions, a brother of Congressman Pete Sessions, interviewed a Venezuelan named Leamsy Salazar at the request of Sidney Powell's team.[657] Salazar's affidavit became one of the predicates for Powell's claims of election fraud.[658]

November 14, 2020 - President Trump announced a new campaign legal team that included Rudy Giuliani, Sidney Powell, Victoria Toensing, Joe diGenova, and others.[659]

Mid-November 2020 - Sidney Powell led the Trump campaign team's filing of sixty-two "kraken" lawsuits[660] that challenged the election results.[661]

November 17, 2020 - President Trump fired the head of CISA,[662] who several days prior had publicly stated that there was no evidence of election fraud.[663]

November 18, 2020 - Kenneth Chesebro, an outside legal advisor, sent to Trump's campaign attorney his first memo that outlined an alternate electors strategy and the potential role for Vice President Pence as a person who could unilaterally decide what to do with alternate electoral votes.[664]

November 19, 2020 - Rudy Giuliani, Sidney Powell, and others held a press conference,[665] during which they falsely claimed that there was foreign election interference, specifically with the manipulation of voting equipment.

November 25, 2020 - Pres. Donald Trump pardoned his former national security advisor, Michael Flynn.[666]

November 25–December 3, 2020 - Rudy Giuliani traveled to Pennsylvania,[667] Arizona,[668] Georgia,[669] and Michigan[670] to hold public hearings, during which he alleged that state legislators had allowed election fraud.

December 1, 2020 - Attorney General Barr announced that the DOJ had not found any evidence of massive election fraud, which Trump's allies had claimed.[671]

December 6, 2020 - Kenneth Chesebro sent his second memo about the alternate electors plan.[672] On that and the following days, Mark Meadows exchanged[673] emails[674] and texts[675] with various people about coordinating an alternate electors scheme.

December 6, 2020 - Donald Trump and John Eastman called the RNC chairwoman, Ronna McDaniel, to secure her assistance in recruiting alternate electors.[676]

December 8, 2020 - The US House of Representatives approved a military spending bill for 2021 pursuant to the National Defense Authorization Act.[677] The congressional

must-pass bill also included Countering America's Adversaries through Sanctions Act sanctions, which included[678]
   a. sanctions on Turkey for its purchase of the Russian-made S-400 air defense system,
   b. sanctions on the construction of Russia's Nord Stream 2 pipeline to Germany,
   c. a mandated congressional stop of President Trump's ordered withdrawal of thousands of US forces from NATO-allied Germany.

President Trump would veto the legislation but would be overridden by the Congress.[679]

Around December 8–13, 2020 - Trump's campaign team recruited[680] and coordinated[681] the actions of alternate electors.

December 14, 2020 - Legitimate state electors convened in all states to formalize Joe Biden's victory.[682] That same day alternate electors[683] gathered[684] in seven battleground states, creating alternate certificates of Trump's victory. That day Rudy Giuliani appeared on Steve Bannon's podcast to promote the concept of alternate electors to listeners.[685]

December 14, 2020 - Attorney General Barr announced that he would be resigning on December 23, 2020.[686]

Mid-December 2020 – All but one "kraken" lawsuits filed by Donald Trump's campaign team were[687] dismissed.[688]

December 18, 2020 - Sidney Powell, Michael Flynn, Patrick Byrne, and Rudy Giuliani met with Donald Trump and his staff at the White House.[689] During the meeting Powell, Flynn, and Byrne suggested seizing voting machines with the help of the National Guard and appointing Powell as a special counsel to investigate alleged election fraud.[690] At the end of the night, Trump tweeted, "Be there, will be wild!" calling his supporters to a rally on January 6 in Washington, DC.[691]

December 21, 2020 - President Trump met with eleven Republican congressmen and VP Mike Pence in the White House. Rudy Giuliani and Mark Meadows were also present.[692]

December 22, 2020 - Donald Trump pardoned George Papadopoulos,[693] the former Trump campaign advisor who had been entangled in the 2016 Russian election interference effort. Papadopoulos had previously pleaded guilty for lying to the FBI about his connections to Russian operatives.

December 23, 2020 - Donald Trump pardoned his former campaign manager, Paul Manafort, and a longtime ally, Roger Stone.[694] Both had been[695] implicated[696] in crimes connected to the 2016 Russian election interference effort.

December 23, 2020 - John Eastman wrote a two-page memo with a scenario for January 6, in which he described the roles of the vice president and Republican congressmen for the alternate electors during the joint session on January 6.[697]

December 23, 2020–January 3, 2021 - Donald Trump pressured Attorney General Barr's successor, Jeffrey Rosen, demanding:[698]

Just say the election was corrupt and leave the rest to me and the Republican Congressmen.

As Rosen resisted, the president threatened to replace him with a more compliant person. In response, top DOJ officials told the president they would resign en masse if he fired Rosen.[699]

2021

January 1, 2021 - President Trump, once again, pressured Vice President Pence to play along with the alternate electors plot.[700] When Pence refused, Trump chided him for being "too honest."[701]

January 2, 2021 - Donald Trump called to the secretary of state of Georgia and asked him to "find" 11,780 votes,[702] which could have given Trump a one-vote advantage over Joe Biden to win in Georgia.

January 3, 2021 - John Eastman wrote a six-page memo outlining various scenarios for the January 6 joint congressional session.[703]

January 4, 2021 - Donald Trump and John Eastman met with Mike Pence to once again pressure him to participate in their alternate electors plot.[704] Pence refused.

January 5–6, 2021 - Donald Trump released several[705] tweets[706] and public statements[707] pressuring Mike Pence to disrupt the counting of the electoral votes.

January 6, 2021 - Supporters of President Trump attacked the Capitol building in an attempt to prevent confirmation of Joe Biden as the next president.[708]

January 9, 2021 - Former secretary of state Rex Tillerson and former national security advisor John Bolton told in an interview to *Foreign Policy* magazine that President Trump had repeatedly personally intervened in the Halkbank case.[709]

January 19, 2021 - Donald Trump pardoned his former advisor Steve Bannon.[710]

January 20, 2021 - Donald Trump pardoned GOP operative Paul Erickson,[711] who had helped Russian spy Maria Butina infiltrate both the NRA and conservative circles.

February 18, 2021 - Lobbyist Imaad Zuberi was sentenced to twelve years in prison for illegal campaign contributions, money laundering, and obstruction of justice.[712]

April 28, 2021 - The FBI executed a search warrant at Rudy Giuliani's home and office. That same day the FBI also seized Victoria Toensing's phone.[713]

April 28, 2021 - Ukraine's Cabinet of Ministers dismissed the Naftogaz board, then fired the CEO, Andriy Kobolev, replacing him with his former advisor, Yuri Vitrenko.[714]

June 29, 2021 - Bloomberg reported that the SDNY was investigating Rudy Giuliani for potentially lobbying for the Turkish government.[715]

September 10, 2021 - Igor Fruman pleaded guilty to making straw donations.[716]

October 22, 2021 - Lev Parnas was found guilty of campaign finance violations and making straw donations.[717]

2022

February 24, 2022 - Russia launched a massive attack on Ukraine, reigniting the conflict that had simmered since 2014.[718]

July 15, 2022 - Sezgin Baran Korkmaz was extradited from Austria to the United States.[719]

November 14, 2022 - The SDNY announced that criminal charges on Giuliani for foreign lobbying were "not forthcoming."[720]

2023

January 17, 2023 - The Supreme Court of the United States heard oral arguments from Halkbank lawyers, who claimed that the bank was a branch of the Turkish government and therefore immune from prosecution.[721]

April 19, 2023 – The Supreme Court relegated the Halkbank case to the US Court of Appeals for the Second Circuit for additional judicial review.[722]

July 15, 2023 - An FBI whistleblower filed a report asserting that, throughout 2021–2022, he was obstructed and harassed for investigating Rudy Giuliani.[723]

August 1, 2023 - Donald Trump was indicted by Special Counsel Jack Smith for his role in the effort to disrupt the certification of the 2020 election results.[724]

August 15, 2023 - Donald Trump and his eighteen allies, including Rudy Giuliani, Sidney Powell, Kenneth Chesebro, and John Eastman, were indicted in Georgia for their efforts to overturn the 2020 election results.[725]

October 3, 2023 - Sidney Powell pleaded guilty to charges brought by Georgia prosecutors and agreed to cooperate with investigators.[726]

October 20, 2023 - Kenneth Chesebro pleaded guilty to charges brought by Georgia prosecutors and agreed to cooperate with investigators.[727]

ENDNOTES

CHAPTER 1

1. Patricia Hurtado et al., "Gold Trader at Heart of Turkey Graft Scandal Charged in U.S.," Bloomberg News, March 21, 2016, https://www.bloomberg.com/news/articles/2016-03-22/gold-trader-charged-in-u-s-with-violating-iran-sanctions.
2. Tom Stocks et al., "Reza Zarrab: The Money Launderer Who Wanted to Be Jacques Cousteau," OCCRP, September 20, 2020, https://www.occrp.org/en/the-fincen-files/reza-zarrab-the-money-launderer-who-wanted-to-be-jacques-cousteau.
3. "Manhattan U.S. Attorney Announces Arrest of Turkish National for Conspiring to Evade U.S. Sanctions against Iran, Money Laundering, and Bank Fraud," United States Attorney's Office, Southern District of New York, press release, March 21, 2016, https://www.justice.gov/usao-sdny/pr/manhattan-us-attorney-announces-arrest-turkish-national-conspiring-evade-us-sanctions.
4. "Government's Memorandum of Law in Opposition to Defendant Reza Zarrab's Motion for Bail, United States v. Reza Zarrab," No 15 Cr 867-RMB (S.D.N.Y. May 25, 2016), retrieved from *New York Times* website, https://int.nyt.com/data/documenttools/2016-05-25-preet-bharara-motion-to-deny-reza-zarrab-bail-details-allegations/81b866d2668aa6c0/full.pdf.
5. Tom Stocks et al., "By Suitcase and by Wire: How Reza Zarrab Smuggled Russia's Money," Courthouse News Service, September 20, 2020, https://www.courthousenews.com/by-suitcase-and-by-wire-how-reza-zarrab-smuggled-russias-money/.
6. Christian Berthelsen, "Where Is Reza Zarrab?" Bloomberg News, November 16, 2017, https://www.bloomberg.com/politics/articles/2017-11-16/mystery-deepens-on-eve-of-u-s-bribery-trial-roiling-turkey.
7. Behiye Taner, "Turkish Gold Sales to Iran Soar as Sanctions Bite," Reuters, May 17, 2020, https://www.reuters.com/article/us-gold-turkey-iran-idINBRE84G0QR20120517/.
8. "Timeline: Sanctions on Iran," Al Jazeera, October 17, 2012, https://www.aljazeera.com/economy/2012/10/17/timeline-sanctions-on-iran.
9. Humeyra Pamuk, "Exclusive: Turkish Gold Trade Booms to Iran, via Dubai," Reuters, October 23, 2012, https://www.reuters.com/article/us-emirates-iran-gold-idUSBRE89M0SW20121023/.
10. Pamuk, "Turkish Gold."
11. Tom Hays and Larry Neumeister, "Turkish Businessman Describes $50M Bribe at Sanctions Trial," Associated Press, November 29, 2017, https://apnews.com/general-news-c610ae89f2194717954ff92280448583.

12   Adam Klasfeld and Tom Stocks, "'The Government Is in on It': An Insider's Account of the Reza Zarrab Conspiracy," Courthouse News Service, September 20, 2020, https://www.courthousenews.com/the-government-is-in-on-it-an-insiders-account-of-the-reza-zarrab-conspiracy-hold-for-sunday/.

13   Stocks et al., "Suitcase."

14   "Indictment, United States of America v. Reza Zarrab, Camelia Jamshidy and Hossein Najafzadeh," No 15 Cr 867-RMB (S.D.N.Y. June 16, 2016), https://www.justice.gov/usao-sdny/file/834156/dl.

15   *New York Times*, "Government's Memorandum."

16   Asli Kandemir, "Exclusive: Turkey to Iran Gold Trade Wiped Out by New U.S. Sanction," Reuters, February 15, 2013, https://www.reuters.com/article/us-iran-turkey-sanctions-idUSBRE91E0IN20130215/.

17   Jonathan Schanzer and Emanuele Ottolenghi, "Turkey's Teflon Don," *Foreign Policy*, March 31, 2014, https://foreignpolicy.com/2014/03/31/turkeys-teflon-don/.

18   Stocks et al., "Suitcase."

19   *New York Times*, "Government's Memorandum."

20   "Superseding Indictment, United States of America v. Reza Zarrab, Mehmet Hakan Atilla, Mehmet Zafer Caglayan, Suleyman Aslan, Levent Balkan, Abdullah Happani, Mohammad Zarrab, Camelia Jamshidy and Hossein Najafzadeh," No S4 15 Cr. 867 (RMB) (S.D.N.Y. September 6, 2017), https://www.justice.gov/usao-sdny/press-release/file/994976/dl.

21   Elias Groll, "Turkish Gold Dealer Pleads Guilty in Politically Explosive Sanctions Trial," *Foreign Policy*, November 28, 2017, https://foreignpolicy.com/2017/11/28/turkish-gold-dealer-pleads-guilty-in-politically-explosive-sanctions-trial-iran-zarrab-erdogan/.

22   *New York Times*, "Government's Memorandum."

23   Benjamin Weiser, "Erdogan Helped Turks Evade Iran Sanctions, Reza Zarrab Says," *New York Times*, November 30, 2017, https://www.nytimes.com/2017/11/30/world/europe/erdogan-turkey-iran-sanctions.html.

24   Berivan Orucoglu, "Why Turkey's Mother of All Corruption Scandals Refuses to Go Away," *Foreign Policy*, January 6, 2015, https://foreignpolicy.com/2015/01/06/why-turkeys-mother-of-all-corruption-scandals-refuses-to-go-away/#cookie_message_anchor.

25   Tim Arango, "Corruption Scandal Is Edging Near Turkish Premier," *New York Times*, December 25, 2013, https://www.nytimes.com/2013/12/26/world/europe/turkish-cabinet-members-resign.html.

26   Constanze Letsch, "Turkish Ministers' Sons Arrested in Corruption and Bribery Investigation," *Guardian*, December 17, 2013, https://www.theguardian.com/world/2013/dec/17/turkish-ministers-sons-arrested-corruption-investigation.

27   Orucoglu, "Why Turkey's Mother."

28   Charles Recknagel, "Turkish Corruption Investigation Throws Government Into Crisis," RFERL, December 19, 2013, https://www.rferl.org/a/turkey-corruption-scandal-crisis/25206516.html.

29   "Turkey PM Erdogan Condemns 'Dirty' Corruption Probe," BBC News, December 18, 2013, https://www.bbc.com/news/world-europe-25437624.

30   Arango, "Corruption Scandal."

31   Serkan Demirtas, "Blame Game," DW, December 28, 2013, https://www.dw.com/en/erdogan-points-fingers-in-corruption-scandal/a-17328957.

32   Dexter Filkins, "A Mysterious Case Involving Turkey, Iran, and Rudy Giuliani," *New Yorker*, April 14, 2017, https://www.newyorker.com/news/news-desk/a-mysterious-case-involving-turkey-iran-and-rudy-giuliani.

33 Basak Özay, "Government in Crisis," DW, December 26, 2013, https://www.dw.com/en/turkey-rocked-by-corruption-scandal/a-17324458.

34 Mark Lowen, "Turkey's Erdogan Battles 'Parallel State,'" BBC News, December 17, 2014, https://www.bbc.com/news/world-europe-30492348.

35 Thomas Seibert, "Turkish Corruption Scandal," DW, January 6, 2014, https://www.dw.com/en/erdogan-family-drawn-into-corruption-probe/a-17344379.

36 "TSK: Siyasi tartışma içinde yer almak istemiyoruz" ["TSK: We do not want to take part in political discussions"], BBC News Turkey, December 27, 2013, https://www.bbc.com/turkce/haberler/2013/12/131227_tsk_aciklama.

37 Selin Girit, "Reza Zarrab: Gold Trader's US Legal Saga Grips Turkey," BBC News, November 29, 2017, https://www.bbc.com/news/world-europe-42149917.

38 Orhan Coskunand and Humeyra Pamuk, "Turkey Vows No Cover-Up Despite Purge of Graft Investigators," Reuters, December 24, 2013, https://www.reuters.com/article/idUSDEE9BN0C7/.

39 "Turkish Prosecutor Dismissed, Charged with Official Interference," Voice of America, December 26, 2013, https://www.voanews.com/a/turkish-prosecutor-is-dismissed-charges-official-interference/1818052.html.

40 "Turkish Bar Union Files Lawsuit against Regulation Lifting Investigation Secrecy," *Hurriyet Daily News*, December 24, 2013, https://www.hurriyetdailynews.com/turkish-bar-union-files-lawsuit-against-regulation-lifting-investigation-secrecy--60003.

41 Tim Arango, "Prosecutor Overseeing Turkish Graft Inquiry Is Removed from Case," *New York Times*, December 27, 2013, https://www.nytimes.com/2013/12/28/world/europe/turkey-corruption-scandal.html.

42 "Turkish Corruption Probe Row Deepens," BBC News, January 7, 2014, https://www.bbc.com/news/world-europe-25637710.

43 "No Suspects Left in Jail in Turkey's Corruption Probe," *Hurriyet Daily News*, March 2, 2014, https://www.hurriyetdailynews.com/no-suspects-left-in-jail-in-turkeys-corruption-probe-63045.

44 "Star Witness in Iran Sanctions Case Admits in Court to Paying Bribes," RFERL, December 5, 2017, https://www.rferl.org/a/star-witness-iran-sanctions-case-admits-in-court-paying-bribes-release-prison-turkey-2013-reza-zarrab-attila/28897250.html.

45 Nick Tattersall and Daren Butler, "Turkey Dismisses Corruption Case That Has Dogged PM Erdogan," Reuters, May 2, 2014, https://www.reuters.com/article/us-turkey-corruption-idUSBREA410NE20140502/.

46 Jonathan Schanzer, "The Biggest Sanctions-Evasion Scheme in Recent History," *Atlantic*, January 4, 2018, https://www.theatlantic.com/international/archive/2018/01/iran-turkey-gold-sanctions-nuclear-zarrab-atilla/549665/.

CHAPTER 2

1 Angèle Pierre, "Turkey: 10 Years after the Gezi Uprising, a Generation in Turmoil," *Le Monde*, May 28, 2023, https://www.lemonde.fr/en/international/article/2023/05/28/turkey-10-years-after-the-gezi-uprising-a-generation-in-turmoil_6028243_4.html.

2 Tim Arango and Ceylan Yeginsu, "Peaceful Protest over Istanbul Park Turns Violent as Police Crack Down," *New York Times*, May 31, 2013, https://www.nytimes.com/2013/06/01/world/europe/police-attack-protesters-in-istanbuls-taksim-square.html.

3   Constanze Letsch, "Turkey Protests Spread after Violence in Istanbul over Park Demolition," *Guardian*, May 31, 2013, https://www.theguardian.com/world/2013/may/31/istanbul-protesters-violent-clashes-police.

4   Constanze Letsch, "Turkey: Erdogan under New Pressure to Quit as Protesters Take to the Streets," *Guardian*, December 28, 2013, https://www.theguardian.com/world/2013/dec/28/erdogan-pressure-quit-turkey-protests.

5   "Anti-Erdogan Protest in Istanbul," DW, December 22, 2013, https://www.dw.com/en/anti-government-protesters-clash-with-police-in-turkey-over-corruption-scandal/a-17316868.

6   "Recep Tayyip Erdogan Wins Turkish Presidential Election," BBC News, August 10, 2014, https://www.bbc.com/news/world-europe-28729234.

7   Zeynep Bilginsoy, "How Turkey's Failed Coup Unfolded, Hour by Hour," Associated Press, July 14, 2017, https://apnews.com/article/ankara-istanbul-turkey-middle-east-europe-6cc9e69a1c5d4da1b6f509ce1152b0ed.

8   Judith Vonberg et al., "47,155 Arrests: Turkey's Post-Coup Crackdown by the Numbers," CNN, April 15, 2017, https://edition.cnn.com/2017/04/14/europe/turkey-failed-coup-arrests-detained/index.html.

9   "Turkish Leader Declares State of Emergency after Failed Coup," CBS News, July 20, 2016, https://www.cbsnews.com/news/turkey-closing-hundreds-schools-anti-coup-measure/.

10 Alastair Jamieson, "Turkey's Erdogan to Build More Prisons as Post-Coup Purge Persists," NBC News, September 16, 2018, https://www.nbcnews.com/news/world/turkey-s-erdogan-build-more-prisons-post-coup-purge-persists-n909486.

11 Amberin Zaman, "Turkey Silences More Journalists in Latest Post-Coup Crackdown," interviewed by Hari Sreenivasan, PBS *NewsHour*, November 2, 2016, audio, 08:09, https://www.pbs.org/newshour/show/turkey-silences-journalists-latest-post-coup-crackdown#audio.

12 "Turkey Sacks 4,400 More Civil Servants, Including Teachers and Police," Reuters, February 8, 2017, https://www.reuters.com/article/idUSKBN15N0KS/.

13 "Turkey: Crackdown on Kurdish Opposition," Human Rights Watch, March 20, 2017, https://www.hrw.org/news/2017/03/20/turkey-crackdown-kurdish-opposition.

14 Carlotta Gall, "Erdogan's Purges Leave Turkey's Justice System Reeling," *New York Times*, June 21, 2019, https://www.nytimes.com/2019/06/21/world/asia/erdogan-turkey-courts-judiciary-justice.html.

15 Kareem Fahim, "Turkey's Erdogan Declares Victory in Referendum over Presidential Powers," *Washington Post*, April 16, 2017, https://www.washingtonpost.com/world/turks-to-decide-whether-to-give-erdogan-vastly-increased-powers/2017/04/15/e79812b6-1bda-11e7-bcc2-7d1a0973e7b2_story.html.

16 "Foreign Agents Registration Act Home, Frequently Asked Questions," U.S. Department of Justice, accessed June 16, 2024, https://www.justice.gov/nsd-fara/frequently-asked-questions.

17 "Foreign Agents Registration Act Home," U.S. Department of Justice, accessed June 16, 2024, https://www.justice.gov/nsd-fara.

18 Adam Klasfeld, "Boom Times for Turkey's Lobbyists in Trump's Washington," Courthouse News Service, October 31, 2019, https://www.courthousenews.com/boom-times-for-turkeys-lobbyists-in-trumps-washington/.

19 U.S. Department of Justice, *Exhibit A to Registration Statement Pursuant to the Foreign Agents Registration Act of 1938, as amended, filed by Gephardt Group, LLC*, Registration No 5874, July 21, 2008, https://efile.fara.gov/docs/5874-Exhibit-AB-20080721-2.pdf.

20 U.S. Department of Justice, *Exhibit A to Registration Statement Pursuant to the Foreign Agents Registration Act of 1938, as amended, filed by Greenberg Traurig, LLP*, Registration No 5712, August 12, 2014, https://efile.fara.gov/docs/5712-Exhibit-AB-20140812-19.pdf.

21 U.S. Department of Justice, *Exhibit A to Registration Statement Pursuant to the Foreign Agents Registration Act of 1938, as amended, filed by Amsterdam & Partners LLP*, Registration No 6325, October 26, 2015, https://efile.fara.gov/docs/6325-Exhibit-AB-20151026-1.pdf.

22 U.S. Department of Justice, *Exhibit A to Registration Statement Pursuant to the Foreign Agents Registration Act of 1938, as amended, filed by Mercury*, Registration No 6170, March 16, 2016, https://efile.fara.gov/docs/6170-Exhibit-AB-20160316-16.pdf.

23 Liz Essley Whyte, "The Bizarre American Lobbying War over Turkish-Run Schools," *Politico Magazine*, February 1, 2018, https://www.politico.com/magazine/story/2018/02/01/the-bizarre-american-lobbying-war-over-turkish-run-schools-216562/.

24 "Brian D Ballard," Open Secrets, accessed June 16, 2024, https://www.opensecrets.org/revolving-door/ballard-brian-d/summary?id=80743.

25 Theodoric Meyer, "The Most Powerful Lobbyist in Trump's Washington," *Politico Magazine*, April 2, 2018, https://www.politico.com/magazine/story/2018/04/02/most-powerful-lobbyist-in-trump-washington-217759/.

26 Brody Mullins and Julie Bykowicz, "Florida Lobbyist Thrives in Trump-Era Washington," *Wall Street Journal*, October 21, 2020, https://www.wsj.com/articles/florida-lobbyist-thrives-in-trump-era-washington-11603285219.

27 Alex Leary, "Brian Ballard Gets RNC Finance Post," *Tampa Bay Times*, April 3, 2017, https://www.tampabay.com/brian-ballard-gets-rnc-finance-post/2319028/.

28 U.S. Department of Justice, *Exhibit A to Registration Statement Pursuant to the Foreign Agents Registration Act of 1938, as amended, filed by Ballard Partners*, Registration No 6415, May 19, 2017, https://efile.fara.gov/docs/6415-Exhibit-AB-20170519-3.pdf.

29 U.S. Department of Justice, *Exhibit A to Registration Statement Pursuant to the Foreign Agents Registration Act of 1938, as amended, filed by Ballard Partners*, Registration No 6415, August 28, 2017, https://efile.fara.gov/docs/6415-Exhibit-AB-20170828-5.pdf.

30 Eric Lipton and Benjamin Weiser, "Turkish Bank Case Showed Erdogan's Influence with Trump," *New York Times*, October 29, 2020, https://www.nytimes.com/2020/10/29/us/politics/trump-erdogan-halkbank.html.

31 U.S. Department of Justice, *Exhibit B to Registration Statement Pursuant to the Foreign Agents Registration Act of 1938, as amended, filed by Greenberg Traurig*, Registration No 5712, May 30, 2017, https://efile.fara.gov/docs/5712-Exhibit-AB-20170530-31.pdf.

32 Martin Pengelly, "'Donald Kept Our Secret': Mar-a-Lago Stay Saved Giuliani from Drink and Depression, Book Says," *Guardian*, August 24, 2022, https://www.theguardian.com/books/2022/aug/24/donald-trump-secret-mar-a-lago-stay-rudy-giuliani-drink-depression-wife-andrew-kirtzman-book.

33 Elizabeth Olson, "Wake Up Call: Giuliani Joins Greenberg Traurig, and Other News," Bloomberg Law, January 20, 2016, https://news.bloomberglaw.com/business-and-practice/wake-up-call-giuliani-joins-greenberg-traurig-and-other-news.

34 Benjamin Weiser and Patrick Kingsley, "Why Giuliani Held a Secret Meeting With Turkey's Leader," *New York Times*, April 20, 2017, https://www.nytimes.com/2017/04/20/nyregion/rudy-giuliani-reza-zarrab-iran-sanctions-case.html.

35 Larry Neumeister, "Lawyer: Giuliani Eyes 'Diplomatic' End to Turkish Man's Case," Associated Press, April 4, 2017, https://apnews.com/general-news-41ac6765f41b434282817a4aa418533c.

36 Weiser and Kingsley, "Secret Meeting."

37 Lipton and Weiser, "Turkish Bank Case."
38 Stephanie Baker, "Where Rudy Giuliani's Money Comes From," *Bloomberg News,* April 5, 2019, https://www.bloomberg.com/news/features/2019-04-05/where-rudy-giuliani-s-money-comes-from.
39 Benjamin Weiser, "Reza Zarrab Testifies That He Bribed Turkish Minister," *New York Times,* November 29, 2017, https://www.nytimes.com/2017/11/29/world/europe/reza-zarrab-turkey-trial.html.
40 Kelly Bloss et al., "Notorious Money Launderer Reza Zarrab's Lavish Life and New Business in Miami," OCCRP, December 7, 2021, https://www.occrp.org/en/how-iran-used-an-international-playboy-to-launder-oil-money/notorious-money-launderer-reza-zarrabs-lavish-life-and-new-business-in-miami.
41 Ryan Lucas, "Gold Trader Reza Zarrab Agrees to Cooperate with U.S. in Sanctions Evasion Case," interview by Robert Siegel, *All Things Considered,* NPR, November 29, 2017, audio, 3:50, https://www.npr.org/2017/11/29/567313598/gold-trader-reza-zarrab-agrees-to-cooperate-with-u-s-in-sanctions-evasion-case.
42 Katie Zavadski, "Did the Feds Flip Turkish Businessman Reza Zarrab—and Could He Bring Down Michael Flynn?" *Daily Beast,* November 16, 2017, https://www.thedailybeast.com/did-the-feds-flip-turkish-businessman-reza-zarraband-could-he-bring-down-michael-flynn.
43 Benjamin Weiser and Patrick Kingsley, "Signs of Possible Guilty Plea in Turkish Gold Trader Case," *New York Times,* October 31, 2017, https://www.nytimes.com/2017/10/31/nyregion/zarrab-turkish-gold-trader.html.
44 "Man Accused in Iran Sanctions Case Reported Working with U.S. Prosecutors," RFERL, November 17, 2017, https://www.rferl.org/a/turkish-iranian-businessman-zarrab-gold-trade-erdogan-ties-iran-sanctions-case-reported-cooperating-us-prosecutors/28859053.html.
45 U.S. Department of Justice, *Exhibit A to Registration Statement Pursuant to the Foreign Agents Registration Act of 1938, as amended, filed by King & Spalding LLP,* Registration No 6501, December 21, 2017, https://efile.fara.gov/docs/6501-Exhibit-AB-20171221-1.pdf.
46 U.S. Department of Justice, *Letter to King & Spalding LLC,* "Re: Obligation to Register Pursuant to the Foreign Agents Registration Act," December 7, 2017, https://www.justice.gov/nsd-fara/page/file/1282106/dl.
47 Glenn Thrush and Julie Hirschfeld Davis, "Trump Picks Christopher Wray to Be F.B.I. Director," *New York Times,* June 7, 2017, https://www.nytimes.com/2017/06/07/us/politics/christopher-wray-fbi-director.html.
48 "Reza Zarrab Case: Gold Trader Implicates Turkish President Erdogan," BBC News, November 30, 2017, https://www.bbc.com/news/world-europe-42189802.
49 Weiser, "Erdogan."
50 Klasfeld, "Boom Times."

CHAPTER 3

1 Rachel Maddow, "How Mike Flynn's Position on Turkey Turned on a Dime . . . a Lot of Dimes," MSNBC, December 18, 2018, video, 27:18, https://youtu.be/Qn4tzinaRNQ?si=aiS1h9dYxP6sg2M-.
2 James V. Grimaldi et al., "Ex-CIA Director: Mike Flynn and Turkish Officials Discussed Removal of Erdogan Foe from U.S," *Wall Street Journal,* March 24, 2017, https://www.wsj.com/articles/ex-cia-director-mike-flynn-and-turkish-officials-discussed-removal-of-erdogan-foe-from-u-s-1490380426.

3   Julia Ainsley, "Mike Flynn Business Partner Bijan Kian Now Subject of Mueller Probe," NBC News, November 22, 2017, https://www.nbcnews.com/news/us-news/mike-flynn-business-partner-bijan-kian-now-subject-mueller-probe-n823366.

4   "Ex-Trump Aide Mike Flynn 'Offered $15m by Turkey for Gulen,'" BBC News, November 11, 2017, https://www.bbc.com/news/world-asia-41947451.

5   Tim Weiner, "Director of C.I.A. to Leave, Ending Troubled Tenure," *New York Times*, December 29, 1994, https://archive.nytimes.com/www.nytimes.com/library/magazine/home/122994mag-woolsey.html.

6   Jeremy Diamond, "Former CIA Chief under Clinton Joins Trump Campaign", CNN, September 12, 2016, https://edition.cnn.com/2016/09/12/politics/james-woolsey-clinton-cia-director-backs-trump/.

7   Mark Hosenball and Steve Holland, "Trump Being Advised by Ex-U.S. Lieutenant General Who Favours Closer Russia Ties," Reuters, February 26, 2016, https://www.reuters.com/article/us-usa-election-trump-advisor-idUSKCN0VZ2ZB/.

8   "Trump Transition Aide Bijan Kian Played Key Role in Flynn's Turkish Work," CBS News, June 13, 2017, https://www.cbsnews.com/news/trump-transition-aide-bijan-kian-played-key-role-in-flynns-turkish-work/.

9   Peter Kenyon, "In Turkey, the Man to Blame for Most Everything Is a U.S.-Based Cleric," *Morning Edition*, NPR, September 4, 2016, audio, 3:28, https://www.npr.org/sections/parallels/2016/09/04/492105146/in-turkey-the-man-to-blame-for-most-everything-is-a-u-s-based-cleric.

10 Grimaldi et al., "Ex-CIA Director."

11 Steve Herman, "Turkey Warns of Consequences If Extradition Request Not Heeded," Voice of America, August 1, 2016, https://www.voanews.com/a/turkish-lawmakers-us-warn-consequences-extradition-request-gulen/3445122.html.

12 Michael Werz and Max Hoffman, "The Process behind Turkey's Proposed Extradition of Fethullah Gülen," Center for American Progress, September 7, 2016, https://www.americanprogress.org/article/the-process-behind-turkeys-proposed-extradition-of-fethullah-gulen/.

13 Grimaldi et al., "Ex-CIA Director."

14 "Austria Extradites Turkish Businessman Wanted for Money Laundering," OCCRP, July 20, 2022, https://www.occrp.org/en/daily/16589-austria-extradites-turkish-businessman-wanted-for-money-laundering.

15 Rachel Weiner, "Without Testimony from Michael Flynn, Judge Is Skeptical of Case against Ex-Business Partner," *Washington Post*, July 18, 2019, https://www.washingtonpost.com/local/public-safety/without-testimony-from-michael-flynn-judge-is-skeptical-of-case-against-ex-business-partner/2019/07/18/eaaec884-a998-11e9-86dd-d7f0e60391e9_story.html.

16 Nathan Layne, "Exclusive—While Advising Trump in 2016, Ex-CIA Chief Proposed Plan to Discredit Turkish Cleric," Reuters, October 26, 2017, https://www.reuters.com/article/us-usa-trump-woolsey-exclusive-idUSKBN1CV2RF/.

17 Layne, "Advising Trump."

18 James Woosley, "WSJ Exclusive: Ex-CIA Head Woolsey on Flynn, Covert Plan," interview by John Bussey, *Wall Street Journal*, video, 11:30, March 25, 2017, https://www.youtube.com/watch?v=hWDxZSz41Eg.

19 Layne, "Advising Trump."

20 Peter Baker and Matthew Rosenberg, "Michael Flynn Was Paid to Represent Turkey's Interests during Trump Campaign," *New York Times*, March 10, 2017, https://www.nytimes.com/2017/03/10/us/politics/michael-flynn-turkey.html.

21 Stef W. Kight, "Timeline: Michael Flynn's Secret Work for Turkey," *Axios*, December 1, 2017, https://www.axios.com/2017/12/15/timeline-michael-flynns-secret-work-for-turkey-1513303955.

22 Baker and Rosenberg, "Michael Flynn."

23 Jerry Dunleavy, "DOJ Celebrates after Appeals Court Reinstates Conviction of Flynn Business Partner," *Washington Examiner*, March 19, 2021, https://www.washingtonexaminer.com/news/715759/doj-celebrates-after-appeals-court-reinstates-conviction-of-flynn-business-partner/.

24 Adam Rawnsley, "Michael Flynn Biz Partner Bijan Kian Charged in Scheme to Send Cleric Back to Turkey," *Daily Beast*, December 17, 2018, https://www.thedailybeast.com/michael-flynn-biz-partner-bijan-kian-charged-with-illegal-lobbying-for-turkey.

25 "Indictment, United States of America v. Bijan Rafiekian and Ekim Alptekin," No 1:18-CR-457-AJT (Eastern District of Virginia December 12, 2018), https://www.justice.gov/opa/press-release/file/1120621/dl.

26 Michael Flynn, "Our Ally Turkey Is in Crisis and Needs Our Support," opinion, *Hill*, November 8, 2016, https://thehill.com/blogs/pundits-blog/foreign-policy/305021-our-ally-turkey-is-in-crisis-and-needs-our-support/.

27 "Turkey Blames U.S.-Based Muslim Cleric for Russian Envoy's Killing," RFERL, December 21, 2016, https://www.rferl.org/a/turkey-blames-us-based-muslim-cleric-gulen-russian-envoy-karlov-assassination/28188195.html.

28 Carlotta Gall, "U.S. Is 'Working On' Extraditing Gulen, Top Turkish Official Says," *New York Times*, December 16, 2018, https://www.nytimes.com/2018/12/16/world/europe/fethullah-gulen-turkey-extradite.html.

29 Nathan Layne, "Flynn's Former Business Partner Charged with Secret Lobbying for Turkey," Reuters, December 17, 2018, https://www.reuters.com/article/us-turkey-usa-gulen/flynns-former-business-partner-charged-with-secret-lobbying-for-turkey-idUSKBN1OG1T3/.

30 James V. Grimaldi et al., "Mueller Probes Flynn's Role in Alleged Plan to Deliver Cleric to Turkey," *Wall Street Journal*, November 10, 2017, https://www.wsj.com/articles/mueller-probes-flynns-role-in-alleged-plan-to-deliver-cleric-to-turkey-1510309982.

31 Carol E. Lee and Julia Ainsley, "Mueller Probing Possible Deal between Turks, Flynn during Presidential Transition," NBC News, November 10, 2017, https://www.nbcnews.com/news/us-news/mueller-probing-possible-deal-between-turks-flynn-during-presidential-transition-n819616.

32 Dan Mangan and Kevin Breuninger, "Michael Flynn Sentencing Delayed as Judge Tells Ex-Trump Official: 'You Sold Your Country Out,'" CNBC, December 18, 2018, https://www.cnbc.com/2018/12/18/judge-tells-michael-flynn-you-sold-your-country-out-at-hearing.html.

33 Grimaldi et al., "Mueller Probes Flynn's Role."

34 Barbara Leonard, "Buddha Bar," Courthouse News Service, September 16, 2020, https://www.courthousenews.com/buddha-bar/.

35 "Игорь Фруман" ["Igor Fruman"], *Фокус [Focus]*, March 23, 2011, https://focus.ua/people/176133.

36 Aubrey Belford and Veronika Melkozerova, "Meet the Florida Duo Helping Giuliani Investigate for Trump in Ukraine," OCCRP, July 22, 2019, https://www.occrp.org/en/investigations/meet-the-florida-duo-helping-giuliani-dig-dirt-for-trump-in-ukraine.

37. Aubrey Belford and Adam Klasfeld, "Behind Trump's Turkish 'Bromance': Oligarchs, Crooks, and a Multi-Million-Dollar Lobbying Deal," OCCRP, September 18, 2020, https://www.occrp.org/en/investigations/behind-trumps-turkish-bromance-oligarchs-crooks-and-a-multi-million-dollar-lobbying-deal.

38. Ben Schreckinger and Darren Samuelsohn, "Giuliani Ukraine Associate Had Checkered Past Even before Indictment," *Politico*, October 17, 2019, https://www.politico.com/news/2019/10/17/lev-parnas-giuliani-ukraine-past-049677.

39. Lev Parnas and Jerry Langton, *Shadow Diplomacy: Lev Parnas and His Wild Ride from Brooklyn to Trump's Inner Circle* (Bronxkill Publishing, 2024), chap. 3, Kindle.

40. Parnas and Langton, *Shadow Diplomacy*, chap. 4, Kindle.

41. Jane Musgrave and John Pacenti, "Lev Parnas' Life in Boca Raton: Suburban Dad Got His Start in Penny Stocks on 'Maggot Mile,'" *Palm Beach Post*, January 24, 2020, https://www.palmbeachpost.com/story/news/2020/01/24/lev-parnasrsquo-life-in-boca-raton-suburban-dad-got-his-start-in-penny-stocks-on-lsquomaggot-milersquo/112176048/.

42. Jeff Ostrowski and Wayne Washington, "Lev Parnas in Palm Beach County: Unpaid Bills, Failed Business Deals," *Florida Times Union*, October 24, 2019, https://www.jacksonville.com/story/news/politics/2019/10/25/lev-parnas-in-palm-beach-county-unpaid-bills-failed-business-deals/2439171007/.

43. Open Secrets, Search results for "Donors—Lev Parnas," accessed June 17, 2024, https://www.opensecrets.org/search?order=asc&q=lev+parnas&sort=D&type=donors.

44. Aubrey Belford and Adam Klasfeld, "Parnas' Adventures in MAGAland," OCCRP, September 18, 2020, https://www.occrp.org/en/investigations/sidebar/parnas-adventures-in-magaland.

45. Julie Bykowicz et al., "Indicted Florida Pair Known for Flashy Style, Claim of Trump Ties," *Wall Street Journal*, October 10, 2019, https://www.wsj.com/articles/indicted-florida-pair-known-for-flashy-style-claim-of-trump-ties-11570757074.

46. Laure Mandeville, "Au Hilton, l'attente fiévreuse des fans de Donald Trump" ["At the Hilton, the feverish wait of Donald Trump fans"], *Le Figaro*, November 9, 2016, https://www.lefigaro.fr/elections-americaines/2016/11/09/01040-20161109ARTFIG00009-les-fans-de-trump-reunis-au-hilton.php.

47. Ben Schreckinger, "Inside Donald Trump's Election Night War Room," *GQ*, November 7, 2017, https://www.gq.com/story/inside-donald-trumps-election-night-war-room.

48. Darren Samuelson and Ben Schreckinger, "Indicted Giuliani Associate Attended Private '16 Election Night Party for 'Friend' Trump," *Politico*, October 11, 2019, https://www.politico.com/news/2019/10/11/lev-parnas-giuliani-trump-private-party-044698.

49. "Mubariz Gurbanoglu," profile by *Forbes*, accessed June 17, 2024, https://www.forbes.com/profile/mubariz-gurbanoglu/?sh=5621f7b7394b.

50. "Lev Parnas Talks Turkey," OCCRP, September 18, 2020, video, 10:30, https://www.youtube.com/watch?v=ctLbglsQqwM.

51. Belford and Klasfeld, "Behind Trump's Turkish 'Bromance.'"

52. "Erdoğan Makes "Grey Wolf" Sign at Rally," Ahval News, March 10, 2018, https://ahvalnews.com/recep-tayyip-erdogan/erdogan-makes-grey-wolf-sign-rally.

53. "Turkey's Çavuşoğlu Flashes Nationalist Sign at Armenian Protesters," Ahval News, April 24, 2022, https://ahvalnews.com/1915/turkeys-cavusoglu-flashes-nationalist-sign-armenian-protesters.

54. "France Bans Turkish Ultra-Nationalist Grey Wolves," DW, April 11, 2020, https://www.dw.com/en/france-bans-turkish-ultra-nationalist-grey-wolves-group/a-55503469.

55 Patrick Keddie, "France Has Banned the 'Grey Wolves' – but Who Are They?" Al Jazeera, November 24, 2020, https://www.aljazeera.com/features/2020/11/24/france-has-banned-the-grey-wolves-but-who-are-they.

56 Ezel Sahinkaya, "Shadowy Turkish Ultra-Nationalist Group under Scrutiny in Europe," Voice of America, December 8, 2020, https://www.voanews.com/a/extremism-watch_shadowy-turkish-ultra-nationalist-group-under-scrutiny-europe/6199344.html.

57 Nazlan Ertan, "Will Turkey's Grey Wolves Land on EU Terror List," *Al-Monitor*, May 20, 2021, https://www.al-monitor.com/originals/2021/05/will-turkeys-grey-wolves-land-eu-terror-list#ixzz8dRLeBIJT.

58 Abdullah Bozkurt, "Mansimov Jailed in Turkey over Erdoğan's Fears and His Allies' Desire to Seize the Billionaire's Assets," Nordic Monitor, May 20, 2021, https://nordicmonitor.com/2020/06/mansimov-jailed-over-erdogans-whims-and-fears-or-lust-to-seize-billionaires-assets/.

59 "Lev Parnas Talks Turkey," OCCRP.

60 Aubrey Belford and Adam Klasfeld, "The Oligarchs and the Watergate: Behind Trump's Turkey 'Bromance,'" Courthouse News Service, September 18, 2020, https://www.courthousenews.com/oligarchs-and-a-multimillion-dollar-lobbying-deal/.

61 Belford and Klasfeld, "Oligarchs and the Watergate.'"

62 Belford and Klasfeld, "Behind Trump's Turkish 'Bromance.'"

63 Adam Klasfeld and Aubrey Belford, "Adventures in MAGA-land with Lev Parnas," Courthouse News Service, September 18, 2020, https://www.courthousenews.com/adventures-in-maga-land-with-lev-parnas/.

64 Aaron Gideon Parnas, *Trump First: How the President and His Associates Turned Their Backs on Me and My Family* (Independently published, 2020), chap. 4, Kindle.

65 "Russia: The World's Richest Government," *Forbes,* April 1, 2008, https://www.forbes.com/2008/03/28/russia-billionaires-duma-biz-cz_hb_0401russiapols.html?sh=513acbf68f3b.

66 Belford and Klasfeld, "Behind Trump's Turkish 'Bromance.'"

67 Belford and Klasfeld, "Oligarchs and the Watergate.'"

68 Belford and Klasfeld, "Behind Trump's Turkish 'Bromance.'"

69 Belford and Klasfeld, "Oligarchs and the Watergate.'

70 Federal Election Commission, search result for individual contributions "Contributor details - Lev Parnas, Recipient name or ID - Republican National Committee (C00003418)," accessed June 17, 2024, https://www.fec.gov/data/receipts/individual-contributions/?committee_id=C00003418&contributor_name=lev+parnas.

71 Belford and Klasfeld, "Behind Trump's Turkish 'Bromance.'"

72 Debra J. Saunders, "Steve Wynn Named RNC Finance Chairman," *Las Vegas Review Journal*, January 30, 2017, https://www.reviewjournal.com/news/politics-and-government/nevada/steve-wynn-named-rnc-finance-chairman/.

73 Belford and Klasfeld, "Behind Trump's Turkish 'Bromance.'"

74 Belford and Klasfeld, "Behind Trump's Turkish 'Bromance.'"

75 U.S. Department of Justice, *Exhibit A to Registration Statement Pursuant to the Foreign Agents Registration Act of 1938, as amended, filed by Ballard Partners*, Registration No 6415, April 24, 2018, https://efile.fara.gov/docs/6415-Exhibit-AB-20180424-10.pdf.

76 U.S. Department of Justice, *Exhibit A to Registration Statement Pursuant to the Foreign Agents Registration Act of 1938, as amended, filed by Ballard Partners*, Registration No 6415, May 19, 2017, https://efile.fara.gov/docs/6415-Exhibit-AB-20170519-3.pdf.

77 Belford and Klasfeld, "Behind Trump's Turkish 'Bromance.'"

78   U.S. Department of Justice, *Exhibit A to Registration Statement Pursuant to the Foreign Agents Registration Act of 1938, as amended*, filed by Ballard Partners, Registration No 6415, August 28, 2017, https://efile.fara.gov/docs/6415-Exhibit-AB-20170828-5.pdf.

CHAPTER 4

1   Isaac Arnsdorf, "The 'International Man of Mystery' Linked to Flynn's Lobbying Deal," ProPublica, June 27, 2017, https://www.propublica.org/article/the-international-man-of-mystery-linked-to-flynns-lobbying-deal.
2   Isaac Arnsdorf, "Flynn's Turkish Lobbying Linked to Russia," *Politico*, April 25, 2017, https://www.politico.com/story/2017/04/25/michael-flynn-turkey-russia-237550.
3   Borzou Daragahi, "The Man at the Center of This Trump Scandal Wants to Clear His Name," *Buzzfeed News*, June 20, 2017, https://www.BuzzFeednews.com/article/borzoudaragahi/the-man-at-the-center-of-this-trump-scandal-wants-to-clear.
4   Isaac Arnsdorf, "Trump Adviser Linked to Turkish Lobbying," *Politico*, November 14, 2016, https://www.politico.com/story/2016/11/donald-trump-turkey-lobbying-231354.
5   Isaac Arnsdorf, "Michael Flynn's Turkish Lobbying Linked to Russia," *Politico*, April 25, 2017, https://www.politico.eu/article/michael-flynns-turkish-lobbying-linked-to-russia/.
6   Arnsdorf, "Michael Flynn's Turkish lobbying linked to Russia."
7   "About Us," Turkish Heritage Organization, retrieved from the Wayback Machine, version from October 31, 2015, https://web.archive.org/web/20151031081337/www.turkheritage.org/en/about-us.
8   Mahir Zeynalov, "How Erdogan's Family Uses Non-Profits in D.C. for Lobbying," *Huffington Post*, October 21, 2016, https://www.huffpost.com/entry/how-erdogans-family-uses-non-profits-in-dc-for_b_580a249ae4b0b1bd89fdb11a.
9   WikiLeaks, "Berat's Box," search results for "Danismaz," retrieved from the Wayback Machine, version from November 4, 2020, https://web.archive.org/web/20201104043047/https://wikileaks.org/berats-box/?q=Danismaz&mfrom=&mto=&title=&notitle=&date_from=&date_to=&nofrom=&noto=&count=50&sort=0#searchresult.
10 WikiLeaks, "Berat's Box," email from Halil Danismaz to Berat Albayrak sent on March 17, 2015, retrieved from the Wayback Machine, version from June 30, 2022, https://web.archive.org/web/20220630100808/https://wikileaks.org/berats-box/emailid/26786.
11 WikiLeaks, "Berat's Box," email from Halil Danismaz to Berat Albayrak and Bilal Erdogan sent on June 24, 2013, retrieved from the Wayback Machine, version from February 14, 2022, https://web.archive.org/web/20220214210513/https://wikileaks.org/berats-box/emailid/36106.
12 Chuck Ross, "Revealed: Turkey's Plan to 'Camouflage' Its Lobbying Activities in the US," *Daily Caller*, March 15, 2017, https://dailycaller.com/2017/03/15/revealed-turkeys-plan-to-camouflage-its-lobbying-activities-in-the-us/.
13 Halil Danismaz, "The U.S. and NATO Need Turkey," ideas, *Time*, August 22, 2016, https://time.com/4457369/the-u-s-and-nato-need-turkey/.
14 Halil Danismaz, "The U.S. Should Recommit to Its Relationship with Turkey," opinion, *Washington Post*, September 26, 2016, https://www.washingtonpost.com/opinions/the-us-should-recommit-to-its-relationship-with-turkey/2016/09/26/136fb45e-81d8-11e6-9578-558cc125c7ba_story.html.
15 Michael Rubin, "Will Erdogan Bring Assassinations Here?" *Newsweek*, November, 29, 2016, https://www.newsweek.com/michael-rubin-will-erdogan-bring-assassinations-here-526379.
16 Zeynalov, "Erdogan's Family."

17 Federal Election Commission, search result for individual contributions "Contributor details - danismaz," accessed June 17, 2024, https://www.fec.gov/data/receipts/individual-contributions/?contributor_name=danismaz.

18 "About Us," Turkish Coalition of America, accessed June 17, 2024, https://tc-america.org/about.htm.

19 "New Milestone Established by the Five Turkish American PACs," News & Events, Turkish Coalition of America, accessed June 17, 2024, https://www.tc-america.org/news-events/events/new-milestone-established-by-the-five-turkish-american-pacs-1092.htm.

20 Open Secrets, Turkish Coalition USA PAC Donations 2016, accessed June 17, 2024, https://www.opensecrets.org/orgs/recipients?candscycle=2016&id=D000029539&toprecipscycle=2016.

21 "Members of the Caucus on U.S.-Turkey Relations and Turkish Americans Bicameral—114th Congress," Turkish Coalition of America, accessed June 17, 2024, https://www.tc-america.org/files/caucus-list-2016-01-11.pdf.

22 "2018 Annual Report," Turkish Coalition of America, accessed June 17, 2024, https://www.tc-america.org/files/TCA-Annual-Report-2018.pdf.

23 "Contributions in the Name of Another Are Strictly Prohibited," Federal Election Commission, accessed June 18, 2024, https://www.fec.gov/updates/contributions-in-the-name-of-another-are-strictly-prohibited/.

24 WikiLeaks, "Berat's Box," email from Halil Danismaz to Berat Albayrak and Bilal Erdogan sent on March 17, 2015, retrieved from the Wayback Machine, version from June 30, 2022, https://web.archive.org/web/20220630100808/https://wikileaks.org/berats-box/emailid/26846.

25 U.S. Department of Justice, *Short Form Registration Statement Pursuant to the Foreign Agents Registration Act of 1938, as amended, filed by Lydia Borland*, Registration No 6210, March 3, 2014, https://efile.fara.gov/docs/6210-Short-Form-20140303-2.pdf.

26 Catie Edmondson and Rick Gladstone, "House Passes Resolution Recognizing Armenian Genocide," *New York Times,* October 29, 2019, https://www.nytimes.com/2019/10/29/us/politics/armenian-genocide-resolution.html.

27 Julie Tsirkin and Dareh Gregorian, "Senate Passes Resolution Recognizing Armenian Genocide," NBC News, December 12, 2019, https://www.nbcnews.com/politics/congress/senate-passes-resolution-recognizing-armenian-genocide-n1100886.

28 "Indictment, United States of America v. Bijan Rafiekian, Kamil Ekim Alptekin," No 1:18-CR-457 (AJT), (Eastern District of Virginia December 12, 2018), https://www.justice.gov/opa/press-release/file/1120621/dl.

29 Brian Melley et al., "Prosecutors: Political Donor Sought to Silence Witnesses," Associated Press, November 22, 2019, https://apnews.com/article/39237ec8a9d0458e9d23588fcc82ac30.

30 "2018 Annual Report," Turkish Coalition of America, page 21, accessed June 17, 2024, https://www.tc-america.org/files/TCA-Annual-Report-2018.pdf.

31 "TCA Celebrates African American-Turkish Connections through Art Exhibition," Monthly Newsletter February 2018, Turkish Coalition of America, accessed June 18, 2024, https://www.tc-america.org/newsletters/tca-newsletter-february-2018.html.

32 "The First Turkish-American Delegate to Nominate a Candidate for President of the U.S," *Turk of America*, 13, no. 40 (March–April 2014): 34, https://issuu.com/turkofamerica/docs/ilovepdf.com/36.

33 WikiLeaks, "Berat's Box," email from Berat Albayrak to Halil Danismaz sent on June 9, 2013, retrieved from the Wayback Machine, version from October 21, 2021, https://web.archive.org/web/20211021214300/https://wikileaks.org/berats-box/emailid/37348.

34 Melley et al., "Prosecutors."

35 "Board of Director," MUSIAD USA, accessed June 18, 2024, https://musiadus.org/board-of-director-2/.

36 "Murat Guzel, Treasurer," TASC, retrieved from the Wayback Machine, version from August 10, 2020, https://web.archive.org/web/20200810015221/https://ourtasc.org/murat-guzel/.

37 Ian J. Lynch, "Turkish Lobbying Efforts to Influence U.S. Senator Lindsey Graham," Ahval News, November 25, 2019, https://ahvalnews.com/us-turkey/turkish-lobbying-efforts-influence-us-senator-lindsey-graham.

38 Nicholas Morgan, "Will the Biden Administration Act against the Pro-Erdoğan Influence in U.S. Politics?," Ahval News, March 5, 2021, https://ahvalnews.com/us-turkey/will-biden-administration-act-against-pro-erdogan-influence-us-politics.

39 Bilal Kenasari and Sorwar Alam, "Turkish-American Taxpayers Criticize US Aid to PYD/PKK," Anadolu Ajansı, March 1, 2018, https://www.aa.com.tr/en/americas/turkish-american-taxpayers-criticize-us-aid-to-pyd-pkk/1077000#.

40 Kenasari and Alam, "Turkish-American Taxpayers."

41 Patrick Wintour, "Erdoğan Accuses US of Planning to Form 'Terror Army' in Syria,", *Guardian*, January 15, 2018, https://www.theguardian.com/world/2018/jan/15/turkey-condemns-us-plan-for-syrian-border-security-force.

42 "Turkey Flies Planes, Drives Vans in New York to Remind U.S. of Coup Attempt," Ahval News, January 15, 2020, https://ahvalnews.com/2016-coup/turkey-flies-planes-drives-vans-new-york-remind-us-coup-attempt.

43 Melley et al., "Prosecutors."

44 Federal Election Commission, search result for individual contributions "Contributor details - murat guzel," accessed June 18, 2024, https://www.fec.gov/data/receipts/individual-contributions/?contributor_name=murat+guzel.

45 Federal Election Commission, search result for individual contributions "Recipient Name or ID - TURKISH COALITION USA PAC (TC-USA PAC) (C00432526), Report time period - 2015-2016, 2017-2018," accessed June 18, 2024, https://www.fec.gov/data/receipts/?cycle=2018&data_type=processed&committee_id=C00432526&two_year_transaction_period=2016&two_year_transaction_period=2018&line_number=F3X-11AI.

46 Melley et al., "Prosecutors."

47 Jim Mustian and Alan Suderman, "Trump Donor Charged with Obstructing Inauguration Inquiry," Associated Press, January 7, 2020, https://apnews.com/article/0310f2dc07b1b047e86301042db6bd7c.

48 Alan Suderman and Jim Mustian, "'Mercenary' Donor Sold Access for Millions in Foreign Money," Associated Press, November 30, 2020, https://apnews.com/article/imaad-zuberi-sold-donor-access-5a6b71bd05ddf2c1655847bb064edcc9.

49 Federal Election Commission, search result for individual contributions "Contributor details - imaad zuberi, avenue ventures, willa rao," accessed June 18, 2024, https://www.fec.gov/data/receipts/individual-contributions/?contributor_name=Imaad+zuberi&contributor_name=avenue+ventures&contributor_name=willa+rao.

50 Suderman and Mustian, "Mercenary."

51 Mike Ives, "Donor to Trump Inauguration Sentenced to 12 Years in Federal Inquiry," *New York Times*, February 19, 2021, https://www.nytimes.com/2021/02/19/us/politics/imaad-zuberi-sentence.html.

52 Melley et al., "Prosecutors."

53   Federal Election Commission, search result for individual contributions "Recipient Name or ID - NRCC (C00075820), Contributor details - MURAT GUZEL," accessed June 18, 2024, https://www.fec.gov/data/receipts/individual-contributions/?committee_id=C00075820&contributor_name=MURAT+GUZEL.

54   Suderman and Mustian, "Mercenary."

55   Constanze Letsch and Ian Traynor, "Turkey Election: Ruling Party Loses Majority as Pro-Kurdish HDP Gains Seats," *Guardian*, June 7, 2015, https://www.theguardian.com/world/2015/jun/07/turkey-election-preliminary-results-erdogan-akp-party.

56   Suderman and Mustian, "Mercenary."

57   Federal Election Commission, search result for individual contributions "Recipient Name or ID - ENGEL FOR CONGRESS (C00236513), Contributor details - imaad zuberi, asifa zuberi, avenue ventures, willa rao," accessed June 18, 2024, https://www.fec.gov/data/receipts/individual-contributions/?committee_id=C00236513&contributor_name=Imaad+zuberi&contributor_name=asifa+zuberi&contributor_name=avenue+ventures&contributor_name=willa+rao.

58   Federal Election Commission, search result for individual contributions "Recipient Name or ID - ROAD TO FREEDOM CAMPAIGN COMMITTEE (C00200865), ROAD TO FREEDOM POLITICAL ACTION COMMITTEE (C00486043), Contributor details - imaad zuberi, Asifa zuberi, avenue ventures, willa rao," accessed June 18, 2024, https://www.fec.gov/data/receipts/individual-contributions/?committee_id=C00200865&committee_id=C00486043&contributor_name=Asifa+zuberi&contributor_name=avenue+ventures&contributor_name=imaad+zuberi&contributor_name=willa+rao.

59   Federal Election Commission, search result for individual contributions "Recipient Name or ID - LINDSEY GRAHAM 2016 (C0057857), FRIENDS OF LINDSEY GRAHAM (C00705574), Contributor details - asifa zuberi, avenue ventures, imaad zuberi, willa rao," accessed June 18, 2024, https://www.fec.gov/data/receipts/individual-contributions/?committee_id=C00578757&committee_id=C00705574&contributor_name=asifa+zuberi&contributor_name=avenue+ventures&contributor_name=imaad+zuberi&contributor_name=willa+rao.

60   Dan Friedman, "'This Is How America Work': Mind-Boggling New Allegations about a Donor to Trump's Inauguration,", *Mother Jones*, March 19, 2020, https://www.motherjones.com/politics/2020/03/this-is-how-america-work-mind-boggling-new-allegations-about-a-donor-to-trumps-inauguration/.

61   Christian Berthelsen and Caleb Melby, "Fundraiser Lobbied for Foreign Countries, U.S. Says," Bloomberg News, March 17, 2020, https://www.bloomberg.com/news/articles/2020-03-18/fundraiser-secretly-lobbied-u-s-officials-for-foreign-countries.

62   Erin Banco and Pilar Melendez, "Feds Charge Trump Donor Imaad Zuberi with Hiding Work as Foreign Agent," *Daily Beast*, October 22, 2019, https://www.thedailybeast.com/imaad-zuberi-who-donated-dollar900000-to-trumps-inaugural-committee-indicted-by-feds.

63   "Political Donor Sentenced to 12 Years in Prison for Lobbying and Campaign Contribution Crimes, Tax Evasion, and Obstruction of Justice," Office of Public Affairs U.S. Department of Justice, press release, February 18, 2021, https://www.justice.gov/opa/pr/political-donor-sentenced-12-years-prison-lobbying-and-campaign-contribution-crimes-tax.

64   Michael Gartland and Chris Sommerfeldt, "FBI Probe into Adams' Campaign Puts Spotlight on Turkish Influence Group Tied to Erdoğan," *New York Daily News,* December 11, 2023, https://www.nydailynews.com/2023/12/11/fbi-probe-into-adams-campaign-puts-spotlight-on-turkish-influence-group-tied-to-erdogan/.

65. Süleyman Arıoğlu, "Babası Rabia Özden'i reddetti" ["Her father rejected Rabia Özden"], *Haber 7*, February 10, 2008, https://www.haber7.com/yasam/haber/299208-babasi-rabia-ozdeni-reddetti.

66. "Mektupla tanıştı Kartal'da nişanlandı" ["They met through a letter and got engaged in Kartal"], *Hurriyet*, March 24, 2005, https://www.hurriyet.com.tr/gundem/mektupla-tanisti-kartal-da-nisanlandi-38710623.

67. "Factbox: The Man Who Tried to Kill Pope John Paul," Reuters, January 18, 2010, https://www.reuters.com/article/us-turkey-agca-factbox-idUSTRE60H1PH20100118/.

68. Sebnem Arsu, "Man Who Shot Pope in 1981 Is Freed," *New York Times*, January 18, 2010, https://www.nytimes.com/2010/01/19/world/europe/19pope.html.

69. Ross, "Camouflage."

70. Ross, "Camouflage."

71. Roger Sollenberger and Kathleen O'Neill, "Exclusive: How a Pro-Trump Black Group Became an Off-the-Books Turkish Lobbying Campaign," *Salon*, September 4, 2020, https://www.salon.com/2020/09/04/exclusive-how-a-pro-trump-black-group-became-an-off-the-books-turkish-lobbying-campaign/.

72. Roger Sollenberger et al., "She Shunned Islam and Was Embraced by Trump World. Now, She's Turned against Them," *Buzzfeed News*, February 5, 2020, https://www.BuzzFeednews.com/article/rogersollenberger/she-shunned-islam-and-was-embraced-by-trump-world-now-shes.

73. Jeremy Diamond, "Donald Trump Joins His 'Diversity Coalition' for Photo Op," CNN, April 18, 2016, https://edition.cnn.com/2016/04/18/politics/donald-trump-diversity-coalition-meet/index.html.

74. SeriouslyUS? (@USseriously), "Wait, what? Just now on @msnbc, I saw an interview with Rabia Kazan, who was apparently dating Robert Hyde,the Giuliani associate who surveilled Marie Yovanovitch?! Kazan is one of those weird characters in MAGA world. I've been saving photos of her in case she'd pop up somewhere," Twitter, January 16, 2020, 5:57 p.m., https://twitter.com/usseriously/status/1217913778697842691.

75. Tim Dickinson, "Step 1: Rub Elbows at Mar-a-Lago. Step 2: 'Gram the Hell Out of It," *Rolling Stone*, March 19, 2019, https://www.rollingstone.com/politics/politics-news/brazil-mar-a-lago-party-810354/.

76. "Mehmet Ali Ağca'nın eski nişanlısı Trump'ın yanından çıktı" ["Mehmet Ali Ağca's ex-fiancee left Trump's side"], OdaTV, August 11, 2018, https://www.odatv.com/guncel/mehmet-ali-agcanin-eski-nisanlisi-trumpin-yanindan-cikti-144419.

77. Veronica Stracqualursi, Paul LeBlanc, and Caroline Kelly, "Who Is Robert Hyde, the Latest Figure to Emerge in Ukraine Scandal?," CNN, January 15, 2020, https://edition.cnn.com/2020/01/15/politics/who-is-robert-hyde-trump-ukraine/index.html.

78. Dareh Gregorian, "Who Is Robert Hyde? The Latest Character in the Trump Impeachment Saga Has a Wild Backstory," NBC News, January 15, 2020, https://www.nbcnews.com/politics/trump-impeachment-inquiry/who-robert-hyde-latest-character-trump-impeachment-scandal-has-wild-n1116656.

79. Erica Orden and Kara Scannell, "Trump Supporter and Giuliani Associate Discussed Surveilling Yovanovitch," CNN, January 14, 2020, https://edition.cnn.com/2020/01/14/politics/robert-hyde-marie-yovanovitch/index.html.

80. Donald K. Sherman and Matt Corley, "Before Pro-Trump Group Gave Away Cash, It Told the IRS It Wouldn't," CREW, March 9, 2020, https://www.citizensforethics.org/reports-investigations/foia-requests/pro-trump-group-gave-away-cash-irs/.

81. Sherman and Corley, "Pro-Trump."

82 David Weigel, "What Makes a Black Cleveland Pastor Back Donald Trump?," *Washington Post*, July 17, 2016, https://www.washingtonpost.com/politics/what-makes-a-black-cleveland-pastor-back-donald-trump/2016/07/17/adf6e2f2-4c6f-11e6-aa14-e0c1087f7583_story.html.

83 Naomi Jagoda, "Trump Signs Order Aimed at Revitalizing Economically Distressed Communities," December 12, 2018, https://thehill.com/policy/finance/420968-trump-to-sign-executive-order-aimed-at-revitalizing-distressed-communities/.

84 Roger Sollenberger and Kathleen O'Neill, "The Turkey Hustle: How a Pro-Trump Black Group Became Unofficial Lobbyists for Erdogan," *Salon*, September 5, 2020, https://www.salon.com/2020/09/05/the-turkey-hustle-how-a-pro-trump-black-group-became-unofficial-lobbyists-for-erdogan/.

85 Sollenberger et al., "She Shunned Islam."

86 Sollenberger and O'Neill, "Turkey Hustle."

87 Sollenberger and O'Neill, "Turkey Hustle."

88 Roger Sollenberger, "Pro-Trump Black Group That Solicited Foreign Investors Is Now under FBI Investigation," *Salon*, February 24, 2021, https://www.salon.com/2021/02/24/pro-trump-black-group-that-solicited-foreign-investors-is-now-under-fbi-investigation/.

89 Harut Sassounian, "Pro-Trump Black American Group's Controversial Link to Turkey—Part II," *Armenian Weekly*, September 21, 2020, https://armenianweekly.com/2020/09/21/pro-trump-black-american-groups-controversial-link-to-turkey-part-ii/.

90 "Members of the Congressional Caucus on U.S.-Turkey Relations and Turkish Americans Bicameral—115th Congress, Listing by State as of January 1, 2018," Turkish Coalition of America, accessed June 18, 2024, https://www.tc-america.org/files/caucus-list-2018-01-08.pdf.

91 Zach Everson, "Why Instagram Is the Best Window into Trump-Era Corruption," *Fast Company*, May 26, 2018, https://www.fastcompany.com/40577887/why-instagram-is-the-best-window-into-trump-era-corruption.

92 Sollenberger and O'Neill, "Turkey Hustle."

93 Sollenberger and O'Neill, "Exclusive: How a Pro-Trump."

94 "15 U.S. Companies to Invest in Turkey Following Brunson's Release—AA," Ahval News, October 14, 2018, https://ahvalnews.com/foreign-investment/15-us-companies-invest-turkey-following-brunsons-release-aa.

95 Sollenberger, "Pro-Trump Black Group."

96 Sollenberger and O'Neill, "Exclusive: How a Pro-Trump."

97 Sollenberger and O'Neill, "Exclusive: How a Pro-Trump."

98 Sollenberger, "Pro-Trump Black Group."

99 "'Turkish 'Gang of Five' Are Guaranteed Income While Businesses Struggle to Survive Lockdown," Ahval News, May 2, 2021, https://ahvalnews.com/gang-five/turkish-gang-five-are-guaranteed-income-while-businesses-struggle-survive-lockdown.

100 K. Murat Yıldız, "'The Gang of Five': Nepotism, Corruption and Tender-Rigging in Erdoğan's Turkey," *Duvar English*, February 10, 2021, https://www.duvarenglish.com/the-gang-of-five-nepotism-corruption-and-tender-rigging-in-erdogans-turkey-news-56200#google_vignette.

101 Sollenberger, "Pro-Trump Black Group."

102 Sherman and Corley, "Pro-Trump."

103 Chandelis Duster and Maegan Vazquez, "Controversial Organization Led by Trump Allies Has Tax-Exempt Status Revoked by IRS," CNN, August 28, 2020, https://edition.cnn.com/2020/08/28/politics/urban-revitalization-coalition-irs-tax-exempt-status/index.html.

104 Duster and Vazquez, "Controversial Organization."

105 Sollenberger, "Pro-Trump Black Group."
106 Sollenberger and O'Neill, "Turkey Hustle."
107 Sollenberger et al., "She Shunned Islam."
108 "Middle Eastern Women's Coalition Endorses President Donald Trump," Middle Eastern Women's Coalition press release, PR Newswire, December 6, 2018, https://www.prnewswire.com/news-releases/middle-eastern-womens-coalition-endorses-president--donald-trump-300761582.html.
109 Middle Eastern Women's Coalition (@mewomenscoalition), first post, "Ola Hawatmeh Vice President of MEWC @styleola," Instagram, December 15, 2018, https://www.instagram.com/p/Bra_VyoAShz/.
110 "Middle Eastern Women's Coalition Endorses President Donald Trump," Middle Eastern Women's Coalition press release, PR Newswire, December 6, 2018, https://www.prnewswire.com/news-releases/middle-eastern-womens-coalition-endorses-president--donald-trump-300761582.html.
111 "Rabia Kazan Moms for America Buffalo Mom Talk," Mom Talk, May 18, 2019, video, 10:12, https://www.youtube.com/watch?v=3SWq_Gdn_Vk.
112 "Rabia Kazan: President Trump Breaking 'Silence' on Abuse of Women Under Sharia Law," Breitbart News, December 13, 2018, video, 1:27, https://www.youtube.com/watch?v=O2iDcAJv_ao.
113 Sollenberger et al., "She Shunned Islam."
114 "Rabia Kazan Moms for America Buffalo Mom Talk," Mom Talk.
115 "2020 Kickoff Trump—Rabia Kazan—Virginia Women for Trump -...," US Politics CHANNEL, March 9, 2019, video, 7:37, https://www.youtube.com/watch?v=LrXawcvSZzM.
116 Zach Everson, "Spa by Ivanka Trump Instagram Accounts Debut," 1100 Pennsylvania, December 19, 2018, https://www.1100pennsylvania.com/p/spa-by-ivanka-trump-instagram-accounts?s=r.
117 Zach Everson, "LePage's Hotel Expenses May Be Revealed Soon," 1100 Pennsylvania, January 7, 2019, https://www.1100pennsylvania.com/p/lepages-hotel-expenses-may-be-revealed.
118 "Meet Newest Moms for America Advisory Board Member Rabia Kazan," Moms for America, March 27, 2019, https://momsforamerica.us/advisory-board-member-rabia-kazan/.
119 Daniel Lippman and Tina Nguyen, "The Mystery of Rudy Giuliani's Spokeswoman," *Politico*, December 10, 2019, https://www.politico.com/news/2019/12/10/christianne-allen-giuliani-079762.
120 Lippman and Nguyen, "Mystery of Rudy Giuliani's Spokeswoman."
121 Sollenberger et al., "She Shunned Islam."
122 Sollenberger, "Pro-Trump Black Group."
123 Martha Boneta (@martha_boneta_fain), "So incredibly honored to visit with Rahmi Koc, businessman, philanthropist who sailed around the world for 2 years and he is incredibly handsome too!" Instagram, February 26, 2019, https://www.instagram.com/p/BuWOM-IBOtk.
124 Sollenberger et al., "She Shunned Islam.".
125 Jeffrey Toobin, "The Dirty Trickster," *New Yorker*, May 23, 2008, https://www.newyorker.com/magazine/2008/06/02/the-dirty-trickster.
126 Devlin Barrett, Rosalind S. Helderman, Lori Rozsa, and Manuel Roig-Franzia, "Longtime Trump Adviser Roger Stone Indicted by Special Counsel in Russia Investigation," *Washington Post*, January 25, 2019, https://www.washingtonpost.com/politics/longtime-trump-adviser-roger-stone-indicted-by-special-counsel-in-russia-investigation/2019/01/25/93a4d8fa-2093-11e9-8e21-59a09ff1e2a1_story.html.

127 Kevin Breuninger, "Trump Ally Roger Stone's Legal Fund Hits $100,000 Target—and Another Crowdfunding Page Is in the Works as Mueller Trial Approaches," CNBC, March 21, 2019, https://www.cnbc.com/2019/03/21/trump-ally-roger-stones-crowdfunding-page-hits-100000-target.html.

128 Sollenberger et al., "She Shunned Islam."

129 Sollenberger et al., "She Shunned Islam."

130 Sollenberger et al., "She Shunned Islam."

131 Sollenberger and O'Neill, "Exclusive: How a Pro-Trump."

132 "Who Can and Can't Contribute," Federal Election Commission, accessed June 18, 2024, https://www.fec.gov/help-candidates-and-committees/candidate-taking-receipts/who-can-and-cant-contribute/.

133 "Foreign Nationals," Federal Election Commission, accessed June 18, 2024, https://www.fec.gov/updates/foreign-nationals/.

134 Federal Election Commission, search result for individual contributions "Contributor details - rabia kazan, Report time period - 2019 - 2020," accessed June 18, 2024, https://www.fec.gov/data/receipts/individual-contributions/?contributor_name=rabia+kazan&two_year_transaction_period=2020&min_date=01/01/2019&max_date=12/31/2020.

135 Sollenberger et al., "She Shunned Islam."

136 Robin Wright, "Turkey, Syria, the Kurds, and Trump's Abandonment of Foreign Policy," *New Yorker*, October 20, 2019, https://www.newyorker.com/magazine/2019/10/28/turkey-syria-the-kurds-and-trumps-abandonment-of-foreign-policy.

137 Dana Farrington, "Trump Impeachment: A Guide to Key People, Facts and Documents," NPR, October 28, 2019, https://www.npr.org/2019/10/28/771287237/trump-impeachment-inquiry-a-guide-to-key-people-facts-and-documents.

138 Sollenberger et al., "She Shunned Islam."

139 Klasfeld, "Boom Times."

140 "Indictment, United States of America v. Bijan Rafiekian and Ekim Alptekin," No 1:18-CR-457-AJT (Eastern District of Virginia December 12, 2018), https://www.justice.gov/opa/press-release/file/1120621/dl.

141 Heidi Przybyla and Anna Schecter, "Donald Trump's Longtime Business Connections in Turkey Back in the Spotlight," NBC News, October 9, 2019, https://www.nbcnews.com/politics/trump-impeachment-inquiry/donald-trump-s-longtime-business-connections-turkey-back-spotlight-n1064011.

142 U.S. Department of Justice, *Exhibit A to Registration Statement Pursuant to the Foreign Agents Registration Act of 1938, as amended, filed by Mercury Public Affairs, LLC*, Registration No 6170, February 22, 2018, https://efile.fara.gov/docs/6170-Exhibit-AB-20180222-34.pdf.

143 Philip Rucker, "Trump Adviser Bryan Lanza Joins Private Strategy Firm," *Washington Post*, February 22, 2017, https://www.washingtonpost.com/news/powerpost/wp/2017/02/22/trump-adviser-bryan-lanza-joins-private-strategy-firm/.

144 U.S. Department of Justice, *Short Form Registration Statement Pursuant to the Foreign Agents Registration Act of 1938, as amended, filed by Bryan Lanza*, Registration No 6170, February 22, 2018, https://efile.fara.gov/docs/6170-Short-Form-20180222-148.pdf.

CHAPTER 5

1 "Donald Trump: 'No New Business Deals' during Presidency," BBC News, December 13, 2016, https://www.bbc.com/news/business-38297701.
2 "Donald Trump: 'No New Business Deals' during Presidency," BBC News.
3 Ivanka Trump, "Thank you Prime Minister Erdogan for joining us yesterday to celebrate the launch of #TrumpTowers Istanbul!" (@IvankaTrump, April 20, 2012) https://twitter.com/IvankaTrump/status/193337302066540545.
4 The Trump Organization, "Donald J. Trump and Ivanka Trump Visit Istanbul to Celebrate the Opening of Highly Anticipated Trump Towers Mall," PR Newswire, May 9, 2012, https://www.prnewswire.com/news-releases/donald-j-trump-and-ivanka-trump-visit-istanbul-to-celebrate-the-opening-of-highly-anticipated-trump-towers-mall-150816665.html.
5 "Erdoğan Trump için ne demişti?" ["What did Erdogan say about Trump?"], Ileri Haber, November 9, 2016, https://www.ilerihaber.org/icerik/erdogan-trump-icin-ne-demisti-62765.html.
6 Drew Harwell and Anu Narayanswamy, "A Scramble to Assess the Dangers of President-Elect Donald Trump's Global Business Empire," Washington Post, November 20, 2016, https://www.washingtonpost.com/business/economy/a-scramble-to-assess-the-dangers-of-president-elects-global-business-empire/2016/11/20/1bbdc2a2-ad18-11e6-a31b-4b6397e625d0_story.html.
7 Przybyla and Schecter, "Donald Trump's Longtime Business Connections."
8 "Aydin Dogan," profile by Forbes, accessed June 19, 2024, https://www.forbes.com/profile/aydin-dogan/?sh=4bda28a33d95.
9 "First Customer of Trump Towers Comes from Baku," Hurriyet, April 27, 2009, https://www.hurriyet.com.tr/gundem/first-customer-of-trump-towers-comes-from-baku-11517099.
10 Berthelsen, "Where Is Reza Zarrab?"
11 Arnsdorf, "International Man of Mystery."
12 WikiLeaks, "Berat's Box," email from Halil Danismaz to Berat Albayrak and Bilal Erdogan sent on June 24, 2013, retrieved from the Wayback Machine, version from February 14, 2022, https://web.archive.org/web/20220214210513/https://wikileaks.org/berats-box/emailid/36106.
13 Zeynalov, "Erdogan's Family."
14 Stocks et al., "Government."
15 Stocks et al., "Government."
16 Ercan Ersoy, "Turkish First Lady's Charity Got Millions from Accused Fraudster," Bloomberg News, May 26, 2016, https://www.bloomberg.com/news/articles/2016-05-26/turkish-first-lady-s-charity-got-millions-from-accused-fraudster.
17 Christian Berthelsen, "Erdogan Links Alleged in U.S. Documents before Iran Trial," Bloomberg News, November 3, 2017, https://www.bloomberg.com/politics/articles/2017-11-03/erdogan-links-alleged-in-new-u-s-documents-before-iran-trial.
18 Weiser, "Erdogan."
19 Weiser, "Erdogan."
20 Rachel Maddow, "Trump Saw Turkey Conflict in Bannon Interview," MSNBC, November 17, 2016, video, 1:00, https://www.msnbc.com/rachel-maddow/watch/trump-cited-turkey-conflict-of-interest-in-bannon-interview-811054147563.
21 Frances Stead Sellers, "How 'Thin-Skinned' Donald Trump Uses Insults, Threats and Lawsuits to Quiet Critics," Washington Post, July 14, 2016, https://www.washingtonpost.com/politics/how-thin-skinned-donald-trump-uses-insults-threats-and-lawsuits-to-quiet-critics/2016/07/14/252ae148-1b83-11e6-8c7b-6931e66333e7_story.html.

22 Brody Mullins, "Trump's Long Trail of Litigation," *Wall Street Journal*, March 13, 2016, https://www.wsj.com/articles/trumps-long-trail-of-litigation-1457891191.

23 Michelle Lee, "Fact Check: Has Trump Declared Bankruptcy Four or Six Times?" *Washington Post*, September 26, 2016, https://www.washingtonpost.com/politics/2016/live-updates/general-election/real-time-fact-checking-and-analysis-of-the-first-presidential-debate/fact-check-has-trump-declared-bankruptcy-four-or-six-times/.

24 Amber Phillips, "'They're Rapists.' President Trump's Campaign Launch Speech Two Years Later, Annotated," *Washington Post*, June 16, 2017, https://www.washingtonpost.com/news/the-fix/wp/2017/06/16/theyre-rapists-presidents-trump-campaign-launch-speech-two-years-later-annotated/.

25 Jonathan Martin and Alexander Burns, "Blaming Muslims after Attack, Donald Trump Tosses Pluralism Aside," *New York Times*, June 13, 2016, https://www.nytimes.com/2016/06/14/us/politics/donald-trump-hillary-clinton-speeches.html.

26 Michael D. Shear et al., "Trump Retreats on Separating Families, but Thousands May Remain Apart," *New York Times*, June 20, 2018, https://www.nytimes.com/2018/06/20/us/politics/trump-immigration-children-executive-order.html.

27 Alan Yuhas and Mazin Sidahmed, "Is This a Muslim Ban? Trump's Executive Order Explained," *Guardian*, January 31, 2017, https://www.theguardian.com/us-news/2017/jan/28/trump-immigration-ban-syria-muslims-reaction-lawsuits.

28 Michelle Ye Hee Lee, "The White House's Facile Comparison of the Trump- Russia and Clinton-Ukraine Stories," *Washington Post*, July 25, 2017, https://www.washingtonpost.com/news/fact-checker/wp/2017/07/25/the-white-houses-facile-comparison-of-the-trump-russia-and-clinton-ukraine-stories/.

29 Colin Dwyer, "President Trump Accuses Obama of 'Wire Tapping,' Provides No Evidence," NPR, March 4, 2017, https://www.npr.org/sections/thetwo-way/2017/03/04/518478158/president-trump-accuses-obama-of-wire-tapping-provides-no-evidence.

30 "The Saga of 'Pizzagate': The Fake Story That Shows How Conspiracy Theories Spread," BBC News, December 2, 2016, https://www.bbc.com/news/blogs-trending-38156985.

31 "Hillary Clinton's Health Scare: Real Concerns vs. Conspiracy Theories," NBC News, September 12, 2016, video, 3:08, https://www.nbcnews.com/video/hillary-clinton-s-health-scare-real-concerns-vs-conspiracy-theories-762920003562.

32 Tal Kopan, "Son of Trump Security Adviser Spread Baseless 'Pizza Gate' Conspiracy," CNN, December 5, 2016, https://edition.cnn.com/2016/12/05/politics/mike-flynn-jr-son-pizza-gate-conspiracy-theory-donald-trump/index.html.

33 Kelly Bjorklund, "Trump's Inexplicable Crusade to Help Iran Evade Sanctions," *Foreign Policy*, January 9, 2021, https://foreignpolicy.com/2021/01/09/trump-help-iran-evade-sanctions-turkey-halkbank/.

34 John Bolton, "Trump Wanted to Make an Impression on Erdoğan," interview by Alexander Sarovic, *Der Spiegel*, March 3, 2021, https://www.spiegel.de/international/world/john-bolton-on-halkbank-trump-wanted-to-make-an-impression-on-erdogan-a-f14f84bf-7632-430f-a786-abc6000e2524.

35 Krishnadev Calamur, "The Turkish President's Arch-Nemesis," *Atlantic*, July 18, 2016, https://www.theatlantic.com/news/archive/2016/07/fethullah-gulen-reading-list/491720/.

36 Kenyon, "In Turkey."

37 "Islamic Scholar Gulen Criticizes Turkish Gov't Response to Gezi Protests," *Hürriyet Daily News*, March 20, 2014, https://www.hurriyetdailynews.com/islamic-scholar-gulen-criticizes-turkish-govt-response-to-gezi-protests-63849.

38 John Hannah, "The End of Erdogan?" *Foreign Policy*, December 20, 2013, https://foreignpolicy.com/2013/12/20/the-end-of-erdogan-2/.

39 Gulsen Solaker, "Turkey's Erdogan Calls on U.S. to Extradite Rival Gulen," Reuters, April 29, 2014, https://www.reuters.com/article/cnews-us-turkey-erdogan-idCABREA3S0A120140429/.

40 Sebnem Arsu and Brian Knowlton, "Turks to Seek Extradition of Preacher Living in U.S.," *New York Times*, April 29, 2014, https://www.nytimes.com/2014/04/30/world/middleeast/turkish-leader-seeks-extradition-of-muslim-preacher-in-us.html.

41 Karen DeYoung, "Turkish Evidence for Gulen Extradition Pre-Dates Coup Attempt," *Washington Post*, August 19, 2016, https://www.washingtonpost.com/world/national-security/turkish-evidence-for-gulen-extradition-pre-dates-coup-attempt/2016/08/19/390cb0ec-6656-11e6-be4e-23fc4d4d12b4_story.html.

42 U.S. Department of Justice, *Exhibit A to Registration Statement Pursuant to the Foreign Agents Registration Act of 1938, as amended, filed by Amsterdam & Partners LLP*, Registration No 6325, October 26, 2015, https://efile.fara.gov/docs/6325-Exhibit-AB-20151026-1.pdf.

43 Holly K. Hacker, "Top Texas Charter School Network Accused of Bias, Self-Dealing," *Dallas Morning News*, May 24, 2016, https://www.dallasnews.com/news/2016/05/24/top-texas-charter-school-network-accused-of-bias-self-dealing/.

44 Kiah Collier, "Turkey Follows through with Complaint against Harmony," *Texas Tribune*, May 24, 2016, https://www.texastribune.org/2016/05/24/turkey-follows-through-complaint-against-harmony/.

45 Dan Frosch, "Turkey Links Texas Charter Schools to Dissident," *Wall Street Journal*, May 24, 2016, https://www.wsj.com/articles/turkey-links-texas-charter-schools-to-dissident-1464121659.

46 Robert R. Amesterdam, "Why Should Turkish Cleric Fethullah Gulen Operate Charter Schools on U.S. Military Bases?" opinion, *Hill*, March 31, 2016, https://thehill.com/blogs/congress-blog/foreign-policy/274675-why-should-turkish-cleric-fethullah-gulen-operate-charter/.

47 Grimaldi et al., "Mueller Probes Flynn's Role."

48 Flynn, "Our Ally Turkey."

49 "Turkey Blames U.S.-Based Muslim Cleric for Russian Envoy's Killing," RFERL.

50 Gall, "Extraditing Gulen."

51 Carol D. Leonnig et al., "Giuliani Pressed Trump to Eject Muslim Cleric from U.S., a Top Priority of Turkish President, Former Officials Say," *Washington Post*, October 15, 2019, https://www.washingtonpost.com/politics/giuliani-pressed-trump-to-eject-muslim-cleric-from-us-a-top-priority-of-turkish-president-former-officials-say/2019/10/15/bf43d1ec-ef68-11e9-b648-76bcf86eb67e_story.html.

52 Leonnig et al., "Giuliani Pressed Trump."

53 Philip Bump, "What Are the Problems Trump Told Erdogan He Has 'Worked Hard to Solve'?" *Washington Post*, October 17, 2019, https://www.washingtonpost.com/politics/2019/10/17/what-are-problems-trump-told-erdogan-he-has-worked-hard-solve/.

54 Ryan Broderick, "Turkish Trolls Working for Erdogan Hijacked American Right-Wing Media—and Rudy Giuliani's Brain," *Buzzfeed News*, October 18, 2019, https://www.buzzfeednews.com/article/ryanhatesthis/giuliani-turkey-gulen-erdogan-conspiracy-theory.

55 Josh Dawsey et al., "Inside Giuliani's Dual Roles: Power-Broker-for-Hire and Shadow Foreign Policy Adviser," *Washington Post*, December 8, 2019, https://www.washingtonpost.com/politics/inside-giulianis-dual-roles-power-broker-for-hire-and-shadow-foreign-policy-adviser/2019/12/08/f9ab9c4c-1773-11ea-9110-3b34ce1d92b1_story.html.

56 Leonnig et al., "Giuliani Pressed Trump."

57   Jennifer Jacobs et al., "Trump Explored Cutting Grants for Schools Tied to Erdogan Foe," Bloomberg News, October 28, 2019, https://www.bloomberg.com/news/articles/2019-10-28/trump-explored-cutting-grants-for-schools-tied-to-erdogan-foe.

58   Jacobs et al., "Trump Explored."

59   Bill Chappell, "Turkey's Erdogan Suggests Swap: Jailed U.S. Pastor for Turkish Cleric," NPR, September 29, 2017, https://www.npr.org/sections/thetwo-way/2017/09/29/554451339/turkeys-erdogan-suggests-swap-jailed-u-s-pastor-for-turkish-cleric.

60   Joyce Lee and Dalton Bennett, "The Assassination of Jamal Khashoggi," Washington Post, April 1, 2019, video, 24:50, https://www.washingtonpost.com/graphics/2019/world/assassination-of-jamal-khashoggi-documentary/.

61   Gul Tuysuz et al., "Trump Suggests 'Rogue Killers' behind Jamal Khashoggi's Disappearance," CNN, October 15, 2018, https://edition.cnn.com/2018/10/15/middleeast/saudi-us-khashoggi-turkey-intl/index.html.

62   Aaron Blake, "The Ugly Story of Trump and Jamal Khashoggi Is Confirmed," Washington Post, February 27, 2021, https://www.washingtonpost.com/politics/2021/02/26/why-intel-report-jamal-khashoggi-is-so-damning-trump/.

63   Patricia Zengerle, "U.S. Lawmakers Demand Accountability for Killing of Saudi Journalist," Reuters, January 10, 2019, https://www.reuters.com/article/us-saudi-khashoggi-congress-idUSKCN1P5026/.

64   "Jamal Khashoggi Disappearance: US Asks Turkey for Recording Evidence," BBC News, October 17, 2018, https://www.bbc.com/news/world-europe-45897153.

65   Carol E. Lee et al., "To Ease Turkish Pressure on Saudis over Killing, White House Weighs Expelling Erdogan Foe," NBC News, November 15, 2018, https://www.nbcnews.com/politics/national-security/white-house-weighs-booting-erdogan-foe-u-s-appease-turkey-n933996.

66   Lee et al., "Turkish Pressure."

67   Lee et al., "Turkish Pressure."

68   Tim Lister, "Trump Administration Working to Extradite Turkish Cleric, Foreign Minister Says," CNN, December 16, 2018, https://edition.cnn.com/2018/12/16/world/turkey-cavusoglu-cleric-gulen/index.html.

69   Lister, "Trump Administration."

70   Jeff Mason, "Trump Willing to Look at Extraditing Turkish Cleric, but Noncommittal," Reuters, December 18, 2018, https://www.reuters.com/article/idUSKBN1OH29C/.

71   Lee et al., "Turkish Pressure."

72   Lee et al., "Turkish Pressure."

73   "Turkey Orders 532 Arrests over Fethullah Gulen Links," Al Jazeera, April 26, 2021, https://www.aljazeera.com/news/2021/4/26/turkey-orders-532-arrests-in-military-probe-over-gulen-links.

74   Edward Wong et al., "Trump Calls Relations with Saudi Arabia 'Excellent,' While Congress Is Incensed," New York Times, October 11, 2018, https://www.nytimes.com/2018/10/11/us/politics/trump-jamal-khashoggi-turkey-saudi.html.

75   Mark Landler and David D. Kirkpatrick, "Turkey's President Says Recording of Khashoggi's Killing Was Given to U.S.," New York Times, November 10, 2018, https://www.nytimes.com/2018/11/10/world/middleeast/jamal-khashoggi-murder-turkey-recordings.html.

76   "A Pastor becomes a Pawn in a Spat between America and Turkey," Economist, September 30, 2017, https://www.economist.com/erasmus/2017/09/30/a-pastor-becomes-a-pawn-in-a-spat-between-america-and-turkey.

77. "Congressional Leaders Seek Release of American Pastor Unjustly Detained in Turkey," Senate Foreign Relations Committee, February 16, 2017, https://www.foreign.senate.gov/press/dem/release/congressional-leaders-seek-release-of-american-pastor-unjustly-detained-in-turkey.
78. Weiser and Kingsley, "Secret Meeting."
79. "Lev Parnas Talks Turkey," OCCRP.
80. Philip Bump, "Turkey, Iran, Gold, Giuliani and Trump: A Guide to the Case of Reza Zarrab," *Washington Post*, October 10, 2019, https://www.washingtonpost.com/politics/2019/10/10/turkey-iran-gold-giuliani-trump-guide-case-reza-zarrab/.
81. Nick Wadhams, "Trump Repeatedly Pressed Tillerson to Intervene in Zarrab Case," Bloomberg News, October 12, 2019, https://www.bloomberg.com/news/articles/2019-10-12/trump-repeatedly-pressed-tillerson-to-intervene-in-zarrab-case.
82. Christian Berthelsen and Bob Van Voris, "Turkish Banker's Lawyers Launch Attack on Trader's Testimony," Bloomberg News, December 5, 2017, https://www.bloomberg.com/politics/articles/2017-12-05/turkish-banker-s-lawyers-launch-methodical-attack-on-gold-trader.
83. "Turkey's Diplomatic Crisis Is Hastening an Economic One," *Economist*, August 9, 2018, https://www.economist.com/europe/2018/08/09/turkeys-diplomatic-crisis-is-hastening-an-economic-one.
84. U.S. Department of Justice, *Supplemental Statement Pursuant to the Foreign Agent Registration Act of 1938, as amended, filed by Ballard Partners*, Registration No 6415, November 30, 2018, https://efile.fara.gov/docs/6415-Supplemental-Statement-20181130-3.pdf.
85. "Turkey's Diplomatic Crisis Is Hastening an Economic One," *Economist*.
86. John Bolton, *The Room Where It Happened: A White House Memoir* (Simon & Schuster, 2020), chap. 7, Kindle.
87. "Turkey's Diplomatic Crisis Is Hastening an Economic One," *Economist*.
88. Laura Koran, "Trump Threatens to Sanction Turkey If They Don't Release US Pastor," CNN, July 26, 2018, https://edition.cnn.com/2018/07/26/politics/trump-threatens-turkey-sanctions-brunson/index.html.
89. U.S. Department of Justice, *Supplemental Statement Pursuant to the Foreign Agent Registration Act of 1938, as amended, filed by Ballard Partners*, Registration No 6415, November 30, 2018, https://efile.fara.gov/docs/6415-Supplemental-Statement-20181130-3.pdf.
90. Dan Friedman, "How Jay Sekulow Got Involved in US Foreign Policy," *Mother Jones*, October 24, 2019, https://www.motherjones.com/politics/2019/10/how-another-trump-lawyer-became-involved-in-us-foreign-policy/.
91. Charlie Savage, "For Jay Sekulow, New Trump Lawyer, Public Stumble Is Out of Character," *New York Times*, June 19, 2017, https://www.nytimes.com/2017/06/19/us/politics/jay-sekulow-trump-lawyer.html.
92. Euan McKirdy, "Trump Presses Turkey's Erdogan to Release Jailed US Pastor," CNN, May 17, 2017, https://edition.cnn.com/2017/05/17/politics/trump-erdogan-white-house-meeting-andrew-brunson/.
93. Colin Wilhelm and Nahal Toosi, "US Sanctions Turkish Officials over Detained Pastor," *Politico*, August 1, 2018, https://www.politico.eu/article/donald-trump-administration-to-sanction-turkish-officials-over-imprisonment-of-american-pastor-andrew-brunson/.
94. "Turkey's Diplomatic Crisis Is Hastening an Economic One," *Economist*.
95. Jim Tankersley et al., "Trump Hits Turkey When It's Down, Doubling Tariffs," *New York Times*, August 10, 2018, https://www.nytimes.com/2018/08/10/us/politics/trump-turkey-tariffs-currency.html.

96   Aubrey Belford et al., "Turkish Tycoon, Trump Fundraiser and Ex-CIA Chief Involved in 2018 Attempt to Free U.S. Pastor Held in Turkey," OCCRP, March 24, 2021, https://www.occrp.org/en/investigations/turkish-tycoon-trump-fundraiser-and-ex-cia-chief-involved-in-2018-attempt-to-free-us-pastor-held-in-turkey.

97   Philip Rucker, "Former CIA Director James Woolsey Quits Trump Transition Team," *Washington Post*, January 5, 2017, https://www.washingtonpost.com/news/powerpost/wp/2017/01/05/former-cia-director-james-woolsey-quits-trump-transition-team/.

98   Alex Asenstadt and Gabby Orr, "Trump Recruitment Failure Sets Off Alarms over 2020," *Politico*, March 1, 2019, https://www.politico.com/story/2019/03/01/trump-2020-super-pac-1197066.

99   Desmond Butler and Michael Biesecker, "Giuliani Pals Leveraged GOP Access to Seek Ukraine Gas Deal," Associated Press, December 23, 2019, https://apnews.com/article/russia-fl-state-wire-trump-impeachment-michael-pence-tx-state-wire-7f97eac651e7ada92fed6480e70dce1b.

100 Belford et al., "Turkish Tycoon."

101 "President Trump Addresses U.N. General Assembly—FULL SPEECH (C-SPAN)," C-SPAN, September 25, 2018, video, 35:04, https://www.youtube.com/watch?v=KfVdIKaQzW8.

102 "Turkey—President Addresses General Debate, 73rd Session," United Nations, September 25, 2018, video, 27:11, https://www.youtube.com/watch?v=k4_WJIpp2jk.

103 Carol E. Lee and Courtney Kube, "Secret Deal with Turkey Paves Way for American Pastor's Release," NBC News, October 11, 2018, https://www.nbcnews.com/politics/white-house/secret-deal-turkey-paves-way-american-pastor-s-release-n919041.

104 U.S. Department of Justice, *Supplemental Statement Pursuant to the Foreign Agent Registration Act of 1938, as amended, filed by Ballard Partners*, Registration No 6415, November 30, 2018, https://efile.fara.gov/docs/6415-Supplemental-Statement-20181130-3.pdf.

105 Donald J. Trump (@realDonadlTrump), "There was NO DEAL made with Turkey for the release and return of Pastor Andrew Brunson. I don't make deals for hostages. There was, however, great appreciation on behalf of the United States, which will lead to good, perhaps great, relations between the United States & Turkey!" Twitter, October 13, 2018, 11:17 a.m., https://twitter.com/realdonaldtrump/status/1051114825391239169.

106 Lee and Kube, "Secret Deal with Turkey."

107 "15 U.S. Companies to Invest in Turkey Following Brunson's Release—AA," Ahval News.

108 Bolton, "Trump Wanted to Make an Impression on Erdoğan."

109 Makini Brice and Tuvan Gumrukcu, "U.S., Turkey Lift Sanctions in Sign of Easing Tensions," Reuters, November 2, 2018, https://www.reuters.com/article/us-turkey-security-usa-sanctions-idUSKCN1N71K2/.

110 Joe Deaux, "Trump Cuts Tariffs on Turkish Steel Imports in Half, to 25%," Bloomberg News, May 16, 2019, https://www.bloomberg.com/news/articles/2019-05-17/trump-cuts-tariffs-on-turkish-steel-imports-in-half-to-25.

111 "Who Are the Kurds?" BBC News, October 15, 2019, https://www.bbc.com/news/world-middle-east-29702440.

112 Henri Barkey and Direnç Kadioglu, "The Turkish Constitution and the Kurdish Question," Carnegie Endowment for International Piece, August 1, 2011, https://carnegieendowment.org/research/2011/08/the-turkish-constitution-and-the-kurdish-question?lang=en.

113 "Turkey PM Erdogan Apologises for 1930s Kurdish Killings," BBC News, November 23, 2011, https://www.bbc.com/news/world-europe-15857429.

114 "Timeline: PKK Attacks in Turkey," Al Jazeera, October 19, 2011, https://www.aljazeera.com/news/2011/10/19/timeline-pkk-attacks-in-turkey.

115 "What Is the PKK, the Kurdish Rebel Group behind Bomb Blast in Turkey?," Reuters, October 2, 2023, https://www.reuters.com/world/middle-east/what-is-pkk-kurdish-rebel-group-behind-bomb-blast-turkey-2023-10-02/.

116 "Foreign Terrorist Organizations," U.S. Department of State, accessed June 19, 2024, https://www.state.gov/foreign-terrorist-organizations/.

117 "Inclusion of the Kurdish Workers' Party on the European List of Terrorist Organisations," Parliamentary question—H-0428/2002, European Parliament, accessed June 19, 2024, https://www.europarl.europa.eu/doceo/document/H-5-2002-0428_EN.html?redirect.

118 "The Kurds of Turkey: Killings, Disappearances and Torture," Human Rights Watch, March 1993, https://www.hrw.org/sites/default/files/reports/TURKEY933.PDF.

119 "Factbox: The Kurdish Struggle for Rights and Land," Reuters, October 9, 2019, https://www.reuters.com/article/idUSKBN1WO19W/.

120 Constanze Letsch, "Kurdish Leader Abdullah Ocalan Declares Ceasefire with Turkey," *Guardian*, March 21, 2013, https://www.theguardian.com/world/2013/mar/21/pkk-leader-ocalan-declares-ceasefire.

121 "Syria's War: Who Is Fighting and Why," *Vox*, April 7, 2017, video, 6:45, https://youtu.be/JFpanWNgfQY?si=lNJR0wi6DERYqCxi.

122 Mariya Petkova, "What Has Russia Gained from Five Years of Fighting in Syria?," Al Jazeera, October 1, 2020, https://www.aljazeera.com/features/2020/10/1/what-has-russia-gained-from-five-years-of-fighting-in-syria.

123 "Syria's War: Who Is Fighting and Why," Vox.

124 Julian Borger and Fazel Hawramy, "US Providing Light Arms to Kurdish-Led Coalition in Syria, Officials Confirm," *Guardian*, September 29, 2016, https://www.theguardian.com/world/2016/sep/29/syria-us-arms-supply-kurds-turkey.

125 Jen Kirby, "9 Questions about Turkey, Syria, and the Kurds You Were Too Embarrassed to Ask,", *Vox*, October 16, 2019, https://www.vox.com/world/2019/10/16/20908262/turkey-syria-kurds-trump-invasion-questions.

126 Nicole Gaouette, "Republican Anger Grows as Trump Disavows Kurds by Saying They Didn't Help during WWII," CNN, October 10, 2019, https://www.cnn.com/2019/10/09/politics/turkey-syria-us-anger-ramifications/index.html.

127 Rodi Said, "Syria's Kurds Rebuked for Seeking Autonomous Region," Reuters, March 17, 2016, https://www.reuters.com/article/us-mideast-crisis-syria-federalism-idUSKCN0WJ1EP/.

128 Michael R. Gordon and Eric Schmitt, "Trump to Arm Syrian Kurds, Even as Turkey Strongly Objects," *New York Times*, May 9, 2017, https://www.nytimes.com/2017/05/09/us/politics/trump-kurds-syria-army.html.

129 Patrice Taddonio, "Flashback: How US-Backed Kurds Defeated ISIS in Kobani, Syria," PBS *Frontline*, October 9, 2019, https://www.pbs.org/wgbh/frontline/article/flashback-how-us-backed-kurds-defeated-isis-in-kobani-syria/.

130 "Turkey v Syria's Kurds: The Short, Medium and Long Story," BBC News, October 23, 2019, https://www.bbc.com/news/world-middle-east-49963649.

131 Jamie Dettmer, "Turkey Ramps Up Pressure on Washington to Abandon Syrian Kurds," Voice of America, February 24, 2017, https://www.voanews.com/a/turkey-ramp-up-pressure-washington-abandon-syrian-kurds/3738502.html.

132 Thomson Reuters, "Turkey Tells U.S. to End Support for Syrian Kurd Militia or Risk Confrontation," CBC News, January 25, 2018, https://www.cbc.ca/news/world/turkey-syria-kurds-us-1.4503855.

133 Kareem Shaheen, "Turkey Sends Tanks into Syria in Operation Aimed at Isis and Kurds," *Guardian*, August 24, 2016, https://www.theguardian.com/world/2016/aug/24/turkey-launches-major-operation-against-isis-in-key-border-town.

134 Ryan Browne and Barbara Starr, "Turkish Operation in Syria Undercuts US Gains in ISIS Fight," CNN, February 28, 2018, https://www.cnn.com/2018/02/28/politics/turkey-syria-us-isis-gains-undermined/index.html.

135 Thomas Gibbons-Neff, "U.S. Special Operations Forces Begin New Role alongside Turkish Troops in Syria," *Washington Post*, September 16, 2016, https://www.washingtonpost.com/news/checkpoint/wp/2016/09/16/u-s-special-operations-forces-begin-new-role-alongside-turkish-troops-in-syria/.

136 Bolton, *Room Where It Happened*, chap. 7, Kindle.

137 Julian Borger, "Mattis Resignation Triggered by Phone Call between Trump and Erdoğan," *Guardian*, December 21, 2018, https://www.theguardian.com/us-news/2018/dec/21/james-mattis-resignation-trump-erdogan-phone-call.

138 Mark Landler et al., "Trump to Withdraw U.S. Forces from Syria, Declaring 'We Have Won against ISIS,'" *New York Times*, December 19, 2018, https://www.nytimes.com/2018/12/19/us/politics/trump-syria-turkey-troop-withdrawal.html.

139 Borger, "Mattis Resignation Triggered by Phone Call between Trump and Erdoğan."

140 Daniel Bush, "Read James Mattis' Full Resignation Letter," PBS, December 20, 2018, https://www.pbs.org/newshour/politics/read-james-mattis-full-resignation-letter.

141 Landler et al., "Trump to Withdraw U.S. Forces from Syria, Declaring 'We Have Won against ISIS.'"

142 Lindsey Graham (@LindseyGrahamSC), "Letter from @SenatorShaheen @marcorubio @SenTomCotton @SenAngusKing @SenJoniErnst and me to President Trump on withdrawal from Syria," Twitter, December 19, 2018, 12:27 a.m., https://twitter.com/LindseyGrahamSC/status/1075578496733364226.

143 Felicia Sonmez, "After Lunch with Trump, Lindsey Graham Shifts Course on Syria: 'I Think the President's Taking This Really Seriously,'" *Washington Post*, December 30, 2018, https://www.washingtonpost.com/politics/after-lunch-with-trump-lindsey-graham-shifts-course-on-syria-i-think-the-presidents-taking-this-really-seriously/2018/12/30/3b889f98-0c76-11e9-8938-5898adc28fa2_story.html.

144 Lindsey Graham (@LindseyGrahamSC), "I learned a lot from President @realDonaldTrump about our efforts in Syria that was reassuring. (1/3)," Twitter, December 30, 2018, 9:08 p.m., https://twitter.com/LindseyGrahamSC/status/1079514527392247809.

145 Carlotta Gall, "In Turkey, Senator Calls for Slower, Smarter U.S. Withdrawal From Syria," *New York Times*, January 19, 2019, https://www.nytimes.com/2019/01/19/world/middleeast/turkey-lindsey-graham.html.

146 Carol E. Lee and Courtney Kube, "Chaos in Syria, Washington after Trump Call with Erdogan Unleashed Turkish Military," NBC NEWS, October 7, 2019, https://www.nbcnews.com/politics/national-security/chaos-syria-washington-after-trump-call-erdogan-unleashed-turkish-military-n1063516.

147 Tamara Qiblawi and Alessandria Masi, "Kurdish Humanitarian Groups Left to Fend for Themselves as Northern Syria Goes from Refuge to Frontline," CNN, October 17, 2019, https://edition.cnn.com/2019/10/17/middleeast/syria-kurdish-turkey-displaced-intl/index.html.

148 "Syria: Turkey Threatens to Send Millions of Refugees to Europe If War against Kurds Interfered With," *Channel 4 News*, October 10, 2019, video, 28:09, https://www.youtube.com/watch?v=rJA1DcAh2KM.

149 "Turkey's Erdogan Threatens to Send Syrian Refugees to Europe," Reuters, October 10, 2019, https://www.reuters.com/article/us-syria-security-turkey-europe/turkeys-erdogan-threatens-to-send-syrian-refugees-to-europe-idUSKBN1WP1ED/.

150 Jacey Fortin, "Trump Says the Kurds 'Didn't Help' at Normandy. Here's the History," *New York Times*, October 10, 2019, https://www.nytimes.com/2019/10/10/world/middleeast/trump-kurds-normandy.html.

151 Holmes Lybrand, "Fact-Checking Trump's Claim That Kurds Did Not Help the US in WWII and Normandy Invasion," CNN, October 11, 2019, https://edition.cnn.com/2019/10/10/politics/donald-trump-world-war-two-kurds-syria-fact-check/index.html.

152 Fortin, "Trump Says the Kurds 'Didn't Help' at Normandy. Here's the History."

153 Siobhán O'Grady, "Actually, President Trump, Some Kurds Did Fight in World War II," *Washington Post*, October 10, 2019, https://www.washingtonpost.com/world/2019/10/10/actually-president-trump-some-kurds-did-fight-world-war-ii/.

154 David Jackson and John Fritze, "As Turkey Pounds Syria, Trump Downplays Ties to Kurds: 'They Didn't Help Us in the Second World War,'" *USA Today*, October 9, 2019, https://www.usatoday.com/story/news/politics/2019/10/09/donald-trump-turkey-invasion-kurd-held-syria-bad-idea/3920404002/.

155 Toluse Olorunnipa and Seung Min Kim, "Republicans Deliver Rare Rebuke of Trump, Slamming His Syria Withdrawal Decision," *Washington Post*, October 7, 2019, https://www.washingtonpost.com/politics/mcconnell-joins-other-republicans-in-rebuking-trumps-syria-withdrawal/2019/10/07/aef0d11e-e914-11e9-9306-47cb0324fd44_story.html.

156 "Lindsey Graham Addresses Trump: 'I Will Hold You Accountable' over Treatment of Kurdish Allies," CBS News, October 17, 2019, https://www.cbsnews.com/news/lindsey-graham-on-turkey-watch-live-stream-as-graham-speaks-on-sanctions-bill-today-today-2019-10/.

157 Donald J. Trump (@realDonaldTrump), "As I have stated strongly before, and just to reiterate, if Turkey does anything that I, in my great and unmatched wisdom, consider to be off limits, I will totally destroy and obliterate the Economy of Turkey (I've done before!). They must, with Europe and others, watch over…," Twitter, October 7, 2019, 12:38 p.m., https://twitter.com/realDonaldTrump/status/1181232249821388801.

158 Jeremy Bowen, "Turkey's Erdogan 'Threw Trump's Syria Letter in Bin,'" BBC News, October 17, 2019, https://www.bbc.com/news/world-middle-east-50080737.

159 Kevin Breuninger, "Trump Halts Trade Negotiations with Turkey, Raises Its Steel Tariffs to 50%," CNBC News, October 14, 2019, https://www.cnbc.com/2019/10/14/trump-halting-trade-negotiations-with-turkey-raising-its-steel-tariffs-to-50percent.html.

160 Donald J. Trump (@realDonaldTrump), "Statement from President Donald J. Trump Regarding Turkey's Actions in Northeast Syria," Twitter, October 14, 2019, 4:55 p.m., https://twitter.com/realDonaldTrump/status/1183833640507269120.

161 Julian Borger and Michael Safi, "Trump Claims Kurds 'No Angels' as He Boasts of His Own 'Brilliant' Strategy," *Guardian*, October 16, 2019, https://www.theguardian.com/us-news/2019/oct/16/trump-claims-kurds-are-much-safer-as-us-troops-leave-syria.

162 Geoffrey Berman, *Holding the Line: Inside the Nation's Preeminent US Attorney's Office and Its Battle with the Trump Justice Department* (Penguin Press, 2022), chap. 21, Kindle.

163 "Superseding Indictment, United States of America v. TURKIYE HALK BANKASI A . S, a/k/a 'Halkbank,'" No S6 15 Cr. 867 (RMB) (S.D.N.Y. October 15, 2019), https://www.justice.gov/opa/press-release/file/1210396/dl.

164 Berman, *Holding the Line: Inside the Nation's Preeminent US Attorney's Office and Its Battle with the Trump Justice Department*, chap. 21, Kindle.

165 Josh Wingrove, "Trump Says U.S. Lifting Turkey Sanctions as Cease-Fire Holds," Bloomberg News, October 23, 2019, https://www.bloomberg.com/news/articles/2019-10-23/trump-says-u-s-lifting-turkey-sanctions-as-cease-fire-holds.

CHAPTER 6

1 Nate Raymond, "U.S. Arrests Turkish Businessman Accused of Evading Iran Sanctions," Reuters, March 21, 2016, https://www.reuters.com/article/idUSKCN0WN295/.

2 Isobel Finkel and Christian Berthelsen, "U.S. Arrests Top Turkish Banker in Iran Sanctions Probe," Bloomberg News, March 28, 2017, https://www.bloomberg.com/news/articles/2017-03-28/halkbank-deputy-g-m-arrested-in-u-s-in-iran-financing-probe.

3 "Superseding Indictment."

4 Carlotta Gall and Benjamin Weiser, "The Talk of Turkey? A Politically Charged Trial in New York," *New York Times*, November 26, 2017, https://www.nytimes.com/2017/11/26/world/europe/erdogan-reza-zarrab-trial.html.

5 Berthelsen, "Where Is Reza Zarrab?"

6 Nina Agrawal, "Turkish Gold Trader Reza Zarrab Makes Plea Deal in Iran Sanctions Case," *Los Angeles Times*, November 28, 2017, https://www.latimes.com/nation/nationnow/la-na-reza-zarrab-trial-20171128-story.html.

7 Weiser, "Erdogan."

8 World Bank, "Report No: 73647-TU Project appraisal document on proposed loans in the amount US$201 million to TURKIYE CUMHURIYETI ZIRAAT BANKASI A.S. (US$67 million) TURKIYE VAKIFLAR BANKASI T.A.O. (US$67 million) TURKIYE HALK BANKASI A.S. (US$67 million) with the guarantee of the Republic of Turkey and proposed grants from the Global Environment Facility Trust Fund in the amount US$3.64 million to TURKIYE CUMHURIYETI ZIRAAT BANKASI A.S. (US$ 0.9 million) TURKIYE VAKIFLAR BANKASI T.A.O. (US$0.9 million) TURKIYE HALK BANKASI A.S. (US$0.9 MILLION) The Republic of Turkey (US$0.94 million) for the small and medium enterprises energy efficiency project, February 28, 2013," World Bank Group, accessed June 20, 2024, https://documents1.worldbank.org/curated/en/431451468172773840/pdf/736470PAD0P1220Official0Use0Only090.pdf.

9 Christian Berthelsen, "Erdogan Was Target in Bribery Inquiry, Turkish Officer Says," Bloomberg News, December 11, 2017, https://www.bloomberg.com/politics/articles/2017-12-11/erdogan-was-a-target-in-bribery-inquiry-turkish-officer-says.

10 Benjamin Weiser, "Officer Said He Fled Turkey, Carrying Evidence of Corruption," *New York Times*, December 11, 2017, https://www.nytimes.com/2017/12/11/world/europe/turkey-trial-zarrab.html.

11 Adam Klasfeld, "Testimony Ends with Assassination Tale," Courthouse News Service, December 7, 2017, https://www.courthousenews.com/turkish-gold-traders-dramatic-testimony-ends-at-knifepoint/.

12 Klasfeld, "Testimony Ends with Assassination Tale."

13 "Zarrab Trial in U.S. Is a 'Clear Plot against Turkey', Government Says," Reuters, November 20, 2017, https://www.reuters.com/article/us-usa-turkey-zarrab-idUSKBN1DK1A6/.

14 "Zarrab Trial in U.S. Is a 'Clear Plot against Turkey', Government Says," Reuters.

15. Tracy Connor, "Turkey Targets Riches of U.S. Witness Who Named Erdogan in Scheme," NBC News, December 1, 2017, https://www.nbcnews.com/news/us-news/juror-be-booted-turkish-conspiracy-trial-sleeping-n825736.
16. Weiser, "Reza Zarrab Testifies."
17. Connor, "Turkey Targets Riches of U.S. Witness."
18. Hulya Polat, "Turkish Officials Lash Out against Bribery Claims in New York Trial," Voice of America, November 30, 2017, https://www.voanews.com/a/turkey-officials-lash-out-against-bribey-claims-in-new-york-trial/4144237.html.
19. "Superseding Indictment."
20. "Turkey Signs Deal to Get Russian S-400 Air Defence Missiles," BBC News, September 12, 2017, https://www.bbc.com/news/world-europe-41237812.
21. Lipton and Weiser, "Turkish Bank Case."
22. David Ignatius, "The Man at the Crux of the U.S.-Turkey Dispute Is about to Go on Trial," *Washington Post*, October 12, 2017, https://www.washingtonpost.com/opinions/global-opinions/the-man-at-the-crux-the-of-us-turkey-dispute-is-about-to-go-on-trial/2017/10/12/92c4c7a2-af96-11e7-be94-fabb0f1e9ffb_story.html.
23. Lipton and Weiser, "Turkish Bank Case."
24. Nicole Hong, "Turkish Official Asked U.S. Attorney General to Release Reza Zarrab," *Wall Street Journal* PRO Central Banking, November 16, 2016, https://www.wsj.com/articles/turkish-official-asked-u-s-attorney-general-to-release-reza-zarrab-1479255405.
25. Ignatius, "The Man at the Crux of the U.S.-Turkey Dispute."
26. Joseph Hincks, "World Leaders React to Donald Trump Winning the U.S Election," *Time*, November 9, 2016, https://time.com/4563879/donald-trump-president-reactions-world-leaders/.
27. Weiser and Kingsley, "Secret Meeting."
28. Josh Dawsey et al., "Trump Asked Tillerson to Help Broker Deal to End U.S. Prosecution of Turkish Trader Represented by Giuliani," *Washington Post*, October 10, 2019, https://www.washingtonpost.com/politics/trump-asked-tillerson-to-help-broker-deal-to-end-us-prosecution-of-turkish-trader-represented-by-giuliani/2019/10/10/fbe16976-eb6b-11e9-9306-47cb0324fd44_story.html.
29. Bjorklund, "Trump's Inexplicable Crusade."
30. Bjorklund, "Trump's Inexplicable Crusade."
31. Bjorklund, "Trump's Inexplicable Crusade."
32. Bjorklund, "Trump's Inexplicable Crusade."
33. Bjorklund, "Trump's Inexplicable Crusade."
34. Şebnem Arsu et al., "Shedding Light on an Alleged Plot to Evade Iran Sanctions," *Spiegel International*, February 26, 2021, https://www.spiegel.de/international/world/erdogans-bad-bank-on-trial-shedding-light-on-an-alleged-plot-to-evade-iran-sanctions-a-bd705f81-bfcd-42fc-b3b1-55bdbe2c8339.
35. Bolton, *Room Where It Happened*, chap. 7, Kindle.
36. Alan Yuhas, "US Attorney Preet Bharara Fired after Refusing Jeff Sessions' Order to Resign," *Guardian*, March 11, 2017, https://www.theguardian.com/us-news/2017/mar/11/preet-bharara-us-attorney-refuses-resign-jeff-sessions.
37. Preet Bharara, "That Time President Trump Fired Me (with Leon Panetta)", September 20, 2017, *Stay Tuned with Preet*, produced by CAFE Studios, podcast, audio, 46:50, https://podcasts.apple.com/us/podcast/stay-tuned-with-preet/id1265845136?i=1000392484145.

38 Bharara, "That Time President Trump Fired Me."
39 Bharara, "That Time President Trump Fired Me."
40 Bharara, "That Time President Trump Fired Me."
41 Dan Balz, "Watergate Happened 50 Years Ago. Its Legacies Are Still with Us," *Washington Post*, June 12, 2022, https://www.washingtonpost.com/politics/2022/06/12/watergate-trust-government-reforms/.
42 "Attorney General Jeff Sessions Appoints Geoffrey S. Berman as Interim United States Attorney," United States Attorney's Office Southern District of New York, press release, January 3, 2018, https://www.justice.gov/usao-sdny/pr/attorney-general-jeff-sessions-appoints-geoffrey-s-berman-interim-united-states.
43 Larry Neumeister, "NY Prosecutor's Colleagues Say He's No Trump Puppet," Associated Press, February 26, 2019, https://apnews.com/general-news-14a7553e29fb4868b047706b1d722a52.
44 "Information, United States v. Michael Cohen," No 18 Cr. 602 (WHP) (S.D.N.Y. August 21, 2018), https://www.justice.gov/usao-sdny/press-release/file/1088966/dl.
45 "Information, United States v. Imaad Zuberi," No 20 Cr. 011 (CM) (S.D.N.Y. July 1, 2020), http://cdn.cnn.com/cnn/2020/images/01/07/zuberi.sdny.pdf.
46 "Sealed Indictment, United States of America v. Lev Parnas, Igor Fruman, David Correia, and Andrey Kukushkin," No 19 Cr. 725 (S.D.N.Y. October 10, 2019), https://www.justice.gov/usao-sdny/press-release/file/1208281/dl.
47 "Superseding Indictment, United States of America v. TURKIYE HALK BANKASI A . S, a/k/a 'Halkbank,'" No S6 15 Cr. 867 (RMB) (S.D.N.Y. October 15, 2019), https://www.justice.gov/opa/press-release/file/1210396/dl.
48 Berman, *Holding the Line: Inside the Nation's Preeminent US Attorney's Office and Its Battle with the Trump Justice Department*, chap. 21, Kindle.
49 Bolton, *Room Where It Happened*, chap. 7, Kindle.
50 "Turkey's Diplomatic Crisis Is Hastening an Economic One," *Economist*.
51 Bolton, *Room Where It Happened*, chap. 7, Kindle.
52 Berman, *Holding the Line: Inside the Nation's Preeminent US Attorney's Office and Its Battle with the Trump Justice Department*, chap. 21, Kindle.
53 Lipton and Weiser, "Turkish Bank Case."
54 Berman, *Holding the Line: Inside the Nation's Preeminent US Attorney's Office and Its Battle with the Trump Justice Department*, chap. 21, Kindle.
55 Berman, *Holding the Line: Inside the Nation's Preeminent US Attorney's Office and Its Battle with the Trump Justice Department*, chap. 21, Kindle.
56 Department of Treasury, *Letter from Frederick W. Vaughan, Deputy Assistant Secretary, Office of Legislative Affairs to The Honorable Ron Wyden, Ranking Member, Committee on Finance*, November 20, 2019, https://www.finance.senate.gov/imo/media/doc/112019%20Treasury%20Response%20Letter%20to%20Wyden%20RE%20Halkbank.pdf.
57 Nick Wadhams et al., "Trump-Erdogan Call Led to Lengthy Quest to Avoid Halkbank Trial," Bloomberg News, October 16, 2019, https://www.bloomberg.com/news/articles/2019-10-16/trump-erdogan-call-led-to-lengthy-push-to-avoid-halkbank-trial.
58 Berman, *Holding the Line: Inside the Nation's Preeminent US Attorney's Office and Its Battle with the Trump Justice Department*, chap. 21, Kindle.
59 Berman, *Holding the Line: Inside the Nation's Preeminent US Attorney's Office and Its Battle with the Trump Justice Department*, chap. 21, Kindle.
60 Berman, *Holding the Line: Inside the Nation's Preeminent US Attorney's Office and Its Battle with the Trump Justice Department* , chap. 21, Kindle.

61. Berman, *Holding the Line: Inside the Nation's Preeminent US Attorney's Office and Its Battle with the Trump Justice Department*, chap. 21, Kindle.
62. Lipton and Weiser, "Turkish Bank Case."
63. Berman, *Holding the Line: Inside the Nation's Preeminent US Attorney's Office and Its Battle with the Trump Justice Department*, chap. 21, Kindle.
64. Lipton and Weiser, "Turkish Bank Case."
65. Bjorklund, "Trump's Inexplicable Crusade."
66. "'Barr Did the Bidding of the President and Politicized the DOJ' Says Fmr. U.S. Attorney," MSNBC, September 16, 2022, video, 12:14, https://youtu.be/E9AKYpMy_xg.
67. Rosalind S. Helderman et al., "Trump Ousts Manhattan U.S. Attorney Who Investigated President's Associates," *Washington Post*, June 20, 2020, https://www.washingtonpost.com/politics/geoffrey-berman-us-attorney-william-barr-trump/2020/06/20/fcbfa3b4-b30f-11ea-8758-bfd1d045525a_story.html.
68. Katie Benner and Michael S. Schmidt, "Justice Dept. Official and Liaison to Special Counsel to Step Down," *New York Times*, December 11, 2019, https://www.nytimes.com/2019/12/11/us/politics/justice-ocallaghan-mueller.html.
69. Berman, *Holding the Line: Inside the Nation's Preeminent US Attorney's Office and Its Battle with the Trump Justice Department*, chap. 21, Kindle.
70. Berman, *Holding the Line: Inside the Nation's Preeminent US Attorney's Office and Its Battle with the Trump Justice Department*, chap. 21, Kindle.
71. Berman, *Holding the Line: Inside the Nation's Preeminent US Attorney's Office and Its Battle with the Trump Justice Department*, chap. 21, Kindle.
72. Maggie Haberman and Katie Benner, "Trump Administration Sues to Try to Delay Publication of Bolton's Book,", *New York Times*, June 16, 2020, https://www.nytimes.com/2020/06/16/us/politics/john-bolton-book-publication.html.
73. Berman, *Holding the Line: Inside the Nation's Preeminent US Attorney's Office and Its Battle with the Trump Justice Department*, chap. 21, Kindle.
74. Benner and Schmidt, "Justice Dept. Official."
75. Carol E. Lee, Ken Dilania, and Peter Alexander, "Barr Takes Control of Legal Matters of Interest to Trump, Including Stone Sentencing," NBC News, February 11, 2020, https://www.nbcnews.com/politics/justice-department/barr-takes-control-legal-matters-interest-trump-including-stone-sentencing-n1135231.
76. Eileen Sullivan and Michael D. Shear, "Trump Praises Barr for Rejecting Punishment Recommended for Stone," *New York Times*, February 12, 2020, https://www.nytimes.com/2020/02/12/us/politics/trump-stone.html.
77. Lee et al., "Barr Takes Control."
78. Dartunorro Clark et al., "All Four Roger Stone Prosecutors Resign from Case after DOJ Backpedals on Sentencing Recommendation," NBC News, February 11, 2020, https://www.nbcnews.com/politics/politics-news/doj-backpedalling-sentencing-recommendation-trump-ally-roger-stone-n1134961.
79. Dan Mangan, "Attorney General Barr Orders Review of Criminal Case against Former Trump Aide Michael Flynn," CNBC, February 14, 2020, https://www.cnbc.com/2020/02/14/william-barr-orders-review-of-trump-aide-michael-flynn-case.html.
80. Lee et al., "Barr Takes Control."
81. Berman, *Holding the Line: Inside the Nation's Preeminent US Attorney's Office and Its Battle with the Trump Justice Department*, chap. 23, Kindle.

82 "Attorney General William P. Barr on the Nomination of Jay Clayton to Serve as U.S. Attorney for the Southern District of New York," Office of Public Affairs, U.S. Department of Justice, press release, June 19, 2020, https://www.justice.gov/opa/pr/attorney-general-william-p-barr-nomination-jay-clayton-serve-us-attorney-southern-district.

83 Geoffrey Berman, "Legal Matters: The DOJ, Politics, and the Law with Geoffrey Berman," Interview by Robert Weisberg, David Sklansky, Introduction by Sharon Driscoll, Stanford Lawyer Magazine, December 14, 2020, https://law.stanford.edu/stanford-lawyer/articles/legal-matters-the-doj-politics-and-law/.

84 "Statement on U.S. Attorney Geoffrey S. Berman on Announcement by Attorney General Barr," United States Attorney's Office, Southern District of New York, press release, June 19, 2020, https://www.justice.gov/usao-sdny/pr/statement-us-attorney-geoffrey-s-berman-announcement-attorney-general-barr.

85 Office of the Attorney General, *Letter from Attorney General William P. Barr to Geoffrey S. Berman*, June 20, 2020, https://context-cdn.washingtonpost.com/notes/prod/default/documents/febfd776-1bc3-4e20-9a88-0e944ba99e3c/note/97ee92d4-dea5-42f0-9f25-8240522ebff1.#page=1.

86 "Statement of Geoffrey S. Berman," United States Attorney's Office, Southern District of New York, press release, June 20, 2020, https://www.justice.gov/usao-sdny/pr/statement-geoffrey-s-berman.

87 Michael D. Shear and Matt Apuzzo, "F.B.I. Director James Comey Is Fired by Trump," *New York Times*, May 9. 2017, https://www.nytimes.com/2017/05/09/us/politics/james-comey-fired-fbi.html.

88 Washington Post Staff, "Read the Full Testimony of FBI Director James Comey in Which He Discusses Clinton Email Investigation," *Washington Post*, May 3, 2017, https://www.washingtonpost.com/news/post-politics/wp/2017/05/03/read-the-full-testimony-of-fbi-director-james-comey-in-which-he-discusses-clinton-email-investigation/.

89 Committee on the Judiciary, U.S. House of Representatives, *Interview of: Geoffrey Berman*, July 9, 2020, retrieved from the Wayback Machine version July 13, 2020, https://web.archive.org/web/20200713215354/https://judiciary.house.gov/uploadedfiles/berman_transcript.pdf.

90 Paul Rosenzweig, "Why Bill Barr Got Rid of Geoffrey Berman," *Atlantic*, June 21, 2020, https://www.theatlantic.com/ideas/archive/2020/06/why-bill-barr-got-rid-geoffrey-berman/613339/.

91 "Trump Denies Firing Manhattan Prosecutor Berman," Reuters, June 20, 2020, video, 0:22, https://youtu.be/rw8ZMfNhjVs?si=q3NoY5IQzxVtdbKU.

92 Schmidt et al., "Giuliani."

93 "Transcript: John Bolton Interview with ABC News' Martha Raddatz," ABC News, June 21, 2020, https://abcnews.go.com/Politics/transcript-john-bolton-interview-abc-news-martha-raddatz/story?id=71287825:.

CHAPTER 7

1 Devlin Barrett et al., "Two Business Associates of Trump's Personal Attorney Giuliani Have Been Arrested on Campaign Finance Charges," *Washington Post*, October 10, 2019, https://www.washingtonpost.com/politics/two-business-associates-of-trumps-personal-lawyer-giuliani-have-been-arrested-and-are-in-custody/2019/10/10/9f9c101a-eb63-11e9-9306-47cb0324fd44_story.html.

2   Ari Shapiro and Dave Blanchard, "How a Complicated Web Connects 2 Soviet-Born Businessmen with the Impeachment Inquiry," NPR, October 23, 2019, https://www.npr.org/2019/10/23/771849041/how-a-complicated-web-connects-2-soviet-born-businessmen-with-the-impeachment-in.

3   Ema O'Connor, "A Lawyer for Giuliani's Ukrainian Associate Tried to Argue He Was Not a Flight Risk. It Did Not Go Well," *Buzzfeed News*, November 1, 2019, https://www.buzzfeednews.com/article/emaoconnor/igor-fruman-giuliani-ukraine-flight-risk-bail.

4   Karoun Demirjian and Josh Dawsey, "House Panels Subpoena Giuliani for Documents in Ukraine Probe," *Washington Post*, September 30, 2019, https://www.washingtonpost.com/national-security/house-panels-subpoena-giuliani-for-documents-in-ukraine-probe/2019/09/30/0a951ccc-e3bc-11e9-b403-f738899982d2_story.html.

5   "Giuliani Subpoenaed for Ukraine Documents as Next Step in Impeachment Inquiry, Committees Also Send Document Requests and Deposition Notices to Three Giuliani Associates," U.S. House of Representatives, Committee on Foreign Affairs, press release, September 30, 2019, retrieved from the Wayback Machine version October 4, 2019, https://web.archive.org/web/20191004160409/https://foreignaffairs.house.gov/2019/9/giuliani-subpoenaed-for-ukraine-documents-as-next-step-in-impeachment-inquiry.

6   Paul LeBlanc, "Rudy Giuliani Said He Was Flying to Vienna Just before Associates Were Arrested before Reportedly Trying to Go to Vienna," CNN, October 11, 2019, https://edition.cnn.com/2019/10/10/politics/rudy-giuliani-vienna-flight-associates-arrested/index.html.

7   Parnas and Langton, *Shadow Diplomacy*, chap. 3, Kindle.

8   Parnas and Langton, *Shadow Diplomacy*, chap. 4, Kindle.

9   Adam Entous, "How Lev Parnas Became Part of the Trump Campaign's 'One Big Family,'" *New Yorker*, October 15, 2019, https://www.newyorker.com/news/news-desk/why-lev-parnas-worked-for-rudy-giuliani-and-donald-trump.

10 Jeff Ostrowski and Wayne Washington, "Ties to Giuliani Raise Scrutiny of Flop Wannabe Movie Mogul," *Palm Beach Post*, October 29, 2019, https://www.palmbeachpost.com/story/news/politics/2019/10/29/ties-to-giuliani-raise-scrutiny-of-flop-wannabe-movie-mogul/2393176007/.

11 Schreckinger and Samuelsohn, "Giuliani Ukraine."

12 Todd Prince, "Lev Parnas's South Florida Stomping Ground a Mecca for Financial Scams," RFERL, November 10, 2019, https://www.rferl.org/a/lev-parnas-south-florida-boca-raton-financial-scams/30262945.html.

13 Musgrave and Pacenti, "Lev Parnas' Life."

14 Schreckinger and Samuelsohn, "Giuliani Ukraine."

15 Jeff Ostrowski and Wayne Washington, "Ties to Giuliani Raise Scrutiny of Flop Wannabe Movie Mogul," *Palm Beach Post*, October 29, 2019, https://www.palmbeachpost.com/story/news/politics/2019/10/29/ties-to-giuliani-raise-scrutiny-of-flop-wannabe-movie-mogul/2393176007/.

16 Karen Freifeld and Aram Roston, "Exclusive: Trump Lawyer Giuliani Was Paid $500,000 to Consult on Indicted Associate's Firm," Reuters, October 15, 2019, https://www.reuters.com/article/us-usa-trump-whistleblower-giuliani-excl-idUSKBN1WU07Z/.

17 Michael Sallah and Emma Loop, "Two Key Players in the Ukraine Controversy Spent Lavishly as They Dug for Dirt on Biden," *Buzzfeed News*, October 9, 2019, https://www.buzzfeednews.com/article/mikesallah/ukraine-spending-trump-parnas-fruman.

18 Schreckinger and Samuelsohn, "Giuliani Ukraine."

19 Paul Sonne et al., "Lev Is Talking. So Where Is Igor?" *Washington Post*, January 21, 2020, https://www.washingtonpost.com/world/national-security/lev-is-talking-so-where-is-igor/2020/01/21/7e0d586c-0c9e-11ea-a49f-9066f51640f6_story.html.

20. "Игорь Фруман" ["Igor Fruman"], *Фокус [Focus]*, March 23, 2011, https://focus.ua/people/176133.
21. Belford and Melkozerova, "Meet."
22. Paul Sonne, et al., "Lev Is Talking."
23. "Lev Talks Turkey," OCCRP.
24. Samantha J. Gross and David Smiley, "Guiliani's Associates Sought Cannabis Licenses in Florida before Arrest," *Tampa Bay Times*, October 17, 2019, https://www.tampabay.com/florida-politics/buzz/2019/10/17/guilianis-associates-sought-cannabis-licenses-in-florida-before-arrest/.
25. Butler and Biesecker, "Giuliani Pals."
26. Christopher Miller et al., "There's a Village in Ukraine Where Rudy Giuliani Is the Honorary Mayor. That's Not the Weird Part of This Story," *Buzzfeed News*, October 26, 2019, https://www.buzzfeednews.com/article/christopherm51/fiddlers-on-the-roof-ukraine-impeachment.
27. Entous, "One Big Family."
28. Ben Meiselas, Brett Meiselas, and Jordan Meiselas, "Lev Remembers: Inside the Trump Cult with Lev Parnas," June 15, 2021, *The MeidasTouch Podcast*, produced by MeidasTouch Network, podcast, audio, 1:37:08, https://podcasts.apple.com/us/podcast/lev-remembers-inside-the-trump-cult-with-lev-parnas/id1510240831?i=1000525573987.
29. Ben Meiselas et al., "Lev Remembers."
30. Andrew Kaczynski, "2014 Photo of Trump and Indicted Giuliani Associate Took Place at Ivanka Trump Hosted Fashion Show," CNN, October 18, 2019, https://edition.cnn.com/2019/10/18/politics/parnas-trump-doral-kfile/index.html.
31. Entous, "One Big Family."
32. Entous, "One Big Family."
33. Sean Sullivan, "Donald Trump Repeatedly Interrupted by Protesters during Rowdy Miami Rally," *Washington Post*, October 23, 2015, https://www.washingtonpost.com/news/post-politics/wp/2015/10/23/donald-trump-repeatedly-interrupted-by-protesters-during-rowdy-miami-rally/.
34. Belford and Klasfeld, "Parnas' Adventures."
35. Klasfeld and Belford, "Adventures in Maga-Land."
36. Bykowicz et al., "Indicted Florida Pair."
37. Entous, "One Big Family."
38. Federal Election Commission, search result for individual contributions, "Contributor details - Lev Parnas," accessed June 22, 2024, https://www.fec.gov/data/receipts/individual-contributions/?contributor_name=lev+parnas.
39. Samuelsohn and Schreckinger, "Indicted Guiliani Associate."
40. Mandeville, "Au Hilton."
41. Entous, "One Big Family."
42. Eric Pooley, "Mayor of the World," Person of the Year 2001, *Time*, December 31, 2001, https://content.time.com/time/specials/packages/article/0,28804,2020227_2020306,00.html.
43. "Giuliani Becomes Honorary Knight," ABC News, February 13, 2002, https://abcnews.go.com/US/story?id=91907&page=1.
44. Calvin Woodward, "Giuliani at Justice Department Was a Reagan Loyalist Who Didn't Always Follow the Program," Law.com, May 21, 2007, https://www.law.com/dailyreportonline/almID/1202552592917/.

45   Erica Orden and Kara Scannell, "Rudy Giuliani's SDNY Saga: from Top Prosecutor to Subject of Scrutiny," CNN, January 15, 2020, https://edition.cnn.com/2020/01/15/politics/rudy-giuliani-sdny-prosecutor-investigation-scrutiny/index.html.

46   Michael Winerip, "High-Profile Prosecutor," *New York Times Magazine,* June 9, 1985, https://www.nytimes.com/1985/06/09/magazine/high-profile-prosecutor.html.

47   Michael Ellison, "Giuliani to Quit Senate Race," *Guardian,* May 20, 2000, https://www.theguardian.com/world/2000/may/20/uselections2000.usa1.

48   John Solomon and Matthew Mosk, "Giuliani's Road to Private Sector Wealth," NBC News, May 13, 2007, https://www.nbcnews.com/id/wbna18636813.

49   "Mexico Hopes Giuliani Can Ride to Rescue," *Chicago Tribune,* December 24, 2002, https://www.chicagotribune.com/2002/12/24/mexico-hopes-giuliani-can-ride-to-rescue/.

50   Andrew Roth, "Unravelling Rudolph Giuliani's Labyrinthine Ties to Ukraine," *Guardian,* October 30, 2019, https://www.theguardian.com/us-news/2019/oct/30/unravelling-rudolph-giulianis-labyrinthine-ties-to-ukraine.

51   John Cassidy, "Has Rudy Giuliani Been Done in by His Own Buck-Raking?," *New Yorker,* November 17, 2016, https://www.newyorker.com/news/john-cassidy/has-rudy-giuliani-been-done-in-by-his-own-buck-raking.

52   Mary Jacoby, "Qatar Contract Offers Glimpse into Giuliani Firm," *Wall Street Journal,* November 7, 2007, https://www.wsj.com/articles/SB119440640166884884.

53   JoAnne Allen, "Giuliani to Run in 2008," Reuters, August 9, 2007, https://www.reuters.com/article/us-usa-politics-giuliani-idUSN1518266220070215/.

54   Haroon Siddique, "Giuliani Abandons White House Bid," *Guardian,* January 30, 2008, https://www.theguardian.com/world/2008/jan/30/uselections2008.rudygiuliani.

55   Pengelly, "Donald Kept Our Secret."

56   "Judith Giuliani Discusses Marriage to Rudy Giuliani in Exclusive 'Inside Edition' Interview," CBS News, September 13, 2022, https://www.cbsnews.com/newyork/news/judith-giuliani-rudy-giuliani-inside-edition-interview/.

57   Devlin Barrett, "How Rudy Giuliani, Once a National Hero, Ruined His Own Reputation," review of *Giuliani: The Rise and Tragic Fall of America's Mayor,* by Andrew Kirtzman, *Washington Post,* September 16, 2022, https://www.washingtonpost.com/outlook/2022/09/16/how-rudy-giuliani-once-national-hero-ruined-his-own-reputation/.

58   Rupert Neate, "Donald Trump Announces US Presidential Run with Eccentric Speech," *Guardian,* June 16, 2015, https://www.theguardian.com/us-news/2015/jun/16/donald-trump-announces-run-president.

59   Julia Manchester, "Rudy Giuliani (Sort of) Endorses Donald Trump," CNN, April 19, 2016, https://edition.cnn.com/2016/04/19/politics/donald-trump-rudy-giuliani-endorsement/index.html.

60   Dan Solomon, "What Does a Donald Trump Rally in Austin Look Like?" *Texas Monthly,* August 24, 2016, https://www.texasmonthly.com/the-daily-post/what-does-a-donald-trump-rally-in-austin-look-like/.

61   Ryan Blethen, "5 Takeaways from Donald Trump's Rally in Everett," *Seattle Times,* August 31, 2016, https://www.seattletimes.com/seattle-news/politics/5-takeaways-from-donald-trumps-rally-in-everett/.

62   Joshua Berlinger, "'Make Mexico Great Again Also': The Newest Trump Hat," CNN, September 1, 2016, https://edition.cnn.com/2016/09/01/politics/new-trump-hat-trnd/index.html.

63   "Rudy Giuliani Becomes Pitchman for LifeLock," ABC News, March 20, 2013, https://abcnews.go.com/Business/giuliani-pitchman-lifelock/story?id=18774357.

64 "RNC 2016 Schedule of Events and Speakers," *Politico*, July 18, 2016, https://www.politico.com/story/2016/07/rnc-2016-schedule-of-events-and-speakers-225704.

65 David A. Fahrenthold, "Trump Recorded Having Extremely Lewd Conversation about Women in 2005," *Washington Post*, October 8, 2016, https://www.washingtonpost.com/politics/trump-recorded-having-extremely-lewd-conversation-about-women-in-2005/2016/10/07/3b9ce776-8cb4-11e6-bf8a-3d26847eeed4_story.html.

66 Meg Anderson and Amita Kelly, "Here Are the 30+ Republicans Calling for Trump to Step Aside", NPR, October 8, 2016, https://www.npr.org/2016/10/08/497225589/here-are-the-30-republicans-calling-for-trump-to-step-aside.

67 Scott Detrow, "Donald Trump's Lone Surrogate on TV Struggled to Defend Him," NPR, October 9, 2016, https://www.npr.org/2016/10/09/497270514/donald-trumps-lone-surrogate-on-tv-struggled-to-defend-him.

68 Jose A. DelReal, "Giuliani, Suggesting Trump May Have 'Exaggerated' in Lewd Comments, Says, 'Talk and Action Are Two Different Things,'" *Washington Post*, October 9, 2016, https://www.washingtonpost.com/news/post-politics/wp/2016/10/09/giuliani-talk-and-action-are-two-different-things/.

69 Abby Phillip, "Trump Names Rudy Giuliani as Cybersecurity Adviser," *Washington Post*, January 12, 2017, https://www.washingtonpost.com/news/powerpost/wp/2017/01/12/trump-names-rudy-giuliani-as-cybersecurity-adviser/.

70 Steve Holland, "Giuliani Is a Leading Candidate to Be Trump's Secretary of State—Source," Reuters, November 15, 2016, https://www.reuters.com/article/us-usa-trump-state-department-giuliani-idUSKBN13A07H/.

71 Louis Nelson, "Conway: Giuliani 'Possibly' Tapped for National Intelligence Director," *Politico*, November 22, 2016, https://www.politico.com/blogs/donald-trump-administration/2016/11/conway-giulianipossibly-tapped-for-national-intelligence-director-231739.

72 Louis Nelson, "Giuliani on Being Attorney General: Nobody Knows the DOJ Better Than Me," *Politico*, November 10, 2016, https://www.politico.com/story/2016/11/rudy-giuliani-trump-cabinet-attorney-general-231170.

73 "Lev Talks Turkey," OCCRP.

74 Bykowicz et al., "Indicted Florida Pair."

75 Belford and Klasfeld, "Parnas' Adventures."

76 Entous, "One Big Family."

77 Entous, "One Big Family."

78 Michael Warren, "Giuliani's Journey to the Center of Trump's Impeachment Battle Started with a Phone Call in 2018," CNN, September 30, 2019, https://edition.cnn.com/2019/09/29/politics/giuliani-journey-trump-impeachment-ukraine-phone-call/index.html.

79 U.S. Department of Justice, *Exhibit A to Registration Statement Pursuant to the Foreign Agents Registration Act of 1938, as amended, filed by Ballard Partners*, Registration No 6415, May 19, 2017, https://efile.fara.gov/docs/6415-Exhibit-AB-20170519-3.pdf.

80 U.S. Department of Justice, *Exhibit A to Registration Statement Pursuant to the Foreign Agents Registration Act of 1938, as amended, filed by Ballard Partners*, Registration No 6415, August 28, 2017, https://efile.fara.gov/docs/6415-Exhibit-AB-20170828-5.pdf.

81 Weiser and Kingsley, "Secret Meeting."

82 Weiser and Kingsley, "Secret Meeting."

83 "Lev Parnas Releases Recording of Trump Dinner: Full Video," CBS News, January 25, 2020, video, 1:23:15, https://youtu.be/_sxSGKB3Sj0.

84. Kenneth P. Vogel and Eric Lipton, "Recording Shows That the Swamp Has Not Been Drained," *New York Times*, January 26, 2020, https://www.nytimes.com/2020/01/26/us/politics/trump-recording-donors.html.

85. Rosalind S. Helderman et al., "At Donor Dinner, Giuliani Associate Said He Discussed Ukraine with Trump, According to People Familiar with His Account," *Washington Post*, November 12, 2019, https://www.washingtonpost.com/politics/at-donor-dinner-giuliani-associate-said-he-discussed-ukraine-with-trump-according-to-people-familiar-with-his-account/2019/11/12/2a1f28e0-0558-11ea-b17d-8b867891d39d_story.html.

86. Jacob Pramuk, "Rudy Giuliani Is Joining President Trump's Personal Legal Team for the Mueller Probe," CNBC, April 19, 2018, https://www.cnbc.com/2018/04/19/rudy-giuliani-is-joining-president-trumps-personal-legal-team-for-the-mueller-probe.html.

87. Nathan Vardi, "The Company He Keeps," *Forbes*, October 28, 2006, https://www.forbes.com/forbes/2006/1113/138.html?sh=235c8f4c4b00.

88. Theodoric Meyer and Marianne Levine, "Trump Inaugural Fundraiser Now Lobbying on Pensions," *Politico*, August 23, 2019, https://www.politico.com/newsletters/politico-influence/2018/08/23/trump-inaugural-fundraiser-now-lobbying-on-pensions-326415.

89. Anna Massoglia (@annalecta), "President Trump—an @FEC-registered 2020 presidential candidate barred from asking for donations over $5k—on stage at his hotel for the America First Action Super PAC's $250,000-a-head fundraiser at Trump Intl Hotel tonight in DC with Donald Trump Jr, who runs Trump's businesses," Twitter, June 19, 2018, 11:08 p.m., retrieved from the Wayback Machine version September 13, 2020, https://web.archive.org/web/20200913211309/https://twitter.com/annalecta/status/1009256676350922753.

90. Andrew Kaczynski et al., "Inauguration Galas, an Intimate Dinner, and a White House Party: Trump's 10 Interactions with Indicted Giuliani Associates," CNN, November 12, 2019, https://edition.cnn.com/2019/11/12/politics/kfile-trump-interactions-giuliani-associates/index.html.

91. Rebecca Ballhaus et al., "Lev Parnas Paid His Way into Donald Trump's Orbit," *Wall Street Journal*, January 19, 2020, https://www.wsj.com/articles/lev-parnas-paid-his-way-into-donald-trumps-orbit-11579469071.

92. Escott, "Private Photos of Indicted Donor Depict Ties to Trump, Giuliani," *Wall Street Journal*, October 21, 2019, video, 5:41, https://www.wsj.com/video/private-photos-of-indicted-donor-depict-ties-to-trump-giuliani/7EED4946-5201-4D70-A8FF-0516DCC1488F.

93. Eric Lutz, "Giuliani Throws Parnas under the Bus: 'I Feel Sorry for Him,'" *Vanity Fair*, January 23, 2020, https://www.vanityfair.com/news/2020/01/rudy-giuliani-throws-lev-parnas-under-bus-i-feel-sorry-for-him.

94. Erin Laviola, "Svetlana Parnas, Lev Parnas' Wife: 5 Fast Facts," *Heavy*, December 3, 2022, https://heavy.com/news/2019/10/svetlana-lev-parnas-wife/.

95. Parnas, *Trump First*, chap. 1, Kindle.

CHAPTER 8

1. Parnas, *Trump First*, chap. 1, Kindle.
2. Joshua Goodman, "Sources: Venezuela Wooed Texas Republican to Ease Sanctions," Associated Press, June 22, 2020, https://apnews.com/article/15ea6f405e859acadf969696d286b94a.
3. Goodman, "Sources: Venezuela Wooed."
4. "Exxon Owed $1.6bn by Venezuela for 2007 Nationalisation," BBC News, October 10, 2014, https://www.bbc.com/news/business-29561345.

5   Patrick Gillespie et al., "Venezuela: How a Rich Country Collapsed," CNN, July 30, 2017, https://money.cnn.com/2017/07/26/news/economy/venezuela-economic-crisis/index.html.

6   Goodman, "Sources: Venezuela Wooed."

7   Goodman, "Sources: Venezuela Wooed."

8   "The Collapse of Venezuela, Explained," Vox, August 25, 2017, video, 7:30, https://www.youtube.com/watch?v=S1gUR8wM5vA.

9   Joe Sterling et al., "Deadly Election Day in Venezuela as Protesters Clash with Troops," CNN, July 30, 2017, https://edition.cnn.com/2017/07/30/americas/venezuela-on-edge-vote/index.html.

10 "Treasury Sanctions Eight Members of Venezuela's Supreme Court of Justice," U.S. Department of the Treasury, press release, May 18, 2017, https://home.treasury.gov/news/press-releases/sm0090.

11 Alexandra Ulmer and David Lawder, "Trump Slaps Sanctions on Venezuela; Maduro Sees Effort to Force a Default," Reuters, August 25, 2017, https://www.reuters.com/article/world/trump-slaps-sanctions-on-venezuela-maduro-sees-effort-to-force-default-idUSL2N1LB12B/.

12 Roberta Rampton and Alexandra Ulmer, "U.S. Imposes Fresh Sanctions on Venezuela, Pence Calls for More Action," Reuters, May 7, 2018, https://www.reuters.com/article/world/u-s-imposes-fresh-sanctions-on-venezuela-pence-calls-for-more-action-idUSKBN1I81S1/.

13 "US Imposes Sanctions on Venezuela's First Lady Cilia Flores," BBC News, September 25, 2018, https://www.bbc.com/news/world-latin-america-45644074.

14 "Pete Sessions, Federal Congressional Candidacy Data, 2018 Election Cycle," Open Secrets, accessed June 22, 2024, https://www.opensecrets.org/members-of-congress/industries?cid=N00005681&cycle=2018&newMem=N&recs=20&type=I.

15 Patricia Zengerle, "Senate Revises Russia Sanctions Bill, Sends It to House," Reuters, June 29, 2017, retrieved from the Wayback Machine, version November 11, 2021, https://web.archive.org/web/20211111131239/https://www.reuters.com/article/us-usa-sanctions-house-idUSKBN19K2CQ.

16 Tom Benning, "Texas Republican Pete Sessions Carries Big Oil's Fight against Parts of Russia Sanctions Bill," *Dallas Morning News*, July 7, 2017, https://www.dallasnews.com/news/politics/2017/07/07/texas-republican-pete-sessions-carries-big-oil-s-fight-against-parts-of-russia-sanctions-bill/.

17 Benning, "Texas Republican."

18 U.S. Department of the Treasury, Office of Foreign Assets Control, *Executive Order 13827 of March 19, 2018, Taking Additional Steps to Address the Situation in Venezuela*, accessed June 22, 2024, https://ofac.treasury.gov/media/5486/download?inline.

19 Joshua Goodman, "Texas Republican Made Secret Peacemaking Trip to Venezuela," Associated Press, April 5, 2018, https://apnews.com/general-news-e7fa47d52c0c4839a7f83f7674664249.

20 Katie Leslie. "U.S. Rep. Pete Sessions Took Secret Trip to Venezuela That His Office Says Was Peace Mission," *Dallas Morning News*, April 6, 2018, https://www.dallasnews.com/news/politics/2018/04/06/u-s-rep-pete-sessions-took-secret-trip-to-venezuela-that-his-office-says-was-peace-mission/.

21 Goodman, "Sources: Venezuela Wooed."

22 Patricia Mazzei, "Venezuelan Oil Company Sues Miami Ex-Congressman over $50 Million Deal,"*New York Times*, May 13, 2020, https://www.nytimes.com/2020/05/13/us/david-rivera-venezuela-oil-pdvsa.html.

23 Joshua Goodman and Terry Spencer, "Ex-Miami US Rep. David Rivera Arrested in Venezuela Probe," Associated Press, December 6, 2022, https://apnews.com/article/venezuela-miami-arrests-criminal-investigations-david-rivera-a81683364212d7c86068839290bd8630.

24 Bill Chappell, "A Former Florida Congressman Is Arrested on Charges of Lobbying for Venezuela," NPR, December 6, 2022, https://www.npr.org/2022/12/06/1141028977/venezuela-lobbying-florida-rep-david-rivera-arrested-indicted.

25 Rosalind S. Helderman et al., "Trump's Lawyer and the Venezuelan President: How Giuliani Got Involved in Back-Channel Talks with Maduro," *Washington Post*, December 30, 2019, https://www.washingtonpost.com/politics/trumps-lawyer-and-the-venezuelan-president-how-giuliani-got-involved-in-back-channel-talks-with-maduro/2019/12/29/289dc6aa-235f-11ea-86f3-3b5019d451db_story.html.

26 Indictment, United States v. David Rivera and Esther Nuhfer, No. 22-20552-Cr-GAYLES/TORRES (S.D. Fla. November 16, 2022), https://www.politico.com/f/?id=00000184-e9f4-d144-a1d7-edf49b970000.

27 Aram Roston, "Exclusive: Meeting Maduro—Inside a U.S. Businessman's Oil Deal with Venezuela," Reuters, February 28, 2019, https://www.reuters.com/article/us-venezuela-politics-sargeant-exclusive-idUSKCN1QH0JS/.

28 Nicholas Confessore et al., "Trump, Venezuela and the Tug-of-War over a Strongman," *New York Times*, November 1, 2020, https://www.nytimes.com/2020/11/01/us/trump-venezuela-maduro.html.

29 Helderman et al., "Trump's Lawyer."

30 "Nicolás Maduro: Corruption and Chaos in Venezuela," U.S. Department of State, fact sheet, August 6, 2019, https://2017-2021.state.gov/nicolas-maduro-corruption-and-chaos-in-venezuela-2/.

31 Lucia Kassai et al., "Venezuela Taps Obscure Driller to Replace Big-Name Oil Firms," Bloomberg News, January 4, 2019, https://www.bloomberg.com/news/articles/2019-01-04/venezuela-taps-obscure-driller-to-replace-big-name-oil-compānies.

32 Luc Cohen and Brian Ellsworth, "Venezuela's PDVSA Inks Oil Deal with Firm Part-Owned by Florida Republican," Reuters, January 7, 2019, https://www.reuters.com/article/venezuela-oil-idUSL1N1Z600N/.

33 Confessore et al., "Trump, Venezuela."

34 U.S. Department of the Treasury, Office of Foreign Assets Control, *Executive Order 13857 of January 25, 2019, Taking Additional Steps to Address the National Emergency with Respect to Venezuela*, accessed June 22, 2024, https://ofac.treasury.gov/media/5491/download?inline.

35 Roston, "Exclusive: Meeting Maduro."

36 Confessore et al., "Trump, Venezuela."

37 "U.S. Bringing 'Maximum Pressure' on Venezuela: Sanctions Official," Reuters, March 29, 2019, https://www.reuters.com/article/us-usa-venezuela-pressure-idUSKCN1RA0A3/.

38 Sasha Ingber, "Venezuelan Supreme Court Judge Denounces Maduro Government, Flees to U.S.," NPR, January 7, 2019, https://www.npr.org/2019/01/07/682865392/venezuela-supreme-court-judge-denounces-government-flees-to-u-s.

39 "Venezuela President Maduro Sworn in for Second Term," BBC News, January 10, 2019, https://www.bbc.com/news/world-46821653.

40 Confessore et al., "Trump, Venezuela."

41 Kenneth P. Vogel, "While Working for Trump, Giuliani Courts Business Abroad," *New York Times*, December 12, 2018, https://www.nytimes.com/2018/12/12/us/politics/giuliani-consulting-abroad.html.

42 Vogel, "While Working for Trump."

43 Indictment, United States v. Raul Gorrin Belisario, No. 18-cr-80160-WPD (S.D. Fla. November 16, 2018), https://www.justice.gov/criminal/criminal-fraud/file/1120281/dl?inline.

44 Confessore et al., "Trump, Venezuela."

45 U.S. Department of Justice, *Short Form Registration Statement Pursuant to the Foreign Agents Registration Act of 1938, as Amended, Filed by RobeRT Daniel Stryk*, Registration No. 6399, January 24, 2020, https://efile.fara.gov/docs/6399-Short-Form-20200124-164.pdf.

46 Ryan Nicol, "Attorney Chris Kise to Help Nicolás Maduro Administration Fight U.S. Sanctions," Florida Politics, January 28, 2020, https://floridapolitics.com/archives/317253-kise-maduro-us-sanctions/.

47 Confessore et al., "Trump, Venezuela."

48 Vicky Ward, "Exclusive Photos of Giuliani in Spain Show Lev Parnas Has Lots More to Share," CNN, February 7, 2020, https://edition.cnn.com/2020/02/07/politics/lev-parnas-exclusive-images-giuliani/index.html.

49 Nathan Jaccard et al., "Jet-Setting Venezuelan Businessman in Corruption Probe Linked to Luxembourg Firms," OCCRP, February 11, 2021, https://www.occrp.org/en/openlux/jet-setting-venezuelan-businessman-in-corruption-probe-linked-to-luxembourg-firms.

50 El Pitazo and OCCRP, "Plunging Venezuela into the Dark," OCCRP, June 12, 2019, https://www.occrp.org/en/investigations/plunging-venezuela-into-the-dark.

51 Ward, "Exclusive Photos."

52 Jay Weaver et al., "Venezuelan Tied to Epic Corruption Case Funneled Millions into Secretive Luxembourg Companies," *Miami Herald*, March 30, 2021, https://www.miamiherald.com/news/nation-world/world/americas/article249091760.html.

53 Ward, "Exclusive Photos."

54 Kenneth P. Vogel and Ben Protess, "Giuliani Represented Venezuelan Investor in Discussion with Justice Dept," *New York Times*, November 26, 2019, https://www.nytimes.com/2019/11/26/us/politics/giuliani-venezuelan-businessman.html.

55 Rebecca Klar, "Giuliani Lobbied DOJ for Venezuelan Businessman Who Claimed to Help Guaidó: Report," *Hill*, January 22, 2020, https://thehill.com/policy/international/americas/479339-giuliani-lobbied-doj-for-venezuelan-businessman-who-claimed-to/.

56 Jeremy Herb, "Gowdy Worked with Giuliani on Legal Matter Ahead of Impeachment Proceedings, New Documents Show," CNN, July 16, 2020, https://edition.cnn.com/2020/07/16/politics/trey-gowdy-rudy-giuliani-impeachment-proceedings/index.html.

57 Vogel and Protess, "Giuliani Represented Venezuelan."

58 Aram Roston et al., "Exclusive: Giuliani Told U.S. His Client Deserves Leniency for Financing Venezuela's Opposition—Parnas," Reuters, January 22, 2020, https://www.reuters.com/article/idUSKBN1ZL1AQ/.

CHAPTER 9

1. Ellen Nakashima et al., "Whistleblower Complaint about President Trump Involves Ukraine, According to Two People Familiar with the Matter," *Washington Post*, September 19, 2019, https://www.washingtonpost.com/national-security/whistleblower-complaint-about-president-trump-involves-ukraine-according-to-two-people-familiar-with-the-matter/2019/09/19/07e33f0a-daf6-11e9-bfb1-849887369476_story.html.

2. Julian E. Barnes et al., "Whistle-Blower Complaint Is Said to Involve Trump and Ukraine," *New York Times*, September 19, 2019, https://www.nytimes.com/2019/09/19/us/politics/intelligence-whistle-blower-complaint-trump.html.

3. "Office of the Intelligence Community Inspector General," Office of the Director of National Intelligence, accessed June 22, 2024, https://www.dni.gov/index.php/who-we-are/organizations/icig/icig-who-we-are.

4. Gregory Korte, "The Whistle-Blower Complaint against Trump, Annotated," Bloomberg News, September 26, 2019, https://www.bloomberg.com/graphics/2019-trump-ukraine-whistleblower-complaint-transcript.

5. Korte, "Whistle-Blower."

6. Ayesha Rascoe, "Who Was on the Trump-Ukraine Call?" NPR, November 7, 2019, https://www.npr.org/2019/11/07/775456663/who-was-on-the-trump-ukraine-call.

7. Deb Riechmann, "Anatomy of the Phone Call Now Imperiling Trump's Presidency," Associated Press, October 12, 2019, https://apnews.com/article/donald-trump-ap-top-news-politics-michael-pence-impeachments-ab67c31d9b3c4acdada93a624052ddc4.

8. Josh Williams et al., "Full Document: Trump's Call with the Ukrainian President," *New York Times*, September 25, 2019, https://www.nytimes.com/interactive/2019/09/25/us/politics/trump-ukraine-transcript.html.

9. Karoun Demirjian et al., "Trump Ordered Hold on Military Aid Days before Calling Ukrainian President, Officials Say," *Washington Post*, September 23, 2019, https://www.washingtonpost.com/national-security/trump-ordered-hold-on-military-aid-days-before-calling-ukrainian-president-officials-say/2019/09/23/df93a6ca-de38-11e9-8dc8-498eabc129a0_story.html.

10. Caitlin Emma and Connor O'Brien, "Trump Slow-Walks Ukraine Military Aid Meant to Contain Russia," *Politico*, August 29, 2019, https://www.politico.eu/article/donald-trump-slow-walks-ukraine-military-aid-meant-to-contain-russia/.

11. Demirjian et al., "Trump."

12. Eileen Sullivan, "How CrowdStrike Became Part of Trump's Ukraine Call," *New York Times*, September 25, 2019, https://www.nytimes.com/2019/09/25/us/politics/crowdstrike-ukraine.html.

13. Scott Pelley, "Why President Trump Asked Ukraine to Look into a DNC 'Server' and CrowdStrike," CBS News, February 16, 2020, https://www.cbsnews.com/news/trump-crowdstrike-ukraine-server-conspiracy-theory-60-minutes-2020-02-16/.

14. Jane C. Timm, "Does Ukraine Have the DNC Server Like Trump Says? We Fact Checked That," NBC News, November 22, 2019, https://www.nbcnews.com/politics/trump-impeachment-inquiry/fact-check-trump-s-false-claims-about-ukraine-dnc-server-n1089596.

15. Pelley, "Why."

16. Jason Koebler, "Trump's Stupid 'Where Is the DNC Server?' Conspiracy Theory, Explained", *Vice*, July 16, 2018, https://www.vice.com/en/article/zmkxp9/dnc-server-conspiracy-theory-russian-hack-explained.

17 Jane C. Timm, "Trump Promotes Conspiracy Theory: Clinton's Deleted Emails Are in Ukraine," NBC News, September 25, 2019, https://www.nbcnews.com/politics/trump-impeachment-inquiry/trump-promotes-conspiracy-theory-clinton-s-deleted-emails-are-ukraine-n1058726.

18 Craig Timberg et al., "In Call to Ukraine's President, Trump Revived a Favorite Conspiracy Theory about the DNC Hack," *Washington Post,* September 25, 2019, https://www.washingtonpost.com/technology/2019/09/25/trumps-mention-crowdstrike-call-with-ukraines-president-recalls-russian-hack-dnc/.

19 Timm, "Does Ukraine?"

20 Zack Beauchamp, "The Trump-Ukraine 'Transcript,' Explained," *Vox,* September 25, 2019, https://www.vox.com/policy-and-politics/2019/9/25/20883420/full-transcript-trump-ukraine-zelensky-white-house.

21 Robbie Gramer and Amy Mackinnon, "U.S. Ambassador to Ukraine Recalled in 'Political Hit Job,' Lawmakers Say," *Foreign Policy,* May 7, 2019, https://foreignpolicy.com/2019/05/07/us-ambassador-to-ukraine-recalled-in-political-hit-job-lawmakers-say-marie-yovanovitch-lutsenko-right-wing-media-accusations-congress-diplomats-diplomacy/.

22 Polina Ivanova et al. "What Hunter Biden Did on the Board of Ukrainian Energy Company Burisma," Reuters, October 18, 2019, https://www.reuters.com/article/us-hunter-biden-ukraine-idUSKBN1WX1P7/.

23 Glenn Kessler, "Correcting a Media Error: Biden's Ukraine Showdown Was in December 2015," *Washington Post*, October 2, 2019, https://www.washingtonpost.com/politics/2019/10/02/correcting-media-error-bidens-ukraine-showdown-was-december/.

24 Christopher Miller, "Why Was Ukraine's Top Prosecutor Fired? The Issue at the Heart of the Dispute Gripping Washington," *RFE/RL*, September 24, 2019, https://www.rferl.org/a/why-was-ukraine-top-prosecutor-fired-viktor-shokin/30181445.html.

25 Monica Alba and Carol E. Lee, "Trump Allies Pushed Biden-Ukraine Allegations at Key Moments in Campaign Timeline," NBC News, September 30, 2019, https://www.nbcnews.com/politics/2020-election/trump-allies-pushed-biden-ukraine-allegations-key-moments-campaign-timeline-n1060106.

26 Miller, "Why."

27 Oliver Bullough, "The Money Machine: How a High-Profile Corruption Investigation Fell Apart," *Guardian*, April 12, 2017, https://www.theguardian.com/world/2017/apr/12/the-money-machine-how-a-high-profile-corruption-investigation-fell-apart.

28 Geoff Bennett et al., "Trump Blames Energy Secretary Rick Perry for Ukraine Call at Center of Impeachment Inquiry", NBC News, October 6, 2019, https://www.nbcnews.com/politics/trump-impeachment-inquiry/trump-blames-energy-secretary-rick-perry-ukraine-call-center-impeachment-n1062931.

29 Simon Shuster and Ilya Marritz, "Rick Perry's Ukrainian Dream," ProPublica, September 10, 2020, https://www.propublica.org/article/rick-perrys-ukrainian-dream.

30 "Read: Testimony of Alexander Vindman, the White House's Ukraine Specialist," NPR, November 8, 2019, https://www.npr.org/2019/11/08/777514772/read-testimony-of-alexander-vindman-the-white-houses-ukraine-specialist.

31 "Read," NPR.

32 Williams et al., "Full Document."

33 Shane Harris, "Intelligence Director Coats to Resign Next Month, Trump Says," *Washington Post*, July 28, 2019, https://www.washingtonpost.com/world/national-security/intelligence-director-coats-expected-to-resign/2019/07/28/34e361e2-b16b-11e9-8e94-71a35969e4d8_story.html.

34 Michael Poznansky, "Dan Coats Just Resigned as Director of National Intelligence. Here's Why That Matters," *Washington Post*, July 30, 2019, https://www.washingtonpost.com/politics/2019/07/30/dan-coats-just-resigned-director-national-intelligence-heres-why-that-matters/.

35 Maggie Haberman et al. "Dan Coats to Step Down as Intelligence Chief; Trump Picks Loyalist for Job," *New York Times*, July 28, 2019, https://www.nytimes.com/2019/07/28/us/politics/dan-coats-intelligence-chief-out.html.

36 Jonathan Bernstein, "Trump's Choice to Lead U.S. Intelligence Is Not Qualified," opinion, Bloomberg News, July 29, 2019, https://www.bloomberg.com/view/articles/2019-07-29/john-ratcliffe-is-not-a-qualified-replacement-for-dan-coats.

37 Katrina Mulligan, "Dan Coats Resignation: Trump Values Leaders Who Protect Him over Those Who Defend America," opinion, *USA Today*, July 29, 2019, https://www.usatoday.com/story/opinion/2019/07/29/donald-trump-dni-dan-coats-john-ratcliffe-intelligence-column/1857031001/.

38 Martin Matishak, "Trump Announces Departure of No. 2 Intelligence Official Sue Gordon,", *Politico*, August 8, 2019, https://www.politico.com/story/2019/08/08/sue-gordon-national-intelligence-trump-1453555.

39 Barnes et al., "Whistle-Blower."

40 "Trump Names Counterterrorism Chief as Acting Director of National Intelligence," Reuters, August 8, 2019, https://www.reuters.com/article/us-usa-trump-intelligence-idUSKCN1UY2UJ/.

41 Robert S. Litt, "Unpacking the Intelligence Community Whistleblower Complaint," *Lawfare*, September 17, 2019, https://www.lawfaremedia.org/article/unpacking-intelligence-community-whistleblower-complaint.

42 Kevin Liptak et al., "Whistleblower Timeline: Team Trump Contacts and Ukraine," CNN, November 13, 2019, https://edition.cnn.com/2019/09/20/politics/whistleblower-timeline-ukraine-team-trump/index.html.

43 Zachary B. Wolf, "Quick Timeline of Trump-Ukraine Events That Led to Impeachment Hearings," CNN, November 13, 2019, https://edition.cnn.com/2019/11/13/politics/trump-impeachment-key-moments/index.html.

44 "Three House Committees Launch Wide-Ranging Investigation into Trump-Giuliani Ukraine Scheme," U.S. House of Representatives, Committee on Foreign Affairs, press release, September 9, 2019, https://web.archive.org/web/20190910070148/https://foreignaffairs.house.gov/2019/9/three-house-committees-launch-wide-ranging-investigation-into-trump-giuliani-ukraine-scheme.

45 Olivia Gazis, "Adam Schiff Subpoenas Acting Intel Chief over Whistleblower Complaint," CBS News, September 13, 2019, https://www.cbsnews.com/news/adam-schiff-subpoenas-acting-intel-chief-over-whistleblower-complaint/.

46 Office of the Director of National Intelligence, Office of General Counsel, *Letter from Jason Klitenic, General Counsel, to the Honorable Adam Schiff, Chairman, Permanent Select Committee on Intelligence, United States House of Representatives*, September 17, 2019, http://cdn.cnn.com/cnn/2019/images/09/17/sept..17.letter.pdf.

47 "Transcript: Representative Adam Schiff on 'Face the Nation,'" September 15, 2019", CBS News, September 15, 2019, https://www.cbsnews.com/news/transcript-representative-adam-schiff-on-face-the-nation-september-15-2019/.

48 Alan Cullison et al., "Trump Repeatedly Pressed Ukraine President to Investigate Biden's Son," *Wall Street Journal*, September 21, 2019, https://www.wsj.com/articles/trump-defends-conversation-with-ukraine-leader-11568993176.

49   Anya van Wagtendonk, "Biden Wants Trump to Release a Transcript of the Call That Led to a Whistleblower Complaint," *Vox*, September 21, 2019, https://www.vox.com/policy-and-politics/2019/9/21/20877393/whistleblower-complaint-joe-biden-transcript-ukraine-call-donald-trump-2020-election.

50   Seung Min Kim et al., "Trump Denies Explicitly Tying U.S. Military Aid to Demand for Ukrainian Probe of Biden," *Washington Post*, September 23, 2019, https://www.washingtonpost.com/politics/white-house-press-secretary-noncommittal-about-releasing-transcript-of-trump-call-with-ukrainian-president/2019/09/23/fec1be30-ddeb-11e9-b199-f638bf2c340f_story.html.

51   "Letter: Pelosi Hints at 'Whole New Stage of Investigation' If Trump Blocks Whistleblower," CBS News, September 23, 2019, https://www.cbsnews.com/sanfrancisco/news/trump-whistleblower-speaker-nancy-pelosi-letter-to-congress/.

52   Kim et al., "Trump."

53   "Trump Insists Phone Call with Ukraine's Zelensky 'Was Perfect' | AFP," *AFP News Agency*, September 26, 2019, video, 0:46, https://youtu.be/BfXozwNoNd0.

54   Liptak et al., "Whistleblower Timeline."

55   Williams et al., "Full Document."

56   Nicholas Fandos, "Nancy Pelosi Announces Formal Impeachment Inquiry of Trump," *New York Times*, September 24, 2019, https://www.nytimes.com/2019/09/24/us/politics/democrats-impeachment-trump.html.

CHAPTER 10

1   Vicky Ward, "Exclusive: After Private White House Meeting, Giuliani Associate Lev Parnas Said He Was on a 'Secret Mission' for Trump, Sources Say," CNN, November 15, 2019, https://edition.cnn.com/2019/11/15/politics/parnas-trump-special-mission-ukraine/index.html.

2   "House Releases Additional Documents Turned over by Lev Parnas," *Washington Post*, January 15, 2020, https://www.washingtonpost.com/context/house-releases-additional-documents-turned-over-by-lev-parnas/7de4189b-00cf-487f-b4cc-f7236c937b42/?itid=lk_inline_manual_4.

3   Lev Parnas, "Exclusive: Rachel Maddow Interviews Lev Parnas—Part 1 | Rachel Maddow | MSNBC," interview by Rachel Maddow, MSNBC, January 22, 2020, video, 48:50, https://www.youtube.com/watch?v=DVnZVuhOycs.

4   Jacob Shamsian, "Meet Victoria Toensing and Joseph diGenova, the Republican Power Couple Caught up in the FBI's Rudy Giuliani Investigation," *Business Insider*, May 4, 2021, https://www.businessinsider.com/victoria-toensing-joseph-digenova-rudy-giuliani-allies-fbi-investigation-2021-5.

5   Darren Samuelsohn, "Forget Rudy: Here Are Trump's Fiercest Defenders," *Politico*, June 9, 2018, https://www.politico.com/story/2018/06/09/trump-lawyers-joseph-digenova-victoria-toensing-634996.

6   Miriam Elder, "At Least the Married Lawyers Who Helped Bring Us the Impeachment Scandal Are Having Fun," *Buzzfeed News*, December 11, 2019, https://www.buzzfeednews.com/article/miriamelder/victoria-toensing-joe-digenova-ukraine-giuliani.

7   Maggie Haberman et al., "Trump Won't Hire Two Lawyers Whose Appointments Were Announced Days Ago," *New York Times*, March 25, 2018, https://www.nytimes.com/2018/03/25/us/politics/trump-digenova-toensing.html.

8   Evan Perez and Eli Watkins, "Trump Not Bringing On Attorney diGenova Just Days after His Hiring Was Announced," CNN, March 25, 2018, https://edition.cnn.com/2018/03/25/politics/joseph-digenova-trump-legal-team/index.html.

9. Lis Power and Tyler Monroe, "Joe diGenova and Victoria Toensing Have Made over Ninety Appearances on Fox in 2019," *Media Matters*, September 30, 2019, https://www.mediamatters.org/fox-news/joe-digenova-and-victoria-toensing-have-made-over-90-appearances-fox-2019.

10. "Rachel Maddow Interviews Lev Parnas. Transcript: 1/15/20, The Rachel Maddow Show," MSNBC, January 15, 2020, https://www.msnbc.com/transcripts/rachel-maddow-show/2020-01-15-msna1322756.

11. Adam Entous, "The Ukrainian Prosecutor behind Trump's Impeachment," *New Yorker*, December 16, 2019, https://www.newyorker.com/magazine/2019/12/23/the-ukrainian-prosecutor-behind-trumps-impeachment.

12. Parnas, "Exclusive."

13. Ken Dilanian, "McMaster Removes Flynn Pick Derek Harvey from National Security Council", NBC News, July 27, 2017, https://www.nbcnews.com/politics/donald-trump/mcmaster-removes-flynn-pick-derek-harvey-national-security-council-n787146.

14. Kyle Cheney and Andrew Desiderio, "House Releases New Impeachment Evidence Linking Nunes Aide to Parnas," *Politico*, January 17, 2020, https://www.politico.com/news/2020/01/17/devin-nunes-aide-lev-parnas-100732.

15. Paul Sonne et al., "Nunes Aide Communicated with Parnas about Ukraine Campaign, Messages Show," *Washington Post*, January 17, 2020, https://www.washingtonpost.com/national-security/nunes-aide-communicated-with-parnas-about-ukraine-campaign-messages-show/2020/01/17/398ea1f6-3984-11ea-a01d-b7cc8ec1a85d_story.html.

16. Timothy Bella, "'He Knows Who I Am': Lev Parnas Says Devin Nunes Was 'Involved in Getting All This Stuff on Biden,'" *Washington Post*, January 16, 2020, https://www.washingtonpost.com/nation/2020/01/16/parnas-nunes-ukraine/.

17. Sonne et al., "Nunes Aide."

18. Amber Phillips, "The Devin Nunes–Ukraine Allegations, Explained," *Washington Post*, January 18, 2020, https://www.washingtonpost.com/politics/2019/11/25/devin-nunes-ukraine-allegations-explained/.

19. Josh Lederman and Phil Helsel, "New Evidence Shows Nunes Aide Communicated with Parnas on Ukraine," NBC News, January 17, 2020, https://www.nbcnews.com/politics/politics-news/new-evidence-shows-nunes-aide-communicated-parnas-ukraine-n1118251.

20. Austin Wright and Nolan D. McCaskill, "Nunes Apologizes for Going Directly to White House with Monitoring Claims," *Politico*, March 23, 2017, https://www.politico.com/story/2017/03/nunes-apologizes-after-going-directly-to-white-house-with-monitoring-claims-236415.

21. Natasha Bertrand and Darren Samuelsohn, "Lawyers for Ukrainian Oligarch Have Another Client: The Columnist Who Pushed Biden Corruption Claims," *Politico*, October 24, 2019, https://www.politico.com/news/2019/10/24/ukraine-oligarch-lawyers-joe-digenova-victoria-toensing-056643.

22. Jan Wolfe and Karen Freifeld, "Giuliani Associate Will Have Tough Time Keeping Documents from Prosecutors—Experts," Reuters, October 25, 2019, https://www.reuters.com/article/idUSKBN1X4287/.

23. Karen Freifeld and Aram Roston, "Exclusive: Trump Lawyer Giuliani Was Paid $500,000 to Consult on Indicted Associate's Firm," Reuters, October 15, 2019, https://www.reuters.com/article/us-usa-trump-whistleblower-giuliani-excl-idUSKBN1WU07Z/.

24. Andrew E. Kramer, "Ukraine Ousts Viktor Shokin, Top Prosecutor, and Political Stability Hangs in the Balance," *New York Times*, March 29, 2016, https://www.nytimes.com/2016/03/30/world/europe/political-stability-in-the-balance-as-ukraine-ousts-top-prosecutor.html.

25. James Politi et al., "Envoys Pushed to Oust Ukraine Prosecutor before Biden," *Financial Times*, October 3, 2019, https://www.ft.com/content/e1454ace-e61b-11e9-9743-db5a370481bc.

26. "U.S. Ambassador Upbraids Ukrainian Prosecutors Over Anticorruption Efforts", *RFE/RL*, September 25, 2015, https://www.rferl.org/a/us-ambassador-upbraids-ukraine-over-corruption-efforts/27271294.html.

27. Council on Foreign Relations, "Former Vice President Biden on U.S.-Russia Relations," C-SPAN, January 23, 2018, video, 1:19:21, https://www.c-span.org/video/?440141-2/vice-president-biden-us-russia-relations.

28. Nik Martin, "Ukraine's Chief Prosecutor Fired," DW, March 29, 2016, https://www.dw.com/en/ukraine-mps-fire-corruption-tainted-prosecutor/a-19148870.

29. Josh Cohen, "Why Poroshenko's Support for Shokin Is Dangerous," Atlantic Council, November 15, 2015, https://www.atlanticcouncil.org/blogs/ukrainealert/why-poroshenko-s-support-for-shokin-is-dangerous/.

30. "Ukrainian Protesters Demand Dismissal of Prosecutor-General," *RFE/RL*, March 28, 2016, https://www.rferl.org/a/ukraine-protest-prosecutor-shokin-dismissal/27639981.html.

31. Kramer, "Ukraine."

32. Anders Aslund, "Shokin's Revenge: Ukraine's Odious Prosecutor General Fires Honest Deputy before Parliament Sacks Him," Atlantic Council, March 29, 2016, https://www.atlanticcouncil.org/blogs/ukrainealert/shokin-s-revenge-ukraine-s-odious-prosecutor-general-fires-honest-deputy-before-parliament-sacks-him/.

33. Vicky Ward, "Exclusive: Giuliani Associate Willing to Tell Congress Nunes Met with Ex-Ukrainian Official to Get Dirt on Biden," CNN, November 23, 2019, https://edition.cnn.com/2019/11/22/politics/nunes-vienna-trip-ukrainian-prosecutor-biden/index.html.

34. Congressional Record—House, *Report of Expenditures for Official Foreign Travel, Permanent Select Committee on Intelligence, House of Representatives, Expended between Oct. 1 and Dec. 31, 2018,* March 4, 2019, retrieved from the Wayback Machine, version November 27, 2019, https://web.archive.org/web/20191127063520/https://clerk.house.gov/foreign/reports/2019q1mar04.pdf.

35. Ward, "Exclusive: Giuliani Associate."

36. Ward, "Exclusive: Giuliani Associate."

37. Belford and Melkozerova, "Meet."

38. "Part Two of the Lev Parnas Interview. Transcript: 1/16/20, The Rachel Maddow Show," MSNBC, January 16, 2020, https://www.msnbc.com/transcripts/rachel-maddow-show/2020-01-16-msna1323171.

39. Catherine Kim, "New Evidence Shows a Nunes Aide in Close Conversation with Parnas," *Vox*, January 18, 2020, https://www.vox.com/policy-and-politics/2020/1/18/21071683/trump-impeachment-devin-nunes-lev-parnas-intelligence-committee-evidence.

40. Aaron Blake, "New Text Messages Put Devin Nunes on the Hot Seat," *Washington Post*, January 18, 2020, https://www.washingtonpost.com/politics/2020/01/18/new-text-messages-put-devin-nunes-hot-seat/.

41. U.S. House of Representatives, Judiciary Committee, *Excerpts of Text Messages between Lev Parnas and Derek Harvey*, January 17, 2020, retrieved from the Wayback Machine, version January 18, 2020, https://web.archive.org/web/20200118063457/https://judiciary.house.gov/uploadedfiles/document_production_lev_parnas_january_17_2020_whatsapp_excerpts_harvey_with_attachments.pdf.

42. Ellen Nakashima et al., "Giuliani Pressed State Department, White House to Grant Visa to Former Ukrainian Official," *Washington Post*, October 19, 2019, https://www.washingtonpost.com/national-security/giuliani-pressed-state-department-white-house-to-grant-visa-to-former-ukrainian-official/2019/10/18/a105e588-f217-11e9-89eb-ec56cd414732_story.html.

43 Mary Clare Jalonick and Eric Tucker, "Democrats Release New Documents on Eve of Impeachment Trial," Associated Press, January 15, 2020, https://apnews.com/article/bd8dcfc961eb84ccf311dd58f01162bb.

44 Jalonick and Tucker, "Democrats."

45 Manu Raju et al., "Giuliani Pushed Trump Administration to Grant a Visa to a Ukrainian Official Promising Dirt on Democrats," CNN, October 18, 2019, https://edition.cnn.com/2019/10/18/politics/giuliani-shokin-state-visa-george-kent/index.html.

46 Jalonick and Tucker, "Democrats."

47 "Profile: Ukraine's Firebrand Ex-minister Lutsenko," BBC News, January 11, 2014, https://www.bbc.com/news/world-europe-25695982.

48 "Ukraine Ex-Interior Minister Yuri Lutsenko Arrested,"BBC News, December 28, 2010, https://www.bbc.com/news/world-europe-12085959.

49 "Yanukovych Pardons Tymoshenko Ally Lutsenko, Five Others," RFE/RL, April 7, 2013, https://www.rferl.org/a/ukraine-yanukovych-lutsenko-pardon/24950001.html.

50 "Update: Lutsenko Planning to Challenge Criminal Case against Him in Court," Kyiv Post, November 9, 2010, https://archive.kyivpost.com/article/content/ukraine-politics/update-lutsenko-planning-to-challenge-criminal-cas-89332.html.

51 "Lutsenko Pardoned in Ukraine," DW, April 7, 2013, https://www.dw.com/en/ukraine-prisoner-lutsenko-receives-presidential-pardon/a-16725920.

52 "Ukrainian President's Ally Approved for Top Prosecutor's Post," RFE/RL, May 12, 2016, https://www.rferl.org/a/ukraine-prosecutor-general-lutsenko-no-legal-background/27731069.html.

53 Viola Gienger, Ryan Goodman, "Timeline: Trump, Giuliani, Biden, and Ukrainegate," Just Security, January 31, 2020, https://www.justsecurity.org/66271/timeline-trump-giuliani-bidens-and-ukrainegate/.

54 Entous, "Ukrainian Prosecutor."

55 Michael Sallah and Emma Loop, "Two Key Players in the Ukraine Controversy Spent Lavishly as They Dug for Dirt on Biden," BuzzFeed News, October 9, 2019, https://www.buzzfeednews.com/article/mikesallah/ukraine-spending-trump-parnas-fruman.

56 Entous, "Ukrainian Prosecutor."

57 Sallah and Loop, "Two Key Players."

58 Kenneth P. Vogel et al., "How a Shadow Foreign Policy in Ukraine Prompted an Impeachment Inquiry," New York Times, September 28, 2019, https://www.nytimes.com/2019/09/28/us/politics/how-a-shadow-foreign-policy-in-ukraine-prompted-impeachment-inquiry.html.

59 Rebecca Ballhaus et al., "Giuliani Associates Urged Ukraine's Prior President to Open Biden, Election Probes," Wall Street Journal, November 9, 2019, https://www.wsj.com/articles/giuliani-associates-urged-ukraines-prior-president-to-open-biden-election-probes-11573247707.

60 Entous, "Ukrainian Prosecutor."

61 Entous, "Ukrainian Prosecutor."

62 "Rachel Maddow," MSNBC.

63 Andrew E. Kramer et al., "Secret Ledger in Ukraine Lists Cash for Donald Trump's Campaign Chief," New York Times, August 14, 2016, https://www.nytimes.com/2016/08/15/us/politics/what-is-the-black-ledger.html.

64 "FAQ," National Anti-Corruption Bureau of Ukraine, accessed June 23, 2024, https://nabu.gov.ua/en/about-the-bureau/zasadi-roboti/zapytannya-vidpovidi/.

65 "Competence," National Anti-Corruption Bureau of Ukraine, accessed June 23, 2024, https://nabu.gov.ua/en/about-the-bureau/zasadi-roboti/pidslidnist/.

66   Vitaly Chervonenko, "Кто кому в Украине антикоррупционер" [Who is an anti-corruption fighter to whom in Ukraine?]," BBC News, November 21, 2017, https://www.bbc.com/ukrainian/features-russian-42067223.

67   "Луценко: ажиотаж вокруг проверки НАБУ 'ненормальный'" [Lutsenko: the hype around the NABU inspection is "abnormal"]," BBC News, November 17, 2017, https://www.bbc.com/ukrainian/news-russian-42028531.

68   Roman Olearchyk and Neil Buckley, "Ukraine Revolution and President Face Tough Test," *Financial Times*, December 8, 2017, https://www.ft.com/content/3d85a4f6-dc0e-11e7-a039-c64b1c09b482.

69   Entous, "Ukrainian Prosecutor."

70   Ben Protess et al., "Giuliani Pursued Business in Ukraine While Pushing for Inquiries for Trump," *New York Times*, November 27, 2019, https://www.nytimes.com/2019/11/27/nyregion/giuliani-ukraine-business-trump.html.

71   Protess et al., "Giuliani Pursued Business."

72   diGenova & Toensing, LLP, *Retainer Letter for Yuri Lutsenko, Prosecutor General of Ukraine, and Konstantyn Kulyk, Deputy Chief, Dept. of Int'l Legal Cooperation Prosecutor General's Office of Ukraine Dated from April 12, 2019*, uploaded by *Daily Beast*, https://www.documentcloud.org/documents/6568847-DiGenova-Toensing-retainer-Lutsenko.html.

73   Entous, "Ukrainian Prosecutor."

74   Gregg Re, "Clinton-Ukraine Collusion Allegations 'Big' and 'Incredible,' Will Be Reviewed, Trump Says," *Fox News*, April 25, 2019, https://www.foxnews.com/politics/trump-barr-will-look-at-incredible-possibility-of-ukraine-clinton-collusion.

75   diGenova & Toensing, LLP, *Retainer Letter for Mr. Viktor Shokin Dated from April 15, 2019*, uploaded by *Daily Beast*, https://www.documentcloud.org/documents/6568846-DiGenova-Toensing-retainer-Shokin.html.

76   Molly K. McKew, "Did Russia Affect the 2016 Election? It's Now Undeniable," *Wired*, February 16, 2018, https://www.wired.com/story/did-russia-affect-the-2016-election-its-now-undeniable/.

77   John Solomon, "Joe Biden's 2020 Ukrainian Nightmare: A Closed Probe Is Revived," *Hill*, April 1, 2019, https://thehill.com/opinion/white-house/436816-joe-bidens-2020-ukrainian-nightmare-a-closed-probe-is-revived/.

78   James Risen, "Joe Biden, His Son and the Case against a Ukrainian Oligarch," *New York Times*, December 8, 2015, https://www.nytimes.com/2015/12/09/world/europe/corruption-ukraine-joe-biden-son-hunter-biden-ties.html.

79   Bullough, "Money Machine."

80   "Hunter Biden Joins the Team of Burisma Holdings," Burisma, press release, May 12, 2014, retrieved from the Wayback Machine, version June 6, 2014, https://web.archive.org/web/20140606004334/http://burisma.com/hunter-biden-joins-the-team-of-burisma-holdings/.

81   Ivanova, "What Hunter Biden Did."

82   Council on Foreign Relations, "Former Vice President."

83   Leigh Ann Caldwell et al., "Giuliani Says State Dept Vowed to Investigate after He Gave Ukraine Docs to Pompeo," October 3, 2019, https://www.nbcnews.com/politics/trump-impeachment-inquiry/giuliani-says-state-dept-vowed-investigate-after-he-gave-ukraine-n1061931.

84   Entous, "Ukrainian Prosecutor."

85   Entous, "Ukrainian Prosecutor."

86 "Zelenskiy Wins Ukraine's Presidential Election with 73%," Associated Press, April 23, 2019, https://apnews.com/article/26e344daaf68479b8aea88653985e54d.

87 Protess et al., "Giuliani Pursued Business."

CHAPTER 11

1 "House Releases," *Washington Post*.

2 "House Releases," *Washington Post*.

3 Daryna Krasnolutska et al., "Ukraine Prosecutor Says No Evidence of Wrongdoing by Bidens," Bloomberg News, May 16, 2019, https://www.bloomberg.com/news/articles/2019-05-16/ukraine-prosecutor-says-no-evidence-of-wrongdoing-by-bidens.

4 Entous, "Ukrainian Prosecutor."

5 Kateryna Chursina and Daryna Krasnolutska, "Ukraine Top Prosecutor Wants to Keep Job under New President," Bloomberg News, May 15, 2019, https://www.bloomberg.com/news/articles/2019-05-15/ukraine-s-top-prosecutor-wants-to-keep-job-under-new-president.

6 Entous, "Ukrainian Prosecutor."

7 "House Releases," *Washington Post*.

8 Tom Winter et al., "Giuliani Sought Private Meeting with Ukrainian President, Documents Show," NBC News, January 14, 2020, https://www.nbcnews.com/politics/trump-impeachment-inquiry/giuliani-sought-private-meeting-ukrainian-president-documents-show-n1115691.

9 "House Releases," *Washington Post*.

10 Kenneth P. Vogel, "Rudy Giuliani Plans Ukraine Trip to Push for Inquiries That Could Help Trump," *New York Times*, May 9, 2019, https://www.nytimes.com/2019/05/09/us/politics/giuliani-ukraine-trump.html.

11 Winter et al., "Giuliani Sought."

12 "Rachel Maddow," MSNBC.

13 Matt Zapotosky et al. "Prosecutors Flagged Possible Ties between Ukrainian Gas Tycoon and Giuliani Associates," *Washington Post*, October 22, 2019, https://www.washingtonpost.com/politics/prosecutors-flagged-possible-ties-between-ukrainian-gas-tycoon-and-giuliani-associates/2019/10/22/4ee22e7c-f020-11e9-b648-76bcf86eb67e_story.html.

14 Belford and Melkozerova, "Meet."

15 Katelyn Polantz et al., "How Two Businessmen Hustled to Profit from Access to Rudy Giuliani and the Trump Administration," CNN, October 23, 2019, https://www.cnn.com/2019/10/23/politics/parnas-fruman-hustle-profit-access-giuliani/index.html.

16 Vijai Maheshwari, "The Comedian and the Oligarch", *Politico*, April 17, 2019, https://www.politico.eu/article/volodymyr-zelenskiy-ihor-kolomoisky-the-comedian-and-the-oligarch-ukraine-presidential-election/.

17 "Ukraine's Biggest Lender Privatbank Nationalised," BBC News, December 19, 2016, https://www.bbc.com/news/business-38365579.

18 Graham Stack, "Oligarchs Weaponized Cyprus Branch of Ukraine's Largest Bank to Send $5.5 Billion Abroad," OCCRP, April 19, 2019, https://www.occrp.org/en/investigations/oligarchs-weaponized-cyprus-branch-of-ukraines-largest-bank-to-send-5-billion-abroad.

19 Constant Méheut, "Ukraine's Arrest of Powerful Oligarch Is Latest Sign of Anti-Corruption Efforts," *New York Times*, September 4, 2023, https://www.nytimes.com/2023/09/04/world/europe/ihor-kolomoisky-arrest-corruption.html.

20 Betsy Swan, "Billionaire Ukrainian Oligarch Ihor Kolomoisky under Investigation by FBI," *Daily Beast*, April 7, 2019, https://www.thedailybeast.com/billionaire-ukrainian-oligarch-ihor-kolomoisky-under-investigation-by-fbi.

21 Michael Sallah and Tanya Kozyreva, "With Deutsche Bank's Help, Ukrainian Oligarchs Leave a Trail of Ruin in US," OCCRP, September 22, 2020, https://www.occrp.org/en/the-fincen-files/with-deutsche-banks-help-ukrainian-oligarchs-leave-a-trail-of-ruin-in-us.

22 Josh Rogin, "In May, Ukrainian Oligarch Said Giuliani Was Orchestrating a 'Clear Conspiracy against Biden,'" opinion, *Washington Post*, October 3, 2019, https://www.washingtonpost.com/opinions/2019/10/03/may-ukrainian-oligarch-said-giuliani-was-orchestrating-clear-conspiracy-against-biden/.

23 Jo Becker et al., "Why Giuliani Singled Out Two Ukrainian Oligarchs to Help Look for Dirt", *New York Times*, November 25, 2019, https://www.nytimes.com/2019/11/25/us/giuliani-ukraine-oligarchs.html.

24 Ben Schreckinger, "Ukraine Scandal Ropes in the Usual Suspects", *Politico*, October 3, 2019, https://www.politico.eu/article/ukraine-scandal-ropes-in-the-usual-suspects-digenova-toensing-firtash/.

25 Belford and Melkozerova, "Meet."

26 Michael Sallah, Tanya Kozyreva, Aubrey Belford, "Two Unofficial US Operatives Reporting to Trump's Lawyer Privately Lobbied a Foreign Government in a Bid to Help the President Win in 2020," *BuzzFeed News*, July 22, 2019, https://www.buzzfeednews.com/article/mikesallah/rudy-giuliani-ukraine-trump-parnas-fruman.

27 Rosalind S. Helderman and Tom Hamburger, "Giuliani Associates Claimed to Have Sway with Both Foreign Billionaires and Trump Administration Officials," *Washington Post*, October 26, 2019, https://www.washingtonpost.com/politics/giuliani-associates-claimed-to-have-sway-with-both-foreign-billionaires-and-trump-administration-officials/2019/10/26/c564139e-f791-11e9-8cf0-4cc99f74d127_story.html.

28 Sallah et al., "Two Unofficial US Operatives."

29 Rudy Giuliani (@RudyGiuliani), "Billionaire Ukrainian Oligarch Ihor Kolomoisky Under Investigation by FBI He has now returned to Ukraine from exile in Israel and the first thing he did is threaten American citizens. This is real test for President. Will he be arrested?" Twitter, May 18, 2019, 11:30 a.m., https://twitter.com/rudygiuliani/status/1129756189707984898?lang=en.

30 "House Releases," *Washington Post*.

31 Becker et al., "Why."

32 Roston et al., "Exclusive: Giuliani."

33 Tom Winter et al., "Who Is Dmytro Firtash? The Man Linked to $1 Million Loan to Giuliani Ally Has a Shadowy Past," NBC News, January 25, 2020, https://www.nbcnews.com/politics/politics-news/who-dmytro-firtash-man-linked-1-million-loan-giuliani-ally-n1121561.

34 Becker et al., "Why."

35 "Six Defendants Indicted in Alleged Conspiracy to Bribe Government Officials in India to Mine Titanium Minerals," Office of Public Affairs, U.S. Department of Justice, press release, April 2, 2014, https://www.justice.gov/opa/pr/six-defendants-indicted-alleged-conspiracy-bribe-government-officials-india-mine-titanium.

36 Ostap Yarysh, "Austria: Firtash Extradition to US Blocked by 'Extensive' Bid to Reopen Case," Voice of America, July 16, 2019, https://www.voanews.com/a/europe_austria-firtash-extradition-us-blocked-extensive-bid-reopen-case/6171994.html.

37 Winter et al., "Who Is Dmytro Firtash?"

38. Becker et al., "Why."
39. Julia Manchester, "Giuliani Attacks Davis for Representing Indicted Ukrainian Figure," *Hill*, March 11, 2019, https://thehill.com/hilltv/rising/433224-giuliani-attacks-davis-for-representing-indicted-Russian-figure/.
40. Tom Winter, "DOJ: Ex-Manafort Associate Firtash Is Top-Tier Comrade of Russian Mobsters," NBC News, July 26, 2017, https://www.nbcnews.com/news/us-news/doj-ex-manafort-associate-firtash-top-tier-comrade-russian-mobsters-n786806.
41. Stephen Grey et al., "Special Report-Putin's Allies Channelled Billions to Ukraine Oligarch," Reuters, November 26, 2014, https://www.reuters.com/article/russia-capitalism-gas-special-report-pix-idUSL3N0TF4QD20141126/.
42. Winter et al., "Who Is Dmytro Firtash?"
43. Todd Prince, "Dmytro Firtash: Who Is the Ukrainian Tycoon Wanted by the U.S. on Bribery Charges?," *RFE/RL*, June 25, 2019, https://www.rferl.org/a/dmytro-firtash-who-is-the-ukrainian-tycoon-wanted-by-the-u-s-on-bribery-charges-/30020239.html.
44. Simon Shuster, "Exclusive: How a Ukrainian Oligarch Wanted by U.S. Authorities Helped Giuliani Attack Biden," *Time*, October 15, 2019, https://time.com/5699201/exclusive-how-a-ukrainian-oligarch-wanted-by-u-s-authorities-helped-giuliani-attack-biden/.
45. Grey et al., "Special Report-Putin's Allies."
46. Grey et al., "Special Report-Putin's Allies."
47. Agustino Fontevecchia and Yuri Aksyonov, "When an Oligarch Is Not a Billionaire: The Case of Ukraine's Dmitry Firtash," *Forbes*, March 15, 2014, https://www.forbes.com/sites/afontevecchia/2014/03/14/when-an-oligarch-is-not-a-billionaire-the-case-of-ukraines-dmitry-firtash/?sh=339165f31b33.
48. Oliver Bullough, "Gas-Powered Kingmaker: How the UK Welcomed Putin's Man in Ukraine," *Guardian*, March 8, 2022, https://www.theguardian.com/news/2022/mar/08/gas-powered-kingmaker-uk-welcomed-putin-dmitry-firtash-ukraine.
49. "Six Defendants," Office of Public Affairs, U.S. Department of Justice.
50. David M. Herszenhorn, "At Request of U.S., Austria Arrests Ukrainian Businessman," *New York Times*, March 13, 2014, https://www.nytimes.com/2014/03/14/world/europe/ukrainian-billionaire-arrested-in-austria.html.
51. Alexander Weber and Boris Groendahl, "Firtash Stays in Custody as $174 Million Bail Is Set," *Bloomberg News*, March 14, 2014, https://www.bloomberg.com/news/articles/2014-03-14/firtash-stays-in-custody-as-174-million-bail-is-set?embedded-checkout=true.
52. Winter et al., "Who Is Dmytro Firtash?"
53. Simona Weinglass, "Inside Anatevka, the Curious Chabad Hamlet in Ukraine Where Giuliani Is 'Mayor,'" *The Times of Israel*, January 31, 2020, https://www.timesofisrael.com/inside-anatevka-the-curious-chabad-hamlet-in-ukraine-where-giuliani-is-mayor/.
54. Parnas, "Exclusive."
55. Becker et al., "Why."
56. Rosalind S. Helderman et al., "How Giuliani's Outreach to Ukrainian Gas Tycoon Wanted in U.S. Shows Lengths He Took in His Hunt for Material to Bolster Trump," *Washington Post*, January 15, 2020, https://www.washingtonpost.com/politics/how-giulianis-outreach-to-ukrainian-gas-tycoon-wanted-in-us-shows-lengths-he-took-in-his-hunt-for-material-to-bolster-trump/2020/01/15/64c263ba-2e5f-11ea-bcb3-ac6482c4a92f_story.html.

57 Aruna Viswanatha et al., "Two Giuliani Associates Who Helped Him on Ukraine Charged with Campaign-Finance Violations," *Wall Street Journal*, October 10, 2019, https://www.wsj.com/articles/two-foreign-born-men-who-helped-giuliani-on-ukraine-arrested-on-campaign-finance-charges-11570714188?mod=hp_lead_pos1.

58 Helderman et al., "How Giuliani's Outreach."

59 Philip Bump, "Lev Parnas's Handwritten Notes about Giuliani's Ukraine Push, Annotated," *Washington Post*, January 15, 2019, https://www.washingtonpost.com/politics/2020/01/15/lev-parnass-handwritten-notes-about-giulianis-ukraine-push-annotated/.

60 Philip Bump, "Ukraine Efforts Seem to Extend Further than We Knew," *Washington Post*, November 25, 2019, https://www.washingtonpost.com/politics/2019/11/25/tendrils-giulianis-unofficial-ukraine-efforts-seem-extend-further-than-we-knew/.

61 Bump, "Ukraine Efforts."

62 Kramer et al., "Secret Ledger."

63 Sergii Leshchenko, "Sergii Leshchenko: The True Story of Yanukovych's Black Ledger," *Kyiv Post*, November 24, 2019, https://archive.kyivpost.com/article/opinion/op-ed/sergii-leshchenko-the-true-story-of-yanukovychs-black-ledger.html.

64 Simon Shuster, "How Paul Manafort Helped Elect Russia's Man in Ukraine", *Time*, October 31, 2019, https://time.com/5003623/paul-manafort-mueller-indictment-ukraine-russia/.

65 Kramer et al., "Secret Ledger."

66 Rachel Weiner, "Paul Manafort Made More than $60 Million in Ukraine, Prosecutors Say," *Washington Post*, July 30, 2018, https://www.washingtonpost.com/local/public-safety/paul-manafort-made-more-than-60-million-in-ukraine-prosecutors-say/2018/07/30/dfe5b47c-9417-11e8-810c-5fa705927d54_story.html.

67 Spencer S. Hsu et al. "Paul Manafort Sentenced to a Total of 7.5 Years in Prison for Conspiracy and Fraud, and Charged with Mortgage Fraud in N.Y.," *Washington Post*, March 13, 2019, https://www.washingtonpost.com/local/legal-issues/paul-manafort-faces-sentencing-in-washington-in-mueller-special-counsel-case/2019/03/12/d4d55dd4-44d0-11e9-aaf8-4512a6fe3439_story.html.

68 "Corrected: Austrian Court Clears Way for U.S. Extradition of Ukrainian Tycoon Firtash," Reuters, June 26, 2019, https://www.reuters.com/article/us-ukraine-usa-firtash-idUSKCN1TQ1AV/.

69 Helderman et al., "How Giuliani's Outreach."

70 Parnas and Langton, *Shadow Diplomacy*, chap. 1, Kindle.

71 Helderman et al., "How Giuliani's Outreach."

72 Shuster, "Exclusive."

73 "Rachel Maddow," MSNBC.

74 Helderman et al., "How Giuliani's Outreach."

75 U.S. Department of Justice, *Amendment to Registration Statement Pursuant to the Foreign Agents Registration Act of 1938, as Amended, Filed by Davis, Goldberg & Galper, PLLC*, Registration No. 6394, July 23, 2019, https://efile.fara.gov/docs/6394-Amendment-20190723-3.pdf.

76 Bertrand and Samuelsohn, "Lawyers."

77 Winter et al., "Who Is Dmytro Firtash?"

78 William K. Rashbaum and Ben Protess, "Giuliani Is Unlikely to Face Criminal Charges in Lobbying Inquiry," *New York Times*, August 3, 2022, https://www.nytimes.com/2022/08/03/us/giuliani-charges-lobbying-inquiry-trump.html.

79 Winter et al., "Who Is Dmytro Firtash?"

80 Shuster, "Exclusive."
81 "Rachel Maddow," MSNBC.
82 John Solomon, "How Mueller Deputy Andrew Weissmann's Offer to an Oligarch Could Boomerang on DOJ," opinion, *Hill*, July 22, 2019, https://thehill.com/opinion/white-house/454185-how-mueller-deputy-andrew-weissmanns-offer-to-an-oligarch-could-boomerang/.
83 Zapotosky et al., "Prosecutors."
84 U.S. Department of Justice, FOIA Library, *Former Attorney General William Barr's Calendar, May 15, 2019–May 4, 2020*, FOIA-2020-00677, pg. 107, https://www.justice.gov/oip/foia-library/foia-processed/general_topics/bill_barrs_calendars_04_29_21/dl.
85 Zapotosky et al., "Prosecutors."
86 Helderman et al., "How Giuliani's Outreach."
87 *Witness statement of Viktor Mikolajovich Shokin, September 4, 2019*, Factcheck.org, accessed June 24, 2024, https://cdn.factcheck.org/UploadedFiles/427618359-Shokin-Statement-1.pdf.
88 *Witness Statement*, FactCheck.org.
89 Helderman et al., "How Giuliani's Outreach."
90 John Solomon, "Solomon: These Once-Secret Memos Cast Doubt on Joe Biden's Ukraine Story," opinion, *Hill*, September 26, 2019, https://thehill.com/opinion/campaign/463307-solomon-these-once-secret-memos-cast-doubt-on-joe-bidens-ukraine-story/.
91 Williams et al., "Full Document."
92 "Read: Whistleblower Whistleblower Complaint Regarding President President Trump and Ukraine," CNN, September 26, 2019, https://edition.cnn.com/2019/09/26/politics/read-whistleblower-complaint-trump-ukraine/index.html.
93 "'I Wouldn't Cooperate with Adam Schiff': Giuliani | ABC News," ABC News, September 29, 2019, video, 14:53, https://www.youtube.com/watch?v=g3O2Ss0t31k.
94 "Giuliani: Democrats Stepped into More than They Realize," Fox News, September 25, 2019, video, 13:26, https://www.youtube.com/watch?v=pPsiSM4H8ZY.
95 "Giuliani Slams 'Swamp Media,' Says It's Time to Fight back against Dems," Fox News, October 2, 2019, video, 13:25, https://www.youtube.com/watch?v=fuX6YQBLOa0.
96 "Exclusive: Giuliani Reacts to Impeachment Inquiry after Series of Hearings," Fox News, November 23, 2019, video, 14:22, https://www.youtube.com/watch?v=u8WJtT3vINE.
97 "Giuliani Admits to Forcing Out Yovanovitch: 'She's Corrupt,'" Fox News, December 16, 2019, video, 9:22, https://www.youtube.com/watch?v=qFCeznGIXKs.
98 "Giuliani: I Can't Sit by and Watch My Country Be Sold Out by Joe Biden," Fox News, January 24, 2020, video, 12:59, https://www.youtube.com/watch?v=hCm9HkVaVYk.
99 "Rudy Giuliani Lays Out the Biden's Corruption in Ukraine", Fox News, February 9, 2020, video, 12:49, https://www.youtube.com/watch?v=vxvoFfjn2do.
100 "Rachel Maddow," MSNBC.
101 "Giuliani Subpoenaed," U.S. House of Representatives Committee on Foreign Affairs.
102 Helderman et al., "How Giuliani's Outreach."
103 Zapotosky et al., "Prosecutors."
104 John Santucci et al., "Pence, Giuliani Defy Demands by Congress for Documents," ABC News, October 15, 2019, https://abcnews.go.com/Politics/pence-giuliani-defy-demands-congress-documents/story?id=66293635.

105 Devan Cole, "*New York Times*: Giuliani Traveled to Hungary and Ukraine to Meet with Ex-Prosecutors in Effort to Defend Trump," CNN, December 4, 2019, https://edition.cnn.com/2019/12/04/politics/rudy-giuliani-ukraine-visit-interviews-documentary/index.html.

106 Natasha Bertrand and Theodoric Meyer, "Trump Let OANN in the White House. Now It's Biden's Problem," *Politico*, March 24, 2021, https://www.politico.com/newsletters/transition-playbook/2021/03/24/bidens-oann-conundrum-492230.

107 Christopher Miller, "Rudy Giuliani Flew into Ukraine in a Budget Flight. He Left on a Private Jet," *BuzzFeed News*, December 18, 2019, https://www.buzzfeednews.com/article/christopherm51/snakes-on-a-plane.

108 Michael Caputo, "'The Ukraine Hoax: Impeachment, Biden Cash, Mass Murder' Debuting This Weekend on OAN," interviewed by Jack Posobiec, OAN, January 24, 2020, https://www.youtube.com/watch?v=AvWddGJJtE4.

109 Christopher Miller, "Rudy Giuliani Made a Surprise Visit to Kyiv and Nobody There Is Happy about It," *BuzzFeed News*, December 5, 2019, https://www.buzzfeednews.com/article/christopherm51/rudy-giuliani-kyiv-ukraine-impeachment.

110 Cole, "*New York Times*."

111 Entous, "Ukrainian Prosecutor."

112 Kenneth P. Vogel and Benjamin Novak, "Giuliani, Facing Scrutiny, Travels to Europe to Interview Ukrainians," *New York Times*, December 4, 2019, https://www.nytimes.com/2019/12/04/us/politics/giuliani-europe-impeachment.html.

113 Bermet Talant, "Right-Wing TV Channel Offers Improbable Account of Giuliani's Visit to Kyiv," *Kyiv Post*, December 9, 2019, https://www.kyivpost.com/post/9344.

114 Anne Applebaum, "The Science of Making Americans Hurt Their Own Country," *Atlantic*, March 19, 2021, https://www.theatlantic.com/ideas/archive/2021/03/russia-studied-how-get-americans-make-mistakes/618328/.

115 Olivia Rubin et al., "Giuliani in Ukraine with Conservative News Outlet in Effort to Discredit Impeachment Probe," *ABC News*, December 5, 2019, https://abcnews.go.com/Politics/rudy-giuliani-ukraine-impeachment-marches-forward-washington/story?id=67519317.

116 Matt Gertz, "Likely Russia-Backed OAN Film Features Ukrainian Sanctioned for Trying to Influence 2020 Election, Devin Nunes," Media Matters, March 19, 2021, https://www.mediamatters.org/one-america-news-network/inside-2020-oan-documentary-may-have-been-aided-russian-proxies.

117 "OAN Investigates," OAN, December 16, 2019, retrieved from the Wayback Machine, version December 17, 2019, https://web.archive.org/web/20191217054223/https://www.oann.com/oaninvestigates/.

118 Rudy Giuliani (@RudyGiuliani), "Working on an important project with @OANN, intended to bring before the American people information Schiff (recently disclosed investor in Franklin Templton) 'Star chamber' proceedings have covered up. Stay tuned," Twitter, December 3, 2019, 9:52 a.m., https://twitter.com/RudyGiuliani/status/1201846610956824576.

119 Donald J. Trump (@realDonaldTrump), "@OANN is doing incredible reporting. If Lamestream Media did the same, they would get respect back. At All-Time Low!" Twitter, December 27, 2019, 11;28 p.m., https://twitter.com/realDonaldTrump/status/1210749216307286016.

120 Vandana Rambaran, "Giuliani Says His Ukraine Trip This Week Is Linked to TV Documentary Defending Trump," Fox News, December 4, 2019, https://www.foxnews.com/media/giuliani-says-hes-meeting-with-ukrainians-for-documentary-arguing-trump-was-framed.

121 Rachel Frazin, "Giuliani Meets with Fired Ukrainian Prosecutor Who Pushed Biden, 2016 Claims: Report," *Hill*, December 4, 2019, https://thehill.com/policy/national-security/473014-giuliani-meets-with-fired-ukrainian-prosecutor-who-pushed-biden-2016/?_recirculation=1&jwsource=cl.

122 Michael Calderone, "'Stunning Piece of Propaganda': Journalists Blast One America News Series," *Politico*, December 19, 2019, https://www.politico.com/news/2019/12/19/journalists-blast-one-america-news-series-giuliani-087893.

123 Aaron Blake, "One America News's Ukraine-Rudy Giuliani Exposé Is a Stunning Piece of Propaganda," *Washington Post*, December 16, 2019, https://www.washingtonpost.com/politics/2019/12/16/one-america-newss-ukraine-rudy-giuliani-expose-is-stunning-piece-propaganda/.

124 "Statement by NCSC Director William Evanina: Election Threat Update for the American Public," Office of the Director of National Intelligence, press release, August 7, 2020, retrieved from the Wayback Machine, version August 7, 2020, https://web.archive.org/web/20200807184418/https://www.dni.gov/index.php/newsroom/press-releases/item/2139-statement-by-ncsc-director-william-evanina-election-threat-update-for-the-american-public.

125 "Treasury Sanctions Russia-Linked Election Interference Actors," U.S. Department of the Treasury, press release, September 10, 2020, https://home.treasury.gov/news/press-releases/sm1118.

126 Josh Rogin, "Secret CIA Assessment: Putin 'Probably Directing' Influence Operation to Denigrate Biden," opinion, *Washington Post*, September 22, 2020, https://www.washingtonpost.com/opinions/2020/09/22/secret-cia-assessment-putin-probably-directing-influence-operation-denigrate-biden/.

127 Shane Harris et al., "White House Was Warned Giuliani Was Target of Russian Intelligence Operation to Feed Misinformation to Trump," *Washington Post*, October 15, 2020, https://www.washingtonpost.com/national-security/giuliani-biden-ukraine-russian-disinformation/2020/10/15/43158900-0ef5-11eb-b1e8-16b59b92b36d_story.html.

128 Julian E. Barnes et al., "Trump Said to Be Warned That Giuliani Was Conveying Russian Disinformation," *New York Times*, October 15, 2020, https://www.nytimes.com/2020/10/15/us/politics/giuliani-russian-disinformation.html.

129 Harris et al., "White House."

130 Ryan Lucas, "Giuliani Distances Himself from Ukrainian Sanctioned by U.S. as Russian Agent," NPR, September 11, 2020, https://www.npr.org/2020/09/11/911957914/giuliani-distances-himself-from-ukrainian-sanctioned-by-u-s-as-russian-agent.

131 Dana Bash et al., "Pelosi Calls Out 'President's Betrayal of His Oath of Office' in Announcing Formal Impeachment Inquiry," CNN, September 24, 2019, https://edition.cnn.com/2019/09/24/politics/democrats-impeachment-strategy/index.html.

132 Elaina Plott Calabro, "Rudy Giuliani: 'You Should Be Happy for Your Country That I Uncovered This,'" *Atlantic*, September 26, 2019, https://www.theatlantic.com/politics/archive/2019/09/giuliani-ukraine-trump-biden/598879/.

CHAPTER 12

1 International Energy Agency, *Ukraine Energy Policy Review 2006* (Paris, OECD/IEA, 2006), pg. 5.

2 Grey et al., "Special Report-Putin's Allies."

3   Andrew E. Kramer, "Ukraine Gas Deal Draws Attention to Secretive Importer," *New York Times*, February 1, 2006, https://www.nytimes.com/2006/02/01/business/worldbusiness/ukraine-gas-deal-draws-attention-to-secretive.html.

4   "Factbox: RUE: A Mystery Player in Russia-Ukraine Gas Row," Reuters, January 3, 2009, https://www.reuters.com/article/us-russia-ukraine-gas-rosukrenergo-sb-idUSTRE5021BN20090103/.

5   Isobel Koshiw, "Dmytro Firtash: The Oligarch Who Can't Come Home," *Kyiv Post*, December 9, 2016, https://www.kyivpost.com/post/7532.

6   "Putin, in Ukraine, Praises Government Days before Election," RFE/RL, October 26, 2004, https://www.rferl.org/a/1055534.html.

7   Nick Paton Walsh, "Putin's Kiev Visit 'Timed to Influence Ukraine Poll,'" *Guardian*, October 27, 2004, https://www.theguardian.com/world/2004/oct/27/ukraine.russia.

8   Askold Krushelnycky, "Ukraine: Voters Brace for Presidential Runoff amid Allegations of Dirty Tricks," RFE/RL, November 19, 2004, https://www.rferl.org/a/1055970.html.

9   Peter Finn, "Yushchenko Was Poisoned, Doctors Say," *Washington Post*, December 12, 2004, https://www.washingtonpost.com/archive/politics/2004/12/12/yushchenko-was-poisoned-doctors-say/38b08066-c0b6-4c82-bb87-f109592fd390/.

10 "Widespread Campaign Irregularities Observed in Ukrainian Presidential Election," OSCE, press release, November 1, 2004, https://www.osce.org/odihr/elections/56794.

11 "Commission Declares Yanukovych the Winner," RFE/RL, November 24, 2004, https://www.rferl.org/a/1056036.html.

12 Steven Lee Myers, "Ukrainian Court Orders New Vote for Presidency, Citing Fraud," *New York Times*, December 4, 2004, https://www.nytimes.com/2004/12/04/world/europe/ukrainian-court-orders-new-vote-for-presidency-citing-fraud.html.

13 "Ukraine Readies for Election Re-Run," Al Jazeera, December 4, 2004, https://www.aljazeera.com/news/2004/12/4/ukraine-readies-for-election-re-run.

14 "Yushchenko Wins Ukraine's Presidency," *Guardian*, December 27, 2004, https://www.theguardian.com/world/2004/dec/27/ukraine.

15 Koshiw, "Dmytro Firtash."

16 Koshiw, "Dmytro Firtash."

17 Evgeny Golovatyuk, "Путь Фирташа от помидоров до тюрьмы" [Firtash's journey from tomatoes to prison], *Liga*, February 23, 2017, https://project.liga.net/projects/firtash/.

18 Igor Oryol, "Круг замкнулся. Зачем государство забирает у Фирташа облгазы и возвращает себе монополию на рынке распределения газа" [The circle is closed. Why is the state taking away regional gas companies from Firtash and regaining its monopoly on the gas distribution market?], *Forbes Ukraine*, May 26, 2022, https://forbes.ua/ru/inside/kolo-zamknulosya-navishcho-derzhava-zabirae-u-firtasha-oblgazi-i-povertae-sobi-monopoliyu-na-rinku-rozpodilu-gazu-26052022-6249.

19 "SBU: Firtash, Top Associates Accused of Embezzling Millions of Hryvnias Worth of State Gas," *Kyiv Independent*, May 15, 2023, https://kyivindependent.com/sbu-gas-scandal-firtash/.

20 "Gas Crises between Russia and Ukraine," Reuters, January 12, 2009, https://www.reuters.com/article/us-russia-ukraine-gas-timeline-sb-idUSTRE50A1A720090111/.

21 "Russia, Ukraine Sign Deal to Settle Gas Dispute," PBS, January 19, 2009, https://www.pbs.org/newshour/economy/europe-jan-june09-gas_01-19.

22 "Russia, Ukraine Sign Deal, End Gas Dispute," NBC News, January 18, 2009, https://www.nbcnews.com/id/wbna28720641.

23 Grey et al., "Special Report-Putin's Allies."

24 Shuster, "How Paul Manafort."

25 Tom Bergin and Stephen Grey, "Opaque Middlemen Exact High Price in Russia's Deals with the West," Reuters, December 19, 2014, https://www.reuters.com/investigates/special-report/russia/.

26 Bergin and Grey, "Opaque Middlemen."

27 Ian Traynor and Oksana Grytsenko, "Ukraine Suspends Talks on EU Trade Pact as Putin Wins Tug of War," *Guardian*, November 21, 2013, https://www.theguardian.com/world/2013/nov/21/ukraine-suspends-preparations-eu-trade-pact.

28 Steven Pifer and Hannah Thoburn, "Viktor Yanukovych: Losing Europe . . . and Losing the Ukrainian Public?" Brookings Institution, November 18, 2013, https://www.brookings.edu/articles/viktor-yanukovych-losing-europe-and-losing-the-ukrainian-public/.

29 Elizabeth Piper, "Special Report: Why Ukraine Spurned the EU and Embraced Russia," Reuters, December 19, 2013, https://www.reuters.com/article/us-ukraine-russia-deal-special-report-idUSBRE9BI0DZ20131219/.

30 "Ukraine Protests after Yanukovych EU Deal Rejection," BBC News, November 30, 2013, https://www.bbc.com/news/world-europe-25162563.

31 David M. Herszenhorn, "Unrest Deepens in Ukraine as Protests Turn Deadly," *New York Times*, January 22, 2014, https://www.nytimes.com/2014/01/23/world/europe/ukraine-protests.html.

32 Ian Traynor, "Ukraine's Bloodiest Day: Dozens Dead as Kiev Protesters Regain Territory from Police," *Guardian*, February 21, 2014, https://www.theguardian.com/world/2014/feb/20/ukraine-dead-protesters-police.

33 Laura Smith-Spark, et al., "Ukraine Government Resigns, Parliament Scraps Anti-Protest Laws amid Crisis," CNN, January 28, 2014, https://edition.cnn.com/2014/01/28/world/europe/ukraine-protests/index.html.

34 William Booth, "Ukraine's Parliament Votes to Oust President; Former Prime Minister Is Freed from Prison," *Washington Post*, February 22, 2014, https://www.washingtonpost.com/world/europe/ukraines-yanukovych-missing-as-protesters-take-control-of-presidential-residence-in-kiev/2014/02/22/802f7c6c-9bd2-11e3-ad71-e03637a299c0_story.html.

35 Howard Amos et al., "Ukraine's New Government Is Not Legitimate—Dmitry Medvedev," *Guardian*, February 24, 2014, https://www.theguardian.com/world/2014/feb/24/ukraine-viktor-yanukovych-arrest-warrant.

36 Shaun Walker, "Ukraine's Former PM Rallies Protesters after Yanukovych Flees Kiev," *Guardian*, February 23, 2014, https://www.theguardian.com/world/2014/feb/22/ukraine-president-yanukovych-flees-kiev.

37 "Putin: Russia Helped Yanukovych to Flee Ukraine," BBC News, October 24, 2014, https://www.bbc.com/news/world-europe-29761799.

38 "Toppled 'Mafia' President Cost Ukraine up to $100 Billion, Prosecutor Says," Reuters, April 30, 2014, https://www.reuters.com/article/us-ukraine-crisis-yanukovich-idUSBREA3T0K820140430/.

39 "EU Freezes Assets of Ukrainians for Fund Misuse," Associated Press, March 5, 2014, https://apnews.com/article/8981d717fc9f4eba8e9625a0c9e702f2.

40 Michael Shields and Angelika Gruber, "Ukrainian Gas Oligarch Firtash Arrested in Vienna on FBI Warrant," Reuters, March 13, 2014, https://www.reuters.com/article/us-ukraine-austria-firtash-idUSBREA2C14V20140313/.

41 Elizabeth Landau et al., "In Crimea, Worlds Collide," CNN, March 6, 2014, https://edition.cnn.com/2014/03/05/world/europe/ukraine-crimea-local-color/index.html.

42 "Pro-Russian Separatists Declare 'Independence' for Donetsk," France 24, April 7, 2014, https://www.france24.com/en/20140407-pro-russian-separatists-declare-independence-donetsk-ukraine.

43 Paul Kirby, "Russia's Gas Fight with Ukraine," BBC News, October 31, 2014, https://www.bbc.com/news/world-europe-29521564.

44 Viacheslav Shramovych, "Ukraine's Deadliest Day: The Battle of Ilovaisk, August 2014," BBC News, August 28, 2014, https://www.bbc.com/news/world-europe-49426724.

45 Shaun Walker, "Ukraine Ceasefire 'Agreed for East of Country' at Minsk Peace Talks," *Guardian*, September 5, 2014, https://www.theguardian.com/world/2014/sep/05/ukraine-ceasefire-east-minsk-peace-talks.

46 Laura Smith-Spark and Nic Robertson, "What Happens after Ukraine Peace Deal?" CNN, February 12, 2015, https://edition.cnn.com/2015/02/12/europe/ukraine-what-happens-next/index.html.

47 "Ukraine-Russia Crisis: What Is the Minsk Agreement?" *Al Jazeera*, February 9, 2022, https://www.aljazeera.com/news/2022/2/9/what-is-the-minsk-agreement-and-why-is-it-relevant-now.

48 David M. Herszenhorn, "Merkel and Hollande Fail to 'Achieve Miracles' on Ukraine," *Politico*, October 20, 2016, https://www.politico.eu/article/angela-merkel-and-francois-hollande-fail-to-achieve-miracles-on-ukraine/.

49 Steven Erlanger and David M. Herszenhorn, "I.M.F. Prepares $18 Billion in Loans for Ukraine," *New York Times*, March 27, 2014, https://www.nytimes.com/2014/03/28/world/europe/ukraine-bailout.html.

50 Natalia Zinets, "IMF Agrees $14–18 Billion Bailout for Ukraine," Reuters, March 27, 2014, https://www.reuters.com/article/us-ukraine-crisis-imf-idUSBREA2Q1OH20140327/.

51 Svitlana Pyrkalo, "EBRD, Ukraine Agree Naftogaz Reform, Sign US$ 300 Million Loan for Winter Gas Purchase," European Bank for Reconstruction and Development, October 23, 2015, https://www.ebrd.com/news/2015/ebrd-ukraine-agree-naftogaz-reform-sign-us-300-million-loan-for-winter-gas-purchases.html.

52 OECD Anti-Corruption Network for Eastern Europe and Central Asia, *Support to Ukraine in the Area of Anti-Corruption*, 2021, https://www.oecd.org/corruption/anti-bribery/corruption/acn/Support-to-Ukraine-in-the-area-of-Anti-Corruption-professional-development-of-NABU-and-SAPO.pdf.

53 Daryna Krasnolutska and Kateryna Chursina, "EBRD Approves $300 Million Loan for Ukraine Winter Gas," Bloomberg News, September 30, 2015, https://www.bloomberg.com/news/articles/2015-09-30/ebrd-approves-300-million-loan-for-ukraine-winter-gas-purchase.

54 Pyrkalo, "EBRD, Ukraine Agree."

55 "Ukraine's Government Appoints New Supervisory Board of Naftogaz," Naftogaz Group, November 22, 2017, https://www.naftogaz.com/en/news/kabmin-zatverdyv-novyy-sklad-naglyadovoi-rady-naftogazu.

56 Simon Shuster and Ilya Marritz, "Exclusive: As Energy Secretary, Rick Perry Mixed Money and Politics in Ukraine. The Deals Could Be Worth Billions," *Time*, September 10, 2020, https://time.com/5887230/rick-perry-deals-energy-ukraine/.

57 Shuster and Marritz, "Rick Perry's."

58 "In Light of New Evidence of Trump Administration Wrongdoing Uncovered during Senate Republican Investigation, Wyden Requests Inspector General Investigation," United States Senate Committee on Finance, September 23, 2020, https://www.finance.senate.gov/ranking-members-news/in-light-of-new-evidence-of-trump-administration-wrongdoing-uncovered-during-senate-republican-investigation-wyden-requests-inspector-general-investigation.

59 Kenneth P. Vogel et al., "Rick Perry's Focus on Gas Company Entangles Him in Ukraine Case," *New York Times*, October 7, 2019, https://www.nytimes.com/2019/10/07/us/politics/rick-perry-ukraine.html.

60. Shuster and Marritz, "Exclusive."
61. "U.S. Senate Confirms Trump Pick Perry as Energy Secretary," Reuters, March 2, 2017, https://www.reuters.com/article/us-usa-trump-perry-idUSKBN1692NE/.
62. Niraj Chokshi, "Perry Ranks among Top Longest-Serving U.S. Governors," *Texas Tribune*, January 20, 2015, https://www.texastribune.org/2015/01/20/perry-ranks-among-top-longest-serving-us-governors/.
63. Patrick Svitek, "Rick Perry Resigns from Board of Dallas Company Building Dakota Access Pipeline," *Texas Tribune*, January 5, 2017, https://www.texastribune.org/2017/01/05/perry-tapped-energy-secretary-resigns-pipeline-com/.
64. Shuster and Marritz, "Exclusive."
65. Emily S. Rueb, "'Freedom Gas,' the Next American Export," *New York Times*, May 29, 2019, https://www.nytimes.com/2019/05/29/us/freedom-gas-energy-department.html.
66. Shuster and Marritz, "Exclusive."
67. "Lake Charles LNG Export Project," NS Energy, July 1, 2022, https://www.nsenergybusiness.com/projects/lake-charles-lng-export-project/.
68. "Lake Charles," NS Energy.
69. Butler and Biesecker, "Giuliani Pals."
70. Brian Bonner, "Kobolyev Says Naftogaz's Achievements under Attack," *Kyiv Post*, February 12, 2019, https://archive.kyivpost.com/business/kobolyev-says-naftogazs-achievements-under-attack.html.
71. Ben Protess and Kenneth P. Vogel, "Recording Surfaces of Another Trump Meeting with Parnas and Fruman," *New York Times*, January 30, 2020, https://www.nytimes.com/2020/01/30/us/politics/trump-parnas-fruman-tape.html.
72. Timothy Puko, "Perry Wanted U.S. Energy Veterans on Naftogaz Board, Messages Say," *Wall Street Journal*, November 5, 2019, https://www.wsj.com/articles/perry-wanted-u-s-energy-veterans-on-naftogaz-board-messages-say-11573004023.
73. "In Light of New Evidence," United States Senate Committee on Finance.
74. "SigmaBleyzer Overview," Pitchbook, accessed June 26, 2024, https://pitchbook.com/profiles/investor/10990-27#overview.
75. Justin Miller, "Rick Perry Exports His Pay-to-Play Politics to Ukraine," *Texas Observer*, November 13, 2019, https://www.texasobserver.org/rick-perry-exports-his-pay-to-play-politics-to-ukraine/.
76. Open Secrets, Donor Lookup, search results for "Donors - Michael Bleyzer,", accessed June 26, 2024, https://www.opensecrets.org/donor-lookup/results?name=Michael+Bleyzer.
77. Desmond Butler et al., "After Boost from Perry, Backers Got Huge Gas Deal in Ukraine," Associated Press, November 11, 2019, https://apnews.com/article/global-trade-tx-state-wire-russia-united-states-joe-biden-6d8ae551fb884371a2a592ed85a74426.
78. Shuster and Marritz, "Exclusive."
79. "Energy Department Releases New Batch of Ukraine Documents," American Oversight, February 4, 2020, https://www.americanoversight.org/energy-department-releases-new-batch-of-ukraine-documents.
80. "Ukraine-Related Documents Obtained by American Oversight," American Oversight, accessed June 26, 2024, https://www.americanoversight.org/ukraine-related-documents-obtained-by-american-oversight.
81. "U.S. SigmaBleyzer Ready to Invest $100 Mln in Production of Fossil Fuel in Ukraine—Regulator," Intefax-Ukraine, June 25, 2018, https://en.interfax.com.ua/news/economic/514314.html.

82   Shuster and Marritz, "Exclusive."
83   Ilya Marritz and Simon Shuster, "The Perry Deals," September 10, 2020, *Trump, Inc.*, produced by Katherine Sullivan, ProPublica, WNYC Studios, podcast, audio, 37:15, https://www.wnycstudios.org/podcasts/trumpinc/episodes/trump-inc-rick-perry-naftogaz.
84   Federal Election Commission, search result for individual contributions "Contributor details - Kelcy Warren, recipient name or ID - Perry for President Inc (C00500587), Opportunity and Freedom PAC (C00573634), Opportunity and Freedom I (C00580092)," accessed June 26, 2024, https://www.fec.gov/data/receipts/individual-contributions/?committee_id=C00500587&committee_id=C00573634&committee_id=C00580092&contributor_name=kelcy+warren.
85   Katie Glueck, "Rick Perry's Super PAC Haul: $16.8 Million," *Politico*, July 10, 2015, https://www.politico.com/story/2015/07/rick-perrys-2016-fundraising-super-pac-16-million-119969.
86   Marritz and Shuster, "The Perry Deals."
87   Shuster and Marritz, "Rick Perry's."
88   Open Secrets, Donor Lookup, search results for "Donors - Alex Cranberg," accessed June 26, 2024, https://www.opensecrets.org/donor-lookup/results?name=alex+cranberg&order=desc&sort=D.
89   Butler et al., "After Boost."
90   Federal Election Commission, search result for individual contributions "Contributor details - Alex Cranberg, recipient name or ID - Perry for Congress (C00309260), Perry for President (C00500587)," accessed June 26, 2024, https://www.fec.gov/data/receipts/individual-contributions/?committee_id=C00309260&committee_id=C00500587&contributor_name=Alex+cranberg.
91   Mark Maremont and Neil King Jr., "Campaign to Pony up for Flight Costs," *Wall Street Journal*, October 20, 2011, https://www.wsj.com/articles/SB10001424052970203752604576641510355515144.
92   Butler et al., "After Boost."
93   Butler et al., "After Boost."
94   Butler et al., "After Boost."
95   "DOE Records of Senior Officials' Ukraine-Related Communications,", American Oversight, accessed June 26, 2024, https://www.documentcloud.org/documents/6768042-DOE-Records-of-Secretary-Perry-s-Ukraine-Related.
96   Butler et al., "After Boost."
97   Butler et al., "After Boost."
98   Kevin Bogardus and Kelsey Brugge, "Inside Rick Perry's Private Meetings on Ukraine," *E&E News by Politico*, October 18, 2019, https://www.eenews.net/articles/inside-rick-perrys-private-meetings-on-ukraine/.
99   Butler et al., "After Boost."
100 Shuster and Marritz, "Exclusive."
101 Shuster and Marritz, "Exclusive."
102 Philip Bump, "In His April Call with Trump, Zelensky Inadvertently Offered Trump Leverage," *Washington Post,* November 15, 2019, https://www.washingtonpost.com/politics/2019/11/15/his-april-call-with-trump-zelensky-inadvertently-offered-trump-leverage/.
103 Miller, "Rick Perry."
104 Desmond Butler et al., "Profit, Not Politics: Trump Allies Sought Ukraine Gas Deal," Associated Press, October 8, 2019, https://apnews.com/article/c77aa80dc3d0480ebff9c2f902446630.

105 Puko, "Perry."

106 Puko, "Perry."

107 Butler et al., "Profit."

108 Shuster and Marritz, "Rick Perry's."

109 Shuster and Marritz, "Exclusive."

110 Marritz and Shuster, "The Perry Deals."

111 Scott Waldman, "This Energy Expert Was on Perry's List for Ukraine," *E&E News by Politico*, November 18, 2019, https://www.eenews.net/articles/this-energy-expert-was-on-perrys-list-for-ukraine/.

112 Dmitry Ryasnoy, "Черный доктор: как Александр Янукович реанимирует энергетический бизнес" [Black doctor: How Alexander Yanukovych is resuscitating the energy business], *Экономическая правда [Economic Truth]*, October 19, 2016, https://www.epravda.com.ua/rus/publications/2016/10/19/608240/.

113 Dmitry Ryasnoy, "Янукович продал 'Донбассэнерго' нардепу от БПП" [Yanukovych sold Donbasenergo to the MP from the BPP], *Экономическая правда [Economic Truth]*, July 12, 2018, https://www.epravda.com.ua/rus/news/2018/07/12/638656/.

114 Marritz and Shuster, "The Perry Deals."

115 Marritz and Shuster, "The Perry Deals."

116 Shuster and Marritz, "Rick Perry's."

117 Greg Miller, "Two Volatile Meetings at the White House Have Become Central to the Impeachment Inquiry," *Washington Post*, October 29, 2019, https://www.washingtonpost.com/national-security/two-volatile-meetings-at-the-white-house-have-become-central-to-the-impeachment-inquiry/2019/10/29/aae1836e-fa7d-11e9-8190-6be4deb56e01_story.html.

118 Sec. Rick Perry, "Productive discussion at the The [sic]White House with Ambassador Bolton, Ambassador Sondland, Ambassador Volker and Ukrainian Security and Defense Council Chair Oleksandr Danylyuk today about opportunities for increased energy security cooperation with Ukraine under the Zelenskyy Administration," Facebook, July 10, 2019, retrieved from the Wayback Machine, version March 18, 2023, https://web.archive.org/web/20230318192917/https://m.facebook.com/SecretaryPerry/photos/productive-discussion-at-the-the-white-house-with-ambassador-bolton-amb assador-s/1060840157437890/.

119 Miller, "Two Volatile Meetings."

120 Shuster and Marritz, "Exclusive."

121 Shuster and Marritz, "Exclusive."

122 Shuster and Marritz, "Exclusive."

123 Marritz and Shuster, "The Perry Deals."

124 Butler and Biesecker, "Giuliani Pals."

125 Bonner, "Kobolyev."

CHAPTER 13

1 "LLCs: The Perfect Mechanism to Funnel Secret (and Perhaps Foreign) Money into Elections," Campaign Legal Center, July 30, 2018, https://campaignlegal.org/update/llcs-perfect-mechanism-funnel-secret-and-perhaps-foreign-money-elections.

2 "Company Overview," Global Energy Producers LLC, uploaded by Courthouse News Service, 2020, https://www.courthousenews.com/wp-content/uploads/2020/01/gep-exec-summ.pdf.

3   Protess and Vogel, "Recording Surfaces."
4   "Lev Parnas Releases Recording," CBS News.
5   Peter Overby, "Giuliani Leads GOP Rivals in Texas Fundraising," *Morning Edition*, NPR, November 19, 2007, audio, 5:12, https://www.npr.org/2007/11/19/16411602/giuliani-leads-gop-rivals-in-texas-fundraising.
6   Meyer and Levine, "Trump Inaugural Fundraiser Now Lobbying on Pensions."
7   Russ Buettner, "Giuliani's Tie to Texas Law Firm May Pose Risk," *New York Times*, May 2, 2007, https://www.nytimes.com/2007/05/02/us/politics/02giuliani.html.
8   Stephanie Baker, "Giuliani Keeps the Hustle Going, Even as Trump Is Impeached," Bloomberg News, December 19, 2019, https://www.bloomberg.com/news/features/2019-12-19/giuliani-keeps-the-hustle-going-even-as-trump-is-impeached.
9   Josh Gerstein, "Former Aide to Rep. Pete Sessions Testifies at Trial of Giuliani Associate," *Politico*, October 18, 2021, https://www.politico.com/news/2021/10/18/former-sessions-aide-testifies-giuliani-associate-516208.
10 Balthaus et al., "Lev Parnas Paid."
11 "Company Overview," Global Energy Producers LLC.
12 Dan Friedman, "Billionaire Oil Magnate Funded Travel by Lev Parnas," *Mother Jones*, January 16, 2020, https://www.motherjones.com/politics/2020/01/billionaire-oil-magnate-funded-travel-by-lev-parnas/.
13 Scott Waldman, "Meet the Top Gun Pilot Ensnared by Trump's Impeachment," *E&E News by Politico*, February 24, 2020, https://www.eenews.net/articles/meet-the-top-gun-pilot-ensnared-by-trumps-impeachment/.
14 "Company Overview," Global Energy Producers LLC.
15 Rueb, "'Freedom Gas.'"
16 "Rachel Maddow," MSNBC.
17 "Lev Parnas' Entire Interview with Anderson Cooper (Part 1)," CNN, January 16, 2020, video, 8:07, https://www.youtube.com/watch?v=9JKraI_Rh6g.
18 "Lev Parnas' Entire Interview with Anderson Cooper (Part 2)," CNN, January 17, 2020, 8:14, https://www.youtube.com/watch?v=QUXht__f3Rk.
19 Ben Meiselas et al., "Lev Remembers."
20 Puko, "Perry."
21 Anthony Adragna and Ben Lefebvre, "Rick Perry Won't Comply with Subpoena in Impeachment Probe," *Politico*, October 18, 2019, https://www.politico.com/news/2019/10/18/rick-perry-subpoena-impeachment-051335.
22 Josh Dawsey, "'Talk to Rudy': Testimony from Diplomats Highlights Giuliani's Central Role in Driving Ukraine Policy," *Washington Post*, November 6, 2019, https://www.washingtonpost.com/politics/talk-to-rudy-testimony-from-diplomats-highlights-giulianis-central-role-in-driving-ukraine-policy/2019/11/06/a7ce7aea-0010-11ea-9777-5cd51c6fec6f_story.html.
23 Timothy Puko and Rebecca Ballhaus, "Rick Perry Called Rudy Giuliani at Trump's Direction on Ukraine Concerns," *Wall Street Journal*, October 16, 2019, https://www.wsj.com/articles/rick-perry-called-rudy-giuliani-at-trumps-direction-on-ukraine-concerns-11571273635.
24 Shane Harris and Aaron C. Davis, "With Revised Statement, Sondland Adds to Testimony Linking Aid to Ukraine Investigations That Trump Sought," *Washington Post*, November 5, 2019, https://www.washingtonpost.com/world/national-security/with-revised-testimony-sondland-ties-trump-to-quid-pro-quo/2019/11/05/3059b3b8-ffec-11e9-9518-1e76abc088b6_story.html.

25 Matthew Chance and Marshall Cohen, "Exclusive: New Audio of 2019 Phone Call Reveals How Giuliani Pressured Ukraine to Investigate Baseless Biden Conspiracies," CNN, June 8, 2021, https://edition.cnn.com/2021/06/07/politics/rudy-giuliani-ukraine-call-investigate-biden/index.html?fbclid=IwAR1KbDujl6H4S8rZAZCydC0hegVTZRiPzW1p0eo2oc6d2T78uU4DkXHms64.

26 Charlie Savage and Josh Williams, "Read the Text Messages between U.S. and Ukrainian Officials," *New York Times,* October 4, 2019, https://www.nytimes.com/interactive/2019/10/04/us/politics/ukraine-text-messages-volker.html.

27 Alayna Treene and Jonathan Swan, "Scoop: Trump Pins Ukraine Call on Energy Secretary Rick Perry," *Axios,* October 5, 2019, https://www.axios.com/2019/10/05/trump-blamed-rick-perry-call-ukraine-zelensky.

28 Williams et al., "Full Document."

29 Daniel Bush, "'Everyone Was in the Loop.' Sondland Confirms Quid Pro Quo," PBS, November 20, 2019, https://www.pbs.org/newshour/politics/sondland-confirms-quid-pro-quo-but-denies-he-heard-it-from-trump.

30 Ben Lefebvre and Daniel Lippman, "Perry Pressed Ukraine on Corruption, Energy Company Changes", *Politico,* October 5, 2019, https://www.politico.com/news/2019/10/05/rick-perry-ukraine-trump-030230.

31 "Lev Parnas Releases Recording," CBS News.

32 Emma Loop, "A Former Member of Congress Involved in Trump's Ukraine Saga Could Be Close to Getting His Job Back," *BuzzFeed News,* March 4, 2020, https://www.buzzfeednews.com/article/emmaloop/pete-sessions-ukraine-parnas-fruman-trump-republican-primary.

33 Protess and Vogel, "Recording Surfaces."

34 Kara Scannell and Marshall Cohen, "New Parnas Video Places Giuliani Associates at Mar-a-Lago with Trump," CNN, January 30, 2020, https://edition.cnn.com/2020/01/30/politics/parnas-video-mar-a-lago-trump/index.html.

35 Loop, "Former Member."

36 Gerstein, "Former Aide."

37 Federal Election Commission, search result for individual contributions "Contributor details - Lev Parnas, Igor Fruman, Recipient name or ID - Pete Sessions for Congress (C00303305)," accessed June 27, 2024, https://www.fec.gov/data/receipts/individual-contributions/?committee_id=C00303305&contributor_name=Igor+Fruman&contributor_name=Lev+Parnas.

38 Gromer Jeffers Jr., "Pete Sessions Downplays Meeting with Soviet-Born Businessmen Caught in Trump Impeachment Inquiry," *Dallas Morning News,* October 4, 2019, https://www.dallasnews.com/news/politics/2019/10/04/pete-sessions-downplays-meeting-soviet-born-businessman-caught-trump-impeachment-inquiry/.

39 Helderman et al., "Trump's Lawyer."

40 Betsy Swan and Adam Rawnsley, "Exclusive: Giuliani Ally Pete Sessions Was Eyed for Top Slot in Ukraine," *Daily Beast,* November 14, 2019, https://www.thedailybeast.com/giuliani-ally-pete-sessions-was-eyed-for-top-slot-in-ukraine.

41 "Rachel Maddow," MSNBC.

42 Schmidt et al., "Giuliani."

43 Erica Orden, "Parnas Recording Shows Trump Talking with Indicted Businessmen the President Has Said He Doesn't Know," CNN, January 26, 2020, https://edition.cnn.com/2020/01/25/politics/recording-trump-lev-parnas-igor-fruman-ukraine-ambassador/index.html.

44 "Yovanovitch Says Washington Will Continue to Support NABU, SAPO despite Scandal", Ukrinform, December 5, 2017, https://www.ukrinform.net/rubric-polytics/2357769-yovanovitch-says-washington-will-continue-to-support-nabu-sapo-despite-scandal.html.

45 Philip Bump, "How Ukraine's Top Prosecutor Went after Marie Yovanovitch, Step by Step," *Washington Post*, January 15, 2020, https://www.washingtonpost.com/politics/2020/01/15/how-ukraines-top-prosecutor-went-after-marie-yovanovitch-step-by-step/.

46 Entous, "Ukrainian Prosecutor."

47 Susan Simpson, "Giuliani's FARA Problem," Just Security, May 11, 2021, https://www.justsecurity.org/76075/giulianis-fara-problem/.

48 Simpson, "Giuliani's."

49 Colby Itkowitz et al., "Parnas Used Access to Trump's World to Help Push Shadow Ukraine Effort, New Documents Show," *Washington Post*, January 15, 2020, https://www.washingtonpost.com/politics/parnas-used-access-to-trumps-world-to-help-push-shadow-ukraine-effort-new-documents-show/2020/01/15/f350dd78-37f1-11ea-bf30-ad313e4ec754_story.html.

50 Simpson, "Giuliani's."

51 Simpson, "Giuliani's."

52 John Solomon, "Top Ukrainian justice Official Says Us Ambassador Gave Him a Do Not Prosecute List," *Hill*, March 20, 2019, https://thehill.com/hilltv/rising/434875-top-ukrainian-justice-official-says-us-ambassador-gave-him-a-do-not-prosecute/.

53 Andy Heil and Christopher Miller, "U.S. Rejects Ukraine Top Prosecutor's 'Don't Prosecute' Accusation," *RFE/RL*, March 21, 2019, https://www.rferl.org/a/us-rejects-top-ukrainian-prosecutors-dont-prosecute-accusation/29834853.html.

54 "House Releases," *Washington Post*.

55 Bump, "How Ukraine's Top Prosecutor."

56 Will Sommer et al., "Fox News Internal Document Bashes Pro-Trump Fox Regulars for Spreading 'Disinformation,'" *Daily Beast*, February 6, 2020, https://www.thedailybeast.com/fox-news-internal-document-bashes-john-solomon-joe-digenova-and-rudy-giuliani-for-spreading-disinformation.

57 Abigail Tracy, "'There Is No Other Reason': Sources Blame the White House, and a Fox News-Fueled Conspiracy Theory, for the Sudden Ouster of Masha Yovanovitch,"*Vanity Fair*, May 8, 2019, https://www.vanityfair.com/news/2019/05/donald-trump-fox-news-us-ambassdor-ukraine-masha-yovanovitch.

58 "Updated Timeline: Messages about Yovanovitch Surveillance Happened Same Week as Giuliani-Pompeo Calls," American Oversight, January 15, 2020, https://www.americanoversight.org/messages-to-parnas-suggest-yovanovitch-surveillance-happened-same-week-as-giuliani-pompeo-calls.

59 Ryan Saavedra (@RealSaavedra), "Laura Ingraham: 'In May 2018, former Congressman Pete Sessions sent Secretary of State Pompeo an urgent letter imploring him to remove the U.S. Ambassador to Ukraine Marie Yovanovitch. . . . She's reportedly demonstrated clear anti-Trump bias,'" Twitter, March 23, 2019, 5:24 p.m., https://twitter.com/RealSaavedra/status/1109551528589746176.

60 Simpson, "Giuliani's."

61 Ryan Broderick, "Here's What Giuliani's Associate Lev Parnas Was Sharing on WhatsApp as He Investigated the Ukraine Conspiracy Theory," *BuzzFeed News*, January 16, 2020, https://www.buzzfeednews.com/article/ryanhatesthis/heres-what-giulianis-associate-lev-parnas-was-sharing-on.

62 "House Releases," *Washington Post*.

63 Simpson, "Giuliani's."

64 "House Releases," *Washington Post*.

65 Donald Trump Jr. (@DonaldJTrumpJr), "We need more @RichardGrenell's and less of these jokers as ambassadors. Calls Grow To Remove Obama's U.S. Ambassador To Ukraine," Twitter, March 24, 2019, 1:12 p.m., https://twitter.com/DonaldJTrumpJr/status/1109850575926108161?s=20.

66 Ryan Broderick and Lam Thuy Vo, "Twitter Has Suspended Several Accounts That Tweeted "I Hired Donald Trump to Fire People Like Yovanovitch,'" *BuzzFeed News*, November 15, 2019, https://www.buzzfeednews.com/article/ryanhatesthis/donald-trump-fire-people-like-yovanovitch-coordinated.

67 Broderick and Vo, "Twitter."

68 Julie Millican and Julie Tulbert, "How Conservative Writer John Solomon Served as the Conduit for Rudy Giuliani's Ukraine Conspiracy Theories," Media Matters, October 17, 2019, https://www.mediamatters.org/john-solomon/how-conservative-writer-john-solomon-served-conduit-rudy-giulianis-ukraine-conspiracy?fbclid=IwAR1eIqNHPvp3rsdPctO6X5ty9VggV8WPcOKeyHieryl9qhCwkdhLNxPxotY.

69 Jake Pearson et al., "How a Veteran Reporter Worked with Giuliani's Associates to Launch the Ukraine Conspiracy," ProPublica, October 25, 2019, https://www.propublica.org/article/how-a-veteran-reporter-worked-with-giuliani-associates-to-launch-the-ukraine-conspiracy.

70 Sommer et al., "Fox News."

71 Power and Monroe, "Joe diGenova."

72 Millican and Tulbert, "How Conservative Writer."

73 "Updates Timeline," American Oversight.

74 "State Department Records of Giuliani and Ukraine-Related Communications with Department Officials, Including Secretary Pompeo," American Oversight, November 22, 2019, https://www.documentcloud.org/documents/6557889-State-Department-Records-of-Giuliani-and-Ukraine.

75 Michael Rothfeld et al., "Robert Hyde, Erratic Ex-Landscaper, Is Unlikely New Impeachment Figure," *New York Times*, January 15, 2020, https://www.nytimes.com/2020/01/15/nyregion/robert-hyde-impeachment-parnas.html.

76 Lucien Bruggeman, "Robert Hyde, a New Character in Impeachment Drama, Is a Trump Devotee with Checkered Past," ABC News, January 17, 2020, https://abcnews.go.com/Politics/robert-hyde-character-impeachment-drama-trump-devotee-checkered/story?id=68307023.

77 "Materials Provided by Giuliani Associate Lev Parnas to the House," *Washington Post*, January 14, 2020, https://www.washingtonpost.com/context/materials-provided-by-giuliani-associate-lev-parnas-to-the-house/2bcc0ac0-c46d-4ef3-ba90-49ecdcc918e2/?itid=lk_inline_manual_19.

78 Gregorian, "Robert Hyde."

79 Halle Kiefer, "Ukraine's New President? A Comedian Whose Only Political Experience Is Playing Ukraine's President," *Vulture by New York Magazine*, April 22, 2019, https://www.vulture.com/2019/04/comedian-volodymyr-zelensky-elected-to-ukraine-presidency.html.

80 "Ukraine Prosecutor General Lutsenko Admits U.S. Ambassador Didn't Give Him a Do Not Prosecute List," *UNIAN*, April 18, 2019, https://www.unian.info/politics/10520715-ukraine-prosecutor-general-lutsenko-admits-u-s-ambassador-didn-t-give-him-a-do-not-prosecute-list.html.

81 "House Releases," *Washington Post*.

82 Simpson, "Giuliani's."

83 Richard Cowan et al., "'I Was Very Concerned': Former U.S. Ambassador Yovanovitch in Impeachment Spotlight," Reuters, November 15, 2019, https://www.reuters.com/article/usa-trump-impeachment-yovanovitch-idINKBN1XP158/.

84 Josh Rogin, "U.S. Ambassador to Ukraine Is Recalled after Becoming a Political Target," opinion, *Washington Post*, May 7, 2019, https://www.washingtonpost.com/opinions/2019/05/07/us-ambassador-ukraine-is-recalled-after-becoming-political-target/.

85 Katherine Faulders et al., "'Take Her Out': Recording Appears to Capture Trump at Private Dinner Saying He Wants Ukraine Ambassador Fired," ABC News, January 25, 2020, https://abcnews.go.com/Politics/recording-appears-capture-trump-private-dinner-ukraine-ambassador/story?id=68506437.

86 "Кабмин инициирует пересмотр контрактов с правлением 'Нафтогазу України'" [The Cabinet of Ministers initiates a review of contracts with the management of Naftogaz of Ukraine], *Gordon*, January 16, 2019, https://gordonua.com/news/politics/kabmin-iniciiruet-peresmotr-kontraktov-s-pravleniem-naftogazu-ukrani-664539.html.

87 Bonner, "Kobolyev."

88 Butler and Biesecker, "Giuliani Pals."

89 Bogardus and Brugger, "Inside."

90 Puko, "Perry."

91 "Naftogaz Creates Gas and Oil Divisions," Naftogaz Group, January 17, 2019, https://www.naftogaz.com/en/news/naftogaz-stvoryv-dyviziony-gaz-ta-nafta.

92 Butler and Biesecker, "Giuliani Pals."

93 Butler and Biesecker, "Giuliani Pals."

94 Butler et al., "Profit."

95 Butler and Biesecker, "Giuliani Pals."

96 Butler et al., "Profit."

97 Butler and Biesecker, "Giuliani Pals."

98 Butler et al., "Profit."

99 Butler and Biesecker, "Giuliani Pals."

100 Butler and Biesecker, "Giuliani Pals."

101 Jay Root, "Perry's New Campaign Guru: Jeff Miller," *Texas Tribune*, August 8, 2014, https://www.texastribune.org/2014/08/08/look-perrys-new-guru-jeff-miller/.

102 Benjamin Storrow, "Longtime Aide Cashes in after Fixing Perry's 'Oops' Image," *E&E News by Politico*, December 12, 2017, https://www.eenews.net/articles/longtime-aide-cashes-in-after-fixing-perrys-oops-image/.

103 Butler et al., "After Boost."

104 Butler and Biesecker, "Giuliani Pals."

105 Butler and Biesecker, "Giuliani Pals."

106 Jake Pearson, "Want to Meet with the Trump Administration? Donald Trump Jr.'s Hunting Buddy Can Help," ProPublica, July 22, 2019, https://www.propublica.org/article/trump-inc-podcast-tommy-hicks-jr-donald-trump-jr-hunting-buddy.

107 Michael Warren and Fredreka Schouten, "'It's Been a Disaster.' Inside the Trump Super PAC Struggles," CNN, June 8, 2019, https://edition.cnn.com/2019/06/07/politics/trump-super-pac-america-first/index.html.

108 Tarini Parti, "Trump's 'Low-Profile' 'Ultimate Loyalist' Now Has More Power Ahead of 2020," *BuzzFeed News*, February 11, 2019, https://www.buzzfeednews.com/article/tariniparti/trump-tommy-hicks-rnc-co-chair.

109. Kevin McCoy, "The Middleman: How Lev Parnas Joined Team Trump and Became Rudy Giuliani's Fixer in Ukraine," January 24, 2020, https://www.usatoday.com/in-depth/news/2020/01/24/lev-parnas-ex-giuliani-ally-could-key-figure-trump-impeachment/4531125002/.
110. Butler and Biesecker, "Giuliani Pals."
111. Rogin, "U.S. Ambassador."
112. "House Releases," *Washington Post*.
113. Desmond Butler and Michael Biesecker, "Ukrainian Leader Felt Trump Pressure before Taking Office," Associated Press, October 24, 2019, https://apnews.com/article/donald-trump-ap-top-news-elections-joe-biden-politics-b048901b635f423db49a10046daaf8a8.
114. Rene Marsh and Michael Warren, "Trump Administration Knew in May Zelensky Felt Pressured to Investigate Bidens," CNN, November 18, 2019, https://edition.cnn.com/2019/11/18/politics/ukraine-zelensky-pressure-trump-investigations/index.html.
115. "Full Transcript of Testimony of Fiona Hill, Former Top Russia Adviser to the White House," *Washington Post*, November 8, 2019, https://www.washingtonpost.com/context/full-transcript-of-testimony-of-fiona-hill-former-top-russia-adviser-to-the-white-house/289badae-624a-4258-8fca-ad19d817a30f/.
116. Butler et al., "After Boost."
117. Butler et al., "Profit."
118. "Giuliani Subpoenaed," U.S. House of Representatives Committee on Foreign Affairs.
119. Viswanatha et al., "Two Giuliani Associates."
120. Seth Hettena, "How the Trump Team Tried to Silence Lev Parnas," *Rolling Stone*, August 30, 2020, https://www.rollingstone.com/politics/politics-features/lev-parnas-rudy-trump-giuliani-impeachment-1051683/.
121. Dan Friedman, "Here Are Rudy Giuliani's Various Claims about His Ties to the Two Men Arrested Wednesday," *Mother Jones*, October 11, 2019, https://www.motherjones.com/politics/2019/10/rudy-giuliani-claims-lev-parnas-igor-fruman-ukraine-donald-trump/.
122. Scannell and Cohen, "New Parnas Video."
123. Kaczynski et al., "Inauguration Galas."
124. Viswanatha et al., "Two Giuliani Associates."
125. Natasha Bertrand and Darren Samuelsohn, "Here's What the Parnas Revelations Mean for Trump," *Politico*, January 16, 2020, https://www.politico.com/news/2020/01/16/lev-parnas-revelations-trump-100216.
126. Katherine Faulders and Trish Turner, "Meet the Legal Team Defending Former Trump Campaign Chairman Paul Manafort," ABC News, August 15, 2018, https://abcnews.go.com/Politics/meet-legal-team-defending-trump-campaign-chairman-paul/story?id=57179421.
127. Michael Biesecker et al., "Florida Men Tied to Giuliani, Ukraine Probe Arrested," Associated Press, October 11, 2019, https://apnews.com/article/indictments-campaign-finance-fl-state-wire-impeachments-elections-c9125e9ccd894965bbf2860100366779.
128. "Part Two of the Lev Parnas Interview," MSNBC.
129. Kara Scannell and Vicky Ward, "From Pot to Impeachment: The High-Wire Legal Act from Lev Parnas' Attorney," CNN, January 20, 2020, https://edition.cnn.com/2020/01/20/politics/joseph-bondy-lev-parnas-attorney/index.html.
130. Aram Roston, "Exclusive: Giuliani Associate Parnas Will Comply with Trump Impeachment Inquiry—Lawyer," Reuters, November 5, 2019, https://www.reuters.com/article/us-usa-trump-impeachment-parnas-exclusiv-idUSKBN1XE297/.

131 Kenneth P. Vogel, "Democrats Release More Material from Lev Parnas on Ukraine Campaign," *New York Times*, January 17, 2020, https://www.nytimes.com/2020/01/17/us/politics/democrats-lev-parnas-material.html.

132 "Lev Parnas and Igor Fruman Charged with Conspiring to Violate Straw and Foreign Donor Bans," United States Attorney's Office, Southern District of New York, press release, October 10, 2019, https://www.justice.gov/usao-sdny/pr/lev-parnas-and-igor-fruman-charged-conspiring-violate-straw-and-foreign-donor-bans.

133 Josh Gerstein, "Former Trump Super PAC Official Testifies at Trial of Giuliani Associate," *Politico*, October 19, 2021, https://www.politico.com/news/2021/10/19/former-trump-superpac-official-testifies-giuliani-516254.

134 Lachlan Markay, "Rudy's Ukraine Henchmen Made Big Donation to Pro-Trump PAC," *Daily Beast*, September 26, 2019, https://www.thedailybeast.com/rudy-giulianis-ukraine-henchmen-made-big-donation-to-pro-trump-pac.

135 Brendan Fischer, "New Wire Transfer Records Reveal Shady Foreign Ties to a Pro-Trump Super PAC," Campaign Legal Center, June 21, 2019, https://campaignlegal.org/update/new-wire-transfer-records-reveal-shady-foreign-ties-pro-trump-super-pac.

136 Colin Moynihan, "Ex-Giuliani Ally Gained Easy Access to Trump's Orbit, Texts Show," *New York Times*, October 21, 2021, https://www.nytimes.com/2021/10/21/nyregion/lev-parnas-trump-giuliani.html.

137 Federal Election Campaign Act (FECA) of 1971, 52 U.S.C. §30121.

138 "Lev Parnas," United States Attorney's Office, Southern District of New York.

139 Sealed Indictment, United States of America v. Lev Parnas, Igor Fruman, David Correia, and Andrey Kukushkin, No. 19 Cr. 725 (S.D.N.Y. October 10, 2019), https://www.justice.gov/usao-sdny/press-release/file/1208281/dl.

140 Olivia Beavers, "Former Pete Sessions Staffer to Comply with Subpoena in Federal Probe Investigating Giuliani, Associates," *Hill*, October 23, 2019, https://thehill.com/policy/national-security/467114-former-pete-sessions-staffer-to-comply-with-subpoena-in-federal/.

141 Rebecca Ballhaus, "Ex-Rep. Sessions Subpoenaed over Interactions with Giuliani, Giuliani Associates," *Wall Street Journal*, October 15, 2019, https://www.wsj.com/articles/ex-rep-sessions-subpoenaed-over-interactions-with-giuliani-giuliani-associates-11571176908.

142 Superseding Indictment, United States v. Lev Parnas, Igor Fruman, David Correia, and Andrey Kukushkin, No. S1 19 Cr. 725 (JPO) (S.D.N.Y. September 17, 2020), https://www.justice.gov/usao-sdny/press-release/file/1317711/dl.

143 Congress of the United States, Permanent Select Committee on Intelligence, *Subpoena Issued to Secretary of Energy Rick Perry*, October 10, 2019, uploaded by *New York Times*, https://int.nyt.com/data/documenthelper/1887-rick-perry-subpoena/1555d936b37778a1c6a7/optimized/full.pdf.

144 Gregory Wallace, Kylie Atwood, "Rick Perry Says He'll Cooperate with Congress on Ukraine Questions," CNN, October 2, 2019, https://edition.cnn.com/2019/10/02/politics/perry-ukraine/index.html.

145 Adragna and Lefebvre, "Rick Perry."

146 Puko and Ballhaus, "Rick Perry."

147 Steve Holland and Timothy Gardner, "Trump Says U.S. Energy Secretary Perry to Step Down at End of the Year," Reuters, October 17, 2019, https://www.reuters.com/article/us-usa-trump-perry-idUSKBN1WW2VN/.

148 Holland and Gardner, "Trump."

149 Butler et al., "Profit."

150 Anthony Adragna and Ben Lefebvre, "How Rick Perry Waltzed past the Impeachment Probe," *Politico*, February 5, 2020, https://www.politico.com/news/2020/02/05/how-rick-perry-waltzed-past-the-impeachment-probe-110827.

151 "In Light of New Evidence," United States Senate Committee on Finance.

152 Shuster and Marritz, "Exclusive."

153 Desmond Butler and Michael Biesecker, "Ukrainian Gas Chief Meets with Prosecutors Probing Giuliani," Associated Press, December 4, 2019, https://apnews.com/article/9872f7d6720a5f253b350da4bd3d6883.

154 Tom Hamburger, Rosalind S. Helderman, "Federal Prosecutors to Interview Ukrainian Gas Executive as Part of Probe into Giuliani and His Associates," *Washington Post*, November 19, 2019, https://www.washingtonpost.com/politics/federal-prosecutors-set-to-interview-ukrainian-gas-executive-as-part-of-probe-into-giuliani-and-his-associates/2019/11/19/f8d3a600-0b22-11ea-97ac-a7ccc8dd1ebc_story.html.

155 Shuster and Marritz, "Exclusive."

156 Shuster and Marritz, "Exclusive."

157 Rachel Adams-Heard, "Ex-Energy Secretary Rick Perry Joins Energy Transfer Board," Bloomberg News, January 3, 2020, https://www.bloomberg.com/news/articles/2020-01-03/ex-energy-secretary-rick-perry-joins-energy-transfer-board.

158 "Кабмин ввел в наблюдательный совет Нафтогаза американца Бенша" [The Cabinet of Ministers appointed American Bensh to the Naftogaz Supervisory Board], *Украинские Национальные Новости [Ukrainian National News]*, March 19, 2020, https://unn.ua/ru/news/kabmin-vviv-do-naglyadovoyi-radi-naftogazu-amerikantsya-bensha.

159 "Ukraine, U.S. Agree on Annual Supplies of 6–8 BCM of LNG for Hub Creation," Interfax-Ukraine, March 13, 2020, https://en.interfax.com.ua/news/economic/646778.html.

160 "Govt Approves Memo with Louisiana Natural Gas Exports on Possible LNG Shipments from U.S. to Ukraine," Interfax-Ukraine, May 27, 2020, https://en.interfax.com.ua/news/economic/665111.html.

161 Shuster and Marritz, "Rick Perry's."

162 Shuster and Marritz, "Rick Perry's."

163 Shuster and Marritz, "Rick Perry's."

164 Amos Hochstein, "Amos J. Hochstein: Naftogaz Faces Increasing Sabotage from Corrupt Forces," opinion, *Kyiv Post*, October 12, 2020, https://archive.kyivpost.com/article/opinion/op-ed/amos-hochstein-why-im-leaving-the-supervisory-board-of-naftogaz.html.

165 "Роберт Бенш, член наглядової ради НАК, заявив, що голова наглядової ради Клер Споттісвуд не допускає його до виконання обов'язків всупереч міжнародним нормам та законодавству України" [Robert Bensh, a member of the Supervisory Board of the Ukrainian National Academy of Sciences, said that the chariman of the Supervisory Board, Claire Spottiswoode, does not allow him to perform his duties contrary to international norms and the legislation of Ukraine], Naftogaz, May 6, 2021, retrieved from the Wayback Machine, version May 6, 2021, https://web.archive.org/web/20210506125523/https://www.naftogaz.com/www/3/nakweb.nsf/0/9F43264214054DC5C22586CD0029CF97?OpenDocument&year=2021&month=05&nt=Новини&fbclid=IwAR3Knz7es3JkpLUhYtIgYzpMWPdvvxkqgapSYXHRjxUR9fh9XQDqGiorQo8.

166 "Независимые члены набсовета 'Нафтогаза' назвали причину отставки" [Independent members of the Naftogaz supervisory board named the reason for their resignation], *Экономическая правда [Economic Truth]*, September 8, 2021, https://www.epravda.com.ua/rus/news/2021/09/8/677617/.

167 Igor Oryol, "Правительство наконец-то назначило наблюдательный совет «Нафтогаза». Кто эти люди и почему это важно" [The government has finally appointed a supervisory board for Naftogaz. Who are these people and why is it important?], *Forbes Ukraine*, January 24, 2023, https://forbes.ua/ru/money/uryad-nareshti-priznachiv-naglyadovu-radu-naftogazu-khto-tsi-lyudi-y-chomu-tse-vazhlivo-24012023-11291.

168 Shuster and Marritz, "Rick Perry's."

169 "Naftogaz and Symbio Infrastructure Agree on Deliveries of Low Carbon Canadian LNG and Green Hydrogen to Ukraine," Naftogaz Group, June 13, 2022, https://www.naftogaz.com/en/news/naftogaz-and-symbio-infrastructure-agree-on-deliveries-of-low-carbon-canadian-lng-and-green-hydrogen.

170 Shuster and Marritz, "Rick Perry's."

171 "DOE Records of Senior Officials' Ukraine-Related Communications," American Oversight, February 4, 2020, https://www.documentcloud.org/documents/6768042-DOE-Records-of-Secretary-Perry-s-Ukraine-Related.

172 Butler et al., "After Boost."

173 Shuster and Marritz, "Exclusive."

174 Adragna and Lefebvre, "How Rick Perry Waltzed."

CHAPTER 14

1 Rosalind S. Helderman et al., "Impeachment Inquiry Puts New Focus on Giuliani's Work for Prominent Figures in Ukraine," *Washington Post*, October 2, 2019, https://www.washingtonpost.com/politics/impeachment-inquiry-puts-new-focus-on-giulianis-work-for-prominent-figures-in-ukraine/2019/10/01/b3c6d08c-e089-11e9-be96-6adb81821e90_story.html.

2 Baker, "Where Rudy Giuliani's Money Comes From."

3 Dawsey et al., "Inside Giuliani's Dual Roles."

4 "Giuliani Involved in Legal Controversy in Romania," CNN, November 4, 2019, video, 7:14, https://www.youtube.com/watch?v=ofs7b6w1Pts.

5 Baker, "Where Rudy Giuliani's Money Comes From."

6 "Giuliani Lays Out Security Plan with President Vázquez in Uruguay," MercoPress, November 15, 2018, https://en.MercoPress.com/2018/11/15/giuliani-lays-out-security-plan-with-president-vazquez-in-uruguay.

7 Dom Phillips and Nayara Felizardo, "Rudy Giuliani's $1.6 Million Amazon Adventure Has Become an Issue in the Brazilian Election," Intercept, October 5, 2018, https://theIntercept.com/2018/10/05/rudy-giuliani-amazon-contract-brazil-election/.

8 Vogel, "While Working for Trump."

9 Kenneth P. Vogel et al., "Giuliani Mixes His Business with Role as Trump's Lawyer," *New York Times*, October 18, 2019, https://www.nytimes.com/2019/10/18/us/politics/giuliani-business.html.

10 Baker, "Where Rudy Giuliani's Money Comes From."

11 Baker, "Where Rudy Giuliani's Money Comes From."

12 Andrew Desiderio and Kyle Cheney, "Gordon Sondland Says Giuliani Pushed Ukraine Probes at Trump's Direction," *Politico*, October 17, 2019, https://www.politico.com/news/2019/10/17/gordon-sondland-to-break-from-trump-in-impeachment-testimony-000288.

13   Christina Wilkie, "Giuliani and Sondland Hijacked Ukraine Policy to Push for Investigations, Trump Impeachment Witness Fiona Hill Says," CNBC, November 21, 2019, https://www.cnbc.com/2019/11/21/trump-impeachment-fiona-hill-says-giuliani-sondland-hijacked-ukraine-policy.html.

14   Trevor Potter and Delaney Marsco, "We Have No Idea Who Is Paying Rudy Giuliani," *Washington Post,* October 10, 2019, https://www.washingtonpost.com/outlook/2019/10/10/we-have-no-idea-who-is-paying-rudy-giuliani/.

15   U.S. Office of Government Ethics, *Compilation of Federal Ethics Laws* (OGE, 2023), https://www.oge.gov/web/oge.nsf/0/3D3B3F1EE20BA918852585BA0063A592/$FILE/Compilation%20of%20Federal%20Ethics%20Laws%20(2023).pdf.

16   Parnas, *Trump First,* chap. 5, Kindle.

17   Protess et al., "Giuliani Pursued Business."

18   Entous, "Ukrainian Prosecutor."

19   Christopher Miller, "Details of a Fateful Call between Rudy Giuliani and the Ukrainians Have Been Secret for Years. Here's the Full Transcript," *BuzzFeed News,* April 30, 2021, https://www.buzzfeednews.com/article/christopherm51/rudy-giuliani-ukraine-phone-call-transcript.

20   Bump, "Lev Parnas's Handwritten Notes."

21   Zapotosky et al., "Prosecutors."

22   Helderman et al., "Trump's Lawyer."

23   Weaver et al., "Venezuelan."

24   Rosalind S. Helderman et al., "A Wealthy Venezuelan Hosted Giuliani as He Pursued Ukraine Campaign. Then Giuliani Lobbied the Justice Department on His Behalf," *Washington Post,* November 26, 2019, https://www.washingtonpost.com/politics/a-wealthy-venezuelan-hosted-giuliani-as-he-pursued-ukraine-campaign-then-giuliani-lobbied-the-justice-department-on-his-behalf/2019/11/26/272105a2-0ec5-11ea-b0fc-62cc38411ebb_story.html.

25   Evan Perez and, David Shortell, "Barr Dropped into Giuliani Meeting at Justice Department in Previously Undisclosed Encounter," CNN, January 17, 2020, https://edition.cnn.com/2020/01/17/politics/barr-giuliani-justice-department-meeting/index.html.

26   U.S. Department of Justice, FOIA Library, *Former Attorney General,* pg. 110.

27   Leonnig et al., "Giuliani Pressed Trump."

28   Jo Becker et al., "Giuliani Pressed for Turkish Prisoner Swap in Oval Office Meeting," *New York Times,* October 10, 2019, https://www.nytimes.com/2019/10/10/us/politics/giuliani-trump-rex-tillerson.html.

29   Weiser, "Erdogan."

30   Lucien Bruggeman and Soo Rin Kim, "Rudy Giuliani's High-Dollar Foreign Clients Could Present Legal Problems: Experts," ABC News, October 30, 2019, https://abcnews.go.com/Politics/rudy-giulianis-high-dollar-foreign-clients-present-legal/story?id=66613693.

31   Baker, "Where Rudy Giuliani's Money Comes From."

32   Josh Dawsey et al. "Giuliani Works for Foreign Clients While Serving as Trump's Attorney," *Washington Post,* July 10, 2018, https://www.washingtonpost.com/politics/giuliani-works-for-foreign-clients-while-serving-as-trumps-attorney/2018/07/09/e21554ae-7988-11e8-80be-6d32e182a3bc_story.html.

33   Marianne Levine and Lili Bayer, "Trump Lawyer Giuliani Got Paid to Lobby Romanian President," *Politico,* August 29, 2018, https://www.politico.eu/article/rudy-giuliani-trump-lawyer-paid-to-criticize-romanian-anti-corruption-drive-klaus-iohannis/.

34 Marianne Levine, "Democratic Senators Ask DOJ to Examine Giuliani's Foreign Work," *Politico*, September 6, 2018, https://www.politico.com/story/2018/09/06/rudy-giuliani-foreign-work-democrats-809127.

35 Benjamin Din, "Giuliani: 'I Never, Ever Represented a Foreign National,'" *Politico*, April 29, 2021, https://www.politico.com/news/2021/04/29/giuliani-denial-trump-fbi-ukrainan-485091.

36 Protess et al., "Giuliani Pursued Business."

37 Rebecca Ballhaus, "Giuliani Weighed Doing Business with Ukrainian Government," *Wall Street Journal*, November 27, 2019, https://www.wsj.com/articles/giuliani-weighed-doing-business-with-ukrainian-government-11574890951.

38 Parnas and Langton, *Shadow Diplomacy*, chap. 1, Kindle.

39 Vogel and Protess, "Giuliani Represented Venezuelan."

40 U.S. Department of Justice, FOIA Library, *Former Attorney General*, pg. 110.

41 Helderman et al., "Wealthy Venezuelan."

42 Michael Warren, "Rudy Giuliani Hires Watergate Prosecutor as Attorney in Impeachment Inquiry," CNN, October 1, 2019, https://edition.cnn.com/2019/10/01/politics/giuliani-hires-watergate-prosecutor/index.html.

43 Helderman et al., "Wealthy Venezuelan."

44 Friedman, "Here Are Rudy Giuliani's Various Claims."

45 Nicole Hong and William K. Rashbaum, "Lawyer for Man Who Worked with Giuliani Ties Case to Trump," *New York Times*, October 23, 2019, https://www.nytimes.com/2019/10/23/nyregion/lev-parnas-igor-fruman-campaign-finance.html.

46 Ian MacDougall, "Did Rudy Giuliani Nullify His Attorney-Client Protections?," ProPublica, October 2, 2019, https://www.propublica.org/article/did-rudy-giuliani-nullify-his-attorney-client-protections.

47 Miriam Elder, "Rudy Giuliani Won't Say If He Has an Agreement with Trump to Act as His Lawyer," *BuzzFeed News*, October 2, 2019, https://www.buzzfeednews.com/article/miriamelder/rudy-giuliani-trump-lawyer.

48 Martin Pengelly, "Trump Calls Rudy Giuliani a 'Great Guy' as Impeachment Pressure Mounts," *Guardian*, October 12, 2019, https://www.theguardian.com/us-news/2019/oct/12/rudy-giuliani-donald-trump.

CHAPTER 15

1 Belford and Klasfeld, "Behind Trump's Turkish 'Bromance.'"

2 Darren Samuelsohn and Marc Caputo, "Trump Pleads for Cash at Closed Donor Retreat," *Politico*, March 3, 2017, https://www.politico.com/story/2017/03/trump-donors-republican-senate-235678.

3 Marc Caputo, "Trump Lobbyist Ballard Named RNC's Regional Finance Vice-Chair," *Politico Pro*, April 3, 2017, https://subscriber.politicopro.com/article/2017/04/trump-lobbyist-ballard-named-rncs-regional-finance-vice-chair-110940.

4 Belford and Klasfeld, "Behind Trump's Turkish 'Bromance.'"

5 Simon Shuster, "How Putin's Oligarchs Got Inside the Trump Team," *Time*, September 20, 2018, https://time.com/5401645/putins-oligarchs/.

6 S. Rep. No 116-XX, *Report of the Select Committee on Intelligence, United States Senate, on Russian Active Measures Campaigns and Interference in the 2016 U.S. Election, vol. 5, Counterintelligence Threats and Vulnerabilities*, 718–19 (2020), https://www.intelligence.senate.gov/sites/default/files/documents/report_volume5.pdf.

7   Special Counsel Robert S. Mueller III, *Report on the Investigation into Russian Interference in the 2016 Presidential Election,* U.S. Department of Justice, Washington D.C., March 2019, 163–64, https://www.justice.gov/archives/sco/file/1373816/dl.

8   Zinaida Paramonova, "Who Is the Russian Oligarch Caught Criticising Putin in Leaked Audio?," *Novaya Gazeta Europe*, March 31, 2023, https://novayagazeta.eu/articles/2023/03/31/who-is-the-russian-oligarch-caught-criticising-putin-in-leaked-audio-en.

9   Belford and Klasfeld, "Behind Trump's Turkish 'Bromance.'"

10 Michael Dobbs, "The 1991 Coup Attempt That the Soviet President Barely Survived," *Washington Post*, August 30, 2022, https://www.washingtonpost.com/history/2022/08/30/coup-attempt-mikhail-gorbachev/.

11 David Remnick, "Yeltsin Elected President of Russia," *Washington Post*, June 14, 1991, https://www.washingtonpost.com/wp-srv/inatl/longterm/russiagov/stories/pres061491.htm.

12 Camille Grand, "Defence Spending: Sustaining the Effort in the Long-Term," *NATO Review*, July 3, 2023, https://www.nato.int/docu/review/articles/2023/07/03/defence-spending-sustaining-the-effort-in-the-long-term/index.html.

13 Greg Rosalsky, "How 'Shock Therapy' Created Russian Oligarchs and Paved the Path for Putin," *Planet Money*, NPR, March 22, 2022, https://www.npr.org/sections/money/2022/03/22/1087654279/how-shock-therapy-created-russian-oligarchs-and-paved-the-path-for-putin.

14 Mark Galeotti, "Gangster's Paradise: How Organised Crime Took over Russia," *Guardian*, March 23, 2018, https://www.theguardian.com/news/2018/mar/23/how-organised-crime-took-over-russia-vory-super-mafia.

15 Andrew E. Kramer, "The Euro in 2010 Feels Like the Ruble in 1998," *New York Times*, May 12, 2010, https://www.nytimes.com/2010/05/12/business/global/12iht-ruble.html.

16 Gregory Feifer, "What Happened to Russian Democracy?" *All Things Considered*, NPR, March 8, 2007, https://www.npr.org/2007/03/08/7762959/what-happened-to-russian-democracy.

17 "Yeltsin: A Flawed Leader Who Shattered Soviet Union," Reuters, August 9, 2007, https://www.reuters.com/article/us-russia-yeltsin-obituary/yeltsin-a-flawed-leader-who-shattered-soviet-union-idUSL1023841420070423/.

18 Von Jörg R. Mettke, "The Rise and Fall of the Drunken Czar," *Spiegel International*, April 24, 2007, https://www.spiegel.de/international/world/boris-yeltsin-rip-the-rise-and-fall-of-the-drunken-czar-a-479096.html.

19 Mark Tran, "Yeltsin Resigns," *Guardian*, December 31, 1999, https://www.theguardian.com/world/1999/dec/31/russia.marktran.

20 Anders Åslund, "The Illusions of Putin's Russia," Atlantic Council, May 6, 2019, https://www.atlanticcouncil.org/blogs/ukrainealert/the-illusions-of-putin-s-russia/.

21 Alan Cullison et al., "In Putin's Past, Glimpses of Russia's Hardline Future," *Wall Street Journal*, December 21, 2007, https://www.wsj.com/articles/SB119820263246543973.

22 Mark Tran, "Who Is Vladimir Putin?,"*Guardian*, August 9, 1999, https://www.theguardian.com/world/1999/aug/09/russia.marktran1.

23 Steven Lee Myers, "Russia Closes File on Three 1999 Bombings," *New York Times*, May 1, 2003, https://www.nytimes.com/2003/05/01/world/russia-closes-file-on-three-1999-bombings.html.

24 Susan B. Glasser and Peter Baker, "Chechnya War a Deepening Trap for Putin," *Washington Post*, September 12, 2004, https://www.washingtonpost.com/archive/politics/2004/09/13/chechnya-war-a-deepening-trap-for-putin/9e793e43-740b-4730-9b5b-89dca8055618/.

25 Jill Dougherty, "Putin Marks Victory in Dagestan; Russia Bombs Chechen Bases," CNN, August 26, 1999, http://edition.cnn.com/WORLD/europe/9908/26/russian.dagestan/.

26 "Putin's Revenge, Part One," *Frontline*, PBS, February 8, 2019, video, 53:07, https://www.youtube.com/watch?v=o2L8qINZD3Q.

27 Vladimir Putin et al., *First Person: An Astonishingly Frank Self-Portrait by Russia's President*, trans. Catherine Fitzpatric (PublicAffairs, 2000).

28 "March 26, 2000: Vladimir Putin Elected President of Russia | F. Rewind," *Firstpost*, March 26, 2023, video, 1:44, https://www.youtube.com/watch?v=F6xeTr5ggKU.

29 Ian Traynor, "Putin's Men Raid Dissenting TV Offices," *Guardian*, May 12, 2000, https://www.theguardian.com/world/2000/may/12/russia.iantraynor.

30 David Hoffman, "Masked Gunmen Raid Russian Media Group Critical of the Kremlin," *Washington Post*, May 12, 2000, https://www.washingtonpost.com/archive/politics/2000/05/12/masked-gunmen-raid-russian-media-group-critical-of-the-kremlin/16af5f7c-c98c-4112-baad-5e9be904219a/.

31 "Rise and Fall of the Most Popular Independent TV Channel in Russia," Редакция *[Redatsiya]*, April 25, 2021, video, 1:50:22, https://www.youtube.com/watch?v=MbPdOY3H04w.

32 "Ten Years Ago, Russia's Independent NTV, the Talk of the Nation, Fell Silent," RFE/RL, April 14, 2011, https://www.rferl.org/a/russia_independent_ntv_fell_silent/3557594.html.

33 David Hoffman, "Probers Jail Top Russian Media Mogul," *Washington Post*, June 14, 2000, https://www.washingtonpost.com/wp-srv/WPcap/2000-06/14/060r-061400-idx.html?itid=lk_inline_manual_11.

34 Jonas Bernstein, "Why They're Praying for Russia's NTV," *Wall Street Journal*, April 6, 2001, https://www.wsj.com/articles/SB986512509488938348.

35 "Ten Years Ago," RFE/RL.

36 Alan Cullison, "Gazprom Supplants NTV Board Members, Threatening the Network's Independence," *Wall Street Journal*, April 4, 2001, https://www.wsj.com/articles/SB986296385516160163?mod=article_inline.

37 Luke Harding, "Boris Berezovsky: A Tale of Revenge, Betrayal and Feuds With Putin", *Guardian*, March 23, 2013, https://www.theguardian.com/world/2013/mar/23/boris-berezovsky-vladimir-putin-feud.

38 Ian Traynor, "Victory for Putin in Battle for 'Russia's BBC1,'" *Guardian*, September 5, 2000, https://www.theguardian.com/world/2000/sep/05/iantraynor.

39 Ian Traynor, "Putin Gained from Aeroflot Scam, Says Media Mogul," *Guardian*, November 16, 2000, https://www.theguardian.com/world/2000/nov/16/russia.iantraynor?INTCMP=ILCNETTXT3487.

40 Miriam Elder, "Boris Berezovsky: Kingmaker Reduced to a Shadow in Exile," *Guardian*, March 23, 2013, https://www.theguardian.com/world/2013/mar/23/boris-berezovsky-kingmaker-vladimir-putin.

41 Traynor, "Putin Gained."

42 Elder, "Boris Berezovsky."

43 Masha Gessen, "The Wrath of Putin," *Vanity Fair*, March 2, 2012, https://www.vanityfair.com/news/politics/2012/04/vladimir-putin-mikhail-khodorkovsky-russia.

44 Susan B. Glasser and Peter Baker, "Russian Tycoon and Putin Critic Arrested in Raid," *Washington Post*, October 25, 2003, https://www.washingtonpost.com/archive/politics/2003/10/26/russian-tycoon-and-putin-critic-arrested-in-raid/22e60f62-2db0-4dc3-b95c-cc90c0cbc1bf/.

45 Henry Foy, "'We Need to Talk about Igor': The Rise of Russia's Most Powerful Oligarch," *Financial Times*, March 1, 2018, https://www.ft.com/content/dc7d48f8-1c13-11e8-aaca-4574d7dabfb6.

46 "Ousting the Oligarchs," *Guardian*, May 31, 2005, https://www.theguardian.com/world/2005/may/31/russia.

47 Raymond Bonner, "Russian Gangsters Exploit Capitalism to Increase Profits," *New York Times*, July 25, 1999, https://www.nytimes.com/1999/07/25/world/russian-gangsters-exploit-capitalism-to-increase-profits.html.

48 Galeotti, "Gangster's Paradise."

49 Tatiana Stanovaya, "The Putin Regime Cracks," Carnegie Endowment for International Peace, May 7, 2020, https://carnegieendowment.org/research/2020/02/the-putin-regime-cracks?lang=en.

50 Andrei Soldatov and Irina Borogan, *The New Nobility: The Restoration of Russia's Security State and the Enduring Legacy of the KGB* (PublicAffairs, 2010), introduction, Kindle.

51 Calder Walton, "What Comes after Putin's Rule in Russia. The West Should Beware," *Time*, June 2, 2023, https://time.com/6284209/after-vladimir-putins-rule-in-russia/.

52 Edward Lucas, "State Security, Post-Soviet Style," review of *The New Nobility*, by Andrei Soldatov and Irina Borogan, *Wall Street Journal*, September 17, 2010, https://www.wsj.com/articles/SB10001424052748703466704575489774021664514.

53 OECD, *OECD Factbook 2014: Economic, Environmental and Social Statistics* (OECD Publishing, 2014), pg. 123, http://dx.doi.org/10.1787/factbook-2014-en.

54 Anders Aslund et al., "Russia's Response to the Financial Crisis," Carnegie Endowment for International Peace, May 4, 2010, https://carnegieendowment.org/events/2010/05/russias-response-to-the-financial-crisis?lang=en.

55 Luke Harding, "Russia Close to Economic Collapse as Oil Price Falls, Experts Predict," *Guardian*, November 20, 2008, https://www.theguardian.com/world/2008/nov/20/oil-russia-economy-putin-medvedev.

56 Philip P. Pan, "Russian Elite Look to Kremlin as Wealth Dries Up," NBC News, October 17, 2008, https://www.nbcnews.com/id/wbna27232646.

57 "Russia: Layoffs, Wage Cuts and Arrears Are Rising," *New York Times*, November 25, 2008, https://www.nytimes.com/2008/12/25/news/25iht-25oxan-ruble.18922683.html.

58 "Numbers Illustrate Russian Economy's Weakness," *New York Times*, November 9, 2009, https://www.nytimes.com/2009/02/19/business/worldbusiness/19iht-ruble.4.20313245.html.

59 Gregory Feifer, "Corruption in Russia, Part 2: Law Enforcers Often the Worst Offenders," RFE/RL, November 28, 2009, https://www.rferl.org/a/Law_Enforcers_Often_The_Worst_Offenders/1890104.html.

60 Gregory Feifer, "Corruption in Russia, Part 1: A Normal Part of Everyday Life," RFE/RL, November 27, 2009, https://www.rferl.org/a/Corruption_in_Russia_Part_1_A_Normal_Part_Of_Everyday_Life_/1889394.html.

61 Michael Schwirtz and David M. Herszenhorn, "Voters Watch Polls in Russia, and Fraud Is What They See," *New York Times*, December 5, 2011, https://www.nytimes.com/2011/12/06/world/europe/russian-parliamentary-elections-criticized-by-west.html.

62 Gregory L. White and Rob Barry, "Russia's Dubious Vote," *Wall Street Journal*, December 28, 2011, https://www.wsj.com/articles/SB10001424052970203391104577124540544822220.

63 Ellen Barry, "Rally Defying Putin's Party Draws Tens of Thousands," *New York Times*, December 10, 2011, https://www.nytimes.com/2011/12/11/world/europe/thousands-protest-in-moscow-russia-in-defiance-of-putin.html.

64 Tom Parfitt, "Anti-Putin Protesters March through Moscow," *Guardian*, February 4, 2012, https://www.theguardian.com/world/2012/feb/04/anti-putin-protests-moscow-russia.

65 Ellen Barry and Michael Schwirtz, "Arrests and Violence at Overflowing Rally in Moscow," *New York Times*, May 6, 2012, https://www.nytimes.com/2012/05/07/world/europe/at-moscow-rally-arrests-and-violence.html.

66 David M. Herszenhorn and Ellen Barry, "Putin Contends Clinton Incited Unrest over Vote," *New York Times*, December 8, 2011, https://www.nytimes.com/2011/12/09/world/europe/putin-accuses-clinton-of-instigating-russian-protests.html.

67 Elise Labott, "Clinton Cites 'Serious Concerns' about Russian Election," CNN, December 6, 2011, https://edition.cnn.com/2011/12/06/world/europe/russia-elections-clinton/index.html.

68 "Moscow Court Jails Seven Anti-Putin Bolotnaya Activists," BBC, February 24, 2014, https://www.bbc.com/news/world-europe-26323760.

69 Karoun Demirjian, "Meanwhile in Russia, Putin Passes Law against Protests," *Washington Post*, July 22, 2014, https://www.washingtonpost.com/news/worldviews/wp/2014/07/22/meanwhile-in-russia-putin-passes-law-against-protests/.

70 Priyanka Boghani, "Putin's Legal Crackdown on Civil Society," *Frontline*, PBS, January 13, 2015, https://www.pbs.org/wgbh/frontline/article/putins-legal-crackdown-on-civil-society/.

71 Grey et al., "Special Report-Putin's Allies."

72 Piper, "Special Report."

73 Jamila Trindle, "The Loan That Launched a Crisis," *Foreign Policy*, February 21, 2014, https://foreignpolicy.com/2014/02/21/the-loan-that-launched-a-crisis/.

74 David M. Herszenhorn, "Thousands Demand Resignation of Ukraine Leader," *New York Times*, December 1, 2013, https://www.nytimes.com/2013/12/02/world/europe/thousands-of-protesters-in-ukraine-demand-leaders-resignation.html.

75 Ora John Reuter and David Szakonyi, "In Russia, the Political Impact of Social Media Varies by Platform," *Washington Post*, December 31, 2014, https://www.washingtonpost.com/news/monkey-cage/wp/2014/12/31/in-russia-the-political-impact-of-social-media-varies-by-platform/.

76 Shaun Walker, "Founder of Vkontakte Leaves after Dispute with Kremlin-Linked Owners," *Guardian*, April 2, 2014, https://www.theguardian.com/media/2014/apr/02/founder-pavel-durov-leaves-russian-social-network-site-vkontakte.

77 Reuter and Szakonyi, "In Russia."

78 Walker, "Founder."

79 "Pro-Kremlin Tycoon Usmanov Buys Up Russian Social Media," RFE/RL, September 16, 2014, https://www.rferl.org/a/usmanov-tycoon-vkontakte-mailru-purchase-durov/26587475.html.

80 Aleksandra Garmazhapova, "Где живут тролли. И кто их кормит" [Where do trolls live? And who feeds them], *Новая Газета* [*Novaya Gazeta*], September 7, 2013, https://novayagazeta.ru/articles/2013/09/07/56253-gde-zhivut-trolli-i-kto-ih-kormit.

81 Max Seddon, "Documents Show How Russia's Troll Army Hit America," *BuzzFeed News*, June 2, 2014, https://www.buzzfeednews.com/article/maxseddon/documents-show-how-russias-troll-army-hit-america.

82 "Who Is Yevgeny Prigozhin, the Man behind the Wagner Group?," *Economist*, September 29, 2022, https://www.economist.com/the-economist-explains/2022/09/29/who-is-yevgeny-prigozhin-the-man-behind-the-wagner-group.

83 Mick Krever, Anna Chernova, "Wagner Chief Admits to Founding Russian Troll Farm Sanctioned for Meddling in US Elections," CNN, February 14, 2023, https://edition.cnn.com/2023/02/14/europe/russia-yevgeny-prigozhin-internet-research-agency-intl/index.html.

84. Maria Lipman, "Media Manipulation and Political Control in Russia," Carnegie Russia Eurasia Center, February 3, 2009, https://carnegieendowment.org/posts/2009/02/media-manipulation-and-political-control-in-russia?lang=en&center=russia-eurasia.

85. Garmazhapova, "Где живут тролли. И кто их кормит."

86. Steven Lee Myers, Ellen Barry, "Putin Reclaims Crimea for Russia and Bitterly Denounces the West," *New York Times*, March 18, 2014, https://www.nytimes.com/2014/03/19/world/europe/ukraine.html.

87. Andrew E. Kramer and Michael R. Gordon, "Russia Sent Tanks to Separatists in Ukraine, U.S. Says," *New York Times*, June 13, 2014, https://www.nytimes.com/2014/06/14/world/europe/ukraine-claims-full-control-of-port-city-of-mariupol.html.

88. Seddon, "Documents Show."

89. Chris Elliott, "The Readers' Editor on . . . Pro-Russia Trolling below the Line on Ukraine Stories," *Guardian*, May 4, 2014, https://www.theguardian.com/commentisfree/2014/may/04/pro-russia-trolls-ukraine-guardian-online.

90. Ellen Nakashima, "Inside a Russian Disinformation Campaign in Ukraine in 2014," *Washington Post*, December 25, 2017, https://www.washingtonpost.com/world/national-security/inside-a-russian-disinformation-campaign-in-ukraine-in-2014/2017/12/25/f55b0408-e71d-11e7-ab50-621fe0588340_story.html.

91. Adam Entous et al., "Kremlin Trolls Burned across the Internet as Washington Debated Options," *Washington Post*, December 25, 2017, https://www.washingtonpost.com/world/national-security/kremlin-trolls-burned-across-the-internet-as-washington-debated-options/2017/12/23/e7b9dc92-e403-11e7-ab50-621fe0588340_story.html.

92. "Russia Flaunts Grip on Crimea with Prime Minister's Visit," Reuters, March 31, 2014, https://www.reuters.com/article/world/russia-flaunts-grip-on-crimea-with-prime-minister-s-visit-idUSDEEA2U07X.

93. "Russia Flaunts," Reuters.

94. Myers and Barry, "Putin Reclaims."

95. Jeffrey Herf, "Trump's Refusal to Acknowledge Defeat Mirrors the Lie That Fueled the Nazi Rise," *Washington Post*, November 23, 2020, https://www.washingtonpost.com/outlook/2020/11/23/trumps-refusal-acknowledge-defeat-mirrors-lie-that-fueled-nazi-rise/.

96. John Herbst and Sergei Erofeev, *The Putin Exodus: The New Russian Brain Drain* (Atlantic Council, 2019), https://www.atlanticcouncil.org/wp-content/uploads/2019/09/The-Putin-Exodus.pdf.

97. Mikhail Bushuev, "The Man Who Dared to Criticize Putin," DW, February 27, 2020, https://www.dw.com/en/boris-nemtsov-the-man-who-dared-to-criticize-vladimir-putin/a-52561085.

98. Tim Lister et al., "Russian Opposition Leader Alexey Navalny Dupes Spy into Revealing How He Was Poisoned," CNN, December 21, 2020, https://www.cnn.com/2020/12/21/europe/russia-navalny-poisoning-underpants-ward/index.html.

99. Andrew Roth and Luke Harding, "Alexei Navalny Detained at Airport on Return to Russia," *Guardian*, January 17, 2021, https://www.theguardian.com/world/2021/jan/17/alexei-navalny-detained-at-airport-on-return-to-russia.

100. Lucy Papachristou, "What We Know about Alexei Navalny's Death in Arctic Prison," Reuters, February 19, 2024, https://www.reuters.com/world/europe/alexei-navalnys-death-what-do-we-know-2024-02-18/.

CHAPTER 16

1. Seddon, "Documents Show."
2. Elliott, "Readers' Editor."
3. Mary Ellen Connell and Ryan Evans, *Russia's "Ambiguous Warfare" and Implications for the U.S. Marine Corps*, CNA, May 2015, https://www.cna.org/archive/CNA_Files/pdf/dop-2015-u-010447-final.pdf.
4. "Senate Intel Committee Releases Bipartisan Report on Russia's Use of Social Media," U.S. Select Committee on Intelligence, press release, October 8, 2019, https://www.intelligence.senate.gov/press/senate-intel-committee-releases-bipartisan-report-russia's-use-social-media.
5. S. Rep. No 116-XX, *vol. 2, Russia's Use of Social Media with Additional Views* (2019), https://www.intelligence.senate.gov/sites/default/files/documents/Report_Volume2.pdf.
6. Thomas Grove and Robin Pomeroy "Armenia Says Will Join Russia-Led Customs Union," Reuters, September 3, 2013, https://www.reuters.com/article/us-armenia-russia-customsunion-idUSBRE9820U520130903/.
7. Will Cathcart, "Putin's Power Grab: First Armenia, Now Ukraine," *Daily Beast*, December 4, 2013, https://www.thedailybeast.com/putins-power-grab-first-armenia-now-ukraine.
8. Piper, "Special Report."
9. Julian Borger et al., "EU and US Impose Sweeping Economic Sanctions on Russia," *Guardian*, July 29, 2014, https://www.theguardian.com/world/2014/jul/29/economic-sanctions-russia-eu-governments.
10. Rupert Wiederwald, "Austria's FPÖ under Scrutiny for Russia Ties," DW, May 21, 2019, https://www.dw.com/en/austrias-far-right-fpö-party-under-scrutiny-for-ties-to-russia/a-48822539.
11. Roman Kupchinsky, "Russia/Ukraine: Questions Raised about Gas Deal Intermediary," January 4, 2006, https://www.rferl.org/a/1064405.html.
12. Benjamin Fox, "Russia Invites EU Far-Right to Observe Crimea Vote," *EUobserver*, March 13, 2014, https://euobserver.com/news/123453.
13. "Crimean 'Referendum at Gunpoint' Is a Myth—Intl Observers," RT, March 16, 2014, https://www.rt.com/news/international-observers-crimea-referendum-190/.
14. "Ukraine Should Never Have Had Crimea—Austrian Presidential Candidate," Sputnik International, March 12, 2014, https://sputnikglobe.com/20160312/crimea-cession-ukraine-mistake-1036191955.html.
15. Robbie Gramer, "Austrian Far-Right Politicians Travel to Moscow to Grease Ties between Trump, Putin," *Foreign Policy*, December 19, 2016, https://foreignpolicy.com/2016/12/19/austrian-far-right-politicians-travel-to-moscow-to-grease-ties-between-trump-putin-meet-michael-flynn-politics-europe/.
16. Martin Laine et al., "Kremlin-Linked Group Arranged Payments to European Politicians to Support Russia's Annexation of Crimea," OCCRP, February 3, 2023, https://www.occrp.org/en/investigations/kremlin-linked-group-arranged-payments-to-european-politicians-to-support-russias-annexation-of-crimea.
17. Gramer, "Austrian."
18. Nicola Slawson, "Austrian President Approves Far-Right Freedom Party Joining Coalition Government," *Guardian*, December 16, 2017, https://www.theguardian.com/world/2017/dec/16/austrian-president-approves-far-right-freedom-party-role-in-coalition-government.
19. Souad Mekhennet and Rick Noack, "Austria's Political Crisis Refocuses Attention on the Far Right's Ties to Russia," *Washington Post*, May 21, 2019, https://www.washingtonpost.com/world/national-security/austrias-political-crisis-refocuses-attention-on-the-far-rights-ties-to-russia/2019/05/21/5e34de0a-71af-11e9-8be0-ca575670e91c_story.html.

20 Boris Groendahl, "Ukrainian Oligarch Firtash Loses Fight over U.S. Extradition," Bloomberg, June 25, 2019, https://www.bloomberg.com/news/articles/2019-06-25/firtash-extradition-to-u-s-allowed-by-top-austrian-court.

21 Ostap Yarysh, "Austria: Firtash Extradition to US Blocked by 'Extensive' Bid to Reopen Case," VOA, July 16, 2019, https://www.voanews.com/a/europe_austria-firtash-extradition-us-blocked-extensive-bid-reopen-case/6171994.html.

22 Lili Bayer, "Why Putin Needs Orbán," *Politico*, February 1, 2017, https://www.politico.eu/article/why-vladimir-putin-needs-viktor-orban-russia-hungary/.

23 Tim Gosling, "Hungary's Energy Dalliance with Russia," *Politico*, April 17, 2020, https://www.politico.eu/article/hungary-energy-dalliance-with-russia/.

24 Anthony Faiola, "From Russia with Love: An Energy Deal for Hungary," *Washington Post*, February 16, 2015, https://www.washingtonpost.com/world/europe/from-russia-with-love-an-energy-deal-for-hungary/2015/02/16/05216670-b134-11e4-bf39-5560f3918d4b_story.html.

25 Rick Lyman and Alison Smale, "Defying Soviets, Then Pulling Hungary to Putin," *New York Times*, November 7, 2014, https://www.nytimes.com/2014/11/08/world/europe/viktor-orban-steers-hungary-toward-russia-25-years-after-fall-of-the-berlin-wall.html.

26 Gergely Szakacs, "Europe 'Shot Itself in Foot' with Russia Sanctions: Hungary PM", Reuters, August 15, 2014, https://www.reuters.com/article/idUSKBN0GF0ES/.

27 Zoltan Simon, "Orban Says He Seeks to End Liberal Democracy in Hungary," Bloomberg News, July 28, 2014, https://www.bloomberg.com/news/articles/2014-07-28/orban-says-he-seeks-to-end-liberal-democracy-in-hungary.

28 Romain Geoffroy and Maxime Vaudano, "What Are Marine Le Pen's Ties to Vladimir Putin's Russia?" *Le Monde*, April 21, 2022, https://www.lemonde.fr/en/les-decodeurs/article/2022/04/21/what-are-marine-le-pen-s-ties-to-vladimir-putin-s-russia_5981192_8.html.

29 Paul Sonne, "A Russian Bank Gave Marine Le Pen's Party a Loan. Then Weird Things Began Happening," December 27, 2018, https://www.washingtonpost.com/world/national-security/a-russian-bank-gave-marine-le-pens-party-a-loan-then-weird-things-began-happening/2018/12/27/960c7906-d320-11e8-a275-81c671a50422_story.html.

30 David Gilbert, "Russia's Fake News Machine Is Now Targeting the French Election," April 21, 2017, https://www.vice.com/en/article/paz4vg/russias-fake-news-machine-is-now-targeting-the-french-election.

31 Gabriel Gatehouse, "Marine Le Pen: Who's Funding France's Far Right?" BBC, April 3, 2017, https://www.bbc.com/news/world-europe-39478066.

32 "The Latest: Le Pen Vows to Pull France Out of EU, NATO," Associated Press, February 5, 2017, https://apnews.com/article/0bb51aea51214887ad2c2454cd54a32a.

33 David D. Kirkpatrick, "Signs of Russian Meddling in Brexit Referendum," *New York Times*, November 15, 2017, https://www.nytimes.com/2017/11/15/world/europe/russia-brexit-twitter-facebook.html.

34 Patrick Wintour and Rowena Mason, "Nigel Farage's Relationship with Russian Media Comes under Scrutiny," *Guardian*, March 31, 2014, https://www.theguardian.com/politics/2014/mar/31/nigel-farage-relationship-russian-media-scrutiny.

35 UK Parliament, *Written Evidence Submitted by Ben Nimmo and Dr Jonathan Eyal, Russia's Information Warfare—Airbrushing Reality*, March 14, 2016, https://committees.parliament.uk/writtenevidence/65511/pdf/.

36 "The Anti Man," *Economist*, September 19, 2015, https://www.economist.com/britain/2015/09/19/the-anti-man.

37 "Montenegro: Russians behind Coup Attempt", DW, November 6, 2016, https://www.dw.com/en/russians-behind-montenegro-coup-attempt-says-prosecutor/a-36284714.

38 Stevo Vasiljevic, "Russians, Opposition Figures Sentenced over Role in 2016 Montenegro Coup Attempt," Reuters, May 9 2019, https://www.reuters.com/article/us-montenegro-court-idUSKCN1SF144/.

39 Alina Polyakova et al., "The Kremlin's Trojan Horses," Atlantic Council, November 15, 2016, https://www.atlanticcouncil.org/in-depth-research-reports/report/kremlin-trojan-horses/.

40 Markos Kounalakis et al., "The Kremlin's Trojan Horses 2.0: Russian Influence in Greece, Italy, and Spain," Atlantic Council, November 15, 2017, https://www.atlanticcouncil.org/in-depth-research-reports/report/the-kremlin-s-trojan-horses-2-0/.

41 Alina Polyakova et al., "The Kremlin's Trojan Horses 3.0: Russian Influence in Denmark, the Netherlands, Norway, and Sweden," Atlantic Council, December 4, 2018, https://www.atlanticcouncil.org/in-depth-research-reports/report/the-kremlins-trojan-horses-3-0/#netherlands.

42 "Russia behind Hack on German Parliament, Reports," DW, December 11, 2016, https://www.dw.com/en/russia-behind-hack-on-german-parliament-paper-reports/a-36729079.

43 David D. Kirkpatrick, "British Cybersecurity Chief Warns of Russian Hacking," New York Times, November 14, 2017, https://www.nytimes.com/2017/11/14/world/europe/britain-russia-cybersecurity-hacking.html.

44 Kevin Collier and Jason Leopold, "Russian Hackers Targeted Swedish News Sites in 2016, State Department Cable Says," Buzzfeed News, August 10, 2018, https://www.buzzfeednews.com/article/kevincollier/2016-sweden-ddos-expressen-hack-russia-cables.

45 Robert Windrem, "Timeline: Ten Years of Russian Cyber Attacks on Other Nations," NBC News, December 18, 2016, https://www.nbcnews.com/storyline/hacking-in-america/timeline-ten-years-russian-cyber-attacks-other-nations-n697111.

46 Missy Ryan, "Russia Spent Millions on Secret Global Political Campaign, U.S. Intelligence Finds," Washington Post, September 13, 2022, https://www.washingtonpost.com/national-security/2022/09/13/united-states-russia-political-campaign/.

47 Pavel K. Baev, "How Bad Judgement Calls Brought a Chain of Blunders: Soviet Responses to the Iranian Revolution," Brookings Institution, March 7, 2019, https://www.brookings.edu/articles/how-bad-judgement-calls-brought-a-chain-of-blunders-soviet-responses-to-the-iranian-revolution/.

48 Anthony Austin, "Soviet Reassessing Its Position on Iran," New York Times, September 13, 1979, https://www.nytimes.com/1979/09/13/archives/soviet-reassessing-its-position-on-iran-critical-remarks-about.html.

49 Ali Fatollah-Nejad, "Four Decades Later, Did the Iranian Revolution Fulfill Its Promises?" Brookings Institution, July 11, 2019, https://www.brookings.edu/articles/four-decades-later-did-the-iranian-revolution-fulfill-its-promises/.

50 Michael Dobbs, "Soviets Agree to Strengthen Iran's Military," Washington Post, June 22, 1989, https://www.washingtonpost.com/archive/politics/1989/06/23/soviets-agree-to-strengthen-irans-military/949c9c68-f810-4448-a75d-b87f6abaa21c/.

51 "Iran Criticizes Russia for Missile Deal Ban," VOA, September 22, 2010, https://www.voanews.com/a/iran-criticizes-russia-for-missile-deal-ban-103623094/172331.html.

52 "Treasury Announces Additional Sanctions against Iranian Engineering and Shipping Firms," U.S. Department of the Treasury, press release, March 28, 2012, https://home.treasury.gov/news/press-releases/tg1509.

53 "Treasury Sanctions Iranian Government and Affiliates," U.S. Department of the Treasury, press release, November 8, 2012, https://home.treasury.gov/news/press-releases/tg1760.

54. Kandemir, "Turkey."
55. Najmeh Bozorgmehr, "Inflation and Weak Rial Push Iran's Middle Class towards Poverty," *Financial Times*, October 25, 2013, https://www.ft.com/content/4d017b7a-3cc2-11e3-86ef-00144feab7de.
56. Borzou Daragahi, "How Iran Can Evade Sanctions This Time," *Atlantic*, May 22, 2018, https://www.theatlantic.com/international/archive/2018/05/iran-sanctions-trump-nuclear-turkey/560819/.
57. "Iran Nuclear Deal: What It All Means," BBC News, November 23, 2021, https://www.bbc.com/news/world-middle-east-33521655.
58. Jackie Northam, "Lifting Sanctions Will Release $100 Billion to Iran. Then What?" *All Things Considered*, NPR, July 16, 2015, https://www.npr.org/sections/parallels/2015/07/16/423562391/lifting-sanctions-will-release-100-billion-to-iran-then-what.
59. Jennifer R. Williams, "A Comprehensive Timeline of the Iran Nuclear Deal," Brookings Institution, July 21, 2015, https://www.brookings.edu/articles/a-comprehensive-timeline-of-the-iran-nuclear-deal/.
60. Elizabeth Whitman, "What Sanctions against Iran Won't Be Lifted? Bans for Terrorism Support, Human Rights Abuses to Remain Intact," *International Business Times*, July 14, 2015, https://www.ibtimes.com/what-sanctions-against-iran-wont-be-lifted-bans-terrorism-support-human-rights-abuses-2008066.
61. Nicole Grajewski, "The Evolution of Russian and Iranian Cooperation in Syria," Center for Strategic & International Studies, November 17, 2021, https://www.csis.org/analysis/evolution-russian-and-iranian-cooperation-syria.
62. Farnaz Fassihi and Jay Solomon, "Syria Regime Rocked by Protests," *Wall Street Journal*, March 26, 2011, https://www.wsj.com/articles/SB10001424052748704517404576222350109783770.
63. Bassem Mroue, "Syrian Tanks Attack Towns That Held Protests," NBC News, May 29, 2011, https://www.nbcnews.com/id/wbna43209537.
64. "Syria's War Explained from the Beginning," Al Jazeera, April 14, 2018, https://www.aljazeera.com/news/2018/4/14/syrias-war-explained-from-the-beginning.
65. C. J. Chivers and Eric Schmitt, "Saudis Step up Help for Rebels in Syria with Croatian Arms," *New York Times*, February 25, 2013, https://www.nytimes.com/2013/02/26/world/middleeast/in-shift-saudis-are-said-to-arm-rebels-in-syria.html.
66. "General Assembly Passes Resolution on Syria as Deaths Mount," CNN, February 16, 2012, https://edition.cnn.com/2012/02/16/world/meast/syria-unrest/index.html.
67. "Isis Rebels Declare 'Islamic State' in Iraq and Syria", BBC News, June 13, 2014, https://www.bbc.com/news/world-middle-east-28082962.
68. Denver Nicks, "U.S. Forms Anti-ISIS Coalition at NATO Summit,"*Time*, September 5, 2014, https://time.com/3273185/isis-us-nato/.
69. Joe Parkinson and Dion Nissenbaum, "U.S., Allies Training Kurds on Using Sophisticated Weaponry against Islamic State," *Wall Street Journal*, September 21, 2014, https://www.wsj.com/articles/u-s-allies-training-kurds-on-using-sophisticated-weaponry-against-islamic-state-1411339625.
70. Vivian Salama and Sameer N. Yacoub, "Iraq Crisis Deepens; US Directly Arms Kurds," Associated Press, August 11, 2014, https://apnews.com/article/e063e183e0684966ba64b16dd889deb8#.
71. "Erdogan 'Condemns' US for Backing YPG," DW, May 28, 2016, https://www.dw.com/en/turkish-president-erdogan-condemns-us-for-backing-kurdish-fighters-in-syria/a-19291004.

72   "Russia Joins War in Syria: Five Key Points," BBC News, October 1, 2015, https://www.bbc.com/news/world-middle-east-34416519.

73   Alexander Pearson and Lewis Sanders IV, "Syria: What Do Key Foreign Powers Want?," DW, January 23, 2019, https://www.dw.com/en/syria-conflict-what-do-the-us-russia-turkey-and-iran-want/a-41211604.

74   "Russian and Iranian Leaders Discuss Syria in Tehran," Al Jazeera, November 23, 2015, https://www.aljazeera.com/news/2015/11/23/russian-and-iranian-leaders-discuss-syria-in-tehran.

75   Martin Chulov and Kareem Shaheen, "Syrian Rebels Decry Russian Airstrikes: 'We Have Not Had ISIS Here in over a Year,'" *Guardian*, October 11, 2015, https://www.theguardian.com/world/2015/oct/11/syrian-rebels-decry-russian-airstrikes-we-have-not-had-isis-here-in-over-a-year.

76   "Strikes on Schools and Hospitals in Syria 'War Crimes,'" Al Jazeera, February 16, 2016, https://www.aljazeera.com/news/2016/2/16/strikes-on-schools-and-hospitals-in-syria-war-crimes.

77   Martin Chulov and Shiv Malik, "Four Syrian Hospitals Bombed since Russian Airstrikes Began, Doctors Say," *Guardian*, October 22, 2015, https://www.theguardian.com/world/2015/oct/22/three-syrian-hospitals-bombed-since-russian-airstrikes-began-doctors-say.

78   Chase Winter, "Russian Strikes in Syria Kill 18,000," DW, October 1, 2018, https://www.dw.com/en/russian-airstrikes-in-syria-reportedly-killed-18000-people/a-45702091.

79   Rick Noack, "This Map Helps Explain Why Some European Countries Reject Refugees, and Others Love Them," *Washington Post*, September 8, 2015, https://www.washingtonpost.com/news/worldviews/wp/2015/09/08/this-map-helps-explain-why-some-european-countries-reject-refugees-and-others-love-them/.

80   Michael Martinez, "Syrian Refugees: Which Countries Welcome Them, Which Ones Don't," CNN, September 10, 2015, https://edition.cnn.com/2015/09/09/world/welcome-syrian-refugees-countries/index.html.

81   Melissa Eddy, "Violent Backlash against Migrants in Germany as Asylum-Seekers Pour In," *New York Times*, August 13, 2015, https://www.nytimes.com/2015/08/14/world/europe/germany-migrants-attacks-asylum-seekers-backlash.html.

82   Riham Alkousaa, "Germany's Far-Right AfD Calls for Repatriation of Syrian Refugees," Reuters, November 9, 2017, https://www.reuters.com/article/us-europe-migrants-germany-syria/germanys-far-right-afd-calls-for-repatriation-of-syrian-refugees-idUSKBN1D92QI/.

83   Yoruk Bahceli, "Wilders Tells Dutch Parliament Refugee Crisis Is 'Islamic Invasion,'" Reuters, September 10, 2015, https://www.reuters.com/article/world/wilders-tells-dutch-parliament-refugee-crisis-is-islamic-invasion-idUSKCN0RA14A/.

84   "Hungarian Prime Minister Says Migrants Are 'Poison' and 'Not Needed,'" *Guardian*, July 27, 2016, https://www.theguardian.com/world/2016/jul/26/hungarian-prime-minister-viktor-orban-praises-donald-trump.

85   Marcus Walker, "Austria's Right-Wing Parties Enjoy Strong Showing in Parliamentary Elections," *Wall Street Journal*, October 16, 2017, https://www.wsj.com/articles/austria-expected-to-shift-right-in-election-marked-by-fierce-immigration-debate-1508067711.

86   Krishnadev Calamur, "Why Sweden's Far Right Is on the Rise," *Atlantic*, September 8, 2018, https://www.theatlantic.com/international/archive/2018/09/sweden-election/569500/.

87   "Russian Bombing in Syria 'Fuels Refugee Crisis' Says US Official as Airstrike Kills 39," *Guardian*, January 9, 2016, https://www.theguardian.com/world/2016/jan/09/imprecise-russian-bombing-syria-fuelling-refugee-crisis-us-official.

88   "Breedlove: Russia Using Refugees as 'Weapon,'" DW, March 2, 2016, https://www.dw.com/en/nato-commander-russia-uses-syrian-refugees-as-weapon-against-west/a-19086285.

89 Judit Szakács and Éva Bognár, *The Impact of Disinformation Campaigns about Migrants and Minority Groups in the EU* (European Parliament, 2021), https://www.europarl.europa.eu/RegData/etudes/IDAN/2021/653641/EXPO_IDA(2021)653641_EN.pdf.

90 Sebnem Arsu, "Turkish Premier Urges Assad to Quit in Syria," *New York Times*, November 22, 2011, https://www.nytimes.com/2011/11/23/world/middleeast/turkish-leader-says-syrian-president-should-quit.html.

91 "Syrian Rebels Will Attend Russia-Backed Astana Peace Talks," France 24, January 16, 2017, https://www.france24.com/en/20170116-syria-rebels-will-attend-astana-peace-talks.

92 Alexey Eremenko and Ziad Jaber, "Syria Peace Talks: Why Were Some Nations Invited and Others Not?," NBC News, January 23, 2017, https://www.nbcnews.com/news/world/syria-peace-talks-why-were-some-nations-invited-others-not-n710791.

93 Karen DeYoung and Greg Miller, "First Sign of Enhanced U.S.-Russia Relations under Trump: An Invite to Syria Talks," *Washington Post*, January 13, 2017, https://www.washingtonpost.com/world/national-security/first-sign-of-enhanced-us-russia-relations-under-trump-an-invite-to-syria-talks/2017/01/13/81d443d6-d9b9-11e6-9f9f-5cdb4b7f8dd7_story.html.

94 Eremenko and Jaber, "Syria Peace Talks."

95 Patrick Wintour, "Russia in Power-Broking Role as Syria Peace Talks Begin in Astana," *Guardian*, January 23, 2017, https://www.theguardian.com/world/2017/jan/22/russia-syria-talks-astana-kazakhstan-#_=_.

96 Bayram Balci, "Turkey's Relations with the Syrian Opposition," Carnegie Endowment for International Peace, April 13, 2012, https://carnegieendowment.org/research/2012/04/turkeys-relations-with-the-syrian-opposition?lang=en.

97 Gordon Lubold and Dion Nissenbaum, "Turkey to Join Coalition's Airstrikes against ISIS," *Wall Street Journal*, August 26, 2015, https://www.wsj.com/articles/turkey-to-join-coalitions-airstrikes-against-isis-1440535062.

98 Rikar Hussein and Mutlu Civiroglu, "Kurds in Northern Syria Fear New Turkish Incursion," VOA, June 28, 2017, https://www.voanews.com/a/kurds-in-northern-syria-fear-new-turkish-incursion/3920315.html.

99 Wright, "Trump's Abandonment of Foreign Policy."

100 Arwa Ibrahim, "Syria's Kurds Forge 'Costly Deal' with Al-Assad as US Pulls Out," Al Jazeera, October 15, 2019, https://www.aljazeera.com/news/2019/10/15/syrias-kurds-forge-costly-deal-with-al-assad-as-us-pulls-out.

101 Tom Balmforth et al., "Russia Lands Forces at Former U.S. Air Base in Northern Syria," Reuters, November 15, 2019, https://www.reuters.com/article/us-syria-security-russia-idUSKBN1XP0XN/.

102 Ishaan Tharoor, "How the Rivalry between Russians and Turks Shaped the World," *Washington Post*, December 19, 2016, https://www.washingtonpost.com/news/worldviews/wp/2015/10/09/how-the-rivalry-between-russians-and-turks-shaped-the-world/.

103 "Putin, Turkish Premier to Discuss Economic, Military Cooperation," RFE/RL, July 18, 2005, https://www.rferl.org/a/1059986.html.

104 Sebnem Arsu, "Turkey's Pact with Russia Will Give It Nuclear Plant," *New York Times*, May 12, 2010, https://www.nytimes.com/2010/05/13/world/europe/13turkey.html.

105 Mansur Mirovalev, "Russians Pay the Price of New Anti-Turkish Measures," Al Jazeera, December 28, 2015, https://www.aljazeera.com/features/2015/12/28/russians-pay-the-price-of-new-anti-turkish-measures.

106 Sergey Markedonov and Natalya Ulchenko, "Turkey and Russia: An Evolving Relationship," Carnegie Endowment for International Peace, August 19, 2011, https://carnegieendowment.org/research/2011/08/turkey-and-russia-an-evolving-relationship?lang=en.

107 "Russian Tourists Flooding into Turkey," *Hurriyet Daily News*, October 31, 2014, https://www.hurriyetdailynews.com/russian-tourists-flooding-into-turkey--73719.

108 "Kremlin Says Turkish Pipeline Deal Moving Ahead Despite 'Difficulties,'" RFE/RL, September 24, 2015, https://www.rferl.org/a/kremlin-says-turkish-pipeline-deal-moving-ahead-despite-difficulties/27267089.html.

109 Mirovalev, "Russians Pay."

110 Bayram Balci, "Turkey's Relations with the Syrian Opposition", Carnegie Endowment for International Peace, April 13, 2012, https://carnegieendowment.org/research/2012/04/turkeys-relations-with-the-syrian-opposition?lang=en.

111 Jeffrey Mankoff and Olga Oliker, "Turkey's Downing of a Russian Jet," CSIS, November 25, 2015, https://www.csis.org/analysis/turkeys-downing-russian-jet.

112 Don Melvin et al., "Putin Calls Jet's Downing 'Stab in the Back'; Turkey Says Warning Ignored," CNN, November 24, 2015, https://www.cnn.com/2015/11/24/middleeast/warplane-crashes-near-syria-turkey-border/index.html.

113 Andrew Roth, "Putin Signs Sweeping Economic Sanctions against Turkey," *Washington Post*, November 28, 2015, https://www.washingtonpost.com/world/putin-signs-sweeping-economic-sanctions-against-turkey/2015/11/28/f3f5fff4-9603-11e5-befa-99ceebcbb272_story.html.

114 Emre Peker et al.,, "Putin Says Moscow to Drop Gas Pipeline to Europe," *Wall Street Journal*, December 1, 2014, https://www.wsj.com/articles/putin-and-erdogan-seek-closer-economic-ties-1417448097.

115 Alec Luhn and Ian Black, "Erdoğan Has Apologised for Downing of Russian Jet, Kremlin Says," *Guardian*, June 27, 2016, https://www.theguardian.com/world/2016/jun/27/kremlin-says-erdogan-apologises-russian-jet-turkish.

116 "Russia Closes 'Crisis Chapter' with Turkey," Al Jazeera, June 29, 2016, https://www.aljazeera.com/news/2016/6/29/russia-closes-crisis-chapter-with-turkey.

117 Hüseyin Hayatsever, "Çavuşoğlu Sputnik'e konuştu: Türkiye ve Rusya, Suriye'de savaşı durdurmaya odaklanmalı"[Çavuşoğlu spoke to Sputnik: Türkiye and Russia should focus on stopping the war in Syria], *Sputnik Türkiye*, October 8, 2016, https://sputniknews.com.tr/20161008/cavusoglu-sputnik-turkiye-rusya-suriye-1025196595.html.

118 Belford and Klasfeld, "Behind Trump's Turkish 'Bromance.'"

119 Hayatsever, "Çavuşoğlu."

120 "Russian, Turkish Leaders Agree to Close 'Crisis Chapter' in Ties: Kremlin," Reuters, June 29, 2016, https://www.reuters.com/article/us-russia-turkey-relations-idUSKCN0ZF16M/.

121 Ishaan Tharoor, "Turkey's Erdogan Turned a Failed Coup into His Path to Greater Power," *Washington Post*, July 17, 2017, https://www.washingtonpost.com/news/worldviews/wp/2017/07/17/turkeys-erdogan-turned-a-failed-coup-into-his-path-to-greater-power/.

122 "Turkey Declares 'State of Emergency' after Failed Coup," Al Jazeera, July 21, 2016, https://www.aljazeera.com/news/2016/7/21/turkey-declares-state-of-emergency-after-failed-coup.

123 Gulsen Solaker and Ece Toksabay, "Turkey's Emergency Rule Expires as Erdogan's Powers Expand,"Reuters, July 18, 2018, https://www.reuters.com/article/idUSKBN1K824B/.

124 "Turkey's Coup Attempt: What You Need to Know," BBC News, July 17, 2016, https://www.bbc.com/news/world-europe-36816045.

125 Paul Kirby, "Turkey Coup Attempt: Who's the Target of Erdogan's Purge?" BBC News, July 20, 2016, https://www.bbc.com/news/world-europe-36835340.

126 Josh Keller et al., "The Scale of Turkey's Purge Is Nearly Unprecedented," *New York Times*, August 2, 2016, https://www.nytimes.com/interactive/2016/08/02/world/europe/turkey-purge-erdogan-scale.html.

127 Kirby, "Turkey Coup Attempt."

128 Gall, "Erdogan's Purges."

129 "How Turkey's Courts Turned on Erdogan's Foes," Reuters, May 4, 2020, https://www.reuters.com/investigates/special-report/turkey-judges/.

130 Rod Nordland, "Turkey's Free Press Withers as Erdogan Jails 120 Journalists," *New York Times*, November 17, 2016, https://www.nytimes.com/2016/11/18/world/europe/turkey-press-erdogan-coup.html.

131 Constanze Letsch, "Turkey Shuts Fifteen Media Outlets and Arrests Opposition Editor," *Guardian*, October 31, 2016, https://www.theguardian.com/world/2016/oct/30/turkey-shuts-media-outlets-terrorist-links-civil-servants-press-freedom.

132 "Turkish Media Group Bought by Pro-Government Conglomerate," *New York Times*, March 21, 2018, https://www.nytimes.com/2018/03/21/world/europe/turkey-media-erdogan-dogan.html.

133 "Turkey Leads the World in Jailed Journalists," *Economist*, January 16, 2019, https://www.economist.com/graphic-detail/2019/01/16/turkey-leads-the-world-in-jailed-journalists.

134 Ayla Albayrak and Joe Parkinson, "Turkey's Government Forms 6,000-Member Social Media Team," *Wall Street Journal*, September 16, 2013, https://www.wsj.com/articles/SB10001424127887323527004579079151479634742.

135 Maya Kosoff, "Turkey Blocks Wikipedia amid Dissent Crackdown," *Vanity Fair*, May 1, 2017, https://www.vanityfair.com/news/2017/05/turkey-blocks-wikipedia-amid-dissent-crackdown.

136 Zeynep Bilginsoy and Mehmet Guzel, "Turkey: Social Media Law's Passage Raises Censorship Worries," Associated Press, July 29, 2020, https://apnews.com/article/turkey-istanbul-international-news-legislation-social-media-9abc40bdd22f6c8df763bad0b4c55924.

137 Dorian Jones, "Turkey Slammed over Proposed Social Media Controls," VOA, October 12, 2022, https://www.voanews.com/a/turkey-slammed-over-proposed-social-media-controls-/6786926.html.

138 Firat Kozok and Beril Akman, "New Turkey Law Mandates Jail Time for Spreading 'Disinformation,'" Bloomberg News, October 13, 2022, https://www.bloomberg.com/news/articles/2022-10-13/turkey-criminalizes-spread-of-false-information-on-internet.

139 Ali Kucukgocmen, "Top European Court Says Turkey Should Change Law on Insulting President," Reuters, October 19, 2021, https://www.reuters.com/world/middle-east/top-european-court-says-turkey-should-change-law-insulting-president-2021-10-19/.

140 Ceylan Yeginsu and Safak Timur, "Turkey's Post-Coup Crackdown Targets Kurdish Politicians," *New York Times*, November 4, 2016, https://www.nytimes.com/2016/11/05/world/europe/turkey-coup-crackdown-kurdish-politicians.html.

141 Ömer Taşpınar and Gönül Tol, "Turkey and the Kurds: From Predicament to Opportunity," Brookings Institution, January 22, 2014, https://www.brookings.edu/articles/turkey-and-the-kurds-from-predicament-to-opportunity/.

142 Yeginsu and Timur, "Turkey's Post-Coup."

143 Patrick Kingsley, "Amid Turkey's Purge, a Renewed Attack on Kurdish Culture," *New York Times*, June 29, 2017, https://www.nytimes.com/2017/06/29/world/middleeast/amid-turkeys-purge-a-renewed-attack-on-kurdish-culture.html?smid=tw-share.

144 "Turkey Referendum Grants President Erdogan Sweeping New Powers," BBC News, April 16, 2017, https://www.bbc.com/news/world-europe-39617700.

145 Reuben Silverman, "What Happens When a Turkish President Loses an Election? No One Knows,"*Foreign Policy*, April 22, 2023, https://foreignpolicy.com/2023/04/22/turkey-presidential-election-erdogan-akp-personality-cults-military-earthquake-economy/.

146 Kareem Shaheen, "Erdoğan Rejoins Turkey's Ruling Party in Wake of Referendum on New Powers," *Guardian*, May 2, 2017, https://www.theguardian.com/world/2017/may/02/erdogan-rejoins-ruling-party-as-new-presidential-powers-take-effect.

147 OSCE, Republic of Turkey Constitutional Referendum *16 April 2017, OSCE/ODIHR Limited Referendum Observation Mission Final Repo*RT, June 2017, https://www.osce.org/files/f/documents/6/2/324816.pdf.

148 "Lack of Equal Opportunities, One-Sided Media Coverage and Limitations on Fundamental Freedoms Created Unlevel Playing Field in Turkey's Constitutional Referendum, International Observers Say,", OSCE, April 17, 2017, https://www.osce.org/odihr/elections/turkey/311726.

149 Jennifer Amur, "Why Turkish Opposition Parties Are Contesting the Referendum Results," *Washington Post*, April 17, 2017, https://www.washingtonpost.com/news/worldviews/wp/2017/04/16/heres-why-turkish-opposition-parties-are-contesting-the-referendum-results/.

150 Shadia Nasralla et al., "Observer Says 2.5 Million Turkish Referendum Votes Could Have Been Manipulated," Reuters, April 18, 2017, https://www.reuters.com/article/us-turkey-politics-referendum-observers-idUSKBN17K0JW/.

151 Kara Fox et al., "Turkey Referendum: Erdogan Declares Victory," CNN, April 17, 2017, https://edition.cnn.com/2017/04/16/europe/turkey-referendum-results-erdogan/index.html.

152 Diego Cupolo, "What Turkey's Election Observers Saw," *Atlantic*, April 21, 2017, https://www.theatlantic.com/international/archive/2017/04/turkey-erdogan-referendum-kurds-hdp-fraud/523920/.

153 Patrick Kingsley, "Videos Fuel Charges of Fraud in Erdogan's Win in Turkey Referendum," *New York Times*, April 18, 2017, https://www.nytimes.com/2017/04/18/world/europe/turkey-referendum-is-haunted-by-allegations-of-voter-fraud.html.

154 Patrick Kingsley, "Erdogan Claims Vast Powers in Turkey after Narrow Victory in Referendum," *New York Times*, April 16, 2017, https://www.nytimes.com/2017/04/16/world/europe/turkey-referendum-polls-erdogan.html.

155 Shaun Walker and Jennifer Rankin, "Erdoğan and Putin Discuss Closer Ties in First Meeting since Jet Downing," *Guardian*, August 9, 2016, https://www.theguardian.com/world/2016/aug/09/erdogan-meets-putin-leaders-seek-mend-ties-jet-downing-russia-turkey.

156 Tim Hume, "Turkey's Erdogan, Russia's Putin Reset Relationship after Jet Shootdown," CNN, August 9, 2016, https://edition.cnn.com/2016/08/09/world/turkey-russia-erdogan-putin-meeting/index.html.

157 "Russia Warned Turkey of Imminent Army Coup, Says Iran's FNA," TASS, July 20, 2016, https://tass.com/world/889638.

158 "Turkey's Erdogan: The West Is Taking Sides with Coup," Al Jazeera, August 2, 2016, https://www.aljazeera.com/news/2016/8/2/turkeys-erdogan-the-west-is-taking-sides-with-coup.

159 Michael Birnbaum and Karen DeYoung, "The Aftermath of Turkey's Failed Coup Threatens Its Ties with Western Allies," *Washington Post*, September 21, 2016, https://www.washingtonpost.com/world/europe/the-aftermath-of-turkeys-failed-coup-threatens-its-ties-with-western-allies/2016/09/20/314bb754-6e0d-11e6-993f-73c693a89820_story.html.

160 Tulay Karadeniz and Humeyra Pamuk, "Turkey's Erdogan Slams West for Failure to Show Solidarity over Coup Attempt," Reuters, July 29, 2016, https://www.reuters.com/article/us-turkey-security-idUSKCN10912T/.

161 Keller et al., "Scale of Turkey's Purge."

162 Jennifer Rankin and Kareem Shaheen, "Turkey Reacts Angrily to Symbolic EU Parliament Vote on Its Membership," *Guardian*, November 24, 2016, https://www.theguardian.com/world/2016/nov/24/eu-parliament-votes-freeze-membership-talks-turkey.

163 Tim Arango and Ceylan Yeginsu, "Turks Can Agree on One Thing: U.S. Was behind Failed Coup," *New York Times*, August 2, 2016, https://www.nytimes.com/2016/08/03/world/europe/turkey-coup-erdogan-fethullah-gulen-united-states.html.

164 *New York Times*, "Government."

165 Lipton and Weiser, "Turkish Bank."

166 "Remarks by Vice President Biden and President Erdogan of Turkey in Pool Spray," The White House Office of the Vice President, press release, August 25, 2016, https://obamawhitehouse.archives.gov/the-press-office/2016/08/25/remarks-vice-president-biden-and-president-erdogan-turkey-pool-spray.

167 "Superseding Indictment."

168 "Turkey Signs Deal to Get Russian S-400 Air Defence Missiles," BBC.

169 Patrick Tucker, "Why the S-400 and the F-35 Can't Get Along," *Defense One*, July 17, 2019, https://www.defenseone.com/technology/2019/07/why-s-400-and-f-35-cant-get-along/158504/.

170 Idrees Ali and Phil Stewart, "U.S. Removing Turkey from F-35 Programme after Its Russian Missile Defence Purchase," Reuters, July 18, 2019, https://www.reuters.com/article/us-turkey-security-usa-idUSKCN1UC2DD/.

171 "Turkey and Russia Cosy up over Missiles," *Economist*, May 4, 2017, https://www.economist.com/europe/2017/05/04/turkey-and-russia-cosy-up-over-missiles.

172 Suzan Fraser, "AP Explains: Why NATO Member Turkey Wants Russian Missiles," Associated Press, July 18, 2019, https://apnews.com/general-news-2ec55ffb87ec494095560a1e062faf80#.

173 "Countering America's Adversaries through Sanctions Act-Related Sanctions," U.S. Department of the Treasury, Office of Foreign Assets Control, accessed July 4, 2024, https://ofac.treasury.gov/sanctions-programs-and-country-information/countering-americas-adversaries-through-sanctions-act-related-sanctions.

174 Firat Kozok, "Russia Is Wiring Dollars to Turkey for $20 Billion Nuclear Plant," Bloomberg News, July 29, 2022, https://www.bloomberg.com/news/articles/2022-07-29/russia-is-wiring-dollars-to-turkey-for-20-billion-nuclear-plant.

175 Michael R. Gordon, "Russia and I.M.F. Agree on a Loan for $10.2 Billion," *New York Times*, February 23, 1996, https://www.nytimes.com/1996/02/23/world/russia-and-imf-agree-on-a-loan-for-10.2-billion.html.

176 Daniel Williams, "Russia, IMF Reach Bailout Agreement," *Washington Post*, July 13, 1998, https://www.washingtonpost.com/archive/politics/1998/07/14/russia-imf-reach-bailout-agreement/9d97f8f8-5f03-4cfe-9b2d-cde4fd6046b4/.

177 Serge F. Kovaleski, "Populist Elected in Venezuela," *Washington Post*, December 7, 1998, https://www.washingtonpost.com/wp-srv/inatl/daily/dec98/07/venezuela120798.htm.

178 Clifford Krauss, "New President in Venezuela Proposes to Rewrite the Constitution," *New York Times*, February 4, 1999, https://www.nytimes.com/1999/02/04/world/new-president-in-venezuela-proposes-to-rewrite-the-constitution.html.

179 Rory Carroll, "Hugo Chávez Wins Referendum Allowing Indefinite Re-Election," *Guardian*, February 16, 2009, https://www.theguardian.com/world/2009/feb/16/hugo-chavez-indefinite-rule.

180 Serge F. Kovaleski, "Venezuelan Vote Gives President New Powers," *Washington Post*, December 16, 1999, https://www.washingtonpost.com/wp-srv/WPcap/1999-12/16/111r-121699-idx.html.

181 Carroll, "Hugo Chávez."

182 "Factbox: Venezuela's State Takeovers under Chavez," Reuters, April 6, 2011, https://www.reuters.com/article/us-venezuela-nationalizations-idUSTRE73P7N620110426/.

183 "The Troubling Trend of Nationalization," NBC News, May 2, 2006, https://www.nbcnews.com/id/wbna12600039.

184 "Chavez Drives Exxon and ConocoPhillips from Venezuela," Reuters, August 9, 2007, https://www.reuters.com/article/uk-venezuela-nationalization-oil-idUKN2637895020070626/.

185 Mark Weisbrot and Luis Sandoval, *The Venezuelan Economy in the Chávez Years*, Center for Economic and Policy Research, July 2007, https://cepr.net/documents/publications/venezuela_2007_07.pdf.

186 Ewen MacAskill and Duncan Campbell, "Bush Bans Arms Sales to Chávez," *Guardian*, May 15, 2006, https://www.theguardian.com/world/2006/may/16/usa.venezuela.

187 "Chavez Thanks Russia for Arms," Al Jazeera, July 28, 2006, https://www.aljazeera.com/news/2006/7/28/chavez-thanks-russia-for-arms.

188 Nick Paton Walsh, "Moscow Snubs US to Sell Arms to Venezuela," *Guardian*, July 27, 2006, https://www.theguardian.com/world/2006/jul/27/venezuela.russia.

189 Walsh, "Moscow."

190 "U.S. Troops Start Training Exercise in Georgia," Reuters, July 15, 2008, https://www.reuters.com/article/us-georgia-usa-exercises-idUSL1556589920080715/.

191 Luke Harding and Ian Traynor, "Russians March into Georgia as Full-Scale War Looms," *Guardian*, August 11, 2008, https://www.theguardian.com/world/2008/aug/11/georgia.russia13#top.

192 "Russia Has Become a Crucial Ally of Venezuela's Dictatorship", *Economist*, January 29, 2022, https://www.economist.com/the-americas/2022/01/29/russia-has-become-a-crucial-ally-of-venezuelas-dictatorship.

193 Mike Eckel, "Venezuela Convulses and Russia Frets: What Does Moscow Stand to Lose If the Maduro Government Falls?" RFE/RL, April 30, 2019, https://www.rferl.org/a/explainer-venezuela-coup-bad-news-moscow/29913164.html.

194 Daniel Wallis, "Venezuela's Maduro: From Bus Driver to Chavez's Successor," Reuters, March 6, 2013, https://www.reuters.com/article/us-venezuela-chavez-maduro-idUSBRE9250PO20130306/.

195 Sara Schaefer Muñoz and Anatoly Kurmanaev, "Fears of Venezuela Default Grow amid Drop in Oil Prices," *Wall Street Journal*, January 21, 2016, https://www.wsj.com/articles/fears-of-venezuela-default-grow-amid-drop-in-oil-prices-1453422852.

196 Larry Elliott, "Opec Bid to Kill off US Shale Sends Oil Price Down to 2009 Low," *Guardian*, December 7, 2015, https://www.theguardian.com/business/2015/dec/07/opec-plan-kill-us-shale-oil-price-down-seven-year-low.

197 Gillian B. White and Bourree Lam, "What's at Stake in Venezuela's Economic Crisis," *Atlantic*, July 5, 2016, https://www.theatlantic.com/business/archive/2016/07/venezuela-economic-crisis/490031/.

198 Elena Ianchovichina and Harun Onder, "Dutch Disease: An Economic Illness Easy to Catch, Difficult to Cure," Brookings Institution, October 31, 2017, https://www.brookings.edu/articles/dutch-disease-an-economic-illness-easy-to-catch-difficult-to-cure/.

199 "How Chávez and Maduro Have Impoverished Venezuela," *Economist*, April 6, 2017, https://www.economist.com/finance-and-economics/2017/04/06/how-chavez-and-maduro-have-impoverished-venezuela.

200 Matt O'Brien, "Venezuela Is on the Brink of a Complete Economic Collapse," *Washington Post*, January 29, 2016, https://www.washingtonpost.com/news/wonk/wp/2016/01/29/venezuela-is-on-the-brink-of-a-complete-collapse/.

201 Andrew Rosati, "Venezuela Doesn't Have Enough Money to Pay for Its Money," Bloomberg News, April 27, 2016, https://www.bloomberg.com/news/articles/2016-04-27/venezuela-faces-its-strangest-shortage-yet-as-inflation-explodes.

202 Alan Taylor, "Venezuela Gripped by Weeks of Anti-Government Protest," *Atlantic*, February 27, 2014, https://www.theatlantic.com/photo/2014/02/venezuela-gripped-by-weeks-of-anti-government-protest/100689/.

203 Sibylla Brodzinsky, "'We Are like a Bomb': Food Riots Show Venezuela Crisis Has Gone beyond Politics," *Guardian*, May 20, 2016, https://www.theguardian.com/world/2016/may/20/venezuela-breaking-point-food-shortages-protests-maduro.

204 Andrew Cawthorne, "Year of Protests and Crisis in Volatile Venezuela," Reuters, November 30, 2017, https://www.reuters.com/article/us-global-poy-venezuela-idUSKBN1DU1KQ/.

205 "Venezuelans Take to the Streets for Mass Protest," DW, September 2, 2016, https://www.dw.com/en/venezuelans-stage-mass-protest-demanding-recall-to-oust-president/a-19521847.

206 Gillian B. White and Bourreê Lam, "What's at Stake in Venezuela's Economic Crisis," *Atlantic*, July 5, 2016, https://www.theatlantic.com/business/archive/2016/07/venezuela-economic-crisis/490031/.

207 Graham Kates, "How Russian Oil Giant Rosneft Could Claim U.S. Oil," CBS News, March 9, 2017, https://www.cbsnews.com/news/rosneft-russian-oil-could-claim-us-oil-trump-cfius/.

208 Marianna Parraga and Alexandra Ulmer, "Special Report—Vladimir's Venezuela: Leveraging Loans to Caracas, Moscow Snaps up Oil Assets," Reuters, August 11, 2017, https://www.reuters.com/article/us-venezuela-russia-oil-specialreport-idUKKBN1AR14U/.

209 "Factbox—Oil, Loans, Military: Russia's Exposure to Venezuela," Reuters, January 24, 2019, retrieved from the Wayback Machine, version January 24, 2019, https://web.archive.org/web/20190124191929/https://www.reuters.com/article/us-venezuela-politics-russia-factbox-idUSKCN1PI1T4/.

210 Polina Ivanova and Maria Tsvetkova, "Venezuela to Move State Oil Firm PDVSA Office from Lisbon to Moscow," Reuters, March 1, 2019, https://www.reuters.com/article/uk-venezuela-politics-russia-pdvsa-idUKKCN1QI4BE/.

211 Maria Tsvetkova and Anton Zverev, "Exclusive: Kremlin-Linked Contractors Help Guard Venezuela's Maduro—Sources," Reuters, January 25, 2019, https://www.reuters.com/article/us-venezuela-politics-russia-exclusive/exclusive-kremlin-linked-contractors-help-guard-venezuelas-maduro-sources-idUSKCN1PJ22M/?il=0.

212 Nathaniel Reynolds, "Putin's Not-So-Secret Mercenaries: Patronage, Geopolitics, and the Wagner Group," Carnegie Endowment for International Peace, July 8, 2019, https://carnegieendowment.org/research/2019/07/putins-not-so-secret-mercenaries-patronage-geopolitics-and-the-wagner-group?lang=en.

213 "Full Transcript of Testimony of Fiona Hill," *Washington Post*.

214 Sibylla Brodzinsky, "Venezuelans Warn of 'Dictatorship' after Officials Block Bid to Recall Maduro," *Guardian*, October 21, 2016, https://www.theguardian.com/world/2016/oct/21/venezuela-president-maduro-recall-referendum.

215 Angela Dewan, "Turkey Referendum: What Happened and What Comes Next," CNN, April 18, 2017, https://edition.cnn.com/2017/04/17/europe/turkey-referendum-explainer/index.html.

216 Jennifer L. McCoy, "Venezuela's Controversial New Constituent Assembly, Explained," *Washington Post*, August 1, 2017, https://www.washingtonpost.com/news/monkey-cage/wp/2017/08/01/venezuelas-dubious-new-constituent-assembly-explained/.

217 William Neuman and Nicholas Casey, "Venezuela Election Won by Maduro amid Widespread Disillusionment," *Washington Post*, May 20, 2018, https://www.nytimes.com/2018/05/20/world/americas/venezuela-election.html.

218 "Voters Had Genuine Choice in Turkish Elections, but Incumbent President and Ruling Party Enjoyed Undue Advantage, Including in Media, International Observers Say," *OSCE*, June 25, 2018, https://www.osce.org/odihr/elections/turkey/385704.

219 Ellen Scholl, "Hot Commodities: The 'Mending Fences' Edition," Lawfare Institute, October 14, 2016, https://www.lawfaremedia.org/article/hot-commodities-mending-fences-edition.

220 "Twenty-Third World Energy Congress Programme," World Energy Council, October 9–13, 2016, https://www.worldenergy.org/assets/downloads/FINAL_Programme_World-Energy-Congress_2016-1.pdf.

221 "World Energy Congress: Putin, Erdogan Meet in Istanbul," Al Jazeera, October 10, 2016, https://www.aljazeera.com/economy/2016/10/10/world-energy-congress-putin-erdogan-meet-in-istanbul.

222 Nicolás Maduro (@NicolasMaduro), "Extraordinaria jornada de trabajo con el Presidente de Turquía . . . hemos decidido ampliar las relaciones e inversiones entre nuestros países" [Extraordinary working day with the President of Turkey . . . we have decided to expand relations and investments between our countries], Twitter, October 10, 2016, 7:11 a.m., https://twitter.com/NicolasMaduro/status/785422478671831040.

223 "President Maduro Meets World Leaders in Turkey," PDVSA, press release, October 10, 2016, http://www.pdvsa.com/index.php?option=com_content&view=article&id=6994:president-maduro-meets-world-leaders-in-turkey&catid=10&Itemid=908&lang=en.

224 Nailia Bagirova et al., "Venezuela's Maduro Says Oil Producers Close to Output Cap Deal," Reuters, October 22, 2016, https://www.reuters.com/article/us-oil-opec-maduro-idUSKCN12M0MF/.

225 Michael Smith and Monte Reel, "Venezuela's Trade Scheme WITH Turkey Is Enriching a Mysterious Maduro Crony," Bloomberg News, April 25, 2019, https://www.bloomberg.com/news/features/2019-04-25/venezuela-turkey-trading-scheme-enriches-mysterious-maduro-crony.

226 Patricia Laya and Andrew Rosati, "Venezuela Has 20 Tons of Gold Ready to Ship. Address Unknown," Bloomberg News, January 29, 2019, https://www.bloomberg.com/news/articles/2019-01-30/venezuela-has-20-tons-of-gold-ready-to-ship-destination-unknown.

227 Jamie Dettmer, "Mystery Deepens over Venezuela's Gold," VOA, February 1, 2019, https://www.voanews.com/a/mystery-deepens-over-venezuela-gold/4769065.html.

228 Irek Murtazin, "Золотой рейс" [Golden flight], *Novaya Gazeta*, January 31, 2019, https://novayagazeta.ru/articles/2019/01/31/79378-zolotoy-reys.

229 Patricia Laya and Ben Bartenstein, "Iran Is Hauling Gold Bars Out of Venezuela's Almost-Empty Vaults," Bloomberg News, April 30, 2020, https://www.bloomberg.com/news/articles/2020-04-30/iran-is-hauling-gold-bars-out-of-venezuela-s-almost-empty-vaults.

230 Mehdi Jedinia et al., "What's behind Iran's Fuel Shipment to Venezuela?" VOA, May 31, 2020, https://www.voanews.com/a/extremism-watch_whats-behind-irans-fuel-shipment-venezuela/6190247.html.

231 "Iranian Warships Seem Bound for Venezuela," *Economist*, June 19, 2021, https://www.economist.com/the-americas/2021/06/19/iranian-warships-seem-bound-for-venezuela.

232 Mayela Armas et al., "Venezuela Central Bank Gold Reserves Fall as Maduro Seeks Cash," Reuters, September 7, 2021, https://www.reuters.com/article/venezuela-gold-idUSL1N2Q92BL/.

233. Deisy Buitrago and Vivian Sequera, "Iran, Venezuela Eye Trade Increase, Sign Petrochemical Deal," Reuters, June 12, 2023, https://www.reuters.com/world/iranian-president-caracas-kicking-off-regional-tour-2023-06-12/.

CHAPTER 17

1. Luke Harding, "Bush Backs Ukraine and Georgia for Nato Membership," *Guardian*, April 1, 2008, https://www.theguardian.com/world/2008/apr/01/nato.georgia.
2. "Russia Recognizes Abkhazia, South Ossetia," RFE/RL, August 26, 2008, https://www.rferl.org/a/Russia_Recognizes_Abkhazia_South_Ossetia/1193932.html.
3. "Russia Has Become a Crucial Ally of Venezuela's Dictator," *Economist*, January 29, 2022, https://www.economist.com/the-americas/2022/01/29/russia-has-become-a-crucial-ally-of-venezuelas-dictatorship.
4. Chris McGreal, "FBI Breaks up Alleged Russian Spy Ring in Deep Cover," *Guardian*, June 28, 2010, https://www.theguardian.com/world/2010/jun/29/fbi-breaks-up-alleged-russian-spy-ring-deep-cover.
5. Scott Shane and Benjamin Weiser, "Spying Suspects Seemed Short on Secrets," *New York Times*, June 29, 2010, https://www.nytimes.com/2010/06/30/world/europe/30spy.html.
6. Brett Forrest, "The Big Russian Life of Anna Chapman, Ex-Spy," *Politico*, January 4, 2012, https://www.politico.com/states/new-york/albany/story/2012/01/the-big-russian-life-of-anna-chapman-ex-spy-069297.
7. "Russian Spies Living among Us: Inside the FBI's 'Operation Ghost Stories,'" produced by Resa Matthews and Anthony Venditti, October 13, 2020, CBS News, video, 43:25, https://www.cbsnews.com/news/russian-spies-operation-ghost-stories-fbi-declassified/.
8. "Factbox: 'Haven't We Met?'—U.S. Case Alleges Use of Spycraft," Reuters, June 29, 2010, https://www.reuters.com/article/us-russia-usa-spying-contest-factbox-idUSTRE65S36A20100629/.
9. Tom Parfitt et al., "Spy Swap: US and Russia Hand over Agents in Full Media Glare," *Guardian*, June 9, 2010, https://www.theguardian.com/world/2010/jul/09/russian-spies-swap-us.
10. S. Rep. No 116-XX, 5:578.
11. S. Rep. No 116-XX, 5:620.
12. Amber Phillips, "The NRA-ification of the Republican Party," *Washington Post*, August 14, 2015, https://www.washingtonpost.com/news/the-fix/wp/2015/08/14/the-nra-ification-of-the-republican-party/.
13. "How the NRA Hijacked the Republican Party," Reuters, January 18, 2013, https://www.reuters.com/article/idUS381701105220130118/.
14. "ОБЩЕРОССИЙСКАЯ ОБЩЕСТВЕННАЯ ОРГАНИЗАЦИЯ «ПРАВО НА ОРУЖИЕ»" [All-Russian Public Organization for Improving Weapons Culture "Right to Weapons"], RBC, accessed July 5, 2024, https://companies.rbc.ru/id/1112202000877-obschestvennaya-organizatsiya-obscherossijskaya-obschestvennaya-organizatsiya-po-povyisheniyu-oruzhejnoj-kulturyi-pravo-na-oruzhie/.
15. Glenn Kates, "Russian Gun Lobby Seeks Right to Bear Arms," RFE/RL, December 20, 2012, https://www.rferl.org/a/russia-gun-laws-newtown-massacre/24804185.html.
16. S. Rep. No 116-XX, 5:570.
17. Sam Foster, "Licensed to Kill?," *Guardian*, January 10, 2011, https://www.theguardian.com/world/2011/jan/10/gun-ownership-laws-around-the-world.
18. S. Rep. No 116-XX, 5:571.
19. S. Rep. No 116-XX, 5:571.

20 S. Rep. No 116-XX, *5:581*.

21 S. Rep. No 116-XX, *5:581*.

22 S. Rep. No 116-XX, *5:581*.

23 S. Rep. No 116-XX, *5:582*.

24 "Bolton Relationship with Butina to Get Closer Scrutiny from House," produced by Rachel Maddow, MSNBC, January 24, 2019, video, 9:49, https://www.msnbc.com/rachel-maddow/watch/bolton-relationship-with-butina-to-get-closer-scrutiny-from-house-1431017539593.

25 "John Bolton's Message on Russian Gun Rights," Everytown for Gun Safety, August 21, 2018, video, 3:15, https://www.youtube.com/watch?v=EytAMUUH9Yc.

26 S. Rep. No 116-XX, *5:585*.

27 "Edward Royce," Ballotpedia, accessed July 12, 2024 https://ballotpedia.org/Edward_Royce.

28 S. Rep. No 116-XX, *5:582*.

29 Affidavit in Support of an Application for a Criminal Complaint, No. 18 Cr 218-TSC (D.D.C. July 16, 2018), https://www.justice.gov/d9/press-releases/attachments/2018/07/16/butina_mariia_-_affidavit_-_july_2018_0_0.pdf.

30 S. Rep. No 116-XX, *5:573*.

31 Tom Hamburger et al., "Inside Trump's Financial Ties to Russia and His Unusual Flattery of Vladimir Putin," *Washington Post*, January 17, 2017, https://www.washingtonpost.com/politics/inside-trumps-financial-ties-to-russia-and-his-unusual-flattery-of-vladimir-putin/2016/06/17/dbdcaac8-31a6-11e6-8ff7-7b6c1998b7a0_story.html.

32 Neil MacFarquhar, "A Russian Developer Helps Out the Kremlin on Occasion. Was He a Conduit to Trump?," *New York Times*, July 16, 2017, https://www.nytimes.com/2017/07/16/world/europe/aras-agalarov-trump-kremlin.html.

33 Michael Crowley, "When Donald Trump Brought Miss Universe to Moscow," *Politico*, May 15, 2016, https://www.politico.com/story/2016/05/donald-trump-russia-moscow-miss-universe-223173.

34 Jim Zarrolli,"At the 2013 Miss Universe Contest, Trump Met Some of Russia's Rich and Powerful," *Morning Edition*, NPR, audio, 3:52, https://www.npr.org/2017/07/17/537277074/at-the-2013-miss-universe-contest-trump-met-some-of-russias-rich-and-powerful.

35 Hamburger et al., "Inside Trump's Financial Ties."

36 Jeremy B. Merrill (@jeremybmerrill), "1/ How long was Trump in Moscow for the Miss Universe pageant? You know, when *that* alleged tape was supposedly filmed? Apparently 37 hrs 45 min. I know that because I FOIA'd it," Twitter, May 1, 2018, 7:00 p.m., https://twitter.com/jeremybmerrill/status/991437347987382272.

37 "Emin—In Another Life (ft. Donald Trump and Miss Universe'1 3 Contestants) Official Video," EminOfficial, November 20, 2013, video, 3:40, https://www.youtube.com/watch?v=iuZUNjFsgS8.

38 Donald Trump, interview by Thomas Roberts, MSNBC, August 1, 2017, https://www.msnbc.com/thomas-roberts/watch/watch-donald-trump-s-full-2013-interview-736112707862.

39 Ken Dilanian and Allan Smith, "Scuttled Trump Tower Moscow Project Back in Limelight after Cohen Guilty Plea," NBC News, November 29, 2018, https://www.nbcnews.com/politics/donald-trump/scuttled-trump-tower-moscow-project-back-limelight-after-cohen-guilty-n941796.

40 Alan Cullison and Brett Forrest, "Trump Tower Moscow? It Was the End of a Long, Failed Push to Invest in Russia," *Wall Street Journal*, November 29, 2018, https://www.wsj.com/articles/trump-tower-moscow-it-was-the-end-of-a-long-failed-push-to-invest-in-russia-1543532455.

41 Hamburger et al., "Inside Trump's Financial Ties."

42 Karen Yourish et al., "A Timeline Showing the Full Scale of Russia's Unprecedented Interference in the 2016 Election, and Its Aftermath," *New York Times*, September 20, 2018, https://www.nytimes.com/interactive/2018/09/20/us/politics/russia-trump-election-timeline.html?mtrref=www.google.com&assetType=REGIWALL.

43 Rosalind S. Helderman and Tom Hamburger, "Music Promoter Dangled Possible Putin Meeting for Trump during Campaign," *Washington Post*, December 14, 2017, https://www.washingtonpost.com/politics/music-promoter-dangled-possible-putin-meeting-for-trump-during-campaign/2017/12/14/38d6a8e2-dec5-11e7-89e8-edec16379010_story.html.

44 S. Rep. No 116-XX, *5:420*.

45 Timothy L. O'Brien, "Trump, Russia and a Shadowy Business Partnership," Bloomberg News, June 21, 2017, https://www.bloomberg.com/opinion/articles/2017-06-21/trump-russia-and-those-shadowy-sater-deals-at-bayrock.

46 James S. Henry, "The Curious World of Donald Trump's Private Russian Connections," *American Interest*, December 19, 2016, https://www.the-american-interest.com/2016/12/19/the-curious-world-of-donald-trumps-private-russian-connections/.

47 O'Brien, "Trump, Russia."

48 Abigail Abrams, "The Attorney General Said There Was 'No Collusion.' But Trump Associates Still Interacted with Russians More than 100 Times," *Time*, April 18, 2019, https://time.com/5572821/donald-trump-russia-contacts/.

49 Azeen Ghorayshi et al., "These Secret Files Show How the Trump Moscow Talks Unfolded While Trump Heaped Praise on Putin," *Buzzfeed News*, February 5, 2019, https://www.buzzfeednews.com/article/azeenghorayshi/trump-tower-moscow-the-secret-files-cohen-sater-putin.

50 S. Rep. No 116-XX, *5:430–31*.

51 Kevin Drum, "Here's the Letter of Intent for the Trump Moscow Project," *Mother Jones*, December 19, 2018, https://www.motherjones.com/kevin-drum/2018/12/heres-the-letter-of-intent-for-the-trump-moscow-project/.

52 Mueller, Report, 71.

53 Chase Peterson-Withorn, "Michael Cohen Says Trump Ran for President as a 'Marketing Opportunity.' If So, It Isn't Working," *Forbes*, February 27, 2019, https://www.forbes.com/sites/chasewithorn/2019/02/27/michael-cohen-says-trump-ran-for-president-as-a-marketing-opportunity-if-so-it-isnt-working/.

54 S. Rep. No 116-XX, *5:427–28*.

55 S. Rep. No 116-XX, *5:439*.

56 S. Rep. No 116-XX, *5:443–44*.

57 S. Rep. No 116-XX, *5:445–48*.

58 Nabi Abdullaev, "U.S. Companies to Talk Business with Putin in St. Petersburg," *Forbes*, May 31, 2017, https://www.forbes.com/sites/riskmap/2017/05/31/us-companies-to-talk-business-with-putin-in-st-petersburg/.

59 Azeen Ghorayshi et al., "These Secret Files Show How the Trump Moscow Talks Unfolded While Trump Heaped Praise On Putin", *Buzzfeed News*, February 5, 2019, https://www.buzzfeednews.com/article/azeenghorayshi/trump-tower-moscow-the-secret-files-cohen-sater-putin.

60 S. Rep. No 116-XX, *5:450–51*.

CHAPTER 18

1. S. Rep. No 116-XX, *2:30*.
2. Elliott, "Readers' Editor."
3. S. Rep. No 116-XX, *2:29–30*.
4. Shaun Walker, "The Russian Troll Factory at the Heart of the Meddling Allegations," *Guardian*, April 2, 2015, https://www.theguardian.com/world/2015/apr/02/putin-kremlin-inside-russian-troll-house.
5. Walker, "Russian Troll."
6. Indictment, United States of America v. Internet Research Agency LLC, Concord Management and Consulting LLC, Concord Catering, Yevgeniy Viktorovich Prigozhin, Mikhail Ivanovich Bystrov, Mikhail Leonidovich Burchik, Aleksandra Yuryevna Krylova, Anna Vladislavovna Bogacheva, Sergey Pavlovich Polozov, Maria Anatolyevna Bovda, Robert Sergeyevich Bovda, Dzheykhun Nasimi Ogly Aslanov, Vadim Vladimirovich Podkopaev, Gleb Igorevich Vasilenko, Irina Viktorovna Kaverzina, Vladimir Venkov, No. 18 Cr 32-DLF (D.D.C. February 16, 2018), retrieved from the Wayback Machine, version February 17, 2018, https://web.archive.org/web/20180217195723/https://www.justice.gov/file/1035477/download.
7. "Расследование РБК: как «фабрика троллей» поработала на выборах в США" [RBC investigation how the "troll farm" worked in the U.S. elections], RBC, October 17, 2017, https://www.rbc.ru/technology_and_media/17/10/2017/59e0c17d9a79470e05a9e6c1?from=center_1.
8. Indictment, United States of America v. Internet Research Agency LLC et al.
9. S. Rep. No 116-XX, *2:45*.
10. "Population under Age 18 Declined Last Decade," United States Census Bureau, August 12, 2021, https://www.census.gov/library/stories/2021/08/united-states-adult-population-grew-faster-than-nations-total-population-from-2010-to-2020.html.
11. Simon Kemp, "Digital in 2017: Global Overview," We Are Social, January 25, 2017, slide 52, https://wearesocial.com/sg/blog/2017/01/digital-in-2017-global-overview/.
12. "Расследование РБК," RBC.
13. Hanna Levintova, "Russian Journalists Just Published a Bombshell Investigation about a Kremlin-Linked 'Troll Factory,'" *Mother Jones*, October 18, 2017, https://www.motherjones.com/politics/2017/10/russian-journalists-just-published-a-bombshell-investigation-about-a-kremlin-linked-troll-factory/.
14. "Расследование РБК," RBC.
15. Tim Lister and Clare Sebastian, "Stoking Islamophobia and Secession in Texas—from an Office in Russia," CNN, October 6, 2017, https://edition.cnn.com/2017/10/05/politics/heart-of-texas-russia-event/index.html.
16. Claire Allbright, "A Russian Facebook Page Organized a Protest in Texas. A Different Russian Page Launched the Counterprotest," *Texas Tribune*, November 1, 2017, https://www.texastribune.org/2017/11/01/russian-facebook-page-organized-protest-texas-different-russian-page-l/.
17. Ryan Lucas, "How Russia Used Facebook to Organize Two Sets of Protesters," *All Things Considered*, NPR, November 1, 2017, https://www.npr.org/2017/11/01/561427876/how-russia-used-facebook-to-organize-two-sets-of-protesters.
18. S. Rep. No 116-XX, *2:47*.
19. Alicia Parlapiano and Jasmine C. Lee, "The Propaganda Tools Used by Russians to Influence the 2016 Election," *New York Times*, February 16, 2018, https://www.nytimes.com/interactive/2018/02/16/us/politics/russia-propaganda-election-2016.html.

20 Tony Romm, "'Pro-Beyoncé' vs. 'Anti-Beyoncé': 3,500 Facebook Ads Show the Scale of Russian Manipulation," *Washington Post*, May 10, 2018, https://www.washingtonpost.com/news/the-switch/wp/2018/05/10/here-are-the-3400-facebook-ads-purchased-by-russias-online-trolls-during-the-2016-election/.

21 Kevin Poulsen et al., "Exclusive: Russians Appear to Use Facebook to Push Trump Rallies in Seventeen U.S. Cities," *Daily Beast*, September 20, 2017, https://www.thedailybeast.com/russians-appear-to-use-facebook-to-push-pro-trump-flash-mobs-in-florida.

22 Aric Toler, "Florida Trump Flash Mobs Organized by the Russian 'Troll Factory,'" Bellingcat, September 20, 2017, https://www.bellingcat.com/news/americas/2017/09/20/florida-trump-flash-mobs-organized-russian-troll-factory/.

23 Indictment, United States of America v. Internet Research Agency LLC et al.

24 Philip Bump, "Timeline: How Russian Trolls Allegedly Tried to Throw the 2016 Election to Trump," *Washington Post*, February 16, 2018, https://www.washingtonpost.com/news/politics/wp/2018/02/16/timeline-how-russian-trolls-allegedly-tried-to-throw-the-2016-election-to-trump/.

25 Deanna Paul, "Russians Used a Photo of His Father as Pro-Trump Propaganda. He Saw It in the Mueller Report," *Washington Post*, April 22, 2019, https://www.washingtonpost.com/history/2019/04/22/russians-used-photo-his-father-pro-trump-propaganda-he-saw-it-mueller-report/.

26 Parlapiano and Lee, "Propaganda Tools."

27 Donie O'Sullivan et al., "Her Son Was Killed—Then Came the Russian Trolls," CNN, June 29, 2018, https://edition.cnn.com/2018/06/26/us/russian-trolls-exploit-philando-castiles-death/index.html.

28 S. Rep. No 116-XX, *2:34*.

29 S. Rep. No 116-XX, *vol. 1, Russian Efforts against Election Infrastructure, with Additional Views*, 6, 22 (2019), https://www.intelligence.senate.gov/sites/default/files/documents/Report_Volume1.pdf.

30 S. Rep. No 116-XX, *1:13*.

31 S. Rep. No 116-XX, *1:7*.

32 S. Rep. No 116-XX, *1:8*.

33 S. Rep. No 116-XX, *1:10*.

34 S. Rep. No 116-XX, *1:23*.

35 S. Rep. No 116-XX, *1:5*.

36 S. Rep. No 116-XX, *1:23*.

37 S. Rep. No 116-XX, *5:170*.

38 David Smith, "WikiLeaks Emails: What They Revealed about the Clinton Campaign's Mechanics," *Guardian*, November 6, 2016, https://www.theguardian.com/us-news/2016/nov/06/wikileaks-emails-hillary-clinton-campaign-john-podesta.

39 Kyle Cheney and Sarah Weaton, "The Most Revealing Clinton Campaign Emails in WikiLeaks Release," *Politico*, October 7, 2016, https://www.politico.com/story/2016/10/john-podesta-wikileaks-hacked-emails-229304.

40 Smith, "WikiLeaks Emails."

41 "Eighteen Revelations from WikiLeaks' Hacked Clinton Emails," BBC News, October 27, 2016, https://www.bbc.com/news/world-us-canada-37639370.

42 Cheney and Weaton, "Most Revealing."

43 Ellen Nakashima, "Russian Government Hackers Penetrated DNC, Stole Opposition Research on Trump," *Washington Post*, June 14, 2016, https://www.washingtonpost.com/world/national-security/russian-government-hackers-penetrated-dnc-stole-opposition-research-on-trump/2016/06/14/cf006cb4-316e-11e6-8ff7-7b6c1998b7a0_story.html.

44 "Full Text of Donald Trump Jr. Emails about Meeting with Russian Lawyer," *Wall Street Journal*, July 11, 2017, https://www.wsj.com/articles/full-text-of-donald-trump-jr-emails-about-meeting-with-russian-lawyer-1499792757.

45 "Full Text of Donald Trump Jr. Emails," *Wall Street Journal*.

46 Jan Diehm and Sean O'Key, "The Email Exchange Trump Jr. Released, in Chronological Order," CNN, July 7, 2017, https://edition.cnn.com/interactive/2017/07/politics/donald-trump-jr-full-emails/.

47 Jon Swaine and Scott Stedman, "Revealed: Russian Billionaire Set Up US Company before Trump Tower Meeting," *Guardian*, October 18, 2018, https://www.theguardian.com/us-news/2018/oct/18/russian-billionaire-aras-agalarov-company-trump-tower-meeting.

48 S. Rep. No 116-XX, *5:348–49*.

49 S. Rep. No 116-XX, *5:367–69*.

50 Alex Horton, "The Magnitsky Act, Explained," *Washington Post*, July 14, 2017, https://www.washingtonpost.com/news/the-fix/wp/2017/07/14/the-magnitsky-act-explained/.

51 "Magnitsky Sanctions Listings," Office of Foreign Assets Control, U.S. Department of the Treasury, press release, April 12, 2013, https://ofac.treasury.gov/recent-actions/20130412.

52 "Announcement of Sanctions under the Sergei Magnitsky Rule of Law Accountability Act," U.S. Department of the Treasury, press release, May 20, 2014, https://home.treasury.gov/news/press-releases/jl2408.

53 Ben Schreckinger, "The Putin Obsession That Led to Trump Jr.'s Meeting," *Politico*, July 14, 2017, https://www.politico.eu/article/the-putin-obsession-that-led-to-trump-jr-s-meeting/.

54 S. Rep. No 116-XX, *5:367*.

55 Eric Tucker, "Trump Tower Meeting Emails 'Really Bad,' Aide Told Trump," Associated Press, April 25, 2019, https://apnews.com/article/215ffd4a7c25473abd5a0b1781bb947b.

56 Ashley Parker and David E. Sanger, "Donald Trump Calls on Russia to Find Hillary Clinton's Missing Emails," *New York Times*, July 27, 2016, https://www.nytimes.com/2016/07/28/us/politics/donald-trump-russia-clinton-emails.html.

57 S. Rep. No 116-XX, *5:232*.

58 Eric Lichtblau, "Computer Systems Used by Clinton Campaign Are Said to Be Hacked, Apparently by Russians," *New York Times*, July 29, 2016, https://www.nytimes.com/2016/07/30/us/politics/clinton-campaign-hacked-russians.html.

59 Mark Hosenball et al., "Exclusive: Clinton Campaign Also Hacked in Attacks on Democrats," Reuters, July 30, 2016, https://www.reuters.com/article/us-usa-cyber-democrats-investigation-exc-idUSKCN1092HK/.

60 S. Rep. No 116-XX, *5:181*.

61 S. Rep. No 116-XX, *5:182*.

62 Alvin Chang, "How Russian Hackers Stole Information from Democrats, in Three Simple Diagrams," *Vox*, July 16, 2018, https://www.vox.com/policy-and-politics/2018/7/16/17575940/russian-election-hack-democrats-trump-putin-diagram.

63 S. Rep. No 116-XX, *5:182*.

64 "2016 Presidential Campaign Hacking Fast Facts," CNN, October 23, 2023, https://edition.cnn.com/2016/12/26/us/2016-presidential-campaign-hacking-fast-facts/index.html.

65 Stephen Braun, "Hacked Emails Show Democratic Party Hostility to Sanders," Associated Press, July 23, 2016, https://apnews.com/events-united-states-presidential-election-c62ff2b1605346f99c4d3e43e6099fd1.

66 Nakashima, "Russian Government."

67 Andrew Roth, "Russia Denies DNC Hack and Says Maybe Someone 'Forgot the Password,'" *Washington Post*, June 15, 2016, https://www.washingtonpost.com/news/worldviews/wp/2016/06/15/russias-unusual-response-to-charges-it-hacked-research-on-trump/.

68 "Interview with Texas Congressman Michael McCaul; Colin Powell: Trump Is a 'National Disgrace," CNN, September 14, 2016, http://edition.cnn.com/TRANSCRIPTS/1609/14/sitroom.02.html.

69 Louis Nelson, "RNC Denies It Was Hacked," *Politico*, September 14, 2016, https://www.politico.com/story/2016/09/republican-national-committee-was-hacked-rep-mccaul-says-228183.

70 Theodore Schleifer, "GOP Congressman: I 'Misspoke' When I Said RNC Was Hacked," CNN, September 14, 2016, https://edition.cnn.com/2016/09/14/politics/michael-mccaul-rnc-hacked/index.html.

71 Dustin Volz and Jonathan Landay, "Russia Hacked Republican State Campaigns but Not Trump's—FBI Head," Reuters, January 11, 2017, https://www.reuters.com/article/us-usa-russia-cyber-rnc-idUSKBN14U2DD/.

72 Nicole Gaouette, "FBI's Comey: Republicans Also Hacked by Russia," CNN, January 10, 2017, https://edition.cnn.com/2017/01/10/politics/comey-republicans-hacked-russia/index.html.

73 David E. Sanger and Matt Flegenheimer, "Russian Hackers Gained 'Limited' Access to R.N.C., Comey Says," *New York Times*, January 10, 2017, https://www.nytimes.com/2017/01/10/us/politics/russia-hack-hearing-clapper-rogers-brennan.html.

74 Sanger and Flegenheimer, "Russian Hackers."

75 Daniella Diaz, "Graham: Russians Hacked My Campaign Email Account," CNN, December 14, 2016, https://edition.cnn.com/2016/12/14/politics/lindsey-graham-hacking-russia-donald-trump/index.html.

76 Peter W. Stevenson, "Rubio: Russia's Election Hacking Went beyond Just Clinton and Trump—to Me," *Washington Post*, March 30, 2017, https://www.washingtonpost.com/news/the-fix/wp/2017/03/30/we-just-found-out-that-russias-election-hacking-went-beyond-clinton-and-trump/.

77 Michael Riley and Jordan Robertson, "Russian Hacks on U.S. Voting System Wider than Previously Known," Bloomberg News, June 13, 2017, https://www.bloomberg.com/politics/articles/2017-06-13/russian-breach-of-39-states-threatens-future-u-s-elections.

78 Michael Riley, "Russian Hackers of DNC Said to Nab Secrets from NATO, Soros," Bloomberg News, August 11, 2016, https://www.bloomberg.com/news/articles/2016-08-11/russian-hackers-of-dnc-said-to-scoop-up-secrets-from-nato-soros.

79 Robert Barnes et al., "Powell Emails Were Leaked on a Site Linked to the Russian Government," *Washington Post*, September 14, 2016, https://www.washingtonpost.com/politics/powell-emails-were-leaked-on-a-site-linked-to-the-russian-government/2016/09/14/fb217992-7ab0-11e6-beac-57a4a412e93a_story.html.

80 Nakashima, "Russian Government."

81 Jen Kirby, "DNC Hacker Guccifer 2.0 Is Reportedly a Member of Russian Military Intelligence," *Vox*, March 22, 2018, https://www.vox.com/2018/3/22/17153918/dnc-hacker-guccifer-2-0-russia-mueller.

82 Kevin Poulsen and Spencer Ackerman, "Exclusive: 'Lone DNC Hacker' Guccifer 2.0 Slipped up and Revealed He Was a Russian Intelligence Officer," *Daily Beast*, October 25, 2018, https://www.thedailybeast.com/exclusive-lone-dnc-hacker-guccifer-20-slipped-up-and-revealed-he-was-a-russian-intelligence-officer.

83 S. Rep. No 116-XX, *5:207*.

84 S. Rep. No 116-XX, *5:212*.

85 Michael D. Shear and Matthew Rosenberg, "Released Emails Suggest the D.N.C. Derided the Sanders Campaign," *New York Times*, July 22, 2016, https://www.nytimes.com/2016/07/23/us/politics/dnc-emails-sanders-clinton.html.

86 Maquita Peters, "Leaked Democratic Party Emails Show Members Tried to Undercut Sanders," NPR, July 23, 2016, https://www.npr.org/sections/thetwo-way/2016/07/23/487179496/leaked-democratic-party-emails-show-members-tried-to-undercut-sanders.

87 David E. Sanger and Charlie Savage, "U.S. Says Russia Directed Hacks to Influence Elections," *New York Times*, October 7, 2016, https://www.nytimes.com/2016/10/08/us/politics/us-formally-accuses-russia-of-stealing-dnc-emails.html.

88 Paul Farhi, "A Caller Had a Lewd Tape of Donald Trump. Then the Race to Break the Story Was On," *Washington Post*, October 7, 2016, https://www.washingtonpost.com/lifestyle/style/the-caller-had-a-lewd-tape-of-donald-trump-then-the-race-was-on/2016/10/07/31d74714-8ce5-11e6-875e-2c1bfe943b66_story.html.

89 Laura Koran et al., "WikiLeaks Posts Apparent Excerpts of Clinton Wall Street Speeches," CNN, October 8, 2016, https://edition.cnn.com/2016/10/07/politics/john-podesta-emails-hacked/index.html.

90 Cheney and Weaton, "Most Revealing."

91 Sam Frizell, "What Leaked Emails Reveal about Hillary Clinton's Campaign," *Time*, October 7, 2016, https://time.com/4523749/hillary-clinton-wikileaks-leaked-emails-john-podesta/.

92 Katiana Krawchenko et al., "The John Podesta Emails Released by WikiLeaks," CBS News, June 25, 2024, https://www.cbsnews.com/news/the-john-podesta-emails-released-by-wikileaks/.

93 Patrick Healy and Jonathan Martin, "In Second Debate, Donald Trump and Hillary Clinton Spar in Bitter, Personal Terms," *New York Times*, October 9, 2016, https://www.nytimes.com/2016/10/10/us/politics/presidential-debate.html.

94 "Feds Found RNC-Related Cyberattack Months Ago but It Didn't Raise Serious Concerns, Sources Say," ABC News, December 12, 2016, https://abcnews.go.com/Politics/feds-found-rnc-related-cyberattack-months-ago-raise/story?id=44130951.

95 Michael Weiss and Kimberly Dozier, "How Russian Hackers Can Blackmail Donald Trump—and the GOP," *Daily Beast*, December 10, 2016, https://www.thedailybeast.com/how-russian-hackers-can-blackmail-donald-trumpand-the-gop.

96 Tami Abdollah, "Study Links Russian Tweets to Release of Hacked Emails," Associated Press, October 11, 2019, https://apnews.com/political-news-a4af9a6635bd4e0889f7b968c8b3b357.

97 Ben Popken et al., "Trump Campaign Planned for WikiLeaks Dump, Tried to Acquire Clinton Emails, Mueller Report Finds," NBC News, April 18, 2019, https://www.nbcnews.com/politics/donald-trump/trump-campaign-planned-wikileaks-dump-tried-acquire-clinton-emails-mueller-n996081.

98 Chuck Todd et al., "How Team Trump Capitalized on Russia's Interference in 2016," NBC News, July 16, 2018, https://www.nbcnews.com/politics/first-read/how-team-trump-capitalized-russia-s-interference-2016-n891661.

99   Lauren Gambino, "Roger Stone: Trump Adviser Found Guilty on All Counts in WikiLeaks Hacking Case," *Guardian*, November 15, 2019, https://www.theguardian.com/us-news/2019/nov/15/roger-stone-guilty-verdict-wikileaks-hacking-case-latest-news.

100 Darren Samuelsohn and Josh Gerstein, "What Roger Stone's Trial Revealed about Donald Trump and WikiLeaks," *Politico*, November 12, 2019, https://www.politico.com/news/2019/11/12/roger-stone-trial-donald-trump-wikileaks-070368.

101 Julia Ioffe, "The Secret Correspondence between Donald Trump Jr. and WikiLeaks," *Atlantic*, November 13, 2017, https://www.theatlantic.com/politics/archive/2017/11/the-secret-correspondence-between-donald-trump-jr-and-wikileaks/545738/.

102 S. Rep. No 116-XX, *5:944*.

CHAPTER 19

1   Rosalind S. Helderman and Tom Hamburger, "Guns and Religion: How American Conservatives Grew Closer to Putin's Russia," *Washington Post*, April 30, 2017, https://www.washingtonpost.com/politics/how-the-republican-right-found-allies-in-russia/2017/04/30/e2d83ff6-29d3-11e7-a616-d7c8a68c1a66_story.html.

2   Matthew Rosenberg et al., "Wife of Former N.R.A. President Tapped Accused Russian Agent in Pursuit of Jet Fuel Payday," *New York Times*, September 2, 2018, https://www.nytimes.com/2018/09/02/us/politics/maria-butina-russian-spy.html?partner=rss&emc=rss.

3   Igor Derysh, "Maria Butina's Boyfriend Claimed He Set Up Trump-Russia NRA 'Conduit' as Campaign Funds Flowed," *Salon*, December 12, 2018, https://www.salon.com/2018/12/12/maria-butinas-boyfriend-claimed-he-set-up-trump-russia-nra-conduit-as-campaign-funds-flowed/.

4   Amy Knight, "Maria Butina's Boss Alexander Torshin: The Kremlin's No-Longer-Secret Weapon," *Daily Beast*, December 15, 2018, https://www.thedailybeast.com/butina-boss-alexander-torshin-the-kremlins-no-longer-secret-weapon.

5   Helderman and Hamburger, "Guns and Religion."

6   Matthew Rosenberg et al., "Beyond the N.R.A.: Maria Butina's Peculiar Bid for Russian Influence," *New York Times*, August 4, 2018, https://www.nytimes.com/2018/08/04/us/politics/maria-butina-nra-russia-influence.html.

7   Tim Dickinson, "Read Maria Butina's Influence Plot in Her Own Words," *Rolling Stone*, April 26, 2019, https://www.rollingstone.com/politics/politics-news/maria-butina-diplomacy-project-redacted-text-827034/.

8   Dickinson, "Read Maria Butina's."

9   Desmond Butler, "Woman Held as Russian Spy Was a Graduate Student at an American University Working on a Sensitive Cybersecurity Project," *Business Insider*, October 29, 2018, https://www.businessinsider.com/ap-russian-held-as-agent-studied-us-groups-cyberdefenses-2018-10.

10 Rosalind S. Helderman et al., "Before Her Arrest as an Alleged Russian Agent, Maria Butina's Proud Defense of Her Homeland Drew Notice at American University," *Washington Post*, July 25, 2018, https://www.washingtonpost.com/politics/before-her-arrest-as-an-alleged-russian-agent-maria-butinas-proud-defense-of-her-homeland-drew-notice-at-american-university/2018/07/25/957c1812-8c2a-11e8-a345-a1bf7847b375_story.html.

11 Tom Winter, "Alleged Russian Operative Mariia Butina Negotiating with Prosecutors," NBC News, November 16, 2018, https://www.nbcnews.com/politics/justice-department/alleged-russian-spy-mariia-butina-negotiating-prosecutors-n937206.

12 S. Rep. No 116-XX, *5:589*.

13 Lucia Graves and Peter Stone, "True Romance? The Intriguing Tale of the Russian Agent and Her Republican Lover," *Guardian*, March 27, 2019, https://www.theguardian.com/us-news/2019/mar/27/russia-trump-maria-butina-paul-erickson.

14 Devlin Barrett and Rosalind S. Helderman, "Boyfriend of Admitted Russian Agent Charged with Fraud," *Washington Post*, February 6, 2019, https://www.washingtonpost.com/world/national-security/boyfriend-of-admitted-russian-agent-charged-with-fraud/2019/02/06/c503afe4-2a6a-11e9-984d-9b8fba003e81_story.html.

15 S. Rep. No 116-XX, *5:573*.

16 Rosalind S. Helderman, "Lawyer for Alleged Russian Agent Maria Butina Says Texts Show Claim That She Offered Sex for Job Is 'Sexist Smear,'" *Washington Post*, August 24, 2018, https://www.washingtonpost.com/politics/lawyer-for-alleged-russian-agent-maria-butina-says-texts-show-claim-that-she-offered-sex-for-job-is-sexist-smear/2018/08/24/ffafde94-a719-11e8-97ce-cc9042272f07_story.html.

17 Pete Madden et al., "Lover or Cover? Maria Butina and the Romance at the Heart of an Alleged Russian Influence Operation," ABC News, August 28, 2018, https://abcnews.go.com/Politics/lover-cover-romance-heart-alleged-russian-influence-operation/story?id=57437405.

18 Betsy Swan and Erin Banco, "Feds Target Butina's GOP Boyfriend as Foreign Agent," *Daily Beast*, December 5, 2018, https://www.thedailybeast.com/feds-target-butinas-gop-boyfriend-as-foreign-agent.

19 Allegra Kirkland, "Meet the Operative Who Was Alleged Conduit between Mariia Butina and GOP," Talking Points Memo, July 17, 2018, https://talkingpointsmemo.com/muckraker/paul-erickson-center-nexus-between-butina-russia-gop.

20 Tim Mak, "The Kremlin and GOP Have a New Friend—and Boy, Does She Love Guns,"*Daily Beast*, February 23, 2017, https://www.thedailybeast.com/the-kremlin-and-gop-have-a-new-friendand-boy-does-she-love-guns.

21 S. Rep. No 116-XX, *5:589*.

22 Denise Clifton and Mark Follman, "The Very Strange Case of Two Russian Gun Lovers, the NRA, and Donald Trump," *Mother Jones*, May/June 2018, https://www.motherjones.com/politics/2018/03/trump-russia-nra-connection-maria-butina-alexander-torshin-guns/.

23 S. Rep. No 116-XX, *5:593*.

24 Tim Mak, "Maria Butina, Accused of Being Russian Agent, Has Long History of Urging Protest," *All Things Considered*, NPR, audio, 3:43, https://www.npr.org/2018/09/19/647174528/maria-butina-accused-of-being-russian-agent-has-long-history-of-urging-protest.

25 Mark Follman, "Trump Spoke to a Russian Activist about Ending Sanctions—Just Weeks after Launching His Campaign,", *Mother Jones*, March 9, 2018, https://www.motherjones.com/politics/2018/03/trump-spoke-to-a-russian-activist-about-ending-sanctions-just-weeks-after-launching-his-campaign/.

26 Matt Taibbi, "The Overstock CEO's Wild Maria Butina Story Raises Serious Questions," *Rolling Stone*, September 4, 2019, https://www.rollingstone.com/politics/politics-features/maria-butina-russia-spy-fbi-860256/.

27 Michael Corkery, "Overstock C.E.O. Takes Aim at 'Deep State' after Romance with Russian Agent," *New York Times*, August 15, 2019, https://www.nytimes.com/2019/08/15/business/overstock-paul-byrne-maria-butina-affair.html.

28 S. Rep. No 116-XX, *5:627*.

29 Corkery, "Overstock."

30 Mak, "Kremlin and GOP."

31. Rosalind S. Helderman et al., "'She Was like a Novelty': How Alleged Russian Agent Maria Butina Gained Access to Elite Conservative Circles," *Washington Post*, June 17, 2018, https://www.washingtonpost.com/politics/she-was-like-a-novelty-how-alleged-russian-agent-maria-butina-gained-access-to-elite-conservative-circles/2018/07/17/1bb62bbc-89d2-11e8-a345-a1bf7847b375_story.html.

32. Jamie Dettmer, "Russian Spies Hide in Plain Sight," VOA, July 24, 2018, https://www.voanews.com/a/russian-spies-hide-in-plain-sight/4497252.html.

33. Helderman et al., "'She Was like a Novelty.'"

34. S. Rep. No 116-XX, *5:560*.

35. Helderman et al., "'She Was like a Novelty.'"

36. S. Rep. No 116-XX, *5:589*.

37. S. Rep. No 116-XX, *5:592–95, 622–29*.

38. S. Rep. No 116-XX, *5:598–99*.

39. Pete Madden and Matthew Mosk, "NRA Says 2015 Moscow Trip Wasn't 'Official.' Emails, Photos Reveal Gun Group's Role," ABC News, January 30, 2019, https://abcnews.go.com/Politics/nra-2015-moscow-trip-wasnt-official-emails-photos/story?id=60715741.

40. David A. Graham, "The End of the David Clarke Era," *Atlantic*, August 15, 2018, https://www.theatlantic.com/politics/archive/2018/08/david-clarke-era-milwaukee-sheriff/567595/.

41. S. Rep. No 116-XX, *5:599*.

42. S. Rep. No 116-XX, *5:602–3, 607*.

43. S. Rep. No 116-XX, *5:600*.

44. Betsy Swan, "NRA Heavyweight Wanted Access to Putin: Leaked Email," *Daily Beast*, January 30, 2019, https://www.thedailybeast.com/nra-heavyweight-wanted-access-to-putin-leaked-email.

45. S. Rep. No 116-XX, *5:609*.

46. Merrill Fabry, "This Is How the National Prayer Breakfast Got Its Start," *Time*, February 4, 2016, https://time.com/4202899/national-prayer-breakfast-history/.

47. S. Rep. No 116-XX, *5:609, 631–32*.

48. S. Rep. No 116-XX, *5:596*.

49. S. Rep. No 116-XX, *5:611*.

50. S. Rep. No 116-XX, *5:626–27*.

51. S. Rep. No 116-XX, *5:624*.

52. Stephen Collinson, "Donald Trump: Presumptive GOP Nominee; Sanders Takes Indiana," CNN, May 4, 2016, https://edition.cnn.com/2016/05/03/politics/indiana-primary-highlights/index.html.

53. Alexandra Jaffe, "NRA Endorses Donald Trump at National Convention," NBC News, May 20, 2016, https://www.nbcnews.com/politics/2016-election/trump-aims-assure-wary-gun-rights-supporters-nra-speech-n577296.

54. S. Rep. No 116-XX, *5:615–19*.

55. Rosenberg et al., "Beyond the N.R.A."

56. S. Rep. No 116-XX, *5:625*.

57. S. Rep. No 116-XX, *5:628*.

58. Steven Mufson and Tom Hamburger, "Trump Adviser's Public Comments, Ties to Moscow Stir Unease in Both Parties," *Washington Post*, August 5, 2016, https://www.washingtonpost.com/business/economy/trump-advisers-public-comments-ties-to-moscow-stir-unease-in-both-parties/2016/08/05/2e8722fa-5815-11e6-9aee-8075993d73a2_story.html.

59 Julia Ioffe, "Who Is Carter Page?," *Politico*, September 23, 2016, https://www.politico.com/magazine/story/2016/09/the-mystery-of-trumps-man-in-moscow-214283/.

60 David Cohen, "Conway Denies Trump Campaign Ties to Russia Figure," *Politico*, September 25, 2016, https://www.politico.com/story/2016/09/carter-page-trump-conway-228641.

61 S. Rep. No 116-XX, *5:628–30*.

62 S. Rep. No 116-XX, *5:630*.

63 Andrew Prokop, "Maria Butina, Explained: The Accused Russian Spy Who Tried to Sway Us Politics through the NRA," *Vox*, July 19, 2018, https://www.vox.com/2018/7/19/17581354/maria-butina-russia-nra-trump.

64 S. Rep. No 116-XX, *5:630–31*.

65 Helderman et al., "'She Was like a Novelty.'"

66 Rosenberg et al., "Beyond the N.R.A."

67 Gary Fields, "Concerns over Prayer Breakfast Lead Congress to Take It Over," Associated Press, January 29, 2023, https://apnews.com/article/politics-united-states-government-james-lankford-mark-pryor-religion-2d3d2b1ca91fe7919427df5fe4489f0d.

68 Kenneth P. Vogel and Elizabeth Dias, "At Prayer Breakfast, Guests Seek Access to a Different Higher Power," *New York Times*, July 27, 2018, https://www.nytimes.com/2018/07/27/us/politics/national-prayer-breakfast.html.

69 S. Rep. No 116-XX, *5:630–33*.

70 Clifton and Follman, "Very Strange Case."

71 S. Rep. No 116-XX, *5:633–34*.

72 S. Rep. No 116-XX, *5:634*.

73 Mak, "Kremlin and GOP."

74 Helderman et al., "'She Was like a Novelty.'"

75 Jason Leopold and Anthony Cormier, "Here Is the Money Trail from the Russian 'Agent' and Her Republican Partner," *BuzzFeed News*, July 31, 2018, https://www.buzzfeednews.com/article/jasonleopold/maria-butina-paul-erickson-suspicious-bank-money-russia.

76 Kara Scannell et al., "The Russian Accused of Using Sex, Lies and Guns to Infiltrate US Politics," CNN, July 22, 2018, https://edition.cnn.com/2018/07/19/politics/maria-butina-paul-erickson-russian-sex-lies-guns/index.html.

77 Pete Madden et al., "Lover or Cover? Maria Butina and the Romance at the Heart of an Alleged Russian Influence Operation," ABC News, August 28, 2018, https://abcnews.go.com/Politics/lover-cover-romance-heart-alleged-russian-influence-operation/story?id=57437405.

78 "Russian National Charged in Conspiracy to Act as an Agent of the Russian Federation within the United States," Office of Public Affairs, U.S. Department of Justice, press release, July 16, 2018, https://www.justice.gov/opa/pr/russian-national-charged-conspiracy-act-agent-russian-federation-within-united-states.

79 Matthew Rosenberg, "Maria Butina Pleads Guilty to Role in a Russian Effort to Influence Conservatives," *New York Times*, December 13, 2018, https://www.nytimes.com/2018/12/13/us/politics/butina-guilty.html.

80 Carrie Johnson, "Judge Orders Maria Butina, Linked to Russian Spy Agency, Jailed Ahead of Trial," July 18, 2018, *All Things Considered*, NPR, audio 3:37, https://www.npr.org/2018/07/18/630094267/maria-butina-was-in-contact-with-russian-intelligence-feds-say-in-new-documents.

81 Sarah N. Lynch, "Exclusive: Alleged Russian Agent Butina Met with U.S. Treasury, Fed Officials," Reuters, July 23, 2018, https://www.reuters.com/article/uk-usa-russia-butina-exclusive-idUKKBN1KC0DE/.

82 Sharon LaFraniere and Eileen Sullivan, "Maria Butina Sentenced for Role in Russian Influence Campaign," *New York Times*, April 26, 2019, https://www.nytimes.com/2019/04/26/us/politics/maria-butina-trump.html.

83 Lafraniere and Sullivan, "Maria Butina."

84 "Russian National Sentenced to Eighteen Months in Prison for Conspiring to Act as an Agent of the Russian Federation within the United States," Office of Public Affairs, U.S. Department of Justice, press release, April 26, 2019, https://www.justice.gov/opa/pr/russian-national-sentenced-18-months-prison-conspiring-act-agent-russian-federation-within.

85 Sara Murray et al., "Maria Butina Released from Federal Prison, Deported to Russia," CNN, October 25, 2019, https://edition.cnn.com/2019/10/25/politics/maria-butina-released/index.html.

86 Valerie Hopkins, "After Fifteen Months in U.S. Prisons, She Now Sits in Russia's Parliament," *New York Times*, November 19, 2021, https://www.nytimes.com/2021/11/19/world/europe/maria-butina-russia-duma.html.

87 "Treasury Designates Russian Oligarchs, Officials, and Entities in Response to Worldwide Malign Activity," U.S. Department of the Treasury, press release, April 6, 2018, https://home.treasury.gov/news/press-releases/sm0338.

88 "US Boyfriend of Russian Agent Maria Butina Charged with Fraud," *Guardian*, February 7, 2019, https://www.theguardian.com/us-news/2019/feb/07/us-boyfriend-of-russian-agent-maria-butina-charged-with.

89 "Man Romantically Linked to Russian Spy Is Sentenced to Seven Years in Fraud Case," *Washington Post*, July 6, 2020, https://www.washingtonpost.com/national/man-romantically-linked-to-russian-spy-senteced-for-fraud/2020/07/06/489095c8-bd97-11ea-8cf5-9c1b8d7f84c6_story.html.

90 Stephen Groves, "Trump Pardons Ex-Boyfriend of Deported Russian Agent," Associated Press, January 20, 2021, https://apnews.com/article/donald-trump-sioux-falls-maria-butina-us-news-russia-bc8e1858b424ca5d5d6119a53facfcdd.

91 S. Rep. No 116-XX, 5:531.

92 Ali Watkins, "A Former Trump Adviser Met with a Russian Spy," *BuzzFeed News*, April 3, 2017, https://www.buzzfeednews.com/article/alimwatkins/a-former-trump-adviser-met-with-a-russian-spy.

93 Rosalind S. Helderman, "Memo Points to FBI's Sustained Interest in Carter Page, Ex-Adviser to Trump," *Washington Post*, February 2, 2018, https://www.washingtonpost.com/politics/memo-points-to-fbis-ongoing-interest-in-trump-adviser-carter-page/2018/02/02/89bfdee2-077c-11e8-8777-2a059f168dd2_story.html.

94 S. Rep. No 116-XX, 5:532.

95 Kevin G. Hall, "Why Did FBI Suspect Trump Campaign Adviser Was a Foreign Agent?" McClatchy *DC*, April 14, 2017, https://www.mcclatchydc.com/news/politics-government/white-house/article144722444.html.

96 Tom McCarthy, "Who Is Carter Page, the Trump Ex-Adviser at the Center of the Memo Furore?" *Guardian*, February 3, 2018, https://www.theguardian.com/us-news/2018/feb/02/who-is-carter-page-trump-ex-adviser-memo-furore-russia-fbi.

97 Dan Zak, "The Curious Journey of Carter Page, the Former Trump Adviser Who Can't Stay out of the Spotlight," *Washington Post*, November 16, 2017, https://www.washingtonpost.com/lifestyle/style/the-curious-journey-of-carter-page-the-former-trump-adviser-who-cant-stay-out-of-the-spotlight/2017/11/15/f240cc40-c49e-11e7-afe9-4f60b5a6c4a0_story.html.

98 Joe Parkinson and Drew Hinshaw, "Inside the Secretive Russian Security Force That Targets Americans," *Wall Street Journal*, July 7, 2023, https://www.wsj.com/articles/fsb-evan-gershkovich-russia-security-force-dkro-e9cf9a49.

99 Luke Harding, "Enemy of the State," *Guardian*, September 23, 2011, https://www.theguardian.com/world/2011/sep/23/luke-harding-russia.

100 Parkinson and Hinshaw, "Inside."

101 Zachary Cohen, "FBI Documents Detail How the Russians Try to Recruit Spies," CNN, July 6, 2017, https://edition.cnn.com/2017/04/15/politics/russia-spy-recruitment-tactics-fbi-carter-page/index.html.

102 Mueller, Report, 96.

103 Ken Dilanian and Mike Memoli, "Who Is Carter Page and What Does He Have to Do with the Russia Probe?" NBC News, February 5, 2018, https://www.nbcnews.com/politics/donald-trump/who-carter-page-what-does-he-have-do-russia-probe-n844821.

104 S. Rep. No 116-XX, *5:531*.

105 Benjamin Weiser, "Three Men Are Charged with Serving as Secret Agents for Russia in New York," *New York Times*, January 26, 2015, https://www.nytimes.com/2015/01/27/nyregion/3-charged-with-working-as-agents-for-russia-in-new-york.html.

106 S. Rep. No 116-XX, *5:532*.

107 "Evgeny Buryakov Pleads Guilty in Manhattan Federal Court in Connection with Conspiracy to Work for Russian Intelligence," United States Attorney's Office, Southern District of New York, press release, March 11, 2016, https://www.justice.gov/usao-sdny/pr/evgeny-buryakov-pleads-guilty-manhattan-federal-court-connection-conspiracy-work.

108 Sealed Complaint, United States of America v. Evgeny Buryakov, Igor Sporyshev and Victor Podobnyy, No. 15-Cr-73-RMB (S.D.N.Y. January 23, 2015), uploaded by Just Security, https://www.justsecurity.org/wp-content/uploads/2017/11/PodobnyyComplaint-2.pdf.

109 Artin Afkhami, "Timeline of Carter Page's Contacts with Russia [Updated]," Just Security, February 5, 2018, https://www.justsecurity.org/46786/timeline-carter-pages-contacts-russia/.

110 Watkins, "Former Trump Adviser."

111 S. Rep. No 116-XX, *5:533*.

112 "A Transcript of Donald Trump's Meeting with the *Washington Post* Editorial Board," *Washington Post*, March 21, 2016, https://www.washingtonpost.com/blogs/post-partisan/wp/2016/03/21/a-transcript-of-donald-trumps-meeting-with-the-washington-post-editorial-board/.

113 S. Rep. No 116-XX, *5:535–36*.

114 Ioffe, "Who is Carter Page?"

115 S. Rep. No 116-XX, *5:536*.

116 Zachary R Mider, "Trump's New Russia Adviser Has Deep Ties to Kremlin's Gazprom," Bloomberg News, March 30, 2016, https://www.bloomberg.com/politics/articles/2016-03-30/trump-russia-adviser-carter-page-interview.

117 Robert Zubrin, "Trump: The Kremlin's Favorite Candidate,"*National Review*, April 4, 2016, https://www.nationalreview.com/2016/04/trump-kremlins-candidate/.

118 S. Rep. No 116-XX, *5:537*.

119 S. Rep. No 116-XX, *5:544–45*.

120 S. Rep. No 116-XX, 5:541–45.

121 "Советник Трампа и вице-премьер РФ Дворкович пообщались на вечере РЭШ" [Trump's adviser and Russian vice-premier Dvorkovich talked at the NES gathering], *РИА Новости [RIA News]*, July 8, 2016, https://ria.ru/20160708/1461720445.html.

122 S. Rep. No 116-XX, 5:548.

123 "Советник Трампа: в проекте 'Шелкового пути' важно взаимное соблюдение интересов РФ и Китая" [Trump advisor: Mutual respect for the interests of the Russian Federation and China is important in the Silk Road project], TASS, July 7, 2016, https://tass.ru/ekonomika/3438160.

124 "Бывший советник Трампа похвалил Грефа и Сечина" [Former Trump adviser praised Gref and Sechin], RBC, December 12, 2016, https://www.rbc.ru/politics/12/12/2016/584ece9a9a79473cc5427ec4.

125 S. Rep. No 116-XX, 5:548, 557.

126 S. Rep. No 116-XX, 5:549–50.

127 Michael S. Schmidt, "Major Takeaways from Carter Page's Congressional Interview on Russian Election Meddling," *New York Times*, November 7, 2017, https://www.nytimes.com/2017/11/07/us/politics/trump-adviser-carter-page-transcript-meeting-2016-campaign-russia.html.

128 Shaun Walker, "Trump's Foreign Policy Adviser Will Talk about His Foreign Policy—Just Not Today," *Guardian*, July 7, 2016, https://www.theguardian.com/world/2016/jul/07/carter-page-donald-trump-foreign-policy-advisor-russia.

129 Anna Nemtsova, "Why Russia Is Rejoicing over Trump," *Politico*, July 20, 2016, https://www.politico.com/magazine/story/2016/07/2016-trump-putin-russia-gop-platform-214074/.

130 Mufson and Hamburger, "Trump Adviser's."

131 Rebecca Shabad, "Democrats Ask FBI: Did Donald Trump Aides' Russia Connections Lead to Cyberattacks?," CBS News, August 30, 2016, https://www.cbsnews.com/news/democrats-ask-fbi-did-donald-trump-aides-russia-connections-lead-to-cyberattacks/.

132 Dan Friedman, "Carter Page's Mysterious Trip to Budapest Highlights Hungary's Effort to Win Over Trump," *Mother Jones*, November 9, 2017, https://www.motherjones.com/politics/2017/11/carter-pages-mysterious-trip-to-budapest-highlights-hungarys-effort-to-win-over-trump/.

133 "Trump Campaign Adviser Carter Page Held High-Level Meetings with Hungarian Officials in Budapest," ABC News, November 20, 2017, https://abcnews.go.com/Politics/trump-campaign-adviser-carter-page-held-high-level/story?id=51284300.

134 S. Rep. No 116-XX, 5:552–53.

135 Cohen, "Conway."

136 FISA Application for surveillance of Carter Page, Federal Bureau of Investigation, No. 17-cv-597 (FBI) -1, October 2016, uploaded by *New York Times*, https://int.nyt.com/data/documenthelper/95-carter-page-fisa-documents-foia-release/full/optimized.pdf.

137 S. Rep. No 116-XX, 5:557–58.

138 Carter Page, "Full Interview: Carter Page on Russia Contact," interview by Anderson Cooper, CNN, March 4, 2017, video, 25:35, https://www.youtube.com/watch?v=82ZcZ7s-3O8.

139 David A. Graham, "What Carter Page's Testimony Revealed," *Atlantic*, November 7, 2017, https://www.theatlantic.com/politics/archive/2017/11/carter-page-international-man-of-mystery/545159/.

140 "Transcript of Donald Trump's Meeting," *Washington Post*.

141 Sharon LaFraniere et al., "How the Russia Inquiry Began: A Campaign Aide, Drinks and Talk of Political Dirt," *New York Times*, December 30, 2017, https://www.nytimes.com/2017/12/30/us/politics/how-fbi-russia-investigation-began-george-papadopoulos.html.

142 Jerry Dunleavy, "Transcript of George Papadopoulos' Private Testimony Released," *Washington Examiner*, March 26, 2019, https://www.washingtonexaminer.com/news/248238/transcript-of-george-papadopoulos-private-testimony-released/.

143 David A. Graham, "Putin's Useful Idiots," *Atlantic*, February 24, 2022, https://www.theatlantic.com/ideas/archive/2022/02/russia-ukraine-war-republican-response/622919/.

144 "Vladimir Putin's Useful Idiots," *Economist*, July 3, 2023, https://www.economist.com/europe/2023/07/03/vladimir-putins-useful-idiots.

145 S. Rep. No 116-XX, *5:473*.

146 Raphael Satter, "Malta Academic in Trump Probe Has History of Vanishing Acts," Associated Press, October 22, 2018, https://apnews.com/article/800354d636af47f3afbd19338a377887.

147 Eileen Sullivan, "Joseph Mifsud, Key to Russia Inquiry, Gets Moment in the Spotlight," *New York Times*, July 24, 2019, https://www.nytimes.com/2019/07/24/us/politics/joseph-mifsud-mueller.html.

148 David D. Kirkpatrick, "The Professor behind the Trump Campaign Adviser Charges," *New York Times*, October 31, 2017, https://www.nytimes.com/2017/10/31/world/europe/russia-us-election-joseph-mifsud.html.

149 S. Rep. No 116-XX, *5:474*.

150 Sharon LaFraniere et al., "A London Meeting of an Unlikely Group: How a Trump Adviser Came to Learn of Clinton 'Dirt,'" *New York Times*, November 10, 2017, https://www.nytimes.com/2017/11/10/us/russia-inquiry-trump.html.

151 S. Rep. No 116-XX, *5:474*.

152 Ali Watkins, "Mysterious Putin 'Niece' Has a Name," *Politico*, November 9, 2017, https://www.politico.com/story/2017/11/09/putin-niece-olga-vinogradova-george-papadopoulos-russia-probe-244758.

153 S. Rep. No 116-XX, *5:475*.

154 S. Rep. No 116-XX, *5:469, 475*.

155 "Co-Founders," Russian International Affairs Council, retrieved from the Wayback Machine, version February 24, 2016, https://web.archive.org/web/20160224225219/http://russiancouncil.ru/en/about-us/founders.

156 "Presidium," Russian International Affairs Council, retrieved from the Wayback Machine, version March 4, 2016, https://web.archive.org/web/20160304080208/http://russiancouncil.ru/en/about-us/presidium/.

157 "Council Members," Russian International Affairs Council, retrieved from the Wayback Machine, version March 15, 2016, https://web.archive.org/web/20160315204644/http://russiancouncil.ru/en/about-us/members_RSMD.

158 S. Rep. No 116-XX, *5:500–506*.

159 S. Rep. No 116-XX, *5:479*.

160 Lichtblau, "Computer."

161 S. Rep. No 116-XX, *5:486*.

162 Lafraniere et al., "How the Russia Inquiry Began."

163 T.A. Frank, "The Surreal Life of George Papadopoulos," *Washington Post Magazine*, May 20, 2019, https://www.washingtonpost.com/news/magazine/wp/2019/05/20/feature/the-surreal-life-of-george-papadopoulos/.

164 S. Rep. No 116-XX, *5:495–96*.

165 S. Rep. No 116-XX, *5:505*.

166 David M. Weinberg, "Know Comment: The Donald's Foreign Policy," *Jerusalem Post*, April 7, 2016, https://www.jpost.com/opinion/know-comment-the-donalds-foreign-policy-450602.

167 "Republican Campaign Advisor George Papadopoulos: Sanctions Have Done Little More than to Turn Russia Towards China," Interfax, September 30, 2016, https://interfax.com/newsroom/exclusive-interviews/876/.

168 S. Rep. No 116-XX, *5:511–15*.

169 S. Rep. No 116-XX, *5:523–24*.

170 "Members List," Russian-American Chamber of Commerce in the USA, retrieved from the Wayback Machine, version October 22, 2016, https://web.archive.org/web/20161022073522/http://www.russianamericanchamber.com/members.

171 S. Rep. No 116-XX, *5:507–9*.

172 S. Rep. No 116-XX, *5:509*.

173 S. Rep. No 116-XX, *5:525*.

174 Matt Apuzzo and Michael S. Schmidt, "Trump Campaign Adviser Met with Russian to Discuss 'Dirt' on Clinton," *New York Times*, October 30, 2017, https://www.nytimes.com/2017/10/30/us/politics/george-papadopoulos-russia.html.

175 Mark Mazzetti and Sharon LaFraniere, "George Papadopoulos, Ex-Trump Adviser, Is Sentenced to Fourteen Days in Jail," *New York Times*, September 7, 2018, https://www.nytimes.com/2018/09/07/us/politics/george-papadopoulos-sentencing-special-counsel-investigation.html.

176 Steve Holland, "Trump Grants Full Pardon to Russia Probe Figure George Papadopoulos," Reuters, December 22, 2020, https://www.reuters.com/article/us-usa-trump-pardons-idUSKBN28X00R/.

177 Alexander Burns and Maggie Haberman, "Donald Trump Hires Paul Manafort to Lead Delegate Effort," *New York Times*, March 28, 2016, https://archive.nytimes.com/www.nytimes.com/politics/first-draft/2016/03/28/donald-trump-hires-paul-manafort-to-lead-delegate-effort/.

178 Franklin Foer, "Paul Manafort, American Hustler," *Atlantic*, March 2018, https://www.theatlantic.com/magazine/archive/2018/03/paul-manafort-american-hustler/550925/.

179 Philip Bump, "Timeline: Paul Manafort's Long History with Oligarch Oleg Deripaska," *Washington Post*, September 20, 2017, https://www.washingtonpost.com/news/politics/wp/2017/03/22/timeline-paul-manaforts-long-murky-history-of-political-interventions/.

180 Foer, "Paul Manafort."

181 Thomas B. Edsall, "Partners in Political PR Firm Typify Republican New Breed," *Washington Post*, April 6, 1985, https://www.washingtonpost.com/archive/politics/1985/04/07/partners-in-political-pr-firm-typify-republican-new-breed/8d0b8c04-fabc-43ae-887b-25c7e8af0ec0/.

182 Eli Lake, "Trump Just Hired His Next Scandal," Bloomberg News, opinion, April 13, 2016, https://www.bloomberg.com/view/articles/2016-04-13/trump-just-hired-his-next-scandal-lobbyist-paul-manafort.

183 Franklin Foer, "Paul Manafort Joined the Trump Campaign in a State of 'Despair and Desperation,'" interview by Dave Davies, *Fresh Air*, NPR, January 29, 2018, https://www.npr.org/2018/01/29/581478324/paul-manafort-joined-the-trump-campaign-in-a-state-of-despair-and-desperation.

184 S. Rep. No 116-XX, *5:34*.

185 Luke Harding, "Russia's Richest Man with a Fortune Made in the Aluminium Wars," *Guardian*, October 21, 2008, https://www.theguardian.com/world/2008/oct/22/oleg-deripaska-russia-oligarch.

186 Harding, "Russia's Richest Man."

187 Misha Glenny et al., "US Refused Oligarch Visa over Alleged Criminal Associations," *Guardian*, October 30, 2008, https://www.theguardian.com/world/2008/oct/31/oleg-deripaska-us-visa-rusal.

188 Foer, "Paul Manafort."

189 "Ukraine Seizes Rusal Alumina Plant, Deripaska-Linked Assets," Bloomberg News, February 17, 2023, https://www.bloomberg.com/news/articles/2023-02-17/ukraine-seizes-rusal-alumina-plant-deripaska-linked-assets.

190 "Ukraine Candidate Vows Prosecutions If Elected," NBC News, October 31, 2004, https://www.nbcnews.com/id/wbna6374820.

191 "About Oleg Deripaska, the Russian Billionaire Who Worked with Paul Manafort," ABC News, March 22, 2017, https://abcnews.go.com/International/oleg-deripaska-russian-billionaire-worked-paul-manafort/story?id=46303922.

192 Rob Davies, "Oleg Deripaska: Putin 'Favourite' with Strong Ties to UK Politics," *Guardian*, March 10, 2022, https://www.theguardian.com/world/2022/mar/10/oleg-deripaska-profile-putin-britain.

193 S. Rep. No 116-XX, 5:35–36.

194 Ilya Marritz, "Let's Recall What Exactly Paul Manafort and Rudy Giuliani Were Doing in Ukraine," ProPublica, March 1, 2022, https://www.propublica.org/article/lets-recall-what-exactly-paul-manafort-and-rudy-giuliani-were-doing-in-ukraine.

195 "Партия регионов Украины и 'Единая Россия' будут сотрудничать"[The Party of Regions of Ukraine and the United Russia will cooperate], RBC, July 3, 2005, https://www.rbc.ru/politics/03/07/2005/5703bafc9a7947afa08c832d.

196 Brett Forrest, "Paul Manafort's Overseas Political Work Had a Notable Patron: A Russian Oligarch", *Wall Street Journal*, August 30, 2017, https://www.wsj.com/articles/paul-manaforts-overseas-political-work-had-a-notable-patron-a-russian-oligarch-1504131910.

197 Forrest, "Paul Manafort's."

198 S. Rep. No 116-XX, 5:37.

199 Jeff Horwitz and Chad Day, "AP Exclusive: Before Trump Job, Manafort Worked to Aid Putin," Associated Press, March 22, 2017, retrieved from the Wayback Machine, version October 1, 2020, https://web.archive.org/web/20201001035848/https://apnews.com/article/122ae0b5848345faa88108a03de40c5a.

200 Kenneth P. Vogel and Andrew E. Kramer, "Russian Spy or Hustling Political Operative? The Enigmatic Figure at the Heart of Mueller's Inquiry," *New York Times*, February 23, 2019, https://www.nytimes.com/2019/02/23/us/politics/konstantin-kilimnik-russia.html.

201 Christopher Miller, "Who Is Paul Manafort's Man in Kyiv? An Interview with Konstantin Kilimnik," RFE/RL, February 23, 2017, https://www.rferl.org/a/paul-manafort-konstantin-kilimnik-trump-campaign-ukraine/28326123.html.

202 Sam Patten, "I Pled Guilty to Robert Mueller. Here's My Story," *Rolling Stone*, September 2, 2023, https://www.rollingstone.com/politics/politics-features/mueller-report-sam-patten-book-excerpt-1234816693/.

203 Vogel and Kramer, "Russian Spy."

204 Mueller, Report, 133–34.

205 S. Rep. No 116-XX, 5:84–89.

206 Jay Nanavati, Supplemental Motion in Limine by Paul J. Manafort Jr. (Attachments: #1 Exhibit A-DD, #2 Exhibit EE-FF, #3 Exhibit GG-YY), United States v. Manafort, 1:18-cr-00083, (E.D. Va. July 26, 2018) ECF No. 153, uploaded by CourtListener, https://www.courtlistener.com/docket/6315908/153/2/united-states-v-manafort/.

207 European Parliament, Delegation to Observe the Parliamentary Elections in Ukraine, *Election Observation Report,* March 26, 2006, 8, https://www.europarl.europa.eu/cmsdata/212701/Election_report_Ukraine_26_March_2006.pdf.

208 Olga Dmitricheva (Chornaya) et al., "Благополучно завершившийся 15 декабря 2001 года процесс создания предвыборного блока «За Единую Украину!» был сложным и многоэтапным" [The process of creating the election bloc 'For a United Ukraine!' successfully completed on December 15, 2001, was complex and multi-stage], *Зеркало Недели [Mirror of the Week],* March 22, 2002, https://zn.ua/internal/pyat_istochnikov,_pyat_sostavnyh_chastey_bloka_za_edinuyu_ukrainu.html.

209 Mary Mycio, "Reformers Gain Seats in Ukraine Parliament Vote," *Los Angeles Times,* April 2, 2002, https://www.latimes.com/archives/la-xpm-2002-apr-02-mn-35812-story.html.

210 Foer, "Paul Manafort."

211 Nanavati, "Supplemetal Motion."

212 Graham Stack, "Exposed: The Ukrainian Politician Who Funded Paul Manafort's Secret EU Lobbying Campaign," OCCRP, November 4, 2019, https://www.occrp.org/en/investigations/exposed-the-ukrainian-politician-who-funded-paul-manaforts-secret-eu-lobbying-campaign.

213 Luke Harding, "Former Trump Aide Approved 'Black Ops' to Help Ukraine President," *Guardian,* April 5, 2018, https://www.theguardian.com/us-news/2018/apr/05/ex-trump-aide-paul-manafort-approved-black-ops-to-help-ukraine-president.

214 Kramer et al., "Secret Ledger."

215 Forrest, "Paul Manafort's."

216 Superseding Indictment, United States of America v. Paul J. Manafort, Jr. and Richard W. Gates III, No. 1:18 Cr. 83, (E.D. Va. February 22, 2018), https://www.justice.gov/archives/sco/file/1038391/dl.

217 S. Rep. No 116-XX, *5:50.*

218 S. Rep. No 116-XX, *5:38.*

219 S. Rep. No 116-XX, *5:42.*

220 Josh Kovensky, "Trump's Campaign Manager Haunted by Past Business," *Kyiv Post,* July 8, 2016, https://archive.kyivpost.com/article/content/ukraine-politics/trumps-campaign-manager-haunted-by-past-business-418137.html.

221 Harding, "Russia's Richest Man."

222 Luke Harding, "Russia's Richest Oligarchs See Assets Fall by 70% in a Year," *Guardian,* April 17, 2009, https://www.theguardian.com/world/2009/apr/18/russia-forbes-rich-annual-survey.

223 Dmitry Zhdannikov and Darya Korsunskaya, "Russia Tycoons Bailout Could Turn into Kremlin Trap," Reuters, October 30, 2008, https://www.reuters.com/article/us-russia-bailout-idUSTRE49T6GN20081030/.

224 Forrest, "Paul Manafort's."

225 Karen Yuan, "A Timeline of Paul Manafort's Career," *Atlantic,* February 6, 2018, https://www.theatlantic.com/membership/archive/2018/02/a-timeline-of-paul-manaforts-career/552437/.

226 Foer, "Paul Manafort."

227 Surf Horizon Limited, Winding up petition submitted on behalf of B-Invest, Grand Court of the Cayman Islands, December 9, 2019, uploaded by *Politico,* https://www.politico.com/f/?id=00000156-9ffd-de38-a3df-bffd9f450000.

228 Foer, "Paul Manafort."

229 S. Rep. No 116-XX, *5:53–54.*

230 Mueller, Report, 135.

231 Julia Ioffe and Franklin Foer, "Did Manafort Use Trump to Curry Favor with a Putin Ally?" *Atlantic*, October 2, 2017, https://www.theatlantic.com/politics/archive/2017/10/emails-suggest-manafort-sought-approval-from-putin-ally-deripaska/541677/.

232 S. Rep. No 116-XX, *5:69–70*.

233 S. Rep. No 116-XX, *5:70*.

234 Philip Bump, "The Government Finally Connects the Line from Trump's Campaign to Russian Intelligence," *Washington Post*, April 15, 2021, https://www.washingtonpost.com/politics/2021/04/15/government-finally-connects-line-trumps-campaign-russian-intelligence/.

235 Mattathias Schwartz, "Exclusive: Paul Manafort Admits He Passed Trump Campaign Data to a Suspected Russian Asset," *Business Insider*, August 8, 2022, https://www.businessinsider.com/paul-manafort-exclusive-interview-trump-campaign-polling-data-russia-kilimnik-2022-8.

236 S. Rep. No 116-XX, *5:71–72*.

237 S. Rep. No 116-XX, *5:74–82*.

238 S. Rep. No 116-XX, *5:67, 85*.

239 Luke Harding and Dan Collyns, "Manafort Held Secret Talks with Assange in Ecuadorian Embassy, Sources Say," *Guardian*, November 27, 2018, https://www.theguardian.com/us-news/2018/nov/27/manafort-held-secret-talks-with-assange-in-ecuadorian-embassy.

240 S. Rep. No 116-XX, *5:82–84*.

241 S. Rep. No 116-XX, *5:99*.

242 S. Rep. No 116-XX, *5:83, 122*.

243 Kramer et al., "Secret Ledger."

244 Maggie Haberman and Jonathan Martin, "Paul Manafort Quits Donald Trump's Campaign after a Tumultuous Run," *New York Times*, August 19, 2016, https://www.nytimes.com/2016/08/20/us/politics/paul-manafort-resigns-donald-trump.html.

245 S. Rep. No 116-XX, *5:93, 97, 112*.

246 Tom Hamburger and Rosalind S. Helderman, "Former Trump Campaign Chairman Paul Manafort Files as Foreign Agent for Ukraine Work", *Washington Post*, June 27, 2017, https://www.washingtonpost.com/politics/former-trump-campaign-chairman-paul-manafort-files-as-foreign-agent-for-ukraine-work/2017/06/27/8322b6ac-5b7b-11e7-9fc6-c7ef4bc58d13_story.html.

247 Benjamin Wallace-Wells, "Paul Manafort Returns to the Center of the Russia Story," *New Yorker*, August 11, 2017, https://www.newyorker.com/news/benjamin-wallace-wells/paul-manafort-returns-to-the-center-of-the-russia-story.

248 Indictment, United States of America v. Paul J. Manafort, Jr. and Richard W. Gates III, No. 1:17 Cr. 201 (D.D.C. October 27, 2017), retrieved from the Wayback Machine, version October 30, 2017, https://web.archive.org/web/20171030131635/https://www.justice.gov/file/1007271/download.

249 Sharon LaFraniere, "Paul Manafort, Trump's Former Campaign Chairman, Guilty of Eight Counts," *New York Times*, August 21, 2018, https://www.nytimes.com/2018/08/21/us/politics/paul-manafort-trial-verdict.html.

250 Katelyn Polantz, "Paul Manafort Pleads Guilty and Agrees to Cooperate with Mueller Investigation," CNN, September 14, 2018, https://edition.cnn.com/2018/09/14/politics/paul-manafort-guilty-plea/index.html.

251 Sharon LaFraniere, "Manafort Breached Plea Deal by Repeatedly Lying, Mueller Says," *New York Times*, November 26, 2018, https://www.nytimes.com/2018/11/26/us/politics/mueller-paul-manafort-cooperation.html.

252 Sharon LaFraniere, "Paul Manafort's Prison Sentence Is Nearly Doubled to 7½ Years," *New York Times*, March 13, 2019, https://www.nytimes.com/2019/03/13/us/politics/paul-manafort-sentencing.html.

253 Tucker Higgins and Jordan Malter, "Special Counsel Robert Mueller's Investigation Could Turn a Profit for the Government, Thanks to Paul Manafort's Asset Forfeiture," CNBC, September 17, 2018, https://www.cnbc.com/2018/09/17/mueller-probe-could-turn-a-profit-thanks-to-manafort-assets.html.

254 "Trump Pardons Paul Manafort, Roger Stone and Charles Kushner," BBC News, December 24, 2020, https://www.bbc.com/news/world-us-canada-55433522.

255 Josh Gerstein, "Trump Pardon Unwinds Some Manafort Forfeitures," *Politico*, February 26, 2021, https://www.politico.com/news/2021/02/26/trump-manafort-pardon-471785.

256 Alana Abramson, "Robert Mueller Indicts Konstantin Kilimnik and Hits Paul Manafort with Another Charge," *Time*, June 8, 2018, https://time.com/5306563/robert-mueller-indicts-konstantin-kilimnik-and-hits-paul-manafort-with-another-charge/.

257 "Treasury Escalates Sanctions against the Russian Government's Attempts to Influence U.S. Elections," U.S. Department of the Treasury, press release, April 15, 2021, https://home.treasury.gov/news/press-releases/jy0126.

258 Peter Stone, "Konstantin Kilimnik: Elusive Russian with Ties to Manafort Faces Fresh Mueller Scrutiny," *Guardian*, November 9, 2018, https://www.theguardian.com/us-news/2018/nov/09/konstantin-kilimnik-russia-trump-manafort-mueller.

259 Natasha Bertrand, "When Trump Won, Putin Deployed His Oligarchs," *Politico*, April 18, 2019, https://www.politico.com/story/2019/04/18/mueller-report-putin-trump-1282648.

260 S. Rep. No 116-XX, *5:703–52*.

261 Gloria Borger, Pamela Brown, Jim Sciutto, Marshall Cohen, Eric Lichtblau, "First on CNN: Russian Officials Bragged They Could Use Flynn to Influence Trump, Sources Say," CNN, May 19, 2017, https://edition.cnn.com/2017/05/19/politics/michael-flynn-donald-trump-russia-influence/index.html.

262 Philip Rucker, "Obama Warned Trump against Hiring Flynn as National Security Adviser, Officials Say," *Washington Post*, May 8, 2017, https://www.washingtonpost.com/news/post-politics/wp/2017/05/08/obama-warned-trump-against-hiring-flynn-as-national-security-adviser-official-confirms/.

263 Kristen Welker et al., "Obama Warned Trump against Hiring Mike Flynn, Say Officials," NBC News, May 8, 2017, https://www.nbcnews.com/news/us-news/obama-warned-trump-against-hiring-mike-flynn-say-officials-n756316.

264 Stephen Braun and Robert Burns, "Flynn, Fired Once by a President, Now Removed by Another," Associated Press, February 14, 2017, https://apnews.com/article/ce90066b4e20483da79adf21910da0c7.

265 Chad Ray and Stephen Braun, "Flynn Files New Financial Form Reporting Ties to Data Firm," Associated Press, August 4, 2017, https://apnews.com/article/bfc2de11c52f40929f24d42e56014014.

266 "Pentagon Investigates Michael Flynn's Foreign Payments," Al Jazeera, April 28, 2017, video, 1:55, https://youtu.be/Ib-J-9f2MpY?si=zbeD4_GiuQ6pTY94.

267 Austin Wright, "Flynn Was Paid $34,000 for Moscow Speech, Documents Show," *Politico*, March 16, 2017, https://www.politico.com/story/2017/03/michael-flynn-paid-moscow-speech-236137.

268 Natasha Bertrand, "Mike Flynn Was Paid by Russia's Top Cybersecurity Firm While He Still Had Top-Secret-Level Security Clearance," *Business Insider*, March 16, 2017, https://www.businessinsider.com/mike-flynn-and-russia-2017-3.

269 "Putin's Dinner with Michael Flynn: 'I Didn't Even Really Talk to Him,'" Reuters, June 4, 2017, https://www.reuters.com/article/us-russia-usa-putin-idUSKBN18V0XZ/.

270 Rosalind S. Helderman and Tom Hamburger, "Trump Adviser Flynn Paid by Multiple Russia-Related Entities, New Records Show," *Washington Post*, March 16, 2017, https://www.washingtonpost.com/politics/new-details-released-on-russia-related-payments-to-flynn-before-he-joined-trump-campaign/2017/03/16/52a4205a-0a55-11e7-a15f-a58d4a988474_story.html.

271 Murray Waas, "Michael Flynn Ignored Official Warnings about Receiving Foreign Payments," *Guardian*, April 8, 2021, https://www.theguardian.com/us-news/2021/apr/08/michael-flynn-ignored-official-warnings-receiving-foreign-payments.

272 Borger et al., "First on CNN."

273 Mueller, Report, 160–61.

274 "Read the Transcripts of Michael Flynn's Calls with Russia's Ambassador to the United States," *Washington Post*, May 29, 2020, https://www.washingtonpost.com/context/read-the-transcripts-of-michael-flynn-s-calls-with-russia-s-ambassador-to-the-united-states/cb3d37df-bf1d-444f-8810-10a7ec613314/?itid=lk_interstitial_manual_40.

275 Carol E. Lee and Paul Sonne, "U.S. Sanctions Russia over Election Hacking; Moscow Threatens to Retaliate," *Wall Street Journal*, December 29, 2016, https://www.wsj.com/articles/u-s-punishes-russia-over-election-hacking-with-sanctions-1483039178.

276 "Read the Transcripts of Michael Flynn's," *Washington Post*.

277 DeYoung and Miller, "First Sign."

278 Emily Tamkin, "After Russians Promise Retaliation, Putin Decides Not to Expel U.S. Diplomats," *Foreign Policy*, December 30, 2016, https://foreignpolicy.com/2016/12/30/after-russians-promise-retaliation-putin-decides-not-to-expel-u-s-diplomats/.

279 "Read the Transcripts of Michael Flynn's," *Washington Post*.

280 Karen DeYoung, "Trump Administration Not Sending a Delegation to Syria Peace Talks," *Washington Post*, January 21, 2017, https://www.washingtonpost.com/world/national-security/trump-administration-not-sending-a-delegation-to-syria-peace-talks/2017/01/21/7e42cc5c-dff8-11e6-ad42-f3375f271c9c_story.html.

281 David Ignatius, "Why Did Obama Dawdle on Russia's Hacking?" opinion, *Washington Post*, January 12, 2017, https://www.washingtonpost.com/opinions/why-did-obama-dawdle-on-russias-hacking/2017/01/12/75f878a0-d90c-11e6-9a36-1d296534b31e_story.html.

282 Greg Miller et al., "National Security Adviser Flynn Discussed Sanctions with Russian Ambassador, despite Denials, Officials Say," *Washington Post*, February 9, 2017, https://www.washingtonpost.com/world/national-security/national-security-adviser-flynn-discussed-sanctions-with-russian-ambassador-despite-denials-officials-say/2017/02/09/f85b29d6-ee11-11e6-b4ff-ac2cf509efe5_story.html.

283 Philip Ewing, "Five Things on Michael Flynn, Russia and Donald Trump," NPR, February 10, 2017, https://www.npr.org/2017/02/10/514551968/5-things-on-michael-flynn-russia-and-donald-trump.

284 Ken Dilanian, "Official: Flynn Discussed Sanctions with Russians before Taking Office," NBC News, February 10, 2017, https://www.nbcnews.com/news/us-news/official-flynn-discussed-sanctions-russians-taking-office-n719271.

285 Chris Cillizza, "Just How Much Trouble Is Michael Flynn In?" *Washington Post*, February 10, 2017, https://www.washingtonpost.com/news/the-fix/wp/2017/02/10/just-how-much-trouble-is-michael-flynn-in/.

286 Adam Entous et al., "Justice Department Warned White House That Flynn Could Be Vulnerable to Russian Blackmail, Officials Say," *Washington Post*, February 13, 2017, https://www.washingtonpost.com/world/national-security/justice-department-warned-white-house-that-flynn-could-be-vulnerable-to-russian-blackmail-officials-say/2017/02/13/fc5dab88-f228-11e6-8d72-263470bf0401_story.html.

287 Jen Kirby, "Here's What Michael Flynn Admitted He Lied to the FBI About," *Vox*, December 1, 2017, https://www.vox.com/policy-and-politics/2017/12/1/16724742/michael-flynn-plead-guilty-lied-fbi.

288 Devlin Barrett and Greg Miller, "Transcripts of Calls between Flynn, Russian Diplomat Show They Discussed Sanctions," *Washington Post*, May 29, 2020, https://www.washingtonpost.com/national-security/transcripts-of-calls-between-flynn-russian-diplomat-show-they-discussed-sanctions/2020/05/29/cc3d29c6-a1f0-11ea-b5c9-570a91917d8d_story.html.

289 Katelyn Polantz, "Mueller Releases Memo Summarizing FBI's Interview with Michael Flynn," CNN, December 18, 2018, https://edition.cnn.com/2018/12/17/politics/mueller-memo-michael-flynn-interview/index.html.

290 Matthew Rosenberg and Mark Mazzetti, "Trump Team Knew Flynn Was under Investigation before He Came to White House," *New York Times*, May 17, 2017, https://www.nytimes.com/2017/05/17/us/politics/michael-flynn-donald-trump-national-security-adviser.html.

291 Del Quentin Wilber et al., "How the Mike Flynn Investigation Began," *Wall Street Journal*, June 1, 2017, https://www.wsj.com/articles/how-the-mike-flynn-investigation-began-1496341010.

292 Greg Miller et al., "Flynn's Swift Downfall: From a Phone Call in the Dominican Republic to a Forced Resignation at the White House," *Washington Post*, February 14, 2017, https://www.washingtonpost.com/world/national-security/flynns-swift-downfall-from-a-phone-call-in-the-dominican-republic-to-a-forced-resignation-at-the-white-house/2017/02/14/17b0d8e6-f2f2-11e6-b9c9-e83fce42fb61_story.html.

293 U.S. Department of Justice, *Registration Statement Pursuant to the Foreign Agents Registration Act of 1938, as Amended, Filed by Flynn Intel Group Inc*, Registration No. 6406, March 7, 2017, https://efile.fara.gov/docs/6406-Registration-Statement-20170307-1.pdf.

294 Rachel Weiner, "Michael Flynn Reviewed FARA Filing He Later Called False, Ex-Lawyer Testifies," *Washington Post*, July 16, 2019, https://www.washingtonpost.com/local/public-safety/michael-flynns-ex-lawyer-testifies-on-the-former-national-security-advisers-consulting-work/2019/07/16/f317b28a-a801-11e9-86dd-d7f0e60391e9_story.html.

295 Philip Ewing, "Michael Flynn Pleaded Guilty. Why Is the Justice Department Dropping the Charges?" NPR, May 8, 2020, https://www.npr.org/2020/05/08/852582068/mike-flynn-pleaded-guilty-why-is-the-justice-department-dropping-the-charges.

296 Darren Samuelsohn, "Mueller Says Flynn's Cooperation 'Complete,'" *Politico*, March 12, 2019, https://www.politico.com/story/2019/03/12/michael-flynn-cooperating-1219273.

297 Morgan Chalfant, "Judge to Flynn: 'Arguably, You Sold Your Country Out,'" *Hill*, December 18, 2018, https://thehill.com/business-a-lobbying/421898-judge-to-flynn-arguably-you-sold-your-country-out/.

298 Spencer S. Hsu, "Michael Flynn Hires Conservative Lawyer and Commentator, Will Continue to Cooperate with Government," *Washington Post*, June 13, 2019, https://www.washingtonpost.com/local/legal-issues/michael-flynn-hires-conservative-lawyer-and-commentator-will-continue-to-cooperate-with-government/2019/06/12/def388c2-8d2d-11e9-8f69-a2795fca3343_story.html.

299 Josh Gerstein, "Michael Flynn Seeking to Withdraw Guilty Plea," *Politico*, January 14, 2020, https://www.politico.com/news/2020/01/14/michael-flynn-guilty-plea-withdraw-099021.

300 Kyle Cheney and Josh Gerstein, "Court-Appointed Adviser Blasts 'Corrupt' DOJ Move to Drop Flynn Case," *Politico*, September 11, 2020, https://www.politico.com/news/2020/09/11/court-corrupt-doj-drop-michael-flynn-case-412555.

301 Caroline Kelly and David Shortell, "Barr Defends Dropping Flynn Case: 'I'm Doing the Law's Bidding,'" CNN, May 7, 2020, https://edition.cnn.com/2020/05/07/politics/barr-flynn-defends-case/index.html.

302 "Ежегодное послание к Владимиру Путину" [Annual address to Vladimir Putin], *Kommersant*, December 19, 2016, https://www.kommersant.ru/doc/3175832.

303 S. Rep. No 116-XX, *5:718*.

304 S. Rep. No 116-XX, *5:719*.

305 Zachary Cohen, "Conflicting Stories about Kushner's Meeting with Russian Banker," CNN, June 2, 2017, https://edition.cnn.com/2017/06/02/politics/jared-kushner-russian-banker-what-we-know/index.html.

306 David Filipov et al., "Explanations for Kushner's Meeting with Head of Kremlin-Linked Bank Don't Match Up," *Washington Post*, June 1, 2017, https://www.washingtonpost.com/politics/explanations-for-kushners-meeting-with-head-of-kremlin-linked-bank-dont-match-up/2017/06/01/dd1bdbb0-460a-11e7-bcde-624ad94170ab_story.html.

307 "Correction: Trump-Russia-Oligarch's Influence Story," Associated Press, July 6, 2018, https://apnews.com/article/5e533f93afae4a4fa5c2f7fe80ad72ac.

308 Mueller, Report, 164.

309 Michelle Caruso-Cabrera, "The $10 Billion Man Out to Change Russia's Image," CNBC, December 11, 2013, https://www.cnbc.com/2013/12/11/russias-kirill-dmitriev-puts-new-twist-on-sovereign-wealth-fund.html.

310 Rachel Weiner, "George Nader Sentenced to Ten Years in Prison for Child Sex Charges," *Washington Post*, June 26, 2020, https://www.washingtonpost.com/local/legal-issues/george-nader-sentenced-to-10-years-in-prison-for-child-sex-charges/2020/06/26/d8b2c2e4-b6f7-11ea-a8da-693df3d7674a_story.html.

311 Dan Mangan, "Mueller Witness George Nader Charged with Transporting Fourteen-Year-Old Boy for Sex, Child Porn," CNBC, July 19, 2019, https://www.cnbc.com/2019/07/19/mueller-witness-george-nader-accused-of-transporting-boy-for-sex-porn.html.

312 Mueller, Report, 147.

313 Mark Mazzetti and Emily B. Hager, "Secret Desert Force Set up by Blackwater's Founder," *New York Times*, May 14, 2011, https://www.nytimes.com/2011/05/15/world/middleeast/15prince.html.

314 Adam Entous et al., "Blackwater Founder Held Secret Seychelles Meeting to Establish Trump-Putin Back Channel," *Washington Post*, April 3, 2017, https://www.washingtonpost.com/world/national-security/blackwater-founder-held-secret-seychelles-meeting-to-establish-trump-putin-back-channel/2017/04/03/95908a08-1648-11e7-ada0-1489b735b3a3_story.html.

315 Keri Geiger and Michael Riley, "Blackwater Founder Said to Have Advised Trump Team," Bloomberg News, April 18, 2017, https://www.bloomberg.com/politics/articles/2017-04-18/blackwater-founder-erik-prince-said-to-have-advised-trump-team.

316 S. Rep. No 116-XX, *5:734*.

317 Mueller, Report, 155.

318 Shane Harris and Karoun Demirjian, "Congressional Democrats Examine Erik Prince's Statements on 2017 Seychelles Meeting for Possible Perjury," *Washington Post*, April 19, 2019, https://www.washingtonpost.com/world/national-security/congressional-democrats-examine-eriks-prince-statements-on-2017-seychelles-meeting-for-possible-perjury/2019/04/19/b7f888da-62cb-11e9-9412-daf3d2e67c6d_story.html.

319 Kevin Collier, "How the Mueller Investigation Was Hampered by Encryption Apps and Disappearing Messages," CNN, April 19, 2019, https://edition.cnn.com/2019/04/19/politics/mueller-investigation-encryption/index.html.

320 Philip Bump, "On a Number of Important Questions, Mueller Never Got Answers," *Washington Post*, April 19, 2019, https://www.washingtonpost.com/politics/2019/04/19/number-important-questions-robert-mueller-never-got-answers/.

321 S. Rep. No 116-XX, *5:722–26*.

322 Julian Borger, "Russia Committed War Crimes in Syria, Finds UN Report," *Guardian*, March 2, 2020, https://www.theguardian.com/world/2020/mar/02/russia-committed-war-crimes-in-syria-finds-un-report.

323 Mueller, Report, 158–59.

324 Sam Berger and Talia Dessel, "Trump's Russia Cover-Up by the Numbers," Moscow Project, accessed July 11, 2024, https://cdn.themoscowproject.org/content/uploads/2019/06/17140607/MoscowProjectContacts-6.17-Final-PDF.pdf.

325 Karen Yourish and Larry Buchanan, "Mueller Report Shows Depth of Connections between Trump Campaign and Russians," *New York Times*, April 19, 2019, https://www.nytimes.com/interactive/2019/01/26/us/politics/trump-contacts-russians-wikileaks.html.

326 Spencer Ackerman, "Intelligence Figures Fear Trump Reprisals over Assessment of Russia Election Role," *Guardian*, December 11, 2016, https://www.theguardian.com/us-news/2016/dec/11/intelligence-agencies-cia-donald-trump-russia.

327 Eli Watkins, "Some of the Times Trump Has Called Russia Probe a 'Witch Hunt,'" CNN, January 11, 2018, https://edition.cnn.com/2018/01/10/politics/donald-trump-witch-hunt-justice-department/index.html.

328 Nancy Benac et al., "Mueller Reveals Trump's Attempts to Choke off Russia Probe," Associated Press, April 18, 2019, https://apnews.com/article/north-america-donald-trump-ap-top-news-politics-russia-48f9d5132d7a4e2d823edad8fc407979.

329 Matt Apuzzo et al., "F.B.I. Is Investigating Trump's Russia Ties, Comey Confirms," *New York Times*, March 20, 2017, https://www.nytimes.com/2017/03/20/us/politics/fbi-investigation-trump-russia-comey.html.

330 Shear and Apuzzo, "F.B.I. Director James Comey."

331 Rebecca R. Ruiz and Mark Landler, "Robert Mueller, Former F.B.I. Director, Is Named Special Counsel for Russia Investigation," *New York Times*, May 17, 2017, https://www.nytimes.com/2017/05/17/us/politics/robert-mueller-special-counsel-russia-investigation.html.

332 Mueller, Report.

333 "Publications," U.S. Senate Select Committee on Intelligence, accessed July 11, 2024, https://www.intelligence.senate.gov/publications/report-select-committee-intelligence-united-states-senate-russian-active-measures.

CHAPTER 20

1 Sylvia Ayuso, "US Imposes More Visa Restrictions on Venezuelan Officials," *El Pais*, February 3, 2015, https://english.elpais.com/elpais/2015/02/03/inenglish/1422969256_026188.html.

2   Kates, "How Russian Oil Giant."

3   Kenneth P. Vogel et al., "Prosecutors Examining Ukrainians Who Flocked to Trump Inaugural," *New York Times*, January 10, 2019, https://www.nytimes.com/2019/01/10/us/politics/ukraine-donald-trump-inauguration.html.

4   Rosalind S. Helderman and Spencer S. Hsu, "American Political Consultant Admits Foreign Money Was Funneled to Trump Inaugural," *Washington Post*, September 1, 2018, https://www.washingtonpost.com/local/public-safety/washington-consultant-for-ukraine-party-set-to-plead-guilty-to-violating-lobbyist-disclosure-law/2018/08/31/172cf2c8-ad23-11e8-a8d7-0f63ab8b1370_story.html.

5   Kenneth P. Vogel, "A Foreigner Paid $200,000 for Tickets to Trump's Inaugural. Now He Says He Was Duped.," *New York Times*, June 18, 2019, https://www.nytimes.com/2019/06/18/us/politics/trump-inaugural-lawsuit-pavel-fuks.html.

6   Bill Allison and John McCormick, "Citgo's Trump Inauguration Gift Surfaces amid National-Security Concern," Bloomberg News, April 19, 2017, https://www.bloomberg.com/politics/articles/2017-04-19/citgo-s-inaugural-gift-surfaces-amid-national-security-concern.

7   Indictment, United States of America v. David Rivera and Esther Nuhfer, No. 22-20552-Cr-GAYLES/TORRES (S.D. Fla. Jul. 6, 2023), uploaded by *Politico*, https://www.politico.com/f/?id=00000184-e9f4-d144-a1d7-edf49b970000.

8   Kenneth P. Vogel et al., "Democratic Donor Who Pivoted to Trump Draws Scrutiny in Inaugural Inquiry," *New York Times*, February 5, 2019, https://www.nytimes.com/2019/02/05/us/politics/imaad-zuberi-trump-inauguration.html.

9   Michael Finnegan, "Fundraiser for Trump and Obama Sentenced to Twelve Years in Prison for Foreign Money Scams," *Los Angeles Times*, February 18, 2021, https://www.latimes.com/california/story/2021-02-18/zuberi-fundraiser-trump-obama-sentenced-prison.

10 Melley et al., "Prosecutors."

11 Kenneth P. Vogel and William K. Rashbaum, "Donor to Trump Inauguration Charged with Obstructing Investigation," *New York Times*, January 7, 2020, https://www.nytimes.com/2020/01/07/us/politics/imaad-zuberi-trump-inauguration.html.

12 Suderman and Mustian, "Mercenary."

13 Belford and Klasfeld, "Behind Trump's Turkish 'Bromance.'"

14 Bethania Palma, "Did Devin Nunes Meet with Michael Flynn and Turkey's Foreign Minister?" Snopes, March 28, 2017, https://www.snopes.com/fact-check/nunes-flynn-turkey-meeting/.

15 Natasha Bertrand, "Devin Nunes Attended a Breakfast with Michael Flynn and Turkey's Foreign Minister Just before the Inauguration," *Business Insider*, November 10, 2017, https://www.businessinsider.com/devin-nunes-michael-flynn-turkey-russia-2017-11.

16 Klasfeld and Belford, "Adventures in Maga-Land."

17 Abdullah Bozkurt, "Mansimov jailed in Turkey."

18 Josh Kovensky (@joshKovensky), "Here's Nasirov pictured at Trump's inauguration. Whether he used state funds to travel there briefly set off a minor scandal in Ukraine," Twitter, January 16, 2020, 6:20 p.m., https://twitter.com/JoshKovensky/status/1217919677004951575.

19 Belford and Klasfeld, "Behind Trump's Turkish 'Bromance.'"

20 Open Secrets, Donor Lookup, search results for "Donors - Lev Parnas,", accessed July 11, 2024, https://www.opensecrets.org/donor-lookup/results?name=lev+parnas&order=asc&sort=N.

21 Rebecca Jacobs and Eli Lee, "Erdogan-Tied Businessman Granted Access to Trump through Donor," Citizens for Ethics, November 7, 2019, https://www.citizensforethics.org/reports-investigations/crew-investigations/turkish-businessman-access-trump-donor/.

22 Jacobs and Lee, "Erdogan-Tied Businessman."

23 Michael Kranish et al., "Inside the Opulent Trump Inaugural Dinner Designed as a Glittery Overture to Foreign Diplomats," *Washington Post*, March 15, 2019, https://www.washingtonpost.com/politics/inside-the-opulent-trump-inaugural-dinner-designed-as-a-glittery-overture-to-foreign-diplomats/2019/03/14/e20c8482-3f5d-11e9-a0d3-1210e58a94cf_story.html.

24 Jacobs and Lee, "Erdogan-Tied Businessman."

25 Kranish et al., "Inside."

26 Jake Horowitz, "Trump-Tied Businessmen Met NSC Officials, Bannon over Venezuela Sanctions, Sources Say," Mic, April 3, 2017, https://www.mic.com/articles/172936/trump-tied-businessmen-met-nsc-officials-bannon-over-venezuela-sanctions-sources-say.

27 Anna Swartz, "Trump Inauguration Donor's Son Was Involved in NSC Meetings on Venezuela Exposed by 'Mic,'" Mic, April 21, 2017, https://www.mic.com/articles/174867/trump-inauguration-donor-wadie-habboush-white-house-nsc-meeting.

28 Nahal Toosi, "Inside the Chaotic Early Days of Trump's Foreign Policy," *Politico*, March 3, 2019, https://www.politico.eu/article/donald-trump-foreign-policy-inside-story-chaotic-early-days/.

29 Kranish et al., "Inside."

30 Jacobs and Lee, "Erdogan-Tied Businessman."

31 "Turkey Sets Conditions in International Agreements in Favor of Businessmen Close to Erdoğan," *Nordic Monitor*, July 6, 2021, https://nordicmonitor.com/2021/07/turkey-sets-conditions-to-international-agreements-in-favor-of-businessmen-close-to-erdogan/.

32 Kadri Gürsel, "Crackdown Shatters AKP 'Anti-Corruption' Taboo," *Al Monitor*, December 19, 2013, retrieved from the Wayback Machine, version May 5, 2021, https://web.archive.org/web/20210505115812/https://www.al-monitor.com/originals/2013/12/corruption-crackdown-damages-akp.html.

33 Letsch, "Turskish Minsters' Sons."

34 Rosenberg et al., "Beyond the N.R.A."

35 Marianne Levine and Theodoric Meyer, "Who Manafort Invited to the Inauguration," *Politico*, August 16, 2018, https://www.politico.com/newsletters/politico-influence/2018/08/16/who-manafort-invited-to-the-inauguration-319828.

36 Vogel et al., "Prosecutors Examining Ukranians."

37 Patten, "I Pled Guilty."

38 S. Rep. No 116-XX, *5:47*.

39 Jon Swaine, "Manafort Associate Paid Trump Inauguration $50,000 in Ukrainian Cash," *Guardian*, August 31, 2018, https://www.theguardian.com/us-news/2018/aug/31/paul-manafort-sam-patten-charged-cambridge-analytica.

40 Ken Dilanian et al., "Manafort-Linked Lobbyist W. Samuel Patten Admits Using Straw Donor to Buy Trump Inaugural Tickets for Russian, Ukrainian," NBC News, August 31, 2018, https://www.nbcnews.com/politics/justice-department/lobbyist-charged-failing-register-foreign-agent-manafort-linked-case-n905386.

41 Todd Carney et al., "A Collusion Reading Diary: What Did the Senate Intelligence Committee Find?" Lawfare Institute, August 21, 2020, https://www.lawfaremedia.org/article/collusion-reading-diary-what-did-senate-intelligence-committee-find.

42 Patten, "I Pled Guilty."

43 Craig Timberg et al., "In the Crowd at Trump's Inauguration, Members of Russia's Elite Anticipated a Thaw between Moscow and Washington," *Washington Post*, January 20, 2018, https://www.washingtonpost.com/politics/amid-trumps-inaugural-festivities-members-of-russias-elite-anticipated-a-thaw-between-moscow-and-washington/2018/01/20/0d767f46-fb9f-11e7-ad8c-ecbb62019393_story.html?hpid=hp_hp-more-top-stories_russiainauguration-245pm:homepage/story.

44 Vogel," Foreigner."

45 Mike Eckel, "Ukrainian Oligarch Wins U.S. Lawsuit against Russian-American Lobbyist over Trump Inauguration Tickets," RFE/RL, July 21, 2022, https://www.rferl.org/a/ukraine-oligarch-lawsuit-trump-inauguration/31953596.html.

46 Baker, "Where Rudy Giuliani's Money Comes From."

47 Kenneth P. Vogel, "Ukraine Role Focuses New Attention on Giuliani's Foreign Work," *New York Times*, June 30, 2019, https://www.nytimes.com/2019/06/30/us/politics/ukraine-giuliani-foreign-work.html.

48 Justin Elliott et al., "Confidential Memo: Company of Trump Inaugural Chair Sought to Profit from Connections to Administration, Foreigners," ProPublica, February 5, 2019, https://www.propublica.org/article/trump-inc-podcast-tom-barrack-colony-company-of-trump-inaugural-chair-sought-to-profit.

49 Colony Northstar, *Strategic Plan for Colony NorthStar, Inc* (Washington D.C., February 2017), uploaded by ProPublica, https://www.documentcloud.org/documents/5726057-Colony-memo-February-2017#document/p4/a480135.

50 Bill Allison, "Trump's Florida Fundraiser Flourishes as New Washington Lobbyist," Bloomberg News, March 5, 2018, https://www.bloomberg.com/politics/articles/2018-03-05/trump-s-florida-fundraiser-flourishes-as-new-washington-lobbyist.

51 Meyer, "Most Powerful Lobbyist."

52 "Donald Trump Says It Is Time to 'Drain the Swamp' in D.C.," CBS News, October 21, 2016, video, 46:06, https://www.youtube.com/watch?v=PxWu69vrdhA.

53 "Lobbyists in (and out of) the Trump Administration," Open Secrets, accessed July 11, 2024, https://www.opensecrets.org/trump/lobbyists.

54 Grimaldi et al., "Ex-CIA Director."

55 Flynn, "Our Ally Turkey."

56 Lee and Ainsley, "Mueller Probing Possible Deal."

57 Neumeister, "Lawyer: Guiliani."

58 U.S. Department of Justice, *Exhibit B to Registration Statement Pursuant to the Foreign Agents Registration Act of 1938, as Amended, Filed by Greenberg Traurig*, Registration No. 5712, May 30, 2017, https://efile.fara.gov/docs/5712-Exhibit-AB-20170530-31.pdf.

59 Benjamin Weiser and Maggie Haberman, "Turk in Iran Sanctions Case Adds Rudy Giuliani to Legal Team," *New York Times*, March 27, 2017, https://www.nytimes.com/2017/03/27/nyregion/reza-zarrab-iran-sanctions-case-rudolph-w-giuliani-to-legal-team.html.

60 U.S. Department of Justice, *Exhibit A to Registration Statement Pursuant to the Foreign Agents Registration Act of 1938, as Amended, Filed by Ballard Partners*, Registration No. 6415, August 28, 2017, https://efile.fara.gov/docs/6415-Exhibit-AB-20170828-5.pdf.

61 Indictment, United States of America v. David Rivera and Esther Nuhfer, No. 22-20552-Cr-GAYLES/TORRES (S.D. Fla. Jul. 6, 2023), uploaded by *Politico*, https://www.politico.com/f/?id=00000184-e9f4-d144-a1d7-edf49b970000.

62 Jay Weaver, "Ex-U.S. Rep. David Rivera Arrested. Charges Tied to $50 Million Venezuela Consulting Deal," *Miami Herald*, December 6, 2022, https://www.miamiherald.com/news/local/article269634466.html.

63 Indictment, United States of America v. David Rivera and Esther Nuhfer.

64 Bill Chappell, "A Former Florida Congressman Is Arrested on Charges of Lobbying for Venezuela," NPR, December 6, 2022, https://www.npr.org/2022/12/06/1141028977/venezuela-lobbying-florida-rep-david-rivera-arrested-indicted.

65 Indictment, United States of America v. David Rivera and Esther Nuhfer.

66 "Exxon Owed $1.6bn by Venezuela for 2007 Nationalisation," BBC.

67 Gary Fineout, "Feds Arrest Ex-Florida Rep. David Rivera on Charges Connected to Venezuela," *Politico*, December 5, 2022, https://www.politico.com/news/2022/12/05/florida-david-rivera-venezuela-arrest-00072467.

68 Indictment, United States of America v. David Rivera and Esther Nuhfer.

69 Weaver, "Ex-U.S. Rep. David Rivera."

70 Goodman, "Sources: Venezuela Wooed."

71 "Venezuela-Related Designations," U.S. Department of the Treasury, Office of Foreign Assets Control, July 26, 2017, https://ofac.treasury.gov/recent-actions/20170726.

72 "Venezuela-Related Designation," U.S. Department of the Treasury, Office of Foreign Assets Control.

73 "Issuance of Venezuela-Related Executive Order and Associated General Licenses," U.S. Department of the Treasury, Office of Foreign Assets Control, August 25, 2017, https://ofac.treasury.gov/recent-actions/20170825.

74 Rachel Wilson, "Florida Lobbyist Turning Trump Ties into Megamillions", Center for Public Integrity, July 5, 2017, https://archive.publicintegrity.org/politics/florida-lobbyist-turning-trump-ties-into-mega-millions/.

75 Goodman, "Sources: Venezuela Wooed."

76 U.S. Senate, *Lobbying Report filed by Ballard Partners*, Senate ID #401104288-315, July 20, 2017, https://lda.senate.gov/filings/public/filing/a4f3b382-69d4-482f-a80d-996c1a75d9d8/print/.

77 Antonio Maria Delgado et al., "This Venezuelan Mogul Met Pence. Is He Trying to Broker an Exit Strategy for Maduro?" *Miami Herald*, December 22, 2017, https://www.miamiherald.com/article190926039.html.

78 Anna Massoglia and Karl Evers-Hillstrom, "Revolving Door Brings Trump-Tied Lobbying Firm Even Closer to the White House," Open Secrets, January 22, 2019, https://www.opensecrets.org/news/2019/01/ballard-partners-revolving-door-white-house/.

79 Delgado et al., "This Venezuelan Mogul."

80 Confessore et al., "Trump, Venezuela."

81 Roston, "Exclusive: Meeting Maduro."

82 Helderman et al., "Trump's Lawyer."

83 Sergii Leshchenko, "Kiev Versus Kiev," *Foreign Policy*, December 20, 2016, https://foreignpolicy.com/2016/12/20/kiev-versus-kiev-poroshenko-ukraine-corruption-nabu/.

84 Parnas and Langton, *Shadow Diplomacy*, chap. 8, Kindle.

85 Paul Sonne et al., "Lev Is Talking."

86 Joseph A. Bondy (@josephabondy), "Here's the 'I don't know him at all, don't know what he's about, don't know where he comes from, know nothing about him' guy, w Lev Parnas & Roman Nasirov, former head of Ukrainian Fiscal Service, at Mar-a-Lago 12/16. @POTUS .@realDonaldTrump @Acosta #LevRemembers #LetLevSpeak," Twitter, January 16, 2020, 7:10 p.m., https://twitter.com/josephabondy/status/1217932038260625410.

87 Josh Kovensky (@joshKovensky), "Here's Nasirov pictured at Trump's inauguration. Whether he used state funds to travel there briefly set off a minor scandal in Ukraine," Twitter, January 16, 2020, 6:20 p.m., https://twitter.com/JoshKovensky/status/1217919677004951575.

88 Parnas, *Trump First*, chap. 4, Kindle.

89 Balthaus et al., "Lev Parnas Paid."

90 Ostrowski and Washington, "Lev Parnas."

91 Yuras Karmanau, "Court Meets on Ukraine Tax Chief's $74M Embezzlement Case," Associated Press, March 6, 2017, https://apnews.com/general-news-86dfb9488db24613a14762541334af93.

92 Nicholas Confessore et al., "The Swamp That Trump Built," *New York Times*, October 10, 2020, https://www.nytimes.com/interactive/2020/10/10/us/trump-properties-swamp.html.

93 U.S. Department of Justice, *Browse Filings - Ballard Partners - Registration #6415*, accessed July 11, 2024, https://efile.fara.gov/ords/fara/f?p=1381:110:26589312515469:::RP,110:P110_USECNTRY:N.

94 Confessore et al., "Swamp."

95 Oleg Sukhov, "Big Target, Big Test," *Kyiv Post*, March 9, 2017, https://archive.kyivpost.com/ukraine-politics/big-target-big-test.html.

96 Vogel," Foreigner."

97 Stephanie Baker, "Trump Wanted $20 Million for 2006 Moscow Deal: Developer," Bloomberg News, February 6, 2019, https://www.bloomberg.com/news/articles/2019-02-06/trump-wanted-20-million-for-2006-moscow-deal-developer-says.

98 Vogel, "Ukraine Role."

99 John Pappas, "Episode 5: 'Inauguration, Inc.,'" *The Weekly*, *New York Times*, June 26, 2019, video, 25:56, https://www.nytimes.com/2019/06/26/the-weekly/trumps-inauguration-the-money-behind-the-most-expensive-us-presidential-debut.html.

100 Dan Friedman, "Ukrainian Oligarch Scrutinized by Robert Mueller Was a Giuliani Client," *Mother Jones*, January 17, 2019, https://www.motherjones.com/politics/2019/01/ukrainian-oligarch-pavel-fuks-scrutinized-by-robert-mueller-was-rudy-giuliani-client/.

101 Escott, "Private Photos."

102 Stephanie Baker and Daryna Krasnolutska, "Rudy Giuliani Has Curious Links to a Jewish Village in Ukraine," Bloomberg News, November 27, 2019, https://www.bloomberg.com/news/articles/2019-11-27/rudy-giuliani-has-curious-links-to-a-jewish-village-in-ukraine.

103 Andrew Kaczynski, "London Trip Photos Show Giuliani with Indicted Associate at Yankees' Game, Ukrainian Charity Event," CNN, October 26, 2019, https://edition.cnn.com/2019/10/26/app-politics-section/kfile-giuliani-london-trip/index.html.

104 Vogel and Protess, "Giuliani Represented Venezuelan."

105 Tom Schoenberg, "Trump Fires Wall Street Enforcer Bharara after He Refuses to Quit," Bloomberg News, March 11, 2017, https://www.bloomberg.com/news/articles/2017-03-11/trump-fires-wall-street-enforcer-bharara-who-refused-to-resign.

106 Alan Feuer et al., "Trump Fires U.S. Attorney in New York Who Investigated His Inner Circle," *New York Times*, June 20, 2020, https://www.nytimes.com/2020/06/20/nyregion/trump-geoffrey-berman-fired-sdny.html.

107 Weiser and Kingsley, "Secret Meeting."

108 Dawsey et al., "Trump Asked Tillerson."
109 Leonnig et al., "Giuliani Pressed Trump."
110 Helderman et al., "Trump's Lawyer."
111 Roston et al., "Exclusive: Giuliani."
112 U.S. Department of Justice, FOIA Library, *Former Attorney General*, pg. 110.
113 Vogel and Protess, "Giuliani Represented Venezuelan."
114 Butler et al., "Profit."
115 Butler and Biesecker, "Giuliani Pals."
116 Simpson, "Giuliani's."
117 Schmidt et al., "Giuliani."
118 Kenneth P. Vogel and Ben Protess, "Lev Parnas Says He Has Recording of Trump Calling for Ambassador's Firing," *New York Times*, January 24, 2020, https://www.nytimes.com/2020/01/24/us/politics/trump-recording-yovanovitch.html.
119 Butler and Biesecker, "Giuliani Pals."
120 Swan and Rawnsley, "Exclusive: Giuliani Ally."
121 Ward, "Exclusive: After Private White House Meeting."
122 Solomon, "Joe Biden's 2020 Ukrainian Nightmare."
123 Solomon, "Solomon: These Once-Secret Memos."
124 Aaron Rupar, "'I Forced Her Out': Giuliani Goes on Fox News and Admits He's Much More than Trump's Lawyer," *Vox*, December 17, 2019, https://www.vox.com/policy-and-politics/2019/12/17/21025974/rudy-giuliani-laura-ingraham-yovanovitch-forced-out.
125 Bertrand and Samuelsohn, "Lawyers."
126 Winter et al., "Who Is Dmytro Firtash?"
127 U.S. Department of Justice, FOIA Library, *Former Attorney General*, pg. 107.
128 Brandon Carter, "Read: House Intel Committee Releases Whistleblower Complaint on Trump-Ukraine Call," NPR, September 26, 2019, https://www.npr.org/2019/09/26/764071379/read-house-intel-releases-whistleblower-complaint-on-trump-ukraine-call.
129 "Giuliani Subpoenaed," U.S. House of Representatives Committee on Foreign Affairs.
130 Sealed Indictment, United States of America v. Lev Parnas, Igor Fruman, David Correia, and Andrey Kukushkin, No. 19 Cr. 725 (S.D.N.Y. October 10, 2019), https://www.justice.gov/usao-sdny/press-release/file/1208281/dl.
131 "Treasury Takes Further Action against Russian-Linked Actors," U.S. Department of the Treasury, press release, January 11, 2021, https://home.treasury.gov/news/press-releases/sm1232.

CHAPTER 21

1 "Three House Committees Launch," U.S. House of Representatives Committee on Foreign Affairs.
2 "Giuliani Subpoenaed," U.S. House of Representatives Committee on Foreign Affairs.
3 Barrett et al., "Two Business Associates."
4 Viswanatha et al., "Two Giuliani Associates."
5 Elaina Plott Calabro, "The Mystery of Rudy Giuliani's Vienna Trip," *Atlantic*, October 10, 2019, https://www.theatlantic.com/politics/archive/2019/10/rudy-giuliani-vienna/599833/.

6 Sealed Indictment, United States of America v. Lev Parnas, Igor Fruman, David Correia, and Andrey Kukushkin, No. 19 Cr. 725 (S.D.N.Y. October 10, 2019), https://www.justice.gov/usao-sdny/press-release/file/1208281/dl.

7 Campaign Legal Center, *Supplement to Federal Election Commission Complaint MUR #7442*, June 20, 2019, https://campaignlegal.org/sites/default/files/2019-06/06-20-19%20 GEP%20LLC%20supplement%20(MUR%207442)%20(final%20with%20exhibits).pdf.

8 Gerstein, "Former Trump."

9 Lachlan Markay, "Rudy's Ukraine Henchmen Made Big Donation to Pro-Trump PAC," *Daily Beast*, September 26, 2019, https://www.thedailybeast.com/rudy-giulianis-ukraine-henchmen-made-big-donation-to-pro-trump-pac.

10 Zoe Tillman et al., "Two Men Who Worked with Rudy Giuliani to Dig Up Dirt on Biden Have Been Arrested," *BuzzFeed News*, October 10, 2019, https://www.buzzfeednews.com/article/zoetillman/lev-parnas-igor-fruman-arrested-giuliani-ukraine.

11 Sealed Indictment, United States of America v. Lev Parnas, Igor Fruman, David Correia, and Andrey Kukushkin, No 19 Cr. 725 (S.D.N.Y. October 10, 2019), https://www.justice.gov/usao-sdny/press-release/file/1208281/dl.

12 Ben Weider, "With Parnas, Fruman Pot Plan up in Smoke, Russian Money Man Turned to California," McClatchy, March 13, 2020, https://www.mcclatchydc.com/news/investigations/article240843881.html.

13 "Lev Parnas and David Correia Charged with Conspiring to Defraud Investors in Their Fraud Insurance Company 'Fraud Guarantee,'" United States Attorney's Office, Southern District of New York, press release, September 17, 2020, https://www.justice.gov/usao-sdny/pr/lev-parnas-and-david-correia-charged-conspiring-defraud-investors-their-fraud-insurance.

14 Campaign Legal Center, *Complaint to the Federal Election Commission,* July 25, 2018, https://campaignlegal.org/sites/default/files/2018-07/SIGNED%20 07-25-18%20GEP%20LLC%20Straw%20Donor%20Complaint.pdf.

15 Follow the Money, *Search for "Igor Fruman,"* accessed July 12, 2024, https://www.followthemoney.org/entity-details?eid=45551111.

16 Federal Election Commission, search result for individual contributions "Contributor details - Lev Parnas, Igor Fruman, Igor Furman," accessed July 12, 2024, https://www.fec.gov/data/receipts/individual-contributions/?contributor_name=Global+energy+producers&contributor_name=igor+fruman&contributor_name=igor+furman&contributor_name=lev+parnas.

17 Ostrowski and Washington, "Lev Parnas."

18 Balthaus et al., "Lev Parnas Paid."

19 Jacob Barker, "Lev Parnas, Trump Accuser, Claims Interest in Downtown St. Louis' Railway Exchange Project," *St. Louis Today*, January 29,2020, https://www.stltoday.com/news/local/metro/lev-parnas-trump-accuser-claims-interest-in-downtown-st-louis-railway-exchange-project/article_e769518b-3c1f-5c84-b987-7a6d0411feee.html.

20 *Mortgage Loan Contract between Seafront Properties and Gregory Abovsky, Lilian Abovsky, Daniel Chernin*, May 15, 2018, uploaded by *Daily Beast*, https://www.documentcloud.org/documents/6431850-Abovsky-loan.html.

21 Greg Farrell et al., "Rudy Giuliani Sidekick Lev Parnas Traces Part of Money Trail to Ukraine," Bloomberg News, January 23, 2020, https://www.bloomberg.com/news/articles/2020-01-23/giuliani-s-sidekick-parnas-traces-part-of-money-trail-to-ukraine.

22 "Yandex Announces Appointment of Greg Abovsky as Chief Operating Officer," Yandex, press release, November 22, 2017, https://yandex.com/company/press_center/press_releases/2017/1122.

23 Kevin Poulson, "Facebook Put User Data within Kremlin's Grasp Last Year," *Daily Beast*, December 19, 2018, https://www.thedailybeast.com/facebook-put-user-data-within-kremlins-grasp-last-year-2.

24 Dylan Myles-Primakoff and Justin Sherman, "Russia's Internet Freedom Shrinks as Kremlin Seizes Control of Homegrown Tech," *Foreign Policy*, October 26, 2020, https://foreignpolicy.com/2020/10/26/russia-internet-freedom-kremlin-tech/.

25 "Yandex Shareholders Approve Governance Changes to Allay Kremlin Fears," Reuters, December 20, 2019, https://www.reuters.com/article/us-russia-yandex-governance-idUSKBN1YO1O9/.

26 "Russian Tech Giant Yandex's Data Harvesting Raises Security Concerns," *Financial Times*, March 28, 2022, https://www.ft.com/content/c02083b5-8a0a-48e5-b850-831a3e6406bb.

27 Fischer, "New Wire Transfer."

28 Campaign Legal Center, Supplement.

29 Anatevka Jewish Refugee Community, "Wonderful shock! Igor Fruman, on behalf of American Friends Of Anatevka, surprised everyone present by announcing their commitment to match every dollar donated to https://www.anatevka.com/campaign/anatevkachallenge/ up to $1 million dollars!!!," Facebook, August 28, 2018, https://www.facebook.com/anatevkajrc/posts/pfbid02NBxcWMNK2S6wsA7vUNTDkNsGLMMSWtUrrKKAnM1x4EA4dE5bhsNLbtsZCVeyKbEcl.

30 Miller et al., "There's a Village."

31 Baker and Krasnolutska, "Rudy Giuliani."

32 "Anatevka Challenge," Anatevka, retrieved from the Wayback Machine, version December 14, 2019, https://web.archive.org/web/20191214150022/https://www.anatevka.com/campaign/anatevkachallenge/.

33 "American Friends of Anatevka Inc.," ProPublica, retrieved from the Wayback Machine, version August 25, 2022, https://web.archive.org/web/20220825121233/https://projects.propublica.org/nonprofits/organizations/822992136/201821309349200627/IRS990EZ.

34 Campaign Legal Center, Complaint.

35 Baker and Krasnolutska, "Rudy Giuliani."

36 Weinglas, "Inside Anatevka."

37 Miller et al., "There's a Village."

38 Ева Ланская [Eva Lanskaya], "It's been nearly a year since Mr. Rudolph Giuliani has expressed his genuine interest in supporting the 'Friends of Anatevka' charity initiative. Since then, the village has undertaken a lot of positive changes. Anyone who'd like to visit the village of Anatevka and make any contribution, as well as talk to the teachers at the school can send a message to our Facebook page, and we will provide you with the contact details of our secretary who'll assist you with arranging the trip. One should always remember that charity work and care for children are above any politics," LiveJournal, February 16, 2020, retrieved from the Wayback Machine, version August 24, 2023, https://web.archive.org/web/20230824061905/https://eva-lanska.livejournal.com/.

39 "Сын Виктора Христенко заключил мирный договор с бывшей женой, писательницей Ланской" [The son of Viktor Khristenko concluded a peace treaty with his ex-wife, writer Lanskaya], *Московский Комсомолец [Moscow's comsomolets]*, December 19, 2012, https://www.mk.ru/social/2012/12/19/789740-syin-viktora-hristenko-zaklyuchil-mirnyiy-dogovor-s-byivshey-zhenoy-pisatelnitsey-lanskoy.html.

40 Roman Anin, "Former Russian Minister Acquired Golf Courses Worth Millions," OCCRP, January 2, 2019, https://www.occrp.org/en/investigations/9072-former-russian-minister-acquired-golf-courses-worth-millions.

41 "How Deputy Prime Minister Golikova Made Fifty Billion Rubles on Russian People's Health," ACF International, October 7, 2022, https://acf.international/news/vice-premer-golikova.

42 Rebecca Davis O'Brien and Rebecca Balthaus, "Giuliani Associate Got $1 Million Loan from Lawyer for Ukrainian Tycoon," *Wall Street Journal*, December 17, 2019, https://www.wsj.com/articles/giuliani-associate-got-1-million-loan-from-lawyer-for-ukrainian-tycoon-11576620716.

43 Winter et al., "Who Is Dmytro Firtash?"

44 Friedman, "Here Are Rudy Giuliani's Various Claims."

45 Viswanatha et al., "Two Giuliani Associates."

46 Jeremy Diamond et al., "Dowd Resigns as Trump's Lawyer amid Disagreements on Strategy," CNN, March 22, 2018, https://edition.cnn.com/2018/03/22/politics/john-dowd-white-house/index.html.

47 John M. Dowd, *Letter to Investigative Counsel, House Permanent Select Committee on Intelligence*, October 3, 2019, https://www.congress.gov/116/meeting/house/110331/documents/HMKP-116-JU00-20191211-SD1331.pdf.

48 Victoria Albert, "Lev Parnas Says Trump Tried to Fire Yovanovitch 'At Least Four or Five Times,'" CBS News, January 16, 2020, https://www.cbsnews.com/news/lev-parnas-rachel-maddow-interview-giuliani-associate-says-trump-tried-to-fire-marie-yovanovitch-at-least-four-times/.

49 Bertrand and Samuelsohn, "Here's What the Parnas Revelations."

50 Faulders and Turner, "Meet."

51 Biesecker, "Florida Men."

52 Hettena, "How the Trump Team."

53 "Part Two of the Lev Parnas Interview," MSNBC.

54 Scannell and Ward, "From Pot to Impeachment."

55 Josh Gerstein, "Indicted Giuliani Associate Igor Fruman Taps Manafort Attorney," *Politico*, October 22, 2019, https://www.politico.com/news/2019/10/22/giuliani-igor-fruman-manafort-todd-blanche-054996.

56 Roston, "Exclusive: Giuliani Associate."

57 Meghan Roos and Naveed Jamali, "Rudy Giuliani Voicemail Hints at Cause of Federal Search Warrant," *Newsweek*, April 28, 2021, https://www.newsweek.com/rudy-giuliani-voicemail-hints-cause-federal-search-warrant-1587304.

58 "Read: Documents from Giuliani Associate Lev Parnas Released by House Impeachment Investigators," CNN, January 14, 2020, https://edition.cnn.com/2020/01/14/politics/read-lev-parnas-house-impeachment-investigators/index.html.

59 Katherine Faulders, "House Intel Committee Possesses Video, Audio Recordings from Giuliani Associate," ABC7, November 25, 2019, https://abc7.com/house-intel-committee-possesses-video-audio-recordings-from-giuliani-associate/5717535/.

60 Amy Mackinnon, "How Rudy Giuliani Opened the Door to the Ukraine Impeachment Inquiry," *Foreign Policy*, November 22, 2019, https://foreignpolicy.com/2019/11/22/rudy-giuliani-ukraine-impeachment-inquiry-trump/.

61 Allan Smith et al., "Giuliani Won't Comply with Congressional Subpoena," NBC News, October 15, 2019, https://www.nbcnews.com/politics/trump-impeachment-inquiry/giuliani-won-t-comply-congressional-subpoena-n1066586.

62 Manu Raju and Jeremy Herb, "Lawyer: Giuliani Associate 'Being Cooperative' with House Impeachment Probe," CNN, October 14, 2019, https://edition.cnn.com/2019/10/14/politics/rudy-giuliani-semyon-kislin-house-impeachment/index.html.

63 Parnas, "Exclusive."

64 "Lev Parnas' Entire Interview (Part 1)," CNN.

65 "Lev Parnas Talks Turkey," OCCRP.

66 Parnas, *Trump First*, chap. 1, Kindle.

67 George Gerstein, "Florida Businessman Pleads Guilty in Fraud Case Involving Giuliani Associates," *Politico*, October 29, 2020, https://www.politico.com/states/florida/story/2020/10/29/florida-businessman-pleads-guilty-in-fraud-case-involving-giuliani-associates-1332553.

68 Shayna Jacobs, "Giuliani Associate Igor Fruman Pleads Guilty in Campaign-Finance Case," *Washington Post*, September 10, 2021, https://www.washingtonpost.com/national-security/igor-fruman-guilty-plea-giuliani/2021/09/10/934a5744-0502-11ec-8c3f-3526f81b233b_story.html.

69 Lauren del Valle, "Lev Parnas Found Guilty on Campaign Finance Charges," CNN, October 22, 2021, https://edition.cnn.com/2021/10/22/politics/lev-parnas-verdict/index.html.

70 Ballhaus, "Ex-Rep. Sessions."

71 Sealed Indictment, United States of America v. Lev Parnas, Igor Fruman, David Correia, and Andrey Kukushkin, No. 19 Cr. 725 (S.D.N.Y. October 10, 2019), https://www.justice.gov/usao-sdny/press-release/file/1208281/dl.

72 Beavers, "Former Pete Sessions Staffer."

73 "Lev Parnas," United States Attorney's Office, Southern District of New York.

74 Mike Spies et al., "The Pro-Trump Super PAC at the Center of the Ukraine Scandal Has Faced Multiple Campaign Finance Complaints," ProPublica, October 18, 2019, https://www.propublica.org/article/the-pro-trump-super-pac-at-the-center-of-the-ukraine-scandal-has-faced-multiple-campaign-finance-complaints.

75 Parnas, *Trump First*, chap. 1, Kindle.

76 Butler et al., "Profit."

77 Vogel et al., "Rick Perry's Focus."

78 Congress of the United States, Permanent Select Committee on Intelligence, Subpoena.

79 Wallace and Atwood, "Rick Perry."

80 Stephanie Ebbs, "Perry Rejects Congressional Subpoena, Insists Resignation Not Related to Ukraine," ABC News, October 18, 2019, https://abcnews.go.com/Politics/perry-rejects-congressional-subpoena-insists-resignation-related-ukraine/story?id=66376371.

81 Holland and Gardner, "Trump."

82 Aruna Viswanatha et al., "Federal Prosecutors Scrutinize Rudy Giuliani's Ukraine Business Dealings, Finances," *Wall Street Journal*, October 14, 2019, https://www.wsj.com/articles/federal-prosecutors-scrutinize-rudy-giuliani-s-ukraine-business-dealings-finances-11571092100.

83 David Smith, "Giuliani under Scrutiny over Dealings Involving Turkey and Ukraine," *Guardian*, October 12, 2019, https://www.theguardian.com/us-news/2019/oct/11/rudy-giuliani-trump-oval-office-turkey-iran-prisoner-swap.

84 Kenneth P. Vogel et al., "Prosecutors Subpoena Trump Fund-Raisers Linked to Giuliani Associates," *New York Times*, November 20, 2019, https://www.nytimes.com/2019/11/20/us/politics/trump-fund-raisers-subpoenaed.html.

85 Aram Roston, "U.S. Prosecutors Seek Information on Payments to Trump Lawyer Giuliani: Subpoena," Reuters, November 25, 2019, https://www.reuters.com/article/us-usa-trump-impeachment-giuliani/u-s-prosecutors-seek-information-on-payments-to-trump-lawyer-giuliani-idUSKBN1XZ2GZ/.

86 Rebecca Davis O'Brien et al., "Federal Subpoenas Seek Information on Giuliani's Consulting Business," *Wall Street Journal*, November 25, 2019, https://www.wsj.com/articles/federal-subpoenas-seek-information-on-giulianis-consulting-business-11574712722.

87 Orden and Scannell, "Rudy Giuliani's SDNY Saga."

88 Larry Neumeister, "Feds: Eighteen Electronic Devices Seized from Giuliani and Firm," Associated Press, May 20, 2021, https://apnews.com/article/ny-state-wire-donald-trump-europe-business-government-and-politics-ee268ae04ecbd716590c8cfb605d9fc7.

89 William K. Rashbaum et al., "F.B.I. Searches Giuliani's Home and Office, Seizing Phones and Computers," *New York Times*, April 28, 2021, https://www.nytimes.com/2021/04/28/nyregion/rudy-giuliani-trump-ukraine-warrant.html.

90 William K. Rashbaum et al., "Giuliani Will Not Face Federal Charges over Lobbying, Prosecutors Say," *New York Times*, November 14, 2022, https://www.nytimes.com/2022/11/14/nyregion/giuliani-federal-charges-lobbying.html.

91 Luc Cohen, "Giuliani Ukraine Probe Ends without Charges, U.S. Prosecutor Says," Reuters, November 14, 2022, https://www.reuters.com/legal/no-criminal-charges-forthcoming-giuliani-probe-prosecutor-says-2022-11-14/.

92 AJ McDougall, "FBI Whistleblower Alleged Bosses 'Suppressed' Trumpworld Probes: Report," *Daily Beast*, August 9, 2023, https://www.thedailybeast.com/fbi-whistleblower-told-congress-his-bosses-had-suppressed-probes-of-trump-allies-like-rudy-giuliani-report.

93 Mattathias Schwartz, "Exclusive: A Veteran FBI Agent Told Congress That Investigations into Giuliani and Other Trump Allies Were Suppressed," *Business Insider*, August 9, 2023, https://www.businessinsider.com/fbi-whistleblower-senate-judiciary-russia-giuliani-leak-trump-allies-fuks-biden-2023-8.

94 "Read the Full Transcript of Top Diplomat Bill Taylor's Impeachment Testimony," NBC News, November 6, 2019, https://www.nbcnews.com/politics/trump-impeachment-inquiry/read-full-transcript-top-diplomat-bill-taylor-s-impeachment-testimony-n1077676.

95 "Read the Full Testimony of Fiona Hill, the President's Former Top Russia Adviser," *Politico*, November 6, 2019, https://www.nbcnews.com/politics/trump-impeachment-inquiry/read-full-transcript-top-diplomat-bill-taylor-s-impeachment-testimony-n1077676.

96 Dana Farrington, "Read: Former Ukraine Ambassador Yovanovitch's Testimony to Congress," NPR, November 4, 2019, https://www.npr.org/2019/11/04/776075849/read-former-ukraine-ambassador-yovanovitchs-testimony-to-congress.

97 Bobby Allyn, "Then-National Security Adviser Called Rudy Giuliani a Hand Grenade' on Ukraine," NPR, August 15, 2019, https://www.npr.org/2019/10/15/770378149/then-national-security-advisor-called-rudy-giuliani-a-hand-grenade-on-ukraine.

98 Eric Tucker, "Trump Pardons Flynn despite Guilty Plea in Russia Probe," Associated Press, November 26, 2020, https://apnews.com/article/donald-trump-pardon-michael-flynn-russia-aeef585b08ba6f2c763c8c37bfd678ed.

99 Doha Madani, "Trump Pardons Roger Stone, Paul Manafort, Charles Kushner and Others," NBC News, December 23, 2020, https://www.nbcnews.com/politics/politics-news/trump-pardons-roger-stone-paul-manafort-charles-kushner-others-n1252307.

100 Vogel and Novak. "Giuliani, Facing Scrutiny."

101 "One America News Investigates with Chanel Rion: Ukrainian Witnesses Destroy Schiff's Case (Part 3)," One America News Network, December 31, 2019, retrieved from the Wayback Machine, https://archive.org/details/youtube-iQ9F9K-FUnU.

102 Ian Bateson, "What Rudy Giuliani's Version of Reality Looks Like from Ukraine," *Washington Post*, December 27, 2019, https://www.washingtonpost.com/opinions/2019/12/27/what-rudy-giulianis-version-reality-looks-like-ukraine/.

103 William K. Rashbaum and Rebecca Davis O'Brien, "Ukrainian Accused of Election Interference Charged with Money Laundering," *New York Times*, December 7, 2022, https://www.nytimes.com/2022/12/07/nyregion/andriy-derkash-money-laundering-ukraine.html.

104 Nico Hines, "Rudy Giuliani Ally Sanctioned for Russian Influence Operation against the U.S.," *Daily Beast*, January 11, 2021, https://www.thedailybeast.com/andrii-telizhenko-rudy-giuliani-ally-sanctioned-for-russian-influence-operation-against-the-us.

105 Calderone, "'Stunning.'"

106 Josh Kovensky, "I Watched OAN's Unhinged Ukraine Impeachment Special So You Don't Have To," Talking Points Memo, December 18, 2019, https://talkingpointsmemo.com/muckraker/i-watched-oans-unhinged-ukraine-impeachment-special-so-you-dont-have-to.

107 Bateson, "What Rudy Giuliani's Version."

108 Dan Friedman, "Giuliani Allies Were Part of a 'Russia-Linked Foreign Influence Network,' the US Government Says," *Mother Jones*, January 11, 2021, https://www.motherjones.com/politics/2021/01/giuliani-allies-were-part-of-russia-linked-foreign-influence-network-us-government-says/.

109 Jeremy Herb and Manu Raju, "House of Representatives Impeaches President Donald Trump," CNN, December 19, 2019, https://edition.cnn.com/2019/12/18/politics/house-impeachment-vote/index.html.

110 Veronica Stracqualursi, "'I'm Not Trying to Pretend to Be a Fair Juror Here': Graham Predicts Trump Impeachment Will 'Die Quickly' in Senate," CNN, December 14, 2019, https://edition.cnn.com/2019/12/14/politics/lindsey-graham-trump-impeachment-trial/index.html.

111 Kyle Cheney et al., "Republicans Defeat Democratic Bids to Hear Witnesses in Trump Trial," *Politico*, January 31, 2020, https://www.politico.com/news/2020/01/31/murkowski-to-vote-against-calling-witnesses-in-impeachment-trial-109997.

112 Richard Cowan, "Breaking with Republicans, Romney Votes 'Guilty' in Trump Impeachment Trial", Reuters, February 6, 2020, https://www.reuters.com/article/us-usa-trump-impeachment-romney-idUSKBN1ZZ2Q6/.

113 Philip Ewing, "'Not Guilty': Trump Acquitted on Two Articles of Impeachment as Historic Trial Closes," NPR, February 5, 2020, https://www.npr.org/2020/02/05/801429948/not-guilty-trump-acquitted-on-2-articles-of-impeachment-as-historic-trial-closes.

114 Kate Sullivan, "Lamar Alexander: Trump's Actions 'Improper' but 'Long Way' from High Crimes and Misdemeanors," CNN, February 1, 2020, https://edition.cnn.com/2020/02/01/politics/lamar-alexander-trump-actions-improper-ukraine/index.html.

115 "Watch: Rep. Collins' Full Closing Statement Ahead of House Impeachment Vote | Trump Impeachment", PBS *NewsHour*, December 18, 2020, video, 4:56, https://www.youtube.com/watch?v=_hD-3Ahgi8k.

116 Paul LeBlanc, "Republican Lawmaker Says Jesus Had 'More Rights' before Crucifixion than Trump in Impeachment Inquiry," CNN, December 18, 2019, https://edition.cnn.com/2019/12/18/politics/trump-impeachment-jesus/index.html.

117 "'This Week' Transcript 11-10-19: Rep. Jackie Speier, Rep. Mac Thornberry, Joint Chiefs Chairman Gen. Mark Milley," ABC News, November 10, 2019, https://abcnews.go.com/Politics/week-transcript-11-10-19-rep-jackie-speier/story?id=66889542.

118 Grace Segers, "Susan Collins Will Vote to Acquit Trump, Saying He's 'Learned' from Impeachment," CBS News, February 4, 2020, https://www.cbsnews.com/news/susan-collins-will-vote-to-acquit-trump-saying-hes-learned-from-impeachment/.

119 Adam Schiff et al. "House Managers: Trump Won't Be Vindicated. The Senate Won't Be, Either," opinion, *Washington Post*, February 5, 2020, https://www.washingtonpost.com/opinions/house-managers-trump-wont-be-vindicated-the-senate-wont-be-either/2020/02/05/1df7bea0-485c-11ea-8124-0ca81effcdfb_story.html.

CHAPTER 22

1 Dareh Gregorian, "Trump Told Bob Woodward He Knew in February That COVID-19 Was 'Deadly Stuff' but Wanted to 'Play It Down,'" NBC News, September 9, 2020, https://www.nbcnews.com/politics/donald-trump/trump-told-bob-woodward-he-knew-february-covid-19-was-n1239658.

2 Tamara Keith, "Timeline: What Trump Has Said and Done about the Coronavirus," NPR, April 21, 2020, https://www.npr.org/2020/04/21/837348551/timeline-what-trump-has-said-and-done-about-the-coronavirus.

3 Thomas Franck, "Trump Says the Coronavirus Is the Democrats' 'New Hoax,'" CNBC, February 28, 2020, https://www.cnbc.com/2020/02/28/trump-says-the-coronavirus-is-the-democrats-new-hoax.html.

4 Peter Baker, "For Trump, Coronavirus Proves to Be an Enemy He Can't Tweet Away," *New York Times*, March 8, 2020, https://www.nytimes.com/2020/03/08/us/politics/trump-coronavirus.html.

5 Libby Cathey, "Timeline: Tracking Trump Alongside Scientific Developments on Hydroxychloroquine," ABC News, August 8, 2020, https://abcnews.go.com/Health/timeline-tracking-trump-alongside-scientific-developments-hydroxychloroquine/story?id=72170553.

6 Meridith McGraw and Sam Stein, "It's Been Exactly One Year since Trump Suggested Injecting Bleach. We've Never Been the Same," *Politico*, April 23, 2021, https://www.politico.com/news/2021/04/23/trump-bleach-one-year-484399.

7 Dakin Andone, "Protests Are Popping up across the US over Stay-at-Home Restrictions," CNN, April 17, 2020, https://edition.cnn.com/2020/04/16/us/protests-coronavirus-stay-home-orders/index.html.

8 David Smith, "Trump Calls Protesters against Stay-at-Home Orders 'Very Responsible,'" *Guardian*, April 18, 2020, https://www.theguardian.com/us-news/2020/apr/17/trump-liberate-tweets-coronavirus-stay-at-home-orders.

9 Lois Beckett, "Armed Protesters Demonstrate against COVID-19 Lockdown at Michigan Capitol," *Guardian*, April 30, 2020, https://www.theguardian.com/us-news/2020/apr/30/michigan-protests-coronavirus-lockdown-armed-capitol.

10 Anne Gearan and John Wagner, "Trump Expresses Support for Angry Antishutdown Protesters as More States Lift Coronavirus Lockdowns," *Washington Post*, May 1, 2020, https://www.washingtonpost.com/politics/trump-expresses-support-for-angry-anti-shutdown-protesters-as-more-states-lift-coronavirus-lockdowns/2020/05/01/25570dbe-8b9f-11ea-8ac1-bfb250876b7a_story.html.

11 Evan Hill et al., "How George Floyd Was Killed in Police Custody," *New York Times*, May 31, 2020, https://www.nytimes.com/2020/05/31/us/george-floyd-investigation.html.

12. "Protests in Minneapolis over Death of George Floyd after Arrest—in Pictures," *Guardian*, May 27, 2020, https://www.theguardian.com/us-news/gallery/2020/may/27/protests-in-minneapolis-over-death-of-george-floyd-after-arrest-in-pictures.

13. Larry Buchanan et al., "Black Lives Matter May Be the Largest Movement in U.S. History," *New York Times*, July 3, 2020, https://www.nytimes.com/interactive/2020/07/03/us/george-floyd-protests-crowd-size.html.

14. Peter Baker, "In Days of Discord, a President Fans the Flames," *New York Times*, May 30, 2020, https://www.nytimes.com/2020/05/30/us/politics/trump-george-floyd-protests.html.

15. Nate Silver, "Our New Polling Averages Show Biden Leads Trump by Nine Points Nationally," *FiveThirtyEight* by ABC News, June 18, 2020, https://fivethirtyeight.com/features/our-new-polling-averages-show-biden-leads-trump-by-9-points-nationally/.

16. Hillel Italie, "AP Sources: Former Trump Adviser John Bolton Has a Book Deal," Associated Press, November 10, 2019, https://apnews.com/article/9d2af632621f453595b9cf3643b936bd.

17. Asawin Suebsaeng and Sam Stein, "Trump Suspects a Spiteful John Bolton Is behind Some of the Ukraine Leaks," *Daily Beast*, October 15, 2019, https://www.thedailybeast.com/trump-suspects-a-spiteful-john-bolton-is-behind-ukraine-leaks.

18. Daniel Lippman et al., "Bolton Bombshell Sets off a Whodunit Frenzy," *Politico*, January 27, 2020, https://www.politico.com/news/2020/01/27/john-bolton-book-impeachment-trial-106714.

19. Deb Riechmann, "Former Staffer: White House Politicized Bolton Book Review," Associated Press, September 23, 2020, https://apnews.com/article/classified-information-national-security-john-bolton-27cbabb9c37bc67d7b457a74cf4b6487.

20. Maanvi Singh, "Trump Administration Sues to Block Publication of John Bolton's Book," *Guardian*, June 17, 2020, https://www.theguardian.com/us-news/2020/jun/16/john-bolton-book-donald-trump-administration-suit.

21. "Judge Rules John Bolton Can Publish Book despite Trump Administration Efforts to Block It," CBS News, June 20, 2020, https://www.cbsnews.com/news/john-bolton-can-publish-book-despite-trump-administration-efforts-to-block-it-judge-rules/.

22. Bolton, *Room Where It Happened*.

23. Bolton, *Room Where It Happened*, chap. 14, Kindle.

24. Bolton, *Room Where It Happened*, chap. 7, Kindle.

25. Smith, "Giuliani."

26. "Transcript: John Bolton interview with ABC News' Martha Raddatz," ABC News.

27. Quint Forgey and Matthew Choi, "'This Is Deadly Stuff': Tapes Show Trump Acknowledging Virus Threat in February," *Politico*, September 9, 2020, https://www.politico.com/news/2020/09/09/trump-coronavirus-deadly-downplayed-risk-410796.

28. Juana Summers, "Timeline: How Trump Has Downplayed the Coronavirus Pandemic," NPR, October 2, 2020, https://www.npr.org/sections/latest-updates-trump-covid-19-results/2020/10/02/919432383/how-trump-has-downplayed-the-coronavirus-pandemic.

29. Jeffrey Kluger, "Tragic Math: The U.S. Exceeds 200,000 COVID-19 Deaths," *Time*, September 22, 2020, https://time.com/5891101/us-coronavirus-deaths-200000/.

30. Gregorian, "Trump Told Bob."

31. Jane C. Timm, "Trump Pushes False Claims about Mail-in Vote Fraud. Here Are the Facts," NBC News, April 10, 2020, https://www.nbcnews.com/politics/donald-trump/trump-pushes-false-claims-about-mail-vote-fraud-here-are-n1180566.

32 Miles Parks, "Fact Check: Trump Spreads Unfounded Claims about Voting by Mail," NPR, June 22, 2020, https://www.npr.org/2020/06/22/881598655/fact-check-trump-spreads-unfounded-claims-about-voting-by-mail.

33 William Barr, "Transcript: NPR's Full Interview with Attorney General William Barr," interview by Steve Inskeep, *Morning Edition*, NPR, June 25, 2020, https://www.npr.org/2020/06/25/883273933/transcript-nprs-full-interview-with-attorney-general-william-barr.

34 Tiffany Hsu, "Conservative News Sites Fuel Voter Fraud Misinformation," *New York Times*, October 25, 2020, https://www.nytimes.com/2020/10/25/business/media/voter-fraud-misinformation.html.

35 John Whitesides and Julia Harte, "Why Vote by Mail Triggered a Partisan Battle Ahead of November's Election," Reuters, April 14, 2020, https://www.reuters.com/article/us-usa-election-absentee-voting-explaine-idUSKCN21W162/.

36 Clint Forgey et al., "Trump Refuses to Back down on Suggestion of Election Delay," *Politico*, July 30, 2020, https://www.politico.com/news/2020/07/30/trump-suggests-delaying-2020-election-387902.

37 Rebecca Shabad, "Trump Floats Delaying the Election, but He Can't Do That," NBC News, July 30, 2020, https://www.nbcnews.com/politics/2020-election/trump-suggests-delaying-2020-election-n1235300.

38 Grace Sparks, "CNN Poll of Polls: Biden Maintains Double-Digit Lead over Trump Nationally, with Coronavirus a Top Issue," CNN, July 20, 2020, https://edition.cnn.com/2020/07/20/politics/poll-of-polls-july-trump-biden-coronavirus/index.html.

39 Donald J. Trump (@realDonaldTrump), "With Universal Mail-In Voting (not Absentee Voting, which is good), 2020 will be the most INACCURATE & FRAUDULENT Election in history. It will be a great embarrassment to the USA. Delay the Election until people can properly, securely and safely vote???" Twitter, July 30, 2020, 9:46 a.m., https://twitter.com/realDonaldTrump/status/1288818160389558273.

40 Michael Crowley, "Trump Won't Commit to 'Peaceful' Post-Election Transfer of Power," *New York Times*, September 23, 2020, https://www.nytimes.com/2020/09/23/us/politics/trump-power-transfer-2020-election.html.

41 Kyle Cheney et al., "Hunter Biden, Rudy, Giuliani, and the 'Hard Drive from Hell,'" *Politico*, October 22, 2020, https://www.politico.com/news/2020/10/22/hunter-biden-giuliani-hard-drive-431022.

42 Nick Aspinwall, "Guo Wengui and Steve Bannon Are Flooding the Zone with Hunter Biden Conspiracies", *Foreign Policy*, November 2, 2020, https://foreignpolicy.com/2020/11/02/guo-wengui-steve-bannon-hunter-biden-conspiracies-disinformation/.

43 EJ Dickson, "Twitter, Facebook Allow Pizzagate-Esque Conspiracy Theories to Spread about Hunter Biden," *Rolling Stone*, October 21, 2020, https://www.rollingstone.com/culture/culture-news/hunter-biden-twitter-facebook-election-conspiracy-theories-1077735/.

44 Jonathan Karl, "Photos Capture Election-Night Tension at White House as Trump Family, Aides Watch Lead Fade Away," ABC News, June 14, 2022, https://abcnews.go.com/Politics/photos-capture-election-night-tension-white-house-trump/story?id=85382786.

45 Chris Stein, "An 'Inebriated' Giuliani Urged Trump to Falsely Claim Victory on Election Night," *Guardian*, June 13, 2022, https://www.theguardian.com/us-news/2022/jun/13/giuliani-inebriated-trump-falsely-claim-victory-election-night.

46 Barbara Sprunt and Ximena Bustillo, "Former Trump Advisers Testify They Urged Him Not to Declare Victory on Election Night," NPR, June 13, 2022, https://www.npr.org/2022/06/13/1104614467/jan-6-jason-miller-ivanka-trump-guiliani.

47 Donald Trump, "Donald Trump 2020 Election Night Speech Transcript," Rev, November 4, 2020, https://www.rev.com/blog/transcripts/donald-trump-2020-election-night-speech-transcript.

48 Christina A. Cassidy, "Report Shows Big Spike in Mail Ballots during 2020 Election," Associated Press, August 16, 2021, https://apnews.com/article/health-elections-coronavirus-pandemic-election-2020-campaign-2016-f6b627a5576014a55a7252e542e46508.

49 Libby Cathey, "Trump Calls for Vote Counting to Stop as Path to Victory Narrows, Biden Urges All to 'Stay Calm,'" ABC News, November 5, 2020, https://abcnews.go.com/Politics/overview-trump-calls-vote-counting-stop-path-victory/story?id=74038071.

50 Jonathan Lemire et al., "Biden Defeats Trump for White House, Says 'Time to Heal,'" Associated Press, November 8, 2020, https://apnews.com/article/joe-biden-wins-white-house-ap-fd58df73aa677acb74fce2a69adb71f9.

51 Donald J. Trump (@realDonaldTrump), "I look forward to Mayor Giuliani spearheading the legal effort to defend OUR RIGHT to FREE and FAIR ELECTIONS! Rudy Giuliani, Joseph diGenova, Victoria Toensing, Sidney Powell, and Jenna Ellis, a truly great team, added to our other wonderful lawyers and representatives!" Twitter, November 15, 2020, 11:12 a.m., https://twitter.com/realDonaldTrump/status/1327811527123103746.

52 Emily Caldwell, "Five Things to Know about Dallas Lawyer Sidney Powell amid Jan. 6 Committee Revelations," *Dallas Morning News*, July 12, 2022, https://www.dallasnews.com/news/elections/2022/07/12/5-things-to-know-about-dallas-lawyer-sidney-powell-amid-jan-6-committee-revelations/.

53 Carrie Johnson, "Flynn Attorney Says She Briefed Trump on Case amid DOJ Intervention," NPR, September 29, 2020, https://www.npr.org/2020/09/29/918314575/flynn-attorney-says-she-briefed-trump-on-case-amid-doj-intervention.

54 "Congress Passes Legislation Standing up Cybersecurity Agency in DHS," Department of Homeland Security, November 13, 2018, https://www.dhs.gov/news/2018/11/13/congress-passes-legislation-standing-cybersecurity-agency-dhs.

55 "Joint Statement from Elections Infrastructure Government Coordinating Council & the Election Infrastructure Sector Coordinating Executive Committees," Cyber Security and Infrastructure Security Agency, press release, November 12, 2020, https://www.cisa.gov/news-events/news/joint-statement-elections-infrastructure-government-coordinating-council-election.

56 Kaitlan Collins and Paul LeBlanc, "Trump Fires Director of Homeland Security Agency Who Had Rejected President's Election Conspiracy Theories," CNN, November 18, 2020, https://www.cnn.com/2020/11/17/politics/chris-krebs-fired-by-trump/index.html.

57 Isaac Chotiner, "William Barr's 'Radical Break' from Precedent, and the Future of the Justice Department," *New Yorker*, November 12, 2020, https://www.newyorker.com/news/q-and-a/william-barrs-radical-break-from-precedent-and-the-future-of-the-justice-department.

58 Mike Balsamo, "In Exclusive AP Interview, AG Barr Says No Evidence of Widespread Election Fraud, Undermining Trump," Associated Press, December 1, 2020, https://www.ap.org/news-highlights/best-of-the-week/2020/exclusive-interview-with-attorney-general-barr-nets-massive-scoop/.

59 Katherine Faulders and Alexander Mallin, "Barr Had 'Intense' Meeting with Trump after AG's Interview Undercutting Voter Fraud Claims: Sources," ABC News, December 2, 2020, https://abcnews.go.com/Politics/barr-intense-meeting-trump-ags-interview-undercutting-voter/story?id=74516139.

60 Meredith Deliso et al., "Election 2020: A Look at Trump Campaign Election Lawsuits and Where They Stand," ABC News, December 12, 2020, https://abcnews.go.com/Politics/election-2020-trump-campaign-election-lawsuits-stand/story?id=74041748.

61 Kate Brumback, "Georgia Hand Tally of Votes Is Complete, Affirms Biden Lead," Associated Press, November 19, 2020, https://apnews.com/article/election-2020-joe-biden-donald-trump-georgia-elections-1a2ea5e8df69614f4e09b47fea581a09.

62 "Completed Wisconsin Recount Confirms Biden's Win over Trump," Associated Press, November 29, 2020, https://apnews.com/general-news-7aef88488e4a801545a13cf4319591b0.

63 Josh Gerstein, "Another Law Firm Bails Out on Trump Campaign," *Politico*, November 13, 2020, https://www.politico.com/news/2020/11/13/law-firm-drops-trump-campaign-436418.

64 Aaron Blake, "Timeline: Trump's Revolving Door of Lawyers," *Washington Post*, November 23, 2020, https://www.washingtonpost.com/politics/2020/11/17/trump-keeps-losing-court-he-keeps-losing-his-lawyers-too/.

65 "Trump Legal Team to File New Ballot Lawsuits," Fox News, November 8, 2020, https://www.foxnews.com/transcript/trump-legal-team-to-file-new-ballot-lawsuits.

66 Philip Bump, "Many Theories, No Evidence: Giuliani Encapsulates the Entire Trump Era," *Washington Post*, June 22, 2022, https://www.washingtonpost.com/politics/2022/06/22/lots-theories-no-evidence-giuliani-encapsulates-entire-trump-era/.

67 Helderman et al., "Trump's Lawyer."

68 Manu Raju et al., "Former Texas Rep. Pete Sessions Was Pushed by Giuliani Associates to Back Effort to Eject Ukraine Ambassador," CNN, October 10, 2019, https://www.cnn.com/2019/10/10/politics/pete-sessions-indictment-giuliani-associates/index.html.

69 Swan and Rawnsley, "Exclusive: Giuliani Ally."

70 Doug Bock Clark et al., "Building the 'Big Lie': Inside the Creation of Trump's Stolen Election Myth," ProPublica, April 26, 2022, https://www.propublica.org/article/big-lie-trump-stolen-election-inside-creation.

71 Exhibit N Redacted Declaration, Wood v. Raffensperger, 1:20-cv-04651 (N.D. Ga. Nov 17, 2020), https://www.courtlistener.com/docket/18632787/6/14/wood-v-raffensperger/.

72 Ali Swenson, "Smartmatic Does Not Own Dominion Voting Systems," Associated Press, November 17, 2020, https://apnews.com/article/fact-checking-9740535009.

73 Philip Bump, "Swing-State Counties That Used Dominion Voting Machines Mostly Voted for Trump," *Washington Post*, December 1, 2020, https://www.washingtonpost.com/politics/2020/12/01/swing-state-counties-that-used-dominion-voting-machines-mostly-voted-trump/.

74 Clark et al., "Building the 'Big Lie.'"

75 Clark et al., "Building the 'Big Lie.'"

76 Emma Brown et al., "The Making of a Myth", *Washington Post*, May 9, 2021, https://www.washingtonpost.com/investigations/interactive/2021/trump-election-fraud-texas-businessman-ramsland-asog/.

77 Mike Giglio, "The Secret Source Who Helped Fuel Trump's Big Lie," *New Yorker*, May 28, 2021, https://www.newyorker.com/news/american-chronicles/the-secret-source-who-helped-fuel-trumps-big-lie.

78 Brown et al., "Making of a Myth."

79 Emma Brown et al., "Sidney Powell's Secret 'Military Intelligence Expert,' Key to Fraud Claims in Election Lawsuits, Never Worked in Military Intelligence," *Washington Post*, December 11, 2020, https://www.washingtonpost.com/investigations/sidney-powell-spider-spyder-witness/2020/12/11/0cd567e6-3b2a-11eb-98c4-25dc9f4987e8_story.html.

80 Brown et al., "Sidney Powell's."
81 "Plot to Overturn the Election (full documentary) | FRONTLINE", *Frontline* PBS, March 29, 2022, video, 53:17, https://www.youtube.com/watch?v=90O-q7dgS-I.
82 Brown et al., "Sidney Powell's."
83 Brown et al., "Sidney Powell's."
84 Aaron Keller, "Here's How Lawyers Destroyed Sidney Powell's 'Wildly Unqualified' Election Malfeasance 'Experts' in Georgia," *Law & Crime*, December 7, 2020, https://lawandcrime.com/2020-election/heres-how-georgias-lawyers-destroyed-sidney-powells-wildly-unqualified-election-malfeasance-experts/.
85 "Watch Again: Trump's Legal Team Holds Press Conference about the Election," *Independent*, November 19, 2020, video, 1:31:04, https://www.youtube.com/watch?v=T8LiGZhK-bg.
86 Ali Swenson, "AP Fact Check: Trump Legal Team's Batch of False Vote Claims," Associated Press, November 19, 2020, https://apnews.com/article/fact-check-trump-legal-team-false-claims-5abd64917ef8be9e9e2078180973e8b3.
87 William Cummings et al., "By the Numbers: President Donald Trump's Failed Efforts to Overturn the Election," *USA Today*, January 6, 2021, https://www.usatoday.com/in-depth/news/politics/elections/2021/01/06/trumps-failed-efforts-overturn-election-numbers/4130307001/.
88 "The Kraken: What Is It and Why Has Trump's Ex-Lawyer Released It?" BBC, November 27, 2020, https://www.bbc.com/news/election-us-2020-55090145.
89 Zach Montellaro and Kyle Cheney, "Pro-Trump Legal Crusade Peppered with Bizarre Blunders," *Politico*, December 3, 2020, https://www.politico.com/news/2020/12/03/sidney-powell-trump-election-lawsuit-442472.
90 Cummings et al., "By the Numbers."
91 Harriet Alexander, "'Your Election Is a Sham': Giuliani Tells Pennsylvania 'I Know Crooks Really Well' as He Appears in Gettysburg," *Independent*, November 25, 2020, https://www.independent.co.uk/news/world/americas/us-election-2020/rudy-giuliani-pennsylvania-election-trump-fraud-b1761888.html.
92 Ryan Randazzo and Maria Polletta, "Arizona GOP Lawmakers Hold Meeting on Election Outcome with Trump Lawyer Rudy Giuliani," Arizona Central, November 30, 2020, https://www.azcentral.com/story/news/politics/elections/2020/11/30/republican-lawmakers-arizona-hold-meeting-rudy-giuliani/6468171002/.
93 "Rudy Giuliani, Others Appear at Hearings at State Capitol over Georgia Election," 11Alive, December 4, 2020, https://www.youtube.com/watch?v=kTTU0qfCtc8.
94 "Rudy Giuliani Testifies in Lansing", *Detroit News*, December 2, 2020, https://www.detroitnews.com/picture-gallery/news/local/michigan/2020/12/03/rudy-giuliani-testifies-lansing/3803464001/.
95 Alexander, "'Your Election Is a Sham.'"
96 "Rudy Giuliani Testifies in Lansing", *Detroit News*.
97 Paul LeBlanc, "Wisconsin Assembly Speaker Says Trump Called Him This Month to Decertify 2020 Election," CNN, July 20, 2022, https://edition.cnn.com/2022/07/20/politics/donald-trump-wisconsin-2020-presidential-election/index.html.
98 Beth LeBlanc, "Trump Campaign Lists Lawmakers' Cells, Misdirects Calls for Chatfield to Former Petoskey Resident," *Detroit News*, January 4, 2021, https://www.detroitnews.com/story/news/politics/2021/01/04/trump-campaign-lists-michigan-lawmakers-cell-numbers-misdirects-private-citizen/4130279001/.

99 Katelyn Polantz, "Judge Rejects Another Trump Attempt to Decertify Georgia Votes," CNN, January 5, 2021, https://edition.cnn.com/2021/01/05/politics/judge-trump-decertify-votes/index.html.

100 Andrew Solender, "Arizona House Speaker Says GOP Rep. Biggs Pressed Him on Decertifying Electors," *Axios*, June 21, 2022, https://www.axios.com/2022/06/21/rusty-bowers-andy-biggs-arizona-trump.

101 H. R. Rep. No. 117-663, *Final Report of the Select Committee to Investigate the January 6th Attack on the United States Capitol*, 300–7 (2022), https://www.govinfo.gov/content/pkg/GPO-J6-REPORT/pdf/GPO-J6-REPORT.pdf.

102 Kate Brumback, "Georgia Again Certifies Election Results Showing Biden Won," Associated Press, December 7, 2020, https://apnews.com/article/election-2020-joe-biden-donald-trump-georgia-elections-4eeea3b24f10de886bcdeab6c26b680a.

103 Linda So and Jason Szep, "U.S. Election Workers Get Little Help from Law Enforcement as Terror Threats Mount," Reuters, September 8, 2021, https://www.reuters.com/investigates/special-report/usa-election-threats-law-enforcement/.

104 Reid J. Epstein, "Two Election Workers Targeted by Pro-Trump Media Sue for Defamation," *New York Times*, December 2, 2021, https://www.nytimes.com/2021/12/02/us/politics/gateway-pundit-defamation-lawsuit.html.

105 Matt Gertz, "Fox News Helped Destroy Shaye Moss' Life. The Network Couldn't Care Less about That," Media Matters, September 22, 2022, https://www.mediamatters.org/january-6-insurrection/fox-news-helped-destroy-shaye-moss-life-network-couldnt-care-less-about.

106 Jason Szep and Linda So, "Trump Campaign Demonized Two Georgia Election Workers—and Death Threats Followed," Reuters, December 1, 2021, https://www.reuters.com/investigates/special-report/usa-election-threats-georgia/.

107 Linda So et al., "Exclusive: Georgia Probe into Trump Examines Chaplain's Role in Election Meddling," Reuters, September 9, 2022, https://www.reuters.com/world/us/exclusive-georgia-probe-into-trump-examines-chaplains-role-election-meddling-2022-09-09/.

108 Oma Seddiq, "Trump Retweets Prominent Attorney Who Says Georgia Gov. Brian Kemp 'Will Soon Be Going to Jail,'" *Business Insider*, December 15, 2020, https://www.businessinsider.com/trump-shares-tweet-claiming-ga-gov-brian-kemp-will-be-going-to-jail-2020-12.

109 Greg Bluestein, "How Brian Kemp Resisted Trump's Pressure to Overturn the Georgia Election Results," *Politico*, March 19, 2022, https://www.politico.com/news/magazine/2022/03/19/brian-kemp-david-perdue-donald-trump-2020-00018601.

110 Danny Hakim and Richard Fausset, "Two Months in Georgia: How Trump Tried to Overturn the Vote," *New York Times*, August 14, 2023, https://www.nytimes.com/2023/08/14/us/trump-georgia-election-results.html.

111 Marianne Levine and James Arkin, "Loeffler, Perdue Call on Georgia's Republican Secretary of State to Resign," *Politico*, November 9, 2020, https://www.politico.com/news/2020/11/09/loeffler-perdue-georgia-secretary-state-resign-435484.

112 Lauren Gambino, "Georgia's Secretary of State Says Lindsey Graham Suggested He Throw out Legal Ballots," *Guardian*, November 17, 2020, https://www.theguardian.com/us-news/2020/nov/16/georgia-brad-raffensperger-lindsey-graham-elections-ballots.

113 Kate Brumback, "Georgia Official Says Graham Asked Him about Tossing Ballots," Associated Press, November 16, 2020, https://apnews.com/article/georgia-official-graham-tossing-ballots-281416294b5c54c6535f8ffaab4322a2.

114 Rachel Treisman, "Georgia Officials Fact-Check an Infamous Trump Phone Call in Real Time," NPR, June 21, 2022, https://www.npr.org/2022/06/21/1106472863/georgia-officials-fact-check-infamous-trump-phone-call-in-real-time.

115 "What Is the Electoral College?" National Archives, accessed July 14, 2024, https://www.archives.gov/electoral-college/about.

116 "New York Election Results and Maps 2020," CNN, accessed July 14, 2024, https://edition.cnn.com/election/2020/results/state/new-york.

117 National Archives, *New York Certificate of Vote 2020*, accessed July 14, 2024, https://www.archives.gov/files/electoral-college/2020/vote-new-york.pdf.

118 "Rhode Island Election Results and Maps 2020," CNN, accessed July 14, 2024, https://edition.cnn.com/election/2020/results/state/rhode-island.

119 National Archives, *Rhode Island Certificate of Vote 2020*, accessed July 14, 2024, https://www.archives.gov/files/electoral-college/2020/vote-rhode-island.pdf.

120 3 U.S.C. § 15 (a).

121 "Frequently Asked Questions," Electoral College, National Archives, accessed July 14, 2024, https://www.archives.gov/electoral-college/faq#no270

122 Jake Tapper and Jamie Gangel, "CNN Exclusive: Jan 6 Investigators Believe Nov. 4 Text Pushing 'Strategy' to Undermine Election Came from Rick Perry," CNN, December 17, 2021, https://edition.cnn.com/2021/12/17/politics/rick-perry-jan-6-text-mark-meadows-nov-4/index.html.

123 Robert Downen and Matthew Choi, "Two Texas Businessmen Pitched Trump on Plan to Overturn 2020 Election, Jan. 6 Report Reveals," *Texas Tribune*, December 23, 2022, https://www.texastribune.org/2022/12/23/texas-businessmen-rick-perry-2020-election-jan-6-report/.

124 H. R. Rep. No. 117-663, *269*.

125 H. R. Rep. No. 117-663, *270*.

126 Alexander, "'Your Election Is a Sham.'"

127 Randazzo and Polletta, "Arizona GOP."

128 Ross Williams, "Georgia Capitol Latest Port in a Storm for Giuliani's State Legislature Tack," Georgia Recorder, December 4, 2020, https://georgiarecorder.com/2020/12/04/georgia-capitol-latest-port-in-a-storm-for-giulianis-state-legislature-tack/.

129 David Mack, "Did Rudy Giuliani Fart Twice at a Michigan Election Fraud Hearing?" *Buzzfeed News*, December 3, 2020, https://www.buzzfeednews.com/article/davidmack/rudy-giuliani-fart.

130 Kenneth Chesebro, *Memorandum—The Real Deadline for Setting a State's Electoral Votes*, November 18, 2020, uploaded by Just Security, https://www.justsecurity.org/wp-content/uploads/2022/06/january-6-clearinghouse-kenneth-chesebro-memorandum-to-james-r.-troupis-attorney-for-trump-campaign-wisconsin-November-18-2020.pdf.

131 Kenneth Chesebro, *Memorandum—Important That All Trump-Pence Electors Vote on December 14*, December 6, 2020, uploaded by New York Times, https://int.nyt.com/data/documenttools/chesebro-dec-6-memo/ce55d6abd79c2c71/full.pdf.

132 Kenneth Chesebro, *Memorandum—Statutory Requirement for December 14 Electoral Votes*, December 9, 2020, uploaded by Just Security, https://www.justsecurity.org/wp-content/uploads/2022/06/january-6-clearinghouse-kenneth-chesebro-memorandum-to-james-r.-troupis-attorney-for-trump-campaign-wisconsin-december-9-2020.pdf.

133 Kenneth Chesebro, *Emails to John Eastman and Rudy Giuliani*, December 13–January 4, 2020, https://www.govinfo.gov/content/pkg/GPO-J6-DOC-Chapman004708/pdf/GPO-J6-DOC-Chapman004708.pdf.

134. "John Eastman's First 'January 6 Scenario' Memo," *Washington Post*, October 29, 2021, https://www.washingtonpost.com/context/eastman-first-version-memo/4aeb9362-1989-4100-8e3f-a130bdd6e83a/.

135. "John Eastman's Second Memo on 'January 6 Scenario,'" *Washington Post*, October 29, 2021, https://www.washingtonpost.com/context/john-eastman-s-second-memo-on-january-6-scenario/b3fd2b0a-f931-4e0c-8bac-c82f13c2dd6f/.

136. Chesebro, Memorandum—Important.

137. Farnoush Amiri, "How the Trump Fake Electors Scheme Became a 'Corrupt Plan,' According to the Indictment," Associated Press, December 18, 2023, https://apnews.com/article/donald-trump-jan-6-investigation-fake-electors-608932d4771f6e2e3c5efb3fdcd8fcce.

138. Chesebro, Memorandum—Statutory.

139. Chesebro, Emails.

140. Chesebro, Emails.

141. "John Eastman's Second Memo," *Washington Post*.

142. "Frequently Asked Questions," Electoral College, National Archives.

143. Maggie Haberman et al., "Previously Secret Memo Laid Out Strategy for Trump to Overturn Biden's Win,", *New York Times*, August 8, 2023, https://www.nytimes.com/2023/08/08/us/politics/trump-indictment-fake-electors-memo.html?partner=slack&smid=sl-share.

144. Erci Cortelessa, "Eastman Told Trump That Pence Plan for Jan. 6 Was Illegal," *Time*, June 16, 2022, https://time.com/6188491/john-eastman-jan-6-testimony-trump/.

145. Indictment, United States of America v. Donald J. Trump, No. 1:23 Cr. 257, (D.D.C. August 1, 2023), https://www.justice.gov/storage/US_v_Trump_23_cr_257.pdf.

146. "Ronna McDaniel Testifies She Was Contacted about Plan for 'Contingent Electors,'" MSNBC, October 13, 2022, video, 1:40, https://www.youtube.com/watch?v=ElwipVAqeu0.

147. Amiri, "How the Trump Fake Electors."

148. Amy Gardner et al., "'Fake' Elector Plot Raised Concerns over Legal Peril, Indictment Shows," *Washington Post*, August 7, 2023, https://www.washingtonpost.com/national-security/2023/08/07/fake-electors-trump-indictment/.

149. Rachel Leingang, "Trump Fake-Elector Scheme: Where Do Seven States' Investigations Stand?," *Guardian*, June 5, 2024, https://www.theguardian.com/us-news/2023/oct/22/trump-fake-elector-scheme-case-tracker.

150. Amy Gardner et al., "Fake Trump Electors in Ga. Told to Shroud Plans in 'Secrecy,' Email Shows," *Washington Post*, June 6, 2022, https://www.washingtonpost.com/politics/2022/06/06/fake-trump-electors-ga-told-shroud-plans-secrecy-email-shows/.

151. Jonathan Oosting, "Ex-GOP Chair: Trump Fake Electors Plotted to Hide Overnight in Michigan Capitol," Bridge Michigan, June 21, 2022, https://www.bridgemi.com/michigan-government/ex-gop-chair-trump-fake-electors-plotted-hide-overnight-michigan-capitol.

152. Farnoush Amiri, "Explainer: How Fake Electors Tried to Throw Result to Trump," Associated Press, February 21, 2022, https://apnews.com/article/capitol-siege-joe-biden-presidential-elections-election-2020-electoral-college-311f88768b65f7196f52a4757dc162e4.

153. Marshall Cohen et al., "Trump Campaign Officials, Led by Rudy Giuliani, Oversaw Fake Electors Plot in Seven States," CNN, January 20, 2022, https://edition.cnn.com/2022/01/20/politics/trump-campaign-officials-rudy-giuliani-fake-electors/index.html.

154. Tom Joscelyn and Norman L. Eisen, "Kenneth Chesebro: A Chief Architect of the False Elector Scheme," Just Security, November 28, 2023, https://www.justsecurity.org/90271/kenneth-chesebro-a-chief-architect-of-the-false-elector-scheme/.

155 Beth Reinhard et al., "As Giuliani Coordinated Plan for Trump Electoral Votes in States Biden Won, Some Electors Balked," *Washington Post*, January 20, 2022, https://www.washingtonpost.com/investigations/electors-giuliani-trump-electoral-college/2022/01/20/687e3698-7587-11ec-8b0a-bcfab800c430_story.html.

156 Mark Joyella, "On Fox News, Stephen Miller Says an Alternate Set of Electors' Will Certify Trump as Winner," *Forbes*, December 14, 2020, https://www.forbes.com/sites/markjoyella/2020/12/14/on-fox-news-stephen-miller-says-an-alternate-set-of-electors-will-certify-trump-as-winner/?sh=473be956711a.

157 Rosalind S. Helderman and, Josh Dawsey, "'Unhinged': The White House Meeting That Preceded Trump's 'Will Be Wild' Tweet," *Washington Post*, July 12, 2022, https://www.washingtonpost.com/national-security/2022/07/12/trump-white-house-meeting-jan-6/.

158 Elise Viebeck et al., "Electoral College Affirms Biden's Victory on a Relatively Calm Day of a Chaotic Election," *Washington Post*, December 14, 2020, https://www.washingtonpost.com/politics/electoral-college-affirms-bidens-victory-on-a-relatively-calm-day-of-a-chaotic-election/2020/12/14/0994b232-3e48-11eb-9453-fc36ba051781_story.html.

159 Andrew Solender, "Trump Repeatedly Advised to Concede in Fall of 2020, Ex-Aides Testify," *Axios*, July 12, 2022, https://www.axios.com/2022/07/12/trump-aides-advised-concede-2020-election.

160 Evan Perez and Devan Cole, "William Barr Says There Is No Evidence of Widespread Fraud in Presidential Election," CNN, December 1, 2020, https://edition.cnn.com/2020/12/01/politics/william-barr-election-2020/index.html.

161 Zoe Tillman, "Trump and His Allies Have Lost Nearly Sixty Election Fights in Court (and Counting)," *BuzzFeed News*, December 14, 2020, https://www.buzzfeednews.com/article/zoetillman/trump-election-court-losses-electoral-college.

162 Jonathan Swan and, Zachary Basu, "Bonus Episode: Inside the Craziest Meeting of the Trump Presidency," *Axios*, February 2, 2021, https://www.axios.com/2021/02/02/trump-oval-office-meeting-sidney-powell.

163 Hugo Lowell, "Revealed: Trump Reviewed Draft Order That Authorized Voting Machines to Be Seized," *Guardian*, February 4, 2022, https://www.theguardian.com/us-news/2022/feb/04/trump-draft-order-voting-machines-white-house-meeting.

164 Swan and Basu, "Bonus Episode."

165 Helderman and Dawsey, "'Unhinged.'"

166 Zachary Cohen, "What We Know about Infamous Oval Office Meeting Held by Trump's Inner Circle in December 2020," CNN, July 12, 2022, https://edition.cnn.com/2022/07/12/politics/trump-oval-office-meeting-december-2020/index.html.

167 Swan and Basu, "Bonus Episode."

168 Donald J. Trump (@realDonaldTrump), "Peter Navarro releases 36-page report alleging election fraud 'more than sufficient' to swing victory to Trump https://washex.am/3nwaBCe. A great report by Peter. Statistically impossible to have lost the 2020 Election. Big protest in D.C. on January 6th. Be there, will be wild!" Twitter, December 29, 2020, 3:42 a.m., https://twitter.com/realDonaldTrump/status/1340185773220515840.

169 Andrew Solender, "Logs Show Ten House Republicans Attended White House Meeting on Pressuring Pence," *Axios*, July 12, 2022, https://www.axios.com/2022/07/12/house-republicans-jan6-white-house.

170 "John Eastman's Second Memo," *Washington Post*.

171 Jonathan Allen, "'Say the Election Was Corrupt': Jan. 6 Panel Details Trump's DOJ Pressure Campaign," NBC News, June 23, 2022, https://www.nbcnews.com/politics/congress/january-6-hearing-trump-pressured-justice-undermine-election-rcna34804.

172　Barbara Sprunt, "Former DOJ Officials Detail Threatening to Resign en Masse in Meeting with Trump," NPR, June 23, 2022, https://www.npr.org/2022/06/23/1107217243/former-doj-officials-detail-threatening-resign-en-masse-trump-meeting.

173　Chesebro, Memorandum—Important.

174　"John Eastman's Second Memo," *Washington Post.*

175　H. R. Rep. No. 117-663, *435.*

176　Martin Pengelly, "Trump Said Pence Was 'Too Honest' over January 6 Plot, Says Ex-Vice-President in Book," review of *So Help Me God,* Michael Pence, *Guardian,* November 9, 2021, https://www.theguardian.com/books/2022/nov/09/trump-pence-honest-jan-6-capitol-attack-lincoln-project-book.

177　Luke Broadwater and Michael S. Schmidt, "Trump, Told It Was Illegal, Still Pressured Pence to Overturn His Loss," *New York Times,* June 16, 2022, https://www.nytimes.com/2022/06/16/us/trump-pence-election-jan-6.html.

178　"Donald J. Trump, Tweets of January 6, 2021," American Presidency Project, January 6, 2021, https://www.presidency.ucsb.edu/documents/tweets-january-6-2021.

179　Brian Bennett, "From Taunts and Lies to an Angry Mob: Jan. 6 Panel Details Trump's Pressure Campaign against Pence," *Time,* June 16, 2022, https://time.com/6188551/pence-pressure-jan-6-trump/.

180　Select Committee to Investigate the January 6th Attack on the United States Capitol, *Select Committee Transcription,* CTRL0000082311, January 2, 2021, https://www.govinfo.gov/app/details/GPO-J6-DOC-CTRL0000082311/summary.

181　H. R. Rep. No. 117-663, *435–62.*

182　"Read Pence's Full Letter Saying He Can't Claim 'Unilateral Authority' to Reject Electoral Votes," PBS, January 6, 2021, https://www.pbs.org/newshour/politics/read-pences-full-letter-saying-he-cant-claim-unilateral-authority-to-reject-electoral-votes.

183　"#StopTheSteal: Timeline of Social Media and Extremist Activities Leading to 1/6 Insurrection," Just Security, February 10, 2021, https://www.justsecurity.org/74622/stopthesteal-timeline-of-social-media-and-extremist-activities-leading-to-1-6-insurrection/.

184　Marissa J. Lang et al., "Trump Supporters Pour into Washington to Begin Demonstrating against Election," *Washington Post,* January 5, 2021, https://www.washingtonpost.com/dc-md-va/2021/01/05/dc-protest-trump-supporters-election/.

185　"Live: Pro-Trump Protesters Hold 'Rally for Revival' at Washington, D.C. Freedom Plaza," *Bloomberg Quicktake,* January 5, 2021, video, 4:21:43, https://www.youtube.com/watch?v=tRUTm-ZIcow.

186　Charlie Savage, "Trump Pardons Michael Flynn, Ending Case His Justice Dept. Sought to Shut Down," *New York Times,* November 25, 2020, https://www.nytimes.com/2020/11/25/us/politics/michael-flynn-pardon.html.

187　Holland, "Trump Grants."

188　Amita Kelly et al., "Trump Pardons Roger Stone, Paul Manafort and Charles Kushner", NPR, December 23, 2020, https://www.npr.org/2020/12/23/949820820/trump-pardons-roger-stone-paul-manafort-and-charles-kushner.

189　Shelly Tan et al., "How One of America's Ugliest Days Unraveled inside and outside the Capitol," *Washington Post,* January 9, 2021, https://www.washingtonpost.com/nation/interactive/2021/capitol-insurrection-visual-timeline/.

190　"Giuliani: 'Let's Have Trial by Combat,'" *Politico,* Febuaury 8, 2021, video, :35, https://www.politico.com/video/2021/02/08/giuliani-lets-have-trial-by-combat-122543.

191 Brian Naylor, "Read Trump's Jan. 6 Speech, a Key Part of Impeachment Trial," NPR, February 10, 2021, https://www.npr.org/2021/02/10/966396848/read-trumps-jan-6-speech-a-key-part-of-impeachment-trial.

192 Naylor, "Read Trump's Jan. 6 Speech."

193 Andrew Restuccia and Siobhan Hughes, "Jan 6. Hearing Witnesses Say Trump Did Too Little to Stop Riot: Live Updates," *Wall Street Journal*, July 25, 2022, https://www.wsj.com/livecoverage/jan-6-hearing-today-trump/card/trump-s-tweet-about-pence-seen-as-critical-moment-during-riot-fmPxoFkeoTKxi0NqPLCL.

194 "Donald Trump Defends Rioters Who Chanted 'Hang Mike Pence' during January 6th Insurrection," CNBC, November 12, 2021, video, 1:09, https://www.youtube.com/watch?v=LOpWCtNqFQM.

195 "'Bring out Pence': Jan. 6 Committee Shows Video of Protesters Threatening Mike Pence," WCPO 9, June 16, 2022, video, 2:06, https://www.youtube.com/watch?v=Ucln7XVN47I.

196 "Capitol Riots: Pro-Trump Protesters Storm the US Legislature—in Pictures," BBC News, January 6, 2021, https://www.bbc.com/news/world-us-canada-55568131.

197 Paul Kane, "Inside the Assault on the Capitol: Evacuating the Senate," *Washington Post*, January 6, 2021, https://www.washingtonpost.com/politics/reporter-senate-evacuated/2021/01/06/3e7d5456-5061-11eb-83e3-322644d82356_story.html.

198 Ashley Parker et al., "How the Rioters Who Stormed the Capitol Came Dangerously Close to Pence," *Washington Post*, January 15, 2021, https://www.washingtonpost.com/politics/pence-rioters-capitol-attack/2021/01/15/ab62e434-567c-11eb-a08b-f1381ef3d207_story.html.

199 Catie Edmondson, "'So the Traitors Know the Stakes': The Meaning of the Jan. 6 Gallows," *New York Times*, June 16, 2022, https://www.nytimes.com/2022/06/16/us/politics/jan-6-gallows.html.

200 Luke Broadwater and Maggie Haberman, "Jan. 6 Panel Presents Evidence of Trump's Refusal to Stop the Riot," *New York Times*, July 21, 2022, https://www.nytimes.com/2022/07/21/us/politics/trump-jan-6.html.

201 Peter Wade, "'Look at All Those People Fighting for Me': Trump 'Gleefully' Watched Jan. 6 Riot, Says Former Press Secretary," *Rolling Stone*, January 6, 2022, https://www.rollingstone.com/politics/politics-news/stephanie-grisham-trump-gleefully-watched-jan-6-1280113/.

202 Patricia Zengerle and Richard Cowan, "Trump Watched Jan. 6 U.S. Capitol Riot Unfold on TV, Ignored Pleas to Call for Peace," Reuters, July 22, 2022, https://www.reuters.com/world/us/us-capitol-probes-season-finale-focus-trump-supporters-three-hour-rage-2022-07-21/.

203 Maggie Haberman and Luke Broadwater, "Trump Said to Have Reacted Approvingly to Jan. 6 Chants About Hanging Pence," *New York Times*, May 25, 2022, https://www.nytimes.com/2022/05/25/us/politics/trump-pence-jan-6.html.

EPILOGUE

1 Senate Document No. 106–21, *Washington's Farewell Address to the People of the United States* (Washington, 2000), https://www.govinfo.gov/content/pkg/GPO-CDOC-106sdoc21/pdf/GPO-CDOC-106sdoc21.pdf.

APPENDIX A

1 "ОБЩЕРОССИЙСКАЯ," RBC.

2 Kates, "Russian Gun Lobby."

3   S. Rep. No 116-XX, *5:578.*
4   S. Rep. No 116-XX, *5:578.*
5   Arango and Yeginsu, "Peaceful Protest."
6   Letsch, "Turkey Protests."
7   Andreas Rinke et al., "Germany's Merkel Calls on Turkey to Remove Hurdles to EU Accession," Reuters, June 24, 2013, https://www.reuters.com/article/us-germany-turkey-merkel-idUSBRE95N11420130624/.
8   WikiLeaks, "Berat's Box," email from Berat Albayrak to Halil Danismaz sent on June 9, 2013, retrieved from the Wayback Machine, version October 21, 2021, https://web.archive.org/web/20211021214300/https://wikileaks.org/berats-box/emailid/37348.
9   WikiLeaks, "Berat's Box," email from Halil Danismaz to Berat Albayrak and Bilal Erdogan sent on June 24, 2013, retrieved from the Wayback Machine, version February 14, 2022, https://web.archive.org/web/20220214210513/https://wikileaks.org/berats-box/emailid/36106.
10 S. Rep. No 116-XX, *5:580.*
11 Jeremy B. Merrill (@jeremybmerrill), "1/ How long was Trump in Moscow for the Miss Universe pageant?"
12 Katie Rogers, "How Trump's 'Miss Universe' in Russia Became Ensnared in a Political Inquiry," *New York Times*, July 11, 2017, https://www.nytimes.com/2017/07/11/us/politics/how-trumps-miss-universe-in-russia-became-ensnared-in-a-political-inquiry.html.
13 "Ukraine Protests," BBC News.
14 Traynor and Grytsenko, "Ukraine Suspends."
15 Piper, "Special Report."
16 S. Rep. No 116-XX, *5:582.*
17 "John Bolton's Message," Everytown for Gun Safety.
18 "Bolton Relationship," MSNBC.
19 Orucoglu, "Why Turkey's Mother."
20 Constanze Letsch, "Leaked Tapes Prompt Calls for Turkish PM to Resign," *Guardian*, February 25, 2014, https://www.theguardian.com/world/2014/feb/25/leaked-tapes-calls-erdogan-resign-turkish-pm.
21 Letsch, "Turkey: Erdogan."
22 Özay, "Government."
23 Ayla Jean Yackley and Ece Toksabay, "Turkish PM Widens Purge, Facing Biggest Threat of His Rule", Reuters, December 20, 2013, https://www.reuters.com/article/idUSBRE9BJ1AM/.
24 "Turkish Corruption," BBC News.
25 Alan Taylor, "Ukraine's President Voted Out, Flees Kiev," *Atlantic*, February 22, 2014, https://www.theatlantic.com/photo/2014/02/ukraines-president-voted-out-flees-kiev/100686/.
26 Carl Schreck, "From 'Not Us' to 'Why Hide It?': How Russia Denied Its Crimea Invasion, Then Admitted It," RFE/RL, February 26, 2019, https://www.rferl.org/a/from-not-us-to-why-hide-it-how-russia-denied-its-crimea-invasion-then-admitted-it/29791806.html.
27 "No Suspects Left," Hurriyet Daily News.
28 Jonathan Stempel and Brendan Pierson, "Gold Trader Says He Paid Bribes to Get out of Turkish Jail after 2013 Arrest," Reuters, December 4, 2017, https://www.reuters.com/article/idUSKBN1DY2GD/.
29 Kaczynski, "2014 Photo."
30 Shields and Gruber, "Ukrainian Gas Oligarch."
31 S. Rep. No 116-XX, *2:30.*

32. S. Rep. No 116-XX, *5:584*.

33. Greg Miller and Adam Goldman, "Head of Pentagon Intelligence Agency Forced Out, Officials Say," *Washington Post*, April 30, 2014, https://www.washingtonpost.com/world/national-security/head-of-pentagon-intelligence-agency-forced-out-officials-say/2014/04/30/ec15a366-d09d-11e3-9e25-188ebe1fa93b_story.html.

34. Braun and Burns, "Flynn, Fired."

35. Margaret Brennan, "Michael Flynn's Security Clearance Suspended by Defense Intelligence Agency," CBS News, February 15, 2017, https://www.cbsnews.com/news/flynns-security-clearance-suspended-by-defense-intelligence-agency/.

36. Charles Riley, "Russia Cuts off Natural Gas Supplies to Ukraine," CNN, June 16, 2014, https://money.cnn.com/2014/06/16/news/ukraine-russia-gas/index.html.

37. S. Rep. No 116-XX, *2:29–30*.

38. "Recep Tayyip Erdogan," BBC News.

39. Klasfeld, "Boom Times."

40. U.S. Department of Justice, *Exhibit A to Registration Statement Pursuant to the Foreign Agents Registration Act of 1938, as Amended, Filed by Greenberg Traurig, LLP*, Registration No. 5712, August 12, 2014, https://efile.fara.gov/docs/5712-Exhibit-AB-20140812-19.pdf.

41. Ceylan Yeginsu, "Erdogan Is Sworn in as President of Turkey," *New York Times*, August 28, 2014, https://www.nytimes.com/2014/08/29/world/europe/erdogan-is-sworn-in-as-president-of-turkey.html.

42. "Jury Convicts Flynn Intel Group Founder of Conspiring to Act as an Undisclosed Agent of Turkey," Office of Public Affairs, U.S. Department of Justice, press release, July 23, 2019, https://www.justice.gov/opa/pr/jury-convicts-flynn-intel-group-founder-conspiring-act-undisclosed-agent-turkey.

43. Baker and Rosenberg, "Michael Flynn."

44. "Turkey's Massive Corruption Case Dropped by Prosecutor," *Hurriyet Daily News*, October 18, 2014, https://www.hurriyetdailynews.com/turkeys-massive-corruption-case-dropped-by-prosecutor-73149.

45. Peker et al., "Putin Says."

46. Knight, "Maria Butina's Boss."

47. S. Rep. No 116-XX, *5:589*.

48. "Расследование РБК," RBC.

49. Indictment, United States of America v. Internet Research Agency LLC et al.

50. Levintova, "Russian Journalists."

51. "Расследование РБК," RBC.

52. Dickinson, "Read Maria Butina's."

53. Clifton and Follman, "Very Strange Case."

54. Lynch, "Exclusive: Alleged Russian Agent."

55. "Here's Donald Trump's Presidential Announcement Speech," *Time*, June 16, 2015, https://time.com/3923128/donald-trump-announcement-speech/.

56. Mak, "Maria Butina, Accused."

57. Follman, "Trump Spoke."

58. Taibbi, "Overstock."

59. Patrick Healy, "Scott Walker Enters 2016 Presidential Race, Pledging Conservative Agenda," *New York Times*, July 13, 2015, https://www.nytimes.com/2015/07/14/us/politics/scott-walker-presidential-campaign.html.

60 S. Rep. No 116-XX, *5:593.*
61 Yourish et al., "Timeline."
62 S. Rep. No 116-XX, *5:596.*
63 U.S. Department of Justice, *Exhibit A to Registration Statement Pursuant to the Foreign Agents Registration Act of 1938, as Amended, Filed by Amsterdam & Partners LLP*, Registration No. 6325, October 26, 2015, https://efile.fara.gov/docs/6325-Exhibit-AB-20151026-1.pdf.
64 S. Rep. No 116-XX, *5:420.*
65 Petkova, "What Has Russia Gained?"
66 Pyrkalo, "EBRD, Ukraine."
67 S. Rep. No 116-XX, *5:429.*
68 Drum, "Here's the Letter."
69 Melvin et al., "Putin Calls."
70 Roth, "Putin Signs."
71 "Russia Closes," Al Jazeera.
72 Belford and Klasfeld, "Behind Trump's Turkish 'Bromance.'"
73 Hayatsever, "Çavuşoğlu."
74 S. Rep. No 116-XX, *5:598-99.*
75 Helderman and Hamburger, "Trump Adviser Flynn."
76 S. Rep. No 116-XX, *5:443–44.*
77 Liz Moyer, "Rudolph Giuliani to Join Greenberg Traurig Law Firm," *New York Times*, January 19, 2016, https://www.nytimes.com/2016/01/20/business/dealbook/rudolph-giuliani-to-join-greenbergtraurig.html.
78 U.S. Department of Justice, *Exhibit A to Registration Statement Pursuant to the Foreign Agents Registration Act of 1938, as Amended, Filed by Mercury*, Registration No. 6170, March 16, 2016, https://efile.fara.gov/docs/6170-Exhibit-AB-20160316-16.pdf.
79 S. Rep. No 116-XX, *5:609.*
80 Hosenball and Holland, "Trump Being Advised."
81 S. Rep. No 116-XX, *5:170.*
82 Smith, "WikiLeaks Emails."
83 Hurtado et al., "Gold Trader."
84 "Manhattan U.S. Attorney," United States Attorney's Office.
85 "Transcript of Donald Trump's Meeting," *Washington Post.*
86 S. Rep. No 116-XX, *5:53–54.*
87 Sollenberger and O'Neill, "Exclusive: How a Pro-Trump."
88 Sollenberger et al., "She Shunned Islam."
89 "Ukraine's Government Appoints," Naftogaz Group.
90 S. Rep. No 116-XX, *5:613.*
91 Ellen Nakashima and Shane Harris, "How the Russians Hacked the DNC and Passed Its Emails to WikiLeaks," *Washington Post*, July 13, 2018, https://www.washingtonpost.com/world/national-security/how-the-russians-hacked-the-dnc-and-passed-its-emails-to-wikileaks/2018/07/13/af19a828-86c3-11e8-8553-a3ce89036c78_story.html.
92 Lister and Sebastian, "Stoking Islamophobia."
93 S. Rep. No 116-XX, *2:47.*
94 Collinson, "Donald Trump."

95 S. Rep. No 116-XX, *5:614–21.*
96 Jaffe, "NRA Endorses."
97 S. Rep. No 116-XX, *5:621.*
98 *New York Times*, "Government."
99 S. Rep. No 116-XX, *5:182.*
100 Chang, "How Russian Hackers."
101 Theodore Schleifer and Eugene Scott, "What Was in the DNC Email Leak?" CNN, July 25, 2016, https://edition.cnn.com/2016/07/24/politics/dnc-email-leak-wikileaks/index.html.
102 Shear and Rosenberg, "Released Emails."
103 "Full Text of Donald Trump Jr. Emails," *Wall Street Journal.*
104 S. Rep. No 116-XX, *5:184.*
105 Benjamin Weiser and Sharon LaFraniere, "Veselnitskaya, Russian in Trump Tower Meeting, Is Charged in Case That Shows Kremlin Ties," *New York Times*, January 8, 2019, https://www.nytimes.com/2019/01/08/nyregion/trump-tower-natalya-veselnitskaya-indictment.html.
106 Carrie Dann et al., "Democratic National Committee Breached by Russian Hackers," NBC News, June 14, 2016, https://www.nbcnews.com/politics/politics-news/democratic-national-committee-breached-russian-hackers-n592061.
107 Nakashima, "Russian Government."
108 Kirby, "DNC Hacker."
109 Luhn and Black, "Erdoğan Has Apologised."
110 Belford and Klasfeld, "Behind Trump's Turkish 'Bromance.'"
111 Hayatsever, "Çavuşoğlu."
112 S. Rep. No 116-XX, *1:6, 22.*
113 "Turkey's Failed Coup Attempt: All You Need to Know," Al Jazeera, July 15, 2017, https://www.aljazeera.com/news/2017/7/15/turkeys-failed-coup-attempt-all-you-need-to-know.
114 "A Look at Turkey's Post-coup Crackdown," Associated Press, August 30, 2018, https://apnews.com/article/dbb5fa7d8f8c4d0d99f297601c83a164.
115 Chris Johnston, "Turkey Coup Attempt: Arrest Warrants Issued for Former Newspaper Staff," *Guardian*, July 27, 2016, https://www.theguardian.com/world/2016/jul/27/turkey-discharges-1700-officers-from-military-after-coup-attempt.
116 Gulsen Solaker et al., "Turkey Orders 2,745 Judges and Prosecutors to Be Detained after Coup: NTV," Reuters, July 16, 2016, https://www.reuters.com/article/idUSKCN0ZW11Z/.
117 "Turkey's Failed Coup Attempt," Al Jazeera.
118 Maddow, "How Mike Flynn's Position."
119 S. Rep. No 116-XX, *5:625.*
120 S. Rep. No 116-XX, *5:627–28.*
121 Shear and Rosenberg, "Released Emails."
122 S. Rep. No 116-XX, *5:626–27.*
123 "DNC 2016 Schedule of Events and Speakers," *Politico*, July 15, 2016, https://www.politico.com/story/2016/07/dnc-2016-schedule-of-events-and-speakers-225617.
124 Sabrina Siddiqui et al., "Hillary Clinton Named Presidential Nominee as Democrats Make History," *Guardian*, July 27, 2016, https://www.theguardian.com/us-news/2016/jul/26/hillary-clinton-presidential-nomination-democratic-convention.
125 Parker and Sanger, "Donald Trump Calls."
126 S. Rep. No 116-XX, *5:232.*

127 Poulsen et al., "Exclusive: Russians,"
128 Toler, "Florida Trump."
129 Indictment, United States of America v. Internet Research Agency LLC et al.
130 Helderman et al., "Before Her Arrest."
131 "Turkey's Erdogan: The West," Al Jazeera.
132 Walker and Rankin, "Erdoğan and Putin."
133 U.S. Department of Justice, *Exhibit A to Registration Statement Pursuant to the Foreign Agents Registration Act of 1938, as Amended, Filed by Flynn Intel Group Inc*, Registration No. 6406, March 7, 2017, https://efile.fara.gov/docs/6406-Exhibit-AB-20170307-2.pdf.
134 Kramer et al., "Secret Ledger."
135 Luke Harding, "How Trump's Campaign Chief Got a Strongman Elected President of Ukraine," *Guardian*, August 16, 2016, https://www.theguardian.com/us-news/2016/aug/16/donald-trump-campaign-paul-manafort-ukraine-yanukovich.
136 "Report: Pro-Russian Party Earmarked $12.7M in Cash for Trump Camp," CBS News, August 15, 2016, https://www.cbsnews.com/news/elections-2016-trump-campaign-chair-paul-manafort-pro-russian-ukraine-party-ties-new-york-times/.
137 Amber Phillips, "Paul Manafort's Complicated Ties to Ukraine, Explained," *Washington Post*, August 19, 2016, https://www.washingtonpost.com/news/the-fix/wp/2016/08/19/paul-manaforts-complicated-ties-to-ukraine-explained/.
138 Nolan D. McCaskill et al., "Paul Manafort Resigns from Trump Campaign," *Politico*, August 19, 2016, https://www.politico.com/story/2016/08/paul-manafort-resigns-from-trump-campaign-227197.
139 Lipton and Weiser, "Turkish Bank."
140 Schleifer, "GOP Congressman."
141 Sibylla Brodzinsky, "Venezuelans Throng Streets of Caracas Seeking Recall Referendum for President," *Guardian*, September 1, 2016, https://www.theguardian.com/world/2016/sep/01/venezuelans-march-caracas-recall-referendum-rally.
142 Grimaldi et al., "Ex-CIA Director."
143 Belford et al., "Turkish Tycoon."
144 Layne, "Advising Trump."
145 Ignatius, "The Man at the Crux of the U.S.-Turkey Dispute."
146 Andrew Cawthorne and Deisy Buitrago, "Venezuela Opposition Fumes as Door Slams on 2016 Maduro Vote," Reuters, September 22, 2016, https://www.reuters.com/article/venezuela-politics/venezuela-opposition-fumes-as-door-slams-on-2016-maduro-vote-idINL2N1BY0IL/.
147 "Venezuela: No Recall Vote for Nicolas Maduro in 2016," Al Jazeera, September 22, 2016, https://www.aljazeera.com/economy/2016/9/22/venezuela-no-recall-vote-for-nicolas-maduro-in-2016.
148 Brodzinsky, "Venezuelans Warn."
149 Ana Vanessa Herrero and Elisabeth Malkin, "Venezuelans Take to Streets to Oppose President Nicolás Maduro," *New York Times*, October 26, 2016, https://www.nytimes.com/2016/10/27/world/americas/nicolas-maduro-venezuela-protests.html.
150 Kaitlyn Folmer et al., "Former Trump Campaign Aide Was in Alleged Russian Agent's Social Network," ABC News, August 4, 2018, https://abcnews.go.com/Politics/trump-campaign-aide-alleged-russian-agents-social-network/story?id=57033322.
151 Emily Stewart, "Alleged Russian Spy Maria Butina Chatted with Former Trump Campaign Aide Ahead of the 2016 Election," *Vox*, August 4, 2018, https://www.vox.com/policy-and-politics/2018/8/4/17651234/maria-butina-jd-gordon-russia-trump.

152 S. Rep. No 116-XX, *1:7.*
153 Carlotta Gall, "Americans Jailed after Failed Coup in Turkey Are Hostages to Politics," *New York Times*, October 7, 2017, https://www.nytimes.com/2017/10/07/world/europe/turkey-american-detainees.html.
154 Sanger and Savage, "U.S. Says."
155 Farhi, "Caller."
156 Jane C. Timm, "Trump on Hot Mic: 'When You're a Star ... You Can Do Anything' to Women", NBC News, October 7, 2016, https://www.nbcnews.com/politics/2016-election/trump-hot-mic-when-you-re-star-you-can-do-n662116.
157 S. Rep. No 116-XX, 1:7.
158 Cawthorne and Buitrago, "Venezuela Opposition."
159 Cengiz Özbek, "The Rise of a New Turkey-Venezuela Alliance," DW, January 30, 2019, https://www.dw.com/en/turkey-and-venezuela-the-rise-of-a-new-alliance/a-47302588.
160 Scholl, "Hot Commodities."
161 Smith and Reel, "Venezuela's Trade Scheme."
162 "President Maduro," PDVSA.
163 "Korkmaz Helped Charter Flight for Venezuela's El Aissami on U.S.-Funded Private Jet—Academic," *Ahval*, June 29, 2021, https://ahvalnews.com/sezgin-baran-korkmaz/korkmaz-helped-charter-flight-venezuelas-el-aissami-us-funded-private-jet.
164 Andrew Wilks, "As Gold Trade Booms, Venezuela Eyes Stronger Turkey Ties," *Al Jazeera*, January 17, 2019, https://www.aljazeera.com/features/2019/1/17/as-gold-trade-booms-venezuela-eyes-stronger-turkey-ties.
165 Dettmer, "Mystery."
166 Wintour, "Russia."
167 Belford and Klasfeld, "Parnas' Adventures."
168 Bykowicz et al., "Indicted Florida Pair."
169 S. Rep. No 116-XX, *5:629.*
170 S. Rep. No 116-XX, *5:630.*
171 Federal Election Commission, search result for individual contributions "Contributor details - Lev Parnas, Report time period - 2015-2016," accessed July 16, 2024, https://www.fec.gov/data/receipts/individual-contributions/?contributor_name=lev+parnas&two_year_transaction_period=2016.
172 Hong, "Turkish Official."
173 Tal Kopan, "WikiLeaks Releases More Dnc Emails near Eve of Election," CNN, November 6, 2016, https://www.cnn.com/2016/11/06/politics/wikileaks-dnc-emails-surprise/index.html.
174 Flynn, "Our Ally Turkey."
175 Prokop, "Maria Butina."
176 S. Rep. No 116-XX, *2:34.*
177 S. Rep. No 116-XX, *5:630–31.*
178 Clifton and Follman, "Very Strange Case."
179 S. Rep. No 116-XX, *5:632.*
180 Benjamin Weiser and Nick Corasaniti, "Preet Bharara Says He Will Stay on as U.S. Attorney under Trump," *New York Times*, November 30, 2016, https://www.nytimes.com/2016/11/30/nyregion/preet-bharara-says-he-will-stay-on-as-us-attorney-under-trump.html.
181 Kates, "How Russian Oil Giant."

182 Mueller, Report, 160.
183 Belford and Klasfeld, "Behind Trump's Turkish 'Bromance.'"
184 Parnas and Langton, *Shadow Diplomacy*, chap. 8, Kindle.
185 Bharara, "That Time President Trump Fired Me."
186 Philip Bump, "Here Are the Times That We Know Lev Parnas Interacted with President Trump," *Washington Post*, January 30, 2020, https://www.washingtonpost.com/politics/2020/01/24/here-are-times-that-we-know-lev-parnas-met-president-trump/.
187 "Ежегодное послание к Владимиру Путину" [Annual address to Vladimir Putin], *Kommersant*, December 19, 2016, https://www.kommersant.ru/doc/3175832.
188 S. Rep. No 116-XX, *5*:718.
189 Lee and Ainsley, "Mueller Probing Possible Deal."
190 Patrick Gillespie and Flora Charner, "Crisis-Ridden Venezuela Gave $500K to Trump Inauguration," CNN, April 20, 2017, https://money.cnn.com/2017/04/20/news/economy/venezuela-trump-inauguration/index.html.
191 "Guns, Oil and Loans: What's at Stake for Russia in Venezuela?," *Moscow Times*, January 25, 2019, https://www.themoscowtimes.com/2019/01/25/guns-oil-and-loans-whats-at-stake-for-russia-venezuela-a64284.
192 "Read the Transcripts of Michael Flynn's," *Washington Post*.
193 Lee and Sonne, "U.S. Sanctions."
194 DeYoung and Miller, "First Sign."
195 Miles Parks, "The Ten Events You Need to Know to Understand the Michael Flynn Story," NPR, December 15, 2017, https://www.npr.org/2017/12/05/568319589/the-10-events-you-need-to-know-to-understand-the-michael-flynn-story.
196 DeYoung and Miller, "First Sign."
197 "Read the Transcripts of Michael Flynn's," *Washington Post*.
198 Nicholas Confessore et al., "How Michael Flynn's Disdain for Limits Led to a Legal Quagmire," *New York Times*, June 18, 2017, https://www.nytimes.com/2017/06/18/us/politics/michael-flynn-intel-group-trump.html.
199 Ignatius, "The Man at the Crux of the U.S.-Turkey Dispute."
200 Balthaus et al., "Lev Parnas Paid."
201 Ostrowski and Washington, "Lev Parnas."
202 Helderman and Hamburger, "Giuliani Associates Claimed."
203 Confessore et al., "Swamp."
204 Volz and Landay, "Russia Hacked."
205 Gaouette, "FBI's Comey."
206 Sanger and Flegenheimer, "Russian Hackers."
207 Sanger and Flegenheimer, "Russian Hackers."
208 Jonathan Landay and Aram Roston, "Trump Backer Erik Prince's Account of Russian Banker Contact Differs from Mueller Report," Reuters, April 19, 2019, https://www.reuters.com/article/us-usa-trump-russia-prince-idUSKCN1RV03F/.
209 Bump, "On a Number of Important Questions."
210 Harris and Demirjian, "Congressional Democrats."
211 Mueller, Report, 155.
212 "Read the Transcripts of Michael Flynn's," *Washington Post*.
213 Kranish et al., "Inside."

214 Palma, "Did Devin Nunes Meet?"
215 Bertrand, "Devin Nunes."
216 Bharara, "That Time President Trump Fired Me."
217 "Brian D Ballard," Open Secrets.
218 Belford and Klasfeld, "Behind Trump's Turkish 'Bromance.'"
219 Nicholas Fandos, "Inauguration Schedule: What Is Happening and When," *New York Times*, January 17, 2017, https://www.nytimes.com/2017/01/17/us/politics/trump-inauguration-schedule.html.
220 Vogel et al., "Democratic Donor."
221 Belford and Klasfeld, "Behind Trump's Turkish 'Bromance.'"
222 "Trump's First Day," *Time*, January 20, 2016, https://time.com/president-donald-trump-inauguration-day-photos/.
223 Wintour, "Russia."
224 Faysal Abbas Mohamad, "The Astana Process Six Years On: Peace or Deadlock in Syria?" Carnegie Endowment for International Peace, August 1, 2023, https://carnegieendowment.org/sada/2023/08/the-astana-process-six-years-on-peace-or-deadlock-in-syria?lang=en.
225 Parks, "Ten Events."
226 "A Timeline of Sally Yates' Warnings to the White House about Mike Flynn," ABC News, May 8, 2017, https://abcnews.go.com/Politics/timeline-sally-yates-warnings-white-house-mike-flynn/story?id=47272979.
227 "Comey Opening Statement for Senate Intelligence Hearing, Annotated," NPR, June 7, 2017, https://www.npr.org/2017/06/07/531643428/comey-opening-statement-for-senate-intelligence-hearing-annotated.
228 Clifton and Follman, "Very Strange Case."
229 Belford and Klasfeld, "Behind Trump's Turkish 'Bromance.'"
230 S. Rep. No 116-XX, 5:634.
231 Belford and Klasfeld, "Behind Trump's Turkish 'Bromance.'"
232 Jacobs and Lee, "Erdogan-Tied Businessman."
233 Kramish et al., "Inside."
234 Swartz, "Trump Inauguration."
235 Horowitz, "Trump-Tied Businessmen."
236 Derek Hawkins, "Flynn Sets Record with Only 24 Days as National Security Adviser. The Average Tenure Is about 2.6 Years," *Washington Post*, February 14, 2017, https://www.washingtonpost.com/news/morning-mix/wp/2017/02/14/flynn-sets-record-with-only-24-days-as-nsc-chief-the-average-tenure-is-about-2-6-years/.
237 Ken Dilanian et al., "Comey Wrote Memo Saying Trump Urged Him to Drop Flynn Investigation: Sources," NBC News, May 18, 2017, https://www.nbcnews.com/news/us-news/comey-wrote-memo-saying-trump-urged-him-drop-flynn-investigation-n760471.
238 Jen Kirby, "Read: James Comey's Memos on Trump Meetings," *Vox*, April 19, 2018, https://www.vox.com/2018/4/19/17260120/james-comey-trump-memos-russia-investigation.
239 Ignatius, "The Man at the Crux of the U.S.-Turkey Dispute."
240 Weiser and Kingsley, "Secret Meeting."
241 Adam Klasfeld, "Turkey's Lobbyists Had Deep Access to Trump White House," Courthouse News Service, October 22, 2019, https://www.courthousenews.com/turkeys-lobbyists-had-deep-access-to-trump-white-house/.
242 Becker et al., "Giuliani Pressed for Turkish."

243 Wadhams, "Trump Repeatedly Pressed Tillerson."
244 Nick Wadhams et al., "Trump Urged Top Aide to Help Giuliani Client Facing DOJ Charges," Bloomberg News, October 9, 2019, https://www.bloomberg.com/news/articles/2019-10-09/trump-urged-top-aide-to-help-giuliani-client-facing-doj-charges.
245 Belford and Klasfeld, "Behind Trump's Turkish 'Bromance.'"
246 Jacobs and Lee, "Erdogan-Tied Businessman."
247 "In Pictures: The Forty Richest Turks," *Forbes*, April 13, 2007, https://www.forbes.com/2007/04/13/turkey-40-richest-cz_fs_0413richturks_slide.html?sh=78bb43b666eb.
248 Levent Kenez, "Turkey Sets Conditions in International Agreements in Favor of Businessmen Close to Erdoğan," *Nordic Monitor*, July 6, 2021, https://nordicmonitor.com/2021/07/turkey-sets-conditions-to-international-agreements-in-favor-of-businessmen-close-to-erdogan/.
249 Gürsel, "Crackdown."
250 U.S. Department of Justice, *Exhibit A to Registration Statement Pursuant to the Foreign Agents Registration Act of 1938, as Amended, Filed by Flynn Intel Group Inc*, Registration No. 6406, March 7, 2017, https://efile.fara.gov/docs/6406-Exhibit-AB-20170307-2.pdf.
251 U.S. Department of Justice, *Supplemental Statement Pursuant to the Foreign Agents Registration Act of 1938, as Amended, Filed by Flynn Intel Group Inc*, Registration No. 6406, March 7, 2017, https://efile.fara.gov/docs/6406-Supplemental-Statement-20170307-1.pdf.
252 Weiner, "Michael Flynn Reviewed."
253 N'dea Akei Yancey-Bragg, "Ukraine: Top Tax Official on Trial for Corruption," OCCRP, March 7, 2017, https://www.occrp.org/en/daily/6168-ukraine-top-tax-official-on-trial-for-corruption.
254 Indictment, United States of America v. David Rivera and Esther Nuhfer.
255 Weaver, "Ex-U.S. Rep. David Rivera."
256 Belford and Klasfeld, "Behind Trump's Turkish 'Bromance.'"
257 U.S. Department of Justice, *Exhibit A to Registration Statement Pursuant to the Foreign Agents Registration Act of 1938, as Amended, Filed by Ballard Partners*, Registration No. 6415, May 19, 2017, https://efile.fara.gov/docs/6415-Exhibit-AB-20170519-3.pdf.
258 U.S. Department of Justice, *Exhibit A to Registration Statement Pursuant to the Foreign Agents Registration Act of 1938, as Amended, Filed by Ballard Partners*, Registration No. 6415, August 28, 2017, https://efile.fara.gov/docs/6415-Exhibit-AB-20170828-5.pdf.
259 Bharara, "That Time President Trump Fired Me."
260 Josh Dawsey et al., "Trump Administration Fires Preet Bharara, High-Profile U.S. Attorney in New York," *Politico*, March 11, 2017, https://www.politico.com/story/2017/03/preet-bharara-fired-trump-us-attorneys-235961.
261 Indictment, United States of America v. David Rivera and Esther Nuhfer.
262 Jay Weaver and Antonio Maria Delgado, "Rivera Didn't Register as Foreign Agent in $50 Million Contract with Venezuela Oil Firm," *Miami Herald*, May 15, 2020, https://www.miamiherald.com/news/nation-world/world/americas/venezuela/article242736076.html.
263 "Turkish Banker Arrested for Conspiring to Evade U.S. Sanctions against Iran and Other Offenses," United States Attorney's Office, Southern District of New York, press release, March 28, 2017, https://www.justice.gov/usao-sdny/pr/turkish-banker-arrested-conspiring-evade-us-sanctions-against-iran-and-other-offenses.
264 Weiser and Haberman, "Turk in Iran."
265 Weiser and Kingsley, "Secret Meeting."

266 Gardiner Harris, "Rex Tillerson's Praise for Turkey Is Met with a List of Complaints,", *New York Times,* March 30, 2017, https://www.nytimes.com/2017/03/30/world/europe/rex-tillerson-turkey.html.
267 Indictment, United States of America v. David Rivera and Esther Nuhfer.
268 "Turkey Referendum Grants," BBC News.
269 "In Light of New Evidence," United States Senate Committee on Finance.
270 Shuster and Marritz, "Exclusive."
271 Viswanatha et al., "Federal Prosecutors Scrutinize."
272 Vogel, "Ukraine Role."
273 Friedman, "Ukrainian Oligarch Scrutinized."
274 Shear and Apuzzo, "F.B.I. Director James Comey."
275 U.S. Department of Justice, *Exhibit A to Registration Statement Pursuant to the Foreign Agents Registration Act of 1938, as Amended, Filed by Ballard Partners,* Registration No. 6415, May 19, 2017, https://efile.fara.gov/docs/6415-Exhibit-AB-20170519-3.pdf.
276 Klasfeld, "Turkey's Lobbyists."
277 Belford and Klasfeld, "Behind Trump's Turkish 'Bromance.'"
278 Peter Hermann and Perry Stein, "Erdogan's Guards Clash with Protesters outside Turkish Ambassador's D.C. Residence," *Washington Post,* May 17, 2017, https://www.washingtonpost.com/local/public-safety/turkeys-presidential-guards-violently-clash-with-protesters-outside-embassy/2017/05/17/8420942a-3b05-11e7-9e48-c4f199710b69_story.html.
279 Don Peck, "Presidential Silence after an Attack on American Soil," *Atlantic,* January 13, 2019, https://www.theatlantic.com/politics/archive/2019/01/trump-stands-by-while-erdogan-orders-attack-protesters/580093/.
280 Mike Levine, "The Russia Probe: A Timeline from Moscow to Mueller," ABC News, July 23, 2019, https://abcnews.go.com/Politics/russia-probe-timeline-moscow-mueller/story?id=57427441.
281 Gienger and Goodman, "Timeline: Trump."
282 Philip Bump, "A Timeline of Giuliani's Dubious Interactions with the Trump Administration," *Washington Post,* April 28, 2021, https://www.washingtonpost.com/politics/2021/04/28/timeline-giulianis-dubious-interactions-with-trump-administration/.
283 Goodman, "Sources: Venezuela Wooed."
284 Delgado et al., "This Venezuelan Mogul."
285 Massoglia and Evers-Hillstrom, "Revolving Door."
286 Confessore et al., "Trump, Venezuela."
287 "In Light of New Evidence," United States Senate Committee on Finance.
288 Maya Shwayder, "Poroshenko Meets Trump in Washington," DW, June 20, 2017, https://www.dw.com/en/ukraines-petro-poroshenko-squeezes-in-last-minute-visit-with-donald-trump/a-39340342.
289 Bogardus and Brugger, "Inside."
290 Leopold and Cormier, "Here Is the Money Trail."
291 Julia Jones and Stefano Pozzebon, "Venezuelans Reject Constitutional Rewrite in Non-Binding Referendum," CNN, July 17, 2017, https://edition.cnn.com/2017/07/17/americas/venezuela-referendum-votes/index.html.
292 Mery Mogollon and Patrick J. McDonnell, "Millions Take Part in Symbolic Referendum Rejecting Plans to Rewrite Venezuela's Constitution," *Los Angeles Times,* July 16, 2017, https://www.latimes.com/world/mexico-americas/la-fg-venezuela-vote-20170716-story.html.

293 McCoy, "Venezuela's Controversial."
294 Emma Bowman, "Several Countries Reject Venezuela's Election to Rewrite Constitution," *The Two-Way*, NPR, July 30, 2017, https://www.npr.org/sections/thetwo-way/2017/07/30/540472340/several-countries-reject-venezuelas-election-to-rewrite-constitution.
295 McCoy, "Venezuela's Controversial."
296 Goodman, "Sources: Venezuela Wooed."
297 U.S. Department of Justice, *Exhibit A to Registration Statement Pursuant to the Foreign Agents Registration Act of 1938, as Amended, Filed by Ballard Partners*, Registration No. 6415, August 28, 2017, https://efile.fara.gov/docs/6415-Exhibit-AB-20170828-5.pdf.
298 "Venezuela-Related Sanctions," U.S. Department of the Treasury, Office of Foreign Asset Control, accessed July 17, 2024, https://ofac.treasury.gov/sanctions-programs-and-country-information/venezuela-related-sanctions.
299 "Superseding Indictment."
300 "Turkey Signs Deal to Get Russian S-400 Air Defence Missiles," BBC.
301 Selcan Hacaoglu, "US Open to Turkey F-35 Talks If Dispute over Russian Air Defenses Is Resolved," Bloomberg News, January 30, 2024, https://www.bloomberg.com/news/articles/2024-01-30/us-ready-to-reopen-turkey-f-35-talks-if-russian-s-400-system-issue-resolved.
302 "Venezuela's Maduro Meets Turkey's Erdogan on European Tour," VOA, October 6, 2017, https://www.voanews.com/a/venezuela-nicolas-maduro-turkey-recep-tayyip-erdogan-meet-european-tour/4059398.html.
303 Benjamin Weiser, "Reza Zarrab, Turk at Center of Iran Sanctions Case, Is Helping Prosecution," *New York Times*, November 28, 2017, https://www.nytimes.com/2017/11/28/world/europe/reza-zarrab-turkey-iran.html.
304 Confessore et al., "Trump, Venezuela."
305 Roston, "Exclusive: Meeting Maduro."
306 "American Friends," ProPublica.
307 Mike Eckel, "Guns, Sex, and a 'Flight Risk': Behind the Charges against Maria Butina," RFE/RL, July 19, 2018, https://www.rferl.org/a/guns-sex-and-a-flight-risk-behind-the-charges-against-maria-butina/29375982.html.
308 Zavadski, "Feds Flip Turkish Businessman."
309 Sophie Balay, "Ukrainian Anti-Graft Prosecutor Indicts Ex Tax Service Chief," OCCRP, November 13, 2017, https://www.occrp.org/en/daily/7250-ukrainian-anti-graft-prosecutor-indicts-ex-tax-service-chief.
310 Zavadski, "Feds Flip Turkish Businessman."
311 U.S. Department of Justice, *Exhibit A to Registration Statement Pursuant to the Foreign Agents Registration Act of 1938, as Amended, Filed by King & Spalding LLP*, Registration No. 6501, December 21, 2017, https://efile.fara.gov/docs/6501-Exhibit-AB-20171221-1.pdf.
312 C. Ryan Barber, "FBI Director Wray Banked $14M from King & Spalding since 2016," Law.com, December 20, 2018, https://www.law.com/nationallawjournal/2018/12/20/fbi-director-wray-banked-14m-from-king-spalding-since-2016/?slreturn=20240617145016.
313 "Reza Zarrab Case: Gold Trader Implicates Turkish President Erdogan," BBC.
314 Weiser, "Erdogan."

315 World Bank, *Project Appraisal Document on Proposed LOANs in the Amount of US$201 Million to Turkiye Cumhuriyeti Ziraat Bankasi A.S. (US$67 Million) Turkiye Vakiflar Bankasi T.A.O. (US$67 Million) Turkiye Halk Bankasi A.S. (US$67 Million) with the Guarantee of the Republic of Turkey and Proposed Grants from the Global Environment Facility Trust Fund in the Amount of US$3.64 Million to Turkiye Cumhuriyeti Ziraat Bankasi A.S. (US$0.9 Million) Turkiye Vakiflar Bankasi T.A.O. (US$0.9 Million) Turkiye Halk Bankasi A.S. (US$0.9 Million) the Republic of Turkey (US$0.94 Million) for the Small and Medium Enterprises Energy Efficiency Project,* February 28, 2013, https://documents1.worldbank.org/curated/en/431451468172773840/pdf/736470PAD0P1220Official0Use0Only090.pdf.

316 Weiser, "Reza Zarrab Testifies."

317 Connor, "Turkey Targets Riches of U.S. Witness."

318 Statement of the offense, United States of America v. Michael T. Flynn, No. 1:17 Cr. 232-RC (D.D.C. December 1, 2017), https://www.justice.gov/archives/sco/file/1015126/dl.

319 Jonathan Dienst and Tracy Connor, "Sessions Uses Executive Authority to Appoint Interim U.S. Attorneys," NBC News, January 3, 2018, https://www.nbcnews.com/news/us-news/sessions-uses-executive-authority-appoint-interim-u-s-attorneys-n834446.

320 Christian Berthelsen, "Federal Prosecutor in N.Y. Wins Term Extension from Judge," Bloomberg News, April 25, 2018, https://www.bloomberg.com/politics/articles/2018-04-25/top-federal-prosecutor-in-n-y-has-term-extended-by-u-s-judge.

321 "Turkish Banker Convicted of Conspiring to Evade U.S. Sanctions against Iran and Other Offenses," Office of Public Affairs, U.S. Department of Justice, press release, January 3, 2018, https://www.justice.gov/opa/pr/turkish-banker-covicted-conspiring-evade-us-sanctions-against-iran-and-other-offenses.

322 Dorian Jones, "Erdogan Accuses US of 'Political Coup Attempt,'" VOA, January 9, 2018, https://www.voanews.com/a/turkish-president-accuses-us-coup-attempt/4199728.html.

323 Шимон Бриман [Simon Briman], "Русскоязычный бизнесмен принял участие во встрече Трампа с потенциальными донорами его кампании 2020 года" [Russian-speaking businessman took part in Trump's meeting with potential donors to his 2020 campaign], *Forum Daily*, March 6, 2018, https://www.forumdaily.com/russkoyazychnyj-biznesmen-prinyal-uchastie-vo-vstreche-trampa-s-potencialnymi-donorami-ego-kampanii-2020-goda/.

324 Nicole Gaouette et al., "Trump Fires Tillerson, Taps Pompeo as Next Secretary of State," CNN, March 13, 2018, https://edition.cnn.com/2018/03/13/politics/rex-tillerson-secretary-of-state/index.html.

325 Nolan D. McCaskill, "Pompeo Confirmed as Secretary of State," *Politico*, April 26, 2018, https://www.politico.com/story/2018/04/26/pompeo-clears-key-senate-hurdle-to-be-secretary-of-state-555908.

326 "Venezuela-Related Sanctions," U.S. Department of the Treasury.

327 Butler et al., "After Boost."

328 Scanneli et al., "Russian Accused."

329 Indictment, United States of America v. David Rivera and Esther Nuhfer.

330 Helderman et al., "Trump's Lawyer."

331 Goodman, "Sources: Venezuela Wooed."

332 "Treasury Designates," U.S. Department of the Treasury.

333 Campaign Legal Center, Complaint.

334 "Turkey's President Erdogan Calls Snap Election in June," BBC, April 18, 2018, https://www.bbc.com/news/world-europe-43814077.

335 Maggie Haberman and Michael S. Schmidt, "Giuliani to Join Trump's Legal Team," *New York Times*, April 19, 2018, https://www.nytimes.com/2018/04/19/us/politics/giuliani-trump.html.

336 Protess and Vogel, "Recording Surfaces."

337 Scannell and Cohen, "New Parnas Video."

338 Sollenberger, "Pro-Trump Black Group."

339 Scanneli et al., "Russian Accused."

340 Zach Everson (@Z_Everson), "The president of the Turkish American Business Association/American Chamber of Commerce in Turkey, Ali Osman Akat, posted a pic an hour ago from the Trump Hotel DC. Unclear, of course, if this pic is fresh or if he's there to meet with @realDonaldTrump. http://bit.ly/2FsR6nj," Twitter, April 30, 2018, 8:46 p.m., https://twitter.com/Z_Everson/status/991101453300387842.

341 Helderman et al., "At Donor Dinner."

342 "Donald Trump Parnas-Yovanovitch Recording Transcript: Trump Discusses Firing Yovanovitch at Donor Dinner—'Take Her Out,'" Rev, January 26, 2020, https://www.rev.com/blog/transcripts/donald-trump-parnas-yovanovitch-recording-transcript-trump-discusses-firing-yovanovitch-at-donor-dinner.

343 Loop, "Former Member."

344 Ben Fox and Matthew Lee, "US Ambassador Pressed Ukraine Corruption Fight before Ouster," Associated Press, September 28, 2019, https://apnews.com/article/16e6c724d3ee40cea4ff82ab5efa7ed6.

345 Aram Roston and Joseph Tanfani, "Exclusive: Texts Tie DeSantis Closely to Trump Insider Lev Parnas in 2018 Race," Reuters, June 21, 2023, https://www.reuters.com/world/us/texts-tie-desantis-closely-trump-insider-lev-parnas-2018-race-2023-05-22/.

346 Roston and Tanfani, "Exclusive."

347 O'Neill, "Exclusive: How."

348 Campaign Legal Center, Supplement.

349 Farrell et al., "Rudy Giuliani Sidekick."

350 *Mortgage Loan Contract*.

351 "Turkish Banker Mehmet Hakan Atilla Sentenced To Thirty-Two Months for Conspiring to Violate U.S. Sanctions against Iran and Other Offenses," United States Attorney's Office, Southern District of New York, press release, May 16, 2018, https://www.justice.gov/usao-sdny/pr/turkish-banker-mehmet-hakan-atilla-sentenced-32-months-conspiring-violate-us-sanctions.

352 Markay, "Rudy's Ukraine Henchmen."

353 Helderman et al., "Trump's Lawyer."

354 "Venezuela-Related Sanctions," U.S. Department of the Treasury.

355 Entous, "Ukrainian Prosecutor."

356 Confessore et al., "Trump, Venezuela."

357 Gerstein, "Former Aide."

358 Shuster and Marritz, "Exclusive."

359 "Louisiana Natural Gas Exports, Inc.," Open Corporates, retrieved from the Wayback Machine, version August 21, 2022, https://web.archive.org/web/20220821154043/https://opencorporates.com/companies/us_la/43098621F.

360 Shuster and Marritz, "Exclusive."

361 Kaczynski et al., "Inauguration Galas."

362 Balthaus et al., "Lev Parnas Paid."

363 Roston and Tanfani, "Exclusive."

364 Adam Klasfeld, "In the Age of Trump, Judge Reflects on D'Souza and the 'New Rudy,'" Courthouse News Service, June 22, 2018, https://www.courthousenews.com/on-the-bench-in-the-age-of-trump/.

365 Gul Tuysuz et al., "Turkey's Erdogan Victorious in Election That Grants Him Unprecedented Power," CNN, June 25, 2018, https://edition.cnn.com/2018/06/24/europe/turkish-election-results-intl/index.html.

366 "U.S. SigmaBleyzer Ready," Interfax-Ukraine.

367 Shuster and Marritz, "Exclusive."

368 Butler et al., "After Boost."

369 Federal Election Commission, search result for individual contributions "Contributor details - Lev Parnas, Igor Fruman, Recipient name or ID - Pete Sessions for Congress (C00303305)," accessed July 18, 2024, https://www.fec.gov/data/receipts/individual-contributions/?committee_id=C00303305&contributor_name=Lev+Parnas&contributor_name=igor+fruman.

370 Dorian Jones, "Turkey's Erdogan Stands Firm with Venezuela's Maduro," VOA, January 25, 2019, https://www.voanews.com/a/turkey-s-erdogan-stands-firm-with-venezuela-s-maduro/4758691.html.

371 "Russian National Charged," Office of Public Affairs.

372 "Turkey's Diplomatic Crisis Is Hastening an Economic One," Economist.

373 Klasfeld, "Turkey's Lobbyists."

374 U.S. Department of Justice, *Supplemental Statement Pursuant to the Foreign Agent Registration Act of 1938, as Amended, Filed by Ballard Partners*, Registration No. 6415, November 30, 2018, https://efile.fara.gov/docs/6415-Supplemental-Statement-20181130-3.pdf.

375 Campaign Legal Center, Complaint.

376 Letter to Judge Oetken from Todd Blanche, United States of America v. Lev Parnas, Igor Fruman, David Correia, and Andrey Kukushkin, No. 19 Cr. 725 (S.D.N.Y. January 28, 2020), https://storage.courtlistener.com/recap/gov.uscourts.nysd.524345/gov.uscourts.nysd.524345.85.0.pdf.

377 Koran, "Trump Threatens to Sanction."

378 Wilks, "As Gold Trade Booms."

379 U.S. Department of Justice, *Supplemental Statement Pursuant to the Foreign Agent Registration Act of 1938, as Amended, Filed by Ballard Partners*, Registration No. 6415, November 30, 2018, https://efile.fara.gov/docs/6415-Supplemental-Statement-20181130-3.pdf.

380 Savage, "For Jay Sekulow."

381 Friedman, "Jay Sekulow."

382 Smith and Reel, "Venezuela's Trade Scheme."

383 Karen DeYoung and Felicia Sonmez, "U.S. Sanctions Two Turkish Officials over Detention of American Pastor," *Washington Post*, August 1, 2018, https://www.washingtonpost.com/politics/treasury-department-imposes-sanctions-on-two-turkish-officials-over-detention-of-american-pastor/2018/08/01/f7705876-95b2-11e8-a679-b09212fb69c2_story.html.

384 Tankersley et al., "Trump Hits Turkey When It's Down."

385 Parnas, *Trump First*, chap. 1, Kindle.

386 Helderman et al., "Trump's Lawyer."

387 Helderman et al., "Trump's Lawyer."

388 Sam Sokol and Anna Myroniuk, "Why Is Rudy Giuliani Close with This Hassidic Ukrainian Rabbi?" *Jerusalem Post*, October 30, 2019, https://www.jpost.com/american-politics/why-is-rudy-giuliani-close-with-this-hassidic-ukrainian-rabbi-606138.

389 Miller et al., "There's a Village."

390 Weinglas, "Inside Anatevka."

391 Baker and Krasnolutska, "Rudy Giuliani."

392 Belford et al., "Turkish Tycoon."

393 "Turkish Businessman Extradited from Austria to Face Money Laundering and Wire Fraud Charges," United States Attorney's Office, District of Utah, press release, July 15, 2022, https://www.justice.gov/usao-ut/pr/turkish-businessman-extradited-austria-face-money-laundering-and-wire-fraud-charges.

394 Farrell et al., "Rudy Giuliani Sidekick."

395 Lee and Kube, "Secret Deal with Turkey."

396 Gienger and Goodman, "Timeline: Trump."

397 "Andrew Brunson: Turkey Releases US Pastor after Two Years," BBC, October 12, 2018, https://www.bbc.com/news/world-europe-45841276.

398 Donald J. Trump (@realDonaldTrump), "There was NO DEAL made with Turkey for the release and return of Pastor Andrew Brunson. I don't make deals for hostages. There was, however, great appreciation on behalf of the United States, which will lead to good, perhaps great, relations between the United States & Turkey!" Twitter, October 13, 2018, 11:17 a.m., https://twitter.com/realdonaldtrump/status/1051114825391239169.

399 "Fifteen U.S. Companies to Invest in Turkey Following Brunson's Release—AA," Ahval News.

400 "Venezuela-Related Sanctions," U.S. Department of the Treasury.

401 Brice and Gumrukcu, "U.S., Turkey Lift Sanctions."

402 "U.S. Government Fully Re-Imposes Sanctions on the Iranian Regime as Part of Unprecedented U.S. Economic Pressure Campaign," U.S. Department of the Treasury, press release, November 5, 2018, https://home.treasury.gov/news/press-releases/sm541.

403 Aykan Erdemir and Merve Tahiroglu, "Trump Waives Iran Sanctions for Turkey," *Foreign Policy*, November 12, 2018, https://foreignpolicy.com/2018/11/12/trump-waives-iran-sanctions-for-turkey/.

404 Brendan Farrington, Gary Fineout, "GOP's DeSantis Defeats Gillum in Florida Governor's Race," Associated Press, November 7, 2018, https://apnews.com/article/263896e7421946b09d7dcf670a15c606.

405 Andrew Eversden and Edgar Walters, "Texas Democrat Colin Allred Defeats GOP Incumbent Pete Sessions in Key U.S. House Race," *Texas Tribune*, November 6, 2018, https://www.texastribune.org/2018/11/06/democrat-colin-allred-leads-gop-congressman-pete-sessions-texas/.

406 Peter Baker et al., "Jeff Sessions Is Forced Out as Attorney General as Trump Installs Loyalist," *New York Times*, November 7, 2018, https://www.nytimes.com/2018/11/07/us/politics/sessions-resigns.html.

407 "In Light of New Evidence," United States Senate Committee on Finance.

408 "Venezuelan Billionaire News Network Owner, Former Venezuelan National Treasurer and Former Owner of Dominican Republic Bank Charged in Money Laundering Conspiracy Involving over $1 Billion in Bribes," Office of Public Affairs, U.S. Department of Justice, press release, November 20, 2018, https://www.justice.gov/opa/pr/venezuelan-billionaire-news-network-owner-former-venezuelan-national-treasurer-and-former.

409 "Transcript: NPR's Full Interview with Trump Lawyer Rudy Giuliani," NPR, February 5, 2020, https://www.npr.org/2020/02/05/802423844/transcript-nprs-full-interview-with-trump-lawyer-rudy-giuliani.

410 Ward, "Exclusive: Giuliani Associate."

411 Lipton and Weiser, "Turkish Bank."
412 Marritz and Shuster, "The Perry Deals."
413 Arsu, "Shedding Light."
414 "Transcript: John Bolton interview with ABC News' Martha Raddatz," ABC News.
415 Selcan Hacaoglu, "Erdogan Receives a Hero's Welcome Fit for Bolivar in Venezuela," Bloomberg News, December 4, 2018, https://www.bloomberg.com/news/articles/2018-12-04/erdogan-receives-a-hero-s-welcome-fit-for-bolivar-in-venezuela.
416 Ward, "Exclusive: Giuliani Associate."
417 Ward, "Exclusive: After Private White House Meeting."
418 Belford and Melkozerova, "Meet."
419 Jagoda, "Trump Signs Order."
420 Rosenberg, "Maria Butina."
421 Bjorklund, "Trump's Inexplicable Crusade."
422 Borger, "Mattis Resignation Triggered by Phone Call between Trump and Erdoğan."
423 Jeremy Diamond and Elise Labott, "Trump Told Turkey's Erdogan in Dec. 14 Call about Syria, 'It's All Yours. We Are Done,'" CNN, December 24, 2018, https://edition.cnn.com/2018/12/23/politics/donald-trump-erdogan-turkey.
424 Colin P. Clarke and Ahmet S. Yayla, "The United States Can't Rely on Turkey to Defeat ISIS," *Foreign Policy*, December 31, 2019, https://foreignpolicy.com/2018/12/31/the-united-states-cant-rely-on-turkey-to-defeat-isis-kurds-syria-ypg-erdogan/.
425 Patrick Kingsley, "Who Are the Kurds, and Why Is Turkey Attacking Them in Syria?," *New York Times*, October 14, 2018, https://www.nytimes.com/2019/10/14/world/middleeast/the-kurds-facts-history.html.
426 Chase Winter, "Explained: Why Turkey Is Targeting Syrian Kurds," DW, October 9, 2019, https://www.dw.com/en/explained-why-turkey-wants-a-military-assault-on-syrian-kurds/a-50731834.
427 Rachel Weiner et al., "Michael Flynn's Business Associates Charged with Illegally Lobbying for Turkey," *Washington Post*, December 18, 2018, https://www.washingtonpost.com/local/legal-issues/michael-flynns-business-partner-charged-with-illegally-lobbying-for-turkey/2018/12/17/46fb3762-020a-11e9-9122-82e98f91ee6f_story.html.
428 Barbara Starr et al., "Trump Orders Rapid Withdrawal from Syria in Apparent Reversal," CNN, December 19, 2018, https://edition.cnn.com/2018/12/19/politics/us-syria-withdrawal/index.html.
429 Philip Ewing, "Defense Secretary Mattis Resigns amid Syria and Afghanistan Tension," NPR, December 20, 2018, https://www.npr.org/2018/12/20/623246756/defense-secretary-mattis-to-retire-in-february-trump-says.
430 Middle Eastern Women Coalition (@mewomenscoalition), "Ola Hawatmeh Vice President of MEWC @styleola," Instagram, December 15, 2018, https://www.instagram.com/p/Bra_VyoAShz/.
431 Cohen and Ellsworth, "Venezuela's PDVSA."
432 "Treasury Targets Venezuela Currency Exchange Network Scheme Generating Billions of Dollars for Corrupt Regime Insiders," U.S. Department of the Treasury, press release, January 8, 2019, https://home.treasury.gov/news/press-releases/sm583.
433 "Venezuela President Maduro Sworn In," BBC News.
434 "Кабмин инициирует," Gordon.
435 "Naftogaz Creates," Naftogaz Group.
436 Bogardus and Brugger, "Inside."

437   Gall, "In Turkey, Senator Calls for Slower, Smarter U.S. Withdrawal from Syria."
438   Lipton and Weiser, "Turkish Bank."
439   Butler and Biesecker, "Giuliani Pals."
440   Andrew E. Kramer et al., "The Ukrainian Ex-Prosecutor behind the Impeachment Furor," *New York Times*, October 5, 2019, https://www.nytimes.com/2019/10/05/world/europe/ukraine-prosecutor-trump.html.
441   Entous, "Ukrainian Prosecutor."
442   Kenneth P. Vogel and Iuliia Mendel, "Biden Faces Conflict of Interest Questions That Are Being Promoted by Trump and Allies," *New York Times*, May 1, 2019, https://www.nytimes.com/2019/05/01/us/politics/biden-son-ukraine.html.
443   "Issuance of a New Venezuela-Realted Executive Order and General Licenses; Related Designation," U.S. Department of the Treasury, Office of Foreign Asset Control, press release, January 28, 2019, https://ofac.treasury.gov/recent-actions/20190128.
444   Ballhaus, "Giuliani Weighed."
445   Protess et al., "Giuliani Pursued Business."
446   Rosalind S. Helderman et al., "Giuliani Was in Talks to Be Paid by Ukraine's Top Prosecutor as They Together Sought Damaging Information on Democrats," *Washington Post*, November 27, 2019, https://www.washingtonpost.com/politics/giuliani-was-in-talks-to-be-paid-by-ukraines-top-prosecutor-as-they-together-sought-damaging-information-on-democrats/2019/11/27/636c3e86-112d-11ea-b0fc-62cc38411ebb_story.html.
447   diGenova & Toensing, LLP, *Retainer Letter for Yuri Lutsenko*.
448   Sollenberger et al., "She Shunned Islam."
449   Pete Madden et al., "Republican Operative Paul Erickson Indicted on Wire Fraud, Money Laundering Charges in South Dakota," ABC News, February 6, 2019, https://abcnews.go.com/US/accused-russian-agent-maria-butinas-boyfriend-paul-erickson/story?id=60900080.
450   Entous, "Ukrainian Prosecutor."
451   Bonner, "Kobolyev."
452   "William P. Barr Confirmed As 85th Attorney General of the United States," Office of Pubic Affairs, U.S. Department of Justice, February 14, 2019, https://www.justice.gov/opa/pr/william-p-barr-confirmed-85th-attorney-general-united-states.
453   Marritz and Shuster, "The Perry Deals."
454   Simpson, "Giuliani's."
455   Simpson, "Giuliani's."
456   Mac William Bishop et al., "A Powerful Ukrainian Is Playing Both Sides of Giuliani's Ukraine Project," NBC News, February 16, 2020, https://www.nbcnews.com/politics/trump-impeachment-inquiry/powerful-ukrainian-playing-both-sides-giuliani-s-ukraine-project-n1136756.
457   Ballhaus et al., "Giuliani Associates."
458   Sollenberger et al., "She Shunned Islam."
459   "US Ambassador Slams Ukraine over Corruption," Associated Press, March 6, 2019, https://apnews.com/article/b126f24a720a4978af37d1aa29b2bf64.
460   Butler et al., "Profit."
461   Yuri Lutsenko, "Senior Ukrainian Official Says He's Opened Probe into US Election Interference," interview by John Solomon, *Hill*, March 20, 2019, https://thehill.com/hilltv/rising/434892-senior-ukrainian-justice-official-says-hes-opened-probe-into-us-election/.

462 John Solomon, "As Russia Collusion Fades, Ukrainian Plot to Help Clinton Emerges," opinion, *Hill*, March 20, 2019, https://thehill.com/opinion/campaign/435029-as-russia-collusion-fades-ukrainian-plot-to-help-clinton-emerges/?rnd=1582113932.

463 Bump, "How Ukraine's Top Prosecutor."

464 Devlin Barrett et al., "Mueller Report Sent to Attorney General, Signaling His Russia Investigation Has Ended," *Washington Post*, March 22, 2019, https://www.washingtonpost.com/world/national-security/mueller-report-sent-to-attorney-general-signaling-his-russia-investigation-has-ended/2019/03/22/b061d8fa-323e-11e9-813a-0ab2f17e305b_story.html.

465 Kevin Breuninger and Mike Calia, "Special Counsel Mueller's Report Has Been Released to the Public—Read Key Findings Here," CNBC, April 18, 2019, https://www.cnbc.com/2019/04/18/special-counsel-muellers-report-has-been-released-to-the-public.html.

466 "Updates Timeline: Messages about Yovanovitch Surveillance Happened Same Week as Giuliani-Pompeo Calls," American Oversight, January 15, 2020, https://www.americanoversight.org/messages-to-parnas-suggest-yovanovitch-surveillance-happened-same-week-as-giuliani-pompeo-calls.

467 Caldwell et al., "Giuliani Says State Dept Vowed."

468 Sollenberger et al., "She Shunned Islam."

469 Wadhams, "Trump-Erdogan Call."

470 Solomon, "Joe Biden's 2020 Ukrainian Nightmare."

471 "State Department Records," American Oversight.

472 Rudy Giuliani, "Giuliani Slams Mueller Leak," interview by Howard Kurtz, *MediaBuzz*, Fox News, April 7, 2019, https://www.foxnews.com/transcript/giuliani-slams-mueller-leak.

473 Murray Waas, "Giuliani Investigators Home in on 2019 Plan to Advance Ukraine Interests in US," *Guardian*, November 4, 2021, https://www.theguardian.com/world/2021/nov/04/giuliani-ukraine-investigators-contracts-prosecutors?CMP=oth_b-aplnews_d-1.

474 "37th Annual Conference on U.S.-Turkey Relations," TAIK, accessed July 19, 2024, https://taik.org.tr/en-US/Events/2822/37th-Annual-Conference-on-U-S-Turkey-Relations.

475 Przybyla and Schecter, "Donald Trump's Longtime Business Connections."

476 "Yalçındağ Takes Helm at Yandex Turkey," *Hurriyet Daily News*, July 11, 2012, https://www.hurriyetdailynews.com/yalcindag-takes-helm-at-yandex-turkey-25292.

477 David D. Kirkpatrick and Eric Lipton, "Behind Trump's Dealings with Turkey: Sons-in-Law Married to Power," *New York Times*, November 12, 2019, https://www.nytimes.com/2019/11/12/us/politics/trump-erdogan-family-turkey.html.

478 Waas, "Giuliani Investigators."

479 "Ukraine Prosecutor General," Unian.

480 Benac et al., "Mueller Reveals."

481 Andrew Higgins and Iuliia Mendel, "Ukraine Election: Volodymyr Zelensky, TV Comedian, Trounces President," *New York Times*, April 21, 2019, https://www.nytimes.com/2019/04/21/world/europe/Volodymyr-Zelensky-ukraine-elections.html.

482 Rogin, "In May."

483 Belford and Melkozerova, "Meet."

484 Simpson, "Giuliani's."

485 Farrington, "Read: Former Ukraine Ambassador."

486 Re, "Clinton-Ukraine."

487 Ryan Lucas, "Russian Agent Maria Butina Sentenced to Eighteen Months Following Guilty Plea,"NPR, April 26, 2019, https://www.npr.org/2019/04/26/716799929/russian-agent-maria-butina-to-be-sentenced-in-federal-court-on-friday.

488 Butler and Biesecker, "Giuliani Pals."

489 Butler and Biesecker, "Giuliani Pals."

490 Warren and Schouten, "'It's Been a Disaster.'"

491 Parti, "Trump's 'Low-Profile."

492 Butler and Biesecker, "Giuliani Pals."

493 Gramer and Mackinnon, "U.S. Ambassador."

494 "House Releases," *Washington Post*.

495 "House Releases," *Washington Post*.

496 Vogel, "Rudy Giuliani Plans."

497 Winter et al.," Giuliani Sought Private Meeting."

498 Charles Creitz, "Giuliani Cancels Ukraine Trip, Says He'd Be 'Walking into a Group of People That Are Enemies of the US,'" Fox News, May 11, 2019, https://www.foxnews.com/politics/giuliani-i-am-not-going-to-ukraine-because-id-be-walking-into-a-group-of-people-that-are-enemies-of-the-us.

499 "Rachel Maddow," MSNBC.

500 "House Releases," *Washington Post*.

501 Krasnolutska et al., "Ukraine Prosecutor."

502 Entous, "Ukrainian Prosecutor."

503 Butler and Biesecker, "Giuliani Pals."

504 Baker and Krasnolutska, "Rudy Giuliani."

505 John Hudson, "Giuliani's Role as Unofficial Envoy Faces Scrutiny with Rough Transcript Release," *Washington Post*, September 25, 2019, https://www.washingtonpost.com/world/national-security/giulianis-role-as-unofficial-envoy-faces-scrutiny-with-rough-transcript-release/2019/09/25/f85dcc9e-f0dd-421b-8941-fcfb5de074db_story.html.

506 Dawsey, "'Talk to Rudy.,'"

507 O'Neill, "Exclusive: How."

508 Vogel, "While Working for Trump."

509 Confessore et al., "Trump, Venezuela."

510 Venture Capital (@kelly2277), "Aaron Parnas was a Summer Associate at @RudyGiuliani's firm, Greenberg Traurig AND a research assistant for a Professor on FEDERAL ELECTION CONTRIBUTION LIMITS IN LIGHT OF CITIZEN UNITED DECISION. . . His father utilized this decision using Aaron Investment 1 - a shell company," Twitter, October 11, 2019, 12:35 a.m., https://twitter.com/kelly2277/status/1182499950267113475.

511 Kiefer, "Ukraine's New President?"

512 Lefebvre and Lippman, "Perry."

513 "U.S. Ambassador to the European Union Gordon Sondland Brings Together U.S. and European Leaders to Advance Transatlantic Relations; Jared Kushner, Jay Leno, President Zelenskyy and Others Attend," Global Public Affairs, U.S. Department of State, June 5, 2019, https://2017-2021-translations.state.gov/2019/06/05/u-s-ambassador-to-the-european-union-gordon-sondland-brings-together-u-s-and-european-leaders-to-advance-transatlantic-relations-jared-kushner-jay-leno-president-zelenskyy-and-others-attend/.

514 Berman, *Holding the Line: Inside the Nation's Preeminent US Attorney's Office and Its Battle with the Trump Justice Department*, chap. 21, Kindle.

515 Berman, *Holding the Line: Inside the Nation's Preeminent US Attorney's Office and Its Battle with the Trump Justice Department*, chap. 21, Kindle.

516 Toma Istomina, "Zelenskiy Fires Fifteen Governors, Proposes Firing Prosecutor General Lutsenko," *Kyiv Post*, June 11, 2019, https://www.kyivpost.com/ukraine-politics/zelenskiy-fires-15-governors-proposes-firing-prosecutor-general-lutsenko.html.

517 Berman, *Holding the Line: Inside the Nation's Preeminent US Attorney's Office and Its Battle with the Trump Justice Department*, chap. 21, Kindle.

518 Lipton and Weiser, "Turkish Bank."

519 Lipton and Weiser, "Turkish Bank."

520 "Pentagon to Give Additional $250 Million in Military Aid to Ukraine", RFE/RL, June 18, 2019, https://www.rferl.org/a/pentagon-to-give-additional-250-million-in-military-aid-to-ukraine/30006853.html.

521 Puko, "Perry."

522 "Corrected: Austrian Court," Reuters.

523 Ward, "Exclusive Photos."

524 Jaccard et al., "Jet-Setting Venezuelan."

525 Weaver et al., "Venezuelan."

526 Andrew Kaczynski, "London Trip Photos Show Giuliani with Indicted Associate at Yankees' Game, Ukrainian Charity Event," CNN, October 26, 2019, https://edition.cnn.com/2019/10/26/app-politics-section/kfile-giuliani-london-trip/index.html.

527 Baker and Krasnolutska, "Rudy Giuliani."

528 Berman, *Holding the Line: Inside the Nation's Preeminent US Attorney's Office and Its Battle with the Trump Justice Department*, chap. 21, Kindle.

529 "'Barr Did the Bidding of the President and Politicized the DOJ' Says Fmr. U.S. Attorney," MSNBC.

530 Helderman et al., "Trump Ousts Manhattan U.S. Attorney."

531 Benner and Schmidt, "Justice Dept. Official."

532 Berman, *Holding the Line: Inside the Nation's Preeminent US Attorney's Office and Its Battle with the Trump Justice Department*, chap. 21, Kindle.

533 Butler et al., "After Boost."

534 Miller, "Two Volatile Meetings."

535 Shuster and Marritz, "Exclusive."

536 Vogel et al., "How a Shadow Foreign Policy."

537 Aaron Blake et al., "The Full Trump-Ukraine Impeachment Timeline," *Washington Post*, January 27, 2020, https://www.washingtonpost.com/graphics/2019/politics/trump-impeachment-timeline/.

538 Chance and Cohen, "Exclusive: New Audio."

539 Solomon, "How Mueller Deputy."

540 U.S. Department of Justice, *Amendment to Registration Statement Pursuant to the Foreign Agents Registration Act of 1938, as Amended, Filed by Davis, Goldberg & Galper, PLLC*, Registration No. 6394, July 23, 2019, https://efile.fara.gov/docs/6394-Amendment-20190723-3.pdf.

541 Shuster, "Exclusive."

542 Becker et al., "Why."

543 "Halkbank Executive Returns to Turkey after Serving U.S. Sentence," Reuters, July 24, 2019, https://www.reuters.com/article/us-turkey-usa-banker/halkbank-executive-returns-to-turkey-after-serving-u-s-sentence-idUSKCN1UJ1MO/.

544 "Hakan Atilla to Head Istanbul Stock Exchange," *Hurriyet Daily News*, October 22, 2019, https://www.hurriyetdailynews.com/hakan-atilla-to-head-istanbul-stock-exchange-147813.

545 "Official Readout: President Trump's July 25 Phone Call with Ukraine's Volodymyr Zelensky," *Washington Post*, September 25, 2019, https://www.washingtonpost.com/context/official-readout-president-trump-s-july-25-phone-call-with-ukraine-s-volodymyr-zelensky/4b228f51-17e7-45bc-b16c-3b2643f3fbe0/?itid=lk_inline_manual_1.

546 Bennett et al., "Trump Blames."

547 Lauren Kent et al., "Rick Perry Says He 'Absolutely' Asked Trump to Call Zelensky—Just Not about the Bidens," CNN, October 7, 2019, https://edition.cnn.com/2019/10/07/politics/rick-perry-trump-zelensky-ukraine-call/index.html.

548 Helderman et al., "Wealthy Venezuelan."

549 Pamela Brown and Caroline Kelly, "Giuliani Says He Met with Ukrainian Official to Discuss Biden," CNN, August 23, 2019, https://edition.cnn.com/2019/08/21/politics/giuliani-ukraine-lawyer-meeting/index.html.

550 Helderman et al., "Wealthy Venezuelan."

551 "Venezuela-Related Sanctions," U.S. Department of the Treasury.

552 Barnes et al., "Whistle-Blower."

553 U.S. Department of Justice, FOIA Library, *Former Attorney General*, pg. 107.

554 Winter et al., "Who Is Dmytro Firtash?"

555 "Новим генпрокурором став колишній член НАЗК" [A former member of the NAZK became the new prosecutor general], *Українська правда [Ukrainian Pravda]*, August 29, 2019, https://www.pravda.com.ua/news/2019/08/29/7224824/.

556 Agnieszka Barteczko et al., "U.S. to Help Poland, Ukraine Disconnect from Russian Gas," Reuters, August 31, 2019, https://www.reuters.com/article/us-poland-usa-energy-idUSKCN1VL0HH/.

557 Shuster and Marritz, "Exclusive."

558 Marritz and Shuster, "The Perry Deals."

559 Winter et al., "Who Is Dmytro Firtash?"

560 Herb, "Gowdy."

561 U.S. Department of Justice, FOIA Library, *Former Attorney General*, pg. 110.

562 Vogel and Protess, "Giuliani Represented Venezuelan."

563 Inspector General of the Intelligence Community, *Letter to the Chairman and the Ranking Member of the Permanent Select Committee on Intelligence, U.S. House of Representatives,* September 9, 2019, retrieved from the Wayback Machine, version September 29, 2019, https://web.archive.org/web/20190920204043/https://intelligence.house.gov/uploadedfiles/20190909_-_ic_ig_letter_to_hpsci_on_whistleblower.pdf.

564 "Three House Committees Launch," U.S. House of Representatives Committee on Foreign Affairs.

565 Philip Ewing, "Trump Fires John in Final Break after Months of Internal Policy Division," NPR, September 10, 2019, https://www.npr.org/2019/09/10/724363700/trump-fires-john-bolton-in-final-break-after-months-of-policy-divisions.

566 David Welna, "The Hold on Ukraine Aid: A Timeline Emerges from Impeachment Probe," NPR, November 27, 2019, https://www.npr.org/2019/11/27/783487901/the-hold-on-ukraine-aid-a-timeline-emerges-from-impeachment-probe.

567. Jacob Pramuk, "Pelosi Announces Impeachment Inquiry into Trump as Pressure Grows over Alleged Abuses of Power," CNBC, September 24, 2019, https://www.cnbc.com/2019/09/24/nancy-pelosi-announces-trump-impeachment-inquiry-by-house-democrats.html.
568. "Read the Trump-Ukraine Phone Call Readout," Politico, September 25, 2019, https://www.politico.com/story/2019/09/25/trump-ukraine-phone-call-transcript-text-pdf-1510770.
569. "Read: Whistleblower Complaint," CNN.
570. Solomon, "Solomon: These Once-Secret Memos."
571. Witness Statement, FactCheck.org.
572. "Giuliani Subpoenaed," U.S. House of Representatives Committee on Foreign Affairs.
573. Helderman et al., "How Giuliani's Outreach."
574. Blake et al., "Full Trump-Ukraine Impeachment."
575. "Trump Withdraws US Troops from Northern Syria," Atlantic Council, October 7, 2019, https://www.atlanticcouncil.org/blogs/menasource/trump-withdraws-us-troops-from-northern-syria/.
576. Shannon Pettypiece and Kristen Welker, "White House Refuses to Cooperate with Impeachment Investigation," NBC News, October 8, 2019, https://www.nbcnews.com/politics/trump-impeachment-inquiry/white-house-refuses-turn-over-documents-democrats-impeachment-inquiry-n1063771.
577. Fortin, "Trump Says the Kurds 'Didn't Help' at Normandy. Here's the History."
578. Jackson and Fritze, "Turkey Pounds Syria."
579. Olorunnipa and Kim, "Republicans Deliver Rare Rebuke of Trump."
580. Steve Holland, "Trump Warned Erdogan in Letter: 'Don't Be a Tough Guy' or 'A Fool,'" Reuters, October 16, 2019, https://www.reuters.com/article/us-syria-security-trump-erdogan-idUSKBN1WV2PM/.
581. "Turkey's Erdogan 'Threw Trump's Syria Letter in Bin,'" BBC News.
582. Barrett et al., "Two Business Associates."
583. LeBlanc, "Rudy Giuliani."
584. Congress of the United States, Permanent Select Committee on Intelligence, Subpoena to Rick Perry.
585. Tucker Higgins, "Energy Secretary Rick Perry Hit with Subpoena in Trump Impeachment Probe," CNBC, October 10, 2019, https://www.cnbc.com/2019/10/10/rick-perry-hit-with-subpoena-in-trump-impeachment-probe.html.
586. Farrington, "Read: Former Ukraine Ambassador."
587. Karoun Demirjian et al., "Trump's Ex-Russia Adviser Told Impeachment Investigators of Giuliani's Efforts in Ukraine," Washington Post, October 15, 2019, https://www.washingtonpost.com/national-security/trumps-former-top-russia-adviser-to-testify-in-house-impeachment-probe/2019/10/14/e6015c1c-ee34-11e9-8693-f487e46784aa_story.html.
588. "U.S. Imposes New Sanctions on Turkey over Syria Offensive," CBS News, October 14, 2019, https://www.cbsnews.com/news/sanctions-on-turkey-trump-imposes-new-sanctions-over-kurdish-offensive-in-northern-syria-2019-10-14/.
589. "Trump Hits Turkey with Sanctions, Calls for Ceasefire," Al Jazeera, October 15, 2019, https://www.aljazeera.com/economy/2019/10/15/trump-hits-turkey-with-sanctions-calls-for-ceasefire.
590. Seung Min Kim and Karen DeYoung, "Trump Calls for Cease-Fire in Northern Syria and Imposes Sanctions on Turkey," Washington Post, October 14, 2019, https://www.washingtonpost.com/politics/trump-says-he-will-soon-issue-order-authorizing-sanctions-on-turkey-over-its-incursion-into-syria/2019/10/14/ec0b9746-eea5-11e9-b2da-606ba1ef30e3_story.html.
591. Borger and Safi, "Trump Claims Kurds 'No Angels.'"

592 "Turkish Bank Charged in Manhattan Federal Court for Its Participation in a Multibillion-Dollar Iranian Sanctions Evasion Scheme," Office of Public Affairs, U.S. Department of Justice, press release, October 15, 2019, https://www.justice.gov/opa/pr/turkish-bank-charged-manhattan-federal-court-its-participation-multibillion-dollar-iranian.

593 U.S. Department of Justice, *Amendment to Registration Statement Pursuant to the Foreign Agents Registration Act of 1938, as Amended, Filed by Ballard Partners*, Registration No. 6415, October 16, 2019, https://efile.fara.gov/docs/6415-Amendment-20191016-21.pdf.

594 Bethan McKernan, Julian Borger, "Pence and Erdoğan Agree on Ceasefire Plan but Kurds Reject 'Occupation,'" *Guardian*, October 17, 2019, https://www.theguardian.com/world/2019/oct/17/us-delegation-seeks-syria-ceasefire-after-trump-undercuts-mission-turkey-mike-pence.

595 Holland and Gardner, "Trump."

596 Adragna and Lefebvre, "Rick Perry."

597 Ryan Goodman and Danielle Schulkin, "Timeline: Trump, Barr, and the Halkbank Case on Iran Sanctions-Busting, Just Security, July 27, 2020, https://www.justsecurity.org/71694/trump-barr-and-the-halkbank-case-timeline/.

598 Murray et al., "Maria Butina."

599 Roos and Jamali, "Rudy Giuliani."

600 David Nakamura et al., "Trump Welcomes Turkey's Erdogan to White House, Offers Thanks for Tentative Cease-Fire in Northern Syria," *Washington Post*, November 13, 2019, https://www.washingtonpost.com/politics/trump-welcomes-turkeys-erdogan-to-white-house-offers-thanks-for-tentative-cease-fire-in-northern-syria/2019/11/13/b08698fc-0628-11ea-b17d-8b867891d39d_story.html.

601 "Transcript: Marie Yovanovitch's Nov. 15 Testimony in Front of the House Intelligence Committee", *Washington Post*, November 16, 2019, https://www.washingtonpost.com/politics/2019/11/16/transcript-marie-yovanovitchs-nov-testimony-front-house-intelligence-committee/.

602 "Read Alexander Vindman's Prepared Opening Statement from the Impeachment Hearing," *New York Times*, November 19, 2019, https://www.nytimes.com/2019/11/19/us/politics/vindman-statement-testimony.html.

603 Gretchen Frazee, "Read Gordon Sondland's Full Opening Testimony in the Trump Impeachment Hearing," PBS, November 20, 2019, https://www.pbs.org/newshour/politics/read-gordon-sondlands-full-opening-testimony-in-the-trump-impeachment-hearing.

604 "Read Fiona Hill's Opening Statement," *New York Times*, November 21, 2019, https://www.nytimes.com/interactive/2019/11/21/us/politics/fiona-hill-opening-statement-ukraine.html.

605 Butler and Biesecker, "Ukrainian Gas Chief."

606 Hamburger and Helderman, "Federal Prosecutors."

607 Miller, "Rudy Giuliani Flew."

608 Caputo, "'Ukraine Hoax.'"

609 Miller, "Rudy Giuliani Made."

610 Ben Lefebvre et al., "Rick Perry dances toward the exits", *Politico*, November 30, 2019, https://www.politico.com/news/2019/11/30/rick-perry-energy-secretary-074410.

611 Simon Shuster, "Exclusive: Lawsuit Raises Questions about Rick Perry's Role in Ukraine's Energy Sector," *Time*, December 16, 2019, https://time.com/5750669/exclusive-lawsuit-raises-questions-about-rick-perrys-role-in-ukraine-energy-sector/.

612 Nicholas Fandos and Michael D. Shear, "Trump Impeached for Abuse of Power and Obstruction of Congress," *New York Times*, December 18, 2019, https://www.nytimes.com/2019/12/18/us/politics/trump-impeached.html.

613 Adams-Heard, "Ex-Energy Secretary."
614 Olesya Astakhova and Can Sezer, "Turkey, Russia Launch TurkStream Pipeline Carrying Gas to Europe," Reuters, January 8, 2020, https://www.reuters.com/article/us-turkey-russia-pipeline-idUSKBN1Z71WP/.
615 Nicholas Fandos and Sheryl Gay Stolberg, "House Delivers Impeachment Charges to Senate, Paving the Way for a Trial," *New York Times*, January 15, 2020, https://www.nytimes.com/2020/01/15/us/politics/impeachment-managers.html.
616 "Wyden Continues Investigation into Trump Interference in Halkbank Case on Behalf of Turkey," United States Senate Committee on Finance, press release, March 11, 2021, https://www.finance.senate.gov/chairmans-news/wyden-continues-investigation-into-trump-interference-in-halkbank-case-on-behalf-of-turkey.
617 Peter Baker, "Impeachment Trial Updates: Senate Acquits Trump, Ending Historic Trial," *New York Times*, February 6, 2020, https://www.nytimes.com/2020/02/05/us/politics/impeachment-vote.html.
618 "Кабмин ввел в наблюдательный совет нафтогаза американца бенша," Украинские Национальные Новости.
619 "Ukraine, U.S. Agree," Interfax-Ukraine.
620 Laya and Bartenstein, "Iran."
621 "Govt Approves Memo," Interfax-Ukraine.
622 Jo Harper, "Ukraine Skeptical of US Gas Imports," DW, July 24, 2020, https://www.dw.com/en/nord-stream-2-ukraine-united-states-lng-poland-fracking/a-54303274.
623 Ben Lefebvre, "Ukraine Gas Company to Add Rick Perry Pick to Board," *Politico*, September 10, 2020, https://www.politico.com/news/2020/09/10/ukraine-gas-company-to-add-rick-perry-pick-to-board-412261.
624 Singh, "Trump Administration."
625 Max Cohen and Matthew Choi, "'Traitor': Pompeo, Mnuchin and Navarro Pile on Bolton," *Politico*, June 18, 2020, https://www.politico.com/news/2020/06/18/peter-navarro-john-bolton-book-328490.
626 Singh, "Trump Administration."
627 "Attorney General William P. Barr on the Nomination of Jay Clayton to Serve as U.S. Attorney for the Southern District of New York," Office of Public Affairs, U.S. Department of Justice.
628 "US Attorney Geoffrey Berman Denies He Is Stepping Down," BBC News, June 20, 2020, https://www.bbc.com/news/world-us-canada-53117951.
629 Feuer et al., "Trump Fires."
630 Andrew Prokop, "The Firing of SDNY US Attorney Geoffrey Berman, Explained," *Vox*, June 22, 2020, https://www.vox.com/2020/6/22/21298917/geoffrey-berman-sdny-fired-barr.
631 Benjamin Weiser et al., "Trump Fired Her Boss. Now She's Taking Cases That Incensed White House," *New York Times*, June 21, 2020, https://www.nytimes.com/2020/06/21/nyregion/us-attorney-trump-audrey-strauss.html.
632 "Transcript: John Bolton interview with ABC News' Martha Raddatz," ABC News.
633 Libby Cathey, "Bolton Book Releases Tuesday Even as Judge Says His Profits Might Be Seized," ABC News, June 23, 2020, https://abcnews.go.com/Politics/bolton-book-set-release-tuesday-judge-profits-seized/story?id=71385543.
634 Jennifer Szalai, "In 'The Room Where It Happened,' John Bolton Dumps His Notes and Smites His Enemies," *New York Times*, June 17, 2020, https://www.nytimes.com/2020/06/17/books/review-room-where-it-happened-john-bolton-memoir.html.

635 Order, United States of America v. Halkbank, No. 15 Cr 867-RMB (S.D.N.Y. July 20, 2020), uploaded by Law.com, https://images.law.com/contrib/content/uploads/documents/389/108696/Halkbank-trial-order.pdf.

636 Lefebvre, "Ukraine Gas Company."

637 "Ukraine Says U.S. Company Refuses to Cooperate over LNG Supply Deal," Reuters, September 11, 2020, https://www.reuters.com/article/usa-ukraine-lng-idUSL8N2G82TT/.

638 "Lev Parnas," United States Attorney's Office, Southern District of New York.

639 Sealed Indictment, United States of America v. Lev Parnas, Igor Fruman, David Correia, and Andrey Kukushkin, No. 19 Cr. 725 (S.D.N.Y. October 10, 2019), https://www.justice.gov/usao-sdny/press-release/file/1208281/dl.

640 Abby Livingston, "Pete Sessions Is 'Congressman 1' in Indictment of Rudy Giuliani Associates, Reports Say," *Texas Tribune*, October 10, 2019, https://www.texastribune.org/2019/10/10/pete-sessions-congressman-1-guliani-associates-indictment/.

641 Sealed Indictment, United States of America v. Lev Parnas, Igor Fruman, David Correia, and Andrey Kukushkin, No. 19 Cr. 725 (S.D.N.Y. October 10, 2019), https://www.justice.gov/usao-sdny/press-release/file/1208281/dl.

642 Jonathan Stempel, "Turkey's Halkbank Urges Dismissal of Iran Sanctions Criminal Case in U.S.," Reuters, September 18, 2020, https://www.reuters.com/article/us-usa-turkey-halkbank-idUSKBN2692FF/.

643 "In Light of New Evidence," United States Senate Committee on Finance.

644 "Kobolyev: Criminal Case Opened against Naftogaz Management," *Kyiv Post*, October 8, 2020, https://archive.kyivpost.com/ukraine-politics/kobolyev-criminal-case-opened-against-naftogaz-management.html.

645 "Ex-U.S. Diplomat Steps Down from Naftogaz Board, Citing Ukrainian Corruption Concerns," RFE/RL October 13, 2020, https://www.rferl.org/a/ex-u-s-diplomat-steps-down-from-naftogaz-board-citing-ukrainian-corruption-concerns/30890034.html.

646 "Intel: Missile Launched on Turkey's Black Sea Coast after Notice of S-400 Test," *Al Monitor*, October 16, 2020, https://www.al-monitor.com/originals/2020/10/turkey-s400-test-sinop-missile-fire.html.

647 "Donald Trump 2020 Election Night Speech Transcript," Rev.

648 Tapper and Gangel, "CNN Exclusive."

649 Deliso et al., "Election 2020."

650 Maryclaire Dale, "Trump's Legal Team Cried Vote Fraud, but Courts Found None," Associated Press, November 22, 2020, https://apnews.com/article/election-2020-donald-trump-pennsylvania-elections-talk-radio-433b6efe72720d8648221f405c2111f9.

651 Theodoric Meyer, "Greenberg Traurig Drops Turkey," *Politico*, November 6, 2020, https://www.politico.com/newsletters/politico-influence/2020/11/06/greenberg-traurig-drops-turkey-791451.

652 Scott Detrow and Asma Khalid, "Biden Wins Presidency, According to AP, Edging Trump in Turbulent Race," NPR, November 7, 2020, https://www.npr.org/2020/11/07/928803493/biden-wins-presidency-according-to-ap-edging-trump-in-turbulent-race.

653 Matt Zapotosky and Devlin Barrett, "Barr Clears Justice Dept. To Investigate Alleged Voting Irregularities as Trump Makes Unfounded Fraud Claims," *Washington Post*, November 9, 2020, https://www.washingtonpost.com/national-security/trump-voting-fraud-william-barr-justice-department/2020/11/09/d57dbe98-22e6-11eb-8672-c281c7a2c96e_story.html.

654 Chotiner, "William Barr's 'Radical Break.'"

655 Downen and Choi, "Two Texas Businessmen."
656 H. R. Rep. No. 117-663, *269–70*.
657 Clark et al., "Building the 'Big Lie.'"
658 "Watch Again," Independent.
659 Donald J. Trump (@realDonaldTrump), "I look forward to Mayor Giuliani spearheading the legal effort to defend OUR RIGHT to FREE and FAIR ELECTIONS! Rudy Giuliani, Joseph diGenova, Victoria Toensing, Sidney Powell, and Jenna Ellis, a truly great team, added to our other wonderful lawyers and representatives!" Twitter, November 15, 2020, 11:12 a.m., https://twitter.com/realDonaldTrump/status/1327811527123103746.
660 "Kraken," BBC.
661 Cummings et al., "By the Numbers."
662 Collins and LeBlanc, "Trump Fires."
663 "Joint Statement," Cyber Security and Infrastructure Security Agency.
664 Chesebro, *Memorandum—The Real Deadline*.
665 "Watch Again," *Independent*.
666 Martin Pengelly, "Trump Pardons Former National Security Adviser Michael Flynn," *Guardian*, November 25, 2020, https://www.theguardian.com/us-news/2020/nov/25/donald-trump-pardons-michael-flynn.
667 Alexander, "'Your Election Is a Sham.'"
668 Randazzo and Polletta, "Arizona GOP."
669 "Rudy Giuliani, Others Appear," 11Alive.
670 "Rudy Giuliani Testifies in Lansing," *Detroit News*.
671 Balsamo, "In Exclusive AP Interview."
672 Chesebro, *Memorandum—Important*.
673 Ryan Goodman et al., "Comprehensive Timeline on False Electors Scheme in 2020 Presidential Election," Just Security, May 15, 2024, https://www.justsecurity.org/81939/timeline-false-electors/.
674 Maggie Haberman and Luke Broadwater, "'Kind of Wild/Creative': Emails Shed Light on Trump Fake Electors Plan," *New York Times*, July 26, 2022, https://www.nytimes.com/2022/07/26/us/politics/trump-fake-electors-emails.html.
675 Jamie Gangel et al., "CNN Exclusive: Mark Meadows' 2,319 Text Messages Reveal Trump's Inner Circle Communications before and after January 6," CNN, April 25, 2022, https://edition.cnn.com/2022/04/25/politics/mark-meadows-texts-2319/index.html.
676 Indictment, United States of America v. Donald J. Trump, No. 1:23 Cr. 257, (D.D.C. August 1, 2023), https://www.justice.gov/storage/US_v_Trump_23_cr_257.pdf.
677 Rebecca Kheel, "House Approves Defense Policy Bill despite Trump Veto Threat," *Hill*, December 8, 2020, https://thehill.com/policy/defense/529290-house-approves-defense-policy-bill-despite-trump-veto-threat/.
678 Congress.gov, "H.R.6395—116th Congress (2019–2020): William M. (Mac) Thornberry National Defense Authorization Act for Fiscal Year 2021," January 1, 2021, https://www.congress.gov/bill/116th-congress/house-bill/6395.
679 Matthew Daly, "In a First, Congress Overrides Trump Veto of Defense Bill," Associated Press, January 1, 2021, https://apnews.com/article/election-2020-donald-trump-defense-policy-bills-85656704ad9ae1f9cf202ee76d7a14fd.
680 Joscelyn and Norman L. Eisen, "Kenneth Chesebro."
681 Cohen, Zachary Cohen, Dan Merica, "Trump campaign officials."

682 Nick Corasaniti and Jim Rutenberg, "Electoral College Vote Officially Affirms Biden's Victory," *New York Times*, December 14, 2020, https://www.nytimes.com/2020/12/14/us/politics/biden-electoral-college.html.

683 Amiri, "How the Trump Fake Electors."

684 Gardner et al., "Fake Trump Electors."

685 Reinhard et al., "As Giuliani Coordinated."

686 Allie Malloy et al., "Attorney General William Barr Resigns," CNN, December 15, 2020, https://edition.cnn.com/2020/12/14/politics/william-barr-out-as-attorney-general/.

687 David Gilbert, "The Kraken Is Dead: Sidney Powell's Final Lawsuit Just Got Dismissed," Vice News, December 10, 2020, https://www.vice.com/en/article/5dpypz/the-kraken-is-dead-sidney-powells-final-lawsuit-just-got-dismissed.

688 Kyle Cheney and Josh Gerstein, "Donald Trump's Brutal Day in Court," *Politico*, December 4, 2020, https://www.politico.com/news/2020/12/04/donald-trump-in-court-443010.

689 Swan and Basu, "Bonus Episode."

690 Helderman and Dawsey, "'Unhinged.'"

691 Dan Barry and Sheera Frenkel, "'Be There. Will Be Wild!': Trump All but Circled the Date," *New York Times*, January 6, 2021, https://www.nytimes.com/2021/01/06/us/politics/capitol-mob-trump-supporters.html.

692 Bryan Metzger, "Eleven House Republicans Attended a White House Meeting with Trump to Strategize about Overturning the Election Results on January 6. Six of Them Later Asked for Pardons," *Business Insider*, July 12, 2022, https://www.businessinsider.com/house-republicans-white-house-meeting-december-21-2020-election-2022-7.

693 Holland, "Trump Grants."

694 Steve Holland, "Trump Pardons Former Campaign Chairman Manafort, Associate Roger Stone," Reuters, December 23, 2020, https://www.reuters.com/article/uk-usa-trump-pardons-idAFKBN28Y02D/.

695 Samuelsohn and Gerstein, "What Roger Stone's Trial Reveals."

696 Eric Tucker, "US Says Russia Was Given Trump Campaign Polling Data in 2016," Associated Press, April 16, 2021, https://apnews.com/article/donald-trump-paul-manafort-russia-campaigns-konstantin-kilimnik-d2fdefdb37077e28eba135e21fce6ebf.

697 "John Eastman's First," *Washington Post*.

698 Allen, "'Say the Election Was Corrupt.'"

699 Sprunt, "Former DOJ Officials."

700 Tim Dickinson, "Trump Told Pence 'You're Too Honest' When He Objected to Jan. 6 Scheme," *Rolling Stone*, August 1, 2023, https://www.rollingstone.com/politics/politics-features/trump-pence-too-honest-jan-6-scheme-1234799181/.

701 Martin Penegelly, "Trump Said Pence Was 'Too Honest' over January 6 Plot, Says Ex-Vice President in Book," *Guardian*, November 9, 2022, https://www.theguardian.com/books/2022/nov/09/trump-pence-honest-jan-6-capitol-attack-lincoln-project-book.

702 Treisman, "Georgia Officials."

703 "John Eastman's Second Memo," *Washington Post*.

704 Broadwater and Schmidt, "Trump, Told It Was Illegal."

705 Nick Niedzwiadek and Kyle Cheney, "Trump Pressures Pence to Throw out Election Results—Even Though He Can't," *Politico*, January 5, 2021, https://www.politico.com/news/2021/01/05/trump-pressures-pence-election-results-455069.

706 "Donald J. Trump, Tweets," American Presidency Project.

707 Naylor, "Read Trump's Jan. 6 Speech."
708 Kat Lonsdorf et al., "A Timeline of the Jan. 6 Capitol Attack—Including When and How Trump Responded," NPR, January 5, 2022, https://www.npr.org/2022/01/05/1069977469/a-timeline-of-how-the-jan-6-attack-unfolded-including-who-said-what-and-when.
709 Bjorklund, "Trump's Inexplicable Crusade."
710 Jonathan Lemire et al., "Trump Pardons Ex-Strategist Steve Bannon, Dozens of Others," Associated Press, January 20, 2021, https://apnews.com/article/steve-bannon-trump-pardons-broidy-66c82f25134735e742b2501c118723bb.
711 Groves, "Trump Pardons."
712 "Political Donor Sentenced," Office of Public Affairs.
713 Rashbaum et al., "F.B.I. Searches."
714 Todd Prince, "Ukraine's 'Internal Threat' on Blinken's Plate after Naftogaz CEO Fired," RFE/RL, May 5, 2021, https://www.rferl.org/a/ukraine-naftogaz-blinken-corruption-zelenskiy-kobolyev/31237722.html.
715 Christian Berthelsen et al., "Giuliani Facing Inquiry into Whether He Lobbied for Turkey," Bloomberg News, June 29, 2021, https://www.bloomberg.com/news/articles/2021-06-29/giuliani-facing-inquiry-into-whether-he-lobbied-trump-for-turkey.
716 Erica Orden, "Giuliani Associate Igor Fruman Pleads Guilty to Solicitation of a Contribution by a Foreign National," CNN, September 10, 2021, https://edition.cnn.com/2021/09/10/politics/igor-fruman-plea/index.html.
717 del Valle, "Lev Parnas."
718 Holly Ellyatt, "Russian Forces Invade Ukraine," CNBC, February 24, 2022, https://www.cnbc.com/2022/02/24/russian-forces-invade-ukraine.html.
719 "Turkish Businessman Extradited," United States Attorney's Office.
720 Rashbaum et al., "Giuliani Will Not Face."
721 Chimène Keitner, "Expert Recap and Analysis of Halkbank Oral Argument at the Supreme Court," Just Security, January 19, 2023, https://www.justsecurity.org/84836/expert-recap-and-analysis-of-halkbank-oral-argument-at-the-supreme-court/.
722 Emma Svoboda, "The Supreme Court Ruled That the FSIA Does Not Apply to Criminal Cases and Remanded Common Law Arguments to the Second Circuit," Lawfare Institute, April 24, 2023, https://www.lawfaremedia.org/article/the-supreme-court's-halkbank-decision-explained.
723 Dan Friedman and David Corn, "A New Rudy Scandal: FBI Agent Says Giuliani Was Co-opted by Russian Intelligence," *Mother Jones*, September 1, 2023, https://www.motherjones.com/politics/2023/09/a-new-rudy-scandal-fbi-agent-says-giuliani-was-co-opted-by-russian-intelligence/.
724 Indictment, United States of America v. Donald J. Trump, No. 1:23 Cr. 257, (D.D.C. August 1, 2023), https://www.justice.gov/storage/US_v_Trump_23_cr_257.pdf.
725 Janie Boschma et al., "Former President Donald Trump's Fourth Indictment, Annotated," CNN, August 15, 2023, https://edition.cnn.com/interactive/2023/08/politics/annotated-trump-indictment-georgia-election-dg/.
726 Kate Brumback, "Sidney Powell Pleads Guilty over Efforts to Overturn Trump's Loss in Georgia and Agrees to Cooperate," Associated Press, October 19, 2023, https://apnews.com/article/sidney-powell-plea-deal-georgia-election-indictment-ec7dc601ad78d756643aa2544028e9f5.
727 Marshall Cohen et al., "Kenneth Chesebro: Pro-Trump Lawyer Pleads Guilty in Georgia Election Subversion Case, Implicates Trump in Fake Elector Conspiracy," CNN, October 20, 2023, https://edition.cnn.com/2023/10/20/politics/kenneth-chesebro-georgia-election-subversion/index.html.

ABOUT THE AUTHOR

Ever since backpacking through Europe in his teenage years, Chad Lewis has sought to understand the world. He focused his studies at the University of Maryland around American foreign policy vis-à-vis post-Soviet politics. He spent over a decade abroad, living in Europe, Russia, and South America, exploring how those parts of the globe differed from America in cultural, socio-economic, and political senses.

The years-long close observation of Russia helped Lewis notice early signs of Kremlin trolls who were promoting Putin's talking points in the Western media. They masqueraded as Americans but had English grammar mistakes common for Russian speakers. Juxtaposing those comments with Russia's increasing foreign aggression, Lewis quickly understood the potential national security ramifications. Concerned, in the fall of 2014 he reached out to the US government and alerted them to his findings. Years later, the intelligence community would admit that the US had fallen victim to a Kremlin disinformation effort.

In 2019, alarm bells rang for Lewis with the arrest of Rudy Giuliani's associates, Lev Parnas and Igor Fruman. While most of the media focused on their connections to Donald Trump's first impeachment, Lewis started weaving isolated reports of their actions into an integrated picture and discovered layers of influence peddling, both domestic and foreign, by Giuliani and his associates. Lewis turned his research into his first book, The Persuasion Game, to illuminate the gravity of the damage done to US institutions by influence peddlers and to protect American democracy from future treachery. He aims to expand upon this subject by launching his new podcast in 2025.

Learn more at chadlewis.net.